Love Between Women

THE CHICAGO SERIES ON SEXUALITY, HISTORY, AND SOCIETY
A SERIES EDITED BY JOHN C. FOUT

Love Between Women

Early Christian Responses to Female Homoeroticism

Bernadette J. Brooten

THE UNIVERSITY OF CHICAGO PRESS
·
CHICAGO & LONDON

Bernadette J. Brooten is the Robert and Myra Kraft and Jacob Hiatt Professor of Christian Studies at Brandeis University in the Department of Near Eastern and Judaic Studies. She is the author of *Women Leaders in the Ancient Synagogue,* and coeditor of *Frauen in der Männerkirche?*

The University of Chicago Press, Chicago 60637
The University of Chicago Press, Ltd., London
© 1996 by The University of Chicago
All rights reserved. Published 1996
Printed and bound by CPI Group (UK) Ltd, Croydon, CR0 4YY
05 04 03 02 01 00 99 98 97 96   1 2 3 4 5
ISBN 978-0-226-07591-4 (cloth)
ISBN 978-0-226-07592-1 (paper)

Library of Congress Cataloging-in-Publication Data

Brooten, Bernadette J.
    Love between women : early Christian responses to female
homoeroticism / Bernadette J. Brooten.
        p.   cm.
    Includes bibliographical references and index.
    1. Lesbianism—Biblical teaching. 2. Bible. N.T. Romans I,
18–32—Criticism, interpretation, etc. 3. Lesbianism—Religious
aspects—Christianity—History of doctrines—Early church, ca.
30–600. 4. Bible. N.T. Romans I, 18–32—Criticism,
interpretation, etc.—History—Early church, ca. 30–600.
5. Lesbianism—Rome. I. Title.
BS2665.6.L47B76   1996
306.76'63'0901—dc20   96-4727
                                                        CIP

Contents

CONTENTS

Illustrations

Following p. 186

Illustrations

Acknowledgments

It has been a privilege to write a book on ancient responses to love between women, a privilege that no one before me has enjoyed. I thank everyone who enabled me to obtain the education necessary to find and interpret rare and sometimes untranslated ancient sources. I express special gratitude to my mother, Sadie Assad Brooten, and my sister, Barbara Brooten Job, who encouraged me to get a good education, as well as to all of my many teachers throughout the years.

I thank those who provided me with institutional and financial support: the Volkswagen Foundation, the Institute for Ecumenical Research of the University of Tübingen, Harvard University, especially Harvard Divinity School, the Bunting Institute of Radcliffe College, the National Endowment for the Humanities, the Milton Fund of the Harvard Medical School, Nancy Ruth, the American Academy of Religion, the American Council of Learned Societies, the American Association of University Women, and Brandeis University. This project required extensive library resources and numerous requests for interlibrary loan. I offer special thanks to the dedicated staff members, as well as to the donors, of the following libraries: the theological, fine arts, and classics libraries of the University of Tübingen, as well as its University Library; the following libraries of Harvard University: Andover-Harvard Library, Houghton Library, the Fogg Art Museum Library, and Widener Library; and the Goldfarb Library of Brandeis University.

I express my deepest gratitude to the outstanding research assistants who collaborated with me. Of these, three deserve special mention owing to the length and intensity of their service: Caroline Johnson, Melanie Johnson-DeBaufre, and Denise Kimber Buell. Their numerous editorial suggestions, their superb bibliographical skills, and their sharp proofreading eyes have improved every page of this book.

I also express special thanks to Inge Baumann, Christina Bucher, Jutta Flatters, and Linda Maloney for their extraordinary help at the beginning of this project.

In addition to these three scholars, numerous other persons have assisted me as research assistants, colleagues, supporters, and friends. They have read chapters of the book, done bibliographical work, cheered me on, helped me to improve my writing, helped me to find funding, and given me the emotional support necessary to write a book on a such a difficult subject. They include: Barbara Geller Nathanson, Mary Nicolini, Saul Olyan, Elaine Pagels, David Pao, Lenore Parker, Ann Pellegrini, Richard Pervo, David Pingree, Tina Pippin, Kate Potter, Jo Anne Preston, Cheryl Qamar, Kathy Randel, Achim Reinstädtler, Jennifer Rike, Barbara Rossing, Jonathan Sarna, Beatrix Schiele, Laurel Schneider, Luise Schottroff, Dieter Schmidt, Mary Schmidt, P. H. Schrijvers, Helen Schüngel-Straumann, Elisabeth Schüssler Fiorenza, Jane Scott, Robin Sebesta, Anne Seelbach, Jane Shaw, Ellen Sheets, Susan Shenkel, Leonore Siegele-Wenschkewitz, Anne Simon, Janet Farrell Smith, Jane McIintosh Snyder, Brita and Krister Stendahl, Stanley Stowers, Jennifer Starr, Constance Studer, J. P. Sullivan, Melinda Taranto Garnis, Richard Tarrant, Thandeka, Ronald Thiemann, Christine Thomas, Bonnie Thurston, Ulrich Tiechy, Mary Ann Tolbert, Prentis Tomlinson, Richard Valantassis, Annewies van den Hoek, Pieter van der Horst, Samantha Waller, Stuart Walker, Roy Ward, Sharon Welch, Mary Ellen Wells, Reinhard Werk, Kathleen O'Brien Wicker, Jodie Wigren, Ute Wild, Demetrius Williams, Bonnie Wisthoff, Bonnie Woods, Susan Yanow, Marcia Yudkin, Berni Zisserson, Ellen Aitken, Rebecca Alpert, Ghazala Anwar, Elsi Arnold, Jane Arnold, Clarissa Atkinson, Harold Attridge, David C. Aune, David E. Aune, Carolann Barrett, Ellen Birnbaum, Gail Birnbaum, Heinz Blanke, Andrea Blome, Marilyn Bodner, Marianne Bonz, Daniel Boyarin, François Bovon, Susan Boynton, Ann Brock, Constance Buchanan, Marga Bührig, Elke Burkholz, Liza Burr, Ron Cameron, Robert Canavello, Katie Cannon, Jacqueline Carr-Hamilton, Elizabeth Castelli, Ruth Clements, Kathleen Corley, Dana Chyung, Elizabeth Clark, Louise Cramer, Emily Culpepper, Mary Rose D'Angelo, Elaine Dearden, Indralakshmi Din-Dayal, Maureen Donohue, Jane Dempsey Douglass, Gordon Duggins, Sarah Duncan, Mereth DunnEstey, Mark Edwards, Irmgard Ehlers, Hannelore Ehrhart, Edouard Fontenot, Georgia Frank, John Gager, Ysabel Geiger, Warren Goldfarb, Deirdre Good, Royal Govain, Arthur Green, Judy Ravesloot Haley, David Halperin, Ann Ellis Hanson, Susan Ashbrook Harvey, John Hermann, Rebecca Hermann, Benjamin Hickman, Martha Himmelfarb, Susan Holman, Marie Howe, Margaret Hutaff, Claudia Janssen, Willa Jarnagin, Else Kähler, Tamar Kamionkowski, Betsy Keats, Jai Keller, Mechthild Kiegel-

ACKNOWLEDGMENTS

mann, Karen King, Cynthia Kittredge, Connie Koenenn, Gisela and Helmut Koester, Rebecca Kowals, Ross Shepard Kraemer, Rebecca Krawiec, Florence Ladd, John Lanci, Bentley Layton, Herta Leistner, Rebecca Lesses, David Levenson, Aline Lukas, Jennifer Berenson Maclean, Patricia Maguire, Shaun Marmon, Dale Martin, Christopher Matthews, Shelly Matthews, Ann Matter, Janet McDaniel, Grace McMillan, Gloria Melnitsky, Margaret Miles, Irene Monroe, and Maria Moonlion. I also express special gratitude to two persons who died before the completion of the book: John Boswell and Nelle Morton.

A word of deep gratitude goes to Sheila Briggs for her encouragement and support at a crucial phase of the work.

I have benefited from presenting portions of my work in classes at the Claremont Graduate School, Harvard Divinity School, and Brandeis University, and I thank the members of those classes for their responses, even though I do not have space to mention all of their names. In addition, I have lectured on material from the book at the University of Utrecht, the Theodor-Heuss-Akademie, the Deutsche Gesellschaft für Pastoralpsychologie, the Evangelische Akademie Arnoldshain, the Evangelische Akademie Bad Boll, the Oxford Patristics Conference, the American Academy of Religion Annual Meeting, the Society of Biblical Literature International Meeting, the Theological Opportunities Program of Harvard Divinity School, the Colloquium of the Bunting Institute of Radcliffe College, the Harvard Gay and Lesbian Studies Lecture Series, the Society of Biblical Literature Annual Meeting, the New Testament Department of Yale University, the Women's Studies Graduate Colloquium of Brandeis University, the Mellon Seminar of Princeton University, a Society of Biblical Literature regional meeting, and the University of Frankfurt.

Finally, I thank John Fout for accepting the book into this series, as well as Doug Mitchell, Matthew Howard, and Carol Saller of the University of Chicago Press for their care in preparing the manuscript for publication.

October 1, 1995

Abbreviations and Technical Terms,
Short Titles, and Keys to Symbols

Translations of ancient sources are my own, unless otherwise indicated. I
have generally used the New Revised Standard Version for biblical quotations, sometimes with slight alterations.

Abbreviations and Technical Terms

Acts	Acts of the Apostles
ANF	The Ante-Nicene Fathers
ANRW	*Aufstieg und Niedergang der römischen Welt*
apud	preserved in the work of, quoted in
BAGD	Walter Bauer, William F. Arndt, F. Wilbur Gingrich, and Frederick W. Danker, *Greek-English Lexicon of the New Testament*
b.	Babylonian Talmud (followed by the name of the tractate)
BASOR	Bulletin of the American Schools of Oriental Research
BCE	Before the Common Era (= BC)
bot.	bottom of the page
BTB	*Biblical Theology Bulletin*
BZNW	Beihefte zur *Zeitschrift für die neutestamentliche Wissenschaft*
c.	century
CBQ	*Catholic Biblical Quarterly*
CChr	Corpus Christianorum
CE	Common Era (= AD)
CIL	*Corpus Inscriptionum Latinarum*
Col	Colossians
1-2 Cor	1-2 Corinthians
CQR	*Church Quarterly Review*
CSEL	Corpus Scriptorum Ecclesiasticorum Latinorum

Deut	Deuteronomy
Eph	Ephesians
esp.	especially
ET	English Translation
et al.	*et alii* ("and others")
ÉTR	*Études théologiques et religieuses*
EvT	*Evangelische Theologie*
Exod	Exodus
f	following verse, page, etc.
ff	following verses, pages, etc.
fol.	folio
Fr., fr., or Fragm.	fragment
FRLANT	Forschungen zur Religion und Literatur des Alten und Neuen Testaments
Gal	Galatians
GCS	Die griechischen christlichen Schriftsteller der ersten Jahrhunderte
Gen	Genesis
Genesis Rabbah	part of Midrash Rabbah
Hab	Habakkuk
HTR	*Harvard Theological Review*
IG	*Inscriptiones Graecae*
JBL	Journal of Biblical Literature
Jer	Jeremiah
JR	Journal of Religion
Ker.	Tractate *Keritot*
KJV	King James Version
LCL	Loeb Classical Library
Lev	Leviticus
Leviticus Rabbah	part of Midrash Rabbah
LPGL	G. W. H. Lampe, *Patristic Greek Lexicon*
LSJ	Liddell-Scott-Jones, *Greek-English Lexicon*
LXX	Septuagint, ancient Greek version of Jewish Bible
m.	Mishnah (followed by the name of the tractate)
Mak.	Tractate *Makkot*
Matt	Matthew, Gospel of
mid.	middle of the page
MT	Masoretic Text of the Hebrew Bible
Ned.	*Nedarim*

ABBREVIATIONS, SHORT TITLES, AND KEYS TO SYMBOLS

no.	number
n.s.	new series
NHS	Nag Hammadi Studies
NovT	*Novum Testamentum*
NRSV	New Revised Standard Version
NPNF	Nicene and Post-Nicene Fathers
NTA	*New Testament Abstracts*
NTS	*New Testament Studies*
OCD	*Oxford Classical Dictionary*
OLD	P. G. W. Glare, ed., *Oxford Latin Dictionary*
OTP	James H. Charlesworth, ed., *The Old Testament Pseudepigrapha*
passim	the cited item occurs frequently throughout the work
P	Papyrus
1–2 Pet	1–2 Peter
PG	J. Migne, ed., *Patrologia Graeca*
Phil	Philippians
PL	J. Migne, ed., *Patrologia Latina*
pl./pls.	plate/plates
pt.	part
PW	Pauly-Wissowa, *Real-Encyclopädie der classischen Altertums-wissenschaft*
PWSup	Pauly-Wissowa, *Real-Encyclopädie der classischen Altertums-wissenschaft*, Supplement
Prov	Proverbs
r	*recto* (the front side of a manuscript, coin, vase, etc.)
RAC	*Reallexikon für Antike und Christentum*
RSV	Revised Standard Version
Rom	Romans
Sanh.	Tractate *Sanhedrin*
SBLDS	Society of Biblical Literature Dissertation Series
SBLTT	Society of Biblical Literature Texts and Translations
SC	Sources chrétiennes
ScEs	*Science et esprit*
Šabb.	Tractate *Šabbat*
Sib. Or.	Sibylline Oracles
Sir	Sirach (Ecclesiasticus)
the Suda	a medieval Greek lexicon
s.v.	*sub verbo* (listed in a lexicon under the word "...")
SVF	Johannes von Arnim, ed., *Stoicorum Veterum Fragmenta*
t.	Tosefta (followed by the name of the tractate)
TBl	*Theologische Blätter*

TDNT	G. Kittel and G. Friedrich, eds., *Theological Dictionary of the New Testament*
1–2 Thess	1–2 Thessalonians
1–2 Tim	1–2 Timothy
Tit	Titus
TS	*Theological Studies*
TWNT	G. Kittel and G. Friedrich, eds., *Theologisches Wörterbuch zum Neuen Testament*
TZ	*Theologische Zeitschrift*
v	*verso* (the reverse side of a manuscript, coin, vase, etc.)
v.	verse
vv.	verses
vol.	volume
Wis	Wisdom of Solomon
WUNT	Wissenschaftliche Untersuchungen zum Neuen Testament
y.	Jerusalem Talmud (followed by the name of the tractate)
ZEE	*Zeitschrift für evangelische Ethik*
ZNW	*Zeitschrift für die neutestamentliche Wissenschaft*

Short Titles

I have used the following short titles for frequently cited works (other, unlisted short titles may appear in the notes when in close proximity to the original full citations):

Aune, "Romans." Aune, David E. "Romans as a *Logos Protreptikos*." In *The Romans Debate*, ed. Karl P. Donfried. Rev. and exp. ed. of the 1977 ed. Peabody, MA: Hendrickson, 1991.

Bassler, "Divine Impartiality." Bassler, Jouette M. "Divine Impartiality in Paul's Letter to the Romans." *NovT* 26 (1984) 43–58.

Betz, *Greek Magical Papyri*. Betz, Hans Dieter, ed. *The Greek Magical Papyri in Translation*. Vol. 1. Chicago: University of Chicago Press, 1986.

Blum, *Studies*. Blum, Claes. *Studies in the Dream-Book of Artemidorus*. Uppsala: Almqvist and Wiksells, 1936.

Boll, *Griechischer Liebeszauber*. Boll, Franz. *Griechischer Liebeszauber aus Ägypten*. Sitzungsberichte der Heidelberger Akademie der Wissenschaften, Philosophisch-historische Klasse, 1910, 2. Abhandlung.

Boswell, *Christianity, Social Tolerance, and Homosexuality*. Boswell, John. *Christianity, Social Tolerance, and Homosexuality: Gay People in Western Europe from the Beginning of the Christian Era to the Fourteenth Century*. Chicago: University of Chicago Press, 1980.

Boswell, *Same-Sex Unions*. Boswell, John. *Same-Sex Unions in Premodern Europe*. New York: Villard, 1994.

Bram, *Ancient Astrology*. Bram, Jean Rhys, trans. *Ancient Astrology: Theory and Practice:* Matheseos Libri viii *by Firmicus Maternus*. Noyes Classical Studies. Park Ridge, NJ: Noyes, 1975.

Colson, *Philo*. Colson, F. H., and G. H. Whitaker, eds. and trans. *Philo*, 10 vols. LCL. Cambridge, MA: Harvard University Press, 1929–62.

Countryman, *Dirt, Greed, and Sex*. Countryman, L. William. *Dirt, Greed, and Sex: Sexual Ethics in the New Testament and Their Implications for Today*. Philadelphia: Fortress, 1988.

Cumont, *L'Égypte des Astrologues*. Cumont, Franz. *L'Égypte des Astrologues*. Brussels: Fondation Égyptologique Reine Élisabeth, 1937.

Dover, *Greek Homosexuality*. Dover, K[enneth] J. *Greek Homosexuality*. 2d rev. ed. Cambridge, MA: Harvard University Press, 1989.

Drabkin and Drabkin, *Caelius Aurelianus* Gynaecia. Drabkin, Miriam F., and Israel E. Drabkin, eds. *Caelius Aurelianus* Gynaecia: *Fragments of a Latin Version of Soranus'* Gynaecia *from a Thirteenth Century Manuscript*. Supplements to the Bulletin of the History of Medicine 13. Baltimore: Johns Hopkins, 1951.

Drabkin, *On Acute and On Chronic Diseases*. Drabkin, I. E., ed. and trans. *Caelius Aurelianus: On Acute Diseases and On Chronic Diseases*. Chicago: University of Chicago Press, 1950.

Foucault, *History*. Foucault, Michel. *The History of Sexuality*. 3 vols. Trans. Robert Hurley. French original, Paris: Editions Gallimard, 1976–84; New York: Random House, 1978–86.

Gager, *Curse Tablets and Binding Spells*. Gager, John, ed. *Curse Tablets and Binding Spells from the Ancient World*. New York: Oxford University Press, 1992. With contributions by Catherine F. Cooper, David Frankfurter, Derek Krueger, and Richard Lim.

Georgi, *Unterweisung*. Georgi, Dieter. *Unterweisung in lehrhafter Form: Weisheit Salomos*. Jüdische Schriften aus hellenistisch-römischer Zeit 3. Gütersloh: Gütersloh/Gerd Mohn, 1980.

Gundel, *Neue astrologische Texte des Hermes Trismegistos*. Gundel, Wilhelm, ed. *Neue astrologische Texte des Hermes Trismegistos: Funde und Forschungen auf dem Gebiet der antiken Astronomie und Astrologie*. Abhandlungen der Bayerischen Akademie der Wissenschaften. Philosophisch-historische Abteilung, n.s. 12. Munich: Bayerische Akademie der Wissenschaften, 1936.

Hallett, "Homoeroticism." Hallett, Judith P. "Female Homoeroticism and the Denial of Roman Reality in Latin Literature." *Yale Journal of Criticism* 3 (1989) 209–27.

Halperin, *One Hundred Years*. Halperin, David M. *One Hundred Years of Homosexuality: And Other Essays on Greek Love*. New York: Routledge, 1990.

Himmelfarb, *Tours of Hell*. Himmelfarb, Martha. *Tours of Hell: An Apocalyptic Form in Jewish and Christian Literature*. Philadelphia: University of Pennsylvania Press, 1983.

Ilberg, *Sorani Gynaeciorum libri iv*. Ilberg, Johannes, ed. *Sorani Gynaeciorum libri iv*. Corpus Medicorum Graecorum 4. Leipzig/Berlin: Teubner, 1927.

Jewett, "Following the Argument." Jewett, Robert. "Following the Argument of Romans." In *The Romans Debate*. Ed. Karl P. Donfried. Rev. and exp. ed. of the 1977 ed. Peabody, MA: Hendrickson, 1991.

Kroll, Skutsch, and Ziegler, *Matheseos libri viii*. Kroll, W[ilhelm], F. Skutsch, and K. Ziegler, eds. *Iulii Firmici Materni Matheseos libri viii*. 2 vols. Leipzig: Teubner, 1897–1913. Reprint, Stuttgart: Teubner, 1968.

Moxnes, "Honor." Moxnes, Halvor. "Honor, Shame, and the Outside World in Romans." In *The Social World of Formative Christianity and Judaism: Essays in Tribute to Howard Clark Kee*. Ed. Jacob Neusner et al. Philadelphia: Fortress, 1988, 207–18.

Olyan, "'And with a Male.'" Olyan, Saul M. "'And with a Male You Shall Not Lie the Lying Down of a Woman': On the Meaning and Significance of Leviticus 18:22 and 20:13." *Journal of the History of Sexuality* 5 (1994) 179–206.

Pack, "Artemidorus." Pack, Roger. "Artemidorus and His Waking World." *Transactions and Proceedings of the American Philological Association* 86 (1955) 280–90.

Pack, *Onirocriticon*. Roger A. Pack, ed. *Artemidori Daldiani Onirocriticon libri v*. Leipzig: Teubner, 1963.

PGM. Preisendanz, Karl, Albert Henrichs, et al., eds. and trans. *Papyri Graecae Magicae*. 2d ed. 2 vols. Stuttgart: Teubner, 1973–74.

Pingree, *Carmen Astrologicum*. Pingree, David, ed. and trans. *Dorothei Sidonii Carmen astrologicum*. Leipzig: Teubner, 1976.

Pingree, *Hephaistionis Apotelesmaticorum.* Pingree, David, ed. *Hephaes-tionis Thebani Apotelesmaticorum.* 2 vols. Leipzig: Teubner, 1973–74.
Pingree, *Yavanajātaka of Sphujidhvaja.* Pingree, David, ed. and trans. *The Yavanajātaka of Sphujidhvaja.* Vol. 2. Cambridge, MA: Harvard University Press, 1978.
PSI. Papiri greci e latini. Vol. 1. Pubblicazioni della Società italiana per la ricerca dei papiri greci e latini in Egitto. Florence: Ariani, 1912. (E.g., no. 28 = *PSI* 1.28)
Robbins, *Tetrabiblos.* Robbins, F. E., ed. and trans. *Ptolemy: Tetrabiblos.* LCL. Cambridge, MA: Harvard University Press, 1940.
Sanday and Headlam, *Commentary.* Sanday, William, and Arthur C. Headlam. *A Critical and Exegetical Commentary on the Epistle to the Romans.* 5th ed. The International Critical Commentary. Edinburgh: Clark, 1902.
Schrijvers, *Erklärung.* Schrijvers, P. H. *Eine medizinische Erklärung der männlichen Homosexualität aus der Antike (Caelius Aurelianus* De morbis chronicis *IV 9).* Amsterdam: Grüner, 1985.
Stowers, *Letter Writing.* Stowers, Stanley K. *Letter Writing in Greco-Roman Antiquity.* Philadelphia: Westminster, 1986.
Suppl. Mag. Daniel, Robert W., and Franco Maltomini, eds. *Supplementum Magicum.* Vol. 1. Abhandlungen der rheinisch-westfälischen Akademie der Wissenschaften, Sonderreihe Papyrologica Coloniensa 16.1. Opladen: Westdeutscher Verlag, 1990. (E.g., Papyrus no. 42 = *Suppl. Mag.*, 1.42.)
Temkin, *Soranus' Gynecology.* Temkin, Owsei, trans. *Soranus' Gynecology.* Baltimore: Johns Hopkins University Press, 1956.
Walton, *Diodorus.* Walton, Francis R., ed. and trans. *Diodorus of Sicily.* Vol. 11. LCL. Cambridge, MA: Harvard University Press, 1957.
White, *Oneirocritica.* White, Robert J. *The Interpretation of Dreams: Oneirocritica by Artemidorus.* Park Ridge, NJ: Noyes, 1975.
Wikan, "Shame." Wikan, Unni. "Shame and Honour: A Contestable Pair." *Man* 19 (1984) 635–52.
Wilckens, *Brief an die Römer.* Wilckens, Ulrich. *Der Brief an die Römer.* Vol. 1. Zurich: Benziger, 1978; Neukirchen-Vluyn: Neukirchener Verlag, 1978.
Winkler, *Constraints.* Winkler, John J. *The Constraints of Desire: The Anthropology of Sex and Gender in Ancient Greece.* New York: Routledge, 1990.

Winston, *Wisdom*. Winston, David. *The Wisdom of Solomon*. Anchor Bible
    43. Garden City: Doubleday, 1979.

Form for Referring to Ancient Writings

My form for referring to ancient authors and their works has been to use
the person's original name where possible (e.g., Soranos, rather than Soranus, and Sokrates, rather than Socrates) and the title in the original language (e.g., Plato, *Nomoi*, rather than *Leges* or *Laws*). In some cases, however, I have used more common English or Latin forms of the names or
titles when absolute accuracy would make it difficult for the reader to find
the citation (e.g., Epiktetos, *Discourses*, rather than the Greek *Arrianou
tōn Epiktētou Diatribōn* or the Latin *Dissertationes ab Arriano digestae*).

Text-critical Symbols for Texts in Original Languages

αβ	Letters that are uncertain in the original manuscript or tablet
. . .	Letters that can no longer be deciphered (each dot stands for one letter)
( )	Letters abbreviated by the scribe
[ ]	Letters missing in the original owing to damage to the manuscript or tablet and filled in by a modern editor
⟨ ⟩	Letters or words mistakenly omitted by the scribe
{ }	Letters or words deleted by a modern editor
⟦ ⟧	Letters or words deleted by the scribe
††	Text-critically corrupt portion of a text

Text-critical Symbols for English Translations

[ ]	Letters missing in the original owing to damage to the manuscript or tablet and filled in by a modern editor; *or* modern editorial explication of the meaning
⟨ ⟩	Letters or words mistakenly omitted by the scribe
††	Text-critically corrupt portion of a text

1

Introduction

E arly Christianity emerged in a world in which people from various walks of life acknowledged that women could have sexual contact with women. Close textual analysis of several early Christian writers demonstrates that they knew more about sexual relations between women than previous scholars have assumed, which accords with a heightened awareness of female homoeroticism within the cultural environment of early Christianity. Whereas pre-Roman-period Greek and Latin literature contains very few references to female homoeroticism, the awareness of sexual relations between women increases dramatically in the Roman period, as a detailed study of astrological texts, Greek love spells, Greek medical writings, ancient dream interpretation, and other sources reveals.

Because a strict distinction between active and passive sexual roles governed the prevailing cultural conceptualizations of sexual relations in the Roman world, it shaped the way that people viewed female homoeroticism.[1] The distinction between active and passive shaped Roman-period

---

1. In some cultures today, the categories active and passive still shape the way people view male same-sex love. See, e.g., Ana Maria Alonso and Maria Teresa Koreck, "Silences: 'Hispanics,' AIDS, and Sexual Practices," *Differences: A Journal of Feminist Cultural Studies* 1:1 (1989) 101–24; reprinted in *The Lesbian and Gay Studies Reader*, ed. Henry Abelove, Michèle Aina Barala, and David M. Halperin (New York: Routledge, 1993) 110–26, esp. 115–20; and Tomás Almaguer, "Chicano Men: A Cartography of Homosexual Identity and Behavior," *Differences: A Journal of Feminist Cultural Studies* 3:2 (1991) 75–100; reprinted in *The Lesbian and Gay Studies Reader*, 255–73.

In the earlier part of the twentieth century, the categories active and passive played a greater role in defining gay male identity in the United States than they do today. See George Chauncey, *Gay New York: Gender, Urban Culture, and the Making of the Gay Male World, 1890–1940* (New York: BasicBooks, 1994); and George Chauncey, "Christian Brotherhood or Sexual Perversion? Homosexual Identities and the Construction of Sexual Boundaries in the

definitions of natural and unnatural: free, adult male citizens ought never be passive, and women should never be active. Should they transgress these boundaries, society deemed their behavior "contrary to nature" (*para physin*). This concept of "unnatural" and its dependence on the active/passive distinction aids us in understanding early Christian condemnations of female homoeroticism and usage of the phrase *para physin*. If early Christians had not condemned sexual relations between women within a gendered framework of active and passive, natural and unnatural, then they would have been unique in the Roman world in so doing.

Roman-period writers presented as normative those sexual relations that represent a human social hierarchy. They saw every sexual pairing as including one active and one passive partner, regardless of gender, although culturally they correlated gender with these categories: masculine as active and feminine as passive. The most fundamental category for expressing this hierarchy was active/passive—a category even more fundamental than gender for these writers. They often defined "passive," that is, penetrated, males as effeminate. Males could be either active or passive (such as when they were boys or slaves), whereas females were always supposed to be passive. The division between active and passive was, therefore, not biological.

Drawing upon a broad range of sources from the Roman world, I illustrate in this book that early Christian views of female homoeroticism closely resembled those of their non-Christian contemporaries. Some prior researchers have tended to take an apologetic pro-Christian stance and to see early Christian sexual values as of a higher moral level than those of their environment. Other researchers have viewed early Christians as proto-Puritanical and repressive in contrast to the more sex-positive pagans around them. My research is more in line with those researchers who see a continuity between non-Christian and Christian understandings of the body.[2] A focus on female homoeroticism makes this continuity clearer than would a focus on male homoeroticism, since nearly all extant sources on sexual relations between women condemn such relations, whereas some Roman-period non-Christian sources express tolerance toward male-male sexual relations, which masks the similarity between Christian and non-Christian understandings of masculinity. Because the reasons for condemning female homoeroticism run deeper than the reasons for promoting

World War I Era," *Journal of Social History* 19 (1985) 189–212; reprinted in *Hidden from History: Reclaiming the Gay and Lesbian Past*, ed. Martin Bauml Duberman, Martha Vicinus, and George Chauncey (New York: Meridian, 1989) 294–317.

2. E.g., Aline Rousselle, *Porneia: On Desire and the Body in Antiquity*, trans. Felicia Pheasant (French original, Paris: Presses Universitaires de France, 1983; London: Basil Blackwell, 1988).

marriage or celibacy (on which there was much debate in the Roman world), there is a cultural continuity of views on female homoeroticism.

Although ancient Christian writers resembled their non-Christian contemporaries in their views on erotic love between women, both groups differed from our own culture in their overall understanding of erotic orientation. Whereas we often dualistically define sexual orientation as either homosexual or heterosexual, they saw a plethora of orientations. (When we in the late twentieth century think about it, we also recognize bisexuals and transsexuals, leading us to speak of a spectrum, rather than a bifurcation.) Their matrix of erotic orientations included whether a person took an active or a passive sexual role, as well as the gender, age, nationality, and economic, legal (slave or free), and social status of the partner. For example, for the second-century astrologer Ptolemy, the configuration of the stars at one's birth determines a person's lifelong erotic orientation. A man born under one configuration is oriented toward females alone; under a second configuration, he desires to play a passive role toward males (i.e., to be penetrated); under a third, he desires to penetrate children; and under a fourth, he will desire males of any age. But the list does not end there. Other configurations give rise to men who desire low-status women, slave-women, or foreigners. In this schema, female homoeroticism constitutes one erotic orientation out of many, rather than a subcategory of two orientations (heterosexual and homosexual). Ptolemy and other authors reveal a gender bias in that they present far more differentiated pictures of the male erotic life than of the female one, even attributing more orientations to men than to women. By keeping in mind the larger picture of ancient classification systems for erotic orientation, the reader will better understand the specific discussions of female homoeroticism that I analyze.

This book contributes to women's history by documenting the existence of woman-woman marriage, of the brutal surgical procedure of selective clitoridectomy for women who displayed "masculine desires," and of women seeking out magical practitioners to help them attract other women. It contributes to the history of sexuality by analyzing the differences between the cultural conceptualizations of female and male homoeroticism in antiquity, by documenting the concept of a long-term or lifelong erotic orientation in ancient astrology and ancient medicine, by demonstrating that nineteenth-century medical writers were not the first to classify homoerotic behavior as diseased, by analyzing the interplay between ancient religious views and understandings of sexual behavior, and by delineating the gendered character of Roman-period understandings of the erotic. It contributes to theology and New Testament studies by explicating the meaning of "unnatural" in Paul of Tarsus and in Clement of Alexandria, by showing Paul's use of natural law theory and of the Jewish law to undergird his teachings about sexual relations and about gender, by clarifying how homoeroticism was an issue of gender in the early church, and by providing a historical-exegetical basis for contemporary church discussions concerning same-sex love. Finally, this project contributes to ancient history generally through the sheer number of sources presented in it. Prior to this study, these sources have never been collected in one place, and some have never been translated.

Terminology

The ancient sources contain terms for female homoeroticism that prior researchers have not systematically studied and that dictionaries have obscured more frequently than explained (as has often been the case with other ancient erotic terms).[3] The ancient and early medieval Greek and Latin nouns designating a woman who has sexual relations with another woman[4] present the contemporary researcher with certain problems of understanding. These nouns include: Greek *hetairistria, tribas, dihetaristria*, and *Lesbia*; and Latin *tribas, frictrix/fricatrix*, and *virago*.[5] The Arabic term *saḥāqa*, which occurs in a translation of a first-century astrologer, is also relevant here. Although Plato uses the term *hetairistria* (related to *hetaira*, which can mean both "courtesan" and "companion"), later writ-

---

3. E.g., LSJ translates τριβάς as "a woman who practises unnatural vice with herself or with other women." This translation depends upon the reader to infer a meaning for "unnatural vice." Further, the sources that LSJ gives for τριβάς do not support the meaning of "one who masturbates." Under ἑταιρίστρια and διεταρίστρια LSJ simply has "= τριβάς." Even the index to *The Latin Sexual Vocabulary* by J. N. Adams does not contain an entry for *tribas* (or for the Greek τριβάς). In spite of this omission, Adams states with confidence (but no evidence), "There is nothing in either context [in the church father Tertullian's writings] to suggest that *frictrix* was a calque on τριβάς" (*The Latin Sexual Vocabulary* [Baltimore: Johns Hopkins University Press, 1982] 184). (In contrast, nineteenth-century scholars recognized the ancient usage of both *frictrix* and *fricatrix* for a woman engaged in sexual contact with another woman; see, e.g., L[udwig] J. K. Mende, *Ausführliches Handbuch der gerichtlichen Medizin für Gesetzgeber, Rechtsgelehrte, Aerzte und Wundärzte*, pt. 4 [Leipzig: Dyk, 1826] 512.) Adams does not go beyond the usual silence on the precise meaning of τριβάς/ *tribas*.
4. I know of no ancient Hebrew or Aramaic noun for such a woman. Hebrew sources use the verb ·ל·ס·ס, "to commit lewdness," "to swing back and forth," for women who engage in sexual relations with other women.
5. The term *subigitatrix* in Plautus, *Persa* 227, might also refer to female homoeroticism, but Saara Lilja suggests that it does not (*Homosexuality in Republican and Augustan Rome* [Commentationes Humanarum Litterarum 74; Helsinki: Finnish Society of Sciences and Letters, 1983] 28). In eighteenth-century Holland, however, the related term *subigatrix* referred to a woman who engaged in erotic behaviors with another woman (Theo van der Meer, "Tribades on Trial: Female Same-Sex Offenders in Late Eighteenth Century Amsterdam," *Journal of the History of Sexuality* 1 [1991] 438).

ers rarely use *hetairistria*. The Greek sources most commonly employ *tribas*, which probably derives from the verb *tribō*, "to rub" (perhaps because women may stimulate one another sexually by rubbing the genital area),[6] but may also derive from *tribakos*, "experienced" (perhaps in the sense of bisexuality, that is, experienced with both women and men). A fifth-century Byzantine dictionary equates the term *dihetaristria* with *tribas*: "women who, like men, are oriented toward female companions for sex, just like *tribades* [plural of *tribas*]."[7] Similarly, a medieval commentator on the second-century author Lucian interprets *hetairistria* as "the same ones whom they also call *tribades*." The commentator then goes on to explain that they "shamefully rub together [*syn*trib*esthai*] with one another."[8] In the same vein, a medieval commentator on the second-century Christian writer Clement of Alexandria equates *tribades, hetairistriai*, and *Lesbiai* (plurals of *hetairistria* and *Lesbia*),[9] which is the earliest known attestation of "Lesbian" (literally, "a female inhabitant of Lesbos") for a woman erotically oriented toward other women.

Latin authors use *tribas* as a loanword, which subtly underscores their view of sexual love between women as a foreign phenomenon, something in which proper Roman matrons would never engage. The early Christian writer Tertullian employs the term *frictrix*, and an ancient astrological work called *The Book of Hermes Trismegistos* uses a variant form of that, namely *fricatrix;* both terms are probably related to the verb *frico*, which means "to rub." The astrologer Firmicus Maternus uses the term *virago*, that is, a female who has masculine qualities, as a gloss on the Greek *tribas*.

All of these nouns demonstrate that people in the ancient Mediterranean had the concept of an erotic orientation with respect to women. They spoke of individual sexual acts and also designated with specific terms women who engaged in those acts.

Furthermore, these terms raise the question whether one term (*tribas, frictrix*, etc.) refers to both female partners in a homoerotic relationship.

6. On Latin (and some Greek) terms to "to rub," "to stimulate" in a sexual sense, see J. N. Adams, *The Latin Sexual Vocabulary* (Baltimore: Johns Hopkins University Press, 1982) 183–85.

7. Hesychios, *Lexikon*, s.v. διεταρίστριαι: γυναῖκες αἱ τετραμμέναι πρὸς τὰς ἑταίρας ἐπὶ συνουσίᾳ, ὡς οἱ ἄνδρες. οἷον τριβάδες (Kurt Latte, ed., *Hesychii Alexandrini Lexicon*, vol. 1 [Copenhagen: Munksgaard, 1953] 451).

8. [Α]ἰσχρῶς ἀλλήλαις συντρίβεσθαι (Hugo Rabe, ed., *Scholia in Lucianum* [Stuttgart: Teubner, 1971] 277). The manuscripts that include this note date from the tenth through the fifteenth centuries.

9. Arethas (whose commentary is dated 914), scholion to *Paidagōgos* 3.3.21.3 (Otto Stählin, ed., *Clemens Alexandrinus*, vol. 1 [GCS; 3d ed.; Berlin: Akademie, 1972] 337). On this passage, see Albio Cesare Cassio, "Post-Classical Λέσβιαι," *Classical Quarterly* n.s. 33 (1983) 296f. For the modern English usage, see R. W. Burchfield, *A Supplement to the Oxford English Dictionary*, vol. 2 (Oxford: Clarendon, 1976) s.v. "lesbian."

The sources that I treat in this book vary on this point. Some sources use, for example, the word *tribades* (plural of *tribas*) to refer to both of the female partners, while others seem to restrict it to the "active" or "masculine" partner.[10]

We have to remember that these same authors use different terms to designate the active and passive male partners in a male-male relationship. For example, they call the active male partner the "lover" (Greek: *erastēs*) and the passive male the "beloved" (Greek: *erōmenos*). Greek and Latin authors also use the terms *kinaidoi* and *cinaedi* respectively to designate passive males as a category of person. According to the cultural ideology behind this terminological distinction, one male partner always plays the active, that is, penetrating role, while the other always plays a passive, receptive role in sexual, particularly anal, intercourse. Social reality was, however, more complex than the ideology.[11] Ancient authors often saw male homoeroticism through the lens of pederasty, within which the adult male was to play the active role and the boy the passive role. While we cannot know whether males always conformed to the ideology, that is, whether the same male always penetrated his partner (rather than alternating roles), this is the model upon which ancient Greek and Latin authors based their terminology for male homoeroticism.

Female homoeroticism presented these authors with a dilemma. If they tried to fit it into a male model of penetrator and penetrated, they encountered the problem that women do not have phalluses, which renders irrelevant the distinction between active and passive. One cultural response to this dilemma was to depict one of the two women as having become like a man, that is, as having a physical organ wherewith to penetrate her female partner (an enlarged clitoris, a dildo, or some unnamed phallus-like appendage). This response, however, created another problem, namely how to designate—and how to evaluate—her "passive" female partner. Was this passive female simply another woman doing what women are supposed to do, namely allowing themselves to be penetrated? In this case she would be socially acceptable, not worthy of the scorn heaped on her "masculine" partner. This solution does not, however, satisfy a number of ancient male authors, who classify both female partners as unnatural, monstrous, or

10. For an analysis of the theoretical reasons for the invisibility in the nineteenth and twentieth centuries of a "feminine lesbian" who has fallen in love with a "masculine one," see Teresa de Lauretis, "Sexual Indifference and Lesbian Representation," *Theatre Journal* 40 (1988) 155–77; reprinted in *The Lesbian and Gay Studies Reader*, ed. Henry Abelove, Michèle Aina Barala, and David M. Halperin (New York: Routledge, 1993), 141–58.

11. For examples in which, even within the context of male-female relations, the man was designated with a passive term, see John Boswell, *Same-Sex Unions in Premodern Europe* (New York: Villard, 1994) 57f, n. 18.

worthy of death. Therefore, some authors classify both females as *tribades*. Perhaps these authors thought of female homoeroticism in terms other than penetrator/penetrated; they may have recognized that women could engage in the broad range of erotic postures and acts known in the ancient world. Or perhaps they saw the "passive" female partner as refusing to conform to the socially acceptable role of allowing herself to be penetrated by a man. In this case, a woman would be called a *tribas* because she did not allow herself to be penetrated by a man and because she was erotically oriented toward women, rather than toward men.

The polemical character of the terminology calls into question the accuracy of ancient authors' depictions of such women. We have no evidence for homoerotically oriented women referring to themselves as *tribades* or *frictrices*. Therefore, we cannot know whether they did or whether these terms were purely the polemical epithets of their opponents. For example, the Latin poet Martial represents a certain Philaenis, "*tribas* of the very *tribades*" as sexually aggressive toward both boys and girls. She "buggers" the boys and batters eleven girls a day, "quite fierce with the erection of a husband." [12] This representation stands out among Roman-period depictions of female homoeroticism in that most writers present adult women sexually encountering other adult women, not girls and certainly not boys. Whereas pederasty served as the model for much of the Greek and Roman discussion of male-male sexual relations (even if it was not the only reality), ancient authors rarely mentioned pederasty in connection with female homoeroticism. How then are we to interpret Martial, and how are we to translate *tribas* in his epigrams? "Lesbian" could hardly be correct, because in our culture "lesbian" does not connote a woman who sexually penetrates boys and girls. The lesbian-feminist political movement promotes sexual relations between consenting adult women and nearly uniformly opposes female-female (and female-male and male-female) pederasty. (In contrast, many gay men and some lesbian women do categorize male-male pederasty as gay, as seen, for example, in support for the North American Man-Boy Love Association, or in the existence of "man-boy love" sections in gay bookstores). Since, however, in antiquity (and throughout history) sexual excesses formed part of the stock polemics against any hated group, perhaps we should translate *tribas* as "lesbian." Christians, Jews, and pagans regularly accused one another of sexual orgies, and yet we still translate the ancient terms for "Christians," "Jews," or "followers of Isis" with their English equivalents, even though we may question whether having sex with one's mother was constitutive of the Greek term for "Christians." The question here is whether Martial's earliest readers took the root

12. Martial, *Epigrammata* 7.67, 70.

meaning of *tribas* to be "a woman sexually oriented toward other women" or "an insatiably phallic woman sexually aggressive toward other women, as well as toward boys and girls." In the first case, Martial's readers may have interpreted his exaggerated depiction of Philaenis's sexual excesses as simply part of his sarcastic, eroticized style. In the second case, they may have seen the adult female homoerotic component of a *tribas* as just one element of a phallic sexual persona. This translation problem in Martial epitomizes a translation dilemma for all of these ancient terms. Throughout this book, I introduce the reader to the ancient terms in the original language and leave them untranslated while I discuss the potential range and nuance of meaning.

For antiquity I generally use the term "homoerotic" rather than "homosexual." "Homoeroticism" has a less fixed meaning than "homosexuality" and is therefore better suited to studying the texts of a culture very different from the contemporary cultures of industrialized nations. Further, in current popular usage, "homosexuality" evokes the image of a man more strongly than that of a woman, which leads to the phrase "homosexuals and lesbians." I use "homoeroticism" to refer to both women and men; when necessary I break it down into "female homoeroticism" and "male homoeroticism" respectively.

Current scholars debate whether we can apply the term "homosexuality" to antiquity. This debate has more than one facet: Did the ancients see individuals as having a sexual orientation at all? And if they did, did they have a concept of a homoerotic orientation that encompassed both women and men? David Halperin, in his book *One Hundred Years of Homosexuality*, has drawn upon the insights of Michel Foucault to argue that homosexuality as a concept, as a characteristic of a person, has existed only for the past one hundred years.[13] Amy Richlin has critiqued this view, especially on the basis of the existence and legal treatment of passive males, called *cinaedi* in Roman society.[14] Like Richlin, I present non-Christian material in this book for a category of persons viewed in antiquity as having

13. David M. Halperin, *One Hundred Years of Homosexuality: And Other Essays on Greek Love* (New York: Routledge, 1990) 15–53. See also Steven Epstein, who notes that our current concept of identity is of very recent vintage. Epstein proposes, however, a "gay 'ethnic' identity" as a means of getting beyond the essentialist/constructionist impasse, which opens the possibility of lesbian, gay, and bisexual history comparable to the histories of ethnic groups, which exist even though ethnic self-understanding and even ethnic boundaries have changed over time ("Gay Politics, Ethnic Identity: The Limits of Social Constructionism," *Socialist Review* 93/94 [May-August 1987] 9–54; reprinted in *Forms of Desire: Sexual Orientation and the Social Constructionist Controversy*, ed. Edward Stein [New York: Routledge, 1992] 239–93, esp. 265–74, 285–93).

14. Amy Richlin, "Not Before Homosexuality: The Materiality of the *Cinaedus* and the Roman Law against Love between Men," *Journal of the History of Sexuality* 3 (1993) 523–73.

a long-term or even lifelong homoerotic orientation. A number of ancient sources that mention female and male homoeroticism together provide further evidence that people in the Roman Empire worked with a concept of homoeroticism that encompassed both women and men. For example, the second-century Christian writer Clement of Alexandria uses one term, *allēlobasia* (literally: "going into one another"), to designate both female and male homoerotic activity. In fact, early Christians, who generally classified both female and male homoerotic activity as sinful, probably played a crucial role in the development of the concept of homosexuality.

Context within Current Scholarship on Same-Sex Love in Antiquity

In this book I build upon the work of other scholars who have studied female homoeroticism in early Christianity and its environment.[15] I have principally benefited from them in that they have done a portion of the groundwork in locating the sources for female homoeroticism, which are

---

15. These include: Ann Pellegrini, "There's No Place Like Home? Lesbian Studies and the Classics," in *Tilting the Tower: Lesbians Teaching Queer Subjects* (New York: Routledge, 1994) 70–82; Boswell, *Same-Sex Unions;* Michael L. Satlow, *Tasting the Dish: Rabbinic Rhetorics of Sexuality* (Brown Judaic Studies 303; Atlanta: Scholars Press, 1995); Michael L. Satlow, "'They Abused Him Like a Woman': Homoeroticism, Gender Blurring, and the Rabbis in Late Antiquity," *Journal of the History of Sexuality* 5 (1994) 1–25; Eva Cantarella, *Bisexuality in the Ancient World*, trans. Cormac Ó Cuilleanáin (New Haven: Yale University Press, 1992); Mary Rose D'Angelo, "Women Partners in the New Testament," *Journal of Feminist Studies in Religion* 6:1 (1990) 65–86; Halperin, *One Hundred Years of Homosexuality;* David M. Halperin, John J. Winkler, and Froma I. Zeitlin, eds., *Before Sexuality: The Construction of Erotic Experience in the Ancient Greek World* (Princeton, NJ: Princeton University Press, 1990); Judith P. Hallett, "Female Homoeroticsm and the Denial of Roman Reality in Latin Literature," *Yale Journal of Criticism* 3 (1989) 209–27; Christine Downing, *Myths and Mysteries of Same-Sex Love* (New York: Continuum, 1989); K[enneth] J. Dover, *Greek Homosexuality* (2d rev. ed.; Cambridge, MA: Harvard University Press, 1989); L. William Countryman, *Dirt, Greed, and Sex: Sexual Ethics in the New Testament and Their Implications for Today* (Philadelphia: Fortress, 1988); David F. Greenberg, *The Construction of Homosexuality* (Chicago: University of Chicago Press, 1988); Geneviève Pastre, *Athènes et "Le péril saphique": Homosexualité féminine en Grèce ancienne*, vol. 1 (Paris: Librairie "Les Mots à la bouche," 1987); Robin Scroggs, *The New Testament and Homosexuality: Contextual Background for Contemporary Debate* (Phildelphia: Fortress, 1983); Saara Lilja, *Homosexuality in Republican and Augustan Rome* (Commentationes Humanarum Litterarum 74; Helsinki: Finnish Society of Sciences and Letters, 1983); John Ungaretti, "De-Moralizing Morality: Where Dover's *Greek Homosexuality* Leaves Us," *Journal of Homosexuality* 8 (1982) 1–17; Peter Coleman, *Christian Attitudes to Homosexuality* (London: SPCK, 1980); John Boswell, *Christianity, Social Tolerance, and Homosexuality: Gay People in Western Europe from the Beginning of the Christian Era to the Fourteenth Century* (Chicago: University of Chicago Press, 1980); Else Kähler, "Exegese zweier neutestamentlicher Stellen (Römer 1,18–32; 1. Korinther 6,9–11)," in *Probleme der Homophilie in medizinischer, theologischer und juristischer Sicht*, ed. Theodor Bovet (Berne: Paul Haupt, 1965) 12–43, esp. 30–32; and Wilhelm Kroll, PW 12.2, s.v. "Lesbische Liebe" (1925) 2100–2102; and PW 2.6, s.v. "Tribas" (1937) 2403. (See also the Bibliography for further literature on the Bible and homosexuality.)

disparate and extremely hard to find. The insightful work of Judith Hallett has proven especially helpful because it provides a theoretical basis for distinguishing between the treatment of female and male homoeroticism in Roman-period sources. In this book, I expand the base of her study. Whereas Hallett focuses on elite Latin authors, I include nonelite sources in Greek, Latin, and Hebrew, which enable us to reconstruct the views of a broader segment of society.

Another scholar whose work has helped me is Mary Rose D'Angelo, who has drawn upon Adrienne Rich's concept of a "lesbian continuum" in order to study female partners in the New Testament.[16] "Lesbian continuum" denotes for Rich a bonding between women, regardless of erotic attraction or behavior. D'Angelo focuses her attention on the missionary pairs Tryphaina and Tryphosa (Rom 16:12) and Euhodia and Syntyche (Phil 4:1), and on Martha and Mary (Luke 10:38–42; John 11:1–12:19), who may have also been missionary partners. She suggests no erotic involvement, but rather examines these women's commitment to each other and to spreading the gospel. D'Angelo's analysis of female-female bonding in early Christianity complements my research.

In contrast to D'Angelo, however, I have not focused on a lesbian continuum in this book, but rather on erotic love between women and on male responses to it, since erotic contact between women elicited such vociferous responses in the early church and its environment.[17] My goal here has been to ascertain the reasons for that vociferousness and to discern how these writers' responses to sexual love between women help us to understand their views on women generally. Against the backdrop of male writers' condemnation and horror of sexual love between women, we can better appreciate the courage of women who committed themselves to female relationships (such as those studied by D'Angelo) that others may have understood as erotic attachments.

John Boswell's groundbreaking and comprehensive books *Christianity, Social Tolerance, and Homosexuality: Gay People in Western Europe from the Beginning of the Christian Era to the Fourteenth Century* (1980) and *Same-Sex Unions in Premodern Europe* (1994), deserve special mention. In the first, he collected and interpreted more Roman-period sources on female

16. Mary Rose D'Angelo, "Women Partners in the New Testament," *Journal of Feminist Studies in Religion* 6:1 (1990) 65–86; Adrienne Rich, "Compulsory Heterosexuality and Lesbian Existence," *Signs* 5 (1980) 631–60; republished with a new foreword and afterward in Adrienne Rich, *Blood, Bread, and Poetry: Selected Prose 1979–1985* (New York: Norton, 1986) 23–75; see also the responses by Martha E. Thompson, *Signs* 6 (1981) 790–94; and by Ann Ferguson, Jacquelyn N. Zita, and Kathryn Pyne Addelson, *Signs* 7 (1981) 159–99.

17. In addition to the more far-ranging term, "lesbian continuum," Rich also speaks of "lesbian existence," which "suggests both the fact of the historical presence of lesbians and our continuing creation of the meaning of that existence" (*Blood, Bread, and Poetry*, 51).

homoeroticism than any scholar since Wilhelm Kroll in the first half of this century.[18] With *Same-Sex Unions*, Boswell provided an invaluable contribution to scholarship with his collection and commentary on a set of medieval Christian liturgical texts. He put forth the thesis that these liturgies served to unite persons of the same sex in long-term love relationships. Both books advanced the scholarship on same-sex love and Christianity far beyond where it had been before his work.[19]

Because the theses of his books do not apply to women, however, Boswell's work requires critique and revision. In *Christianity, Social Tolerance, and Homosexuality*, Boswell argued that in the cities of the Roman Empire people saw "homosexual interest and practice as an ordinary part of the range of human eroticism" and that "[t]he early Christian church does not appear to have opposed homosexual behavior per se."[20] The sources on female homoeroticism that I present in this book run absolutely counter to those two conclusions. Although other feminists and I have critiqued *Christianity, Social Tolerance, and Homosexuality* for its lack of gender analysis,[21] Boswell did not learn from the critique and continued the same pattern in *Same-Sex Unions*. In that book he even wrote of having thought that "no one could possibly argue for falsification of the [gender-imbalanced] historical record even for a worthy cause."[22] On what grounds could he have argued that a focus on sources about women, combined with an analysis of the reasons for their relative paucity, constitutes distortion? Elsewhere, however, although only in a footnote, Boswell implicitly conceded the necessity for gender analysis, although he did not follow through with it: "Roman and Greek writers appear to have found lesbianism peculiar, even when they accepted male homosexuality as ordinary."[23] Boswell failed to explain why Roman and Greek authors employed such terms as "monstrous," "worthy of death," and "contrary to nature" when writing about sexual love between women.

Further, the gender difference in the liturgies presented in *Same-Sex*

18. Hallett's article, " Homoeroticism," however, provides a more convincing framework within which to view the material.

19. Owing to John Boswell's untimely death, I can only offer a posthumous word of gratitude to him. I thank him not only for his scholarship, but also for his interest in my work and especially for his gracious hospitality toward me when I visited him in New Haven in 1983 for the purpose of discussing our common research interests.

20. Boswell, *Christianity, Social Tolerance, and Homosexuality*, 333.

21. E.g., Jane Vanderbosch, "Comment on John Boswell's *Christianity, Social Tolerance, and Homosexuality*," *Signs* 7 (1982) 722–24; and Bernadette J. Brooten, "Paul's Views on the Nature of Women and Female Homoeroticism," in *Immaculate and Powerful: The Female in Sacred Image and Social Reality*, ed. Clarissa W. Atkinson, Constance H. Buchanan, and Margaret R. Miles (Boston: Beacon, 1985) 61–87.

22. Boswell, *Same-Sex Unions*, xxvii.

23. Ibid., 82, n. 150.

Unions in Premodern Europe demands explanation. Almost all of these liturgies focus specifically on men and use pairs of male saints as models for the union. By the title of the book and the gender-neutral style of presentation, Boswell masked the overwhelmingly masculine character of his material. Just as he placed same-sex unions within the context of opposite-sex unions, Boswell needed to discuss male-male unions within the context of male ecclesiastical privilege.[24] Boswell responded to the masculine character of his material by suggesting that women may have been "content to devise their own forms and promises, as they might do today."[25] (This formulation reminds one of whites in the pre–civil rights period speaking of African-Americans as "happy and contented darkies.") The entire thrust of Boswell's book is to lift up the astounding fact of official church recognition of same-sex unions. Why should the official recognition that forms the core of his book have been uninteresting to Christian women? And how did he ascertain that Christian women should have been content to forgo such recognition? Perhaps Christian women who lived in a committed relationship with other women displayed greater skepticism than men toward marriage ceremonies of any kind and preferred to create their own rituals. But in that case, the gender gap is even greater than Boswell presented it. If that were to be Boswell's theory, he would have had to support it with historical documentation and to revise his whole framework to take into account Christian men's desire for and acceptance of ecclesiastical recognition of male-male unions contrasted with Christian women's contented state of privatization and marginalization. Boswell did not put forth this theory, of course, instead assuming a similar location for lesbians and gay men within the church. He even went so far as to suggest that "[t]he general inattention of male churchmen to female homoeroticism may even have been advantageous for women."[26] Although I agree that women in constrained and marginalized circumstances have often devised underground strategies to obtain limited pockets of freedom, Boswell was proposing that women can benefit from ecclesiastical inattention, while in the rest of his book he stressed the value of a tradition of public, ecclesiastical attention.

As part of his attempt to depict early Christianity as accepting of homo-

24. Brent D. Shaw's scathing critique of *Same-Sex Unions* is wrong on some points, but he correctly notes that the texts cited by Boswell "shed more light on a primitive and basic power linkage between men in the ancient Mediterranean, and the rituals attendant on its formation" (*New Republic*, July 18 and 25, 1994, p. 40). Of the many other reviews, see esp. that by Denise Kimber Buell, "Did They or Didn't They?" review of *Same-Sex Unions* by John Boswell, *Harvard Gay and Lesbian Review* 1:4 (1994) 27–29.
25. Boswell, *Same-Sex Unions,* xxviii.
26. Ibid.

sexuality, Boswell pointed to the martyrs Perpetua and Felicitas, noting that the church presented them as paired saints.[27] If Boswell had wished to place Perpetua and Felicitas on a lesbian continuum, examining their connection in terms of bonding together in the face of martyrdom, he might have drawn upon the work of Rich and D'Angelo. But he did not do that. And while Boswell did not explicitly impute to Perpetua and Felicitas a sexual relationship, their serving for him as the feminine counterpart to Saints Serge and Bakchos, who appear in the liturgical texts as the model for male-male unions, creates the impression of church tolerance of erotic love between women. Boswell did not comment on Perpetua's and Felicitas's babies, whose presence attests to their recent erotic relationships with men. Further, Boswell did not address as a problem for an erotic relationship the fact that Felicitas was a slave, while Perpetua was a woman of an elite social stratum. If the relationship were to have been erotic, the power imbalance between a slave woman and an elite woman raises the question whether we would need to classify the sexual contact as sexual abuse, especially since the sexual use of slaves was commonplace in the Roman Empire.

In contrast to Boswell, I do not claim to be writing about both female and male homoeroticism, nor do I claim that my theses apply to both women and men, although I do treat sources on male homoeroticism where they are relevant, and my analysis of gender does contribute to a better understanding of cultural views on masculinity, as well as femininity.

New Testament scholars who have recently focused their attention on homoeroticism within the New Testament have likewise based their theories on male homosexuality. Robin Scroggs's assessment that Paul must have been opposing pederasty's more dehumanizing aspects[28] bears little relation to female homoeroticism, since pederasty was not its principal form. Richard Hays argues that Romans 1 concerns itself with humanity's rebellion against God and that, for Paul, same-sex sexual expression constitutes a "flouting of sexual distinctions . . . fundamental to God's creative design."[29] Hays fails to define those distinctions, to ask why ancient authors view them as natural, or to mention that the Jewish and non-Jewish thinkers who shaped Paul's understanding of nature call for sexual distinctions based on female inferiority. William Countryman correctly recognizes the centrality of impurity for understanding Romans 1.[30] His

27. Ibid., 139–41, 145 (see also fig. 4); Boswell, *Christianity, Social Tolerance, and Homosexuality*, 135f.

28. Robin Scroggs, *The New Testament and Homosexuality: Contextual Background for Contemporary Debate* (Philadelphia: Fortress, 1983).

29. Richard B. Hays, "Relations Natural and Unnatural: A Response to John Boswell's Exegesis of Romans 1," *Journal of Religious Ethics* 14 (1986) 184–215, quote on p. 191.

30. Countryman, *Dirt, Greed, and Sex*, 109–23.

thought-provoking book, *Dirt, Greed, and Sex*, would be even stronger if Countryman delineated more consistently the connections between sexual purity and sexual property by applying gender analysis to the texts. Victor Furnish, however, in his more recent publications, has begun to take the texts' misogyny more seriously.[31] Like their male counterparts, feminist exegetes and historians of women in early Christianity have also largely overlooked the subject of female homoeroticism.[32] Thus, while male scholars writing about sexual relations between males have generally overlooked the gendered and social character of same-sex love, feminist interpreters have largely failed to include female homoeroticism as part of the history of women or as a subject for gender analysis. In contrast, I shall show that the sources on female homoeroticism reveal Roman-period sexual arrangements to be highly gendered, social arrangements.

This Study within the Context of
Ancient Mediterranean Women's History

The women parodied, documented, described, condemned, and addressed in the sources that I analyze here lived in diverse life circumstances. In the highly stratified society of the Roman Empire, we can classify only a tiny percentage of women as upper class. These women enjoyed privileges unparalleled among the vast majority of women in the ancient Mediterranean. The women about whom Martial, Juvenal, or Soranos wrote might have

31. E.g., Victor Paul Furnish, "The Bible and Homosexuality: Reading the Texts in Context," in *Homosexuality in the Church: Both Sides of the Debate*, ed. Jeffrey S. Siker (Louisville, KY: Westminster/John Knox, 1994) 18–35.

32. See, e.g., Beverly Roberts Gaventa, who cites and engages Richard Hays's work on Rom 1:26f in her commentary on Romans, but does not refer to my 1985 article (cited in *New Testament Abstracts*) or otherwise apply a feminist analysis to the passage (in *The Women's Bible Commentary*, ed. Carol A. Newsom and Sharon H. Ringe [London: SPCK; Louisville, KY: Westminster/John Knox, 1992] 316f, 320). Exceptions include Elizabeth A. Castelli, who discusses Rom 1:26f in her feminist commentary on Romans ("Romans," in *Searching the Scriptures*, vol. 2, *A Feminist Commentary*, ed. Elisabeth Schüssler Fiorenza with the assistance of Ann Brock and Shelly Matthews [New York: Crossroad, 1994] 281f); Luise Schottroff, who discusses Rom 1:26f as part of her feminist social history of early Christianity (*Lydia's Impatient Sisters: A Feminist Social History of Early Christianity*, trans. Barbara and Martin Rumscheidt, with a foreword by Dorothee Soelle [Louisville, KY: Westminster/John Knox, 1995] 38f; *Lydias ungeduldige Schwestern: Feministische Sozialgeschichte des frühen Christentums* [Gütersloh: Kaiser/Gütersloher Verlagshaus, 1994] 64f); and Ross S. Kraemer, who includes a little-known love spell commissioned by a woman to attract another woman in *Maenads, Martyrs, Matrons, Monastics: A Sourcebook on Women's Religions in the Greco-Roman World* (Philadelphia: Fortress, 1988) 95, no. 51.

read Martial's or Juvenal's poetry or have called upon the medical services of Soranos. In contrast, the women who heard Paul's letters or early Christian apocalypses read aloud in their church services probably included slaves, freedwomen, and freeborn women engaged in manual labor. The women about whom the second-century Christian writers Clement of Alexandria and Tertullian of Carthage wrote represented a slightly higher economic, social, and educational level of society, because by this time Christianity had come to attract higher-status converts. In addition to social diversity, the sources represent a considerable geographical spread (including the continents of Africa, Asia, and Europe), and thereby ethnic diversity. This broad spread raises the question: About which women's history are we speaking?

This difficulty also presents itself for understanding male ideas about women, since in the Graeco-Roman world, the concept "woman" existed within a complex matrix of citizenship and noncitizenship, freedom and slavery, several economic and social strata, and ethnicity. For example, Aristotle, whose influence extended far beyond his own time, presents "women" as wives of freeborn men. In Aristotle's schema of the household, slaves may be female, but slaves cannot be women. Aristotle, then, and those who followed his mode of thinking, designate as "women" biologically female persons subject to citizen men and set above female and male slaves. "Women" experience both privilege and subjection. Aristotle applies this schema only to Greeks, claiming that barbarians fail to distinguish between females and slaves with the result that for non-Greeks the marital relationship consists of a male slave and a female slave. For Aristotle, the properly run state and the properly run household are organized upon the proper hierarchy. In that hierarchy, slaves are not "women," and wives are not slaves.[33] To the extent to which ancient authors saw *tribades* as "man-like," they may have viewed them as attempting to release themselves from womanly subjection, a womanly subjection associated with the privileges of freeborn persons.

In what follows, I attempt to identify the social location and the ethnic and cultural identity of the author and of the women about whom he is writing, although the sources do not always allow a precise identification. Even though the sources I introduce here represent a broad ethnic and geographical range, I have not found any that clearly represent slave society. The connection drawn in some sources between *tribades* and prosti-

---

33. See, e.g., Aristotle, *Politika* 1.1–2; 1252b–1254a; for an excellent analysis, see Elizabeth V. Spelman, *Inessential Woman: Problems of Exclusion in Feminist Thought* (Boston: Beacon, 1988) 37–56.

tutes might point to enslaved *tribades,* since many prostitutes in antiquity were slaves.[34] The prostitutes who were *tribades* or whom the sources connect with *tribades,* might, however, have been freeborn, higher-earning courtesans who had the economic freedom to choose an erotic relationship with another woman. Thus, the sources, as diverse as they are, may leave us ignorant about homoerotically inclined slave women. And the masculine desires and behavior of which the ancient writers accuse *tribades* are probably counterparts to a womanhood that was never meant to include female slaves. Furthermore, the ancient authors might have applied this concept of womanhood only in a limited way to foreigners and other females of noncitizen families.

So, who were the women toward whom these male writers were responding and what can we know of their life circumstances? The authors themselves constitute the principal hindrance to our knowledge of women who loved women in the Roman world. In no case do we have the direct, unmediated voice of one of these women. Rather, we have a multitude of male sources that portray female homoeroticism in distinctively male terms. Nevertheless, on the basis of a variety of sources from the Roman and early Byzantine periods, we can reconstruct certain aspects of the lives of these women. The awareness of sexual love between women on the part of male authors, ranging from the elite Roman upper classes to both higher- and lower-status provincials,[35] shows that sexual love between women existed both in the city of Rome among elite Roman women and among the lower-status women who comprised the vast majority of women throughout the Roman Empire. The ancient sources range geographically from such great urban areas of the ancient Mediterranean as Rome, Ephesos, Antioch, and Alexandria, to the smaller cities of North Africa and the rural villages of Upper Egypt. Since the extant sources nearly all express disapproval of sexual love between women, fear must have been a common feature of life: fear of discovery, fear of disapproval, fear of reprisals on the part of family members, neighbors, and strangers. In fact, the ancient medical sources for selective clitoridectomy performed on women deemed to have an overly large clitoris or masculine desires give us a sense of the materiality of that fear. The ancient sources for marriage between

34. See, e.g., Hans Herter, "Die Soziologie der antiken Prostitution im Lichte des heidnischen und christlichen Schrifttums," *Jahrbuch für Antike und Christentum* 3 (1960) 70–111, esp. 77–79.

35. Examples of elite Roman writers who address this topic include Seneca the Elder, Martial, and Juvenal. Higher-status provincials showing such awareness include the astrologer and mathematician Ptolemy of Alexandria and the medical writer Soranos of Ephesos. We can also find evidence for this awareness among such lower-status provincials as the Syrian astrologer Vettius Valens or the Christian author of the *Apocalypse of Peter.*

women, however, raise the possibility that many people tolerated female romantic friendship.

This Study within the Context of Lesbian History

What I document in this book is part of lesbian history. I am using the term "lesbian" in its medieval sense of a woman who "behaves like a man" (i.e., usurps a male cultural role) and "is oriented toward female companions for sex."[36] This definition accords with the Roman-period cultural conceptualizations of female homoeroticism in the geographical regions represented in this book. I did not find a historical break in these conceptualizations so sharp as to require me to use different terms for different centuries or regions.

To categorize the analyses of this book as part of lesbian history is not to claim that ancient lesbians thought or lived like contemporary lesbians. For example, I find no evidence of political organizations in antiquity created to promote lesbian rights, nor is there sufficient evidence to speak of a lesbian culture. But these differences also exist today: many lesbians do not promote lesbian civil rights and do not participate in any of the several lesbian cultures in existence. Lesbian existence today encompasses a broad range of political persuasions, stances toward religion, manners of dress and appearance (including the wearing of jeans, hiking boots, lipstick, mink coats, and chiffon dresses), understandings of one's ethnic identity, concepts of the erotic, and forms of relationships.[37] Female romantic friendships and the women in them vary greatly today and have varied over time. In spite of historical differences in the meaning of "lesbian" over time (and within one culture), applying it to the Roman world in the sense in which a medieval commentator applied *Lesbia* to a second-century text opens up the possibility of greater historical depth to current

36. I thank Prof. Thandeka of Williams College for her suggestion that I use a "Kantian theory of knowledge which makes a distinction between the content of concepts (sensations) and the concepts themselves." She proposes that, since the term "lesbian" has remained, even though its content may have shifted from time to time, I can justify its use philosophically, if I clearly define it in a manner suitable to the culture in question (personal correspondence, December 26, 1989).

37. Judith Butler argues that lesbians who conform to a particular concept of what it means to be lesbian are thereby solidifying the constraints imposed upon lesbians in heterosexist and homophobic thought. In her theory, which takes differences among lesbians into account, she proposes that we destabilize the categories of gender and sexual identity that make up heterosexist and homophobic thought ("Imitation and Gender Insubordination," in *Inside/Out: Lesbian Theories, Gay Theories*, ed. Diana Fuss [New York: Routledge, 1991] 13–31; reprinted in *The Lesbian and Gay Studies Reader*, ed. Henry Abelove, Michèle Aina Barala, and David M. Halperin [New York: Routledge, 1993] 307–20).

analyses of lesbian identity and of the religious constructions of gender roles.

To exclude the sources of this study from lesbian history would mean drawing an artificial line. Without Paul, we cannot understand twentieth-century Christian responses to lesbians. Without Roman-period depictions of Sappho, we miss nuances in later cultural representations of Sappho and do not fully comprehend how moderns were able to use Sappho to oppose female poets and to define female deviancy. Without knowledge of the selective clitoridectomy performed on women with "masculine" desires, we might erroneously see nineteenth- and twentieth-century lobotomies and hysterectomies performed on lesbians as absolute innovations. With the material of this book in hand, historians of later periods may now recognize continuations of ancient patterns and practices. This study also gives scholars of later periods of lesbian history a foundation for establishing discontinuities, turning points, and new—more appropriate—periodizations.

Since part of my task in making this contribution to lesbian history is to analyze the specific gender constructions and social-sexual arrangements of the Roman and early Byzantine worlds, I will not use the term "lesbian" in a way that could obscure the historical discontinuities. For example, since some sources appear to use *tribas* to refer to only one of the female partners, I will remind the reader of this discontinuity by using the original term, *tribas*. The historical discontinuities are, however, no greater than with such other terms as "slavery," "marriage," or "family," and yet we have no qualms about applying these terms to historical and cross-cultural phenomena, even though, for example, a "family" can include slaves or not, multiple wives or not, or the legal power of a man to kill family members or not. For this reason, I categorize the material I present here as part of lesbian history, which is as variegated and diverse as any other history.

In keeping with this diversity, recent writers have debated what it means to identify oneself as lesbian, the relationship between lesbian and gender constructions, and in which ways lesbian existence challenges social arrangements.[38] With this study, I intend to contribute historical depth

---

38. See: Linda Garber, ed., *Tilting the Tower: Lesbians Teaching Queer Subjects* (New York: Routledge, 1994); Judith Butler, *Bodies That Matter: On the Discursive Limits of "Sex"* (New York: Routledge, 1993); Henry Abelove, Michèle Aina Barala, and David M. Halperin, eds., *The Lesbian and Gay Studies Reader* (New York: Routledge, 1993); Monika Barz, Herta Leistner, and Ute Wild, *Lesbische Frauen in der Kirche*, with a foreword by Marga Bürig and Else Kähler (2d rev. ed.; Stuttgart: Kreuz, 1993); Irene Monroe, "The Aché Sisters: Discovering the Power of the Erotic in Ritual," in *Women at Worship: Interpretation of North American Diversity*, ed. Marjorie Procter-Smith and Janet R. Walton (Louisville, KY: Westminster/John Knox, 1993) 127–35; Henry L. Minton, ed., *Gay and Lesbian Studies* (New York: Haworth, 1992); Domna Stanton, ed., *Discourses of Sexuality: From Aristotle to AIDS* (Ann Arbor: University of Michigan Press, 1992); Warren J. Blumenfeld, ed., *Homophobia: How We All*

and cultural breadth to that discussion and to analyze the ways in which religious and cultural values affect women's lives by imbuing social arrangements.

Pay the Price (Boston: Beacon, 1992); Julia Penelope, *Call Me Lesbian: Lesbian Lives, Lesbian Theory* (Freedom, CA: Crossing, 1992); Eske Wollrad, Bettina Schelkle, Petra Dlubatz, and Geertje Bolle, "Lesbische Existenz," in *Wörterbuch der Feministischen Theologie* (Gütersloh: Gütersloher Verlagshaus Gerd Mohn, 1991) 243–45; Silvera Makeda, ed., *Piece of My Heart: A Lesbian of Colour Anthology* (Toronto: Sister Vision, 1991); Monique Wittig, *The Straight Mind: And Other Essays*, with a foreword by Louise Turcotte (Boston: Beacon, 1992); Ruth Ginzburg, "Audre Lorde's (Nonessentialist) Lesbian Eros," *Hypatia* 7 (1992) 73–90; Jacquelyn N. Zita, "Male Lesbians and the Postmodernist Body," *Hypatia* 7 (1992) 106–27; *Differences* 3:2: *Queer Theory: Lesbian and Gay Sexualities* (1991); Carla Trujillo, ed., *Chicana Lesbians: The Girls Our Mothers Warned Us About* (Berkeley: Third Woman, 1991); Judith Roof, *A Lure of Knowledge: Lesbian Sexuality and Theory* (New York: Columbia University Press, 1991); Judith Barrington, ed., *An Intimate Wilderness: Lesbian Writers on Sexuality* (Portland, OR: Eighth Mountain, 1991); Diana Fuss, *Inside/Out: Lesbian Theories, Gay Theories* (New York: Routledge, 1991); Judith Butler, *Gender Trouble: Feminism and the Subversion of Identity* (New York: Routledge, 1990); Gloria Anzaldúa, ed., *Making Face, Making Soul/Haciendo Caras: Creative and Critical Perspectives by Women of Color* (San Francisco: Aunt Lute, 1990); Jeffner Allen, ed., *Lesbian Philosophies and Cultures* (Albany: State University of New York Press, 1990); Carter Heyward, *Touching Our Strength: The Erotic as Power and the Love of God* (San Francisco: Harper and Row, 1989); Evelyn Torton Beck, ed., *Nice Jewish Girls: A Lesbian Anthology* (rev. ed.; Boston: Beacon, 1989); Mary E. Hunt, "On Religious Lesbians: Contradictions and Challenges," *Homosexuality, Which Homosexuality? International Conference on Gay and Lesbian Studies*, ed. Dennis Altman et al. (Amsterdam: Schorer, 1989) 97–112; Ann Ferguson, *Blood at the Root: Motherhood, Sexuality and Male Dominance* (London: Pandora, 1989); Christie Balka and Andy Rose, eds., *Twice Blessed: On Being Lesbian, Gay, and Jewish* (Boston: Beacon, 1989); Warren J. Blumenfeld and Diane Raymond, *Looking at Gay and Lesbian Life* (Boston: Beacon, 1988); Pat Califia, *Sapphistry: The Book of Lesbian Sexuality* (3d rev. ed.; Tallahassee, FL: Naiad, 1988); Adrienne Rich, *Blood, Bread, and Poetry: Selected Prose 1979–1985* (New York: Norton, 1986); Barbara Zanotti, ed., *A Faith of One's Own: Explorations by Catholic Lesbians* (Trumansburg, NY: Crossing, 1986); Rosemary Curb and Nancy Manahan, eds., *Lesbian Nuns: Breaking Silence* (Tallahassee, FL: Naiad, 1985); Audre Lorde, *Sister Outsider: Essays and Speeches* (Trumansburg, NY: Crossing, 1984); Trudy Darty and Sandee Potter, *Woman-Identified Women*, with a foreword by Judith Schwarz (Palo Alto, CA: Mayfield, 1984); Carole S. Vance, ed., *Pleasure and Danger: Exploring Female Sexuality* (Boston: Routledge and Kegan Paul, 1984); Robert Nugent, ed., *A Challenge to Love: Gay and Lesbian Catholics in the Church*, with an introduction by Walter F. Sullivan (New York: Crossroad, 1983); Barbara Smith, ed., *Home Girls: A Black Feminist Anthology* (New York: Kitchen Table Press, 1983); Jeannine Gramick, *Homosexuality and the Catholic Church* (Chicago: Thomas More, 1983); Cherríe Morága and Gloria Anzaldúa, eds., *This Bridge Called My Back: Writings by Radical Women of Color* (New York: Kitchen Table Press, 1983); Margaret Cruikshank, *Lesbian Studies: Present and Future* (Old Westbury, NY: Feminist, 1982); Samois, ed., *Coming to Power: Writings and Graphics of Lesbian S/M* (2d rev. ed.; Boston: Alyson, 1982); Susanne v. Paczensky, *Verschwiegene Liebe: Zur Situation lesbischer Frauen in der Gesellschaft* (Munich: Bertelsmann, 1981); E. M. Ettorre, *Lesbians, Women, and Society* (London: Routledge and Kegan Paul, 1980); *Conditions Five* 2:2: *The Black Women's Issue* (1979); Sally Gearheart and William R. Johnson, eds., *Loving Women/Loving Men: Gay Liberation and the Church* (San Francisco: Glide, 1974); Monique Wittig,

But is this book a book about lesbian history and thereby part of the recent burst of research in this area? [39] The problem is more complex than it appears at first sight. Women currently dispute what it means to be a

---

The Lesbian Body (French original, Paris: Editions de Minuit, 1973; New York: William Morrow, 1975; Avon, 1976; Boston: Beacon, 1986); Sidney Abbott and Barbara Love, Sappho Was a Right-on Woman: A Liberated View of Lesbianism (New York: Stein and Day, 1972); and Monique Wittig, Les Guérillères (French original, Paris: Editions de Minuit, 1969; New York: Viking, 1971; Avon, 1973; Boston: Beacon, 1986).

In addition, see the work of Irene Monroe, who delivered a paper at the November 1994 Annual Meeting of the American Academy of Religion on "The African-American Church and Ecclesiastical Heterosexism: Its Effects on African-American Lesbians." Monroe is currently preparing a book-length study that will incorporate the research for that paper.

For theoretical discussions of female bisexuality, see: Marjorie Garber, Vice Versa: Bisexuality and the Eroticism of Everyday Life (New York: Simon and Schuster, 1995); Elizabeth Reba Weise, Closer to Home: Bisexuality and Feminism (Seattle, WA: Seal, 1992), and Loraine Hutchins and Lani Kaahumanu, eds., Bi Any Other Name: Bisexual People Speak Out (Boston: Alyson, 1991).

39. On lesbian history and the history of female homoerotic attraction from the medieval period to the present, see: Neil Miller, Out of the Past: Gay and Lesbian History from 1869 to the Present (New York: Vintage, 1995); Linda Garber, Lesbian Sources: A Bibliography of Periodical Articles, 1970–1990, with an introduction by Lillian Faderman (New York: Garland, 1993); Lillian Faderman, Odd Girls and Twilight Lovers: A History of Lesbian Life in Twentieth-Century America (New York: Columbia University Press, 1991; New York: Penguin, 1991); Martin Duberman, Martha Vicinus, and George Chauncey, eds., Hidden from History: Reclaiming the Gay and Lesbian Past (New York: Meridian, 1989); Monika Kehoe, ed., Historical, Literary, and Erotic Aspects of Lesbianism (New York: Harrington Park, 1986); Judith C. Brown, Immodest Acts: The Life of a Lesbian Nun in Renaissance Italy (New York: Oxford University Press, 1986); E. Ann Matter, "My Sister, My Spouse: Woman-Identified Women in Medieval Christianity," Journal of Feminist Studies in Religion 2:2 (1986) 81–93; republished in Weaving the Visions: New Patterns in Feminist Spirituality, ed. Judith Plaskow and Carol Christ (San Francisco: Harper and Row, 1989); Carroll Smith-Rosenberg, Disorderly Conduct: Visions of Gender in Victorian America (New York: Knopf, 1985); Lillian Faderman, Scotch Verdict: Miss Pirie and Miss Woods v. Dame Cumming Gordon (New York: Quill, 1983); Jonathan Ned Katz, Gay/Lesbian Almanac: A New Documentary (New York: Harper and Row, 1983); Tom Horner, Homosexuality and the Judeo-Christian Tradition: An Annotated Bibliography (American Theological Library Association Bibliography Series 5; Metuchen, NJ: Scarecrow, 1981); Ilse Kokula, Weibliche Homosexualität um 1900 in zeitgenössischen Dokumenten (Munich: Frauenoffensive, 1981); J. R. Roberts, Black Lesbians: An Annotated Bibliography, with a foreword by Barbara Smith (Tallahassee, FL: Naiad, 1981); Lillian Faderman, Surpassing the Love of Men: Romantic Friendship and Love between Women from the Renaissance to the Present (New York: William Morrow, 1981); Lillian Faderman and Brigitte Eriksson, ed. and trans., Lesbian-Feminism in Turn-of-the-Century Germany (Tallahassee, FL: Naiad, 1980); Jonathan Katz, Gay American History: Lesbians and Gay Men in the U.S.A. (San Francisco: Harper and Row, 1976); Vern L. Bullough, Sexual Variance in Society and History (Chicago: University of Chicago Press, 1976); Leslie Parr, editorial supervisor, Lesbianism and Feminism in Germany, 1895–1910 (New York: Arno, 1975); and Jeannette H. Foster, Sex Variant Women in Literature: A Historical and Quantitative Survey (1956; reprint, Baltimore: Diana, 1975).

See also a number of articles in the Journal of the History of Sexuality.

lesbian and who is a lesbian. For example, can we call a woman in a sexual relationship with another woman a lesbian if she rejects the term as a label that she does not wish to have applied to herself? Is a woman a lesbian even if she engages in occasional sexual relations with men? Can women in the West properly term as lesbian Nigerian women in woman-woman marriages? Should we define as lesbian a male-to-female transsexual who so defines herself?[40] The problem becomes more complex when we examine historical materials, especially those from other cultures. If cultures create widely varying sexual arrangements, does it obscure the past to apply to it a term whose meaning has changed over history?

The current debate over the concept of homosexuality is relevant here. David Halperin, for example, argues that applying the concept of homosexuality to antiquity obscures the differences between the ancient Mediterranean world and our own, while John Boswell used the term "homosexual" with ancient and medieval materials.[41] Historiographically, this is a question of periodization, although Halperin, Boswell, and the other debaters have not defined it as such. Halperin argues that the nineteenth-century medicalization of homosexuality and the rise of a homosexual-rights movement created a turning point, a historical break, the beginning of what we might call "The Homosexual Period" within the history of same-sex love.[42] (I will discuss the question of medicalization at greater length in my chapter on ancient medicine.) Boswell argued that there have always been homosexual persons and that more complete historical research might reveal a gay history that so surprises us as to alter our periodization of it. Thus, one could use Boswell's last book to speak of "The Period of Same-Sex Unions."

The questions of periodization and of appropriate terminology pose

40. Jacquelyn N. Zita, "Male Lesbians and the Postmodernist Body," *Hypatia* 7 (1992) 106–27, uses this question to explore the problems of definition posed by this phenomenon. She concludes that postmodern theorists correctly recognize the body as "invented," but thereby pay insufficient attention to the significance of its historical, physical characteristics.

41. Halperin, *One Hundred Years of Homosexuality*, 15–53; Boswell, *Christianity, Social Tolerance, and Homosexuality;* and *Same-Sex Unions.* John Boswell, "Concepts, Experience, and Sexuality," *Differences* 2:1 (1990) 67–87 (see also the literature cited there). See also Ann Pellegrini, "There's No Place Like Home? Lesbian Studies and the Classics," in *Tilting the Tower: Lesbians Teaching Queer Subjects*, ed. Linda Garber (New York: Routledge, 1994) 70–82 (who adapts a Foucault/Halperin model to lesbian studies); and Amy Richlin, "Not Before Homosexuality: The Materiality of the *Cinaedus* and the Roman Law against Love between Men," *Journal of the History of Sexuality* 3 (1993) 523–73 (who critiques Halperin).

42. Eve Kosofsky Sedgwick has criticized Halperin, as well as Michel Foucault, for working with an overly unified concept of "homosexuality as we know it today." She argues that we need to recognize the simultaneous existence of conflicting discourses and conceptualizations within a given period—including our own (*Epistemology of the Closet* [Berkeley: University of California Press, 1990] 44–48).

themselves differently for sexual love between women than for male homoeroticism. To begin with, the terminology for female homoeroticism is
differently distributed through history than that for male homoeroticism.
Writers continually used the term *tribas* and its etymological derivatives
"tribad," "tribadic," and "tribadism"[43] from the Roman period until well
into the twentieth century.[44] And, as we saw above, the Greek word *Lesbia*
occurs in a medieval marginal note on Clement of Alexandria's comment
on women marrying other women, making "lesbian" etymologically the
oldest of any of the terms currently used for persons in same-sex relationships.[45] In contrast, "gay" is several hundred years old, while "homosexual" is a nineteenth-century invention.[46]

Classicists often refrain from using "lesbian" for antiquity because, for
ancient writers, the verbs *lesbiazein* and *lesbizein* (to behave like inhabitants of the Island of Lesbos) generally meant "to perform fellatio."[47]
Thus, Kenneth Dover writes, "I have avoided the words 'lesbian' and 'lesbianism', and for a good reason" and then notes the association of fellatio
with Lesbos.[48] Dover does, however, use the word "homosexual," which
has neither an ancient etymology, being in fact a hybrid of Greek and Latin,
nor a precise ancient equivalent. But the verbs *lesbiazein* and *lesbizein* do
not invalidate my inclusion of material from the Roman period as part of
lesbian history. Historically, we apply new terms to groups of people when
they have so broken with the past as to require them. For example, at a
certain point, ancient Jews who followed Jesus ceased to be Jews and be-

43. Other European languages contain words derived from *tribas*.

44. For examples of American uses of "tribadism" and related words, see Jonathan Ned
Katz, *Gay/Lesbian Almanac: A New Documentary* (New York: Harper and Row, 1983) 197,
350f, and passim. "Tribadism" fell into disuse only a few decades ago.

45. Arethas (914 CE), scholion to *Paidagōgos* 3.3.21.3 (Otto Stählin, ed., *Clemens Alexandrinus*, vol. 1 [GCS; 3d ed.; Berlin: Akademie, 1972] 337).

46. See Jonathan Ned Katz, "The Invention of Heterosexuality," *Socialist Review* 20:1
(1990) 7–34; and Boswell, *Christianity, Social Tolerance, and Homosexuality*, 42f.

47. E.g., Aristophanes (5th C. BCE), *Wasps* 1346; *Frogs* 1308. Lucian of Samosata
(2d C. CE), *The Mistaken Critic* 28, uses λεσβιάζειν . . . καὶ φοινικίζειν to refer to a man,
i.e., others accuse him of "behaving like a Lesbian and a Phoenician" (tantamount to being
both Lesbian and Lebanese), which we should probably take as meaning "one who fellates
and one who performs cunnilingus." For extensive discussion, see H. D. Jocelyn, "A Greek
Indecency and Its Students: ΛΑΙΚΑΖΕΙΝ," *Proceedings of the Cambridge Philological Society*
206, n.s. 26 (1980) 12–66, esp. 30–34; 48 n. 66; 57–61. See also Dover, *Greek Homosexuality*, 182–84; and Judith P. Hallett, "Sappho and Her Social Context: Sense and Sensuality,"
Signs 4 (1979) 451f.

Classicists may also hesitate to use the term "lesbian" for antiquity, because "Lesbian"
connotes first and foremost an inhabitant of Lesbos, such as the lyric poets Alkaios or Sappho.

48. Dover, *Greek Homosexuality*, 182.

came Christians, and English colonists ceased to be English and became American. No one has yet demonstrated a decisive developmental break between late antiquity and the Byzantine period that would require us to speak of *tribades* for antiquity and *Lesbiai* for the Middle Ages. In fact, the Byzantine sources I have cited define as synonymous *tribades, hetairistriai, dihetairistriai*, and *Lesbiai*. The term *Lesbia* in the sense of a woman erotically oriented toward women is not attested until the Byzantine period, because writers only gradually came to decry Sappho as homoerotic, and thereby to associate Lesbos with homoeroticism. This association does have ancient roots, however, for Lucian of Samosata (2d C. CE) defines as *hetairistriai* "masculine-looking women in Lesbos, who are not willing to suffer 'it' from men, but who only consort with women, as though they themselves were men."[49] Further, ancient and medieval writers associate the hellenistic poet Erinna (4th C. BCE) with Lesbos, although she probably came from the Island of Telos.[50] The second-century church father Tatian calls her "Erinna the Lesbian," and an anonymous ancient poem speaks of "the Lesbian honeycomb of Erinna."[51] Since the few remaining fragments of Erinna's poetry display intense emotion toward women, this ancient association of Erinna with Lesbos may have been intentional.[52]

In fact, several terms for female homoeroticism (*tribas, frictrix/fricatrix*, and *Lesbia*) and their modern derivatives have lived long lives.[53] In line with this terminological longevity, sexual love between women may have experienced fewer turning points in history than that between women and men or between men and men.[54] Catharine MacKinnon criticizes a number of historians of sexuality for conceptualizing the field in terms of change, thereby bracketing out the long-term structures of male domi-

49. Lucian of Samosata, *Dialogues of the Courtesans* 5.2; §289: ἐν Λέσβῳ . . . γυναῖκας ἀρρενωπούς, ὑπ' ἀνδρῶν μὲν οὐκ ἐθελούσας αὐτὸ πάσχειν, γυναιξὶ δὲ αὐτὰς πλησιαζούσας ὥσπερ ἄνδρας (M. D. Macleod, ed. and trans., *Lucian*, vol. 7 [LCL; Cambridge, MA: Harvard University Press, 1969] 380) (translation my own).

50. Rudolf Keydell, *Der Kleine Pauly*, s.v. "Erinna."

51. Tatian, *Address to the Greeks* 33; *Anthologia Graeca* 9.190. See also the medieval lexicon, the Suda, s.v. Ἤρυννα, which states that some say that she was from Lesbos, and that she was a friend and contemporary of Sappho.

52. See below for translations of and literature on Erinna.

53. E.g., late eighteenth-century writers in Holland used the term *fricatrices* (Theo van der Meer, "Tribades on Trial: Female Same-Sex Offenders in Late Eighteenth-Century Amsterdam," *Journal of the History of Sexuality* 1 [1991] 438).

54. See Catharine A. MacKinnon, "Does Sexuality Have a History?" in *Discourses of Sexuality: From Aristotle to AIDS*, ed. Domna Stanton (Ann Arbor: University of Michigan Press, 1992) 117–36.

nance and female subordination that so strongly characterize women's experience of sexuality. Contemporary lesbian theorists may have too quickly applied the results of the history of male sexuality to lesbians.[55] For example, no one has demonstrated the level of tolerance for sexual love between women from the Roman through the medieval periods in northern Africa, western Asia, and southern Europe in the way that historians have documented tolerance for sexual relations between males in those periods and regions.[56] If the condemnation of sexual love between women is tied to social structures of male dominance and female subordination throughout those periods and regions, as I will demonstrate that it is in the Mediterranean world of the Roman and early Byzantine periods, then we can expect a lack of major turning points. Although some women's circumstances underwent changes during those periods, the fundamental social structures of male dominance remained intact and the opposition to sexual love between women strong.

The question of erotic orientation versus individual sexual acts also poses itself differently for women than for men. Within a phallocentric framework, identifying objectionable female homoerotic acts is more difficult than recognizing male-male anal or oral intercourse (traditionally known as "sodomitical acts"). Whereas we can define a *kinaidos/cinaedus* as a male who passively receives a male phallus into his body, we cannot so precisely define a *tribas* or *frictrix*. As noted above, since the ancient sources do not clearly define the sexual position and sexual acts of a *tribas*, some sources designate both partners as *tribades*, whereas others call only the "active" partner a *tribas*. And while most sources seem to assume that a *tribas* has sex only with women, according to one source she just prefers women to men. Whereas the ancient authors are rather vague about the sexual acts of a *tribas*, they vividly depict her as one who takes on a male role and male desires.

Historians who have conceptualized female homoeroticism as parallel to male homoeroticism have overlooked crucial historical evidence that could help us understand the history of female homoeroticism and periodize it properly. The selective clitoridectomy performed on women with "masculine desires" is a case in point. Gillian Clark disputes the procedure's relevance for female homoeroticism because the ancient medical writers

55. E.g., Jacquelyn N. Zita, while questioning the postmodern understanding of the lesbian body (using the example of male-to-female transsexuals who identify themselves as lesbian), nevertheless presents a Foucauldian reconstruction of the history of sexuality as authoritative ("Male Lesbians and the Postmodernist Body," *Hypatia* 7 [1992] 108f).

56. Egypt may be an exception, given the evidence for woman-woman marriage and for female homoerotic love spells.

do not explicitly mention *tribades* in their descriptions of the surgery.[57] Only within an adequate framework for interpreting the ancient sources on female homoeroticism can scholars recognize that "masculine desires" is a code word for *tribades*. Later medical texts explicitly connect the selective clitoridectomy with female homoeroticism. But even if medical practitioners occasionally performed the clitoridectomy on women who were sexually aggressive toward men, the procedure's relevance for female homoeroticism remains. As historians—and as observers of the contemporary world—we may have difficulty discerning when a woman suffers an act of hatred or discrimination as a lesbian and when the same act is directed toward her simply as a woman. Future research on the history of the selective clitoridectomy, and on the history of such terms as *Lesbia, tribas, frictrix/fricatrix,* and *saḥāqa,* will help us outline the developments in the history of female homoeroticism. Since cultural constructions of female homoeroticism constitute a subset of cultural constructions of the female, we will need to write that history as part of the history of women.

In another sense, this study contributes to the history of male ideas about lesbians far more than to women's history. The sources bear witness to male constructions of female homoeroticism, rather than to lesbians' perceptions of themselves. To our knowledge, women composed none of the sources that I analyze in this book, although women did commission the love spells, and female scribes may have composed them. I use the sources for two purposes: (1) to understand ancient conceptualizations of female homoeroticism in the context of cultural constructions of the female; and (2) to reconstruct the history of the women against whom these authors were reacting. "Prehistory," the term employed by Mary Daly for the history of women, can help us for this second purpose.[58] With this model, the male silence about the possibility of sexual love between women expressed in the relative paucity of the sources becomes itself a historical datum to be explained. Just as an archaeologist reconstructs the life circumstances of a prehistorical culture on the basis of careful analysis of highly fragmentary evidence, so too shall I make proposals about the life circumstances of ancient women erotically attracted to other women on

57. Gillian Clark, *Women in Late Antiquity: Pagan and Christian Lifestyles* (Oxford: Clarendon, 1993) 90.
58. Mary Daly, *Gyn/Ecology: The Metaethics of Radical Feminism* (Boston: Beacon, 1978) 24; see my use of "prehistory" for early Christian women's history in "Early Christian Women and Their Cultural Context: Issues of Method in Historical Reconstruction," in *Feminist Perspectives on Biblical Scholarship,* ed. Adela Yarbro Collins (Society of Biblical Literature, Biblical Scholarship in North America 10; Chico, CA: Scholars Press, 1985) 66–69.

the basis of male statements about them. At the very minimum, the material I present refutes the view found even in the most recent scholarship that "a Lesbian identity was not an option in late antiquity."[59]

59. Clark, *Women in Late Antiquity,* 90. I am interpreting Clark's term "Lesbian identity" in a nontechnical sense as meaning that women did not have the option of long-term erotic relationships with other women. For a view similar to that of Clark, see Jan Bremmer, "Why Did Early Christianity Attract Upper-class Women?" in *Fructus Centesimus: Mélanges offerts à Gerard J. M. Bartelink à l'occasion de son soixante-cinquième anniversaire,* ed. A. A. R. Bastiaensen, A. Hilhorst, and C. H. Kneepkens (Instrumenta Patristica 19; Dordrecht: Kluwer, 1989) 46.

PART ONE

Female Homoeroticism in the Roman World:
The Cultural Context of Early Christianity

Introduction: Of Sappho, Woman-Woman Marriage, and the Ways of the Egyptians

Monstrous, lawless, licentious, unnatural, and shameful—with these terms male authors throughout the Roman Empire expressed their disgust for sexual love between women. They often represented women who actively sought the love of another woman as physically phallic and culturally masculine. They sometimes classified *tribades* with prostitutes. In short, authors in that period demonstrated both awareness of sexual love between women and disgust for it.

In the chapters of Part I, I analyze four categories of sources for female homoeroticism from the cultural matrix of early Christianity: love spells commissioned by women to attract other women, astrological texts, medical texts, and a dream-classification text. The erotic spells commissioned by individual women whose names we know represent a rare source for the history of ancient women. The other three categories constitute male literary representations of sexual love between women. Before proceeding to this in-depth analysis, I briefly survey a number of other sources on female homoeroticism from the Roman world, which will set the stage for the coming chapters.

Sappho of Lesbos

Many contemporary readers thinking of lesbians in antiquity first think of Sappho, the Greek poet from the island of Lesbos. Since Sappho (7th/6th C. BCE), however, lived long before early Christianity came into the Mediterranean world, I will not interpret her poetry in this book.[1] But because

---

1. The standard edition of Sappho's poetry is: Edgar Lobel and Denys Page, eds., *Poetarum Lesbiorum Fragmenta* (Oxford: Clarendon, 1955). Interpreters who refer to her poems by fragment number are referring to that edition. See also Denys Page, ed., *Supplementum Lyricis Graecis* (Oxford: Clarendon, 1974) 74–76, 87–102, 155, and 158.

educated people in the Roman world appreciated and studied Sappho's poetry, and because her life circumstances elicited much discussion, I will briefly describe Sappho's significance for cultural understandings of female

English translations of Sappho's poetry include: Diane Rayor, *Sappho's Lyre: Archaic Lyric and Women Poets of Ancient Greece*, with a foreword by W. R. Johnson (Berkeley: University of California Press, 1991); Jane McIntosh Snyder, *The Woman and the Lyre: Women Writers in Classical Greece and Rome* (Carbondale: Southern Illinois University Press, 1989) 14–34; Josephine Balmer, *Sappho: Poems and Fragments* (Secaucus, NJ: Meadowland, 1988); Jeffrey M. Duban, *Ancient and Modern Images of Sappho: Translations and Studies in Archaic Greek Love Lyric* (Lanham, MD: University Press of America, 1983); and Mary Barnard, *Sappho: A New Translation*, with a foreword by Dudley Fitts (Berkeley: University of California Press, 1958).

For interpretations of Sappho's poetry and of her history, see: Jane McIntosh Snyder, *Sappho* (New York: Chelsea House, 1994); Eva Stehle, "Sappho's Gaze: Fantasies of a Goddess and Young Man," *Differences* 2:1 (1990) 88–125; John J. Winkler, *The Constraints of Desire: The Anthropology of Sex and Gender in Ancient Greece* (New York: Routledge, 1990) 162–87; André Lardinois, "Lesbische Sappho en Sappho van Lesbos," in *Van Sappho tot de Sade: Momenten in de geschiedenis van de seksualiteit*, ed. J. Bremmer (Amsterdam: Wereldbibliotheek, 1988) 20–35, 180–83; Peter Green, "In Search of Sappho," *Horizon* 8 (1966) 105–11; Sabine Lang, "Sappho—'Lesbierin' oder 'Lesbe' oder: 'Sehr geliebt hab ich, Atthis, dich lange,'" Paper presented at the Lesben-Pfingsttreffen, Hamburg, May 1985; Page duBois, "Sappho and Helen," in *Women in the Ancient World: The Arethusa Papers*, ed. John Peradotto and J. P. Sullivan (Albany: State University of New York Press, 1984) 95–105; Claude Mossé, "Sapho de Lesbos," *L'histoire* no. 63 (1984), 20–23; Jeffrey M. Duban, *Ancient and Modern Images of Sappho: Translations and Studies in Archaic Greek Love Lyric* (Lanham, MD: University Press of America, 1983); Richard Jenkyns, *Three Classical Poets: Sappho, Catullus, and Juvenal* (Cambridge, MA: Harvard University Press, 1982) 1–84; Eric Gans, "The Birth of the Lyric Self: From Feminine to Masculine," *Helios* n.s. 8 (1981) 33–47; Eva Cantarella, *Pandora's Daughters: The Role and Status of Women in Greek and Roman Antiquity*, trans. Maureen B. Fant, with a foreword by Mary R. Lefkowitz (Italian original: Editori Riuniti, 1981; Baltimore: Johns Hopkins University Press, 1987) 71–73; Eva Stehle Stigers, "Sappho's Private World," in *Reflections of Women in Antiquity*, ed. Helene P. Foley (New York: Gordon and Breach, 1981) 45–61; Marion Giebel, *Sappho in Selbstzeugnissen und Bilddokumenten dargestellt* (Hamburg: Rowohlt, 1980); Judith P. Hallett, "Sappho and Her Social Context: Sense and Sensuality," *Signs* 4 (1979) 447–64; Eva Stehle Stigers, "Romantic Sensuality, Poetic Sense: A Response to Hallett on Sappho," *Signs* 4 (1979) 465–71; Paul Friedrich, *The Meaning of Aphrodite* (Chicago: University of Chicago Press, 1978) 104–28; Mary R. Lefkowitz, "Critical Stereotypes and the Poetry of Sappho," *Greek, Roman and Byzantine Studies* 14 (1973) 113–23; Helmut Saake, *Sapphostudien: Forschungsgeschichtliche, biographische und literarästhetische Untersuchungen* (Munich: Schöningh, 1972) (good survey of Sappho research); M. L. West, "Burning Sappho," *Maia* 22 (1970) 307–30; Max Treu, PWSup 11, s.v. "Sappho," (1968) 1222–40; C. M. Bowra, *Greek Lyric Poetry: From Alcman to Simonides* (2d rev. ed.; Oxford: Clarendon, 1961) 176–240; A. J. Beattie, "A Note on Sappho Fr. 1," *Classical Quarterly* n.s. 7, 8 (1957, 1958) 180–83; Reinhold Merkelbach, "Sappho und ihr Kreis," *Philologus* 101 (1957) 1–29; Denys Page, *Sappho and Alcaeus: An Introduction to the Study of Ancient Lesbian Poetry* (Oxford: Clarendon, 1955); Paul Brandt, "Sappho," in *Handwörterbuch der Sexualwissenschaft: Enzyklopädie der natur- und kulturwissenschaftlichen Sexualkunde des Menschen*, ed. Max Marcuse (Bonn:

homoeroticism and for female intellectual life in the Roman and, second-arily, Byzantine periods. The treatment of Sappho and of her life provides a good barometer of sensibilities concerning female homoeroticism in the Roman period. This period saw great appreciation for her poetry and an increasing preoccupation with her love for women, usually expressed in terms of disapproval of that love.

In the twentieth century we have little direct knowledge of Sappho's poetry, because all but a tiny fraction of it is lost; however, in the ancient Mediterranean world, educated people knew and sang her poetry (with musical accompaniment). Numerous ancient writers quoted from her po-etry, including Dionysios of Halikarnassos (1st C. BCE), whose full quota-tion of the poem usually known as the "Hymn to Aphrodite" preserved it for later generations, and Pseudo-Longinos (1st C. CE), who quoted sev-enteen lines of another poem for the purpose of praising its literary quali-ties.[2] Grammarians, stylists, rhetoricians, and specialists in meter took spe-cial interest in Sappho's poetry and preserved a number of lines,[3] while other ancient writers who took an expansive view of world knowledge quoted Sappho with particular frequency.[4] Such Latin poets as Catullus imitated her poetry outright.[5] In later centuries, writers of anthologies, lexicographers, and Byzantine commentators on classical Greek literature

---

Marcus and Weber, 1923) 416f; W. Aly, PW 2/2, s.v. "Sappho," (1920) 2357–85; William K. Prentice, "Sappho," *Classical Philology* 13 (1918) 347–60; and Bernhard Arnold, *Sappho* (Sammlung gemeinverständlicher wissenschaftlicher Vorträge 5th series, no. 118; Berlin: Lü-deritz, 1871).

On Sappho's influence on later poetry, see David M. Robinson, *Sappho and Her Influence* (London: Harrap, 1924).

Recent excavators of the town of Mytilene have discovered a sanctuary of Demeter and Kore, deities whose nocturnal rites were open only to women; see Hector Williams, "Secret Rites of Lesbos," *Archaeology* 47:4 (1994) 34–40.

2. Dionysios of Halikarnassos, *On Literary Composition* 23, 173–79; Pseudo-Longinos, *On the Sublime* 10.1–3.

3. E.g., the grammarians Apollonios Dyskolos, Zenobios, and Herodian; the Greek stylist Hermogenes; the rhetoricians Aelius Aristides and Maximus of Tyre; and the metrist Hephais-tion (all 2d C. CE).

For exact references to these and the authors cited in the following footnotes, see Edgar Lobel and Denys Page, eds., *Poetarum Lesbiorum Fragmenta* (Oxford: Clarendon, 1955); Carlo Gallavotti, *Saffo e Alceo: Testimonianze e frammenti*, 2 vols. (2d enl. ed.; Naples: Li-breria Scientifica Editrice, 1956–57); or Max Treu, *Sappho: Griechisch und Deutsch* (6th ed.; Munich: Heimeran, 1979).

4. E.g., the philosopher Plutarch (1st/2d C. CE) and Athenaios (2d/3d C. CE), who composed a symposium dialogue rich with literary quotations.

5. See Eva Stehle Stigers, "Retreat from the Male: Catullus 62 and Sappho's Erotic Flow-ers," *Ramus* 6 (1977) 83–102; Patricia A. Johnston, "An Echo of Sappho in Catullus 65," *Latomus* 42 (1983) 388–94; and F. E. Brenk, "*Non primus pipiabat:* Echoes of Sappho in Catullus' *passer* Poems," *Latomus* 39 (1980) 702–16.

preserved further precious lines of Sappho's poetry from oblivion.[6] Thus, our limited knowledge of Sappho's poetry derives from these quotations, but also from fragments of her poems written on parchment and papyrus.[7] The papyrus fragments found in the nineteenth century in the ancient town of Oxyrhynchos, Egypt, further demonstrate Sappho's popularity in the Roman period. People who appreciated fine literature appreciated Sappho.

This appreciation had a long tradition. Plato calls Sappho the tenth Muse.[8] The second-century CE medical writer Galen classifies Sappho with Homer: "Homer is called the [male] poet, Sappho the [female] poet."[9] Grammarians such as Terentianus Maurus (2d/3d C. CE) and Marius Victorinus (4th C. CE) refer to Sappho as "most learned" (*doctissima*).[10] From classical Greece to the Roman period, Sappho's intellectual and artistic abilities were beyond dispute.[11]

Like other educated people in the ancient and medieval Mediterranean world, Greek-language Christian writers show familiarity with Sappho's work. Clement of Alexandria (2d/3d C.) quotes a line of her poetry: "Sappho crowns the Muses with the rose: 'For there were no roses from Pieria in the beginning.'"[12] Eusebios of Caesarea (4th C.) states that Sappho

6. E.g., the anthologizer Stobaios (4th/5th C. CE); Eustathios (12th C. CE), a Christian who commented on classical Greek literature; the *Etymologicum Magnum*, a lexicon used by Eustathios; the Byzantine lexicographer Ammonios (of uncertain date); and the *Lexicon of Zonaras* (ca. 13th C.). Photios (9th C.) also showed familiarity with Sappho (*Bibliothēkē* 161.103a; for further references see Gallavotti, *Saffo e Alceo*, no. 85).

7. For a list of the papyrus fragments of her poetry and of ancient commentaries, see Roger A. Pack, *The Greek and Latin Literary Texts from Greco-Roman Egypt* (2d rev. and enl. ed.; Ann Arbor: University of Michigan Press, 1965) 83–85.

8. In the *Anthologia Graeca* 9.506.2; see also 9.571.7.

9. Galen, *Quod animi mores corporis temperamenta sequantur* 4.771.18.

10. See Gallavotti, *Saffo e Alceo*, no. 130.

11. In addition to textual attestations of Sappho's cultural importance, artistic depictions and coins further document her significance. Pollux (2d C. CE) notes in his *Onomastikon* (9.84) that the Mytilenaians minted coins with the image of Sappho; coins from Lesbos containing Sappho's image and dating from the first through the third centuries CE document the accuracy of his claim (Jane McIntosh Snyder, *The Woman and the Lyre: Women Writers in Classical Greece and Rome* [Carbondale: Southern Illinois University Press, 1989], 7; and L. Forrer, "Les portraits de Sappho sur les monnaies," *Revue belge de numismatique* 57 [1901] 413–25). On artistic depictions of Sappho, see Judith Stein, "Portrait of the Poet as Muse: Images of Sappho and Corinne," Paper presented at the Sixth Berkshire Conference of Women Historians, Smith College, Northampton, MA, June 1984; Marion Giebel, *Sappho in Selbstzeugnissen und Bilddokumenten dargestellt* (Hamburg: Rowohlt, 1980); and Helge von Heintze, *Das Bildnis der Sappho* (Mainz: Kupferberg, 1966).

12. Clement of Alexandria, *Paidagōgos*. 2.8.72.3.; see Gallavotti, *Saffo e Alceo*, no. 116; see also *Strōmateis* 4.19.122; Gallavotti, *Saffo e Alceo*, no. 80.

flourished in the second year of the forty-fifth Olympiad (= 598 BCE).[13] Gregory of Nazianzos (4th C.) shows first-hand knowledge of Sappho's poetry.[14] Byzantine Christian scholars acknowledge without further comment Sappho's significance for cultural history. In his widely read chronology of the world (i.e., of the Mediterranean world) the sixth-century historian Joannes Malalas notes that "In those times, Sappho was recognized as the premier poet [f.: *mousikē*]."[15] In the ninth century, Photios, the well-educated Patriarch of Constantinople, mentions "the eighth volume of Sappho," from which we may deduce that many more of Sappho's writings were available to Photios in the ninth century than to us in the twentieth.[16] In the twelfth century, Eustathios of Thessaloniki composed an extensive commentary on Homer's *Iliad*, in which he refers numerous times to Sappho and preserves some lines of her poetry.[17] Latin patristic writers and works that mention Sappho include Jerome (4th/5th C.), Augustine (4th/5th C.), Isidore of Seville (7th C.), Donatus Ortigraphus (after 650, perhaps 815), and the Polythecon (after 1366).[18] All of this shows that for Christian writers who appreciated Greek culture, Sappho was an indisputable part of the landscape, a figure whose writings one could not ignore or dismiss.[19]

13. According to Jerome's translation of Eusebios's *Chronicle;* see Gallavotti, *Saffo e Alceo,* no. 10; or Max Treu, *Sappho: Griechisch und Deutsch* (6th ed.; Munich: Heimeran, 1979) 108f.

14. See Quintino Cataudella, "Saffo e i Bizantini," *Revue des études grècques* 78 (1965) 66–69; and W. J. W. Koster, "Sappho apud Gregorium Naziazenum," *Mnemosyne* ser. 4, vol. 17 (1964) 374.

15. Joannes Malalas, *Chronographia* 72.2.

16. Photios, *Bibliothēkē*, 161.103a; see also 167.114b.

17. Eustathios (12th-C. Christian writer), *Commentary on Homer's* Iliad (M. van der Valk, ed., *Eustathii archiepiscopi Thessalonicensis commentarii ad Homeri Iliadem pertinentes*, 3 vols. [Leiden: Brill, 1971–79], 2.637.14–16, and passim).

18. Jerome, *Prologus in libro Iob de hebraeo translato* 32–34, in *Biblia sacra iuxta vulgatam versionem*, ed. Robert Weber et al., vol. 1 (3d ed.; Stuttgart: Deutsche Bibelgesellschaft, 1983) 731f; Augustine, *De musica* 2.7.14; Giovanni Marzi, ed., *Aurelii Augustini De musica* (Florence: Sansoni, 1969) 206, 208; Isidore of Seville, *Etymologiarum sive originum libri xx* 1.39.7; W. M. Lindsay, ed., *Isidori Hispalensis Episcopi Etymologiarum sive originum libri xx*, vol. 1 (Oxford: Clarendon, 1911); Donatus Ortigraphus, *De littera* 411; John Chittenden, ed., *Donatus Ortigraphus Ars Grammatica* (*Corpus Christianorum Continuatio Mediaeualis* 40D; Turnhout: Brepols, 1982) 23; and *Polythecon* 8.19.411; A. P. Orbán, ed., *Polythecon* (*Corpus Christianorum Continuatio Mediaeualis* 93; Turnhout: Brepols, 1990) 202.

19. Since the Byzantine references to Sappho apparently break off sharply after the twelfth century, scholars have suggested that the Crusaders could have destroyed her writings, along with those of other ancient Greek authors; see e.g., Gy. Moravcsik, who gives a full discussion of the Byzantine reception of Sappho ("Sapphos Fortleben in Byzanz," *Acta Antiqua* 12 [1964] 473–79).

But another side to the history of Sappho is the almost obsessive preoccupation with her erotic inclinations. In the few remaining fragments of
her poetry Sappho writes about love between women and men and love for
a child that was probably her daughter, but her poetry also contains quite
explicit references to her love for women.[20] During Sappho's own lifetime,
we hear neither of disapproval of her erotic inclinations nor of debate about
them, but in later centuries, wild speculation ruled the day. At least six
playwrights in classical Athens composed comedies entitled "Sappho,"
making her the butt of their ribald jokes.[21] The sparse fragments of these
plays that have survived do not, however, present Sappho as sexually involved with women, and one even represents her as having two male lovers.[22] The first-century BCE Latin poet Horace, who praises Sappho as a
poetic model, employs the enigmatic phrase "masculine Sappho,"[23] which
some modern interpreters have taken to refer to the muscularity of her
poetry, the strength of her meter, or to an "artistic sense more comparable
to that of a man than of a weak woman."[24] By sharply distinguishing be-

20. See Fragments 1, 16, 31, 94 (numbered according to the edition of Lobel and Page);
for discussion, see, e.g., K[enneth] J. Dover, *Greek Homosexuality* (2d rev. ed.; Cambridge,
MA: Harvard University Press, 1989) 173–82; and Jane McIntosh Snyder, *The Woman and
the Lyre: Women Writers in Classical Greece and Rome* (Carbondale: Southern Illinois University Press, 1989), 13–28.

21. See Theodor Kock, ed., *Comicorum Atticorum Fragmenta*, vol. 1 (Leipzig: Teubner,
1880; reprint, Utrecht: Hes, 1976) 674, no. 16 (Ameipsias, 5th/4th C. BCE); vol. 2.1 (Leipzig: Teubner, 1884) 94–96, no. 196 (Antiphanes, 4th C. BCE); 246, no. 32 (Amphis, 4th C.
BCE); 262, no. 20 (Ephippos, 4th C. BCE); 464, no. 30 (Timokles, 4th C. BCE); 564, nos. 69f
(Diphilos, 4th/3d C. BCE). The comic poet Epikrates (4th C. BCE) describes Sappho as a
composer of love songs: ibid., vol. 2.1, 284, no. 4. See also Dover, *Greek Homosexuality*, 174.

For the theory of a parody of Sappho in Euripides, see Massimo Di Marco, "Una parodia
di Saffo in Euripide (*Cycl.* 182–186)," *Quaderni Urbinati di Cultura Classica* n.s. 5 (1980)
39–45.

Aristotle's views on Sappho as a woman shaped later thinking about her. At one point he
writes, "[T]he Mytilenaians [honored] Sappho, although she was a woman" (*Technē Rhētorikē* 2.23.11; 1398b). At another point Aristotle quotes Sappho and then goes on to
say, "Virtues and actions are nobler, when they proceed from those who are naturally worthier,
for instance, from a man rather than from a woman" (*Technē Rhētorikē* 1.9.20; 1367a; ET:
John Henry Freese, *Aristotle*, vol. 22, *The "Art" of Rhetoric* [LCL; Cambridge, MA: Harvard
University Press, 1926] 95).

22. See Kock, ed., *Comicorum Atticorum Fragmenta*, vol. 2.1, 564, no. 69f (Diphilos,
4th/3d C. BCE).

23. Horace, *Carmina* 4.9.10; *Epistulae* 1.19.28: *mascula Sappho*; Friedrich Klingner, ed.,
Q. Horati Flacci Opera (Leipzig: Teubner, 1959) 274.28.

24. Adolf Kiessling, *Q. Horatius Flaccus: Briefe* (7th ed. reworked by Richard Heintze;
Berlin: Weidmann, 1961) 184, no. 28. Porphyrion (3d C. CE) commented on this passage
that Sappho was "masculine" either because of her poetic skill or because of her homoeroticism.

tween intellectual and erotic "masculinity," however, these interpreters may be overlooking a connection made by the ancients between the two. Horace elsewhere refers to Sappho's attraction to other women and speaks of the "masculine libido" of a witch named Folia of Arminum. An ancient commentator interprets this "masculine libido" as referring to sex with women and mentions Sappho as an example of that phenomenon.[25] The earliest extant Sappho biography (2d/3d C. CE) notes, "She has been accused by some of immorality [literally: "of being disorderly with respect to her mode of life"] and of being a lover of women."[26] This biography may be drawing upon earlier traditions about Sappho.[27] Both Plutarch (1st/2d C. CE) and Maximus of Tyre (2d C. CE) compare her with Sokrates, who was known for his preference for males.[28] Ovid (1st C. BCE–1st C. CE)

On Horace, see also: W. S. M. Nicoll, "Horace's Judgement on Sappho and Alcaeus," *Latomus* 45 (1986) 603–8; and David A. Campbell, "Aeolium Carmen: Horace's Allusions to Sappho and Alcaeus," *Echos du Monde Classique: Classical News and Views* 22 (1978) 94–98.

25. Horace, *Carmina* 2.13.24f; *Epodi* 5.41f; for the scholion, see Otto Keller, *Pseudacronis Scholia in Horatium Vetustiora*, vol. 1 (Stuttgart: Teubner, 1967) 398.

26. Papyrus Oxyrhynchus 15.1800, fr. 1.16–19: κ[α]τηγορηται/ δ υπ εν[ι]ω[ν] ως ατακτος ου/[σα] τον τροπον και γυναικε/[ρασ]τρια (Bernard P. Grenfell and Arthur S. Hunt, eds. and trans., *The Oxyrhynchus Papyri*, pt. 15 [London: Egypt Exploration Society, 1922] 138f). Max Treu points out that the Oxyrhynchos biography gives two alternate names for Sappho's father, while the medieval Suda gives five (I count seven) additional names (the Suda, s.v. Σαπφώ [Ada Adler, ed., *Suidae Lexicon* (Lexicographici Graeci 1; pt. 4; Leipzig: Teubner, 1935) 322f]), which could mean that at least seven (or nine) different biographies of Sappho existed in late antiquity (Treu, *Sappho: Griechisch und Deutsch* [6th ed.; Munich: Heimeran, 1979] 234).

The Oxyrhynchos biography reflects ancient debates concerning Sappho's physical appearance; it describes Sappho as ugly, small, and dark-complected. Other ancient authors, including Plato (representing the view of Sokrates), Plutarch, Flavius Claudius, Themistios, the Christian writer Eustathios, and the Byzantine writer Anna Commena, describe her as beautiful. The relationship between representations of her physical appearance and of her erotic orientation is a complicated one. E.g., whereas the Oxyrhynchos biography depicts her as ugly, small, dark, and accused of "shameful love," Plutarch dubs her "the beautiful Sappho." He does this in the context of describing Sappho's love-sickness at the appearance of her female beloved, that is, on the assumption of a homoerotic tendency on her part (*Moralia: Erōtikos* 763A).

On this biography in the context of conventions of ancient biographies of Greek poets, see Mary R. Lefkowitz, *The Lives of the Greek Poets* (Baltimore, MD: Johns Hopkins University Press, 1981) 36f.

27. The biographer Chamaileon (mentioned in the same fragment a few lines later) wrote a monograph on Sappho and may have laid the groundwork for later tradition (see Dover, *Greek Homosexuality*, 174).

28. Plutarch, *Moralia: The Oracles at Delphi* 406A; Maximus of Tyre 18.7. Maximus of Tyre speaks of Sokrates' love for "males," which could include boys, but of Sappho's love for "women."

writes that she loved girls.²⁹ According to the Suda, a medieval lexicon that contains many earlier traditions, Sappho was accused by some of "shameful love" for women.³⁰ Thus, writers of the Roman period showed increased preoccupation with Sappho's love for women, often combined with disapproval of that love. This fits in well with a broader development for the Roman period as a whole: an increased attention to and vehement rejection of sexual relations between women.

At several points in history, people have used this negative representation of Sappho's homoeroticism against female poets and intellectuals. Marilyn Skinner has shown that the poetry of Nossis (3d C. BCE), who chose Sappho as her literary model, may have been expunged from ancient anthologies owing to its homoerotic character and the increasing disrepute of Sappho.³¹ The Latin poet Martial (1st/2d C. CE) mentions Sappho in the context of an ironic description of a female intellectual named Theophila, whose chastity Martial seems to need to stress.³² Lucian of Samosata (2d C. CE) writes sarcastically about wealthy women who want to be cultured, who show an interest in philosophy, and who compose songs like Sappho's.³³ And in the seventeenth century, German women who placed themselves in the tradition of Sappho met the stern opposition of German men who disputed their right to compose poetry by representing Sappho as licentious and immoral.³⁴ Discrediting Sappho as a woman who loved women thereby served to discredit women's artistic and intellectual pursuits.

29. Ovid, *Tristia* 2.365f.
30. The Suda, s.v. Σαπφώ, 322f.
31. Marilyn B. Skinner, "Sapphic Nossis," *Arethusa* 22 (1989) 5–18.
32. Martial, *Epigrammata* 7.69.
33. Lucian of Samosata, *On Salaried Posts in Great Houses* 36. See also Philostratos's (2d C. CE) depiction of an intellectual (ἡ σοφή) named Damophyle, who had been with Sappho and imitated her by gathering around herself a group of girls and composing both erotic and hymnic poetry. Philostratos's representation contains within itself the ambiguities of the traditions about Sappho. The verb for Damophyle's associating with Sappho (ὁμιλέω) ranges in meaning from "to be the pupil of" to "to have sexual intercourse with" to "to converse with" or "to be in the company of." Philostratos applies the noun related to this verb (ὁμιλητρία) to the girls that Damophyle gathered around herself. The text tantalizes the reader by equivocating on whether Damophyle was Sappho's lover, her pupil, her friend, or her colleague in poetic endeavors. It also invites multiple interpretations of Damophyle's relationship to the girls she gathered about herself—pederastic or pedagogical? The male model of Greek pederasty shimmers through the text. Philostratos does not outright say that anyone had sex with anyone; he simply employs ambiguous terminology (Philostratos, *The Life of Apollonios of Tyana* 1.31; F. C. Conybeare, ed. and trans., *Philostratus: The Life of Apollonius of Tyana*, vol. 1 [LCL; Cambridge, MA: Harvard, 1912] 84–87).
34. See Marion Giebel, *Sappho in Selbstzeugnissen und Bilddokumenten dargestellt* (Hamburg: Rowohlt, 1980) 135f; and Gisela Brinker-Gabler, *Deutsche Dichterinnen vom 16. Jahrhundert bis zur Gegenwart* (Frankfurt: Fischer, 1978) 34f.

In antiquity, Sappho, as well as other female poets, educated women, or famous women, served as reminders of women's intellectual and artistic abilities. We can discern this function in the lists of educated women, famous women, or female poets occasionally employed by ancient writers, although these writers may not have used them for that purpose. Some authors list Sappho together with one or more of the following female poets: Erinna, Korinna, Telesilla, Nossis, Praxilla, Moiro, Myrtis, and Anyte,[35] or with such other notable women as the warrior Rhodogoune, Queen Semiramis of Assyria, or the lawgiver Demonassa of Cyprus.[36]

Against this background, we can better assess the impact of the Assyrian Christian writer Tatian (2d C.), who drew upon and embellished prior traditions. Tatian defends Christianity against the charge that women, boys, and girls talk nonsense at Christian meetings by attacking non-Christian Greeks for the disgrace their women bring upon them. By way of example, he chastises the sculptors who memorialized the following

35. E.g., *Anthologia Graeca* (Antipatros of Thessalonike) 9.26.4; Clement of Alexandria, *Strōmateis* 4.19.122.4; and Eustathios, *Commentary on Homer's* Iliad; van der Valk, ed., *Eustathii commentarii ad Homeri Iliadem*, 1.509. ET: Diane Rayor, *Sappho's Lyre: Archaic Lyric and Women Poets of Ancient Greece*, with a foreword by W. R. Johnson (Berkeley: University of California Press, 1991) 109–37; Jane McIntosh Snyder, *The Woman and the Lyre: Women Writers in Classical Greece and Rome* (Carbondale: Southern Illinois University Press, 1989) 38–98; Sylvia Barnard, "Hellenistic Women Poets," *Classical Journal* 73 (1977–78) 204–13; and Georg Luck, "Die Dichterinnen der griechischen Anthologie," *Museum Helveticum* 11 (1954) 170–87.

On Erinna, see: Averil and Alan Cameron, "Erinna's Distaff," *Classical Quarterly* n.s. 19 (1969) 285–88; Felix Scheidweiler, "Erinnas Klage um Baukis," *Philologus* 100 (1956) 40–51; Kurt Latte, "Erinna," *Nachrichten der Akademie der Wissenschaften in Göttingen aus dem Jahre 1953*, 1. Philologisch-Historische Klasse (1953) 79–94; and C. M. Bowra, "Erinna's Lament for Baucis," in *Greek Poetry and Life: Essays Presented to Gilbert Murray on His Seventieth Birthday* (Oxford: Clarendon, 1936) 325–42.

On Korinna, see: D[enys] L. Page, ed., *Poetae Melici Graeci* (Oxford: Clarendon, 1962) 325–45; and D[enys] L. Page, *Corinna* (London: Society for the Promotion of Hellenic Studies, 1953) (edition and commentary); and Madelyn Gutwirth, "*Corinne*, or the Appropriation of Allegory," Paper presented at the Sixth Berkshire Conference of Women Historians, Smith College, Northampton, MA, June 1984.

36. E.g., Dio Chrysostom, *Discourses* 64.2. See also the authors who list Sappho together with Alkaios, her fellow lyric poet from Lesbos; with the male lyric poets Pindar, Anakreon, and Simonides; or with the playwrights Euripides, Sophokles, and Menander (e.g., Eustathios, *Commentary on Homer's* Iliad 1.641; 2.194; Himerios [4th-C. teacher of the church fathers Gregory of Nazianzos and Basil the Great], *Declamations and Orations* 17.4; 28.7; and Themistios, *Epitaphios epi tọ patri* 236.c.5).

Pseudo-Lucian (4th C. CE) has a character in a dialogue list Sappho together with the poet Telesilla and the Pythagorean philosopher Theano. The context is what would happen if women could participate in politics; Sappho and these other honored women serve as examples of women eminently capable of speaking on their own behalf (Pseudo-Lucian, *Erōtes* 30).

38

CHAPTER TWO

female poets through statues: Praxilla, Learchis, Sappho the prostitute, Erinna the Lesbian, Myrtis, Myro the Byzantine, Praxagoris, Kleito, Anyte, Telesilla, Nossis, Mnesarchis the Ephesian, Korinna, and Thaliarchis the Argive.[37] With this move, Tatian discredits a long tradition of female intellectual pursuit and accomplishment. He even goes beyond dubbing Sappho a prostitute and calls her a "love-crazy harlot of a woman, who sang her own licentiousness."[38] Discrediting the intellectual achievements of Sappho by attacking her sexual life may well have contributed to the loss of nearly all of Sappho's writings, as well as those of other women associated with her in any way.[39]

Throughout history scholars have devised ingenious methods for rescuing Sappho the poet from the disrepute into which she had fallen. The conflicting stories about Sappho's erotic life led to numerous permutations over the centuries, of which I will review just a few. In the fourth or third century BCE, a hellenistic historian by the name of Nymphodoros argued that, in addition to the poet Sappho, there had existed a prostitute named Sappho, who fell in love with a young man named Phaon. Nymphodoros may have himself invented this bifurcation of Sappho, perhaps to rescue the poet from ill repute.[40] The Phaon legend played a significant role in how subsequent generations viewed Sappho. In the "Letter of Sappho to Phaon," attributed to Ovid (1st C. BCE–1st C. CE), the Roman-period "Sappho" speaks of her tragic love for Phaon, a handsome ferryman, and of her plan to cast herself off the White Rock of Leukas as a result of her unrequited love.[41] This letter enjoyed widespread distribution and shaped

37. Tatian, *Address to the Greeks* 33.

38. Tatian, *Address to the Greeks* 33: γύναιον πορνικὸν ἐρωτομανές, καὶ τὴν ἑαυτῆς ἀσέλγειαν ᾖδει (Molly Whittaker, ed. and trans., *Tatian:* Oratio ad Graecos *and Fragments* [Oxford: Clarendon, 1982] 62).

39. Some have claimed that Christians actually burned Sappho's books as immoral, but the evidence for this is sparse and late; see Henry Tristam, "The Burning of Sappho," *Dublin Review* 197 (1935) 137–49. Snyder, *The Woman and the Lyre,* 10, agrees that the ancient evidence does not support the hypothesis of systematic burning. Discrediting these poets' characters and their writings could, however, have resulted in the neglect of their work, which is as certain a road to oblivion as burning.

40. Nymphodoros, quoted in Athenaios, *Deipnosophistai* 13.70; 596e. See Max Treu, *Sappho: Griechisch und Deutsch* (6th ed.; Munich: Heimeran, 1979) 235. The playwright Menandros (4th/3d C. BCE) also writes about the story of Sappho, Phaon, and the cliffs, which I shall discuss shortly (fr. 258).

41. *Heroides* 15. The letter may be a later interpolation into Ovid's work; see R[ichard] J. Tarrant, "The Authenticity of the Letter of Sappho to Phaon (*Heroides* XV)," *Harvard Studies in Classical Philology* 85 (1981) 133–53. Only later Ovid manuscripts contain the letter, and an early translation into Greek does not contain it; see Arthur Palmer, ed., *P. Ovidius Nasonis: Heroides with the Greek Translation of Planudes* (Hildesheim: Olms, 1967) 91f. For

later artistic representations of Sappho. The "Letter of Sappho to Phaon" mentions that Sappho once loved Anactoria, Atthis, and other women mentioned in her poems, but had ceased to do so at the point of her love affair with Phaon. Plutarch (1st/2d C. CE) was also familiar with the Leukadian cliff story, but does not seem to see any contradiction between it and his homoerotic interpretation of one of her poems.[42] Seneca the Elder (ca. 55 BCE–40 CE) derides a grammarian named Didymus whose extensive and irrelevant research included a discussion of "whether Sappho was a prostitute."[43] Strabo (1st C. BCE–1st C. CE) repeats the story of Sappho's involvement with Phaon and of her casting herself off the White Rock of Leukas.[44] Like Nymphodoros, Aelian (2d/3d C. CE) speaks of two Sapphos, one the poet and the other a prostitute.[45] The medieval lexicon, the Suda, speaks of two Sapphos from Lesbos, one a poet with three friends toward whom she was accused of having a "shameful love,"[46] even though she was married to a man named Kerkylas from Andros. These names are probably a play on words, since *kerkos* means "penis," and "Andros" means "man"—tantamount to saying that Sappho was married to a Mr. Putzhead from He-mansville.[47] The second Sappho mentioned by the Suda was a harpist who cast herself off the White Rock of Leukas out of love for Phaon.[48]

Centuries later, when Anne LeFèvre Dacier (17th C.) introduced Sappho to a French audience, she fervently insisted upon the historicity of the Phaon legend, thereby opposing any notion of Sappho's involvement with

---

the view that Ovid wrote the piece as a young man, see Heinrich Dörrie, "Sappho an Phaon: Eine Dichtung des jungen Ovid," *Acta Philologica Aenipotana* 3 (1976) 24–26.

See also Ovid, *Tristia* 2.365, in which he writes of Sappho of Lesbos having taught girls to love.

42. Plutarch, *Centuria* 1.29.2. On Plutarch's interpretation of fragment 31, see Dover, *Greek Homosexuality*, 179. Plutarch expresses his great admiration for Sappho's poetry by quoting it numerous times, and in his eyes, Sappho, as the only erotic female poet, was singular among women (Plutarch, *Moralia: On the Pythian Oracle* 406A, 23).

43. Lucius Annaeus Seneca, *Letter to Lucilius* 88.37: *an Sappho publica fuerit* (L. D. Reynolds, ed., *L. Annaei Senecae: Ad Lucilium Epistulae Morales*, vol. 1 [Oxford: Clarendon, 1965] 88.15).

44. Strabo, *Geography* 10.2.9.

45. Claudius Aelian, *Varia historia* 12.19.

46. Atthis, Telesippa, and Megara (the Suda, s.v. Σαπφώ; Ada Adler, ed., *Suidae Lexicon* [Lexicographici Graeci 1; pt. 4; Stuttgart: Teubner, 1935] 322f). On this biography, see Mary R. Lefkowitz, *The Lives of the Greek Poets* (Baltimore, MD: Johns Hopkins University Press, 1981) 64.

47. W. Aly suggests that comic playwrights may have invented the name Kerkylas (PW 2.2, s.v. "Sappho" [1920] 2361).

48. The Suda, s.v. Σαπφώ; Adler, ed., *Suidae Lexicon*, 322f.

women.[49] In the early nineteenth century, a German scholar named Friedrich Gottlieb Welcker attempted to rescue Sappho's womanly honor by opposing any notion of homoerotic activity on her part.[50] Similarly, in the early twentieth century, the influential German classicist Ulrich von Wilamowitz-Moellendorff tried to rescue Sappho's honor by claiming that she was a virtuous married woman and headmistress of a girl's boarding school.[51] Strikingly, the 1913 publication in Berlin of Wilamowitz's piece coincided with an active Berlin lesbian movement at that time.[52] We need further research on how the aforementioned interpretations of Sappho's life circumstances may relate to the interpreters' responses to female romantic friendship in their own societies.

While Sappho interpreters today claim neither that she fell in love with a man named Phaon, nor that she was a prostitute, the precise circumstances of her erotic life still remain in dispute.[53] Since in this study I am not focusing on the historical Sappho, but rather on the reception of Sappho in later centuries, I cannot give a detailed analysis of the historical evidence for her life circumstances. A major direction in current Sappho research is to read the few remaining fragments of her poetry as containing homoerotic allusions.[54] Sexual unorthodoxy runs like a thread through all of these conflict-

49. See Joan DeJean, *Fictions of Sappho 1546–1937* (Chicago: University of Chicago Press, 1989) 58f.

50. F[riedrich] G[ottlieb] Welcker, "Sappho von einem herrschenden Vorurtheil befreyt" (1816), in *Kleine Schriften zur Griechischen Litteraturgeschichte*, pt. 2 (Bonn: Weber, 1845) 5–144; see W. M. Calder, "Welcker's Sapphobild and Its Reception in Wilamowitz," in *Friedrich Gottlieb Welcker: Werk und Wirkung*, ed. Wm. M. Calder et al., *Hermes Einzelschriften* 49 (Wiesbaden: 1986).

51. Ulrich von Wilamowitz-Moellendorff, *Sappho und Simonides: Untersuchungen über griechische Lyriker* (Berlin: Weidmann, 1913) 15–78.

52. Ilse Kokula, *Weibliche Homosexualität um 1900 in zeitgenössischen Dokumenten* (Munich: Frauenoffensive, 1981); Lillian Faderman and Brigitte Eriksson, ed. and trans., *Lesbian-Feminism in Turn-of-the-Century Germany* (Weatherby Lake, MO: Naiad, 1980); and Leslie Parr, editorial supervisor, *Lesbianism and Feminism in Germany, 1895–1910* (New York: Arno, 1975).

53. For the view that Sappho's poetry does not constitute evidence that she personally was homoerotically active, see, e.g., Judith P. Hallett, "Sappho and Her Social Context: Sense and Sensuality," *Signs* 4 (1979) 447–64. For the full spectrum of views, see the literature cited above in n. 1.

54. See, e.g., Jane McIntosh Snyder, *The Woman and the Lyre: Women Writers in Classical Greece and Rome* (Carbondale: Southern Illinois University Press, 1989) 1–37; Dover, *Greek Homosexuality*, 173–82; and Eva Cantarella, *Pandora's Daughters: The Role and Status of Women in Greek and Roman Antiquity*, trans. Maureen B. Fant; with a foreword by Mary R. Lefkowitz (Italian original: Editori Riuniti, 1981; Baltimore: Johns Hopkins University Press, 1987) 78–86. Some contemporary scholars who have read Sappho's poetry as homoerotic have seen that homoeroticism as pathological. See, e.g., George Devereux, "The Nature of Sappho's Seizure in Fr. 31 LP as Evidence of Her Inversion," *Classical Quarterly* n.s. 20

ing images, even those created to rid Sappho of the taint of unorthodoxy. These writers of later generations were apparently unable to accept the love for women expressed in Sappho's poetry as healthy and normal.

This survey of Christian and other ancient and medieval interpretations of Sappho and of her life has illustrated a central research result of my study: that Christian discomfort with love between women differs little from its non-Christian variants. Early Christians and their pagan counterparts used similar language and images to discredit women accused of erotic attraction to other women. Beyond that, the case of Sappho illustrates the close connection between discrediting women's bodies and discrediting women's minds.

Classical and Hellenistic Greek Literature

The earliest clear reference to female homoeroticism in Greek literature seems to be that in Plato's *Symposion*.[55] Aristophanes, in discoursing on the origins of humanity, speaks of *hetairistriai*, women who are attracted to women, as having their origin in primeval beings consisting of two women joined together. This parallels the original creatures who were two men joined together and those who consisted of one woman and one man. Aristophanes imagines that each human being seeks a partner of the gender to which she or he was originally attached. In Plato's last work, the *Laws*,[56] he speaks of sexual relations between men and between women as "contrary to nature" (*para physin*), and adds that "the first who dared to do this acted through lack of self-control with respect to pleasure."[57] Thus, the passage in the *Symposion* presupposes that same-sex love is as natural and normal as love between women and men, while that in the *Laws* does not. The reason for the discrepancy is unclear.

(1970) 17–31. Devereux interprets fragment 31 psychologically, taking Sappho's response to the man as jealousy: "[F]ew women are as obsessed with a (neurotic) feeling of anatomical 'incompleteness'—with the clinically commonplace 'female castration complex'—as the masculine lesbian" (p. 22). For other views of fragment 31, see Odysseus Tsagarakis, "Broken Hearts and the Social Circumstances in Sappho's Poetry," *Rheinisches Museum für Philologie* 129 (1986) 1–17; Richard Jenkyns, *Three Classical Poets: Sappho, Catullus, and Juvenal* (Cambridge, MA: Harvard University Press, 1982) 222–25; and M. Markovich, "Sappho Fr. 31: Anxiety Attack or Love Declaration?" *Classical Quarterly* n.s. 22 (1972) 19–32. On fragment 31, see also A. J. Beattie, "Sappho Fr. 31," *Mnemosyne* S. IV 9 (1956) 103–11.

55. Plato, *Symposion* 191E.

56. Plato, *Nomoi* 1.2; 636B–C; see also 8.5.1; 836A–837A.

57. John Boswell pointed out the possible ambiguity of the phrase παρὰ φύσιν, but did not address himself to the expressions "daring or shameless act" or "lack of self-control." See his *Christianity, Social Tolerance, and Homosexuality: Gay People in Western Europe from the Beginning of the Christian Era to the Fourteenth Century* (Chicago: University of Chicago Press, 1980) 13f, n. 22.

In the third century BCE, Asklepiades composed an epigram on two Samian women, Bitto and Nannion, who did not want to live in accordance with the laws of Aphrodite; instead, deserting sexual activities of which Aphrodite would approve, they turned to other, "not beautiful" ones. Asklepiades calls upon Aphrodite to hate these women, who are fleeing intercourse within her realm. An ancient commentator added as an explanatory note that Asklepiades was accusing them of being *tribades*.[58]

Classical Latin Literature

By portraying female homoeroticism as futile, monstrous, masculine, and foreign, Roman writers "policed and produced a femininity more in line with the ideals of Roman womanhood." Their representation contributed to the proscriptions on erotic love between women, which "were a way to produce properly gendered subjects."[59] The Roman writers that I will review worked in tandem with the marriage legislation of the Emperor Augustus to promote the ideal of a woman willing to receive the male phallus. Augustus elevated male-female marital relations to the level of a state norm with laws that rewarded upper-class persons who married and procreated, that punished those who did not, and that severely punished adulterers.[60] Upper-class Roman women unwilling to marry within their class and give birth to Roman citizens ran contrary to this norm. The poet Ovid, whose work I shall discuss shortly, supported several crucial elements of the cultural construction of womanhood inherent in the Augustan marriage legislation, even while his own erotic writing ran so far afoul of it that he was banished to the Black Sea.[61] Ovid, along with many other upper-

58. *Anthologia Graeca* 5.206; Hugo Stadtmueller, ed., vol. 1 (Leipzig: Teubner, 1894) 168f; see scholion[B]. The designation of the women as Samian may have some connection with Philainis, a woman said to have composed a book on sexual positions. Third-century BCE writers frequently refer to her; ancient sources locate her in Leukas or Samos. Martial and Pseudo-Lucian bring the name Philainis/Philaenis into connection with sexual love between women; see P. Maas, PW 19.2, s.v. "Philainis" (1938) 2122; and below.

Asklepiades's epigram—and this whole chapter—shows that Richard J. Hoffman's thesis that "polytheism was able to embrace the crossing of gender lines and homosexual relationships" does not hold for women ("Vices, Gods, and Virtues: Cosmology as a Mediating Factor in Attitudes toward Male Homosexuality," *Journal of Homosexuality* 9 [1983–84] 27–44, quote on p. 27).

59. I thank Professor Ann Pellegrini of Barnard College for these concise formulations, as well as for her many helpful suggestions on the manuscript of this book.

60. These laws include the *Lex Iulia de maritandis ordinibus* (18 BCE), the *Lex Papia Poppaea* (9 CE), and the *Lex Iulia de adulteriis coercendis* (ca. 16 BCE). See Susan Treggiari, *Roman Marriage: Iusti Coniuges from the Time of Cicero to the Time of Ulpian* (Oxford: Clarendon Press, 1991) 60–80, 277–98, and the primary sources and literature cited there.

61. Ovid's *Amores* was the offending document. See ibid., 291.

class people, rejected the severe strictures placed by the legislation on erotic expression. While Ovid and the state may have disagreed on the state's strict control over marriage, reproduction, and adultery, they agreed on the ideal that a Roman woman be oriented toward a Roman man.

Classicist Judith Hallett has identified three characteristics of representations of female homoeroticism in the elite Latin literature of the Republican and early Imperial periods: masculinization, hellenization, and anachronization. She argues that these techniques imply these authors' refusal to accept female homoeroticism as Roman and as real. She contrasts this Latin refusal with Plato's acknowledgment of female homoeroticism as a real part of his world and with the gradual acceptance of male same-sex love on the part of Latin authors and within Roman culture.[62] Hallett's arguments are, on the whole, insightful and convincing, but the broader context that I provide with this book leads to a nuancing on several points. Since she has covered this ground so well, I shall briefly review the material that she has covered, noting where the broader context that I provide leads me to slightly different interpretations of it.

A comedy of Plautus (ca. 250–184 BCE) provides the earliest extant Latin reference to female homoeroticism. In a brief comic interchange replete with puns, Plautus alludes to the possibility of sexual intercourse between an Athenian courtesan, Phronesium, and her Athenian female slave, Astaphium.[63] Hallett notes the presence of a pun alluding to the slave's forcing sexual intercourse upon her mistress, thereby associating female homoeroticism with a known form of masculine behavior. She does not comment upon Astaphium's slave status or upon the role reversal that a slave's forcing sex upon her mistress implies.[64]

Seneca the Elder (ca. 55 BCE–40 CE) composed one of his fictitious legal controversies around the case of a man who caught two *tribades* in bed, his wife and another woman, and killed them both. One declaimer describes the husband's first reaction: "But I looked first at the man, to see whether he was natural or sewed-on." Another declaimer notes that one would not tolerate the killing of a male adulterer under these circumstances, but adds that if he "had found a pseudo-adulterer. . . ." The reader is left with the shock of the monstrosity, having been led to see that the husband's act was

62. Judith P. Hallett, "Female Homoeroticism and the Denial of Roman Reality in Latin Literature," *Yale Journal of Criticism* 3 (1989) 209–27.

63. Plautus, *Truculentus* 262f; see also Plautus, *Persa* 227 and *Epidicus* 400 for possible allusions to female homoeroticism.

64. On Plautus, see Hallett, "Homoeroticism," 211f; and Saara Lilja, *Homosexuality in Republican and Augustan Rome* (Commentationes Humanarum Litterarum 74; Helsinki: Societas Scientiarum Fennica, 1983) 28, 32.

justified.[65] Masculinization is present in this representation in Seneca's reference to a phallus or phallus-like appendage, while the use of Greek and Greek loanwords constitute hellenization. Hallett notes that the very inclusion of this topic as a fictitious legal discussion places it "at some remove from routine Roman events," since Seneca's *controversiae* often deal with highly unusual events.[66]

For Hallett, Ovid's (43 BCE–18 CE) depictions of female homoeroticism exemplify the hellenizing, masculinizing, and anachronizing tendencies of elite Latin authors. Ovid's comments on Sappho's homoeroticism associate it with the distant Greek past.[67] His *Metamorphoses* contains the Cretan (i.e., Greek) tale of two girls, Iphis and Ianthe, who loved each other and were engaged to marry.[68] Because of her husband's wish to have a boy, Iphis's mother had raised her as a boy and concealed it from her husband. Iphis now bemoans her predicament, saying that the love she possesses is "unheard of," and even "monstrous." [69] If the gods wished to destroy her, she bewails, they should have given her a "natural woe," one "according to custom." [70] Among animals, females do not love females, she says, and, in her despair, she wishes she were no longer female. Iphis knows that she should accept herself as a woman and seek what is in accordance with divine law and love as a woman ought to love. And yet she loves Ianthe, though knowing that "nature does not will it, nature more powerful than them all." [71] It is against the background of the tragedy of freakish circumstances—against divine will, against nature, against custom, unheard of—that the reader is relieved when Isis intervenes and changes Iphis into a boy, making the marriage possible.[72] Masculinization thereby restores the binary opposition seen by Ovid as intrinsic to nature.

Hallett finds in the writings of Seneca the Younger an allusion to female

65. Seneca the Elder, *Controversiae* 1.2.23.

66. Hallett, "Homoeroticism," 212f.

67. Ovid, *Heroides* 15 (if by Ovid), *Tristia* 2.365. See Hallett, "Homoeroticism," 213f; and Lilja, *Homosexuality*, 80.

68. Ovid, *Metamorphoses* 9.666–797. See Hallett, "Homoeroticism," 214; and Lilja, *Homosexuality*, 80.

69. Ovid, *Metamorphoses* 9.727: *prodigiosa* (William S. Anderson, ed., *P. Ovidii Nasonis Metamorphoses* [Leipzig: Teubner, 1982] 227).

70. Ovid, *Metamorphoses* 9.730: *naturale malum . . . et de more* (Anderson, ed., *Metamorphoses*, 228).

71. Ovid, *Metamorphoses* 9.758: *non vult natura, potentior omnibus istis* (Anderson, ed., *Metamorphoses*, 228).

72. The story of Caenis/Caeneus, a woman with no interest in sexual intercourse with men who was changed into a man, should also be mentioned here. Ovid is one of the main sources for the tale: *Metamorphoses* 12.171–535.

homoeroticism.[73] Seneca claims that some women of his time, who have taken on masculine behaviors, now suffer from such masculine diseases as baldness. He does not attribute this to a changed female body: "the genitals [or: "nature"] of the women did not change, but have rather been conquered."[74] For him, the change is psychic, rather than physical. These diseased women "even rival men in their lusts, although born to be passive," and these women, "having devised so deviant a type of shamelessness, enter men."[75] Thus, women who depart from their natural female passivity can enter men. In conjunction with rivaling men's lust, these women of Seneca's time indulge in imitating men in other ways, such as by staying out late at night and drinking, by engaging in wrestling, and by vomiting and using other means to relieve excessive eating.

Even though Seneca does not refer to any sexual love between women, but rather to masculine women who enter men—albeit without a physical change, his juxtapositions nevertheless contribute to the framework of Latin literary representations of female homoeroticism: born to be passive versus rivaling men in their lusts; born to be passive versus devising a deviant type of shamelessness and entering men. Seneca typifies the binary thinking according to which the only alternative to female passivity is the desire and capacity to penetrate.

The poet Phaedrus (died mid-1st C. CE) composed a fable in which he describes the origin of *tribades* and passive males (*molles mares*) as an error on the part of Prometheus, a Greek mythical figure of the remote past (illustrating the themes of hellenization and anachronization).[76] Prometheus had spent the day creating male and female genitals (literally: "natural parts").[77] On returning intoxicated and sleepy from a dinner party, Pro-

---

73. Hallett, "Homoeroticism," 214f.

74. *Epistulae Morales* 95.20: *Non mutata feminarum natura, sed victa est* (Richard M. Gummere, *Seneca*, vol. 6 [LCL; Cambridge, MA: Harvard University Press, 1925] 70). Hallett does not refer to this statement, which runs counter to her interpretation that these Latin authors represent *tribades* as physically masculine. For the meaning of "genitals" for *natura*, see John J. Winkler, *The Constraints of Desire: The Anthropology of Sex and Gender in Ancient Greece* (New York: Routledge, 1990) 217–20; *OLD*, s.v. *natura;* and Lewis and Short, *A Latin Dictionary*, s.v. *natura*. If *natura* were to mean "nature" here, it could still refer to the physical makeup of the women. Gummere preserves the ambiguity of *natura* in his translation: "This does not mean that woman's physique has changed, but that it has been conquered" (p. 71).

75. *Epistulae Morales* 95.20f: *nam cum virorum licentiam aequaverint . . . pati natae. . . . Adeo perversum commentae genus inpudicitiae viros ineunt;* Gummere, *Seneca*, vol. 6, 70; ET: Hallett, "Homoeroticism," 214f.

76. Phaedrus, *Liber Fabularum* 4.16. Phaedrus probably composed the fables of book 4 when he was an old man. See Peter L. Schmidt, *Der Kleine Pauly*, s.v. "Phaedrus."

77. Phaedrus, *Liber Fabularum* 4.16: *naturae partes*.

metheus mistakenly placed female sexual organs on male bodies and male members on women. "Therefore lust now enjoys perverted pleasure."[78] According to Hallett's interpretation, Phaedrus has Prometheus render *tribades* literally masculine in the sense of phallic: a *tribas* possesses a phallus, given her by the Greek Titan Prometheus in the distant past, far removed from the Roman present.[79] To Hallett, these elements epitomize the masculinizing, hellenizing, and anachronizing tendencies of Latin representations of female homoeroticism.[80] Daniel Boyarin, however, has proposed that we interpret the *tribades* in the fable as having *male* bodies with female genitals.[81] Either interpretation corroborates Hallett's theme of masculinization.

Martial (ca. 40–103/4 CE) dedicated two epigrams to Philaenis, "*tribas* of the very *tribades*."[82] He depicts Philaenis as sexually aggressive toward both boys and girls, the latter of whom she, "quite fierce with the erection of a husband," batters eleven in a day.[83] In her other masculine activities, she resembles the penetrating women of Seneca the Younger. Philaenis spends much time on athletics: handball, heavy jumping weights, wrestling. She engages in the pleasure of being whipped by a greasy teacher.[84] Before dining, she vomits seven portions of unmixed wine. After consuming sixteen meat dishes, she returns to the wine. "When, after all of these things, her mind turns back to sex, she does not engage in fellatio, which

78. Phaedrus, *Liber Fabularum* 4.16; ET: Hallett, "Homoeroticism," 209. Note that actual physical organs are involved. Does the author consider them necessary for the female to play the active role in sexual intercourse?

79. Hallett, "Homoeroticism," 209–11.

80. Hallett, "Homoeroticism," 209f.

81. Daniel Boyarin, "Are There Any Jews in 'The History of Sexuality'?" *Journal of the History of Sexuality* 5 (1995) 345, n. 29. Lucian of Samosata (2d C. CE) provides corroboration for Boyarin's interpretation. Lucian writes of male-faced women in Lesbos who "have sex with women, as if they were men" (*Dialogues of the Courtesans* 5; §289). See also the fourth-century CE physiognomic treatise that speaks of women who are masculine in appearance and who have sex with other women (*De physiognomia liber* 85; Jacques André, ed. and trans., *Anonyme Latin: Traité de physiognomonie* [Paris: Les Belles Lettres, 1981] 118).

82. Martial, *Epigrammata* 7.67, 70; 7.70.1: *Ipsarum tribadum tribas* (W. M. Lindsay, *M. Val. Martialis Epigrammata* [2d ed.; Oxford: Clarendon, 1929]). A woman named Philainis (= the latinized "Philaenis") was known in the Greek-speaking world as the author of a book on sexual positions; see P. Maas, PW 19.2, s.v. "Philainis" (1938) 2122. Martial may have had this association in mind. Pseudo-Lucian refers to a woman named Philainis as exemplifying sexual love between women; see below. On Martial's depiction of *tribades*, see Hallett, "Homoeroticism," 215–22.

83. Martial, *Epigrammata* 7.67.1–3: *Pedicat pueros tribas Philaenis / et tentigine saevior mariti / undenas dolat in die puellas.*

84. Cf. Juvenal, *Saturae* 6.422f.

she thinks is not manly enough." Instead she "devours girls' middles."[85] Martial can only scorn the logic of this act, for how could she consider cunnilingus manly? He also says of Philaenis "you rightly call the woman with whom you copulate a girlfriend."[86] Hallett points to the heavy use of Greek loanwords in these two epigrams and to the masculine representation of Philaenis, but notes the absence of the anachronistic tendency found in earlier authors.[87]

In a third epigram,[88] Martial addresses one Bassa, a woman whom he had first thought to be as chaste as the famed Lucretia, for he had never seen Bassa coupling with men and had heard no scandals about her. On the contrary, she was always surrounded by women. But now he realizes that she was a *fututor* (m., "fucker").[89] Her "monstrous lust imitates a man."[90] The possibility of adultery without a man is worthy of the Theban riddle, a mythical Greek riddle from the remote past. As in Martial's representation of Philaenis, Hallett discerns here masculinizing and hellenizing tendencies, but no anachronization, since he depicts Bassa as a personal acquaintance.[91] Hallett argues that Martial probably drew upon both Seneca and Ovid, since they employ similar terms and images.[92]

In addition to the masculinizing and hellenizing motifs noted by Hallett, I draw attention to what seems to be sadomasochistic pleasure at the hand of the trainer, which is designed to evoke special horror in the reader. Could it be that voluntary submission to violence symbolizes Philaenis's control even over violence toward herself? It appears here that a man's violence toward a woman is a cultural outrage only when she allows such violence. By virtue of such autonomy, Philaenis has ceased to be a woman, as culturally defined, and has become a man. To Martial, it can then appear only ridiculous that she shows interest in female genitalia. For how could anyone of sound mind consider cunnilingus (because it can be pleasurable to women?) virile? Thus, for all of her carryings-on, Philaenis is not a real man after all. Martial generates a creative tension in the poems by exagger-

85. Martial, *Epigrammata* 7.67.13–15: *post haec omnia cum libidinatur, / non fellat— putat hoc parum virile—, / sed plane medias vorat puellas.*

86. Martial, *Epigrammata* 7.70.2: *recte, quam futuis, vocas amicam.*

87. In addition to *tribas*, the Greek loanwords in 7.67 are: *harpastum* (l. 4), *haphe* (l. 5), *halter* (l. 6), *palaestra* (l. 7), and *colyphia* (l. 12) (Hallett, "Homoeroticism," 215).

88. Martial, *Epigrammata* 1.90.

89. The verb *futuo* used in line 2 of 7.70, which I have translated as "copulate," is from the same root. Both generally refer to men's copulating with women.

90. Martial, *Epigrammata* 1.90.8: *mentiturque virum prodigiosa Venus* (W. M. Lindsay, ed., *M. Val. Martialis Epigrammata* [Oxford: Clarendon, 1903]).

91. Hallett, "Homoeroticism," 215–17.

92. Ibid., 216f.

ating women's attempts to be virile and then exposing the attempts as ridiculous. But they are not simply laughable. Such behavior is dangerous, and therefore deserves the term "monstrous."

Juvenal's (ca. 67 CE—?) *Sixth Satire* refers to women who set down their litters at the ancient altar of Chastity in Rome: "and in turn they ride horseback, and what is more they throb with the moon as a witness," which may allude to female homoeroticism.[93]

Elsewhere Juvenal has a woman, Laronia, contrast all women with passive males. Unlike men who engage in fellatio with other males, "such an abominable specimen of conduct will not be found among our sex / Tedia does not lick Cluvia, nor Flora Catulla."[94] To Roman women's credit, says Laronia, they not only refrain from oral sex, but also from practicing law, their gender deviance remaining limited to a little wrestling and meat eating.[95]

Juvenal echoes the focus in Seneca the Younger and Martial on meat eating and wrestling as hypermasculine activities, but departs from earlier ascriptions of sexual masculinity to *tribades*. Since, however, Juvenal does not explicitly call Tedia, Cluvia, Flora, or Catulla *tribades*, perhaps he is contrasting male oral sex with the lack of oral sex among women, rather than male versus female homoeroticism.[96] Like Martial, Juvenal presents the female deviants of whom he speaks as part of his own world, rather than of the distant Greek past. Historically, by the first century CE, Martial and Juvenal may have anachronized less because *tribades* had become a more open part of Roman society and denial of their presence had become more difficult.

But in spite of the presence of sexual love between women in Roman society, Plautus, Ovid, Seneca the Elder, Phaedrus, Martial, and Juvenal

93. Juvenal, *Saturae* 6.306–13. 6.311: *inque uices equitant ac Luna teste mouentur* (W. V. Clausen, ed., *A. Persi Flacci et D. Iuni Iuvenalis Saturae* [Oxford: Clarendon, 1959] 82). E. Courtney gives references to metaphors for horse riding applied to sexual activity (*A Commentary on the Satires of Juvenal* [London: Athlone, 1980] 298). Amy Richlin suggests that *mouentur* perhaps here means "reach orgasm" (Amy Richlin, *Juvenal* Satura *VI* [Bryn Mawr, PA: Bryn Mawr College, 1986] 67). Ludwig Friedländer describes the issue here as "tribadic fornication" (*D. Junii Juvenalis Saturarum Libri V: Mit erklärenden Anmerkungen*, vol. 1 [Leipzig: Hirzel, 1895] 319). Hallett does not discuss this passage.

On Juvenal's *Sixth Satire* as an attempt to dissuade men from marrying, see Susanna H. Braund, "Juvenal: Misogynist or Misogamist?" *Journal of Roman Studies* 82 (1992) 71–86.

94. Juvenal, *Saturae* 2.47–50.

95. Juvenal, *Saturae* 2.36–63. Laronia does not necessarily represent Juvenal's view, and it seems nearly certain that he is referring to sexual activity among the women mentioned at 6.306–13.

96. Since, historically, female homoerotic activity in this period could have included oral sex (and, according to Martial, did), Laronia's disavowing its existence among women could have constituted denying the existence of female homoeroticism altogether.

represented it as distant from their society in one or more ways. In contrast, Roman authors displayed some tolerance toward those homoerotic males of their own society who played the active role, although they expressed considerable disdain toward passive citizen males, while expecting male slaves to endure penetration.[97] This differing treatment of female and male homoeroticism is based upon a fundamental asymmetry between the feminine and masculine sexual roles of free persons that we can document throughout the Roman world and will see throughout this book: the permanent passivity expected of women contrasted with the understanding that free men might penetrate either females or males or even be penetrated themselves. This focus on penetration as the principal sexual image led to a simplistic view of female erotic behavior and a complex view of the erotic choices of free men.

Hallett has done an excellent job of analyzing the literary tendencies and intertextual connections among these elite Latin authors. The material that I present in this book demonstrates that the interconnections among these Latin authors are not just literary. Instead, these authors participated in broader cultural patterns of the ancient Mediterranean world as a whole, which included shared assumptions about gender and sexual roles.

The larger Mediterranean context provides us with a broader range of possible interpretations of Roman representations of female homoeroticism. For example, Hallett's focus on Phaedrus, who may depict *tribades* as literally phallic, leads her to interpret Martial's Philaenis as literally phallic. Thus, she renders what I have translated "you rightly call the woman with whom you copulate a girlfriend," as "you rightly call a girlfriend the woman whom you penetrate vaginally with a penis."[98] Hallett apparently infers the phrase "with a penis" from the verb *futuo*, the standard obscene word for the male role in the sexual act.[99] Ancient medical writings, however, demonstrate that the ancients thought that women might derive a

97. See Saara Lilja, *Homosexuality in Republican and Augustan Rome* (Commentationes Humanarum Litterarum 74; Helsinki: Societas Scientiarum Fennica, 1983); and Amy Richlin, "Not Before Homosexuality: The Materiality of the *Cinaedus* and the Roman Law against Love between Men," *Journal of the History of Sexuality* 3 (1993) 523–73.

98. Martial, *Epigrammata* 7.70.2: *recte, quam futuis, vocas amicam;* Hallett, "Homoeroticism," 216.

Peter Howell also sees Martial as envisaging physical penetration in 1.90 (Bassa) and 7.67 (Philaenis). He notes that some women are said to have a clitoris large enough to "be able to copulate, or even sodomise," but sees it as more likely that the use of an artificial phallus is meant. See Howell, *A Commentary on Book One of the Epigrams of Martial* (London: Athlone, 1980) 298.

99. See J. N. Adams, *The Latin Sexual Vocabulary* (Baltimore: Johns Hopkins University Press, 1982) 118–22, who notes that *futuo* can also denote the female part in sexual intercourse between women and men, as in Martial, *Epigrammata* 11.7.13.

capacity to penetrate from an overly large clitoris. Thus, we could interpret Martial's Philaenis as having the ability to copulate, and even to have an erection, with a large clitoris, rather than with a penis.

Denial is another point on which the larger picture of the ancient Mediterranean helps us to understand the elite Latin authors better. In this book I present a range of sources from different social classes and religious and ethnic groups. This documentation of the awareness of sexual love between women shows that the Romans had material cause to feel threatened. Further, the large range of sources allows us to locate the Roman denial response on a spectrum. On the one end of the spectrum we find Roman authors who employ literary techniques to deny the existence of *tribades* among Roman citizen women. Similarly, a Jewish work describes marriage between women as a practice of the Canaanites and Egyptians.[100] Other ancient authors, however, describe the threat of female homoeroticism as one very close to home. Thus, church fathers warn Christian nuns against sexual involvement with other nuns, and Jewish sources express concern about the daughters of Jewish priests or the potential wives of Jewish priests engaging in such behavior. And astrologers present a variety of sexual orientations quite matter-of-factly and must have done so to their clients. Thus, the elite Latin denial of reality has parallels but does not constitute the only response to sexual love between women in the Roman world.

Greek Authors of the Roman Period

Authors writing in Greek in the Roman period echo tendencies we have seen up to this point; they represent sexual love between women as masculine, unnatural, lawless, licentious, and monstrous. The philosopher and biographer Plutarch (ca. 45 to ca. 120 CE) is, however, an important exception. He describes boy-love in the Sparta of the legendary founder of the Spartan constitution, Lykurgos, in rather favorable terms as promoting the education of the youth. By way of side comment, Plutarch adds, "though this love was so approved among them that also the noble and good women loved the virgins; there was no jealous love in it."[101] There is no mention that such love might be perverse or abominable. Nevertheless, we should not assume that Plutarch's admiration of ancient Spartan customs meant that he would have accepted love relations between females, or female sexual autonomy, in his own day.[102]

100. J. H. Weiss, ed., *Sifra* (Vienna: Schlossberg, 1862) on Lev 18:3 (*Aḥarei Mot, Parasha* 9).

101. Plutarch, *Lives: Lykurgos* 18.4.

102. For Plutarch's views on female marital duties, see especially his treatise *Conjugal Precepts* (*Moralia: Conjugal Precepts* 138A–146A). On this work, see Kathleen O'Brien Wicker,

The popular Syrian (or possibly Babylonian) novelist Iamblichos bears witness that, while he considered erotic attraction between women to constitute "wild and lawless amours," he expected his audience to enjoy reading about it.[103] His fast-paced novel, *Babyloniaka*, written during the reign of Marcus Aurelius (161–80), enjoyed a wide audience into the Byzantine period, but is now lost to us. The tenth-century patriarch Photios has, however, written an extensive plot summary. From this we know that Iamblichos wrote about the love of Berenike, the daughter of the king of Egypt, for Mesopotamia, with whom she slept and whom she then married.[104] Iamblichos was one of several second-century authors to write about marriage between women.

A contemporary of Iamblichos, the Syrian satirist and Sophist Lucian of Samosata likewise writes about a woman married to another woman. In his *Dialogues of the Courtesans*, Lucian devotes the fifth dialogue to an experience that the courtesan Leaina has had with her fellow courtesans Megilla

"First-Century Marriage Ethics: A Comparative Study of the Household Codes and Plutarch's Conjugal Precepts," in *No Famine in the Land: Studies in Honor of John L. McKenzie*, ed. James W. Flanagan and Anita Weisbrod Robinson (Claremont, CA: Institute for Antiquity and Christianity, 1975) 141–53. Plutarch advises female subordination, and not female equality or autonomy, in this treatise.

103. Photios, *Bibliothēkē* 94.77a; René Henry, ed. and trans., *Photios: Bibliothèque*, 8 vols. (Paris: Les Belles Lettres, 1959–77), 2 (1960) 44. See also the critical edition of the fragments of Iamblichos by Elmar Habrich, *Iamblichi Babyloniacorum Reliquiae* (Leipzig: Teubner, 1960) 58; and the discussion in Boswell, *Christianity, Social Tolerance, and Homosexuality*, 84. The evidence supports Henry's translation of ἔκθεσμος as "contre nature" or the translation "lawless," rather than Boswell's rendering of it as "inordinate"; see the references for ἔκθεσμος in the standard Greek lexica (LSJ and Preisigke).

On Iamblichos, see Tomas Hägg, *The Novel in Antiquity* (Swedish edition, 1980; Berkeley: University of California Press, 1983) 32–34.

104. Photios, *Bibliothēkē* 94.77a–b, states that Berenike "had an affair with Mesopotamia" (Μεσοποταμίᾳ συνεγίνετο) and that "Berenike married Mesopotamia" (γάμους Μεσοποταμίας ἡ Βερενίκη ποιεῖται) (Henry, *Photios*, 2 [1960] 44, 46). See also Habrich, 58, 64. Since both of these clauses are somewhat ambiguous, scholars differ on whether to read them as referring to sexual love between women. Richard Pervo, John Boswell, Arthur Heiserman, and Erwin Rohde take them as referring to sexual love between Berenike and Mesopotamia, while Gerald N. Sandy, Ursula Schneider-Menzel, and Wilhelm Kroll assume that Berenike sponsored the wedding festivities for Mesopotamia or had them performed. Richard Pervo communicated this to me in a letter of March 17, 1988. Further, see Boswell, *Christianity, Social Tolerance, and Homosexuality*, 84; Heiserman, *The Novel before the Novel: Essays and Discussions about the Beginnings of Prose Fiction in the West* (Chicago: University of Chicago Press, 1977) 61f; Rohde, *Der griechische Roman und seine Vorläufer* (4th ed.; 1914; reprint, Hildesheim: Olms, 1974) 401f; Sandy, in *Collected Ancient Greek Novels*, ed. B. P. Reardon (Berkeley: University of California Press, 1989) 791f; Schneider-Menzel, in *Literatur und Gesellschaft im ausgehenden Altertum*, ed. Franz Altheim (Halle: Niemeyer, 1948) 55, 67; and Kroll, PW 9, s.v. "Iamblichos" (1916) 642.

and Demonassa. Megilla, a wealthy woman from Lesbos,[105] has succeeded in seducing Leaina, in spite of Leaina's shame at the strange activity. It turns out that Megilla sees her true self as Megillos and Demonassa as her wife. She wears a wig to conceal her short hair and says that although she does not have a male organ, she does have some sort of substitute.

The characterization of Megilla, but not Leaina, as masculine is central to Lucian's representation. Megilla loves Leaina "like a man"; Megilla is a woman who is "terribly masculine"; Megilla and Demonassa kiss Leaina "like men"; Megilla's head is closely shaven, "just like the most manly of athletes"; Megilla asks Leaina, "Have you ever seen such a handsome young man?" with reference to herself; she calls herself "Megillos," refusing to be "effeminated"; and she states that she is "all man." [106] This masculinization, however, quite explicitly does not imply a penis. Leaina puts forth three explanations for Megilla's masculine behavior: (1) that, like Achilles, she is a man hiding among the girls; (2) that she is a hermaphrodite, with two sets of genitals; and (3) that, like Teiresias, she has been changed from a man into a woman. Megilla rejects all of these explanations, stressing that she was born just like other women, but that she has "the mind and the desires and everything else of a man." [107] Lucian repeatedly refers in a titillatingly oblique fashion to a penis, but in fact a penis is absent. Megilla says to her lover, Leaina, "I haven't got what you mean . . . I don't need it at all. You'll find I have a much pleasanter method of my own." [108] She tells her, "You'll find I'm as good as any man." [109] Her ability, however, derives not from a penis, but from "something instead of a penis." [110] Thus, for Lucian, sexual love between women does not originate from women's having male genitals. For Lucian, the mind seems to be the most powerful sex organ.

Since, in Lucian's view, a *hetairistria* is not literally a phallic woman, the sexual roles among such women are fluid. Thus, both Megilla and Demon-

105. The combination of a woman from Lesbos with a woman from Corinth must be intentional, since in antiquity people connected both Lesbos and Corinth with sexual adventurousness.

106. Lucian, *Dialogues of the Courtesans* 5.1–3; §§289–91: ὥσπερ ἄνδρα . . . δεινῶς ἀνδρική . . . ὥσπερ οἱ ἄνδρες . . . οἱ σφόδρα ἀνδρώδεις τῶν ἀθλητῶν . . . ἑώρακας ἤδη οὕτω καλὸν νεανίσκον; . . . Μή καταθήλυνέ με . . . τὸ πᾶν ἀνήρ εἰμι (Karl Mras, ed., *Luciani Dialogi Meretricii* [Kleine Texte für Vorlesungen und Übungen 160; Berlin: De Gruyter, 1930] 19–21).

107. Lucian, *Dialogues of the Courtesans* 5.4; §291: ἡ γνώμη δὲ καὶ ἡ ἐπιθυμία καὶ τἆλλα πάντα ἀνδρός ἐστί μοι; ET: M. D. Macleod, trans., *Lucian*, vol. 7 [LCL; Cambridge, MA: Harvard University Press, 1961] 383).

108. Lucian, *Dialogues of the Courtesans* 5.3; §291; ET: Macleod, *Lucian*, vol. 7, 383.

109. Lucian, *Dialogues of the Courtesans* 5.4; §291; ET: Macleod, *Lucian*, vol. 7, 385.

110. Lucian, *Dialogues of the Courtesans* 5.4; §292: τι ἀντὶ τοῦ ἀνδρείου; Mras, *Luciani Dialogi Meretricii*, 22; translation my own.

assa kiss Leaina "like men." They want Leaina to sleep between them, as if they were both going to take an active sexual role with her. Presumably this fluidity of roles applies also to the male-faced women in Lesbos, who "are unwilling to suffer 'it' from men, but only have sex with women, as if they were men."[111] The masculinity is not in their genitals, but in their faces, in their minds, in their desires. They refuse to take the passive role with men. Apparently the autonomy of these Lesbian women constitutes a masculinity so marked that you can see it in their faces.

Like other ancient writers, Lucian depicts this masculine behavior as shameful. Leaina is "ashamed" to speak about her experience, because it is so "strange"; she refuses to tell details, because they are "shameful."[112] This rhetoric of shame is all the more conspicuous, since the families upon whom they might bring shame are strikingly absent. As courtesans, they are already outside a family structure. As wealthy courtesans, Megilla and Demonassa are patently independent. And the male-faced women of Lesbos seem to constitute a regionally separate group. Lucian does not explain why this behavior is shameful or upon whom these women bring shame, because his readers apparently understand that.

Lucian also presupposes that his readers know the meaning of *hetairistria*, the term used by Plato in the myth of the original double human beings seeking the partners from whom they had been separated. In fact, Lucian's dialogue assumes a familiarity with the phenomenon of sexual love between women, even while he tantalizes the reader by having the questioner in the dialogue repeatedly ask what exactly happens and the dialogue partner refuse to give details. The allusion to the women in Lesbos also seems to strike a familiar note with the reader. The familiarity with sexual love between women that Lucian presupposes on the part of his readers accords well with the picture that will emerge throughout this book.

In a fictitious letter purporting to depict life in classical Athens, Lucian's contemporary Alkiphron also takes up the theme of courtesans partying among themselves. He describes one such party replete with homoerotic overtones, even though he depicts the women as having male lovers outside the party.[113] The courtesans perform sensuous dances for one another, wiggling and shaking their hips, buttocks, thighs, and bellies, and judging one another's beauty in the process. Although a male writer has cast this

---

111. Lucian, *Dialogues of the Courtesans* 5.2; §289: γυναῖκας ἀρρενωπούς, ὑπὸ ἀνδρῶν μὲν οὐκ ἐθελούσας αὐτὸ πάσχειν, γυναιξὶ δὲ αὐτὰς πλησιαζούσας ὥσπερ ἄνδρας; Mras, *Luciani Dialogi Meretricii*, 20; translation my own.

112. Lucian, *Dialogues of the Courtesans* 5.1; §289: αἰσχύνομαι . . . ἀλλόκοτον; 5.4; §292: αἰσχρά; Mras, *Luciani Dialogi Meretricii*, 19, 22; translation my own.

113. Alkiphron, *Letters of Courtesans* 14.

fictitious scene of an all-female party, it can nevertheless help us to imagine the homoerotic possibilities of a homosocial environment, even when the women are connected with men. From the literary standpoint, the homoerotically tinged representation of courtesans is worthy of note, since that is a common theme in the ancient sources.

An imitator of Lucian of Samosata composed a dialogue, probably in the early fourth century, on the relative merits of the sexual love of women and the sexual love of boys. The author includes a debate between a Corinthian and an Athenian; the Athenian makes the case for love of boys, while the Corinthian argues for love of women. In the end, even though marriage is necessary to perpetuate the human race, love of boys wins the debate, because "perfect virtue grows least of all among women." [114] In order to ensure the creation of offspring while remaining true to the philosophical ideal of pederasty, the judge of the debate considers pederasty a "privilege only of philosophy," so that only wise men should be allowed to practice it. [115] In the midst of this debate, both sides of which focus entirely on male choice and male prerogative, the Corinthian mocks the pro-pederasty position by suggesting that if we are going to allow pederasty, we might as well allow love between women:

> [B]ut, if males find intercourse with males acceptable, henceforth let women too love each other. Come now, epoch of the future, legislator of strange pleasures, devise fresh paths for male lusts, but bestow the same privilege upon women, and let them have intercourse with each other just as men do. Let them strap to themselves cunningly contrived instruments of licentiousness, those mysterious monstrosities devoid of seed, and let woman lie with woman as does man. Let tribadic licentiousness—that word seldom heard, which I feel ashamed even to utter—freely parade itself, and let our women's chambers emulate Philainis, disgracing themselves with androgynous amours. And how much better that a woman should force her way into the province of male luxury than that the nobility of the male sex should become effeminate and play the part of a woman! [116]

114. Pseudo-Lucian, *Erōtes* 51; ET: M. D. Macleod, ed. and trans., *Lucian*, vol. 8 (LCL; Cambridge, MA: Harvard University Press, 1967) 229.

115. Pseudo-Lucian, *Erōtes* 51.

116. Pseudo-Lucian, *Erōtes* 28: ἐράτωσαν ἀλλήλων καὶ γυναῖκες. ἄγε νῦν, ὦ νεώτερε χρόνε καὶ τῶν ξένων ἡδονῶν νομοθέτα, καινὰς ὁδοὺς ἄρρενος τρυφῆς ἐπινοήσας χάρισαι τὴν ἴσην ἐξουσίαν καὶ γυναιξίν, καὶ ἀλλήλαις ὁμιλησάτωσαν ὡς ἄνδρες· ἀσελγῶν δὲ ὀργάνων ὑποζυγωσάμεναι τέχνασμα, ἀσπόρων τεράστιον αἴνιγμα, κοιμάσθωσαν γυνὴ μετὰ γυναικὸς ὡς ἀνήρ· τὸ δὲ εἰς ἀκοὴν σπανίως ἧκον ὄνομα—αἰσχύνομαι καὶ λέγειν—τῆς τριβακῆς ἀσελγείας ἀνέδην πομπευέτω. πᾶσα δ᾽ ἡμῶν ἡ γυναικωνῖτις ἔστω Φιλαινὶς ἀνδρογύνους ἔρωτας ἀσχημονοῦσα. καὶ πόσῳ κρεῖττον εἰς ἄρρενα τρυφὴν βιάζεσθαι γυναῖκα ἢ τὸ γενναῖον ἀνδρῶν εἰς γυναῖκα θηλύνεσθαι (M. D. Macleod, ed., *Luciani Opera*, vol. 3 [Oxford: Clarendon Press, 1980] 101; ET [slightly altered]: Macleod, *Lucian*, vol. 8, 195).

Pseudo-Lucian represents sexual love between women as simultaneously more shameful than that between males and not as bad as for males to sink to the level of women. On the one hand, the speaker is ashamed even to utter the word "tribadic," which helps to explain the relative rarity of the term *tribas* in ancient literature. But on the other hand, women's taking for themselves the privilege of homoeroticism (which falls within "the province of male luxury") can never be as bad as for men to sink from noble masculinity to the depths of the feminine nature.

Like others in antiquity, Pseudo-Lucian's Corinthian speaker conceptualizes sexual love between women in male terms; for him, one of the women must, by whatever means, become phallic. In an unusual move, he focuses on the lack of procreation represented by sexual love between women; the artificial phallus can ejaculate no seed. Strapping on an artificial phallus signifies women publicly taking on male privilege; for women to become masculine is contrary to nature.[117] That which is most private, the women's chambers, dares to become public. The public parade of tribadic eroticism contrasts with what should be the private women's quarters of women who are vessels receptive to the male seed.[118] Philainis, reported to have written a book on sexual positions, symbolizes the public shame of *tribades*: a woman writing about sex.[119] Like the Philaenis of Martial, this Philainis and her emulators are androgynous, which for Pseudo-Lucian would mean that they share in the male nature.[120]

If the Athenian won the debate in this dialogue, this does not imply that sexual love between women gained any acceptance at all. Whereas the speakers praise pederasty for the male friendship that it enables, they could not see sexual love between women as suitable for philosophers. In the logic of the argument, both sides assume the intellectual and moral inferiority of women. The Corinthian argues that Aphrodite caused women and men to have separate natures, that men are granted the privilege of ejaculating the seed, while women are meant to be vessels to receive it. Therefore, men and women should each retain their own separate natures, women not becoming masculine, and men not becoming soft.[121] Thus, for the "pro-woman" Corinthian, sexual love between women constitutes an absurd attempt of women to enter into the male realm. For the pro-

117. Pseudo-Lucian, *Erōtes* 19.

118. Pseudo-Lucian, *Erōtes* 19.

119. A scholion on Lucian states that the Athenian comic poet Philokrates had written about Philainis as a ἑταιρίστρια καὶ τρίβας (Hugo Rabe, ed., *Scholia in Lucianum* [Leipzig: Teubner, 1906] 205). See P. Maas, PW 19.2, s.v. "Philainis" (1938) 2122, who notes that a number of writers in the third century BCE mention Philainis's book.

120. See Pseudo-Lucian, *Erōtes* 21, in which the Corinthian calls a castrated boy dual-natured, presumably because without a penis he shares in the female nature.

121. Pseudo-Lucian, *Erōtes* 19.

pederasty Athenian, women should "be retained only for childbearing."[122] In fact, both sides agree that women's principal value lies in their ability to help in procreation.

Like other authors we have seen and will see in this book, Pseudo-Lucian speaks of male-male mingling, by which he means pederasty, but of sexual love between adult women, rather than between an adult woman and a girl. But the more egalitarian character of a relationship between adult women does not render it more valuable than pederasty in the eyes of the debaters. In fact, no one speaks on behalf of love between women at all. And in the end, pederasty—the male sexual use of children—wins the highest praise.

Although written in Latin, an anonymous fourth-century physiognomic treatise can be mentioned in this context, because it liberally uses earlier Greek sources.[123] According to the principles of physiognomy, physical characteristics correlate with behavior and character traits. This treatise sharply distinguishes women from men on this basis.[124] It also speaks of "women who have sex with women whose appearance is feminine, but who are more devoted to masculine women, who correspond more to a masculine type of appearance, ⟨who are called [in Greek] 'masculine' (*arrenikai*)⟩."[125] This text echoes tensions about sexual love between women that had already come up in earlier sources: whether women who

122. Pseudo-Lucian, *Erōtes* 38.

123. The treatise uses Pseudo-Aristotle, Loxos, and Polemo. The portion relevant for this study derives from Pseudo-Aristotle (Jacques André, ed. and trans., *Anonyme Latin: Traité de physiognomonie* [Paris: Les Belles Lettres, 1981] 34, who notes that the paragraph I discuss is not preserved in the Pseudo-Aristotle transmitted independently of the treatise [p. 148, n. 7]).

For an excellent discussion of ancient physiognomy, see Maud W. Gleason, "The Semiotics of Gender: Physiognomy and Self-Fashioning in the Second Century C.E.," in *Before Sexuality: The Construction of Erotic Experience in the Ancient Greek World*, ed. David M. Halperin, John J. Winkler, and Froma I. Zeitlin (Princeton: Princeton University Press, 1990) 389–415.

See also Tamsyn S. Barton, *Power and Knowledge: Physiognomics and Medicine under the Roman Empire* (Ann Arbor: University of Michigan Press, 1994), 95–131. Barton provides a helpful analysis of these three ancient disciplines as rhetoric. She also argues against a modern distinction between science and pseudo-science for these fields.

124. *De physiognomia liber* 3–7; André, *Anonyme Latin*, 51–56. I express gratitude to Prof. Georgia Frank for alerting me to this treatise.

125. *De physiognomia liber* 85: *de mulieribus . . . mulieres coire cum mulieribus quarum species est muliebris, masculis autem magis deditas quae magis ad uirilem speciem respondent, ⟨quae ἀρρενικαὶ dicuntur⟩*; André, *Anonyme Latin*, 118.

On this passage, see Aline Rousselle, "Body Politics in Ancient Rome," in *A History of Women*, vol. 1, *From Ancient Goddesses to Christian Saints*, ed. Pauline Schmitt Pantel, trans. Arthur Goldhammer (Italian original: Rome: Laterza, 1990; Cambridge, MA: Belknap Press of Harvard University Press, 1992) 327f. Rousselle notes that in it "overly feminine women are suspected of making love with other women" (p. 328), which suggests that precise gender conformity is essential.

For a further discussion of Pseudo-Aristotle's categorization of gender types, see below.

love other women are masculine or feminine, and whether such women possess the physical means of penetrating another woman. According to this text, some homoerotic women look feminine, while others look masculine. The author presupposes a variety of potential pairs: a feminine woman with a feminine woman, a feminine woman with a masculine woman, and a masculine woman with a masculine woman (since the "women" mentioned at the outset could presumably be either feminine or masculine in appearance). For the anonymous physiognomist, homoerotic women with male genitals constitute a distinct subset of homoerotic women. We will find speculation concerning homoerotic women's genitals and their relative masculinity and femininity frequently throughout this book.

Artistic Representations

Greek vase paintings that document erotic attraction between women should be mentioned here, even though they are from an earlier period.[126] A plate dating to circa 620 BCE from the Greek island of Thera depicts two women, of approximately equal height, in a typical courting position; that is, one is placing her hand below the chin of the other (see fig. 1).[127] An Attic red-figure *kylix*, that is, a drinking vessel for wine, by Apollodoros (ca. 515–495 BCE) shows a nude woman caressing the clitoris of a standing nude woman and stroking the standing woman's inner thigh with her other hand (see fig. 2).[128] Martin Kilmer suggests that the women's visibly erect nipples, which are paralleled in other erotic scenes, contribute to the impression of sexual arousal.[129] Another Attic red-figure *kylix* (ca. 470–460 BCE, perhaps by the Boot Painter), located in the J. Paul Getty Mu-

126. See also the important new study by Gabriele Meixner. In her book *Frauenpaare in kulturgeschichtlichen Zeugnissen* (Munich: Frauenoffensive, 1994), Meixner documents the astounding conclusion of her research that representations of female-female human couples far outnumber female-male couples in prehistoric art.

127. Dover, *Greek Homosexuality*, CE34, discussion on p. 173; G. M. A. Richter, *Korai: Archaic Greek Maidens* (London: Phaidon, 1968) pl. VIII-C.

128. Dover, *Greek Homosexuality*, R207, discussion on p. 173; John Boardman, Eugenio La Rocca, and Antonia Mulas, *Eros in Griechenland* (Munich: List, 1976) 111f; J. D. Beazley, *Paralipomena: Additions to* Attic Black-Figure Vase-Painters *and* Attic Red-Figure Vase-Painters, *Second Edition* (Oxford: Clarendon, 1971) 333. Eva Keuls disputes that this vase depicts a homoerotic scene, suggesting instead that the one woman may be applying perfume to the genitals of the other as a prelude to an encounter with a man (Keuls, *The Reign of the Phallus: Sexual Politics in Ancient Athens* [New York: Harper and Row, 1985] 85, 173, fig. 151). Even if this were the case, however, the woman being perfumed could derive pleasure from the touch.

129. Martin F. Kilmer, *Greek Erotica on Attic Red-Figure Vases* (London: Duckworth, 1993) 27f. Kilmer further suggests that the perfume container ("alabastos") could have stood in for a dildo (p. 28).

58

CHAPTER TWO

seum depicts two nude women on the side of the vase (see fig. 3).[130] One
woman stands, while the other squats and reaches toward the standing
woman's genitals with her fingers. The curators at the Getty have interpreted the gesture as depilation by two *hetairai*, that is, that the squatting
woman is plucking out the pubic hairs of the standing woman. Since ancient Greek women removed their pubic hair by plucking or burning, this
may be the case, or perhaps one could interpret the scene as homoerotic.
An Attic red-figure amphora (ca. 490 BCE, attributed to the Flying Angel
Painter) depicts two nude women with rather visible pubic hair walking
with their arms around each other (see fig. 4).[131] The woman on the left
has a fillet wound around her hair, which could be a gift of affection from
the other woman. Both women are visibly drunk. The woman on the left
is carrying a wine decanter (*oinochoe*) slung horizontally at her side, as if to
indicate that its contents are gone or nearly gone. The woman on the right
holds a Persian-type drinking bowl in her hand; the large size could indicate the large quantity that the women have consumed. The other side
shows a nude woman holding a very long phallus (see fig. 5). Martin
Kilmer has suggested that several additional vase scenes may have female
homoerotic implications. These include nude women bathing together,
dancing with a phallos-bird, and masturbating with a dildo in front of
other women. He further interprets one vase as depicting a woman with
a dildo strapped onto her pelvis, although it could also represent a hermaphrodite.[132]

A South Italian vase from about 350 BCE shows two clothed women, the
one sitting, the other standing facing her at an angle (see fig. 6). The seated
woman reaches up, lightly touching the breast of the other. Eva Keuls suggests that "it is so discreet that its [homoerotic] implication has gone
unnoticed."[133]

Men may have used these vases, especially the drinking vessels for wine,
for their own titillation, although the vases from circa 620 and from around
350 would not have been well-suited to male titillation, since both depict

130. *J. Paul Getty Museum Journal* 12 (1984) 245f: J. Paul Getty Museum, accession no.
83.AE.251; Boot Painter's *kylix*, side A.
131. I thank Dr. John J. Herrmann of the Boston Museum of Fine Arts for his help in
interpreting this painting.
132. Kilmer, *Greek Erotica*, 26–30: R73 (Euthymides [ca. 515–500]), and R152 (Pedi-
eus Painter [ca. 520–505]), R141.3 (Epiktetos [ca. 520–490]). See also the Attic red-figure
pelike (ca. 430 BCE) from Vulci, Etruria (Italy), that depicts two Amazons going into battle
together (now in the Antikensammlung in Munich, reproduced in Meixner, *Frauenpaare*,
p. 104, fig. 39), as well as the Attic neck amphora (Amasis painter, ca. 530 BCE) that represents
two maenads dancing in close embrace (now in the Cabinet des médailles, reproduced in
Meixner, p. 104, fig. 40).
133. Taranto, Southern Italy, Apulian *pelike*, by the Truro painter: Keuls, *The Reign of the
Phallus*, 85; 87, fig. 81; 437, n. 81.

the women as fully clothed. In any case, Kilmer warns against interpreting the depicted sexual acts as representative of women's preferences, suggesting that "they are probably best taken as male fantasy." [134]

As representations of female homoeroticism, these vases share certain features. Unlike many Roman-period writers, the vase painters did not depict the women as in any way masculine or pseudomasculine (the possible depiction of a woman with a dildo strapped onto herself would be an obvious exception). Further, these vases depict adult women, which contrasts with the Greek vases showing male couples, most of which consist of a bearded adult and a beardless youth. [135] Thus, like later representations, the vases do not represent female homoeroticism as pederasty.

In addition to these earlier materials, a funerary relief from the time of the Emperor Augustus (27 BCE – 14 CE) depicting two women with right hands clasped in a *dextrarum iunctio* ("joining of the right [hands]"), the classic gesture of married persons, deserves discussion and further research (see fig. 7). [136] An inscription below the relief identifies one woman as Fonteia Eleusis, a freedwoman (i.e., an emancipated slave), and the other as Fonteia Helena, also a freedwoman. [137] A few centuries later, some un-

---

134. Kilmer, *Greek Erotica*, 30.

135. Dover, *Greek Homosexuality*, pls. between pp. 118 and 119.

136. See the helpful discussion provided by Mary Rose D'Angelo, "Women Partners in the New Testament," *Journal of Feminist Studies in Religion* 6:1 (1990) 65–70. The relief is British Museum Sculpture 2276. See A. H. Smith, *A Catalogue of Sculpture in the Department of Greek and Roman Antiquities: British Museum*, vol. 3 (London: British Museum, 1904) no. 2276, pp. 290f; *Archäologische Zeitung*, n.s., vol. 7 (September 1848) 107; *CIL* 6/3.18524; and Susan Walker and Andrew Burnett, *Augustus: Handlist of the Exhibition and Supplementary Studies* (London: British Museum, 1981) no. 184, pp. 43–47.

On the *dextrarum iunctio*, see Susan Treggiari, *Roman Marriage: Iusti Coniuges from the Time of Cicero to the Time of Ulpian* (Oxford: Clarendon Press, 1991) 149–51, 164f; Reinhard Stupperich, "Zur dextrarum iunctio auf frühen römischen Grabreliefs," *Boreas: Münstersche Beiträge zur Archäologie* 6 (1983) 143–50; Diana E. E. Kleiner, *Roman Group Portraiture: The Funerary Reliefs of the Late Republic and Early Empire* (New York: Garland, 1977) fig. 34; L. Reekmans, "Dextrarum iunctio," *Enciclopedia dell'Arte Antica* (Rome: Enciclopedia Italiana, 1960) 82–85; Louis Reekmans, "La 'dextrarum iunctio' dans l'iconographie romaine et paléochrétienne," *Bulletin de l'institut historique belge de Rome* 31 (1958) 23–95, pls. 1–16; and B. Kötting, "Dextrarum iunctio," *RAC* 3 (1957) 881–88. Stupperich argues that the relief was originally meant to represent a married couple, with the figure on the left being a man. He interprets the clasped right hands as a sign of their marital state. He notes that while artists depicted the *dextrarum iunctio* with the hands in various locations, the clasped hands in this relief are held exceptionally high and demonstratively closely clasped. His only reason for arguing that the relief originally represented a married male-female couple is that "The reverse order [originally two women] seems to be excluded" (p. 148).

137. *Fonteia G(aiae) l(iberta) Eleusis h(uic?) o(lla) Data Fonteia G(aiae) l(iberta) Helena*. Walker and Burnett translate this as: "Fonteia Eleusis, freedwoman of Gaia. The burial urn granted to her. Fonteia Helena, freedwoman of Gaia" (*Augustus*, 43f). They base their rendering of the peculiar *HODATA* on a suggestion by Daniele Manacorda (p. 45).

known person apparently recut the marble stone to transform the woman on the left into a man. The relief and the inscription allow for several interpretations, one of which is that the two women had lived in a relationship that they considered comparable to a Roman marriage, which would correlate with the references to woman-woman marriage in Iamblichos and Lucian.

A recently published wall painting from Pompeii in southern Italy depicts two women having oral sex.[138] The painting was situated in the undressing room (*apodyterium*) of a bath complex at the outskirts of Pompeii, which was preserved by being covered by volcanic ashes following the eruption of Mount Vesuvius in 79 CE. The scene contains four adult nude persons involved in erotic acts on a reclining couch. One man anally (or intercrurally, i.e., between the thighs) penetrates another man, upon whom a woman located below and in front of him performs fellatio. A second woman, behind and below her, performs cunnilingus on her. Notice that the artist represents the male homoerotic act as anal (or intercrural) penetration, but the female homoerotic act as cunnilingus, rather than penetration of some sort. The connecting point between the two homoerotic actions is a male penis being fellated by a woman crouched in front of a man. As an erotic scene involving more than two persons, the painting is reminiscent of other ancient erotic art, some of which demonstrates a fascination with the mechanics of simultaneously giving and receiving pleasure, which an artist can best represent through three or more intertwined participants.[139] Further art historical research may determine the cultural meanings of representing a female homoerotic act as connected to the male sphere through a phallos. Future researchers may also determine whether the representation of the men as erect with their faces toward the viewer and the women as crouched below them with their faces away from the viewer has a cultural valence or results simply from the athletic mechanics of intertwined erotic activity.

138. Luciana Jacobelli, *Le pitture erotiche delle Terme Suburbane di Pompei* (Soprintendenza archeologica di Pompei. Monografie 10; Rome: "L'Erma" di Bretschneider, 1995) scene seven, 54–57, 76–78, fig. 46, pl. 8. I thank Prof. Roy Ward for this reference.

Although the painting is damaged, Jacobelli has identified the acts represented through visual cues within the painting and through ancient parallels. The artist has followed the convention of painting the men in a darker skin color than the women. Furthermore, the location of the heads and outline of the bodies are clear.

Martin F. Kilmer has not found depictions of cunnilingus between women in Greek Attic red-figure vase paintings (*Greek Erotica on Attic Red-Figure Vases* [London: Duckworth, 1993] 70).

139. E.g., scene six in the same *apodyterium* shows a kneeling man penetrating another man, who is himself penetrating a woman from behind (Jacobelli, *Le pitture*, 48–53, fig. 41, pl. 7). For instances of this motif in Greek vase painting, see Kilmer, *Greek Erotica*, 55–58.

Postbiblical Judaism

Since other interpreters have thoroughly researched the ancient Jewish sources on female homoeroticism, I will review these sources only briefly, noting how they fit into the larger picture that I am drawing in this book. The Hebrew Bible does not prohibit sexual relations between women, although it does forbid male-male anal intercourse: "You shall not lie with a male as with a woman; it is an abomination" (NRSV, Lev 18:22); and "If a man lies with a male as with a woman, both of them have committed an abomination; they shall be put to death; their blood is upon them" (NRSV, Lev 20:13).[140]

Saul Olyan has convincingly demonstrated that Lev 18:22 and 20:13 prohibit anal intercourse, but not other male homoerotic acts.[141]

By comparing the Hebrew terminology for the sexual acts prohibited in these verses with that found in other ancient Israelite laws on sexual intercourse, he further demonstrates that Lev 18:22 is directed toward the insertive partner in anal intercourse, but not toward the receptive partner. Olyan posits that at an earlier stage in its history, Lev 20:13 placed a penalty only on the insertive partner. He interprets the awkward change from the singular ("If a man . . .") to the plural ("both of them . . . they . . .") as evidence of a later expansion of the law to include punishment of

---

140. Lev 18:22: MT: וְאֶת־זָכָר לֹא תִשְׁכַּב מִשְׁכְּבֵי אִשָּׁה תּוֹעֵבָה הִוא; LXX: καὶ μετὰ ἄρσενος οὐ κοιμηθήσῃ κοίτην γυναικός· βδέλυγμα γάρ ἐστιν.

Lev 20:13: MT: וְאִישׁ אֲשֶׁר יִשְׁכַּב אֶת־זָכָר מִשְׁכְּבֵי אִשָּׁה תּוֹעֵבָה עָשׂוּ שְׁנֵיהֶם מוֹת יוּמָתוּ דְּמֵיהֶם בָּם; LXX: καὶ ὃς ἂν κοιμηθῇ μετὰ ἄρσενος κοίτην γυναικός, βδέλυγμα ἐποίησαν ἀμφότεροι· θανατούσθωσαν, ἔνοχοί εἰσιν.

141. Saul M. Olyan, "'And with a Male You Shall Not Lie the Lying Down of a Woman': On the Meaning and Significance of Leviticus 18:22 and 20:13," *Journal of the History of Sexuality* 5 (1994) 179–206. These verses have attracted much commentary in recent years; see Olyan for further references. I give prominence here to Olyan, because he has advanced our knowledge of these verses far beyond the prior state of research. I disagree, however, with his closing assessment that the "evidence of the Hebrew Bible is insufficient to support [the] view [that Israelites abhorred male couplings]" (p. 205). Even if the Bible legally prohibits such couplings only at Lev 18:22 and 20:13, the death penalty surely constitutes evidence that the Israelites abhorred it. I do agree with him, though, that before the introduction of this law, there is no legal evidence that Israelites abhorred male-male couplings. In a personal conversation, Olyan clarified that that had been his point (July 13, 1995).

See also Daniel Boyarin, "Are There Any Jews in 'The History of Sexuality'?" *Journal of the History of Sexuality* 5 (1995) 333–55. Boyarin argues that the evidence from the Bible and the Talmud confirms the views of Michel Foucault and David Halperin that sexual identity is not a relevant category for the premodern period. Boyarin notes that the prohibition of male-male anal intercourse left undisturbed other male homoerotic practices, as well as male-male emotional and physical closeness. In addition, see Daniel Boyarin, "'Behold Israel According to the Flesh': On Anthropology and Sexuality in Late Antique Judaisms," *Yale Journal of Criticism* 5 (1992) 27–57.

the receptive partner. He also suggests that the Hebrew term rendered as "abomination" by the NRSV means "the violation of a socially constructed boundary."[142]

If we could establish why ancient Israelites prohibited anal intercourse between males, we might be able to understand why they did not prohibit female homoerotic acts. But the reasons for prohibiting anal intercourse between males are far from clear. Olyan suggests that in their present context within a section of Leviticus dominated by purity concerns, these two laws make most sense when seen as a prohibition against commingling two defiling substances, semen and excrement, in the receptive partner's body.[143] According to this interpretation, there would be no reason to prohibit sexual relations between females, because such relations do not involve the commingling of two defiling substances.[144] Other reasons scholars have proposed for this prohibition include: that the passive male does not conform fully to the class of male human beings,[145] that male-male intercourse involves the wasting of male seed,[146] that ancient Israelites associated male-male intercourse with non-Israelite cultic activity,[147] and that the insertive male did not conform to his class, either because he chose the wrong partner or because he chose the wrong orifice.[148] Since, however, each of these proposals leaves unresolved problems,[149] in the current state of research we cannot definitively explain the lack of a prohibition of female-female sexual contact in ancient Israelite law. In the end, the most plausible explanation may simply be that the lawmakers generally showed greater interest in males and their behavior.

In contrast to the biblical period, in the Roman period, Jews did take up the issue of female homoeroticism. Since in the ancient Mediterranean

142. Olyan, "'And with a Male,'" 180, n. 3.

143. Ibid., 202–6.

144. Ibid., 206. If, however, the Israelite authors of these laws were primarily concerned with the commingling of semen and excrement, why did they not prohibit male-female anal intercourse? Indeed, later rabbis debated male-female anal intercourse and decided to allow it (see below). To his credit, Olyan does mention the lack of a biblical prohibition against anal intercourse with a woman as a counterargument to his own interpretation (p. 203, n. 81).

145. E.g., Thomas M. Thurston, "Leviticus 18:22 and the Prohibition of Homosexual Acts," *Homophobia and the Judaeo-Christian Tradition*, ed. Michael L. Stemmeler and J. Michael Clark (Dallas: Monument, 1990) 7–23; Thurston bases his views on those of Mary Douglas, *Purity and Danger: An Analysis of the Concepts of Pollution and Taboo* (London: Routledge and Kegan Paul, 1966) 41–57.

146. E.g., Howard Eilberg-Schwarz, *The Savage in Judaism: An Anthropology of Israelite Religion and Ancient Judaism* (Bloomington: Indiana University Press, 1990) 183.

147. E.g., Boswell, *Christianity, Social Tolerance, and Homosexuality*, 100.

148. Saul Olyan (personal correspondence of July 17, 1995).

149. See Saul M. Olyan, "'And with a Male,'" 197–204.

world as a whole we see in this period a dramatically increased interest in sexual love between women, Jews resembled their non-Jewish neighbors in expressing awareness of the phenomenon. In their language and rhetoric, Greek-language Jewish sources more closely resemble non-Jewish writings than do early rabbinic ones. Thus, the author of *The Sentences of Pseudo-Phokylides* represents a woman having sexual relations with another woman as imitating a man, which ties in closely with the rhetoric we have seen in the non-Jewish world. This Greek poem, probably written by a Jewish author of the diaspora, contains a long section on proper sexual behavior, marriage, and family life.[150] The author defines intercourse between males as a transgression of nature not found in the animal world.[151] A similar prohibition to women follows in the next line: "And let not women imitate the sexual role [literally, "marriage bed"] of men."[152] The author also warns the reader against letting a son have long, braided, or knotted hair, as long hair is for voluptuous women.[153] Further, beautiful boys are to be protected from male sexual advances and virgins kept locked up until their wedding day.[154] The sexual ethics presented in the poem are thus based on strict gender differentiation in dress and sexual role. Girls are to be kept fit for marriage and, once married, are not to stray outside the boundaries of marriage. The rhetoric of transgressing against nature, of doing acts that animals avoid, and of homoerotic women imitating men ties in with a non-Jewish rhetoric that I document at many points throughout this book and is much in contrast to earlier, biblical perspectives.[155]

I discuss Paul's Letter to the Romans at length below in the context of

150. *The Sentences of Pseudo-Phokylides* 175–227. P[ieter] W. Van der Horst, ed. and trans., *The Sentences of Pseudo-Phocylides* (Studia in Veteris Testamenti Pseudepigrapha 4; Leiden: Brill, 1978) 98–103, 225–57. Van der Horst dates the work to between ca. 30 BCE and 40 CE, and suggests Alexandria as the place of origin (pp. 81–83).

151. *The Sentences of Pseudo-Phokylides* 190f: "Transgress not for unlawful sex the natural limits of sexuality. / For even animals are not pleased by intercourse of male with male" (ET: Van der Horst, *The Sentences of Pseudo-Phokylides,* 101).

152. *The Sentences of Pseudo-Phokylides* 192: μηδέ τι θηλύτεραι λέχος ἀνδρῶν μιμήσαιντο (Van der Horst, *The Sentences of Pseudo-Phokylides,* 100f). Were line 192 not in its present context, it could also refer to a woman imitating a man sexually in another way, such as by masturbating with a dildo. Van der Horst interprets the line as referring to sexual contact between females (pp. 239f).

153. *The Sentences of Pseudo-Phokylides* 210–12.

154. *The Sentences of Pseudo-Phokylides* 213–16.

155. Another Greek-language Jewish source, the Psalms of Solomon 2:14f, speaks of the daughters of Jerusalem having defiled themselves with a "confusion of mingling" (φυρμῷ ἀναμίξεως) (Alfred Rahlfs, ed., *Septuaginta*, vol. 2 [Stuttgart: Deutsche Bibelstiftung, 1935] 472; ET: *OTP,* 2.652). This could refer to incest or to intercourse with animals or with other women.

early Christian teachings.[156] Since, however, Paul was trained as a Pharisee and continued to view himself as "a member of the people of Israel,"[157] we need to consider at least briefly his condemnation of female and male homoeroticism in the context of Judaism. Like *The Sentences of Pseudo-Phokylides*, Paul presents homoerotic behavior as contrary to nature, and he discusses female and male homoeroticism side by side. Paul's Greek terminology also resembles that of *The Sentences of Pseudo-Phokylides* in that both employ the language of "males" and "females," rather than the more usual terms "men" and "women." Both Paul and Pseudo-Phokylides may have employed the term "females" as a parallel to the term "male" found in Lev 18:22 and 20:13, which could mean that they saw themselves as extending the Levitical prohibition of Lev 18:22 to include females.[158] Paul's condemnation, however, differs from *The Sentences of Pseudo-Phokylides* and from all other ancient Jewish discussions of female homoeroticism in that he alone sees it as worthy of death.[159] We might view Paul as the only ancient Jew to extend Lev 20:13 to include women. Whether this stricter view represents a strand of Pharisaic diaspora Jewish thought that has not otherwise survived or whether the greater strictness resulted from changes in thinking due to his belief in Christ, has to remain a matter of speculation.

Like the Sifra, a rabbinic text that I will discuss shortly, Paul associates homoerotic behavior with non-Jewish activities. Paul describes homoerotic behavior as the result of idolatry, including the veneration of images in the form of animals, a practice specifically associated with Egypt,[160] while the Sifra describes male-male and female-female marriage as an Egyptian and/or Canaanite practice.

The Sifra, a rabbinical commentary on Leviticus, is composed of sayings from the tannaitic period (i.e., before ca. 220 CE). As we saw above, Leviticus 18 prohibits sexual relations between males, but not between females. The rabbinic sages whose views Sifra represents apparently believed that female homoeroticism in the form of a long-term commitment was wrong and sought a biblical verse to prove it. They found it in Lev 18:3:

---

156. Rom 1:26f: "Their women exchanged natural intercourse for unnatural, (27) and in the same way also the men, giving up natural intercourse with women, were consumed with passion for one another. Men committed shameless acts with men and received in their own persons the due penalty for their error" (NRSV). See the chapters below on Paul's Letter to the Romans and on Rom 1:18–32.

157. Phil 3:5f.

158. The LXX has ἄρσην. Paul and Pseudo-Phokylides have the plural ἄρσενες and the plural θήλειαι/θηλύτεραι.

159. Rom 1:32.

160. Rom 1:18–23.

> Or: "You shall not do as they do in the land of Egypt . . . and you shall not do as they do in the land of Canaan" (Lev 18:3). One could (interpret it as meaning) that they may not build buildings or plant plants like them. Therefore scripture teaches, "You shall not walk in their statutes" (Lev 18:3). . . . And what did they do? A man married a man and a woman a woman, and a man married a woman and her daughter, and a woman was married to two men.[161]

Since the ancient rabbis took gender markings in biblical formulations very seriously, they could not derive a prohibition of female-female intercourse from Lev 18:22, which speaks of males. Lev 18:3, however, as a general prohibition against imitating the Egyptians and the Canaanites, provided them the means to prohibit female homoeroticism in the form of woman-woman marriage. Michael Satlow suggests that the text does not prohibit female homoeroticism per se, but rather marriage between women, because of the gender blurring that would of necessity occur in marriage between women, but not necessarily in sexual contact between women.[162]

We could also interpret this passage more figuratively as culminating in a series of fictitious scenarios—bizarre forms of marriage—designed to represent the Egyptians and Canaanites as idolaters with idolatrous sexual practices: same-sex marriage, incestuous marriage, and polyandrous marriage. Just as the Romans represented female homoeroticism as a Greek phenomenon, foreign to Roman reality, the Sifra represents it as Egyptian and Canaanite, foreign to the God of Israel. In this interpretation, we would read the text as speaking figuratively about the dangers of assimilation to idolatrous foreign practices, rather than about halakhah (i.e., legal requirements incumbent upon Jews) derived from Lev 18:3.[163]

---

161. Sifra on Lev 18:3 (*Aharei Mot, Parasha* 9): או כמעשה ארץ מצרים וכמעשה ארץ כנען לא תעשו יכול לא יבנו בנינים ולא יטעו נטיעות כמותם תלמוד לומר וכחקותיהם לא תלכו . . . ומה היו עושים האיש נושא לאיש והאשה לאשה. האיש נושא אשה ובתה. והאשה ניסת לשנים

(J. H. Weiss, ed., *Sifra* [Vienna: Schlossberg, 1862]). Translation my own. See *Genesis Rabbah* 26.6 and *Leviticus Rabbah* 23.9, which refer to marriage between males, but not females. See also *b. Hullin* 92b, which prohibits drawing up a marriage contract for males. For discussion, see Boswell, *Same-Sex Unions*, 364–71. For excellent overviews of early rabbinic understandings of the body and of human eroticism, see Daniel Boyarin, *Carnal Israel: Reading Sex in Talmudic Culture* (The New Historicism: Studies in Cultural Poetics 25; Berkeley: University of California Press, 1993); and Michael L. Satlow, *Tasting the Dish: Rabbinic Rhetorics of Sexuality* (Brown Judaic Studies 303; Atlanta: Scholars Press, 1995).

162. Michael L. Satlow, "'They Abused Him Like a Woman': Homoeroticism, Gender Blurring, and the Rabbis in Late Antiquity," *Journal of the History of Sexuality* 5 (1994) 1–25; discussion of this text on pp. 16f. Satlow notes that "of the four liaisons mentioned, only this liaison is nowhere hinted at or mentioned in Lev. 18" (p. 17). Marriage between women may have been the driving force behind this interpretation of Lev 18:3, since the sages could have derived prohibitions of the three other forms of marriage from other biblical verses.

163. See Maimonides, *Mishneh Torah, 'Issurei Bi'ah* (Forbidden Intercourse) 21:8, who uses this passage as the basis of his halakhic discussion of female homoerotic activity among

Whether we read this passage literally or figuratively, the image of the Egyptians allowing marriage between women corresponds with the image of Egypt as the location for woman-woman marriage found in Iamblichos (Mesopotamia marrying Berenike, the queen of Egypt). And, as I discuss below, both the astrologer Ptolemy of Alexandria (in Egypt) and the Christian Clement of Alexandria refer to women marrying other women. Thus, the rabbinic sages give an image of Egypt for which we have contemporaneous corroboration from both within and outside Egypt. Notice also that the Sifra represents such marriages as legally acceptable to their participants and cultures by quoting Lev 18 : 3, which speaks of "their statutes." [164] Even if this were to be a legal fiction, the image of legally sanctioned woman-woman marriage among idolatrous peoples would have carried great rhetorical power for the legally minded rabbis.

While the Sifra represents marriage between women as a foreign practice, the Jerusalem and Babylonian Talmuds represent sexual love between women as something in which Jewish daughters might engage, even daughters of priests and potential wives of priests. The Jerusalem Talmud, the compilation and editing of which was completed around the fifth century CE, refers to women having sexual contact with each other, literally to "rubbing" with each other.[165] The text records a difference of opinion between two rabbinical schools of the first century CE on whether a woman who engaged in sexual contact with another woman (a *mĕsallelet*) was unfit

---

Jewish women. Maimonides interprets marriage between women in the passage to refer generally to sexual contact between women. (See also *Shulchan Aruch*, *'Even Ha'Ezer* 20.2.) For discussion, see Rachel Biale, *Women and Jewish Law: An Exploration of Women's Issues in Halakhic Sources* (New York: Schocken, 1984) 195; and Rebecca T. Alpert, *The Outsider Within: Jewish Lesbians and the Jewish Community* (New York: Columbia University Press, forthcoming). I express gratitude to Rebecca Alpert for making the relevant portion of her manuscript available to me.

164. Further research might corroborate or disconfirm the existence among Canaanites and Egyptians of the other types of marriage represented here.

165. *Y. Giṭṭin* 8:10, 49c.70–71: המסללדת בבנה בית שמאי פוסלין. ובית הלל מכשירין. שתי נשים שהיו מסללדות זו את זו בית שמאי פוסלין ובית הלל מכשירין. "If a woman 'rubs' with her son, the School of Shammai disqualifies [her from eating the priestly due and from marrying a priest]. The School of Hillel allows [her to eat the priestly due and to marry a priest]. If two women 'rub' with each other, the School of Shammai disqualifies [her from eating the priestly due and from marrying a priest]. The School of Hillel allows [her to eat the priestly due and to marry a priest]." Cf. *t. Sota* 5.7: המסללת בבנה קטן. העד בה. בית שמאי פוסלין מן הכהונה ובית הילל מכשירין (Saul Lieberman, ed., *The Tosefta: The Orders of Zeraim, Moed, Nashim, Nezikin*, 4 vols. [New York: Jewish Theological Seminary, 1955–88], 3.2 [1962] 178. Lieberman records המסלסלת as a variant for המסללת. "If a woman 'rubs' with her minor son, and he penetrates her, the School of Shammai disqualifies [her from eating the priestly due and marrying a priest], but the School of Hillel allows [her to eat the priestly due and to marry a priest]." On העד בה as meaning penetration, see Satlow, "'They Abused Him Like a Woman,'" 15f, n. 42.

for the priesthood, that is, unfit to eat the priestly offerings and to marry into the priesthood. The background is that a priest may not marry a woman who has committed harlotry, a woman who has been defiled, or a divorced woman (Lev 21:7), and the high priest must marry a virgin (Lev 21:13). Further, according to the Bible, the daughter of a priest who engages in harlotry is to be burned with fire (Lev 21:9). The question is whether sexual relations between women counts as harlotry, thereby disqualifying those women from marrying a priest and from eating the priestly offerings.[166] According to the text, the School of Shammai says that it does count, while the School of Hillel does not count sexual relations between women as disqualifying a woman from marrying a priest and from eating the priestly offerings.

Because the Babylonian Talmud attributes a parallel tradition to a rabbi who lived in the middle of the third century, the Jerusalem Talmud's attribution of the tradition about women who engage in sexual activity with each other to the first-century Schools of Hillel and Shammai may be anachronistic.[167] The Babylonian Talmud, the final editing of which occurred in the sixth century CE, quotes Rav Huna, a Babylonian rabbi of the mid-third century: "Women who 'rub' with each other are disqualified from the priesthood."[168] It juxtaposes this view with that of Rabbi El'azar, who defines women's 'rubbing' with each other as mere obscenity, rather than as harlotry. Accordingly, in Rabbi El'azar's view, a woman's 'rubbing' with another woman does not disqualify her from the priesthood.[169] Since

166. For more on the rabbinic discussion of the rights and responsibilities of women of the priestly class, see Bernadette J. Brooten, *Women Leaders in the Ancient Synagogue: Inscriptional Evidence and Background Issues* (Brown Judaic Studies 36; Chico, CA: Scholars Press, 1982) 78–83, 245f.

167. Critical scholars of rabbinic literature are generally skeptical about attributions to the Schools of Hillel and Shammai. See Michael L. Satlow, who argues that the Jerusalem Talmud passage is probably "unified and post-tannaitic," i.e., created in the third century or later as one piece. He suggests that the redactors in the Jerusalem Talmud knew of *t. Soṭa* 5.7, eliminated the phrase "he penetrated her," and then added the discussion of female homoerotic activity based on a broader understanding of 'rub,' an understanding that included nonpenetrating sexual activity. Satlow argues that it is implausible that both the tradition in *t. Soṭa* 5.7 and that in the Jerusalem Talmud would have circulated at the same time. He further argues that if the redactors of the Babylonian Talmud had known that the School of Shammai disqualified homoerotic women from the priesthood, they would have cited that tradition, rather than attributing it to the third-century Rav Huna ("'They Abused Him Like a Woman,'" 16, n. 45).

168. *B. Yebamot* 76a: דאמר רב הונא נשים המסוללות זו בזו פסולות לכהונה. In the context, Raba states that the halakhah is not in accordance with Rav Huna.

169. *B. Yebamot* 76a: אבל אשה פריצותא בעלמא. See Rashi on this passage, who interprets המסוללות as meaning, "As in the intercourse of male and female, they rub their femininity [i.e., their genitals] against each other." See Biale, *Women and Jewish Law*, 193.

these traditions parallel those attributed to the Houses of Shammai and
Hillel in the Jerusalem Talmud, and since the editors of the Babylonian
Talmud would probably have cited the ancient and authoritative Houses
of Hillel and Shammai if they had known of their discussions of the issue,
we should probably assume a third-century or later date for this debate on
women's homoerotic contact with each other.

At another point, the Babylonian Talmud quotes Rav Huna's view again.
A man did not allow his daughters to sleep together, and the Talmud asks,
"Shall we say that this supports [the opinion] of Rav Huna? For Rav Huna
stated, 'Women who "rub" with each other are disqualified from the
priesthood.' No. [He prohibited his daughters from sleeping together] in
order that they should not become accustomed to a foreign body." [170] The
text raises the question whether the man kept his daughters from sleeping
together in order to prevent them from engaging in homoerotic, incestuous, sexual contact. But the Talmud answers that the man did not have
that problem in mind, but rather the problem of the daughters' becoming
accustomed to sleeping with another person. The rabbinic sages probably
were thinking of the laws of menstruation, according to which a married
woman has to sleep separately from her husband for a good part of the
month. If a young woman grew used to sleeping with another person, she
might have difficulty abiding by the menstrual laws in the future. In other
words, the talmudic editors quoted Rav Huna's saying for the purpose of
refuting it. [171]

Since both the Jerusalem and the Babylonian Talmuds merely cite the
results of the debate, but do not discuss the reasons for each side's position,
we can only speculate on the conceptualizations of female homoerotic activity with which they were working. One possibility is that those rabbinic
sages who defined the women's homoerotic sexual contact as harlotry
(zěnût), rather than mere obscenity (pěrîsûtā'), assumed that no penetration occurred, while those who defined it as harlotry assumed that the
women used a dildo or possessed the physical capacity to penetrate. [172] If
they assumed a capacity to penetrate, they would have shared this view with
some Latin and Greek writers in this period. However, neither side in this
debate is reported to have distinguished between an active and a passive
partner, which we would expect if penetration were at issue. The sources
seem to assume a mutual activity in which both partners rub and are
rubbed. The medieval Jewish legal thinker Maimonides, who states that

170. B. Šabbat 65a–b: מְסֻלּוֹת—פְּסוּלוֹת: נָשִׁים הַמְסוֹלְלוֹת זוֹ בָּזוֹ—דְּאָמַר רַב הוּנָא. לְרַב הוּנָא לֵיהּ מְסַיְּיע לֵימָא
לִבְהוּ נַהּ!—לָא סָבַר: כִּי הֵיכִי דְּלָא לַיְלְפָן גּוּפָא נוּכְרָאָה.

171. See Alpert, *The Outsider Within;* and Biale, *Women and Jewish Law,* 194f.

172. For rabbinic discussion of a woman using a dildo, see *b. 'Aboda Zara* 44a.

"no intercourse is involved,"[173] supports the interpretation that the activity in question does not involve penetration.

Rachel Biale takes her cue from Maimonides and argues that the rabbinic sages did not see female homoerotic contact as an actual sexual transgression, because they did not conceptualize it as an act of intercourse: "The male sexual experience of heterosexual intercourse is the standard for defining what is a sexual act, and thus what is a sexual transgression."[174]

Both Rachel Biale and Rebecca Alpert stress the differing treatment accorded to sexual love between women and that between men in Jewish sources in this period. Biale suggests that the relative paucity of material on sexual relations between women could be due to the lack of an explicit biblical prohibition, to the fact that "no actual intercourse" is involved, or to the rabbis' lack of access to women's life experiences.

Alpert similarly emphasizes that ancient Judaism was not fundamentally opposed to sexual love between women. She assumes that the rabbinic sages knew that sexual love between women existed but thought that homoerotic women would nevertheless marry men. She argues that the rabbis principally concerned themselves with making sure that women would be prepared for marriage to future husbands, whose needs and desires were of paramount importance to them.[175]

The ancient rabbis thus differ from many of their Greek and Latin contemporaries in their lack of speculation on masculine women and their precise actions, although those who held the views attributed to the School of Shammai and to Rav Huna may have engaged in such speculation. We can best understand the tradition attributed to the School of Hillel and to Rabbi El'azar as based on the view that one need not take female homoerotic contact seriously as a sexual transgression, since it does not involve penetration. The originators of this tradition, along with the final editors of the Babylonian Talmud, thus resemble the Greek and Latin writers, who also focused on penetration by a phallus as the preeminent sexual act.[176]

Several strands of postbiblical Jewish thought concerning female homoeroticism have emerged from this survey: (1) a diaspora, Greek-language prohibition that may constitute an extension of the Levitical prohibition of sexual relations between males to include females; this discourse utilizes such Greek concepts as women imitating men and acts that are "contrary to nature" (Pseudo-Phokylides and Paul); (2) a rabbinic prohibition of marriage between women on the basis of Lev 18:3, an exegetical move

173. Maimonides, *Mishneh Torah,* '*Issurei Bi'ah* (Forbidden Intercourse) 21:8: אֵין שָׁם בִּיאָה.
174. Biale, *Women and Jewish Law,* 197.
175. Alpert, *The Outsider Within.*
176. The Levitical laws' focus on penetration most likely also shaped rabbinic views.

that defines such marriage as a foreign practice (Sifra); (3) the classification of women "rubbing" each other as engaged in by daughters of Jewish priests and potential wives of priests; the definition of this practice as harlotry, that is, as a serious sexual transgression according to Leviticus; and (4) the recognition that daughters of Jewish priests and potential wives of priests might engage in "rubbing" each other; the definition of this practice as mere obscenity, that is, as not coming under Levitical prohibitions. All four of these strands seem to derive from concerns relating to Leviticus.

That Pseudo-Phokylides and Paul both address the issue at around the same time as the Schools of Hillel and Shammai could constitute evidence that some type of rabbinic discussion goes back to the first century after all.[177] The emergent Jewish awareness of sexual relations between women in the Roman period may indicate increased openness on the part of women and possibly a greater frequency of sexual expression within female friendships. While the Greek-language Jewish sources express their condemnations of female homoeroticism in the Greek cultural idiom, the Hebrew and Aramaic ones do not. Thus, the rabbinic sources lack both the concept of the masculine woman and the philosophical concept of "contrary to nature."[178] Nevertheless, the timing of both coincides with increased discussion of female homoeroticism in the Roman period in comparison with earlier eras. In this respect, we can see the several strands of the Jewish discussion as part of a larger discussion within the Roman world.

This survey of a wide variety of sources from classical Greece through the Roman period demonstrates an increasing awareness of sexual love between women, nearly always combined with rejection of such love. Male authors had a difficult time fitting female homoeroticism into a male framework of thinking. Some authors attribute gendered roles to the respective partners in a female homoerotic relationship, while others do not. Some authors describe both partners as culpable, others only the "masculine" partner. Most writers devote far greater attention to sexual relations be-

177. Paul forms an intriguing potential link in the chain of tradition. Paul states that he had been a Pharisee (Phil 3:5), and the Acts of the Apostles has Paul claim that he had studied with Gamaliel (i.e., with Rabban Gamliel the Elder, the grandson of Hillel; Acts 22:3). Acts refers to Gamaliel as a Pharisee (Acts 5:34). Since interpreters are generally skeptical about the historical value of Acts for reconstructing Paul's life, we have to be cautious of taking at face value Paul's claim to have studied with Gamaliel. Nevertheless, if Paul did not study with Gamaliel, he may have studied with another Pharisee who held similar views. Thus, Paul's discussion of female homoeroticism could itself constitute evidence for the antiquity of the Pharisaic/rabbinic discussion of sexual relations between women. Notice, however, that Paul's view is closer to that of the School of Shammai than to that of the School of Hillel.

178. The rabbinic phrase שלא כדרכה ("not according to her manner," used for anal intercourse with a woman; see, e.g., b. Sanhedrin 58b) is not philosophical in the way that φύσις is.

tween males than to those between women, and male homoeroticism finds far greater tolerance in the Roman world than female homoeroticism. Writers employ a variety of techniques to represent such love as bizarre, foreign, and unspeakable.

This broad survey should help to orient the reader as we proceed to a more in-depth consideration of four areas: erotic spells commissioned by women to attract other women, astrology, medicine, and dream interpretation.

⚜ 3 ⚜

"Inflame Her Liver with Love":
Greek Erotic Spells from Egypt

everal ancient erotic spells in which women attempt to attract other women create new hopes for uncovering the history of ancient Mediterranean women. In contrast to the vast majority of sources discussed in this book, here we have documents containing the actual names of women who desired other women. If, however, we believe that these spells can give us profound insight into women's love relationships, we will be disappointed, for the individual women probably did not compose their own spells. Rather, these spells contain highly formulaic language that reveals more about cultural ideology than about individual women's lives.

Because of the limitations of these spells as a source for the history of women, I will focus on them primarily as a source for cultural conceptualizations of the erotic and of women. I will also highlight the instances in which, despite these limitations, these spells can yield historical information. Most important, we find that the male writers who prohibited, satirized, and belittled romantic love between women were responding to social reality.

In order to assess the further implications of these spells for the history of women, we need to understand how ancient people created and employed them. While the exact processes by which interested persons could make use of spells remain obscure, we do know some details. *Magoi*, professionals who specialized in knowing how to perform effective "magical" procedures, codified their knowledge in handbooks. These formularies contain detailed recipes for spells for various occasions that a scribe could copy out, inserting the proper names at the appropriate points. The recipes also often include detailed instructions for specific behavior to accompany the written spell, demonstrating that the spells were not just written and spoken, but also performed.

The instructions of one ancient formulary illustrates this mixture of formulaic words and actions. According to this recipe, intended to bind a woman to a male petitioner, the reader is to make two figures of wax or clay, a male one armed like Ares, holding a sword in his left hand, threatening to thrust it into the right side of the neck of a kneeling female figure with her arms tied behind her back. The formulary says to write specific magical words on particular parts of the woman's body and then to take thirteen copper nails, piercing individual body parts and saying, "I pierce (the name of the body part) of so-and-so, so that she will think of no one, except for me, so-and-so, alone." The formulary then instructs the reader to take a lead tablet,[1] to write the same saying on it, to say it out loud, and to bind the tablet to the figures, tying it with 365 knots and saying, "Abrasax, hold it fast." The lead tablet is to be placed at sunset at the tomb of a person who has died before her or his time or who has died a violent death. (The ghost of such a person is not at rest and, as a roaming ghost, can be counted on to carry out the wishes of the petitioner.) Next to the tablet, the petitioner is to put seasonal flowers and to recite a specific saying.[2]

These formularies by and for the *magoi* resemble other handbooks of the period, such as astrological, medical, or architectural manuals, which also provide instructions on how to practice a craft.[3] Clients commissioned their spells through professionals who wrote out the spells from a formulary and advised clients on the necessary rituals, possibly performing some of the rituals themselves (such as placing the spell in the sarcophagus of a dead person). We should, however, be careful not to absolutize this scenario. For example, sources such as the Jewish writing *Sepher ha-Razim*, which contains a variety of materials and was not directed toward magical practitioners, include recipes for erotic spells.[4] Thus, access to spells may have spilled over the edges of the professional class of *magoi*.

1. On the use of lead in binding spells, see David G. Martinez, *P. Michigan XVI: A Greek Love Charm from Egypt (P. Mich. 757)* (American Studies in Papyrology 30; Atlanta: Scholars Press, 1991) 2–6, who points out that ancient astrologers associated lead with Kronos/Saturn, a maleficent planet, and that lead's "relative worthlessness . . . , coldness . . . , pallid, death-like color. . . , and weight, contribute to the general impression of the chthonic [i.e., earthly, netherworldly] quality of the metal and its appropriateness for forceful magic" (pp. 3f).

2. Karl Preisendanz et al., eds. and trans., *Papyri Graecae Magicae*, 2 vols. (2d ed.; Stuttgart: Teubner, 1973–74) no. 4.296–334 (= *PGM*); ET: Hans Dieter Betz, ed., *The Greek Magical Papyri in Translation*, vol. 1 (Chicago: University of Chicago Press, 1986) 44.

3. See, e.g., those by Vettius Valens, Soranos, and Vitruvius.

4. Mordecai Margolioth, ed., *Sepher ha-Razim* (Jerusalem: Yediot Achronot, 1966), e.g., First Firmament, lines 166–68, p. 75 (a spell for a male petitioner to attract either a woman or a man); Second Firmament, lines 30–37, pp. 82f (a spell for love between a man and a woman); ET: Michael A. Morgan, *Sepher ha-Razim: The Book of the Mysteries* (SBLTT 25, Pseudepigrapha Series 11; Chico, CA: Scholars Press, 1983) 37, 45f (the latter spell is in-

The formularies contain recipes for different types of spells. Erotic spells form a subcategory of the binding spells, through which the petitioner sought to bind another person against his or her will. Of the over 1,500 extant binding spells, erotic spells comprise approximately one quarter, while curse tablets make up the majority.[5] Erotic spells resemble curse tablets in that they may describe the binding and tormenting of the persons toward whom the spells are directed, but they differ from curse tablets in that their ultimate goal is not to harm individuals, but rather to attract their love.[6] In the case of an erotic spell, the binding signifies binding a person to the petitioner with love.

How do erotic spells between women fit into the larger tradition of binding spells? The answer depends on whether women in this period who loved other women modeled their erotic relationships on sexual love between men and women (or on that between males), a question about which other sources from the Roman world leave us confused. Those texts that describe female homoeroticism in terms of an active/passive duality, with one of the women playing a "male" role, may lead us to believe that homoerotic women adapted their sexual relationships to prevailing cultural norms. But legally and culturally, women could not model themselves totally on men. Hence, we find that the first-century Roman poet Martial uses the term *tribas* to describe a woman named Philaenis, who penetrates

---

cluded in John G. Gager, ed., *Curse Tablets and Binding Spells from the Ancient World* [New York: Oxford University Press, 1992] [with contributions by Catherine F. Cooper, David Frankfurter, Derek Krueger, and Richard Lim] no. 31, p. 106).

See also Rebecca Lesses, "Ritual Practices to Gain Power: Adjurations in the Hekhalot Literature, Jewish Amulets, and Greek Revelatory Adjurations" (Ph.D. diss., Harvard University, 1995).

5. See Gager, *Curse Tablets and Binding Spells,* 78. Binding spells could have as their goals such varied purposes as to attract a lover, to curse an enemy, or to cause failure to an opposing team in the circus.

6. See J. C. B. Petropoulos, "The Erotic Magical Papyri," in *Proceedings of the XVIII International Congress of Papyrology,* vol. 2 (Athens: Greek Papyrological Society, 1988) 215–22. Petropoulos divides the erotic spells into attraction spells (ἀγωγαί), which aim to attract/ drive (ἄγειν) the beloved person to oneself, and binding spells (φιλτροκατάδεσμοι), which aim to "tie down" activities and physical functions of the target in order to make her or him fall in love with the person casting the spell. Petropoulos notes that an erotic binding spell "normally involves burning an object (οὐσία) belonging to the victim or transfixing a wax effigy with a needle" (p. 216). The three principal spells that I discuss in this chapter do not fall neatly into one or the other of Petropoulos's categories: the first speaks of both attracting and binding the target; the second of constraining, driving, and forcing her; and the third of making and forcing her. Since none of the three refers to burning a substance or piercing a doll, we could categorize all three as attraction spells, or we could classify at least the first (and possibly the second) as a hybrid form. Petropoulos implicitly recognizes the difficulty inherent in neatly classifying the erotic spells by referring to the many different Greek terms used for them in the ancient recipes.

both girls and boys.[7] At the same time, the Elder Seneca uses the term *tribades* to refer to both partners in a female couple.[8]

This discrepancy between focusing only on the "active" female partner in a woman-woman relationship and on condemning both female partners illustrates the difficulty which ancient authors had in conceptualizing sexual love between women. On the one hand, some tried to present female homoeroticism as fitting into a phallocentric active/passive model of sexual intercourse, complete with an anatomical or artificial penetrating organ. On the other hand, other authors grouped together all women who refused to be penetrated by a man or simply created a female-female relationship, regardless of whether they played an active or passive role. This discrepancy illustrates that female-female relationships did not fit neatly into ancient understandings of sexual relationships as essentially asymmetrical.

Since these binding spells are formulaic, they do not reveal the internal dynamics of these women's relationships. Nevertheless, the spells do provide evidence that: (1) actual historical women in this period desired erotic attachments to other women and were willing to go to some lengths to consummate these relationships; (2) some nonelite women from Upper Egypt (relative backwoods in comparison with the urban centers in which Seneca the Elder, Juvenal, Martial, Paul, or Clement of Alexandria wrote) experienced homoerotic desire; and (3) some social support for woman-woman relationships must have existed for those women who commissioned the spells, at the minimum on the part of the scribes who composed them. The spells also raise intriguing, although ultimately unanswerable, questions about the nature of women's erotic desires.

While we cannot reconstruct precise details of these women's relationships, the cultural ideology pervading the spells invites interpretation. The female homoerotic spells closely resemble other erotic spells (male to female, female to male, male to male) and recipes (to attract either women or men) in their violent imagery of domination and conquest. As I will argue later, John Winkler and John Gager, who have correctly cautioned against taking this imagery too literally, have nevertheless interpreted it too benignly and apologetically. They have failed to integrate into their analysis that recipes for erotic spells, which generally envisage a male client attempting to obtain a female lover, both presupposed and helped to create a larger cultural pattern of the domination of a free male over a female lover, whether free or slave. Women trying to obtain male or female lovers

7. *Epigrammata* 7.67.
8. *Controversiae* 1.2.23.

and men attempting to attract male lovers employed this same cultural pattern in their spells, perhaps because the formularies contained no other model or perhaps because this model reflected their self-understanding.

As repositories of cultural ideology, the three spells discussed below form a valuable complement to the more elite, more urban texts that I discuss elsewhere in this book, because they represent a similar time period,[9] but a different geographical region and a different social stratum from most of these other texts. These spells come from Upper Egypt, far from such great urban centers as Alexandria, Rome, or Ephesos, and both the professionals who copied the spells from handbooks and the persons who commissioned them were most likely from a lower social stratum than many of the authors discussed elsewhere in this book.[10] To be sure, the other authors I discuss cover a broad social and economic spectrum: from such members of the elite as Seneca the Elder, Ovid, Martial, and Juvenal, to those who served the elite, such as the physicians Soranos of Ephesos or Aetios of Amida, down to such craftspeople as the astrologer Vettius Valens or the tentmaker Paul of Tarsus. All of these men, however, participated in the production of culture by means of their literacy, whereas the women who commissioned these binding spells, like many of the other clients of the *magoi*,[11] may or may not have been literate.

In what follows, I first present the extant erotic binding spells in which women seek to bind other women to themselves in an erotic attraction,[12] commenting briefly on each spell. I then put forth proposals as to what they can teach us about cultural conceptualizations of the erotic and, more tentatively, about the life circumstances and hopes of the women who commissioned them. Finally, I discuss whether to categorize these spells as magic or as religion and the spells' relevance for interpreting early Christian sources.

The Female Homoerotic Binding Spells: Texts and Commentary

I.   In a papyrus fragment from a cemetery in Hawara in the Fayyum region, written in a Greek script probably dating to the second century CE,

9. The spells probably date from the second through the third or fourth centuries CE, but the earliest may date from the first century CE.
10. Socially elite individuals in urban areas probably also commissioned similar spells, but the particular value of the three spells under discussion is that they name members of a group underrepresented in the historical record, both regionally and socially.
11. The *magoi* were probably of a status comparable to that of Vettius Valens.
12. See also *PGM* 12.61f, a recipe for a spell that both women and men could use to attract a member of either sex.

CHAPTER THREE

a woman named Herais attempts to attract a woman called Sarapias. This papyrus spell, which is broken off at the bottom, can be found in Karl Preisendanz's collection of Greek magical papyri (*Papyri Graecae Magicae* [= *PGM*] 32).[13]

> I adjure you, Euangelos, by Anoubis and Hermes and all the rest down below [i.e., deities]; attract and bind Sarapias whom Helen bore, to this Herais, whom Thermoutharin bore, now, now; quickly, quickly. By her soul and heart attract Sarapias herself, whom ⟨Helen⟩ bore from her own womb. *maei ote elbōsatok alaoubētō ōeio [. . .] aēn.* Attract and [bind the soul and heart of Sarapias], whom [Helen bore,

13. The papyrus measures 12.6 by 8.4 cm and is written in a rude hand. Principal edition: J. G. Milne, *Archiv für Papyrusforschung und verwandte Gebiete* 5 (1911) no. 312, pp. 393–97; and Richard Wünsch, "Zusatz zu Nr. 312 (S. 393)," *Archiv für Papyrusforschung und verwandte Gebiete* 5 (1911) 397. Republished by Karl Preisendanz et al., eds. and trans., *Papyri Graecae Magicae*, 2 vols. (2d ed.; Stuttgart: Teubner, 1973–74) no. 32; and by Arthur S. Hunt, *Journal of Egyptian Archaeology* 15 (1929) 156f. ET: Betz, *Greek Magical Papyri*, 1:266. Also commented on by: Karl Preisendanz, *Berliner Philologische Wochenschrift* 50 (1930) 749; Karl Preisendanz, *Archiv für Papyrusforschung und verwandte Gebiete* 8 (1927) 128; R. Ganszyniec, "Zu einer Defixion (Papyrus Hawara 312)," *Byzantinisch-Neugriechisches Jahrbuch* 2 (1921) 86; and William Matthew Flinders Petrie, *Hawara, Biahmu, and Arsinoe* (London: Field and Tuer, 1889) 35f.

   Ἐξορκείζ[ω] σε, Εὐάγγελε,
   κατὰ τοῦ Ἀνούβι[δο]ς καὶ
   τοῦ Ἑρμοῦ καὶ [τ]ῶν λοι[πῶν] πάν–
4 των κάτω, ἄξαι καὶ καταδ–
   ῆσαι Σαραπιάδα, ἣν ἔτε–
   κεν Ἑλένη, ἐπ' αὐτὴν Ἡρα–
   είδαν, ἣν ἔτεκεν Θερμο–
8 υθαριν, ἄρτι, ἄρτι, τα–
   χὺ ταχύ. ἐξ ψυχῆς καὶ καρδίας
   ἄγε αὐτὴν τὴν Σαραπιά–
   δ[α], ἣν ἔτεκεν ⟨Ἑλένη⟩ εἰδίᾳ μήτρ–
12 ᾳ, μαει οτε ελβωσατοκ
   αλαουβητω ωειο[
   .αην, ἄξον καὶ κα[τάδησ–
   ον ψυχὴ[ν καὶ καρδίαν Σαραπιάδο–
16 ς, ἣν ἔτεκεν [Ἑλένη, ἐπ' αὐ–
   τὴν Ἡραεί[δαν, ἣν ἔτεκε–
   ν Θερμουθα[ριν μήτ–
   ρᾳ] αὐτῆς, [ἄρτι ἄρτι, ταχὺ ταχύ].

11 ⟨Ἑλένη⟩ (Preisendanz/Henrichs); alternative explanation: the scribe was not sure whether he had given the correct name for the mother and therefore employed the general formula εἰδίᾳ μήτρᾳ (Wünsch)
15 or ονν ψυχὴ [(Milne)
19 or αὐτῆς (Milne, Hunt)

to this] Herais, [whom] Thermoutharin [bore] from her womb [now, now; quickly, quickly].

The spell contains some "mystical" or "magical" language[14] largely indecipherable to us (such as *maei ote*). Ancient creators of binding spells apparently believed that such language was understandable to the divine addressees and would lose its power if translated into Greek. By employing this type of language, practitioners were able to display their knowledge to their underworld addressees and thereby commend themselves to them.

The spell identifies Herais and Sarapias by their mothers, Thermoutharin and Helen respectively, rather than by their fathers. The practice of naming both women and men by means of their mothers' names occurs throughout the binding spells, a point over which scholars have long puzzled,[15] since legal and other types of ancient documents usually identify men by their fathers' names and women by the names of their fathers, their husbands, or both.

The combination of Greek and Egyptian personal names is typical for this period. "Helen" and "Herais" are Greek, while "Thermoutharin" is native Egyptian, and "Sarapias" derives from the Egyptian deity "Sarapis," but has a Greek ending. In spite of the Greek names, the women may ethnically have been native Egyptian (rather than, e.g., Macedonian, Persian, or Jewish—to name three of the other ethnic groups inhabiting Egypt in this period).

Herais appeals to two deities, Anoubis, the Egyptian jackal- or dog-headed deity of the underworld, and Hermes, the Greek messenger deity. "All the rest down below" refers to the other chthonic, or underworld, deities revered in the Roman world. The precise identification of Euangelos has puzzled interpreters. Richard Wünsch has suggested that Euangelos was a superhuman being subordinate to the deity Anoubis, referring to an Euangelos who had once been a deity and had a month named after him in the province of Asia, but, by the time of this papyrus, had been demoted

---

14. Most scholars employ the technical term *voces magicae* for such language; John Gager, who stresses that we cannot distinguish clearly between magic and religion, uses the term *voces mysticae* (*Curse Tablets and Binding Spells,* 9 and passim).

15. See David R. Jordan, "CIL VIII 19525 (B). 2QPVVLVA = Q(VEM) P(EPERIT) VVLVA," *Philologus* 120 (1976) 127–32, who cites the three spells I discuss here. Jordan argues that "[i]dentification ... by ... matrilineal lineage was common on defixiones [binding spells] of the second century A.D. and afterwards" (p. 128). He discusses potential Egyptian or Babylonian influence and quotes U. Wilcken on the possibility of an Egyptian prepatriarchal naming practice that had survived into the Roman period only in religious texts (such as binding spells) (p. 130, n. 8). With Wilcken, Jordan argues for a complete statistical study of Egyptian matrilineal and patrilineal naming practices (p. 130, n. 8).

to the status of a hero.[16] Wünsch's alternative explanation, however, that Euangelos is the name of the dead man upon whom Herais was calling to help her carry out the spell, is more convincing, since other binding spells explicitly call upon dead people to carry out their spells.[17] In this case, Euangelos was the corpse-*daimon*, that is, the soul of a dead person (not necessarily evil in our sense of "demon"), who wandered restlessly. If a person had died unseasonably, that is, as a young person or as a victim of violence, people in the Roman world believed that his or her *daimon* wandered about, but could gain eternal rest through carrying out the demands of a binding spell. By adjuring Euangelos, Herais may have been implicitly promising Euangelos that assisting her (such as by pleading with the underworld deities) would give him eternal rest. Notice that Herais appeals to two male deities and, most likely, to a male corpse-*daimon*, to help her attract a woman, assuming that the deities and the dead would not oppose a homoerotic union.

Notice the repetition in this spell, a feature common to many other binding spells. The spell repeats some form of "attract and bind" three times.[18] This repetition helps us to imagine how the client and/or the practitioner recited the spell aloud, perhaps accompanying it with particular actions. Perhaps Herais, or the practitioner who had supplied her with the spell, spoke it aloud as one of them placed it in the sarcophagus of the dead Euangelos.[19]

In another spell found in the same cemetery, possibly written by the same scribe, a man named Serapiakos tries to attract another man by the name of Amoneios.[20] Although scholars now agree that both the Herais-Sarapias and the Serapiakos-Amoneios spells are indeed homoerotic attraction spells, earlier interpreters disputed this. Richard Wünsch interpreted the spell concerning Herais and Sarapias as a curse spell and argued that Herais was already dead and in the netherworld (as a victim of a curse spell)

16. Richard Wünsch, "Zusatz zu Nr. 312 (S. 393)," *Archiv für Papyrusforschung und verwandte Gebiete* 5 (1911) 397; see also Hermann Usener, *Götternamen: Versuch einer Lehre von der religiösen Begriffsbildung* (Bonn: Cohen, 1896) 268–70; and Jessen, PW 6.1, s.v. "Euangelos" (1907) 844.

17. In fact, the other two female homoerotic spells that I will discuss shortly follow this practice.

18. Beginning in lines 4, 10, and 14.

19. For discussion and examples of depositing spells in graves, see Gager, *Curse Tablets and Binding Spells,* 18–20.

20. *PGM* 32a; ET: Betz, *Greek Magical Papyri,* 1:266. Reminiscent of *PGM* 4.296–334 (discussed above), the papyrus of this spell enclosed a small mud doll, presumably depicting the man whom the spell aimed to attract. See Arthur S. Hunt, "An Incantation in the Ashmolean Museum," *Journal of Egyptian Archaeology* 15 (1929) 155–57, pl. XXXI, fig. 1.

at the time of the spell.²¹ Karl Preisendanz argued that both spells were spells of separation, designed to create enmity between the petitioner and the target, and not attraction spells at all.²² Wünsch's and Preisendanz's interpretations are so unconvincing that they have elicited no further scholarly discussion,²³ but they illustrate the hesitancy of some early interpreters to accept the existence of ancient homoerotic attraction spells. Scholars now recognize several male-male spells as homoerotic, as spells either of attraction or of separation.²⁴

II.   An oval-shaped lead tablet from Hermoupolis Magna (known today as el-Ashmunen) in Upper Egypt contains a sixty-two-line spell inscribed in a third- or fourth-century CE script (see fig. 8). The ten lines at the beginning and the ten lines at the end taper off to form an oval-shaped inscription.²⁵

21. Wünsch construes ἐπ' αὐτήν in line 6 as dependent upon κάτω ἄξαι in line 4 ("Zusatz zu Nr. 312 (S. 393)," 397). Wünsch also argues that a new spell against a different person begins in line 14.

22. Karl Preisendanz, *Berliner Philologische Wochenschrift* 50 (1930) 749. Preisendanz interprets ἐπ' αὐτήν as "against the same" (Herais) rather than "to this" (Herais).

23. Arthur S. Hunt simply notes: "Wünsch was perhaps misled partly by the fact that the two persons named were both female, as in the Ashmolean papyrus they happen both to be male: that, however, is not really material" ("An Incantation in the Ashmolean Museum," 156).

24. In addition to *PGM* 32a, see also *PGM* 66 (on which see L[udwig] Koenen, "Formular eines Liebeszaubers (PGM LXVII: vgl. Tafel V)," *Zeitschrift für Papyrologie und Epigraphik* 8 [1971] 199, n. 1, who argues that the spell is homoerotic; see also Robert W. Daniel, "Intrigue in the Cloister: PGM LXVI," *Zeitschrift für Papyrologie und Epigraphik* 89 [1991] 119f, who doubts the homoerotic character of this spell); Robert W. Daniel and Franco Maltomini, eds., *Supplementum Magicum*, vol. 2 (Abhandlungen der rheinischwestfälischen Akademie der Wissenschaften, Sonderreihe Papyrologica Coloniensia 16.2; Opladen: Westdeutscher Verlag, 1992) no. 54, who think that it is probably homoerotic; and Gager, *Curse Tablets and Binding Spells*, no. 25, who classifies it under "Sex, Love, and Marriage." See also the Coptic text from the Ashmolean museum (1981.940) in which a man tries to obtain a male lover (in Marvin Meyer, Richard Smith, and Neal Kelsey, eds., *Ancient Christian Magic: Coptic Texts of Ritual Power* [San Francisco: HarperSanFrancisco, 1994] no. 84, pp. 177f [ET: David Frankfurter]). A Coptic erotic text published by Paul C. Smither, "A Coptic Love-Charm," *Journal of Egyptian Archaeology* 25 (1939) 173f, may also fall into this category. David Frankfurter has also suggested that *PGM* Ostrakon 1 (vol. 2, p. 233) may be a spell to divide two male lovers (unpublished manuscript).

25. Other spells composed in particular geometric shapes (e.g., *PGM* 1.13–19 [triangles, one pointing up and one down], 7.300 [a continuous circular form around the image of an ibis], 17a.1–18 [a diamond split down the middle], 19a.16–49 [a complex of geometric shapes], and 36.115–33 [triangles and vertical lines of letters]) indicate the relevance of shape in interpreting binding spells, but we can only speculate as to the exact significance of each shape.

82

CHAPTER THREECHAPTER THREE

A woman named Sophia used this tablet to attract another woman, Gorgonia. The *Supplementum Magicum* collection includes this inscription (= *Suppl. Mag.*, 1.42).[26] (The raised numbers indicate the lines of the tablet.)

We also do not know whether the lead was trimmed off to form an oval after the scribe incised the text or whether the scribe followed the form of a precut tablet.

26. The oval-shaped lead tablet measures 18 by 20 cm. Side A contains sixty-two lines of text, while side B has four lines (= side A, lines 1–5). Perhaps the scribe began on side B, quit and then began over again on side A. The tablet is now located in the Biblioteca Medicea Laurenziana in Florence.

Principal edition of side A: Medea Norsa, in *Omaggio della Società italiana per la ricerca dei papiri greci in Egitto al quarto Convegno dei Classicisti tenuto in Firenze dal XVIII al XX aprile del MCMXI* (Florence: Ariani, 1911) no. 5, pp. 20–26; of side B: Franco Maltomini, in *Miscellanea Papyrologica*, ed. Rosario Pintaudi (*Papirologica Florentina*, vol. 7; Florence; Gonnelli, 1980) 176. Side A republished in: *Papiri greci e latini*, vol. 1 (Pubblicazioni della Società italiana per la ricerca dei papiri greci e latini in Egitto; Florence: Ariani, 1912) no. 28, pp. xii–xiii, 63–69 (= *PSI* 1. 28); and sides A and B republished with an English translation in: *Suppl. Mag.*, 1.42. Also commented on by Christine Harrauer, *Meliouchos: Studien zur Entwicklung religiöser Vorstellungen in griechischen synkretistischen Zaubertexten (Wiener Studien*, Beiheft 11; Arbeiten zur antiken Religionsgeschichte 1; Vienna: Verlag der österreichischen Akademie der Wissenschaften, 1987) 83–86; D. R. Jordan, "A Survey of Greek Defixiones Not Included in the Special Corpora," *Greek, Roman, and Byzantine Studies* 26 (1985) no. 151, p. 188 (Jordan refers to the side with four lines as side A and the one with sixty-two lines as side B); S. Eitrem, "Notes on Pap. Soc. It. I 28 and 29," *Aegyptus* 4 (1923) 61–63; R. Ganszyniec, "Zwei magische Hymnen aus Florentiner Papyri," *Byzantinisch-Neugriechische Jahrbücher* 3 (1922) 120; E. Kurtz, "Zu den magischen Hymnen aus Florentiner Papyri," *Byzantinisch-Neugriechische Jahrbücher* 3 (1922) 340; and Richard Wünsch, review of *Omaggio della Società italiana per la ricerca dei papiri greci in Egitto al quarto Convegno dei Classicisti tenuto in Firenze dal XVIII al XX aprile del MCMXI*, *Berliner philologische Wochenschrift* 32 (1912) 3–6.

SIDE A

1   "στυγνοῦ σκότους ἔδρασμα, χαρχαρόστομα σκύλαξ, δρακοντέλιξε, τρικαρανοστρεφῆ,
κευθμωνοδῖτα, μόλε, πνευματηλάτα, σὺν Ἐρινύσιν

4   πικραῖς μάστιξιν ἠγριωμέναις· δράκοντες ἱεροί, μενάδες, φρικτὲ κόραι, μόλετ' αἷς [ἐπα]οιδὰς τὰς ἐμὰς θυμουμέ-
νας· πρὶν ἤ με ἀνάγκῃ τοῦτον ἐκπεῖσαι ται ρωπῇ ποίησον πυρσόπνευ-
στον δαίμων⟨α⟩· ἄκουε καὶ πίησον ἅπαντα ἐν τάχι δρᾶσαι μηδὲν ἐναντι-

8   ωθεὶς ἐμοί· ὑμῖς γάρ ἐσται τῆς γαίης ἀρχηγέται." αλαλαχος αλληχ Ἀρμαχι-
μενευς μαγιμενευς αθινεμβης ασταζαβαθος αρταζαβαθος ωκουμ
φλομ λογχαχιναχανα θου Αζαηλ καὶ Λυκαηλ καὶ Βελιαμ καὶ Βελενηα
καὶ σοχσοχαμ σομοχαν σοζοχαμ ουζαχαμ βαυζαχαμ ουεδδουχ· διὰ τούτου τοῦ

12   ναικυουδαίμονος φλέξον τὴν καρδίαν, τὸ ἧπαρ, τὸ πνεῦμα Γοργονία, ἣν αἴταικεν
Νιλογενία,
ἐπ' ἔρωτι καὶ φιλίᾳ Σοφία, ἣν αἴτεκεν Ἰσάρα· καταναγγάσαται Γοργονία, ἣν
αἴτεκεν Νιλογε–

83

GREEK EROTIC SPELLS FROM EGYPT

"Fundament of the gloomy darkness, jagged-toothed dog, covered
with coiling snakes, turning three heads, traveler in the recesses of the
underworld, come, spirit-driver, with the Erinyes, |⁴ savage with their

νία, βληθῆναι Σοφίᾳ, ἣν αἴταικεν Ἰσάρα, εἰς τὸ βαλανῖον, καὶ γενοῦ βαλάνισσα{ν}·
καῦσον, ποίρω–
σον, φλέξον τὴν ψυχήν, τὴν καρδίαν, τὸ ἧπαρ, τὸ πνεῦμα ἐπ' ἔρωτι Σοφία, ἣν αἴτεγεν
Ἰσάρα· ἄξατε
16 Γοργονία, ἣν αἴτεκεν Νιλογενία, ἄξατε αὐτήν, βασανίσατε αὐτῆς τὸ σῶμα νυκτὸς
καὶ ἡμαίρας, δαμάσα
ται αὐτὴν ἐκπηδῆσῃ ἐκ παντὸς τόπου καὶ πάσης οἰκίας φιλοῦσα⟨ν⟩ Σοφία, {η}ἣν
αἴτεκεν Ἰσάρα, ἐκδότην αὐτὴν
ὡς δούλην ἑαυτὴν αὐτῇ παρέχουσα⟨ν⟩ καὶ τὰ ἑαυτῆς [κ]τήματα πάντα, ὅτι τοῦτο
θέλι καὶ ἐπιτάσσι ὁ μέγας
θεός, ἰαρτανα ουουσιω ιψενθανχωχαινχουεωχ αεηιουω ἰαρτανα ουσιουσιου
ιψοενπευθαδει
20 αννουχεω αεηιουω. ἄναξ μάκαρ ἀθανάτον, Ταρτάρου σκῆπτρα λαβών, στυγνοὺς δὲ
δεινῆς
φοβερᾶς καὶ βιαρπάγου Λήθης, σαί τ' ἐ πικραὶ τρέμουσι Κερβέρε χἐται, σύ τ'
Ἐρινύων μάστιγγος εὐψό–
φους ῥήσσις· τὰ Περσεφόνης λέκτρα σὰς φρένας τέρπεις, ὅταν ἐπ' εὐναῖς ταῖς
ποθουμέναις
χοροῖς, εἴθ' ἄφθιτον Σάραπιν ὃν τρέμι κόσμος, ἴδε σε Ὄσιριν ἄσ{σ}τρον Ἐγύπτου
γαίης· σὸς γὰρ διάκτωρ
24 ἐστὶν πά{ι}σσοφος καὶ πα⟨ῖ⟩ς, σὸς δ' ἐστὶν Ἄνουβις, εὐσεβὴς φθιτῶν κῆρυξ· δεῦρο
ἐλθέ, τὰς ἐμὰς γνώμας
τέλει, ἐπί σαι κρυπτοῖς τοῖσδαι συνβόλοις κλήζω· αχαιφω θωθω αιη ιαη αι ια ηαι
ηια ωθωθ ωφιαχα
εμεν βαρασθρομουαι μωνσυμφιρις τοφαμμιεαρθειαηαιμα σααωωευασε
ενβηρουβα αμεν ου[ρα–]
λις σωθαλις σωθη μου ρακτραθασιμουρ αχωρ αραμε χρειμει μοιτβιψ θαβαψραβου
θλιβαρθ[ιξ]
28 ζαμενηθ ζαταρατα κυφαρταννα αννε Ερεσχιγαλ επλανγαρ⟦βω⟧βωθιθοηαλιθαθθα
διαδ[αξ]
σωθαρα σιερσειρ συμμνθα φρεννωβαθα ωαη[.] λειχοιρετακεστρεν ιωαξειαρνεν
κορυνευκν[υορο]
αλις σωθεωθ δωδεκακιστη ἀκρουροβόρε σωκ[.] ρουμε σουχιαρ ανοχ ανοχ
βριττανδρα σκυλμ[.]
αχαλ βαθραηλ εμαβριμα χρημλα αοστραχιν[.] αμου σαληνασαν τατ χολας
σωρσανγαρ μαδου[ρε]
32 βοασαραουλ σαρουχα σισισρω ζαχαρρω ιβιβι βαρβαλ σοβουχ Ωσιρ ουωαι Αζηλ
αβαδαωτ[.]
ιωβαδαων βερβαισω χιω υ υ υ φθωβαλ λαμαχ χαμαρχωθ βασαρα βαθαραρ
νεαιπεσχιωθ[.]
φορφορ ιυζζε υζε χυχ χυχ χυχ. καταναγγάσαται Γο⟨ρ⟩γονία, ἣν ἄταικεν Νιλογενία,
βληθῆναι Σ[ο–]
φίᾳ, ἣν αἴταικεν Ἰσάρα, εἰς τὸ βαλανῖον αὐτῇ· ναί, κύριε, βασιλεῦ χθονίων θεῶν,
καῦσον, ποίρω[σον,]
36 φλέξον τὴν ψυχήν, τὴν καρδίαν, τὸ ἧπαρ, τὸ πνεῦμα Γοργονία, ἣν αἴτεκεν
Νιλογενία, ἐπ' ἔρωτι [καὶ]

stinging whips; holy serpents, maenads, frightful maidens, come to
my wroth incantations. Before I persuade by force this one and you,
render him immediately a fire-breathing daemon. Listen and do ev-

---

φιλίᾳ Σοφία, ἣν αἴτεκεν Ἰσάρα· ἄξατε αὐτὴν Γοργονία, βασανίσατε αὐτῆς τὸ σῶμα
νυκτὸς καὶ
ἡμαίρα· δαμάσαται αὐτὴν ἐκπηδῆσαι ἐκ παντὸς τόπου καὶ πάσης οἰκίας φιλοῦσα⟨ν⟩
Σοφία, ἣν αἴτε–
κεν Ἰσάρα, ἐκδότην Γοργονία ὡς δούλην ἐ[αυ]τὴ⟨ν⟩ παρέχουσα⟨ν⟩ καὶ τὰ ἑαυτῆς
κτήματα πάντα·

40 ναί, κύριε, βα⟨σι⟩λεῦ χθονίων θεῶν, συντέλεσον τὰ ἐ[γγ]εγραμμένα τῷ πεδάλῳ
    τούτου, ὅτι ἐξορκίζω σαι
    τὸν ὅλον κόσμον, ἀρχὴν μίαν, μεμερισμένον, Θωβαραβαυ Σεμεσειλαμψ σασιβηλ
    σαραηφθω Ιαω ιεου
    ια θυηοηω αεηιουω πανχουχι θασσουθο Σωθ Φρη ιπεχενβωρ Σεσενγεν
    Βαρφαραγγης ωλαμ βωρω
    σεπανσασε θωβαυσθω ιαφθω σου θοου. θιὼ μή μου παρακούσῃς τῆς δεήσεως,
    ἀλλὰ ποίησον Γοργονία, ἣν αἴται–

44 κεν Νιλογενία, κατανάγγασον αὐτὴν βληθῆναι Σοφίᾳ, ἣν αἴτεκεν Ἰσάρα, εἰς τὸ
    βαλανῖον αὐτῇ· καῦσον, πύρωσον,
    φλέξον τὴν καρδίαν, τὸ ἧπαρ, τὸ πνεῦμα Γοργονία, ἣν αἴτεκεν Νιλογενία, ἐπ᾽ ἔρωτι
    καὶ φιλίᾳ Σοφία, ἣν αἴτε–
    κεν Ἰσάρα, ἐπ᾽ ἀγαθῷ· βολχοζη γονστι οφθη, καῦσον, πύρωσον τὴν ψυχήν, τὴν
    καρδίαν, τὸ ἧπαρ, τὸ πνεῦμα
    Γοργονία, ἣν ἔτεκεν Νιλογενία, ἐπ᾽ ἔρωτι καὶ φιλίᾳ Σοφία, ἣν αἴταικεν Ἰσάρα, ὅτι
    τοῦτο θέλι ὁ μέγας

48 θεός, αχχωρ αχχωρ αχχαχ πτουμι χαχχω χαραχωχ χαπτουμη χωραχαραχωρ
    απτουμι
    μηχωχαπτου χαραχπτου χαχχω χαραχω οτεναχωχεν καὶ σισισρω σισι φερμου
    Χμουωρ Ἀρουηρ
    Αβρασαξ Φνουνοβοηλ οχλοβα ζαραχωα βαριχαμω ὃν καλοῦσιν βαχαμ κηβκ.
    καταναγγάσαται Γορ–
    γονία, ἣν αἴταικεν Νιλογενία, βληθῆναι Σοφίᾳ, ἣν ἔτεκεν Ἰσάρα, εἰς τὸ βαλανῖον
    αὐτῇ, φιλῆσε αὐτὴν φίλτρον,

52 πόθον, ἔρωτι ἀκαταπαύστῳ. θηνωρθσι θηνωρ Μαρμαραωθ κρατεοχει ραδαρδαρα
    ξιω χιω χιωχα
    σισεμβρηχ ηχβερηχ χαχ ψεμψοι οψ εμφρη χαλαχ ηρερε τωρχειραμψ μωψ
    μαλαχηρμαλα
    χιβηρθυλιθα χαραβρα θωβωθ· καῦσον, ποίρωσον τὴν ψυχήν, τὴν καρδίαν, τὸ ἧπαρ,
    τὸ πνεῦ–
    μα Γοργονία, ἣν αἴτεγεν Νιλογενία, ἐπ᾽ ἔρωτι καὶ φιλίᾳ Σοφία, ἣν αἴταικεν Ἰσάρα,
    ⟨   ⟩ φίλτρον, πόθον, [. .]

56 ἔρωτι· ηνωρ θηνωρ Αβρασαξ Μιθρα πευχρη Φρη Αρσενοφρη αβαρι μαμαρεμβω Ιαω
    Ιαβωθ·
    ἔξαν, Ἥλιε μελιούχε μελικέτωρ μελιγενέστωρ κμη[.]μ Αβλαναθαναλβα Ακραμμα-
    χαμμαρι Σεσενγεν Βαρφαραγγης, ἄξον Γοργονία, ἣν αἴτεκεν Νιλογενία, ἐπὶ τοῦ ἔ–
    ρωτος Σοφία, ἣν αἴτεκεν Ἰσάρα· καῦσον, ποίρωσον τὴν ψυχήν, τὴν καρδί[αν,]

60   τὸ ἧπαρ, τὸ πνεῦμα, καομένη, πυρουμένη, βασανιζομένη Γοργονία, .
            ἣν αἴτεγεν Νιλογενία, ἕως ἂν βληθῆναι Σοφίᾳ, ἣν αἴτεκεν Ἰσά[ρα,]
            ἲς τὸ βαλανῖον, καὶ κενοῦ βαλάνισσα⟨ν⟩.

erything quickly, in no way opposing me in the performance of this action; |⁸ for you are the governors of the earth.'' *Alalachos allēch Harmachimeneus magimeneus athinembēs astazabathos artazabathos*

SIDE B

στυγνοῦ σκότους ἔδρασμα χαρχαρόστομα σκύλαξ, δρακο[ν–]
64   τέλιξε, τρικαρανοστρεφῆ, κευθμωνοδῖτα, μόλε, πνευμα–
τηλάδα, σὺν Ἐρινύσιν πικραῖς μάστηξιν ἠγριωμαίναις· [δρά–]
κο{κο}ντες ἱεροί, μενάδες.

Since the inscription contains both irregular spelling and numerous grammatical errors (such as confusion between nominative and accusative), I reproduce here—for ease in understanding the text—Daniel and Maltomini's apparatus in *Suppl. Mag.* 1. (For the sake of simplicity I include only their apparatus; for the source of some of these emendations and for alternative emendations, consult the earlier editions).

1f καρχαρόστομε
2 δρακονθελικτέ ?
4f μαινάδες, φρικταὶ
5 ἐς
6 ἐκπεῖσαί ⟨σε⟩ τε ? ῥοπή
7 δαίμονα ποίησον τάχει
8 ὑμεῖς ἐστε
12 νεκυοδαίμονος Γοργονίας ἔτεκεν
13 Σοφίας ἔτεκεν καταναγκάσατε Γοργονίαν ἔτεκεν
14 ἔτεκεν βαλανεῖον
14f πύρωσον
15 Σοφίας ἔτεκεν
16 Γοργονίαν ἔτεκεν ἡμέρας
16f δαμάσατε
17 ἐκπηδῆσαι Σοφίαν ἔτεκεν
18 θέλει ἐπιτάσσει
20 ἀθανάτων Στυγός τε ?
21 σέ θ' αἱ Κερβέρου χαῖται μάστιγας
22 ῥήσσεις λεκτρα: the original scribe inscribed τρ over ρα τερπεις: the original scribe inscribed the second ε over ι, read τέρπει
23 χωρῆς εἴτ' τρέμει εἴτε Αἰγύπτου
25 ἐπεί σε Tablet has τοις δαι; read τοῖσδε συμβόλοις
31 –θραηλ: a corrector inscribed θρα over an original χ
34 καταναγκάσατε Γοργονίαν ἔτεκεν
35 ἔτεκεν βαλανεῖον πύρωσον
36 Γοργονίας ἔτεκεν
37 Σοφίας ἔτεκεν Γοργονίαν
38 ἡμέρας· δαμάσατε Σοφίαν
38f ἔτεκεν
39 Γοργονίαν
40 or βα(σι)λεῦ ? χθονιων: a corrector added χ πετάλῳ τούτῳ σε
42 φρη: a corrector added φ
43 θοου: a corrector added the first ο διὸ Γοργονίαν
43f ἔτεκεν
44 κατανάγκασον ἔτεκεν βαλανεῖον

ōkoum phlom lonchachinachana thou Azaēl and *Lykaēl* and *Beliam*
and *Belenēa* and *sochsocham somochan sozocham ouzacham bauzacham
oueddouch*. By means of this |[12] corpse-daemon inflame the heart,
the liver, the spirit of Gorgonia, whom Nilogenia bore, with love and
affection for Sophia, whom Isara bore. Constrain Gorgonia, whom
Nilogenia bore, to cast herself into the bath-house for the sake of Sophia, whom Isara bore; and you, become a bath-woman. Burn, set on
fire, inflame her soul, heart, liver, spirit with love for Sophia, whom
Isara bore. Drive |[16] Gorgonia, whom Nilogenia bore, drive her, tor-
ment her body night and day, force her to rush forth from every place
and every house, loving Sophia, whom Isara bore, she, surrendered
like a slave, giving herself and all her possessions to her, because this is
the will and command of the great god, *iartana ouousiō ipsenthanchō-
chainchoueōch aeēioyō iartana ousiousiou ipsoenpeuthadei* |[20] *annou-
cheō aeēioyō*. "Blessed lord of the immortals, holding the scepters of
Tartaros and of terrible, fearful Styx (?) and of life-robbing Lethe, the
hair of Kerberos trembles in fear of you, you crack the loud whips of
the Erinyes; the couch of Persephone delights you, when you go to
the longed bed, whether you be the immortal Sarapis, whom the universe fears, whether you be Osiris, star of the land of Egypt; your mes-

---

45 Γοργονίας ἔτεκεν Σοφίας
45f ἔτεκεν
47 Γοργονίας Σοφίας ἔτεκεν θέλει
48 χαχχω: the original scribe inscribed μ over the first χ
50f καταναγκάσατε Γοργονίαν
51 ἔτεκεν βαλανεῖον φιλῆσαι
52 θηνωρ: a corrector added ρ
54 πύρωσον
55 Γοργονίας αιτεγεν: the original scribe inscribed α over ε; read ἔτεκεν Σοφίας ἔτεκεν
57 ἄξον (unless εξαν is a magical word); between ηλιε and μελιουχε there is a space on the
tablet; μελικέρτωρ μελιγενέτωρ
58 The tablet has χαμμα ρι –φαραγγης: a corrector added ϛ Γοργονίαν ἔτεκεν
59 Σοφίας ἔτεκεν πύρωσον
60 πυρουμενη: the original scribe inscribed ου over ω βασανιζομενη: a corrector inscribed ζ (over an original σ?) καομένης, πυρουμένης, βασανιζομένης? these participles
should probably be corrected to the genitive to agree with the following Γοργονίας (also
corrected to the genitive), unless they are in the wrong place and should be corrected to the
accusative after πύρωσον in l. 59 Γοργονίας
61 ἔτεκεν (twice)
62 εἰς βαλανεῖον γενοῦ
63 καρχαρόστομε
63f δρακονθελικτέ?
64 After τρικαρανοστρεφη there is a small horizontal line on the tablet, perhaps to signify
the end of the trimeter
64f πνευματηλάτα
65 μάστιξιν ἠγριωμέναις
66 μαινάδες

senger |²⁴ is the all-wise boy; yours is Anoubis, the pious herald of the dead. Come hither, fulfill my wishes, because I summon you by these secret symbols" *achaiphō thōthō aiē iaē ai ia ēai ēia ōthōth ōphiacha emen barasthromouai mōnsymphiris tophammieartheiaēaima saaōōeuase enbērouba amen ouralis sōthalis sōthe mou raktrathasimour achōr arame chreimiei moitbips thabapsrabou thlibarphix* |²⁸ *zamenēth zatarata kyphartanna anne Ereschigal eplangarbōthithoēalithaththa diadax sōthara sierseir symmytha phrennōbatha ōaē[. .]leichoiretakestreu iōaxeiarneu koryneuknyoro alis sōtheōth dōdekakistē*, swallowing the tip of the tail, *sōk [. .] roume souchiar anoch anoch brittandra skylm[.]achal bathraēl emabrima chrēmla aostrachin* amou salēnasau tat *cholas sōrsangar madoure* |³² *boasaraoul saroucha sisisrō zacharrō ibibi barbal sobouch Ōsir ouōai Azēl abadaōt[. .] iōbadaōn berbaisō chiō y y y phthōbal lamach chamarchōth basara batharar neaipeschiōth [. .] phorphor iyzze yze chych chych chych*. Constrain Gorgonia, whom Nilogenia bore, to cast herself into the bath-house for the sake of Sophia, whom Isara bore, for her. Aye, lord, king of the chthonic gods, burn, set on fire, |³⁶ inflame the soul, the heart, the liver, the spirit of Gorgonia, whom Nilogenia bore, with love and affection for Sophia, whom Isara bore; drive Gorgonia herself, torment her body night and day; force her to rush forth from every place and every house, loving Sophia, whom Isara bore, she, Gorgonia surrendered like a slave, giving herself and all her possessions. |⁴⁰ Aye, lord, king of the chthonic gods, carry out what is inscribed on this tablet, for I adjure you who divided the entire universe, a single realm, *Thōbarabau Semeseilamps sasibēl sarēphthō Iaō ieou ia thyēoēō aeēioyō panchouchi thassoutho Sōth Phrē ipechenbōr Sesengen Barpharaggēs ōlam bōrō sepansase thōbausthō iaphthō sou thoou.* So, do not disobey my request, but cause Gorgonia, whom |⁴⁴ Nilogenia bore, force her to cast herself into the bath-house for the sake of Sophia, whom Isara bore, for her. Burn, set on fire, inflame the heart, the liver, the spirit of Gorgonia, whom Nilogenia bore, with love and affection for Sophia, whom Isara bore, for a good end. *Bolchozē gonsti ophthē*, burn, set on fire the soul, the heart, the liver, the spirit of Gorgonia, whom Nilogenia bore, with love and affection for Sophia, whom Isara bore, because this is the will of the great |⁴⁸ god, *achchōr achchōr achchach ptoumi chachchō charachōch chaptoumē chōracharachōr aptoumi mēchōchaptou charachptou chachchō charachō otenachōcheu* and *sisisrō sisi phermou Chmouōr Harouēr Abrasax Phnounoboēl ochloba zarachōa barichamo* who is called *bacham kēbk.* Force Gorgonia, whom Nilogenia bore, to cast herself into the bath-house for the sake of Sophia, whom Isara bore, for her, so that she love her with passion, |⁵² longing, unceasing love. *Thēnōrthsi thēnōr Marmaraōth krateochei radardara xiō chiō chiōcha sisembrēch ēchberēch chach psempsoi ops emphrē chalach ērere tōrcheiramps mōps malachērmala chibērthylitha charabra thōbōth*, burn, set on fire the soul, the heart, the liver, the spirit of Gorgonia, whom Nilogenia

bore, with love and affection for Sophia, whom Isara bore, --- with
passion, longing, |⁵⁶ love. *Ēnōr thēnōr Abrasax Mithra peuchrē Phrē
Arsenophrē abari mamarembō Iaō Iabōth,* drive, Sun, honey-holder,
honey-cutter, honey-producer, *kmē[ ]m Ablanathanalba Akrammachammari Sesengen Barpharaggēs,* drive Gorgonia, whom Nilogenia
bore, to love Sophia, whom Isara bore; burn, set on fire the soul, the
heart, |⁶⁰ the liver, the spirit of burned, inflamed, tortured Gorgonia,
whom Nilogenia bore, until she casts herself into the bath-house for
the sake of Sophia, whom Isara bore; and you, become a bath-woman.[27]

The dramatic opening (lines 1–8) of this spell forms a metrical invoca-
tory hymn,[28] as do lines 20–25. Lines 1–8[29] contain eleven iambic trimeters,[30] while lines 20–25[31] consist of twelve choliambic[32] lines, although
we need to make some corrections in order for these sections to construe
precisely.[33] This use of poetic form, as well as the sound of the long, otherwise unattested compound words ("jagged-toothed," "covered with
coiling snakes," "turning three heads," "traveler in the recesses of the underworld," "fire-breathing"), creates a heavy effect, suited to these deities
of the underworld.

This spell contains particularly strong evidence that the practitioner employed a formulary to write it. The scribe probably copied the complicated
metrical sections, which either had become metrically corrupted in the
course of time (a corruption that the practitioner did not recognize) or
which the scribe augmented, not realizing that the additions threw off the
meter. The names of Sophia and Gorgonia are not declined (i.e., supple-
mented with endings appropriate to their function within the sentence),

27. Since the three and one-half lines on side B contain more errors than their counterparts
on side A and the scribe did not shape them in the oval form of the text that we find on side
A, they probably represent the scribe's first attempt at the spell.

28. Ὕμνος κλητικός. Another erotic spell containing metrical sections is *Suppl. Mag.*,
1.49.57–61 (iambic trimeters) and 64–73 (dactylic hexameters). Like the metrical sections in
the spell of Sophia, these also required metrical restoration, which I am not printing here.

29. See also the parallel lines on side B of the tablet.

30. Aristotle finds iambic meter (˘– ˘–) particularly useful for satire and ridicule because
it closely resembles common speech (*Poetics* 4). See also *OCD*, s.v. "Iambic Poetry, Greek."

31. This hymn demonstrates that the speaker knows the "symbols" (line 24: secret codes,
watchwords), i.e., the names, the deeds, and the powers of the ruler of the underworld, and
will therefore be heard by the deity.

32. Choliambic meter has a spondee (– –), instead of an iambus, in the last position.

33. See the differing attempts to reconstruct the original meter by Daniel and Maltomini
(*Suppl. Mag.*, 1, pp. 139–41); Kurtz ("Zu den magischen Hymnen aus Florentiner Papyri,"
Byzantinisch-neugriechische Jahrbücher 3 [1922] 340); Ganszyniec ("Zwei magische Hymnen
aus Florentiner Papyri," *Byzantinisch-neugriechische Jahrbücher* 3 [1922] 120); and Wünsch
(review of *Omaggio della Società italiana per la ricerca dei papiri greci in Egitto al quarto
Convegno dei Classicisti tenuto in Firenze dal XVIII al XX aprile del MCMXI, Berliner Philologische Wochenschrift* 32 [1912] 3–6).

adding a fill-in-the-blank character to the spell's composition. Further, the word for "bore" is spelled in five different ways within the same document.[34] Perhaps the formulary contained a symbol as an abbreviation for "bore,"[35] rather than the actual word spelled out, and the scribe transcribed the symbol phonetically. This use of a formulary bears significant implications for interpretation: (1) the spell tells us more about general understandings of erotic desire than about Sophia's specific views; and (2) Sophia must have commissioned the spell from a professional, since the general public would not have had access to formularies.[36]

The spell envisages the public baths as a locus for the desired erotic capture.[37] Five times Sophia calls upon the underworld deities to work through the corpse-*daimon* in a two-step process.[38] On the one hand, the deity is to inflame Gorgonia's inner organs with love for Sophia and then constrain her to cast herself into the bathhouse. Further, the king of the underworld deities is to become a bath-woman, presumably in order better to carry out the spell in close proximity to the targeted woman. Bath attendants in public baths served clients by oiling and washing them, thus having very close physical contact. The burning imagery ("burn," "inflame," "set on fire"), also found in other spells that do not mention bathhouses, is more evocative in the context of the bathing imagery. Visions come to mind: of moist heat and the flushed skin of a person resting in the hot room of the baths, and of the sensuousness of nude bodies and semiclad bodies seated around pools of water.[39] Since people around the ancient Mediterranean also placed binding spells in rivers and wells, apparently in order to come closer to the spirits and the underworld deities,

---

34. Ἔτεκεν (correct), αἴταικεν, αἴτεκεν, αἴτεγεν, and ἄταικεν.

35. E.g., ἣν ἡ Δ (= ἣν ἡ δεῖνα ἔτεκεν). See, e.g., *PGM* 4.350, 527, 2497; 7.389, 471; and D. R. Jordan, "A New Reading of a Papyrus Love Charm in the Louvre," *Zeitschrift für Papyrologie und Epigraphik* 74 (1988) 239.

36. Whether she paid more for such a complicated and long spell we cannot know.

37. For further literature on the importance of bathhouses as places for doing magic, see Betz, *Greek Magical Papyri*, 1:14, n. 16.
Other spells with bath imagery include: *PGM* 2.48f (on throwing a spell into the furnace [ὑποκαύστρα] of a bathhouse), 7.469 (on throwing a love spell into the furnace [ὑποκαυστήριον] of a bathhouse), 36.75 (on gluing a papyrus love spell of attraction to the dry vaulted vapor room of a bath), 36.334f (on placing a love spell of attraction on the flat stone of the bath), *Papyri Demoticae Magicae* 12.147 (in Betz, *Greek Magical Papyri*, 1:171) (on cooking a love spell in [?] the bath).

38. Lines 13–15, 34–36, 44–46, 50–52, 59–62. The order of the two steps varies.

39. See Roy Ward, "Women in Roman Baths," *HTR* 85 (1992) 125–47. Ward argues that women and men bathed together in the period of the Roman Empire; he also notes the reputation of bathhouses as places of sexual play and flirtation.
On contemporary public baths as a site of sensuous pleasures and a place where lesbians meet, see Marcia Freedman's description of the *hammam* in Jerusalem in: Evelyn Torton Beck, ed., *Nice Jewish Girls: A Lesbian Anthology* (Watertown, MA: Persephone, 1982) 216f.

perhaps the watery aspect of bathhouses also contributed to their popularity as locations for the placement or action of binding spells.

The spell calls for the corpse-*daimon* to "inflame the soul, the heart, the liver, the spirit of Gorgonia," a command that is repeated in various forms seven times. Modern readers may conceive of a burning heart, a burning soul, and even a burning spirit, but the image of a burning liver surprises us. People in the Roman world saw the liver as the seat of the passions, and Ovid attests to the liver as susceptible to having a pin driven through it on waxen dolls as part of magical practices.[40]

Terminology of domination, typical for the erotic binding spells as a whole, is more prominent in this than in either of the other two female homoerotic spells. To be sure, some of the spells directed by men toward women contain expressions even more violent than "constrain," "drive," "torment," "force her to rush forth," "surrendered like a slave," and "giving herself and all her possessions." One spell calls upon an angel to drag the woman, in fear, by her hair and her feet to the bedroom of the man, while another demands that Isis, Osiris, Abrasax, and the underworld spirits prevent the woman from sleeping by means of thorns and impalements, and others call for her to be dragged by her inward parts, that is, probably by the genitals. Others echo the language of property and slavery found in the spell of Sophia.[41] I will discuss the meaning of this language for all three spells, following a presentation of the third spell.

III. Two lead tablets, probably from second-century CE Panopolis (earlier known as Achmim) in Upper Egypt, contain what may possibly be a third female homoerotic spell (*Suppl. Mag.*, 1.37; see figs. 9–11).[42] The

---

40. LSJ, s.v. ἧπαρ. Ovid, *Amores* 3.7.27–30; and *Heroides* 6.82–94; ET of Ovid: Gager, *Curse Tablets and Binding Spells*, nos. 142f, pp. 250f. For combinations of organs similar to this spell see, e.g., *Suppl. Mag.*, 1.40.16; and *PGM* 4.1529.

41. *PGM* 7.887–89; *PGM* 36.151–53; *Suppl. Mag*, 1.46 and 50; both spells also speak of dragging the woman by the hair. Examples concerning property: *Suppl. Mag.*, 1.45, 51 and 51.5; *PGM* 17.18f; example calling for the enslavement of a woman by a man: *Suppl. Mag.*, 38.10; example calling for the enslavement of a man by a woman: August Audollent, *Defixionem Tabellae quotquot innotuerunt* . . . (Paris: Fontemoing, 1904; reprint, Frankfurt: Minerva, 1967) no. 271.43f; ET: Gager, *Curse Tablets and Binding Spells*, no. 36, p. 115. (Both of the enslaving spells speak of a long-term relationship.)

42. The Archäologisches Institut of the University of Heidelberg now houses the tablets (measurements: tablet A: 10.2 cm in width and 8.7 cm in height; tablet B: 10.3 cm in width and 8.2 cm in height).

Principal edition: Franz Boll, *Griechischer Liebeszauber aus Ägypten* (Sitzungsberichte der Heidelberger Akademie der Wissenschaften, Philosophisch-historische Klasse, 1910, 2. Abhandlung; Heidelberg: Winter, 1910). Republished with an English translation in Daniel and Maltomini, *Suppl. Mag.*, 1.37; Brigitte Borell, *Statuetten, Gefässe und andere Gegenstände aus Metall (Katalog der Sammlung antiker Kleinkunst des Archäologischen Instituts der Universität Heidelberg 3/1; Mainz: Von Zabern, 1989) no. 56, pp. 53f; pl. 25; and Friedrich Bilabel,

tablets originally formed a diptych, that is, they were nailed together at four points with the writing facing the inside. Perhaps the nailing signified the binding of the woman who was to be attracted.[43]

Sammelbuch Griechischer Urkunden aus Ägypten, vol. 3/1 (Berlin: De Gruyter, 1926) nos. 6224f, p. 34. Also commented on by: D. R. Jordan, "A Survey of Greek Defixiones Not Included in the Special Corpora," Greek, Roman, and Byzantine Studies 26 (1985) nos. 158f, p. 190; David R. Jordan, "CIL VIII 19525 (B). 2QPVVLVA = Q(VEM) P(EPERIT) VVLVA," Philologus 120 (1976) 129; Karl Preisendanz, "Zur synkretistischen Magie im römischen Ägypten," Akten des VIII. Internationalen Kongresses für Papyrologie Wien 1955 (Mitteilungen aus der Papyrussammlung der Österreichischen Nationalbibliothek [Papyrus Erzherzog Rainer] n.s. 5; Vienna: Rohrer Verlag, 1956) p. 114, n. 33; S. Eitrem and Leiv Amundsen, eds., Papyri Osloenes, fasc. 2 (Oslo: Dybwad, 1931) p. 33, n. 1 (Eitrem); Friedrich Pfister, review of Griechischer Liebeszauber by F. Boll, Wochenschrift für klassische Philologie 30 (1913) 1049f; and R. Wünsch, review of Griechischer Liebeszauber by F. Boll, Berliner philologische Wochenschrift 30 (1910) 688f.

43. Suppl. Mag., 1.37, p. 115. Preisendanz had dated the tablets to the 1st C. BCE, while Franz Boll had dated them to the 1st C. CE, a dating accepted by Bilabel. Pfister and Wünsch dated them to the 1st/2d C. CE.

TABLET A

```
1    Ὠρίων Σαραποῦτος,
     ποίησον καὶ ἀνάγκα-
     [drawing of   σον
4    a mummy]  Νίκην
     Ἀπολ-
     λωνοῦ-
     τος ἐ-
8    ρασθῆ-
     ναι Παι-
     τοῦτ[ος,]
     ἣν ἔτ[εκ-]
12   ε Τμεσιῶς.
```

2f ἀνάγκασον (force) Eitrem; ἀναποί[η]σον (stir up) Boll; ἀναπόδ[ι]σον (call back) Wünsch; ἀνάπεισον (persuade) Preisendanz.

TABLET B

```
1    ποίησον Νίκην Ἀ[πολ-]
     λωνοῦτος
     ἐρασθῆναι Παντοῦ-
4    τος ἣν ἔτεκεν
     Τμεσιῶς, ἐπὶ ε''
     μῆνας.
```

5f Daniel and Maltomini find on the photograph of the editio princeps most of a double slash after the E, indicating that the E is meant to be read as the numeral 5. Thus, their reading differs from that of Boll, who had printed ἐπὶ ἑ⟨πτὰ⟩ μῆνας (for seven months), noting an incision to the upper right of the E that could have been the cross bar of a T or a Π.

TABLET A

Horion, son of Sarapous, make and force [drawing of a mummy]
Nike, daughter of Apollonous, to fall in love with Paitous, whom
Tmesios bore.

TABLET B

Make Nike, daughter of Apollonous, fall in love with Pantous, whom
Tmesios bore, for five months.

As in the other two spells, the petitioner directly addresses the corpse-*daimon* (named here Horion, son of Sarapous [f.]), who is to force Nike to fall in love with Pantous/Paitous.[44] The language of force and the language of love occur here in tandem, as in Sophia's spell. This spell is as simple as Sophia's is complex, and yet both communicate the same basic message: oh, spirit of the dead person, force this woman to fall in love with me.

Both Egyptian and Greek names occur in the Pantous/Paitous spell. "Tmesios," a personal name meaning "midwife," is Egyptian.[45] "Horion" and "Sarapous" are probably theophoric ("god-bearing") names, referring to the Egyptian deities Horus and Sarapis respectively. "Apollonous" is a theophoric name derived from the Greek deity Apollo. "Nike" is a Greek name, while "Pantous"/"Paitous" may be Egyptian. Since Nike and her mother both have Greek names, while Pantous and Pantous's mother have clearly or possibly Egyptian names, Nike may have been an ethnic Greek (i.e., Macedonian, a descendant of the successors of Alexander the Great) and Pantous an ethnic Egyptian, but by the second century CE, the names and communities are so intermingled that we cannot ascertain such information with any certainty.

Deciphering the meaning of "for five months" on tablet B has particularly challenged interpreters.[46] While we cannot know for sure, I follow the

44. The drawing of the mummy on tablet A is probably meant to be a picture of the dead man himself.

45. The frequent occurrence of the name "Tmesios" among mummy labels from Panopolis (Achmim) originates perhaps in the particular veneration in Panopolis paid to Heqet, a female deity of childbirth. Apparently parents named their daughters "Tmesios" to honor this deity of childbirth.

46. Prior scholars have discussed the following possible interpretations of $\dot{\epsilon}\pi\dot{\iota}\ \epsilon''\ \mu\hat{\eta}\nu\alpha\varsigma$ (or $\dot{\epsilon}\pi\dot{\iota}\ \dot{\epsilon}\langle\pi\tau\dot{\alpha}\rangle\ \mu\hat{\eta}\nu\alpha\varsigma$ [seven months], as Boll read it): (1) the formulary from which the scribe copied may have promised success *within* five or seven months if he or she properly carried out the magic (Boll, *Griechischer Liebeszauber,* 10f); (2) the love affair would last *for* five or seven months (suggested, but rejected by Boll, *Griechischer Liebeszauber,* 10; accepted by R. Wünsch, review of *Griechischer Liebeszauber* by F. Boll, *Berliner philologische Wochenschrift* 30 [1910] 689; Friedrich Bilabel, *Sammelbuch Griechischer Urkunden aus Ägypten,* vol. 3/1

suggestion that the love relationship was to last for five months, owing to some external circumstances preventing a relationship of longer duration or as a trial period potentially leading to a more permanent arrangement, which I will discuss below.

Many scholars have taken these spells to have been commissioned by a man to attract a woman, but a better analysis reveals both parties on each tablet to have been women.

Franz Boll, who first edited the text, misled later scholars by interpreting Pantous (or, as tablet A has it, Paitous)[47] as a masculine name. When Boll published the tablets in 1910, no other female-female love spells were known, so perhaps it did not even cross Boll's mind that women would commission love spells to attract women. Further, in 1910—as now—relationships between women and men occupied a more prominent place in people's minds than relationships between women, and many people would have preferred not to think about sexual love between women at all.

"Nike," a clearly feminine name, designates the person to be attracted, that is, to be bound by the spell. "Pantous"/"Paitous," the name of the person doing the binding, apparently occurs only in this love spell and not in any other ancient papyrus documents.[48] (Many names, such as "Gorgonia" in the last spell discussed, are attested only once in ancient sources.) In other words, we cannot deduce the gender of Pantous/Paitous from other ancient usages of it.[49] The ending "-ous" can be either feminine or masculine. (Notice "Sarapous," mother of Horion, and "Apollonous," mother of Nike, in this same spell.) The text of the spell itself, however,

---

[Berlin: De Gruyter, 1926] 34; and Daniel and Maltomini, *Suppl. Mag.*, 1, p. 117); and (3) Tmesios had given birth to Pantous *after* seven months of pregnancy (since some ancients believed that seven-month children possessed supernatural power, Boll suggested that such a birth would impress the chthonic powers; Boll, *Griechischer Liebeszauber*, 11; Friedrich Pfister, review of *Griechischer Liebeszauber* by F. Boll, *Wochenschrift für klassische Philologie* 30 [1913] 1050). Eitrem has put forth a variation on the second interpretation, namely that the text refers to a trial marriage (S. Eitrem and Leiv Amundsen, eds., *Papyri Osloenses*, fasc. 2 [Oslo: Dybwad, 1931] 33).

47. The "Pai-" (Greek: ΠΑΙ) on tablet A, line 9, could have originally been "Pan-" (Greek: ΠΑΝ), since the lead is frayed at that spot (Boll, *Griechischer Liebeszauber*, 5). The Ι could thus be the first leg of a partially frayed-away Ν.

48. Friedrich Preisigke, *Namenbuch* (Heidelberg: By the Author, 1922), does not list either form of the name. Daniele Foraboschi, *Onomasticon alterum papyrologicum: Supplemento al Namenbuch di F. Preisigke* (Testi e documenti per lo studio dell'antichità 16. Serie papirologica 2; Milan: Varese Istituto Editoriale Cisalpino, 1971) lists "Pantous" only for this text.

49. P. M. Fraser and E. Matthews, eds., *A Lexicon of Greek Personal Names*, vol. 1, *The Aegean Islands, Cyprus, Cyrenaica* (Oxford: Clarendon, 1987), contains no entry for Παντους or Παιτους. A December 1992 word search of the documents then available on the *Thesaurus Linguae Graecae* and the papyri and inscriptions compiled by the Packard Humanities Institute revealed no further attestations of Pantous or Paitous.

defines Pantous/Paitous as a feminine name through the feminine relative pronoun that comes right after the name on both tablets ("whom [f.] Tmesios bore"). The form of the name could however, point to its being a masculine name, since *Pa* is a masculine Egyptian prefix.[50]

Boll suggests emending the text by altering the feminine form of "whom" (Greek: HN, which is transliterated as *hēn*) to the masculine form (Greek: ON, which is transliterated as *hon*). (*Hēn* on tablet A, line 11, refers back to Paitous, and *hēn* on tablet B, line 4, has Pantous as its antecedent.) Boll argued that the feminine "whom" of tablet A was simply a scribal error and that the scribe had tried to correct the feminine "whom" of tablet B to a masculine "whom" by attempting to alter one letter. Boll offers two slightly visible marks on the lead as evidence for his hypothesis of a scribal correction. On line four of tablet B, the left leg of the Greek letter eta (H) is actually a very narrow loop (see fig. 11 for a close-up of the letter). Boll suggests that the curved incision to the far left and a small mark to the upper right of the curved left leg bear witness to the scribe's rather incompetent attempt to change the eta (H) into an omicron (O) and hence the feminine "whom" into a masculine one.

Contrast Boll's decision in taking these marks on tablet B, line 4, as an attempted omicron with his correct recognition that a mark resembling an iota after *Horiōn* on tablet A, line 1, is actually an accidental scratch. (Thus, *Horiōn* is, as expected, in the vocative, rather than the dative case.) In other words, in the absence of a crucial question of interpretation (such as gender within an erotic spell), Boll does not hesitate to call a scratch a scratch.

Up until the most recent editors, all subsequent scholars preferred the emended text (masculine "whoms") to the one more clearly visible on the tablets (feminine "whoms").[51] Daniel and Maltomini, the tablets' most recent editors, print the feminine "whoms" in their transliteration of the Greek and explain the curved portion of the loop as the scribe's first attempt at the vertical bar of the H and the straight portion of the loop as the second, correct attempt to make the eta's vertical bar. They identify the small horizontal mark to the upper right of the left leg as a discoloration, rather than an incision.[52] In other words, they print *hēn* because the physical evidence does not justify printing *hon*. I follow Daniel and Maltomini's more careful visual observation of the physical surface of the tablet.

Although Daniel and Maltomini recognize that both lead tablets modify Pantous/Paitous with a feminine pronoun, they propose nonetheless that the scribe really meant to write masculine "whoms" and only mistakenly

50. I thank Egyptologist Prof. Robert Ritner of Yale University for pointing this out to me.
51. See above, n. 42.
52. *Suppl. Mag.*, 1, p. 117.

wrote feminine ones. To support their emendation, Daniel and Maltomini refer to four examples of a confusion between feminine and masculine pronouns in magical texts.[53] Their first three examples, however, differ from the spell commissioned by Pantous/Paitous in two respects. First, in each of their examples another pronoun and/or the proper name itself demonstrates that the pronoun in question is erroneous.[54] In the Pantous/Paitous inscription, there is no such corroborating evidence for a hypothetical error. Second, the examples put forth by Daniel and Maltomini contain only one erroneous pronoun per document.[55] In contrast, the Pantous/Paitous documents contain two pronouns defining the gender of Pantous/Paitous, both of which are feminine. It is more plausible to assume that the scribe wrote both pronouns correctly than that he or she made the same mistake twice on two short documents that contain no other mistakes. Daniel and Maltomini's fourth example is misleading and not parallel to the Pantous/Paitous inscription.[56]

Thus, Daniel and Maltomini's alleged parallels do not support their proposal that the scribe of the Pantous/Paitous inscription wrote *hēn*, but meant *hōn*. While the extensive use of formularies in composing ancient magical spells did result in mistakes, this is not such a case. By including

53. Ibid. See also 1.49.26; 52.2; August Audollent, *Defixionum Tabellae quotquot innotuerunt* ... (Paris: Fontemoing, 1904; reprint, Frankfurt: Minerva, 1967) 188.13; and Dierk Wortmann, "Neue magische Gemmen," *Bonner Jahrbuch* 175 (1975) 15.10, pp. 76–81.

54. E.g., in *Suppl. Mag.*, 1.49.26: . . . Ματ]ρῶνα, ἣν ἔτεκεν Ταγένη, οὗ, the name Ματρῶνα (fully legible elsewhere in the document) and the pronoun ἣν both indicate that the οὗ is incorrect.

55. E.g., *Suppl. Mag.*, 1.49, except for the οὗ in line 26, contains the correct pronouns for Ματρῶνα.

56. Wortmann, "Neue magische Gemmen," no. 15, lines 9–11:

9   δειαφύλαξον τὸν Φλαβαίου
10 Λαναδούλκις, ἣν ἔτεν Πουβλ–
11 εἴκια Καλημέρα.

9   διαφύλαξον.
10 ἔτεκεν.

The text, inscribed on a cornelian gem, contains several syntactical difficulties: Φλαβαίου in the genitive, where we would expect an accusative; the placement and function of Λαναδούλκις, which seems to be in the nominative or vocative or is an undeclined foreign name; and the relationship among τὸν, Φλαβαίου, and Λαναδούλκις. Wortmann and his posthumous editors propose several solutions to make sense of these lines: (1) changing the word order, taking Λαναδούλκις (f.) as a nominative, a vocative, or an indeclinable name, and adding ⟨υἱὸν τοῦ⟩ after τόν; and (2) changing Φλαβαίου to Φλαβαίου and construing Λαναδούλκις (f.) as a genitive; and (3) changing Φλαβαίου to Φλαβίου and ἣν to ὃν, which leaves the case and function of Λαναδούλκις unresolved. (Herwig Maehler, one of Wortmann's posthumous editors, has proposed this third solution.) Only the third emendation includes viewing ἣν as incorrect. Thus, we do not need to attribute the syntactical difficulties in this inscription to an erroneous pronoun.

this spell among those commissioned by women to attract other women, I am employing the conservative philological principles of: (1) preferring the most visible letters on the document to a modern editorial emendation; and (2) taking the text as it stands, rather than assuming that the composer made a mistake. Even if the name Pantous/Paitous were to have been masculine in form, the person could still have been a woman, since the pronouns are feminine. Perhaps Pantous/Paitous was a woman taking on a masculine *persona*, much as the Megilla of Lucian's *Dialogues of the Courtesans* reveals herself as Megillos when she introduces her female partner as her wife. The name on the spell could have been a nickname, rather than a given name.[57]

This spell teaches us something not only about the two women involved in the spell, but also about ourselves as scholars. Boll's failure to consider the possibility that this spell could be homoerotic, like Wünsch's and Preisendanz's hesitancy to view the Herais/Sarapias spell as an erotic spell, exemplifies why we lack knowledge of the history of women in the Roman world. Our ignorance does not stem from a lack of sources, but rather from our ignoring and misinterpreting the available sources. That Franz Boll does not consider the possibility that this diptych could be homoerotic is doubly striking, since his great familiarity with ancient astrological texts gave him ample examples of sources on female homoeroticism in this period.

INTERPRETING CULTURAL IDEOLOGY

Can we read the female homoerotic spells as examples of women adopting the violent conceptualization of eroticism abundant in erotic binding spells, or as examples of women breaking out of the model of female subordination (since the spells document women seeking to fulfill their erotic desires)? Several factors complicate this question. First, the language of these spells is culture-bound, and we must read it with cultural sensitivity.[58]

57. I thank Prof. Bentley Layton of Yale University for this suggestion.

58. Sappho's *Hymn to Aphrodite*, with its language of pursuit and hope for the satisfaction of desire, illustrates the conventions of ancient erotic rhetoric:

> For if she runs away, soon she shall run after,
> if she shuns gifts, she shall give,
> if she does not love you, soon she shall even
> against her own will

(Edgar Lobel and Denys Page, eds., *Poetarum Lesbiorum Fragmenta* (Oxford: Clarendon, 1955) fragment 1, pp. 2f; preserved in Dionysios of Halikarnassos, *On Literary Composition* 23, 173–79; ET: Josephine Balmer, *Sappho: Poems and Fragments* [Secaucus, NJ: Meadowland, 1988] 78).

On the other hand, Sappho's poem does not contain the violent imagery of the love spells.

Second, several scholars question whether the ancient binding spells, and particularly the attraction spells, actually signify the domination of the person placing the spell. And third, we do not know the extent to which women actually had a choice in shaping the character of their own attraction spells, since men most often employed and probably created this genre. I will jointly address the questions of culture and of domination in the spells as a whole and then speak more specifically about the women's homoerotic spells.

Contemporary interpreters debate the cultural meaning of the violent language of the erotic binding spells, devoting particular attention to an ancient female clay figurine, pierced through the eyes, mouth, chest, genitals, and other body parts by thirteen nails[59] (in accordance with the recipe of *PGM* 4.296–334 discussed above). In the accompanying binding spell (possibly from Antinoöpolis in Upper Egypt, 3d/4th C.), a man (Sarapamon) attempts to bind a woman (Ptolemais) to himself. He calls upon the dead man, Antinoos, to "[d]rag her by the hair, by the inward parts until she no longer stands aloof from me . . . subject for the entire time of my life, filled with love for me, desiring me, speaking to me all the things she has on her mind."[60]

John Gager and John Winkler have specifically warned against interpreting this figurine too literally and against understanding the violent language of the erotic spells in a way inappropriate to their original cultural context. Gager's volume has great value for research: its comprehensiveness, its insight into the ritual and practical aspects of the binding spells, and its theoretical treatment of the role of binding spells in people's lives. But both Winkler and Gager have displayed an overly apologetic posture vis-à-vis the violent imagery of these spells and of the figurine. They have argued that the spells' primary function was therapeutic for the client, which I hold to be an anachronistic interpretation. Further, their interpretations contain insufficient gender analysis. I will first critique Winkler's and Gager's interpretations and then suggest alternative interpretive possibilities.

Winkler and Gager both focus on the love-sick client. Winkler depicted

59. The figurine, found in Egypt in a clay pot together with a binding spell, and now housed in the Louvre, is pictured in Gager, *Curse Tablets and Binding Spells*, p. 98, fig. 13.
60. *Suppl. Mag.*, 1.47.24–27; ET: Gager, *Curse Tablets and Binding Spells*, no. 28, pp. 97–100. My translation draws upon both that in *Suppl. Mag.* and in Gager, *Curse Tablets and Binding Spells*. The rendering of σπλάγχνα (line 23) as "her heart" in *Curse Tablets and Binding Spells*, instead of "the inward parts" of *Suppl. Mag.*, tones down the spell's violent imagery. Σπλάγχνα can refer to a number of inner organs, including the reproductive organs, which may be the meaning here. Dragging a woman by her genitals is a rather different image than dragging her by the heart. "Obedient" (for the ὑποτεταγμένη of line 26) in *Curse Tablets and Binding Spells* is also somewhat more innocuous than "subject" in *Suppl. Mag.*

the hypothetical scenario of a male client attempting to attract a woman, whereas Gager's remarks concern clients (and targets) of either gender.[61] Winkler correctly stressed that the spells do not seek to harm the target, pointing out that torments such as sleeplessness, dizziness, and loss of appetite are temporary phenomena. He further suggested that the image of slavery used in these spells can mean a desire for a permanent and stable relationship, but gives no arguments to support that view.[62] The image of slavery may indeed have evoked permanence, but we cannot overlook the chilling aspects of that permanence.

Winkler emphasized that Greek erotic literature represents *eros* as a "powerful involuntary attraction, felt as an invasion and described in a pathology of physical and mental disturbance." He further argued that the spells actually contain "patterns of gender-transfer used to hide men's vulnerability and erotic agency." By "erotic agency," Winkler meant that a man composing an erotic spell sought to take himself out of the role of erotic victim in which he "actually" was, and to cast himself into the role of a powerful person. For Winkler, a man commissioning such a spell was actually undertaking a "'kind of last-ditch therapy.'"[63] He presented the love-sick client as undertaking three steps in the process of creating the spell: (1) taking on the role of mastery and control, (2) assuming that he has divine power on his side, and (3) persuading the deity that the intended victim deserves to be punished.[64]

Gager agrees with Winkler's analysis of the therapeutic function of erotic spells, arguing that the true target of the spells is the love-sickness, the passion from which the client suffers. According to Gager, the ancients employed the spells to change the client's internal, rather than external, world:

> [The erotic spells] deal primarily with the inner world of *the client's*
> fantasy and imagination. Their goals are largely realized in the very act

61. Whereas Winkler had emphasized that most of the spells concern men seeking to attract women, Gager stresses that the extant spells document all combinations (male to female, female to male, female to female, male to male, and recipes to target either women or men) (John J. Winkler, *The Constraints of Desire: The Anthropology of Sex and Gender in Ancient Greece* [New York: Routledge, 1990] 90; Gager, *Curse Tablets and Binding Spells*, 80).

62. Winkler, *Constraints*, 96, 97.

63. Ibid., 84, 95, 89 (his quotation marks). Winkler noted that in ancient literature (usually composed by men), the clients are most often female, whereas in the erotic spells, the clients are usually male, and he argued that this contrast or discrepancy makes sense in light of "a cultural habit on the part of men to deal with threats of *erôs* by fictitious denial and transfer" (Ibid., 90).

64. This last step parallels a mentality found among convicted rapists today. See Diana Scully, *Understanding Sexual Violence: A Study of Convicted Rapists* (Perspectives on Gender 3; Boston: Hyman, 1990) 137–41. In the words of one convicted rapist, "I wanted to use and abuse someone as I felt used and abused" (p. 141).

of commissioning and depositing the tablets. Once again, it would be a serious error to read them in an overly literal fashion. It may not be too much to propose that the chthonic powers to whom the tablet is dedicated represent the *client's* sense of domination by psychological forces beyond his or her control; the violent language expresses the turbulence of the erotic passion; and the desire to dominate the target manifests an effort to regain control of oneself.[65]

This argument implies that the spells may have actually worked, but not in the literalistic categories in which we might be inclined to think. In these scholars' view, the clients gain therapeutic relief by creating the spell and imagining themselves as masters, rather than as slaves of passion.

Yet Gager's own collection of ancient testimonies illustrating people's belief that binding spells actually affected the persons targeted[66] contradicts his and Winkler's assessment of the spells' goal as therapy for the client. He himself argues that Pliny the Elder's statement, "There is no one who does not fear to be spellbound by curse-tablets,"[67] probably accurately represents the social views of the first century CE, including those of intellectuals. Pliny's statement demonstrates the anachronism of Gager's and Winkler's focus on the internal world of the client. Gager contradicts himself by arguing that the spells, although public, principally had an internal effect.

A further source for deciding whether people used these spells to effect mainly an internal or an external change is modern Egyptian magical practices. Early twentieth-century anthropological research indicates that Upper Egyptian Muslim and Christian Coptic magical practitioners (some of whose practices resemble the ancient ones described here) have insisted upon their ability to influence external, physical reality.[68] Further, many villagers have accepted their claims. For example, one man targeted by a

65. Gager, *Curse Tablets and Binding Spells*, 82 (emphasis his).

66. Ibid., 243–64.

67. *Naturalis Historia* 28.4.19: *defigi quidem diris deprecationibus nemo non metuit* (W. H. S. Jones, ed., *Pliny: Natural History* [LCL: Cambridge, MA: Harvard University Press, 1963] 14; ET: Gager, *Curse Tablets and Binding Spells*, no. 146, p. 253).

68. See Winifred S. Blackman, *The Fellāḥīn of Upper Egypt: Their Religious, Social, and Industrial Life To-day with Special Reference to Survivals from Ancient Times* (London: Harrap, 1927) esp. 183–200. Blackman describes a Coptic magician who demonstrated his powers to a sceptic by successfully summoning, from within his own private room, a woman from another village (pp. 193f). Blackman also describes the pricking of wax figures with pins: "Wherever the pin or other sharp point is inserted into the figure the person who is represented will feel pain in the corresponding part of his body, until the pin is removed from the clay or wax figure" (p. 197).

Similarities to the ancient spells include using the mother's name, rather than the father's (p. 191), using wax or clay figurines and pins (pp. 196f), and secretly depositing a charm (in this case, one to create hatred, e.g., in a woman whom a man wishes to divorce easily) in a tomb (pp. 190f).

woman with a love-charm "began . . . to desire her as his wife. . . . refusing to eat or sleep, and saying that he must have the girl as his wife."[69] Perhaps ancient Upper Egyptian villagers more closely resembled their modern counterparts than some scholars suppose.[70]

Gager's and Winkler's analogy of therapy is anachronistic. The idea that human beings can best deal with emotions by expressing them probably better represents our own cultural views than those of the ancient Mediterraneans. People must certainly have obtained release from their passions in a variety of ways. (In our world, one person may obtain emotional release through screaming on an amusement park ride, while another screams in a therapist's office.) But the therapy analogy, if it can be applied at all, is probably better suited to such practices in the Roman period as Stoic ethics, with its focus on individual psychology and its subtle techniques for freeing oneself from the overwhelming and irrational power of passion.[71]

By way of further explanation of the violent imagery, Gager argues that the attraction spells probably developed out of more adversarial forms of binding spells from the legal and judicial arenas, whose aggressive language thereby influenced that of the erotic spells.[72] Since most of the erotic spells pertain to relations between men and women, we need to ask why people found the adversarial context and language of binding spells suitable to the erotic experience.

In the eyes of Gager and Winkler, the small figurine of a woman bound and pierced illustrates how the therapy functions. Gager notes that a man says while piercing the figurine: "I pierce whatever part of you so that you will remember me!"[73] The spell does not aim to harm her. Gager suggests that the proper modern analogy for these needles is not "voodoo" dolls from Haiti and other countries, but rather "the therapeutic use of needles

---

69. Blackman, *The Fellāḥīn of Upper Egypt*, 90. Another man discovered a charm that was invalid because it bore the name of his father, rather than of his mother, but which, out of fear, he nevertheless destroyed (pp. 91f). A divorced wife wrote a love charm to make her former husband mad with love for her. The villagers, who knew of the charm, reported to Blackman that the man did everything he could to catch a glimpse of her on market day and that he frequently bought her presents (pp. 95f).

70. For an ancient, albeit novelistic, description of erotic (and other) charms and their effects, see Apuleius, *Metamorphoses* 3.15–25.

71. See Martha Nussbaum, "The Stoics on the Extirpation of the Passions," *Apeiron* 20 (1987) 129–77.

72. See Christopher A. Faraone, "The Agonistic Context of Early Greek Binding Spells," in *Magika Hiera: Ancient Greek Magic and Religion*, ed. Christopher A. Faraone and Dirk Obbink (New York: Oxford University Press, 1990) 3–32. Faraone argues that individuals commissioning spells in the earlier Greek period may often have been in lopsided, competitive contexts and have seen the binding spells as the only way out.

73. See *PGM* 4.296–334.

in Chinese acupuncture."[74] He further puts forth the possibility of a sexual connotation to the piercing needles. Winkler acknowledged that this figurine raises disturbing questions, but argues that "the submission in question is a social protocol, not a sexual practice, and we should at least be cautious about assuming a perfect isomorphism between the public stance and the private posture." He questioned whether *eros* meant "women's bondage, pain, humiliation, submission"[75] and argued that the acts of binding and piercing the figurine do not constitute a man's desire to dominate the woman, but rather to replicate in her his own experience of being dominated by *eros*.

Gager gives no argument as to why acupuncture, rather than voodoo dolls, constitutes the proper modern analogy to the piercing of clay or wax figurines in conjunction with creating erotic spells. Wherein lies the discontinuity between the ancient piercing of figurines and voodoo dolls? Presumably Gager bases his distinction on voodoo dolls as harmful and acupuncture as therapeutic. But in acupuncture, a practitioner pierces the person in need of the therapy, not a doll representing another person, and an acupuncturist makes no claims to change another person's behavior. Further, a social-scientific approach to the study of religion requires, and fairness demands, a fuller explanation as to the difference between contemporary voodoo dolls and the piercing of ancient figurines, especially since Gager himself recognizes that ancient binding spells derive from those forms of binding spells that aimed to harm an opponent or enemy. If Gager's and Winkler's therapy analogy does not hold up, then the acupuncture analogy falls with it, since the point of acupuncture is not to displace one's pain onto another, but to heal, to *relieve* a person from pain.

In spite of my criticisms of Winkler and Gager, I fully agree with them that we must be cautious of interpreting the figurine and the spells too literally. In fact, some of the language, concepts, and practices are so strange to us that we have a very hard time reading them in a fashion suited to their culture. The sheer number of divine beings and spirits invoked in these three spells alone illustrates the very different worldview of the people who commissioned the spells. For them, the world literally teemed with deities and spirits of the dead, beings as real as themselves, capable of acting as agents for or against human beings.

I, however, am more inclined than Winkler and Gager to take these women and men at their word. The petitioners claim that they want an erotic relationship and not simply a change in their internal state of being.

74. Gager, *Curse Tablets and Binding Spells*, 81.
75. Winkler, *Constraints* 96, 95.

For this reason, I assume that Herais, Sophia, and Pantous, like their male counterparts and like the women who sought to attract men, wanted an erotic connection with the targets of their spells (even if the violent imagery is not meant to be taken literally).

On the other hand, Winkler rightly noticed that these spells create a social space for women to have desire and to act upon it.[76] Since a family whose daughter involves herself in an illicit sexual relationship can claim that demonic influence caused her behavior, the spells can have the social effect of preserving the honor of such a family, while allowing a woman errant behavior. Thus, by using these spells, Herais, Sophia, and Pantous / Paitous may have affected their own lives and the lives of others in concrete ways.

The language and imagery of these spells replicate the fundamentally asymmetrical conceptualization of sexual relations found elsewhere in the Roman world and documented in texts discussed throughout this book. The slave imagery present in the spells further underscores the presence of power relations in these texts. We need to remember that those reading and employing these spells knew and/or participated in the Roman institution of chattel slavery, which included sexual access by men to female and male slaves and by women to female slaves.[77] (I do not know of erotic spells commissioned by or directed toward persons identified as slaves; thus, these spells concern the use of slave imagery by persons who are presumably free or freed.) Ancient readers would surely have recognized the social hierarchy implicit in the slave language of these spells.[78]

The male pattern of dominating and punishing a female victim actually

76. Ibid., 97f. In closing, Winkler stated: "These . . . considerations do not—and are not intended to—dispel the anguish roused in us by the Louvre image" (p. 98).

77. On religious language and the sexual use of slaves, see Lawrence Patrick Jones, *A Case Study in "Gnosticism": Religious Responses to Slavery in the Second Century* CE (Ann Arbor, MI: University Microfilms International, 1989). Roman law strictly prohibited sexual contact between married women and any other male, including slaves (*Corpus Iuris Civilis: Digesta* 48.5.6), but such contact doubtlessly occurred anyway. (Jewish law did not prohibit male owners from having sexual access to their female slaves; for proverbial confirmation of the practice, see *m. 'Abot* 2:7.)

In contrast, Roman law did not prohibit the sexual use of female slaves by their mistresses. Although I know of no ancient evidence for sexual relations between female slaveowners and their female slaves, such relations probably also occurred.

78. Many texts of the Roman period, including those of the New Testament, employ slave imagery. On this, see Dale Martin, *Slavery as Salvation: The Metaphor of Slavery in Pauline Christianity* (New Haven, CT: Yale University Press, 1990); and Sheila Briggs, "Can an Enslaved God Liberate? Hermeneutical Reflections on Philippians 2:6–11," in *Interpretation for Liberation*, ed. Katie Geneva Cannon and Elisabeth Schüssler Fiorenza (*Semeia* 47; Atlanta: Scholars Press, 1989) 137–53.

occurs throughout history within patriarchal societies.[79] Ancient martyr-dom accounts contain sexualized images of the torture of women.[80] Such images as enslaving a woman or dragging her by the hair or the inward parts (probably genitals) may shock us, but these images pale in com-parison to the representations of violence and cruelty widespread in the pornography of modern Western societies. Today, pornography includes graphic depictions of the rape, maiming, murder, and beating of women and girls (many of whom participate in the production of the pornography under duress and/or poor working conditions).

What does it mean culturally that these women employed the language of dominance to obtain the desired connection? (We need to remember, of course, that the women commissioning the spells may have had little choice among the available types of spells—especially if they were illiter-ate.)[81] If twentieth-century scholars have difficulty interpreting the image of a man piercing a female figurine or calling upon a spirit to enslave a woman, we may find it even more difficult to understand a woman calling for the sexual enslavement of another woman.

Even in the twentieth century, many contemporary lesbian-feminists in the United States have great difficulty understanding, for example, why lesbians might adopt butch-fem roles (defined loosely: "masculine" and "feminine" lesbians). A woman who identifies herself as a fem, Joan Nestle, interprets her own history:

79. On classical Greece, see Eva C. Keuls, *The Reign of the Phallus: Sexual Politics in An-cient Athens* (New York: Harper and Row, 1985). For an analysis of sexual aggression in Ro-man satire, see Amy Richlin, *The Garden of Priapus: Sexuality and Aggression in Roman Hu-mor* (New Haven: Yale University Press, 1983). Amy Richlin also criticizes the work of Michel Foucault, and of such classicists who follow him as David Halperin and John Winkler, for failing to take sufficient account of the power differential between men and women in their work on ancient sexual behavior and attitudes and for their failure to pay attention to feminist research by classicists ("Zeus and Metis: Foucault, Feminism, Classics," *Helios* 18 [1991] 160–80). Saara Lilja also stresses the aggressive character of Roman attitudes toward sexuality: "Roman sexuality seems to have been characterized by a strong note of violence and aggres-siveness, when compared with the sexuality of the Greeks. . . . It seems as if the originally very rigid and moralistic attitude of the Romans toward sex would all the more easily have leapt to the other extreme of violence and even sadism" (*Homosexuality in Republican and Augustan Rome* [Commentationes Humanarum Litterarum 74; Helsinki: Finnish Society of Sciences and Letters, 1983] 135, 137). On the structural supports for rape in the contemporary United States, see Diana Scully, *Understanding Sexual Violence: A Study of Convicted Rapists* (Per-spectives on Gender 3; Boston: Hyman, 1990).

80. See, e.g., *The Martyrdom of Perpetua and Felicitas* 20; Herbert Musurillo, ed. and trans., *The Acts of the Christian Martyrs* (Oxford: Clarendon, 1972) 128f.

81. The same would apply to men, and especially to illiterate men, but free men enjoyed a level of social power different from that of the women of their own social class, i.e., those to whom they would probably most often direct their spells.

Butch-fem relationships, as I experienced them, were complex erotic and social statements, not phony heterosexual replicas. . . . In the 1950s particularly, butch-fem couples were the front-line warriors against sexual bigotry. Because they were so visibly obvious, they suffered the brunt of street violence. . . . Butches were known by their appearances, fems by their choices. . . . a butch lesbian wearing men's clothes in the 1950s was not a man wearing men's clothes; she was a woman who created an original style to signal to other women what she was capable of doing—taking erotic responsibility. . . . many fems used their appearance to secure jobs that would allow their butch lovers to dress and live the way they both wanted her to. . . . when butches and fems of this style went out together, no one could accuse the fem of passing [as heterosexual]. In fact, the more extremely fem she was, the more obvious was their lesbianism and the more street danger they faced.[82]

Nestle's words should give pause to anyone from outside the lesbian butch-fem experience who thinks that they understand it. She stresses that appearances can deceive. An outsider may not understand that a woman wearing men's clothing has not done so in order to become a man, but rather to communicate complex erotic signals to a female partner. The outsider may not have realized that a lesbian could actually increase her risk of assault by dressing in a culturally more feminine way. Finally, the outsider might miss the clothing's economic aspects: by dressing in a culturally acceptable way, the fem could provide economic support to the couple (a culturally "masculine" role!). In her study of cross-dressing, Marjorie Garber has noted that people usually look through the cross-dresser (i.e., they look through the woman who dresses as a man and see a man), rather than looking carefully at her or him and perceiving the particular sensuousness created by a woman or man who dresses as the other gender.[83] Culturally, a woman in man's clothing is neither a woman, nor a man, but can rather signify a countercultural challenge. As Nestle documents, a lesbian in extremely feminine dress can pose a cultural challenge, for example, by enabling the economic survival of a butch-fem couple.

We can see how a first-person account significantly augments our grasp

82. Joan Nestle, "The Fem Question," in *Pleasure and Danger: Exploring Female Sexuality*, ed. Carole S. Vance (Boston: Routledge and Kegan Paul, 1984) 232–41 (quotes from 232–36). See also Elizabeth Lapovsky Kennedy and Madeline D. Davis, *Boots of Leather, Slippers of Gold: The History of a Lesbian Community* (New York: Penguin Books, 1994); and Neil Miller, *Out of the Past: Gay and Lesbian History from 1869 to the Present* (New York: Vintage Books, 1995) 319–32.

83. Marjorie Garber, *Vested Interests: Cross-Dressing and Cultural Anxiety* (New York: Routledge, Chapman and Hall, 1992).

of the cultural and economic meaning of the fem role.[84] Imagine how many more interpretive clues we need to read the cultural signals of antiquity. Since we have no first-person accounts by Herais, Sophia, and Pantous— or by Sarapias, Gorgonia, and Nike, we can only speculate as to the range of erotic meaning created by the spells' imagery of violence and domination. For example, would an ancient bystander have placed the woman casting the spell in the culturally "masculine" role? Perhaps, but since women also commissioned spells to attract men, the cultural gender of a female spell-caster is not at all clear. And perhaps the ancient outsider interpreted a woman's call for the enslavement of another woman differently than a woman within a homoerotic relationship, since homoerotic women may have used the language and customs of the sexual majority in a countercultural fashion to create their own erotic world of meaning and to ensure their economic and social survival in a world which so disdained their existence (as the sources throughout this book indicate).

On the other hand, perhaps homoerotic women in Upper Egypt did not see themselves as a sexual minority at all, but rather thought of their desire for another woman as a private idiosyncrasy, rather than a countercultural challenge. Maybe for them, a slave was simply a slave—a being totally under their power, one who acquiesces to the mistress's desires in order to survive. I fully recognize that the origin of slave imagery lies in the inhumane institution of slavery that dominated the Roman world. At such a cultural distance, some of the images of these spells disturb us deeply. If we had a better grasp of their meaning for the participants, they might disturb us less—or they might disturb us even more.

Reconstructing Women's History

The greatest contribution of these three spells is that they document the existence of actual women in the Roman world who desired a female partner and went to some lengths to consummate the relationship. Their names—Herais, Sophia, Pantous—constitute the most tangible evidence we have about women who desired other women. Reconstructing the historical situation of these women is more difficult than outlining the cultural ideology inherent in the texts. How did Herais, Sophia, and Pantous envisage that their erotic relationships would take place? Could these women have had long-term romantic relationships with their potential partners, even including marriage or a marriage-like arrangement? Or should we imagine clandestine affairs between these women and their female part-

---

84. For current first-person accounts, see Lesléa Newman, ed., *The Femme Mystique* (Boston: Alyson, 1995).

ners? Were Sarapias, Gorgonia, and Nike married at the time when Herais, Sophia, and Pantous commissioned their spells? While the ancient sources now available to scholars do not allow definitive answers to these questions, I can make suggestions, particularly with the help of other ancient binding spells.

Several ancient erotic binding spells envisage marriage or a long-term relationship as the result of the spell.[85] Both female and male clients express their desire for long-term relationships. For example, in a binding spell found in Hadrumentum in North Africa, probably dating from the third century CE, a woman named Domitiana invokes the divine to attract Urbanus. Her explicit desire is "that he may take her into his house as his wife." In language highly reminiscent of the Septuagint, Domitiana invokes the divine with explicitly Jewish names (e.g., *Iaō*, Greek for YHWH, the ancient Israelite name for God) to "unite him [Urbanus] with Domitiana . . . loving, frantic, tormented with love, passion, and desire for Domitiana . . . unite them in marriage and as spouses in love for all the time of their lives. Make him as her obedient slave, so that he will desire no other woman or maiden apart from Domitiana alone, to whom Candida gave birth, and will keep her as his spouse for all the time of their lives. Now, now! Quickly, quickly!"[86] In another spell, a woman named Dioskourous adjures the spirit of the dead person to make Sarapion love her, adding, "and let him continue loving me, until he arrives in Hades."[87] And a Macedonian woman named Thetima expresses her appeal in this way, "May he indeed not take another wife than myself but let me grow old by the side of Dionusophon."[88] Similarly, an ancient formulary promises the reader who recites a particular love spell many times that the woman so bound

85. Blackman documents that early twentieth-century Upper Egyptian peasant women often used erotic spells to obtain husbands (Winifred S. Blackman, *The Fellāḥīn of Upper Egypt: Their Religious, Social, and Industrial Life To-day with Special Reference to Survivals from Ancient Times* [London: Harrap, 1927] 90).

86. August Audollent, *Defixionum Tabellae quotquot innotuerunt* . . . (Paris: Fontemoing, 1904; reprint, Frankfurt: Minerva, 1967) no. 271.15, 39–47; ET: Gager, *Curse Tablets and Binding Spells*, no. 36, pp. 112–15.

Notice that women, like men, could employ slave imagery. More extensive study would be required to ascertain how this image functioned when employed by women with respect to men. Since Roman law prohibited sexual contact between mistresses and their male slaves (in contrast to the free access of masters to their female and male slaves), the female-to-male image may have carried different cultural connotations than the male-to-female one. See *Corpus Iuris Civilis, Digesta* 48.5.6 (adultery for women is intercourse with any man other than her husband).

87. *PGM* 16.24f; ET: Betz, *Greek Magical Papyri*, 1:252.

88. John G. Gager and his collaborators translate just this sentence of this early unpublished Greek tablet (375–359 BCE), which Emmanuel Voutiras will edit (Gager, *Curse Tablets and Binding Spells*, 85, n. 24).

"will love you all the time of her life."[89] And a third- or fourth-century Egyptian man named Sarapammon desires that a woman named Ptolemais will be "subject for the entire time of my life."[90]

This evidence for clients employing binding spells in order to secure a long-term relationship makes it plausible that Herais, Sophia and Pantous sought enduring connections with Sarapias, Gorgonia, and Nike. Notice the explicit call for "unceasing love" (lines 51f) in Sophia's attempt to attract Gorgonia. This interpretation of the spells implies the public character of their romantic friendships, since long-term relationships can less easily remain secret than brief erotic encounters. Long-term relationships also include the possibility of cohabitation, which can add to the public knowledge about the existence of a relationship. As discussed at several points in this book, Clement of Alexandria, Ptolemy of Alexandria, Iamblichos, the Sifra, and Lucian of Samosata explicitly refer to woman-woman marriage. The first four of these sources locate such marriages in Egypt in the second or early third century CE, while Lucian (2d C. CE) tells of a woman from the island of Lesbos who refers to her female companion from Corinth as her wife. Since the three binding spells under discussion here are all from Egypt and date from similar time periods (Herais: 2d C.; Sophia: 2d or possibly 1st C.; Pantous/Paitous: 3d or 4th C.), they fall into the location and time period for which marriage between women is otherwise attested. Thus, perhaps these three women sought marriage or marriage-like relationships with their partners.

In the spell commissioned by Pantous, she invokes the corpse-*daimon* Horion to make Nike love her for five months. At first sight, the time limitation may seem to exclude the interpretation of the desired relationship as a marriage or marriage-like connection. But S. Eitrem has suggested that this spell may refer to a trial marriage, which, according to some ancient sources, lasted for precisely five months.[91] In a trial marriage, the couple would apparently live together without a contract ("unwritten marriage"; *agraphos gamos*; *agraphōs syneinai*)[92] and only after that would they document the union with a written contract. Pantous could have been hoping to follow the practice of male-female couples in establishing a long-term relationship.

The very act of creating these binding spells, which was probably more

89. *PGM* 7.914f; ET: Betz, *Greek Magical Papyri*, 1:142.

90. *Suppl. Mag.*, 1.47.26; see also Gager, *Curse Tablets and Binding Spells*, no. 28, p. 100.

91. S. Eitrem and Leiv Amundsen, eds., *Papyri Osloenses*, fasc. 2 (Oslo: Dybwad, 1931) p. 33, n. 1 (Eitrem).

92. Hans Julius Wolff, *Written and Unwritten Marriages in Hellenistic and Postclassical Roman Law* (Philological Monographs 9; Haverford, PA: American Philological Association, 1939) 71f.

public than many have assumed, provides further support for the potentially open and public character of the envisaged relationships. (People may have informed others that they had drawn up a spell; some of their ritual actions may have been public; and others may have seen them in the presence of a *magos*.) Drawing up a spell involved not only commissioning a written document, but also carrying out ritual actions, such as speaking the words of the spell out loud, or placing it in a particular location with other objects, such as flowers or a wax or clay figurine.[93] John Gager has particularly emphasized the complex ritual character and the public aspects of binding spells.[94] For example, an inscription from Asia Minor, dated to 156/157 CE, claims that when a man named Ioukoundos became insane, "it was noised abroad by all that he had been put under a spell by his mother-in-law Tatia," who in turn defended herself against these charges.[95] This and other sources bear witness to the public discussion of binding spells.

On the other hand, Herais, Sophia, and Pantous could well have been women in search of a secret adventurous escapade. From an earlier period, Herodas, a hellenistic playwright, describes housewives discussing how to obtain a delightfully firm and smooth leather dildo crafted by a local shoemaker, "a kinder cobbler to a woman you could not possibly find."[96] Herodas thus presents a fictitious, but presumably plausible, scenario of women planning how to derive sexual pleasure from a source other than their husbands, although Herodas's scene is not necessarily homoerotic. Married women plotting together on how to obtain a female lover and conceal the fact from their husbands thus may be a social setting for these love spells.

Since some casters of spells explicitly sought to attract married persons, we can also imagine that Sarapias, Sophia, and Nike were married women. In a Greek spell from Cumae in Italy, the male client desires that his potential partner "first set aside her faithfulness toward her own husband,"[97] while in another spell the male client calls upon the *daimon* not to allow the woman "to think of her [own] husband, [or] her child . . . but let her

93. In the case of the sarcophagus of a person who had died young or who had died a violent death, perhaps the scribe or other professional performed this function. Gager's collection of ancient testimonies bears witness to the public discussion of and knowledge about binding spells (Gager, *Curse Tablets and Binding Spells*, 243–64).

94. Ibid., 20f.

95. Ibid., no. 137.

96. Herodas, *Mimiamboi* 6.72f; A. D. Knox, ed. and trans., *Herodas: The Mimes and Fragments*, with notes by Walter Headlam (Cambridge: Cambridge University Press, 1922) 278f.

97. August Audollent, *Defixionum Tabellae quotquot innotuerunt . . .* (Paris: Fontemoing, 1904; reprint, Frankfurt: Minerva, 1967) no. 198.39f.

come melting for passion and love and intercourse."[98] A male client could have hopes of winning a woman away from her husband. Perhaps these three female clients did as well. But Seneca the Elder's discussion of two *tribades* discovered together in bed by the husband of one of the women, who immediately kills both of them,[99] illustrates the danger of homoerotic activity for married women, even though Seneca's account is fictitious. (In contrast, wives in the ancient Mediterranean world not infrequently had to tolerate their husbands having male lovers.)[100]

Herais, Sophia, and Pantous may well have wanted to establish relationships similar to those between men and women, and they may have imagined themselves as taking a "male," that is, more assertive, role in such relationships. Since, however, women did commission spells to attract men, Herais's, Sophia's, and Pantous's role as clients does not by itself place them in a "masculine" role.

The Erotic Spells, Magic, and Religion

By turning to formulaic spells to attract a female partner, were Herais, Sophia, and Pantous engaging in illicit magic or were they simply participating in the syncretistic, popular religion of their day? If they and others perceived these spells as religious expression, perhaps other practitioners of this religion accorded a certain level of tolerance to these women's homoerotic desires. On the other hand, if they understood these spells as magic, that is, as an illicit phenomenon distinct from religion, their desires may have carried a similarly illicit character.

In general, scholars dispute whether to classify the binding spells as magic or as religion. C. R. Philips argues that the ancient Greeks and Romans neither systematically defined nor systematically repressed what we might call "magic" until the Christian Roman Empire and that current discussion among classicists is unduly shaped by nineteenth-century definitions of magic as either bad religion or bad science. He further notes that Greek and Roman society lacked the social consensus on what constitutes "true religion" that would have been necessary for a definition of

---

98. *PGM* 19a; ET: Betz, *Greek Magical Papyri*, 1:257.

99. *Controversiae* 1.2.23.

100. In a marriage contract from the year 92 BCE, the wife explicitly prohibits the husband from having a boy lover (*Papyrus Tebtynis* 1.104.18–20), which bears witness to the practice of husbands having boy lovers. For further examples, see Eva Cantarella, *Bisexuality in the Ancient World*, trans. Cormac Ó Cuilleanáin (New Haven: Yale University Press, 1992) 171–72.

"magic."[101] Similarly, John Gager and his collaborators avoid using the term "magic" in their volume on curse tablets and binding spells, since they argue that "magic, as a definable and consistent category of human experience, simply does not exist,"[102] but has rather served as a catch-all category for those practices that we do not want to classify as "religion." Along the same lines, Fritz Graf has analyzed the striking similarities between Greek prayers in texts recognized as religious, and prayers or incantations in the corpus of magical papyri.[103]

On the other hand, Hans Dieter Betz argues that we can ascertain genuine differences between magic and religion and that we need to evaluate theologically the practices of both. Betz analyzes evidence that *magoi* of the hellenistic period transformed and legitimated earlier Egyptian magic by adopting terminology and ideas from the Greek mystery cults, but notes that the resulting syncretistic amalgam "destroyed the internal coherence and integrity" of the individual mystery cults.[104] Betz gives as an example the *Mithras Liturgy* in the corpus of magical papyri,[105] which differs from the official cult of Mithras in its lack of "such essentials as the moral ethos, the oaths, the fellowship, and the loyalty among members of the cult, not to speak of the concerns for the welfare of the imperial government and the world community."[106] For Betz: "Magic is the art that makes people who practice it feel better rather than worse, that provides the illusion of security to the insecure, the feeling of help to the helpless, and the comfort of hope to the hopeless. Of course, it is all deception."[107] For Betz, magic differs fundamentally from religion.

101. C[harles] R[obert] Philips, "*Nullum Crimen sine Lege*: Socioreligious Sanctions on Magic," in *Magika Hiera: Ancient Greek Magic and Religion*, ed. Christopher A. Faraone and Dirk Obbink (New York: Oxford University Press, 1991) 260–76. See also Philips's discussion of magic and religion, "The Sociology of Religious Knowledge in the Roman Empire to A.D. 284," in *ANRW* II.16.3 (Berlin: De Gruyter, 1986) 2677–773, esp. 2711–32. On ancient criticism of magic, see G. E. R. Lloyd, *Magic, Reason, and Experience: Studies in the Origin and Development of Greek Science* (Cambridge: Cambridge University Press, 1979) 10–58.
102. Gager, *Curse Tablets and Binding Spells*, v, 24f (quotation on p. 24).
103. Fritz Graf, "Prayer in Magic and Religious Ritual," in Faraone and Obbink, *Magika Hiera*, 188–213.
On the definition of magic in relation to religion, see also Alan F. Segal, "Hellenistic Magic: Some Questions of Definition," in *Studies in Gnosticism and Hellenistic Religions presented to Gilles Quispel on the Occasion of his Sixty-fifth Birthday*, ed. R. Van Den Broek and M. J. Vermaseren (Leiden: Brill, 1981) 349–75.
104. Hans Dieter Betz, "Magic and Mystery in the Greek Magical Papyri," in Faraone and Obbink, *Magika Hiera*, 244–59 (quote on p. 254).
105. *PGM* 4.475–829; ET: Betz, *Greek Magical Papyri*, 1:48–54.
106. Betz, "Magic and Mystery," 254.
107. Betz, *Greek Magical Papyri*, 1:xlviii.

Like Philips, Gager, and Graf, I am unable to discern a clear distinction between magic and religion in the ancient Mediterranean sources that predate Christian theology. Rather, I see the texts that we call "magical," including the over 1,500 extant binding spells, as valuable sources for the popular, often syncretistic religious practices of people of a variety of social classes throughout the ancient Mediterranean.[108] Seeing magic and religion as indistinguishable does not, however, preclude reflecting critically on practices traditionally called either magical or religious. On the necessity of critical interpretation I agree with Betz.[109]

Thus, these three spells provide an excellent witness to the syncretistic religion practiced by those who composed and commissioned them. The spells of both Herais and Sophia appeal to Anoubis, the Egyptian "pious herald of the dead"[110] and protector of necropolises, who is often depicted as a human being with a dog's head. The Herais spell also calls upon Hermes, the Greek messenger deity, and links Anoubis and Hermes with "all the rest down below,"[111] thereby defining Anoubis and Hermes as underworld (or "chthonic") deities. Sophia's spell indirectly refers to Hermes as the "messenger . . . the all-wise boy,"[112] of the Egyptian deity, Osiris. Of the three spells, Sophia's provides the richest array of international divinities and semidivine beings, including Egyptian (Osiris [perhaps defined here as Osiris-Sun],[113] Sarapis, Anoubis, Arsenophre [Arsenouphis], Phre, Harmachimeneus,[114] perhaps Chmouor[115]), Greek (Hermes, Helios, the Erinyes, and Kerberos—the three-headed dog that guards the entrance to the underworld), Hebrew (Azael, Lykael, Beliam [an alternative spelling of

---

108. David Aune proposes seeing magic as a subset of religion: "A particular magical system coheres within a religious structure in the sense that it shares the fundamental religious reality construction of the contextual religion" ("Magic in Early Christianity," in *ANRW* II.23.2 [Berlin: De Gruyter, 1980] 1507–57; quotation on p. 1516).

Another way to approach the problem of religion and magic is from the perspective of social institutions. The *magos* is a private practitioner, rather than a publicly appointed priest or priestess. (For this insight, I am grateful to Prof. Helmut Koester of Harvard Divinity School, who also stresses that the priestly office is often a λειτουργία.) We cannot, however, generally classify religion as public and magic as private, since domestic cults and some oriental religious associations (including early Christian house churches) were either private or represent a gray area between private and public.

109. Betz's criteria and mine differ fundamentally, however; e.g., whereas I ask about the effect on women of particular religious practices and symbolic systems, Betz does not.

110. *Suppl. Mag.*, 1.42.24.

111. *PGM* 32.3f.

112. *Suppl. Mag.*, 1.42.23f.

113. Ibid., 1.42.23: "star of the land of Egypt."

114. Daniel and Maltomini suggest that this name is based on an Egyptian term for "Horos on the Horizon" (Ibid., 1.144).

115. Perhaps derived from Chnum-Horos.

Beliar], Iao), Babylonian (Ereschigal),[116] Persian (Mithras), and Gnostic (Abrasax).[117] Notice the theological tension in Sophia's spell between fearing the deities (traditionally called religion) and commanding them to carry out one's wishes (traditionally called magic).[118] (In addition, the mystical language of this spell contains terms in Hebrew, e.g., *thēnōr* [line 56] = "give light"; and Egyptian, e.g., *chach* [line 53] = "countless.")[119] We might define the religion of Sophia's spell as pantheistic syncretism,[120] a religion shared by people throughout the Roman Empire and expressed in numerous such spells.

Herais, Sophia, and Pantous apparently trusted that this overwhelmingly male pantheon would help them each obtain a female lover. The modern reader may find it striking that the religion of these spells does not prohibit sexual love between women, and its deities express no disapproval of it. This acceptance of female and male homoeroticism is even more striking in light of the drastically asymmetrical understanding of sexual relations found in the spells, an asymmetry that elsewhere forms the basis for rejection of same-sex love.

The Spells and Early Christianity

These spells document that when early Christian authors condemned sexual relations between women, they were responding to a social reality of the Roman world. Strikingly, some of the details of the spells correspond to details of Paul's description of the humans upon whom the wrath of God has been revealed (Rom 1 : 18–32). They venerate a variety of deities, some of them, such as the Greek deity Hermes (called upon by Herais and by Sophia), in the shape of a mortal human being. Others they worship in the shape of a four-footed animal, such as Anoubis (appealed to by Herais and by Sophia), whom Egyptians depicted as dog-headed. Finally, the spells contain evidence for women desiring other women (just as other spells document men "being consumed with passion for one another" [Rom 1 : 27]).[121] Even though these three spells probably all postdate Paul, they

116. Female deity of the underworld, often associated with the Greek Hekate.

117. S. Eitrem points to the different functions that the different deities have in the spell ("Notes on Pap. Soc. It. I 28 and 29," *Aegyptus* 4 [1923] 61f).

118. Especially evident in the choliambic section (lines 20–25).

119. For these and further references, see *Suppl. Mag.*, 1.141–53.

120. See Richard Wünsch, review of *Omaggio della Società italiana per la ricerca dei papiri greci in Egitto al quarto Convegno dei Classicisti tenuto in Firenze dal XVIII al XX aprile del MCMXI*, *Berliner Philologische Wochenschrift* 32 (1912) 6.

121. The Greek word ἐκκαίω (literally: "set on fire," "kindle," "inflame") replicates the frequent imagery of burning found in the erotic spells (καίω, πυρόω, φλέγω).

seem to represent what he would have viewed as the very worst of pagan idolatry, ungodliness, and wickedness.

If these spells resemble erotic spells that women may have commissioned in the Alexandria of the second-century Christian writer Clement, or in the Antioch of the fourth-century church father John Chrysostom, we can better imagine these men's vociferous responses. Clement notes that women marry other women.[122] Had one or more of the women of these spells married another woman? John Chrysostom writes that it is "far more disgraceful when even women seek after these sexual connections, since they ought to feel more shame than men."[123] Herais, Sophia, and Pantous did indeed behave without shame, actively seeking an erotic connection with women whom they desired. These spells provide an invaluable witness to the phenomenon against which early Christian and other ancient writers so vehemently polemicized.

122. Clement of Alexandria, *Paidagogos* 3.3.21.3; see discussion below.
123. John Chrysostom, *Commentary on Romans, Homily 4: PG* 60.417mid.

4

Predetermined Erotic Orientations:
Astrological Texts

Astrological literature contains more references to female homoeroticism than any other type of literature in the Roman world.
This material exhibits broad internal diversity, ranging from technical handbooks for practicing astrologers (Vettius Valens) to theoretical
treatises for elite scientists and philosophers (Ptolemy). The Roman-period
astrologers who produced these texts made predictions about and attempted to understand human behavior based on observation of the heavens, specifically the configurations of the planets and the stars.[1] In casting
a horoscope, an astrologer charted individuals' personalities and futures,
including their sexual behaviors, and also counseled them on how to accept
their lot in life.[2] Female homoeroticism is among the wide range of sexual
possibilities presented in Roman-period astrological texts.

In what follows, I examine these texts as artifacts that both represent and
help to create culture. The horoscopes describe character traits and life
practices that astrologers presumably observed around them, including
women loving women.[3] Regardless of whether these astrologers personally

1. Martin P. Nilsson describes astrology's attraction in antiquity: "For it appealed to the
educated as a science, to the mystics as mysticism, to the broad masses as a convenient form of
fortune-telling" (*Geschichte der griechischen Religion*, 2 vols. [3d ed.; Munich: Beck, 1974],
2.507).

For an introduction to ancient astrology, see Tamsyn Barton, *Ancient Astrology* (London:
Routledge, 1994). See also Tamsyn Barton, *Power and Knowledge: Astrology, Physiognomics,
and Medicine under the Roman Empire* (Ann Arbor: University of Michigan Press, 1994).

2. We cannot be certain to what extent ancient astrologers considered individuals as separate from the collective. Perhaps they understood the variations in sexual behavior as modu-
lations within the universe as a whole, rather than in terms of the individual alone (Robert
Canavello, personal correspondence, October 22, 1993).

3. Franz Cumont uses astrological texts to learn more about Ptolemaic Egypt, about its
government, cities, games, professions, religion, morality, criminal law, etc. His book, *L'Égypte*

knew women who loved women, they deemed female homoeroticism a plausible category for describing a woman's sexual behavior.

As I have shown elsewhere in this book, active and passive constitute foundational categories for Roman-period culture; they are gender-coded as masculine and feminine respectively. In their presentations of a wide range of sexual behaviors and orientations, astrologers often categorized an active sexual role as masculine and a passive sexual role as feminine; for this reason they described passive men as effeminate and active women as masculine. By employing the concept of the masculinization of women and the feminization of men, these astrologers were able to maintain the cultural norm of a hierarchically organized two-gender system while nevertheless being able to account for the numerous, empirically verifiable "exceptions."

The widespread popularity of astrology within both elite and nonelite populations in antiquity makes it a valuable source for determining widely held cultural values in the Roman period. Originally from Babylonia, astrology had gained new appeal in Ptolemaic Egypt, at which time Greek logic and Greek scientific method contributed to its development, and it became the subject of much philosophical debate among educated people. By Roman times, astrology was no longer the sole domain of the scientific elite, but had made its broad influence felt in religion, medicine, philosophy, and other scientific discourse, and in many aspects of daily life. With the introduction of the Julian calendar by the Emperor Augustus, astrology became accessible to the masses.[4] Astrology attracted so many people in the Roman world that even centuries later Christianity could not completely eradicate it.[5]

---

des Astrologues (Brussels: Fondation Égyptologique Reine Élisabeth, 1937), is primarily based upon the *Book of Hermes Trismegistos* (although Cumont's early dating of it is surely wrong; since the work is a composite document, only some parts go back to an early period). Cumont, however, also uses such authors as Vettius Valens and Firmicus Maternus, because he believes to have demonstrated that they preserve earlier material. Cumont's work differs from the present study in that he uses astrological texts as a source for social history, whereas I am examining the ideology of the astrological texts themselves. Social history and ideology-analysis complement one another, of course, and Cumont's recognition that male and female homoeroticism and other forms of sexual unorthodoxy must have been widespread is an important starting point for my study. Cumont bases his view that sexual unorthodoxy was widespread on its frequency within astrological texts.

4. Mathematical calculations concerning the twelve signs of the zodiac were infinitely easier with a solar calendar.

5. The value of astrology was disputed then, as now, but in the Roman period leading scientists accepted it as a serious discipline. Claudius Ptolemy (2d C.), for example, defended astrology against its critics, pointing out that the sun and the moon clearly affect the weather, crops, tides, and animal life. Ptolemy conceded that human scientists cannot make precise predictions about all aspects of astral influence on human life, since such other factors as coun-

Already in the Roman period, elements of astrology and religion intersected, making it difficult for modern scholars to interpret them as mutually exclusive categories. Thus, astrological symbols appear in Christian and
Jewish art and imagery, such as in archaeological remains of synagogue
mosaics. The Dead Sea Scrolls, the Jewish Pseudepigrapha, the Babylonian
Talmud, and ancient Jewish art also employ astrological motifs.[6] And
within the New Testament, the vision of a woman clothed with the sun,
standing on a moon and wearing a crown of twelve stars (Revelation 12),
and the visit to the infant Jesus by wise men who had seen the star in the
east (Matthew 2) illustrate the pervasive influence of astrology.[7] Further,
astrological determinism,[8] the notion that the configuration of stars and
planets preordain one's destiny, raised profound questions about fate and
human freedom that contributed to the philosophical and theological dis-

---

try of origin, rearing, and age also deeply affect human destiny, but he maintained that they
can nevertheless make valuable prognostications. Many astrologers, Ptolemy argued, are not
well trained in astronomy and do not make careful observations. Nevertheless, he asserted,
careless practitioners do not invalidate astrology. Further, they have so many factors to take
into account that they cannot be absolute in their predictions, just as physicians look not only
at the disease, but also at the idiosyncrasy of the patient (*Tetrabiblos* 1.2; see also 1.3 [on the
benefits of prognostication by astronomical means]; 4.10 [on the relationship among astrology, nationality, and age]).

For an analysis of ancient astrology as rhetoric and for the arguments against distinguishing
between science and pseudo-science when studying the ancient world, see Tamsyn S. Barton,
Power and Knowledge: Astrology, Physiognomics, and Medicine under the Roman Empire (Ann
Arbor: University of Michigan Press, 1994) 27–94.

On Christian attitudes toward astrology, see Tamsyn Barton, *Ancient Astrology* (London:
Routledge, 1994) 64–85. On astrology among later Christians, see Ernst Cassirer, *The Individual and the Cosmos in Renaissance Philosophy*, trans. Mario Domandi (New York: Harper
and Row, 1963) 98–103; and Keith Thomas, *Religion and the Decline of Magic* (New York:
Scribner's, 1971) 358–85 (focuses on Christian proponents and opponents of astrology in
the 17th C.). For a critique of Thomas's distinction between magic and religion, see Hildred
Geertz, "An Anthropology of Religion and Magic," *Journal of Interdisciplinary History* 6
(1975) 71–89.

6. See James H. Charlesworth, "Jewish Interest in Astrology during the Hellenistic and
Roman Period," *ANRW* II.20.2 (Berlin: De Gruyter, 1987) 926–50, pls. I–VI. The evidence
cited by Charlesworth includes: 4QCryptic; Treatise of Shem; *b. Šabb.* 156a–156b; and the
signs of the zodiac found in synagogue mosaics in Beth Alpha, Hammat-Tiberias, Naʿaran,
and elsewhere. Charlesworth also refers to evidence for astrology's popularity among early
Christians. See also: Barton, *Ancient Astrology*, 68–70; Rachel Hachlili, "The Zodiac in Ancient Jewish Art: Representation and Significance," *BASOR* 228 (1977) 61–77; Helmut
Koester, *Introduction to the New Testament*, vol. 1 (New York: De Gruyter, 1982) 156–59,
376–79.

7. See also the darkening of the sun in Mark 15:33.

8. Many astrologers today, even though they make statements about causation, view astrology as a matter of analogy, "as above, so below," rather than of determinism. This may be
a development in astrological thinking beyond the fate-oriented view of antiquity.

cussions on these matters. Thus, while religion and astrology may not be synonymous in the Roman period, nevertheless, astrology broadly influenced religious thought and practice.

We need to understand certain basic principles of ancient astrology in order to interpret the texts properly.[9] Since astrology has developed over time, the systems of astrology in the Roman world differed from those in use today. Greek and Roman astrologers knew of five planets (Saturn, Jupiter, Mars, Venus, and Mercury; Neptune, Uranus, and Pluto were discovered only after the invention of the telescope) and two luminaries (the Sun and the Moon), all of which were thought to circle the earth, a motionless globe. Many astrologers assigned gender to the twelve signs of the zodiac, and they believed that a planet or luminary adopted the gender of the sign in which it appeared.[10]

A practicing astrologer in the Roman world drew up a horoscope or birth chart for the native (from Latin: *nativus* [m.]/*nativa* [f.]: a person born [at a particular time], i.e., the client).[11] The horoscope was derived from the heavenly configuration at the time of birth or conception and enabled the astrologer to make predictions concerning such areas of life as health, wealth, marriage, children, and death. It typically consisted of a list of the planets and luminaries and the signs of the zodiac in which they were located. From this list, the astrologer deduced the geometrical relations, known as aspects, between heavenly bodies. Thus, two planets are in sextile aspect when at a 60-degree angle from each other, in quartile or square aspect when at a 90-degree angle from each other, and in trine aspect when at a 120-degree angle from each other. Aspect also functions as a verb in astrological terminology; one heavenly body in a geometrical relation to another is said to aspect it.

The astrologer also ascertained whether a planet was in its own "house," that is, its assigned zodiacal sign.[12] Planets, signs, and their relationships could be especially benefic (lucky) or malefic (unlucky). The astrologer

9. For more detailed explanations of astrological terminology, see Barton, *Ancient Astrology*, 86–156; Jean Rhys Bram, trans., *Ancient Astrology: Theory and Practice: Matheseos libri viii by Firmicus Maternus* (Park Ridge, NJ: Noyes, 1975) "Glossary of Astrological Terms," 333–36; O. Neugebauer and H. B. Van Hoesen, *Greek Horoscopes* (Philadelphia: American Philosophical Society, 1959) "Glossary of Astrological and Technical Terms," 2–13.

10. E.g., Ptolemy and Firmicus Maternus define Aries, Gemini, Leo, Libra, Sagittarius, and Aquarius as masculine, and Taurus, Cancer, Virgo, Scorpio, Capricorn, and Pisces as feminine (Ptolemy, *Tetrabiblos* 1.12; Firmicus Maternus, *Matheseos libri viii* 2.1).

11. Actual Greek horoscopes, found on papyrus and in literary works, can be found in the excellent collection of Neugebauer and Van Hoesen, *Greek Horoscopes*.

12. This contrasts with contemporary astrologers, who designate as "signs" what the ancients called "houses."

based a prognostication on observation of the precise configuration of the heavenly bodies and on consultation of handbooks like those I will discuss in this chapter.

Analyzing the passages on female homoeroticism in these texts is a complicated task. The astrologers that I will discuss all assume that the native is male, unless otherwise stated. Thus, references to female natives appear as asides within the male-centered texts. When the astrologers mention female homoeroticism, they always assess it negatively, although the contexts for the references differ. In some cases, the fragmentary character of the source (e.g., Hermes Trismegistos) or the fact that the source is preserved only in translation or in extensively edited form (e.g., Dorotheos of Sidon) makes it difficult to reconstruct the context, although other ancient astrological sources that are fully extant assist greatly in that task. As I explain below, certain patterns found within these sources illuminate how astrological literature both reflected and helped to sustain Roman-period cultural values and norms about gender and sexual behavior. Some people made life decisions based on astrology, while others may have been influenced simply by hearing about it. I will now discuss each astrologer in approximate chronological order (since scholars can only approximate the dates of some of the works).

Dorotheos of Sidon

Dorotheos of Sidon's astrological didactic poem, *Carmen Astrologicum*, is no longer extant in the original Greek, but such writers as Hephaistion of Thebes and Rhetorios have preserved fragments of the verses, as well as a prose version of the poem. (In fact, Dorotheos exerted extraordinary influence on both ancient and medieval astrologers, many of whom cite him.)[13] David Pingree, editor of the fragments and editor and translator of an Arabic translation, has been able to calculate from particular horoscopes mentioned in the work that Dorotheos must have flourished from 25 to 75 CE.[14] He was thus a contemporary of Paul of Tarsus. Pingree explains that Dorotheos was "extraordinarily influential" in both ancient and me-

---

13. David Pingree, ed. and trans., *The Yavanajātaka of Sphujidhvaja*, vol. 2 (Cambridge, MA: Harvard University Press, 1978) 426f.

14. David Pingree, ed. and trans., *Dorothei Sidonii Carmen Astrologicum* (Leipzig: Teubner, 1976) "Praefatio," VII–X; on Dorotheos, see also: Emilie Boer, *Der Kleine Pauly*, s.v. "Dorotheos von Sidon"; Wilhelm von Christ, *Geschichte der griechischen Literatur*, vol. 2/1, revised by Wilhelm Schmid and Otto Stählin (Handbuch der Altertumswissenschaft 7.2.1; 6th rev. ed.; 1920; reprint, Munich: Beck, 1974) 331; §510; Kuhnert, PW 5, s.v. "Dorotheos" (1905) 1572.

dieval astrology. Examples of his influence can be found in the *Book of Hermes Trismegistos* and the work of Firmicus Maternus, both of which I discuss below.

Dorotheos mentions female homoeroticism several times in two contexts, a chapter on sodomy and one on marriage. In the chapter entitled "Knowledge of Sodomy,"[15] Dorotheos describes women who desire women as parallel with men who desire males (of any age). When Venus and the Moon are in a particular location, then the female native "will be a Lesbian, desirous of women, and if the native is a male, he will be desirous of males."[16] Similarly to Hermes Trismegistos, Dorotheos of Sidon defines the position of Venus as playing an important role in causing natives to be oriented toward members of their own sex.

Dorotheos openly expresses judgment upon the condition: "If the malefics aspect it [Venus], then it [the homoerotic orientation] will be worse. If Venus is under the [Sun's] rays, then it will be worse and more evil."[17] The malefics are the unlucky planets Saturn and Mars. While Dorotheos does not clarify what "worse" might mean for the female native, his description of the male native in the immediately subsequent configuration suggests that a worse and more evil situation is one that involves a more extreme transgression of gender-specific roles. When Venus and Saturn are configured in a particular way, the male native will be "effeminate [and] will be one of those in whom one does [something] like what one does in women."[18] In other words, this native will take the passive role in sexual relations; he will be penetrated.[19] For Dorotheos, effeminacy and male passiveness may well constitute an escalation over simply desiring other males; thus he may view taking the passive role with another male as more evil.

Dorotheos describes another configuration that causes female homoerotic behavior: "If it [Saturn or Mars] is in Capricorn, Aquarius, Aries,

15. *Carmen Astrologicum* 2.7; Pingree, *Carmen Astrologicum* (Arabic translation based on the Pahlavi translation of the Greek original) 52f; ET: Pingree, *Carmen Astrologicum* 206f.

16. *Carmen Astrologicum* 2.7.6; Pingree, *Carmen Astrologicum* (Arabic), 52; ET: Pingree, 206. Pingree translates the Arabic term *saḥāqa* as "Lesbian"; I am following his translation here.

For homoerotic men, the text refers specifically to their desire for "males" (presumably either boys or men; for related configurations, Dorotheos speaks of men's desire for boys).

17. *Carmen Astrologicum* 2.7.7–9; Pingree, *Carmen Astrologicum* (Arabic), 52; ET: Pingree, 206.

18. *Carmen Astrologicum* 2.7.9; Pingree, *Carmen Astrologicum* (Arabic), 52f; ET: Pingree, 206; see also the following two constellations: 2.7.10f; Pingree, *Carmen Astrologicum* (Arabic), 53; ET: Pingree, 206.

19. I am taking "what one does in women" to mean penetration.

Taurus, or Pisces, and the lot of illness is with these two in a feminine sign, if the native is a woman then she will be a Lesbian."[20] He presents this as parallel to males who "will not do to women as they ought to,"[21] that is, penetrate them. Again the condition can be worse: "It will also be thus if Venus is with one of the malefics, and it will be worse than this if Mercury is injured. If Jupiter aspects [something] similar to this, it will relax that misfortune or keep it secret."[22] The last phrase contains an important hint. Dorotheos apparently considered secret homoerotic behavior as a less unfortunate plague for the native than open engagement in same-sex relations. In any case, Dorotheos considers the behavior bad to start with, and certain factors can make it even worse.

Dorotheos goes on to describe three categories of female natives together in one section: (1) those notorious for adultery, (2) those "who do in women the act of men," and (3) those who "will have much intercourse with men."[23] Remember that this combination occurs in a chapter on sodomy. The women "who do in women the act of men" are probably women who penetrate other women. The constellation resulting in the birth of such a woman is a strikingly masculine one. The Sun, the Moon, and Venus are in masculine signs in the cardinal points of the astrological chart,[24] and one of the two luminaries is either in opposition or in quartile aspect to one of the other two. Under this constellation the female native becomes masculine, too, as it were; she performs the "act of men." While the constellations differ for adulterous, homoerotic, and promiscuous women, Dorotheos may have grouped them together because they share an active sexual desire and do not hide it.

Dorotheos mentions female homoeroticism again in his chapter on the lot of marriage. "But if the Moon does not aspect [presumably Venus] while Mars does aspect from quartile," the male native will take pleasure in his wife, but will lose his property because of her, while "if the native is

20. *Carmen Astrologicum* 2.7.12; Pingree, *Carmen Astrologicum* (Arabic), 53; ET: Pingree, 206f. Notice the role played by the lot of illness here. Ptolemy also categorizes a same-sex orientation as a disease of the soul (*Tetrabiblos* 3.14). Dorotheos's system also includes the lot of love, the lot of friendship, the lot of necessity, the lot of soldiering, etc.

21. *Carmen Astrologicum* 2.7.12; Pingree, *Carmen Astrologicum* (Arabic), 53; ET: Pingree, 207.

22. *Carmen Astrologicum* 2.7.13f; Pingree, *Carmen Astrologicum* (Arabic), 53; ET: Pingree, 207.

23. *Carmen Astrologicum* 2.7.15–17; Pingree, *Carmen Astrologicum* (Arabic), 53; ET: Pingree, 207.

24. The astrological chart contained four cardinal points; ancient astrologers sometimes called these the ascendant, midheaven, descendant, and nadir. Midheaven (*Medium Caelum*) is the point in space directly overhead at the time of a person's birth.

female, then the woman is a Lesbian."²⁵ Unlike the juxtaposition of homoerotically inclined women and men in the chapter on sodomy, the connection between the man who loses his property and the Lesbian is unclear.

If Venus has become masculine by appearing in a masculine sign in
midheaven,²⁶ then a woman will be a harlot, "especially if Mars or Mercury
aspects because [this means that] she will be a Lesbian [and] will perform
the act of men; it is worse if the Moon aspects it [Venus] from a masculine
sign."²⁷ Lesbian seems to be a subcategory of harlot in this passage. The
connection between the two may be the public nature of their sexual
activity, or the intensity of their desire, or the frequency of their sexual
activity. Perhaps the combination of Venus and the Moon both being in
masculine signs and their being in aspect to one another leads to a hyper-
masculinization of the female native. This masculinization could connote
greater assertiveness, more public behavior, greater desire for sexual activity, and a more pronounced desire to play the active role.

Two passages convey Dorotheos's negative assessment of female homoeroticism, although they do not address it directly. He describes a configuration with Venus that benefits a woman born under it, "because she will
be one of those who do not perform the act of Venus in an unnatural
way."²⁸ He implies that a woman having relations with another woman
acts unnaturally. Further, if Venus and the Moon are setting, they make
licentious women and soft men, especially when they are aspected by Mars
or Saturn, that is, the malefics.²⁹ The meaning of "licentious" is unclear
here. It could refer to women with an active sexual desire or it might mean
homoerotically inclined women, or both. The juxtaposition of licentious
women and soft men supports the possibility that "licentious" refers to
homoerotic behavior. These two examples illustrate ancient astrologers'
willingness to assess negatively certain types of sexual behavior—occa-

25. *Carmen Astrologicum* 2.4.21; Pingree, *Carmen Astrologicum* (Arabic), 48; ET: Pingree, 202.
26. Midheaven (*Medium Caelum*) is the highest cardinal point on the astrological chart.
27. *Carmen Astrologicum* 2.26.15; Pingree, *Carmen Astrologicum* (Arabic), 75; ET: Pingree, 230. The parallel constellation, Venus in midheaven in a feminine sign, makes a man who
"will not be satisfied and the character of a woman will be in him." At this point, then, the
female and male natives are indeed parallel (*Carmen Astrologicum* 2.26.16; Pingree, *Carmen
Astrologicum* [Arabic], 75; ET: Pingree, 230).
28. *Carmen Astrologicum* 2.26.18; Pingree, *Carmen Astrologicum* (Arabic), 76; ET: Pingree, 230.
29. [T]ὰς μὲν γυναῖκας ἀσελγεῖς ποιοῦσιν, τοὺς δὲ ἄνδρας μαλακούς (Pingree, *Carmen
Astrologicum,* 343; this is from a fragment of Dorotheos preserved in the early seventh-century
astrologer Rhetorios; for the dating see "Praefatio," pp. XII–XIII). Constellations resulting
in pederasts are described in the same fragment.

sionally employing such terms of moral judgment as "licentious"—even though the stars cause this behavior.

Dorotheos attests that certain concepts within astrological thinking are already established by the first century: female homoeroticism is bad, but certain constellations can make it "worse" or "more evil"; those who practice it "perform the act of men"; Venus made masculine can influence the birth of homoerotically inclined female natives; and female homoeroticism is comparable to prostitution. In the next three centuries astrologers repeat and give further documentation for these basic concepts, but they do not alter them.

Manetho

Manetho, an astrologer whose date scholars can only roughly approximate, but who may have lived in the first century CE,[30] composed a didactic poem in Greek entitled *Apotelesmatika* ("Matters Concerning Effects of Certain Constellations on Human Destiny"). In the poem Manetho speaks only once of female homoeroticism. He mentions "*tribades* who perform male functions" being born under a particular configuration of Mercury, Saturn, and Venus.[31] Like other authors discussed in this book, Manetho attributes a male sexual role to the term *tribas*.[32] According to Manetho, then, *tribades* are women who penetrate other women. As we will see in other astrological writings, Venus and Saturn figure prominently in the birth of a *tribas*. Manetho thus provides further evidence for the broad societal awareness of female homoeroticism and of the definition of *tribades* as culturally masculine.

30. David Pingree has posited that a horoscope in the poem dated to May 28 of the year 80 may well be Manetho's own horoscope (Pingree, *Yavanajātaka of Sphujidhvaja*, 2:436). On the other hand, the early fifth-century astrologer Hephaistion is the first to quote Manetho, and Emilie Boer has dated Manetho to the fourth century (*Der Kleine Pauly*, s.v. "Manethon"); Pingree implies that the poem may be a composite Graeco-Egyptian work.

31. Manetho, *Apotelesmatika* 4.358: τριβάδες τ' ἀνδρόστροφα ἔργα τελούσας (Arminius Koechly, ed., *Manethonis Apotelesmaticorum* [*Corpus Epicorum Graecorum* 7; Leipzig: Teubner, 1858] 75; see also the earlier edition by C. A. Mauritius Axtius and Fr. Antonius Rigler, eds., *Manethonis Apotelesmaticorum libri sex* [Cologne: Bachem, 1832] 80). On Manetho, see also Wilhelm Kroll, ed., *Codicum Romanorum*, pt. 2 (*Catalogus Codicum Astrologorum Graecorum* 5.2; Brussels: Lamertin, 1906) 143–54. See also the Italian translation undertaken by Anton Maria Salvini in 1701–2: Rosario Pintaudi, ed., *Anton Maria Salvini: Manetone Degli effetti delle stelle* (Documenti inediti di cultura toscana 1; Florence: Gonnelli, 1976).

32. The phrase ἀνδρόστροφα ἔργα parallels ἀνδρῶν ἔργα in the astrologers Ptolemy (*Tetrabiblos* 3.14; §171), Vettius Valens (*Anthologiai* 2.17; §68), and Hephaistion (*Apotelesmatika* 1.1; §118). See the Latin equivalent, *viriles actus*, in Firmicus Maternus, *Matheseos libri viii* 3.6.30.

124

CHAPTER FOUR

Ptolemy

The next extant astrological references to female homoeroticism appear in the writings of Claudius Ptolemy, the eminent second-century CE Alexandrian astronomer, astrologer, mathematician, and geographer.³³ His major astronomical work, the *Almagest*, established principles that remained normative in the Arab world and Europe until the Copernican revolution. His *Tetrabiblos* ("Four Books"), which enjoyed comparable popularity for a number of centuries, presents systematic criteria for astrological prognostication. In the *Tetrabiblos*, Ptolemy mentions female homoeroticism in two contexts: when he discusses diseases of the soul and when he speaks about marriage.

Ptolemy, like his contemporaries, counted the Sun and the Moon as planets, and assigns them gender along with Saturn, Jupiter, Mars, Venus, and Mercury. He categorizes the Moon and Venus as feminine, owing to their greater share in moisture; and the Sun, Saturn, Jupiter, and Mars as masculine, owing to their greater dryness. (In the ancient Mediterranean, people commonly believed that women's bodies were colder and moister than men's.) He designates Mercury as common, which means both masculine and feminine, since Mercury produces both dryness and moisture.³⁴ Although the Sun and the Moon maintain their assigned genders, those of the other planets are volatile and require constant observation. The planets become masculine or feminine according to their relationship to the Sun and Moon (planets that are morning stars are masculine while the same planets become feminine when they are evening stars) as well as their position on the horizon (in the east, masculine; in the west, feminine).³⁵ Further, planets that occupy a masculine or feminine sign of the zodiac become accordingly masculine or feminine. According to Ptolemy, the zodiacal signs alternate between masculine and diurnal (beginning with Aries) and feminine and nocturnal. Thus, astral masculinity and femininity

33. On Claudius Ptolemy, see Pingree, *Yavanajātaka of Sphujidhvaja*, 2:438; G. E. R. Lloyd, *Greek Science after Aristotle* (New York: Norton, 1973) 113–35; B. L. van der Waerden and F. Lasserre, *Der Kleine Pauly*, s.v. "Klaudios Ptolemaios"; Wilhelm von Christ, *Geschichte der griechischen Literatur*, vol. 2/2, revised by Wilhelm Schmid and Otto Stählin (Handbuch der Altertumswissenschaft 7.2.2; 6th rev. ed.; 1924; reprint, Munich: Beck, 1981) 896–904; §771; E. Konrat Ziegler, B. L. van der Waerden, E[milie] Boer, and Friedrich Lammert, PW 2.23, s.v. "Klaudios Ptolemaios" (1957) 1788–1859; B. L. van der Waerden, PW 2.23.2, s.v. "Ptolemaios I" (1959) 2484.
34. *Tetrabiblos* 1.6; §§19–20; F. E. Robbins, ed. and trans., *Ptolemy: Tetrabiblos* (LCL; Cambridge, MA: Harvard University Press, 1940) 40f. (See also the edition of the *Tetrabiblos* by F[ranz] Boll and E[milie] Boer: *Claudii Ptolemaei opera quae exstant omnia*, vol. 3.1, *Apotelesmatika* [revision of the 1940 Teubner edition; Leipzig: Teubner, 1957].)
35. *Tetrabiblos* 1.6; §20.

are not constant or intrinsic to a planet, but changeable, determined by aspect, position, and characteristics. The planets continually change, becoming now feminine, now masculine as they traverse the heavens. This astral gender fluctuation deeply affects human behavior.[36]

For Ptolemy, activeness and passiveness define what it means to be masculine and feminine. Ptolemy's evaluation of astral masculinity is quite striking: "the male rules and is the first, since also the active is always superior to the passive in power."[37] The widely held ancient view that human females are passive and moist, while human males are active and dry thus finds its counterpart in Ptolemy's theories about the gender of the stars.

Human beings, like the planets, have an assigned gender. But a change in planetary gender can cause sexual behavior appropriate to the opposite sex. Ptolemy defines active male and passive female heterosexual behavior as "natural" (kata physin), although Ptolemy's astrological system casts heterosexuality as anything but a given. Ironically, the positions of the planets determine heterosexual behavior as much as they determine same-sex behavior.

In Tetrabiblos, Ptolemy mentions female homoeroticism in his discussion of "Diseases of the Soul."[38] When Ptolemy describes diseases, which he views as extremes of character, we also get a good picture of his understanding of natural sexual functions and roles. To be naturally active is to be masculine; being naturally feminine means being passive. The soul of every human, male or female, contains an active and a passive part. Diseases such as epilepsy, madness, or demonic seizures constitute a perversion of the active, thinking part of the soul, while excesses and deficiencies in sexual matters pertain to the soul's passive part.

Ptolemy advises the reader to observe the positions of Sun, Moon, Mars, and Venus at the time of a person's birth to ascertain the client's sexual inclinations. When the Sun and the Moon are alone in masculine signs of the zodiac, men exceed in natural sexual inclinations, while women exceed in unnatural ones, "so as merely to increase the virility and activity of the soul."[39] Further, if Mars and/or Venus also become masculine (as a morn-

---

36. In the matter of erotic orientation, the significant point in the fluctuation of gender is the gender of a given planet at the time of one's birth. I have not found a discussion of the influence of later planetary gender fluctuation on erotic orientation (which could mean a fluctuation in human erotic orientation during the course of one's life).

37. Tetrabiblos 1.12; §33: τὸ ποιητικὸν ἀεὶ τοῦ παθητικοῦ πρῶτόν ἐστι τῇ δυνάμει (Robbins, Tetrabiblos, 68f).

38. Tetrabiblos 3.14; §§171–73.

39. Tetrabiblos 3.14; §171: οἱ μὲν ἄνδρες ὑπερβάλλουσι τοῦ κατὰ φύσιν, αἱ δὲ γυναῖκες τοῦ παρὰ φύσιν πρὸς τὸ ἔπανδρον ἁπλῶς τῆς ψυχῆς καὶ δραστικώτερον (Robbins, Tetrabiblos, 368f).

ing star or by entering one of the masculine signs of the zodiac), women lust after unnatural (*para physin*) relations and "cast inviting glances of the eye." Such women, called *tribades*, take the active sexual role with women and perform male functions. If Venus alone is made masculine, such women are secret *tribades*, but if Mars is as well, they live openly and sometimes even call their partners lawful wives.[40] Ptolemy visualizes relationships in which one woman takes on the active male role, while the other woman, not actually under discussion in the *Tetrabiblos*, seems to maintain the natural, feminine, passive role.

The parallel male sexual disease of the soul occurs when the Sun and the Moon are alone in feminine signs and Venus becomes feminine. The men take a passive role in sexual relations, becoming soft, having unnatural (*para physin*) intimate associations and performing female functions. If Venus alone becomes feminine, such men are secret pathics,[41] but if Mars does as well, they are public. Ptolemy asserts that their prostitute-like, base behavior results in their being abused and assaulted, which is only to be expected from such sexual behavior.

The *tribades* and the soft men parallel each other. When the luminaries and Mars and/or Venus become masculine, women become *tribades*, while when the luminaries and Venus or Venus and Mars become feminine, men become soft, passive men. Both act contrary to nature (*para physin*); *tribades* perform male functions as active sexual partners, while soft men play female roles, taking the passive part.

The parallelism is further evident in the planetary influence on persons attracted to members of the opposite sex. Masculinization of the Sun, the Moon, Mars, and/or Venus produces men addicted to natural, that is, heterosexual, intercourse, while with the additional feminization of Venus, women become likewise addicted to sexual intercourse with men.[42]

The structural parallelism here seems perfect. Heterosexually behaving men and *tribades* are produced by planetary masculinity, while heterosexually behaving women and soft men are produced by planetary femininity. The fundamental division is not between males and females, nor between

40. *Tetrabiblos* 3.14; §§171f: αἱ δὲ γυναῖκες πρὸς τὰς παρὰ φύσιν ὁμιλίας λάγναι καὶ ῥιψόφθαλμοι καὶ αἱ καλούμεναι τριβάδες· διατιθέασι δὲ θηλείας, ἀνδρῶν ἔργα ἐπιτελοῦσαι. κἂν μὲν μόνος ὁ τῆς Ἀφροδίτης ἠρρενωμένος ᾖ, λάθρα καὶ οὐκ ἀναφανδόν· ἐὰν δὲ καὶ ὁ τοῦ Ἄρεως, ἄντικρυς ὥστε ἐνίοτε καὶ νομίμας ὥσπερ γυναῖκας τὰς διατιθεμένας ἀναδεικνύειν (Robbins, *Tetrabiblos*, 368–71).

41. *Tetrabiblos* 3.14; §172: οἱ δὲ ἄνδρες μαλακοί τε καὶ σαθροὶ πρὸς τὰς παρὰ φύσιν συνουσίας καὶ γυναικῶν ἔργα, διατιθέμενοι παθητικῶς, ἀποκρύφως μέντοι καὶ λεληθότως (Robbins, *Tetrabiblos*, 370f).

42. A passive verb is used for the natural, excessive female desire. The women become depraved, adulterous, and lustful to be sexually handled in the natural way: *Tetrabiblos* 3.14; §172: πρὸς τὸ διατίθεσθαι κατὰ φύσιν (Robbins, *Tetrabiblos*, 370f).

heterosexual and homosexual, but rather between active and passive. Unlike a soft man or passive woman, both of whom submit to sexual intercourse, a *tribas* takes the lead. She is like a man who causes a woman to submit to him, for she causes a woman to submit to her.

At just the crucial point, however, this cosmetically perfect parallelism breaks down, revealing that active and passive are not parallel at all. This occurs when the behavior is not secret, but rather enters the public realm. When the *tribades* carry out their relations with other women in public, they sometimes designate their partners as lawful wives. The men who submit to shameless acts are like prostitutes and receive the abuse and assault attendant to such behavior. Socially, the two are very different. A man becoming like a woman is not like a woman becoming like a man; he sinks on the social ladder while she attempts to climb it.

Ptolemy also refers to *tribades* in his discussion of marriage. There he places *tribades* in a group with castrated men, further underscoring his view of *tribades* as like men.[43] He also makes systematic comments about how the planets affect men's and women's sexual behavior. The optimum constellation produces men who are pure and solemn in sexual matters, that is, whose only aim is natural, heterosexual intercourse; and women who are temperate and pure.[44] If, however, Saturn is rising and has become masculine, Saturn makes the women either objects of censure themselves or lovers (*erastai*) of those who are objects of censure.[45] The term *erastai* (a masculine plural form—the feminine plural would be *erastriai*) otherwise designates active male lovers.[46] By selecting the word *erastai* to describe women born when Saturn is rising and has become masculine, Ptolemy explicitly defines them as active and masculine.

While Ptolemy divides female sexuality into passive and active behavior, he presents male sexuality as more complex. His work illustrates that the ancient astrologers assigned fewer erotic orientations to women than to men. Astral configurations could create men who played the active role with young males or with males of any age; the passive role with males; or the active role with younger or older women, with low-status women, female slaves, or foreign women. Men could also be inclined toward both the active and the passive roles or toward both females and males. They could

43. *Tetrabiblos* 4.5; §§187–89, esp. §187: ἀποκόπους ἢ τριβάδας (Robbins, *Tetrabiblos*, 404f).
44. Ptolemy does not define these terms for women.
45. *Tetrabiblos* 4.5; §189: ἐπιψόγους ἵστησιν ἢ τῶν ἐπιψόγων ἐραστὰς ἀπεργάζεται (Robbins, *Tetrabiblos*, 406–9). A combination with Jupiter yields greater decency to the diseases, while a combination with Mercury makes them more notorious and makes the native more liable to fail.
46. The passive male beloved is called an ἐρώμενος.

also be eunuchs or incline toward sexual unions with certain female relatives. In contrast, a woman could have a natural attraction toward men (in general, toward particular male relatives, or toward foreigners, low-status men, male slaves, men of superior rank, or masters), could be limited in her reproductive capacities, or she could be a *tribas*. The question of the *tribas*'s partner remains open; Ptolemy devotes no attention to her. The great variety and number of orientations for men illustrate the many sexual outlets of a citizen male in the Roman world, while the lesser number for women corresponds to fewer choices for women, even for citizen women. The greater astrological differentiation for male erotic inclinations also illustrates greater ideological attention to men than to women. Theory concerning male eroticism was much more highly developed than that concerning female erotic behavior. Once again, a structure that on the surface appears to parallel women with men, proves to be asymmetrical at a deeper level, since men have far more sexual options than women.

For Ptolemy, activeness and passiveness are more fundamental than biological maleness and femaleness. Thus, heterosexually behaving men are grouped together with *tribades* (active), while heterosexually behaving women are placed in the same category as soft men (passive). If physiology alone determined behavior or if both genders encompassed a full spectrum of human behavior from soft and passive to ruling and active, then the planets would not require such close observation. But Ptolemy and other ancients presumably observed that females can be active and males passive, a crossover for which a normative cultural definition of women as passive and men as active does not allow. Astrological determinism provides an explanation for the numerous exceptions to the cultural norm. Thus, a highly volatile planetary gender system accounts for highly diverse human sexual behavior.

Vettius Valens

Vettius Valens of Antioch, a contemporary of Ptolemy, completed his *Anthologies* in Greek around the year 175 CE;[47] the work is the fruit of decades of original observation and astrological practice. If Ptolemy represents astrology as the best of ancient science, Vettius Valens gives a glimpse of astrology at the more popular level, for he himself eked out a meager living through practicing his art. Like Ptolemy, Vettius Valens draws upon ear-

---

47. On Vettius Valens, see: Pingree, *Yavanajātaka of Sphujidhvaja*, 2:444f; Emilie Boer, *Der Kleine Pauly*, s.v. "V. Valens Antiochenus"; E. Boer, PW 2.8.1, s.v. "Vettius Valens" (1958) 1871–73; Wilhelm von Christ, *Geschichte der griechischen Literatur*, vol. 2/2, revised by Wilhelm Schmid and Otto Stählin (Handbuch der Altertumswissenschaft 7.2.2; 6th rev. ed.; 1924; reprint, Munich: Beck, 1981) 906; §772.

lier sources for his *Anthologies*. Vettius Valens's *Anthologies* contain horoscopes, as well as an unsystematic treatment of basic astrological principles. Vettius Valens describes female homoerotic behavior as the effect of masculinization when Venus is in trine aspect with Saturn:

> But if they are also in servile signs of the zodiac or divisions of the zodiac, [the natives] have impure passions and unnatural pleasures. When they are in sextile aspect to each other, they have the same nativity plan as when in trine aspect, but faint and weak. When they are eastern [i.e., morning stars] and in the east wind, they masculinize the women not only in their actions, but also in that women, sleeping with women, perform the deeds of men. But the western ones [i.e., evening stars] feminize the men. For at another time, men, sleeping together with men, perform the deeds of women, but they are also often robbed of their generative capacity.[48]

We see here the recurring theme that opposite positions of the stars can cause female masculinization and male feminization. Women who sleep with women are masculine, and men who sleep with men are effeminate. Vettius deems all of this impure and unnatural (*para physin*). When anyone crosses the strict boundary separating women from men, behavior changes drastically. Thus, in Vettius Valens's culture, behavior is divided so sharply along gender lines that when women behave in ways deemed appropriate only to men they are seen as masculinized.

Vettius Valens typifies the assessment of female homoeroticism found in the astrological texts examined in this chapter. He mentions *tribades* in a discussion of injuries and diseases, organized according to the signs of the zodiac, beginning with Aries and proceeding in the usual order through the twelve signs.[49] He postulates as a fixed condition that the Moon is in Leo and the Sun in Cancer; other circumstances change, but not these. Under Capricorn he refers to "women involved in illicit sexual love, *tribades*, licentious ones, servile ones, foul doers"[50] as part of a list that in-

---

48. *Anthologiai* 2.17; §§66–68: ἐὰν δὲ καὶ ἐν λατρώδεσι ζῳδίοις ἢ μοίραις γένωνται, πάθεσιν ἀκαθάρτοις καὶ παρὰ φύσιν ἡδοναῖς χρήσονται. ἐξάγωνοι δὲ πρὸς ἀλλήλους τὴν αὐτὴν ἀποτελεσματογραφίαν τοῖς τριγώνοις ἔχουσιν, ἀμυδρὰν δὲ καὶ ἀσθενῆ. ἐῷοι μὲν ὄντες καὶ ἐν τῷ ἀπηλιώτῃ τὰς γυναῖκας ἀρρενοῦσιν οὐ μόνον ταῖς πράξεσιν, ἀλλὰ καὶ σὺν γυναιξὶ κοιμώμεναι ἀνδρῶν ἔργα ἐπιτελοῦσιν, ἑσπέριοι δὲ θηλύνουσι τοὺς ἄνδρας· ἄλλοτε μὲν γὰρ ἀνδράσι συγκοιμώμενοι γυναικῶν ἔργα ἐπιτελοῦσιν, πολλάκις δὲ καὶ τῶν γονίμων στερίσκονται (David Pingree, ed., *Vettii Valentis Antiocheni Anthologiarum libri novem* [Leipzig: Teubner, 1986] 73). On the morning stars as masculine and the evening stars as feminine, see: Ptolemy, *Tetrabiblos* 1.6; §20.

49. *Anthologiai* 2.37.

50. *Anthologiai* 2.37; §17: γυναῖκες Καυνίαι, τριβάδες, ἀσελγεῖς· λατρευτικοί, αἰσχροποιοί (Pingree, *Vettii Valentis Anthologiarum libri novem*, 105). The manuscript has τριβῶδες, but Wilhelm Kroll, earlier editor of the text, had already corrected it to τριβάδες (Wil-

cludes injuries to the knees, nerves, dullness of sight, madness, troubles with moisture, and phrenitis or inflammation of the brain. The descriptive terms, particularly in a list of injuries and diseases, are derogatory and contain an element of moral condemnation ("illicit," "licentious"). With this, Vettius Valens continues themes set by earlier astrological traditions: *tribades* are masculine and deserving of moral condemnation.

Hermes Trismegistos

The astrological corpus attributed to Hermes Trismegistos, compiled in the seventh century CE, contains material from as early as the second century BCE.[51] Comparable to the Hippokratic corpus of medical writings, the *Book of Hermes Trismegistos (Liber Hermetis Trismegisti)* contains material collected throughout antiquity, making it difficult to date with precision the individual units.[52] The compilation refers twice to female homoeroticism.

The first reference to female homoeroticism in the *Book of Hermes Trismegistos* occurs in the context of a discussion on Venus in several different celestial locations, each of which results in particular sexual propensities on the part of the person born at that time. When "Venus is a morning star

helm Kroll, ed., *Vettii Valentis Anthologiarum Libri* [Berlin: Weidmann, 1908] 111). The γυναῖκες Καννίαι is Pingree's emendation; the manuscript has γυναικοκαυσίαι. The latter contains the same metaphor as ἐκκαίω in Rom 1:27 (in which the men are inflamed with desire for one another) and would mean "inflamed for women," so Pingree's emendation may not be necessary.

51. The *Book of Hermes Trismegistos* is found in the Codex Harleianus of the British Museum. According to an early note, this codex dates from 1431 (Wilhelm Gundel, ed., *Neue astrologische Texte des Hermes Trismegistos: Funde und Forschungen auf dem Gebiet der antiken Astronomie und Astrologie* [Abhandlungen der Bayerischen Akademie der Wissenschaften. Philosophisch-historische Abteilung, n.s. 12; Munich: Bayerische Akademie der Wissenschaften, 1936] 3).

52. Wilhelm Gundel, the editor and commentator of the work, believed that the *Book of Hermes Trismegistos* is a translation of a Greek original, the archetype of which dates to the Ptolemaic period.

David Pingree, however, has disputed Gundel's logic. Pingree agrees with Gundel (on the basis of astronomical calculations) that the essential part of chapter 3 dates from 130 to 60 BCE, but points out that chapter 25 is based upon astronomical observations of the heavens dating to ca. 480 CE. Pingree notes that chapters 27 and 32 of the *Liber Hermetis Trismegisti* (which I cite here) overlap with Firmicus Maternus (4th C.), *Mathesis libri viii* 4.9–15 and 5.5f respectively. Pingree argues, "In those cases in which the *Liber Hermetis* agrees with Firmicus they must both be translating the same Greek source" (Pingree, *Yavanajātaka of Sphujidhvaja*, 2:432f, quote on p. 433). Thus, the material that I cite here is earlier than Firmicus Maternus (4th C. CE), but we do not know how much earlier.

Since chapter 30 of the *Liber Hermetis Trismegisti* (which I will also cite) does not overlap with any other extant ancient astrological material known to Pingree (by far the most knowledgeable historian of ancient astrology), we cannot date it with any precision.

rising in the east . . . if the native is a woman, she becomes a *crissatrix* ["thruster"][53] or a *fricatrix* ["rubber"][54] and is loved by women who are *fricatrices*."[55] Notice that the text envisages both female partners in a sexual act as *fricatrices*, as if there were no active or passive partners. Franz Cumont suggests that *fricatrix* is a translation of the Greek *tribas*, both of which originate from a verb meaning "to rub."[56]

At another point, the *Book of Hermes Trismegistos* groups female homo-eroticism with several other sexual behaviors:

> If, however, the native is a woman, she will be incestuous[57] and exceedingly common or a public prostitute and she will perform

53. Perhaps from *criso*, "To move the haunches as in coitus," *OLD*, s.v. *criso*.

54. From *frico*, " To rub, chafe," *OLD*, s.v. *frico*.

55. *Liber Hermetis Trismegisti* 32, Codex Harleianus fol. 40 v.II; Gundel, *Neue astrologische Texte des Hermes Trismegistos*, 96, lines 25f.

56. Cumont, *L'Égypte des Astrologues*, 183, n. 3. See Petronius, *Satyricon* 92.11, for the verb *fricare* referring to sexual contact between two males.

Two further passages in the *Liber Hermetis Trismegisti* may also concern female homoeroti-cism: (1) *Liber Hermetis Trismegisti* 25, Codex Harleianus fol. 22 r.I: "*cinaedi* [males who play a passive sexual role with other males]; servants [m.] who assist women at their toilet and hairstyling; women who are truly, shall I say, sterile sisters, yet also *trissatrices*" (Gundel, *Neue astrologische Texte des Hermes Trismegistos*, 62, lines 15f; since the scribe could have mistakenly written *trissatrices* instead of *crissatrices*, especially given the presence of *cinaedi* in the group, Cumont emends the *trissatrices* of the codex to *crissatrices*, "swingers" [*L'Égypte des Astrologues*, 183, n. 3]); and (2) *Liber Hermetis Trismegisti* 25, Codex Harleianus fol. 24 v. I–II: *fornicatrices turpia facientes* (Gundel, *Neue astrologische Texte des Hermes Trismegistos*, 68, lines 32f). Cumont takes this phrase as a translation of αἰσχροποιοῦντας (*L'Égypte des Astrologues*, 183, n. 3).

57. Incest occurs quite frequently in the astrological sources, and at a number of points in connection with same-sex love. The connection envisaged by these authors requires detailed research before it can be fully understood, but several of the astrologers' general assumptions about incest can be stated here. These assumptions differ greatly from those of current discussions. The native born under a configuration that denotes incest will be the initiator of such behavior. Power imbalances are not mentioned; thus a woman can be seen as initiating incest with a brother, a son, a nephew, an uncle, or a stepfather, or as corrupting other close relatives or friends (Firmicus Maternus, *Matheseos libri viii* 4.6.4), as if a woman would have the same kind of power over an uncle, a stepfather, or an older brother as she would over her son or a young nephew. Incest is impure and illicit; like same-sex love it constitutes a blurring of boundaries. Thus, these authors do not view incest primarily as a violation of a younger family member, a breach of a child's trust for an older relative, but rather as sexual impurity, equally staining all involved parties with no regard as to who was the perpetrator. While power differences between men and women, expressed as active and passive sexual behavior, are central to the astrological discussion of same-sex love, the power imbalance between adults and children and between men and women is absent from the discussion of incest. A sexual system based on impurity facilitates such a masking of power imbalances, because both parties become impure through the illicit act, regardless of whether each person was even capable of consent or not. For the authors surveyed here, both incest and same-sex love are impure, regardless of who initiated the behavior. Consent and mutuality are irrelevant categories for incest and same-sex love in these texts.

shameful things in life, having intercourse with other women or concubines in the same way as a man.[58]

The common denominator among these behaviors is not obvious. Perhaps shame links them together. The common woman, the prostitute, and the homoerotic woman may also be connected through their public activity.

The text does not spell out precisely what it means for a woman to have intercourse with another woman "in the same way as a man." The phrase suggests penetration, in contrast to the terms *crissatrix* ("thruster") and *fricatrix* ("rubber"), especially since the *Book of Hermes Trismegistos* refers to both female partners as *fricatrices*. I will further analyze this tension as it appears in other astrological writings that provide more context.

Firmicus Maternus

Julius Firmicus Maternus,[59] a Sicilian by birth, began to compose his *Matheseos libri viii* ("Eight Books of the *Mathesis*" or "Theory of Astrology")[60] in 334 CE. He composed the work in Latin, but derived most of it from Greek sources. An aristocratic gentleman of leisure, trained in rhetoric and law, Firmicus Maternus viewed the practice of astrology as a guide for moral living; at one point he even calls astrology a religion.[61] Both female and male homoerotic behavior occur relatively frequently in the work of Firmicus Maternus, who assumed that it is inborn and permanent. Nevertheless, like the astrologers already discussed, Firmicus Maternus describes homoerotic behavior as morally contemptible and transgressive of gender boundaries.

58. *Liber Hermetis Trismegisti* 27, Codex Harleianus fol. 31 r.I: *Si vero nativitas fuerit femina, incesta fit et valde communis vel meretrix publica et inutilia in vita faciet, tamquam vir aliis mulieribus vel concubinis coiens* (Gundel, *Neue astrologische Texte des Hermes Trismegistos*, 80, lines 30–32). I am following Franz Cumont's emendation of *inutilia* ("useless things"). He argues that the translator read ἀχρεῖα ("useless things") for αἰσχρά ("shameful things") (Cumont, *L'Égypte des Astrologues*, 182, n. 1), but since *inutilia* can itself mean "shameful," the emendation is not necessary.

59. On Firmicus Maternus, see Pingree, *Yavanajātaka of Sphujidhvaja*, 2:428; Erich Berneker, *Der Kleine Pauly*, s.v. "Iulius Firmicus Maternus"; Martin Schanz, *Geschichte der römischen Litteratur*, vol. 4/1, revised by Carl Hosius and Gustav Krüger (Handbuch der Altertumswissenschaft 8.2; 3d rev. ed.; 1935; reprint, Munich: Beck, 1980) 129–33; §821; Boll, PW 6, s.v. "Firmicus" (1909) 2365–79.

60. W[ilhelm] Kroll, F. Skutsch, and K. Ziegler, eds., *Iulii Firmici Materni Matheseos libri viii*, 2 vols. (Leipzig: Teubner, 1897–1913; reprint, Stuttgart: Teubner, 1968); ET: Jean Rhys Bram, trans., *Ancient Astrology: Theory and Practice: Matheseos libri viii by Firmicus Maternus* (Noyes Classical Studies; Park Ridge, NJ: Noyes, 1975). Bram's translation contains a good general introduction to ancient astrology, an index of ancient writers on astrology, and a glossary of technical terms. In what follows, I use the edition of Kroll et al. and the translation of Bram, except where I have noted that the translation is my own.

61. *Matheseos libri viii* 2.30.14.

The *Mathesis* is important for ancient astrology both because of the extensive earlier source material it preserves and because it is the last extant astrological work in the West before Christians began to fight more intensively against astrology.[62] Ironically, the *Mathesis* owes its survival at least partially to Christianity, for, in spite of penalties and prohibitions, monks and others continued to copy and later to print the *Mathesis*, and it enjoyed particular popularity in the Renaissance.

The *Mathesis* employs the same division of the twelve signs of the zodiac into masculine and feminine signs as Ptolemy's *Tetrabiblos*.[63] The characteristics of the masculine and feminine signs correspond to those culturally assigned to men and to women in this period. For example, Firmicus describes the masculine Aries as "dominant, fiery, aggressive, . . . with lascivious eyes, restless, impulsive, passionate, lustful."[64] He designates Pisces a feminine sign and describes it as, "damp, watery, . . . fertile, . . . curved, silent."[65] Unlike Ptolemy, Firmicus Maternus does not assign gender to the planets, although the planets do adopt the gender of zodiacal signs as they pass through them.

Like other astrologers, Firmicus Maternus generally presumes that the native is male. The predictions often apply only to men ("governors of individual states," "wife-murderers," "guardians or administrators for women");[66] he mentions women only in passing. He states, "For, as we said in the book of principles, whatever is indicated in the charts of men is also true in women's charts."[67] This does not solve the problem that many points are not transferable and that there are considerable gaps with respect to female experience. Just how the practicing astrologer would use this work to give astrological counsel to women remains unclear, although it has a modern counterpart in contemporary psychological testing, with its greater attention to male experience.

The term *virago*, "masculine woman" (from *vir*, "man"), appears in Firmicus Maternus as a Latin equivalent to *tribas* in Ptolemy and Vettius

62. Firmicus Maternus later converted to Christianity, and in about 346 wrote a polemical attack on the oriental mystery religions (initiation into the secret rites of Isis, Osiris, Serapis, Mithras, etc.), calling upon the emperors Constans and Constantius to eradicate them with force. Both the mystery religions and Christianity offered people a way to escape astrological determinism, so perhaps Firmicus Maternus's intense involvement with these three religious systems indicates a strong interest on his part in questions of free will and determinism.

63. *Matheseos libri viii* 2.1.2; *Tetrabiblos* 1.12; §§32f.

64. *Matheseos libri viii* 2.10.2; ET: Bram, *Ancient Astrology*, 39f.

65. *Matheseos libri viii* 2.10.5; ET: Bram, *Ancient Astrology*, 40.

66. *Matheseos libri viii* 3.2.10; 3.4.36; 3.6.19; ET: Bram, *Ancient Astrology*, 76, 87, 96.

67. *Matheseos libri viii* 5.3.39; ET: Bram, *Ancient Astrology*, 172 (5.3.38). In another passage he adds, "The same is indicated for women with this chart" (*Matheseos libri viii* 8.22.5; ET: Bram, *Ancient Astrology*, 287).

Valens, a point overlooked by previous scholars.[68] Instead, Jean Rhys Bram translates *virago* as "shrew," "shrewish," or "shrewish woman." Most other ancient Latin authors did not translate the Greek *tribas*, but rather used it as a loanword. Firmicus Maternus, however, translates the *tribas* of his sources with *virago*. Notice that *tribas* does not occur in the *Mathesis*, and *virago* occurs where one would expect to find *tribas*. I am suggesting that for Firmicus Maternus, taking a sexually active role was a masculine characteristic, which led him to *virago* as a translation of *tribas*. Further, Firmicus Maternus often parallels *viragines* (pl. of *virago*) and effeminate or homoerotically behaving men.[69] *Virago* is actually quite a good translation of *tribas*. Unlike the *fricatrix* of the *Book of Hermes Trismegistos*, which, like *tribas*, relates to the verb "to rub" (*tribō* in Greek and *frico* in Latin), *virago* is not an etymological translation. But by expressing the gender role transgression of a *tribas*, *virago* sums up the meaning of *tribas* for the societal structures embedded in the astrological texts.

Viragines are the feminine counterpart to *cinaedi* in several passages,[70] but since Firmicus Maternus addresses his book to men and refers to female natives only infrequently, *cinaedi* occur more often than masculine women in his work. Recalling Dorotheos and Ptolemy, he distinguishes between the secretive men (*latentes cinaedi*)[71] and those who are public (*publici cinaedi*),[72] although he does not distinguish between secretive and public behavior for masculine women. Whereas on the female side the primary term for masculinization is *virago*, the male side shows greater differentiation in its categories of effeminacy, including public and private *cinaedi*, eunuchs, and castrated priests of Cybele. The greater range of descriptions for male behavior, as we saw in Ptolemy's *Tetrabiblos*, underscores the *Ma-*

68. The more usual meanings of *virago* are: "A woman having the qualities of a man: a. a physically strong woman. b. a warlike or heroic woman; (esp. applied to goddesses)" (*OLD*, s.v. *virago*). Roman writers saw both physical strength and being warlike as masculine characteristics; hence they could call a servant a *virago* and likewise the deity Pallas Athene.

On "viraginity" as homosexuality in American usage, see Jonathan Ned Katz, *Gay/Lesbian Almanac: A New Documentary* (New York: Harper and Row, 1983) 285–87 (a medical document from 1895).

69. For example, if the Moon is in opposition to Saturn, but Mars is in quartile aspect to the Moon and Saturn and in opposition to Venus, and all these four are in each other's houses, the result is sterile and masculine women (*viragines*) and *cinaedi*.

70. *Matheseos libri viii* 7.25.5; Bram translates *cinaedi* as "male prostitutes" (Bram, *Ancient Astrology*, 262). The term can include men who receive money for sexual services, but is not limited to them. See W. Kroll, PW 11.1, s.v. "Kinaidos" (1921) 459–62. The word is difficult to translate precisely, and I have chosen to leave it untranslated. See also 8.19.7. See further Amy Richlin, "Not Before Homosexuality: The Materiality of the *Cinaedus* and the Roman Law against Love between Men," *Journal of the History of Sexuality* 3 (1993) 523–73.

71. *Matheseos libri viii* 7.25.12; 7.25.19; see also 7.25.21; 7.29.7; 8.29.7.

72. *Matheseos libri viii* 7.25.13; 7.25.20; 7.25.21; 7.25.23; 8.27.8.

thesis's basic orientation toward a male audience in a world that considered men as more important than women.

Firmicus Maternus also considers eunuchs and masculine women together. If Venus is in the seventh house with the Sun, Saturn, and Mercury, or if Venus is in the sixth or twelfth house, eunuchs or masculine women (*mulieres viragines*) are born, as well as those who never have intercourse with men or, if they do, do not conceive or give birth.[73] (Elsewhere, Firmicus Maternus describes two configurations that cause sterile female natives and masculine women,[74] but another configuration causes male natives to marry masculine women and have children from them,[75] so sterility is not intrinsic to being a *virago*. Note that he can imagine *viragines* as married women who can have relationships with men as well as women.)[76] Women who refuse to play a female role parallel emasculated men.[77] At another point, Firmicus speaks of women taking on a male sexual role: "If the Sun and Moon are in masculine signs and Venus is also in a masculine sign in a woman's chart, women will be born who take on a man's character and desire intercourse with women like men."[78] In this same context, he speaks of eunuchs and hermaphrodites who are born when the same planets are in feminine signs, and the Moon and Mars are together on another angle. Thus, if the relevant planets become masculine, women become so as well, and when these planets become feminine, eunuchs or hermaphrodites are born.

Elsewhere, Firmicus Maternus describes a configuration that results in the birth of a *cinaedus* and of female, or passive, prostitutes. A related configuration leads to the birth of men polluted by vice and of masculine female prostitutes (*viragines meretrices*—could these be prostitutes who service women?).[79] He also parallels *cinaedi* and female prostitutes at other points.[80] This parallel may mean that *cinaedi* are effeminate and *meretrices* are hyperfeminine, that is, desirous of sex with many men.

---

73. *Matheseos libri viii* 3.5.23.
74. *Matheseos libri viii* 7.25.4f.
75. *Matheseos libri viii* 3.11.11.
76. See also *Matheseos libri viii* 3.5.23.
77. Firmicus Maternus also speaks of men's bodies having been made effeminate and of men experiencing the passions of effeminate desire (*Matheseos libri viii* 6.11.5: *viri muliebrium libidinum patientur ardores* [Kroll, Skutsch, and Ziegler, *Matheseos libri viii,* 2.94]; see also *Matheseos libri viii* 3.3.11; 4.13.5; 6.30.16).
Like Ptolemy, Firmicus sets up a system that creates the impression of being parallel, but contains a deeper asymmetry.
78. *Matheseos libri viii* 7.25.1: *mulieres quae virili animo succinctae in modum virorum cum mulieribus coire desiderent* (Kroll, Skutsch, and Ziegler, *Matheseos libri viii,* 2.270; ET: Bram, *Ancient Astrology,* 261).
79. *Matheseos libri viii* 8.27.8f.
80. *Matheseos libri viii* 7.25.23; 8.25.4; 8.26.9; 8.27.8; 8.30.2.

As another passage illustrates, the counterpart to hyperfeminine women may be lustful masculine women. One configuration results in public *cinaedi*, another in castrated priests of Cybele (*galli*). If Saturn and Venus are rising morning stars and Mars is located in one of several positions and they are all three located in masculine signs, they make a female native a lustful masculine woman (*libidinosa virago*).[81] There is a parallel here on two counts. First, the men are effeminate or emasculated, while the woman is masculine. Second, the *cinaedi* are public, and the masculine woman is lustful, which may imply a more public expression of her sexual desire.

Firmicus Maternus also mentions masculine women in conjunction with prostitutes. When Mars, Mercury, Venus, and the Moon are together in tropical signs (i.e., Cancer and Capricorn), they produce prostitutes, but the prostitutes' inclinations vary according to the nature of the signs. Surprisingly, if these planets are in feminine signs, they produce prostitutes (*meretrices*), but if they are in masculine signs, they produce masculine women (*viragines*).[82] Strictly speaking, in this context, masculine women seem to be a subcategory of prostitutes, presumably as prostitutes oriented toward women, whereas *meretrices*, prostitutes proper, are those directed toward men. (Perhaps, unlike Ptolemy, Firmicus could not conceive of women marrying women.) In other words, *meretrices*, born when the relevant planets are in feminine signs, are feminine in that they sleep with men and unfeminine in that they are publicly sexual. *Viragines*, born when these planets are in masculine signs, are masculine in that they sleep with women—and perhaps because they do not hide their erotic orientation. In this text, the term *meretrices* as an overarching category, of which *viragines* are a subcategory, may imply public sexual behavior, as such improper for women, rather than monetary exchange. In this interpretation, what would be common to both *meretrices* and *viragines* would be the public nature of their sexual activity.

In addition to two further direct references to masculine women,[83] Firmicus Maternus also mentions a woman who will have the disposition of a masculine woman (*viraginis animus*)[84] and of women who seek to imitate male behavior.[85]

81. *Matheseos libri viii* 7.25.13.
82. *Matheseos libri viii* 7.25.11.
83. *Matheseos libri viii* 4.6.4; 6.30.15.
84. *Matheseos libri viii* 8.9.1. We cannot tell whether she is a masculine woman or just acts like one, or what the precise distinction would be.
85. *Matheseos libri viii* 3.6.30: *alias vero mulieres viriles facit actus appetere* (Kroll, Skutsch, and Ziegler, *Matheseos libri viii*, 1.154). The *viriles actus* are the Latin equivalent of the ἀνδρῶν ἔργα in Ptolemy, *Tetrabiblos* 3.14; §171; Vettius Valens, *Anthologiai* 2.17; §68; and Hephaistion, *Apotelesmatika* 1.1; §118.

Firmicus Maternus also describes a configuration resulting in the public notoriety of a *cinaedus* and adds that in the case of a woman's chart, she will be marked by a similar impure lust.[86] Note the use of "impurity" (*inpuritas*) here, a term used quite frequently throughout the *Matheseos libri viii* for sexual deviance. For example, he describes a constellation under which male natives will be "impure, unchaste, base, entangled in vices of wretched lust and unable to come to natural intercourse, but who are captured by an unnatural [*contra naturam*], inverted passionate desire of lust." [87] In one of Firmicus Maternus's few references directly to women and female sexuality, he describes female homoeroticism as impure: "If Saturn is . . . in quartile aspect, in opposition, or in conjunction with Venus, located, as we said, with Mars, women who have Venus with this combination of stars [or: women who experience sexual desire under this combination of stars] have intercourse with women impurely and unchastely out of lust." [88] Impurity, unchastity, and lust recur as frequently as themes for love between women.

In Firmicus Maternus's astrological system, as in Ptolemy's, gender seems to have been highly volatile. Within a short time, planets became masculine or feminine. A daughter born one day could grow up to be a dutiful, chaste wife who served the wishes of her husband.[89] Born a short time later she could become a masculine woman. The relatively frequent occurrence of sexual deviance in the *Matheseos libri viii* raises the question of just what nature is when so many people are destined by the stars to live contrary to it.

Hephaistion of Thebes

Hephaistion of Thebes composed a three-volume *Apotelesmatika* ("Matters Concerning Effects of Certain Constellations on Human Destiny"— notice that the title is the same as that of the work by Manetho) around 415 in Egypt.[90] Hephaistion's importance for the history of astrology lies

86. *Matheseos libri viii* 8.19.7.

87. *Matheseos libri viii* 5.2.11; translation my own. This same combination of "impure," "natural intercourse," and "unnatural" is also found in Rom 1:24–27.

88. *Matheseos libri viii* 3.6.15: *inpure et inpudice cum mulieribus coibunt libidinis causa* (Kroll, Skutsch, and Ziegler, *Matheseos libri viii*, 1.147; translation revised from Bram.

89. Firmicus Maternus does provide an example of an auspicious birth, "Also she [Venus] binds women to men and men to women with close bonds of affection" (*Matheseos libri viii* 4.19.18; ET: Bram, *Ancient Astrology*, 141). Happy can be the men who have "chaste, amiable wives who serve the wishes of their husbands" (*Matheseos libri viii* 5.4.15; ET: Bram, *Ancient Astrology*, 176).

90. David Pingree, ed., *Hephaestionis Thebani Apotelesmaticorum Libri Tres*, 2 vols. (Leipzig: Teubner, 1973–74). On Hephaistion, see Pingree, *Yavanajātaka of Sphujidhvaja*, 2:

in the earlier sources he preserves, two of which I have discussed here: Ptolemy (*Tetrabiblos*) and Dorotheos of Sidon. His section "Concerning Diseases of the Soul" nearly duplicates Ptolemy's section "Diseases of the Soul."[91] For Hephaistion, as for Ptolemy, women can be born who exceed in unnatural sexual inclinations, that is, their souls become more virile and active. *Tribades* are those who "play the active role with females and perform the deeds of men." Depending on the location of Venus and Mars, they either do this covertly or they do it openly, calling their female partners their "lawful wives."[92]

Like other astrologers, Hephaistion parallels *tribades* with male castrates and males who couple with men. One particular configuration yields on the male side a male castrate or a male who couples with men, and on the female side a woman who is a *tribas* and who couples with women and who performs the deeds of men.[93]

Hephaistion also uses Dorotheos of Sidon and Ptolemy as sources for his section "Concerning Marriage and Wedlock."[94] One constellation results in natives who "manifest the diseases [such as being a *tribas* or a castrate] completely and bring them forward into public places," while under a related constellation persons are born who "manifest hidden diseases or sterile women or persons with no aperture, but if Mars is present as well, castrates or *tribades*."[95] Note that being a *tribas* is here considered a private disease. The juxtaposition of castrates and *tribades*, as well as the distinction between public and private, is familiar to us by now.

At a further point in the section on marriage, Hephaistion apparently associates female homoeroticism with brothels. A rising Saturn that has been made masculine establishes the female natives in brothels or makes

429; Emilie Boer, *Der Kleine Pauly*, s.v. "Hephaistion von Theben"; Wilhelm von Christ, *Geschichte der griechischen Literatur*, vol. 2/2, revised by Wilhelm Schmid and Otto Stählin (Handbuch der Altertumswissenschaft 7.2.2; 6th rev. ed.; 1924; reprint, Munich: Beck, 1981) 1073; §826; F. Boll, PW 8, s.v. "Hephaistion" (1913) 309f. Pingree has established that Hephaistion refers to his own nativity in *Apotelesmatika* 2.1; §32; and 2.2; §23; Pingree has calculated this date as November 26, 380.

91. Hephaistion, *Apotelesmatika* 2.15f; Ptolemy, *Tetrabiblos* 3.14f; §§168–73.

92. Hephaistion, *Apotelesmatika* 2.16; §§8f = Ptolemy, *Tetrabiblos* 3.14; §§171f.

93. Hephaistion, *Apotelesmatika* 1.1; §118: τριβὰς καὶ γυναικὶ συνερχομένη καὶ ἀνδρῶν ἔργα ἐκτελεῖ (Pingree, *Hephaistionis Apotelesmaticorum*, 1.16).

94. Hephaistion, *Apotelesmatika* 2.21 = Dorotheos, *Carmen astrologicum* 2.1; and Ptolemy, *Tetrabiblos* 4.5 (see Pingree, *Hephaistionis Apotelesmaticorum*, "Praefatio" VII, XI).

95. Hephaistion, *Apotelesmatika* 2.21; §19: παντελῶς ἀναδεικνύουσι τὰ πάθη καὶ ἐπὶ δημοσίων τόπων προάγουσιν, . . . κρύφια τὰ πάθη ἢ στείρας καὶ ἀτρήτους, Ἄρεως δὲ προσόντος ἀποκόπους ἢ τριβάδας (Pingree, *Hephaistionis Apotelesmaticorum*, 1.175f). Hephaistion, *Apotelesmatika* 2.21; §19, reproduces practically verbatim Ptolemy, *Tetrabiblos* 4.5; §187. See also the parallel passage on *tribades* in the *Epitome* of Hephaistion (Pingree, *Hephaistionis Apotelesmaticorum*, 2.147; 4.1.107).

them lovers of those who are in brothels; if Jupiter is dominant, the effect is a more honorable form of the disease, but if Mercury is dominant, then a more notorious form of the disease results.[96] (Hephaistion departs from Ptolemy when he speaks of women as lovers of those who are in brothels.) The Greek word for "lovers" designates the active partners in sexual relationships; it occurs here in the masculine form (*erastai;* the feminine would be *erastriai*), but must refer to women, since this paragraph is explicitly about female natives. "Those who are in brothels" are not defined as female or male. Hephaistion could mean either, as long as the female native is the active partner, and the prostitute the passive one.[97] If this passage does refer to female same-sex relations, then its reference to brothels recalls the tone of moral condemnation found in other astrologers, who employ such terms as "impure," "illicit," and "licentious."

In Hephaistion's early fifth-century work we encounter the same astrological tenets documented in first- and second-century astrologers: female homoeroticism is unnatural, masculine, active, sick, and comparable to prostitution, as well as to male castration. Hephaistion also replicates Ptolemy's intriguing reference to public *tribades* who call their partners their "lawful wives."[98] Hephaistion demonstrates that over a period of at least five centuries we can find similar understandings of gender and of female homoeroticism, as well as intriguing hints of a societal institution, marriage between women, that challenged these understandings.

This survey has yielded several surprising findings. Some ancients believed that the stars can cause behavior deemed unnatural—a striking concept if

96. Hephaistion, *Apotelesmatika* 2.21; §§23–25: Γυναῖκας . . . σώφρονας καὶ καθαρίους . . . ὀρεκτικὰς μέν, εὐλαβεῖς δέ. . . . λάγνους καὶ καταφερεῖς. . . . ὁ τοῦ Κρόνου . . . ἀσελγειῶν αἴτιος . . . ἐπὶ τέγους ἵστησιν ἢ τῶν ἐπὶ τέγους ἐραστὰς ἀπεργάζεται . . . πρὸς τὸ εὐσχημονέστερον τῶν παθῶν . . . πρὸς τὸ διαβοητότερον (Pingree, *Hephaistionis Apotelesmaticorum,* 1.176). For discussion of the parallel in Ptolemy, *Tetrabiblos* 4.5; §§188f, see above, pp. 00–000.

97. The difference between Ptolemy and Hephaistion may be a simple problem of transmission. Ptolemy, rather than have Saturn establish the women in brothels or make them lovers of those who are in brothels, has Saturn make them objects of censure or lovers of those who are objects of censure (ἐπιψόγους ἵστησιν ἢ τῶν ἐπιψόγων ἐραστὰς ἀπεργάζεται). This is a difference of only a few letters (Ptolemy: ἐπιψόγους . . . τῶν ἐπιψόγων; Hephastion: ἐπὶ τέγους . . . τῶν ἐπὶ τέγους). Pingree does not list ἐπιψόγους or ἐπιψόγων as manuscript variants for Hephaistion, nor does Robbins list the Hephaistion readings as manuscript variants for Ptolemy, so the confusion may be an old one.

98. The astrologer Rhetorios (6th/7th C.) may also refer to female homoeroticism: Pierre Boudreaux, ed., *Codicum Parisinorum,* pt. 4, with an appendix edited by Franz Cumont (*Catalogus Codicum Astrologorum Graecorum* 8.4; Brussels: Lamertin, 1921), appendix 160.12; 196.8; 197.4). A systematic study of all of the extant astrological texts from antiquity would doubtless yield further sources on *tribades*.

we see the stars as part of nature. Although they considered female homoeroticism unnatural, ancient astrologers mentioned it dozens of times, at-
testing to broad societal recognition of the phenomenon. Further, contrary to the view that the idea of sexual orientation did not develop until
the nineteenth century, the astrological sources demonstrate the existence
in the Roman world of the concept of a lifelong erotic orientation.[99] Because of a particular configuration of the stars, a girl would be born as a
tribas, virago, fricatrix, or *crissatrix;* the stars, then, determined a woman's
erotic inclinations for the duration of her life.

And yet, unlike the twentieth-century binary notion of homosexuality
versus heterosexuality, ancient astrologers conceived of erotic propensities
in a far more complex fashion. Ptolemy, for example, distinguished between active and passive orientations, and he also took account of such
factors as age, wealth, and whether the person to whom one is attracted is
a foreigner.

In other words, astrologers in the Roman world knew of what we might
call sexual orientation, but they did not limit it to two orientations, homosexual and heterosexual. Instead, these ancient writers believed that
configurations of the stars created a broad range of sexual inclinations and
orientations. Their framework for classifying human sexual behavior took
account of factors that most persons of the twentieth century would see as
irrelevant for determining sexual orientation. Thus, passive and active were
more fundamental categories for these astrologers than male and female;
linking passiveness to women and activeness to men, they described passive
men as effeminate and active women as masculine. Such cross-gender behavior often resulted from certain planets, in particular Venus and Mars
(the deities of love and war respectively), becoming feminine or masculine. The astrologers usually explained such transgressions of the strict,
culturally required, gender boundaries as symptomatic of a disease. They
did not prescribe a treatment for this disease. Indeed, astrology generally
aimed to help people understand their preordained lot in life. We can, however, only guess at how astrologers worked with clients preordained toward
homoeroticism.

Nevertheless, they regularly employed terminology that indicated strong
disapproval and even disgust at women becoming masculine and men becoming effeminate, terms such as "impure," "licentious," and "lustful."
The *Book of Hermes Trismegistos,* Dorotheos of Sidon, and Firmicus Maternus all make some kind of connection between prostitutes and women

99. Since contemporary astrologers consider transits and progressions, i.e, the present location of the planets in relation to their location at the time of one's birth, they give less weight
to the birth chart, and this results in "a different sense of what [is] . . . predetermined at birth"
(Robert Canavello, personal correspondence, October 22, 1993).

who have a sexual relationship with another woman; perhaps they are categorized together because they are both public, which transgresses a cultural norm for women.[100] Ptolemy sees public female homoerotic behavior as an escalation over such behavior in private.

The surface impression of a structural parallelism between women and men dissolves as one examines the texts more carefully. Men and male sexuality are more central to these writers than women and female sexuality. A greater range of options occurs for the men, both of the "natural" and of the "unnatural" variety. Further, since being active and assertive has greater value for these writers than being passive, women who have become masculine have adopted that which they have no right to claim, while effeminate men have relinquished the rights and privileges due to their sex. The most influential of the aforementioned astrologers, Ptolemy, makes this clear when he describes the abuse heaped upon passive men, those who perform the deeds of women, and how *tribades* sometimes call their female partners "lawful wives." The men sink socially while the women attempt to rise. The astrologers in question, in mapping out a comprehensive system of astral influence on human behavior, were simultaneously mapping out a comprehensive gender system. The categories of active and passive set the boundaries of masculinity and femininity for all women and men. Through analyzing masculine (active) women and effeminate (passive) men in these astrological texts, we are able to see that the boundaries between "natural" and "unnatural" sexual and gender behavior limit the range of acceptable human expression. Thus we can see how this system affected all women and men.

100. On the public sphere as culturally masculine, see Karen J. Torjesen, "Excavations in the Deep-Structure of the Theological Tradition: The Social Origins of Theology," *Occasional Papers* 14 (Claremont, CA: Institute for Antiquity and Christianity, 1988).

5

Women with Masculine Desires:
Medical Treatments

According to Michel Foucault, representatives of the newly emerging medical profession in the nineteenth century gave a scientific shape to modern conceptions of homosexuality. He and other scholars have claimed that nineteenth-century physicians medicalized homosexuality by developing treatments and etiologies for it, including the theory that it is congenital or acquired through childhood experiences.[1] They maintain that the emerging medical profession applied scientific concepts to acts that previously had been described as sinful or criminal. These scholars, however, have overlooked ancient medical classifications of certain forms of same-sex behaviors and desires as chronic diseases, with corresponding etiologies and treatments (even though they have examined ancient medical texts for other purposes). Contrary to the views of Foucault and others, I will show that some ancient writers saw particular same-sex acts as symptoms of a chronic disease that affected the entirety of one's identity.[2] The patient suffering from such a disease did have an identity,

1. See, e.g., Michel Foucault, *The History of Sexuality*, vol. 1, *An Introduction*, trans. Robert Hurley (French original, Paris: Éditions Gallimard, 1976; New York: Random House, 1978) 36–49, 103–14; and David F. Greenberg, *The Construction of Homosexuality* (Chicago: University of Chicago Press, 1988) 397–433.

For a discussion of the changes that occurred in medical conceptualizations of female homoeroticism during the late nineteenth and early twentieth centuries, see George Chauncey, "From Sexual Inversion to Homosexuality: The Changing Medical Conceptualization of Female 'Deviance,' " *Salmagundi* 58–59 (Fall 1982 / Winter 1983) 114–46; reprinted in *Passion and Power: Sexuality in History*, ed. Kathy Peiss and Christian Simmons (Philadelphia: Temple University Press, 1989) 87–117.

2. Other researchers have already questioned Foucault's thesis on the basis of medical texts from ancient India: Michael J. Sweet and Leonard Zwilling, "The First Medicalization: The Taxonomy and Etiology of Queerness in Classical Indian Medicine," *Journal of the History of Sexuality* 3 (1993) 590–607. The texts that Sweet and Zwilling discuss, the *Caraka* and the

apparently a lifelong one, characterized by behavior considered unnatural (i.e., appropriate for the opposite sex), unless treatment effected a cure. Ancient medical writers did not occupy the same powerful role in society as those in the modern medical profession, but when we approach the ancient Mediterranean world, we have to recognize that same-sex desire and behavior did fall within the realm of medical theory.

I will examine several medical texts from the Roman and early Byzantine periods that address deviant female sexual behavior. According to one view, *tribades*, that is, women who actively seek sexual relations with other women, are mentally ill and need to be treated with mind control. In another model, medical writers prescribe clitoridectomy for women who exhibit masculine desires and behaviors that they attribute to overly large clitorises. These medical diagnoses and treatments share the underlying view that healthy female sexual behavior is passive, while healthy male sexual behavior is active. These medical writers engage in a lively ongoing discussion dating back to pre-Sokratic philosophy on the etiology of male sexual passivity; this discussion at times also applies to women who take on active sexual roles. In what follows, I will focus on female sexuality and women's identity, but also include some material on male same-sex love in order to understand the medical writers' gender map.

Understanding these medical writers is important for understanding early Christianity, because medical theory intersected with and influenced early Christian views of the body. Several recent researchers, most notably Aline Rousselle and Michel Foucault, have argued that medical writers of the Roman period worked with markedly different concepts of the body and of sexuality than are found in the older Hippokratic corpus[3] and that the Roman-period views prepared the way for Christian sexual ethics.

Súsruta, date in their present form from the first two centuries CE, but contain earlier material. This makes them precisely contemporaneous with the principal medical writer that I discuss in this chapter, Soranos of Ephesos, who also refers to earlier sources. Both the *Caraka* and the *Súsruta* refer to "masculine lesbian females," which parallels what is found in Soranos.

3. The Hippokratic corpus is a collection ranging from the 5th C. BCE through possibly the 1st or even 2d C. CE. Ann Ellis Hanson has established that, compared with the Hippokratic corpus, the gynecological literature of the Roman Empire gives some place to women's health outside of their reproductive functions, changes its understanding of the female body, and assumes that some women's sexual behavior approximates that of men in that it does not subsume desire and sexual pleasure under reproduction. In addition, there is a new emphasis on hypersexuality in women. At the same time, Hanson discerns the image of woman as wife and mother to be a constant from classical Greek through Roman gynecology ("The Medical Writers' Woman," in *Before Sexuality: The Construction of Erotic Experience in the Ancient Greek World*, ed. David M. Halperin, John J. Winkler, and Froma I. Zeitlin [Princeton: Princeton University Press, 1990] 309–38). See also Lesley Dean-Jones, "The Politics of Pleasure: Female Sexual Appetite in the Hippokratic Corpus," *Helios* 19 (1992) 72–91.

For a survey of Greek medical writers, see Lesley Dean-Jones, *Women's Bodies in Classical Greek Science* (Oxford: Clarendon; New York: Oxford University Press, 1994).

Rousselle has demonstrated that medical writers of the Roman period urged sexual restraint for both women and men; she sees these medical writings as an important background for understanding early Christian asceticism.[4] Foucault finds in medical and other writings of the first and second centuries a greater focus on self-control and an increasing association of sexual acts with evil and disease. According to Foucault's thesis, this greater emphasis on self-restraint is a stage in the development of a later Christian preoccupation with the evils of sexuality.[5]

Ancient medical writers represent and helped to create the culture in which early Christianity originated, which means that they are significant for Christian history not only because of their later influence, but also because they helped to shape the frameworks of thinking to which early Christians responded. Some writers of the early church read and responded to the medical writers of the early Roman period, such as Tertullian (2d/3d C.), whose framework for his treatise "On the Soul"[6] apparently mirrors that of the second-century medical writer Soranos. Some of the late antique and early medieval medical encyclopedists and compilers were themselves Christian and adopted much of Greek medical learning of the earlier Roman period as their own, thus extending the earlier medical writers' influence among Christians. For example, Aetios of Amida, a Christian

4. Aline Rousselle, *Porneia: On Desire and the Body in Antiquity*, trans. Felicia Pheasant (French original, Paris: Presses Universitaires de France, 1983; Oxford: Blackwell, 1988). Mary Lefkowitz doubts that the ancient medical writers were as representative of broad social attitudes as Rousselle seems to assume, pointing out that only a tiny percentage of the populace could afford physicians (*Times Literary Supplement*, August 19–25, 1988, 912). Leaving aside the question of whether Lefkowitz's criticism undermines Rousselle's main thesis (that the attitudes represented by the medical writers paved the way for early Christian asceticism), the same criticism cannot be leveled against this chapter for two reasons. Perhaps only a small elite agreed with or even knew about the medical classification of women's desire for other women as diseased, but the concepts of femininity and masculinity operative in the medical discussion coincide with those found in a variety of genres of ancient literature. Secondly, some of what I will be discussing comes from handbooks for midwives, who served a larger percentage of the population than highly literate author/physicians. Of course we do not know whether the midwives accepted what they read in these handbooks (or how many midwives could read them), but the potential for the broad dissemination of the medical practices and understandings of the body found in these handbooks is considerable.

5. Foucault, *History*, vol. 3, 235–40; 99–144 (focusing on the 2d-C. medical writers Galen and Soranos).

6. See Heinrich Karpp, "Sorans vier Bücher Περὶ ψυχῆς und Tertullians Schrift De anima," *ZNW* 33 (1934) 31–47. Karpp argues that Soranos's lost work actually formed the basis of Tertullian's *De anima* (see esp. *De anima* 6), and that Tertullian drew upon the authority of Soranos to establish the corporeality of the soul. Karpp hypothesizes that the earliest known Christian psychology is basically pagan psychology which has been Christianized (p. 31). Berthold Altaner and Alfred Stuiber also note that Tertullian used Soranos as a source (*Patrologie* [8th ed.; Freiburg: Herder, 1978] 156), as does Otto Bardenhewer (*Geschichte der altkirchlichen Literatur*, 5 vols. [Freiburg: Herder, 1902–32], 2 [1903] 377).

and personal physician to the Emperor Justinian, abstracted the writings of Soranos, Philoumenos, and Aspasia, among others. The ancient medical writers were learned and probably served the upper class more than any other. Learned and/or wealthy Christians would have had greater access than the majority of early Christians to the medical material that I discuss here. Some treatments and attitudes found in the material may, however, have enjoyed broader circulation through the medical practices of midwives and thus have made their way into the rank and file of early Christians.

Tribades *as Mentally Ill*

One stream of ancient medical writing presents female homoeroticism as a mental illness, specifically as a disease of the soul, which we have also seen in such astrological texts as Ptolemy's *Tetrabiblos*. Among the medical writers, Soranos of Ephesos established an enduring and influential view of *tribades* as women who suffer from a chronic disease of the soul that the physician should treat by mind control. Soranos mentions *tribades* briefly in a lengthy discussion of effeminate men and explains that they have masculine qualities, such as their jealous pursuit of women, whom they prefer to men. Their heavy use of alcohol and impulsive quest for new forms of lust also have cultural overtones of masculinity. A comparison of Soranos's depiction of masculine women and effeminate men reveals that categories of active and passive undergird his analysis of diseased and healthy sexual behavior.

Soranos studied medicine in Alexandria and served as a physician in Rome around the beginning of the second century CE.[7] He was a leading representative of the Methodist school of medicine,[8] which taught that there are three basic bodily statuses and therefore three basic types of disease, each type involving the whole body. Its therapy was based on following a disease through its particular cycle. Given this typological view of disease, Methodists considered a detailed knowledge of anatomy to be unnecessary in treating disease. Soranos, however, was somewhat eclectic and did mention anatomy in his medical writings.[9]

7. See Fridolf Kudlien, *Der Kleine Pauly*, s.v. "Soranos"; Albin Lesky, *Geschichte der griechischen Literatur* (3d ed. rev. and exp.; Berne/Munich: Francke, 1971) 996f; Kind, PW 2.3, s.v. "Soranos" (1929) 1113–30; Wilhelm von Christ, *Geschichte der griechischen Literatur*, vol. 2/2, revised by Wilhelm Schmid and Otto Stählin (Handbuch der Altertumswissenschaft 7.2.2; 6th rev. ed.; 1924; reprint, Munich: Beck, 1981) 910f; §774.

8. See Fridolf Kudlien, *Der Kleine Pauly*, s.v. "Methodiker"; Owsei Temkin, trans., *Soranus' Gynecology* (Baltimore: Johns Hopkins University Press, 1956) xxv–xxx.

9. For a fuller discussion of Soranos's place in ancient medicine, see Paul Burguière, Danielle Gourevitch, and Yves Malinas, *Soranos d'Éphèse: Maladies des femmes*, vol. 1, *Texte établi, traduit et commenté* (Paris: Les Belles Lettres, 1988) VII–XLVI (by Gourevitch).

Soranos discusses *tribades* in his two-part treatise *On Acute and On Chronic Diseases* (*Peri oxeōn kai chroniōn pathōn*), which no longer exists in Greek, although there is a good Latin translation of it by Caelius Aurelianus, a fifth-century medical writer and translator of Greek medical works, from Sicca Veneria in Numidia (eastern Algeria).[10] Caelius Aurelianus was a careful translator, and his primary change was to abridge the text at various points.[11] P. H. Schrijvers, in an excellent commentary on the passage that I am about to discuss, attempts to distinguish between Soranos's original and Caelius Aurelianus's alterations.[12] Schrijvers concludes that the translation is generally accurate, but observes several elements in

10. See Fridolf Kudlien, *Der Kleine Pauly*, s.v. "Caelius Aurelianus"; Martin Schanz, *Geschichte der römischen Literatur*, vol. 4/2, revised by Carl Hosius and Gustav Krüger (Handbuch der Altertumswissenschaft 8.2; 4th rev. ed.; 1935; reprint, Munich: Beck, 1980) 285–89; §1131; M. Wellmann, PW 3, s.v. "Caelius Aurelianus" (1899) 1256–58.

11. Karl Vietmeier, in his extensive study of certain medical terms in Caelius Aurelianus, came to the conclusion that the translation was sufficiently meticulous to allow a retroversion into Greek of the medical terminology, which Vietmeier does in his study (*Beobachtungen über Caelius Aurelianus als Übersetzer medizinischer Fachausdrücke verlorener griechischer Schriften des methodischen Arztes Soranos von Ephesos* [Gütersloh: Thiele, 1937] 99). Schanz and Hosius argue that the translation was generally careful, although abbreviated at points: "eine im allgemeinen treue, hier und da abgekürzte Uebersetzung" (Schanz, *Geschichte der römischen Literatur*, vol. 4/2, 286). M. Wellmann (PW 3, s.v. "Caelius Aurelianus" [1899] 1257) and Valentin Rose (*Anecdota Græca et Græcolatina*, 2 vols. [Berlin: Duemmler, 1864–70], 2.166f) also concur that Caelius Aurelianus was a careful translator. Wellmann's judgment is derived from a comparison of one fragment of Caelius Aurelianus's *Gynaecia* with the extant works of Soranos. See also Schmid/Stählin, however, who describe the Latin as a "complete reworking" of the Greek original, by which they primarily mean that he latinized it (von Christ, *Geschichte der griechischen Literatur*, vol. 2/2, 911). On Caelius Aurelianus as a translator, see also: Gerhard Bendz, *Emendationen zu Caelius Aurelianus* (Publication of the New Society of Letters at Lund 44; Lund: Gleerup, 1954); and Pierre Schmid, *Contributions à la critique du texte de Caelius Aurelianus* (Neuchâtel: Academica Heitz, 1942), neither of whom proposes a new emendation relevant for the texts discussed here.

12. P. H. Schrijvers, *Eine medizinische Erklärung der männlichen Homosexualität aus der Antike: (Caelius Aurelianus De morbis chronicis IV 9)* (Amsterdam: Grüner, 1985) 2 and passim. Schrijvers's other principal contribution is to base his text on the *editio princeps* (major edition) of Johannes Sichardus (Jean Sichard) (Basle 1529) on the grounds that I. E. Drabkin was not conservative enough in his edition (I. E. Drabkin, ed. and trans., *Caelius Aurelianus: On Acute Diseases and On Chronic Diseases* [Chicago: University of Chicago Press, 1950] 900–905). I am following the edition of Schrijvers for *Chronicarum passionum* 4.9; §§131–37, and taking his German translation into account for my English translation, where there are problems with that of Drabkin. For *On Acute Diseases and On Chronic Diseases* as a whole, I am following the edition and translation of Drabkin, which is very competently done. My form of citation follows Drabkin's edition, which subdivides the chapters into paragraphs.

See also the recent edition and German translation of Caelius Aurelianus: Gerhard Bendz, ed., and Ingeborg Pape, German trans., *Caelius Aurelianus: Akute Krankheiten Buch I–III; Chronische Krankheiten Buch I–V*, 2 vols. (*Corpus Medicorum Latinorum* 6.1–2; Berlin: Akademie, 1990–93). Volume 2, which contains the relevant portion on homoeroticism, was not available to me.

the passage that may indicate Christian influence or that otherwise do not seem to fit in with what we know of Soranos.[13] Schrijvers argues that the organization of the treatise, the interest only in sexually passive men (and not in the active male partners in anal intercourse), and the comparison between effeminate men and women who take on an active sex role all clearly go back to Soranos.[14] I agree with Schrijvers that the specific portion of the text on *tribades* seems to represent Soranos's views accurately.

The second treatise, *On Chronic Diseases*, contains a full chapter on effeminate men, who are compared to *tribades* in a small section of the chapter. The treatise *On Chronic Diseases* begins with diseases affecting the head and proceeds downward. Book 4 marks the arrival at the abdominal and anal regions of the body. Within book 4, chapter 6 treats dysentery; chapter 7, diseases of the colon; and chapter 8, worms. Chapter 9 presents the mental disease of soft (*molles*) or passive (*subacti*) men. Given its placement within *On Chronic Diseases*, chapter 9 seems to be an indirect way of discussing anal intercourse, that is, a diseased sexual behavior involving the anus. Soranos focuses on the passive male partners in anal intercourse, considering receptive males unnatural (*non . . . ex natura*) while presuming penetrating males to be healthy.[15] Soranos does not fault nature, but rather "lust, which drove out modesty and subjugated to obscene use even those (bodily) parts which are not meant for such use."[16] In other words, male effeminacy is a disease resulting from the ethical failure of allowing lust free

13. The elements that Caelius Aurelianus may have added include: the strikingly ethical and emotional overtone at several points; the mention of sins/vices (*peccata*) (*Chronicarum passionum* 4.9; §§132f), perhaps implying Christian influence; and the mention of divine providence (4.9; §131), which does not seem to fit within the philosophical framework of the Methodist school of medical thinking (Schrijvers, *Erklärung*, 17–25, 29f, 38).

14. Schrijvers, *Erklärung*, 7f.

15. See *Acutarum passionum* 3.18; §§180f, which advises the medical practitioner not to let the (male) patient suffering from satyriasis have visitors, particularly women and young boys, since even healthy men would often be stimulated by them and would seek sexual gratification. The symptoms of satyriasis include a severe tension in the genitals, with pain, burning, and an itching which leads the patient to sexual lust. The assumption is that men not suffering from satyriasis, i.e., healthy men, are also sexually aroused by both women and young boys. See Schrijvers, *Erklärung*, 7f; and John Boswell, *Christianity, Social Tolerance, and Homosexuality: Gay People in Western Europe from the Beginning of the Christian Era to the Fourteenth Century* (Chicago: University of Chicago Press, 1980) 53, n. 33; 75, n. 67.

16. *Chronicarum passionum* 4.9; §131: *Non enim hoc humanos ex natura venit in mores, sed pulso pudore libido etiam indebitas partes obscoenis usibus subiugavit.*
I am beginning the discussion with the second sentence, because Schrijvers presents convincing arguments that the first sentence may be Caelius Aurelianus's addition to Soranos's original: "Everyone really doubts that so-called effeminate men or pathics, which the Greeks called *malthakoi*, even exist." *Molles sive subactos Graeci malthacos vocaverunt, quos quidem esse nullus facile virorum credit* (4.9; §131). Schrijvers believes that Caelius Aurelianus may have added this sentence to the text of Soranos, possibly to distance himself from the topic,

rein; it is a disease of the soul rather than of the body.[17] The disease typifies chronic diseases with periods of attack followed by periods of remission. At times, natural use of the "Sparta" (probably the penis involved in penetrating activity),[18] cannot satisfy these men. According to Soranos, their dissatisfaction with what is natural contradicts divine providence, which "in-

---

which in the Christianized world of the fifth century was more taboo than in the second century; in the fifth century, male homosexual actions were punishable by death (Schrijvers, *Erklärung*, 12).

17. Schrijvers suggests that at §133 Caelius Aurelianus may have omitted the physiological explanation of male passivity found in (Pseudo)Aristotle, *Problemata* 4.26; 879b–880a, which Soranos, who was erudite and at pains to discuss other scientific views, must have included (Schrijvers, *Erklärung*, 37; see also 15f). According to *Problemata* 4.26 (W. S. Hett, ed. and trans., *Aristotle: Problems*, vol. 1 [LCL; Cambridge, MA: Harvard University Press, 1936] 126–31), the spermatic ducts in some men do not lead to the penis, but rather to the anus. In such men, the anus craves friction in order to be able to emit the semen that has collected there. In some men the spermatic ducts lead solely to the anus, with little or no moisture going into the penis; these men are the "naturally effeminate" (οἱ φύσει θηλυδρίαι), because they are "unnaturally constituted" (παρὰ φύσιν συνεστᾶσιν). Such a man could become a woman (γυνὴ γὰρ ἂν ἐγένετο). (Does "woman" here mean a human being who is penetrated?) In other men the spermatic ducts allow the semen to settle in both the anal and the genital regions; these men desire both active and passive intercourse (ὅσοις δ᾽ ἐπ᾽ ἀμφό-τερα, οὗτοι καὶ δρᾶν καὶ πάσχειν [ἐπιθυμοῦσιν]). If the semen inclines more toward the anus, the man will have a greater desire for passive intercourse, while if it inclines more toward the penis, the man will desire active intercourse. *Problemata* adds that custom or habit can also influence desire, so that habit can become like nature (μᾶλλον τὸ ἔθος ὥσπερ φύσις γίνεται). For example, men may have pleasant recollections of being anally penetrated as boys and, may further "because of their habit, desire the passive state, as if it were natural" (διὰ δὲ τὸ ἔθος ὥσπερ πεφυκότες ἐπιθυμοῦσι πάσχειν). This desire for passivity out of habit is even more likely to occur if a man is lustful (λάγνος) and effeminate (μαλακός, can be the equivalent of *mollis*). Does "effeminate" mean a man with an anatomical tendency toward passivity, i.e., with spermatic ducts leading to the anus?

Perhaps Schrijvers is correct that Caelius Aurelianus omitted Soranos's discussion of the spermatic duct theory of desire for anal intercourse. Caelius Aurelianus did often shorten Soranos's historical treatment of prior scientific views. But Caelius Aurelianus also does not discuss here the physiological explanation for masculine sexual desire in women, namely an overly large clitoris, a fact not noticed by Schrijvers. Caelius Aurelianus definitely knew this theory, because he includes it in his *Gynaecia* (see below), although we do not know whether Caelius Aurelianus did the *Gynaecia* before or after *Chronicarum passionum*. Perhaps Soranos did not include either physiological explanation, preferring to focus on the disease as one of the mind. It is hard to see how Soranos could have given the explanation of the overly large clitoris in one work and then insisted in another work that the disease was one of the mind. Maybe he did not discuss the physiological explanation for male passivity in order to keep the focus on mental illness. On the other hand, *Problemata* 4.26 shows that an ancient author was able to see both physiology and habit or custom as the origin of male passivity. So perhaps Soranos did argue that misplaced spermatic ducts did not lead to male passivity, which was a disease of the mind, but that an overly large clitoris did cause masculine desire in women, which was nevertheless also a disease of the mind.

18. See Schrijvers, *Erklärung*, 16f, for this interpretation.

tended the places of our body for particular functions"[19] (presumably the penis for penetrating a vagina and the anus for excreting). During these periods of attack, the diseased men try to seduce other men by adopting feminine dress and a feminine gait. During periods of remission, these men can suddenly change and take on hypermasculine characteristics and behaviors. Thus, the diseased men alternate between playing the passive role by submitting to anal intercourse and the active role by engaging in penetrating activity, whether with women or boys. Thus, the contrast here is not principally between homosexual and heterosexual, but rather between passive and active behavior.

In the middle of discussing the male disease, *On Chronic Diseases* 4.9 compares the diseased men with *tribades*. This is the only explicit discussion of *tribades* in the chapter:

> For (the effeminate men) are just like the women who are called *tribades*, because they practice both kinds of love, rush to have sex with women more than with men and pursue women with an almost masculine jealousy, and, when they are freed from the disease or temporarily relieved, they seek to accuse others of that from which they are known to suffer, ⟨then, in their baseness of spirit, worn out by their two-fold sexuality⟩, as though often ravished by drunkenness, they, bursting forth into new forms of lust that have been nourished by shameful custom, rejoice in the outrage to their own sex.[20]

19. *Chronicarum passionum* 4.9; §131: *nostri corporis loca divina providentia certis destinavit officiis.* Schrijvers discusses at some length whether this is an addition by Caelius Aurelianus. The problems are the use of "divine providence," which seems to be Stoic (which Soranos was not), and the teleological view of bodily parts, i.e., that bodily parts have a definite end or purpose. Schrijvers concludes that Soranos probably did not have a teleological view of intercourse, but that he did apparently see intercourse in a functional way, i.e., as serving exclusively for reproduction. In sum, Caelius Aurelianus may have slightly reworked Soranos's original for emotional and rhetorical purposes (Schrijvers, *Erklärung*, 17–25).

20. *Chronicarum passionum* 4.9; §132: *nam sicut feminae Tribades appellatae, quod utranque Venerem exerceant, mulieribus magis quam viris misceri festinant et easdem invidentia paene virili sectantur, et cum passione fuerint desertae seu temporaliter relevatae, ea quaerunt aliis obiicere quae pati noscuntur,* †*iuvamini humilitate duplici sexu confectam*†, *velut frequenter ebrietate corruptae in novas libidinis formas erumpentes consuetudine turpi nutritas sui sexus iniuriis gaudent.* (I am following the text of Schrijvers here: *Erklärung,* 31.) Schrijvers does not emend *frequenter* to *frequenti*, as does the Rovillius edition (Lyon, 1566), on the argument that *frequenter* can substitute for the adverb *saepe* in late Latin. Similarly, Schrijvers does not emend *nutritas* to *nutritae*, as do Rovillius and Drabkin, on the argument of the parallel constructions *furorem nutrire* and *amorem nutrire* in Ovid and Statius (Ibid., 34).

Schrijvers's translation of *mulieribus magis quam viris misceri festinant* as "sich eher mit Frauen als mit Männern vereinigen wollen" is too bland a rendering of *festinant* (ibid., 31), hence my "rush. . . ."

My translation of the portion between daggers is based on a suggestion by Richard Tarrant to emend the text to: †*tum in animi humilitate duplici sexu confectae*†. He proposes that the

I will now comment briefly on each aspect of the passage, following the order of the text. Soranos typically begins discussion of a disease by giving the etymology of its name. Here the women are called *tribades*,[21] because they practice both kinds of love, preferring women and pursuing them actively. The women's bisexuality is expressed with two phrases, "both kinds of love" and "two-fold sexuality" (*utraque Venus* and *duplex sexus*).[22] The term *duplex sexus* means, "having within oneself the characteristics of both sexes," since *sexus* refers to the specific qualities associated with being female or male.[23] *Tribades* relate sexually both to women and to men, but their disease lies in their active preference for women. Soranos defines the active pursuit of women as masculine. Just as the men adopt the culturally feminine characteristics of trying to attract men through their clothing and gait, the women take on the culturally masculine characteristic of jealous pursuit.

Tribades are those women who pursue women, not the women who are pursued. Schrijvers's translation of *utraque Venus*, here and in §135, as "Liebe mit beiden Geschlechtern," "love with both sexes," may be correct.[24] I prefer "both kinds of love," which includes not only the love with women and the love with men, but also the more fundamental division between passive and active sexual behavior. In line with the fundamental cultural distinction between active and passive, the women whom the *tribades* pursue are of no interest to the text. The women who play the "male role" are diseased, while their partners are apparently not, since they continue to play the passive, female role.

While *tribades* and *molles* experience intervals of remission, their behavior during remission differs. Whereas the men become hypermasculine, the diseased women accuse other women of being *tribades*. The text does not

---

tum may have dropped out following the *-tur* of *noscuntur* (which itself may be a mistake) (personal conversation, Cambridge, MA, August 28, 1991; I wish to thank Professor Tarrant for his generosity in assisting me with this difficult text). Tarrant is building upon Drabkin's proposal to emend *iuvamini* to *in animi* and *confectam* or *confecta* to *confectae* (Drabkin, *On Acute Diseases and On Chronic Diseases,* 902).

21. Schrijvers proposes that Soranos was probably thinking of *tribas* as related to the adjective *tribakos*, "experienced," rather than as related to the verb *tribo*, "to rub." Thus this etymology of *tribas* emphasizes their bisexuality over their same-sex preference and active behavior. Schrijvers gives as evidence for this understanding of Soranos's etymology Teiresias, who was *doctus*, "learned, experienced" (roughly equivalent to *tribakos*) in the area of *Venus utraque* (cf. *utraque Venus* in this passage), "both kinds of love" (see Ovid, *Metamorphoses* 3.323), because he had been both a woman and a man during his life (Schrijvers, *Erklärung,* 32f).

22. *Duplex sexus* occurs in the text-critically corrupt portion of the text discussed below.

23. *OLD,* s.v. *sexus.*

24. Schrijvers, *Erklärung,* 31, 43.

explicitly describe the *tribades* in remission as being sexually healthy, that is, passive and therefore feminine.[25] Some remission is permanent, thus actually freeing some women from the disease; why and how the women are freed remains unclear. Perhaps the author believes that mind control (*animus coërcendus*), which the text mentions later as the proper medical treatment for the disease,[26] can sometimes effect a total cure.

A corruption in the Latin text after the word "suffer" further complicates interpretation. I follow Richard Tarrant's tentative proposal for solving this text-critical problem.[27] He notes that the portion of the text on *tribades* reveals three phases: (1) attack of the disease; (2) remission from the disease; and (3) renewed attack of the disease. Thus his translation includes a transition back to the renewed attack stage of the disease: "then, in their baseness of spirit, worn out by their two-fold sexuality. . . ."

In contrast, P. H. Schrijvers offers a more complicated and less grammatically persuasive emendation. He proposes that the *tribades* use dildoes: "after a degrading device was produced for their double sexuality."[28]

25. Compare this pattern with that typically found in the ancient astrological texts, which pairs up passive men with hyperactive heterosexual (passive) women; and *tribades* with hyperactive heterosexual (active) men (see below).

26. *Chronicarum passionum* 4.9; §133: *Nam neque ulla curatio corporis depellendae passionis causa recte putatur adhibenda, sed potius animus coërcendus, qui tanta peccatorum labe vexatur.* "For a bodily treatment cannot be successfully applied to drive out the disease; one must, rather, control the mind, which is afflicted by such a deep disgrace." Schrijvers believes that Caelius Aurelianus may have added the second part of the sentence to Soranos's original, since the sharp term *coërcendus* is not characteristic for Caelius Aurelianus's translation of Soranos (Schrijvers, *Erklärung*, 38).

27. Personal conversation, Cambridge, MA, August 28, 1991.

28. Schrijvers prints the following between daggers: *iuvamini humilitate duplici sexu confectam* and emends it to: *iuvamine humilitate duplici sexu confecto*, which is an ablative absolute. According to this reading, *iuvamen* is an aid or dildo. (Greek: ὀλίσβος; see Aristophanes, *Lysistrata* 110, in which a dildo is called a "leathern aid," σκυτίνη (ἐ)πικουρία. The Suda refers to a proverb, Συκίνη ἐπικουρία, "useless aid," upon which Aristophanes may be basing his "leathern aid" [Ada Adler, ed., *Suidae Lexicon* (Lexicographici Graeci 1; pt. 4; Stuttgart: Teubner, 1935) 453]). Schrijvers notes that *iuvamen* is quite common in late Latin and that the normal medical term in Caelius Aurelianus for "aid" is *adiutorium*. Schrijvers suggests that Caelius Aurelianus chose the term *iuvamen* very carefully and that it has a somewhat cynical nuance, as compared with *adiutorium*. Schrijvers suggests that *humilitate* could be an adjective or participle (in the ablative to modify *iuvamine*) and derived from the late Latin verb *humiliare* (but Tarrant argues that this proposal does not stand up morphologically). (Or perhaps it has the sense of "insignificant" or "unimportant," more along the lines of the proverbial συκίνη ἐπικουρία. The dildo would then be a "futile device.") *Duplici sexu* would be a dative form; Schrijvers argues that the word order makes a dative more plausible than an ablative absolute (*duplici sexu confecto* with *iuvamine* as an instrumental ablative) (Schrijvers, *Erklärung*, 31–35).

Drabkin places a larger amount of text between daggers, namely, *ea quaerunt aliis obicere quae pati noscuntur iuvamini humilitate duplici sexu confectam.* His proposed meaning is: "in

Schrijvers's theory is at least plausible, since other ancient texts attest to the existence of dildoes (Greek: *olisboi*),[29] and the Suda, a medieval lexicon known to contain ancient sources, says that *tribades* use dildoes.[30] In one of the dialogues of Lucian of Samosata, a contemporary of Soranos, a courtesan who calls another woman her wife says that she has "something instead of a penis."[31] Greek vase paintings depict individual women with dildoes,[32] although I know of no vase painting that shows one woman penetrating another with a dildo.

Schrijvers's suggestion for interpreting *iuvamen*, "aid, device," as

---

(*or* to overcome) their degradation they seek to blame others for their affliction; then plagued by double sexuality. . . ." His alternative explanation is that *ea . . . noscuntur* may refer to "renewed (heterosexual?) promiscuity" (Drabkin, *On Acute Diseases and On Chronic Diseases*, 902, n. 5). He proposes several emendations: *adiutorio, an iuvenum, iuvenibus,* and *in animi* for *iuvamini*; *humilitati* or *humilitatae* for *humilitate*; and *confectae* for *confectam*.

Schrijvers's emendations and interpretation make more sense, although problems still remain. His interpretation requires only slight emendations of the text, and he is able to produce plausible historical arguments for it. Drabkin's proposal is really not complete. Drabkin gives no philological arguments for his alternative explanation. He is probably suggesting that the *tribades* are parallel to the *molles* in that they engage in excessive heterosexual intercourse during remission.

29. E.g., Herodas, *Mimiamboi* 6f. See K[enneth] J. Dover, *Greek Homosexuality* (1978; reprint, Cambridge, MA: Harvard University Press, 1989) 102; A. Körte, PW 17, s.v. "Olisbos" (1937) 2480–82.

A fragment of the poetry of Sappho contains the word ολισβδοκοισ, probably ὄλισβοδό-κοισ(ι). The term ὀλισβοδόκος must mean "receiver of the dildo." The context is badly damaged, so that the referent is unclear. Giuseppe Giangrande has argued that this word "leaves us in no doubt as to what Sappho and her companions were up to, and confirms the ancient view that Sappho was a τριβάς" ("Sappho and the ὄλισβος," *Emerita* 48 [1980] 249f); see also Giuseppe Giangrande, "A che serviva l' 'olisbos' de Saffo?" *Labeo* 29 (1983) 154–55; and A. Guarino, "Professorenerotismus," *Labeo* 27 (1981) 439f. K. J. Dover, however, suggests that Sappho could be referring to a female enemy who is unable to find a partner, since the referent is unclear and since "the olisbos is associated essentially with solitary female masturbation" (*Greek Homosexuality*, 176, n. 9).

30. The Suda, s.v. Ὄλισβος: αἰδοῖον δερμάτινον, ᾧ ἐχρῶντο αἱ Μιλήσιαι γυναῖκες, ὡς τριβάδες καὶ αἰσχρουργοί· ἐχρῶντο δὲ αὐτοῖς καὶ αἱ χῆραι γυναῖκες. "*Olisbos*: Leathern genitals that the Milesian women, as *tribades* and obscene women [or: masturbating women], used. Widows also used them." The Suda then makes reference to Aristophanes, *Lysistrata* 109f (Ada Adler, ed., *Suidae Lexicon* [Lexicographici Graeci 1; pt. 3; Stuttgart: Teubner, 1933] 518).

31. Lucian of Samosata, *Dialogues of the Courtesans* 5.4; §292: ἔχω γάρ τι ἀντὶ τοῦ ἀνδρείου (M. D. Macleod, ed. and trans., *Lucian*, vol. 7 [LCL; Cambridge, MA: Harvard University Press, 1969] 384; translation my own.

32. For examples, see Eva C. Keuls, "The Dildo: Male Fantasies Projected onto Women," *The Reign of the Phallus* (New York: Harper and Row, 1985) 82–86, pls. 72–77, 80; and John Boardman, *Athenian Red Figure Vases: The Archaic Period* (New York: Oxford University Press, 1975) pls. 71, 99.1, and 176; see also pl. 342. The two-ended dildo in pl. 99 does raise the question of its possible simultaneous use by two women.

"dildo" is quite in line with ancient male thinking about female homo-eroticism and sexuality in general. While ancient female homoerotic behav-ior probably included a full range of sexual expression, the ancient (and often modern) male imagination seems limited to postulating a physical substitute for the penis on the apparent assumption that sex occurs when a male organ penetrates a human orifice. Thus, ancient male representations of female homoeroticism show an obsessive preoccupation with trying to imagine what women could ever possibly do with each other.[33]

The context of the passage does not support Schrijvers's proposal, how-ever, since there is no immediate connection between a dildo and the pre-ceding clause about the women accusing others of having their disease. Further, the connection with the following clause ("as though they . . . rejoice") is unclear, and there is still a syntactical problem.[34] Schrijvers's emendation does not fit properly with the following clause: "After a device was produced, as though they . . . rejoiced." Schrijvers's interpretation as-sumes that the mention of the disease's remission is parenthetical while Tarrant accounts for intervals of attack and remission endemic to chronic diseases.

The remainder of the passage that follows the textual corruption reveals three further characterizations of *tribades*. Firstly, the text represents these women as sex addicts; it compares their pursuit of ever new forms of lust to alcohol addiction. The disease drives these women to rush (*festino*) to have sex with women, to pursue or chase after (*sector*) women, and to burst forth (*erumpo*) into new forms of lust. *Tribades*, overpowered by their dis-ease, live lives that are out of control.

Secondly, Soranos implies human responsibility for the disease of the *tribades*. Earlier in the chapter, Soranos says that nature did not introduce effeminate male practices into "human customs" (*humani mores*);[35] at a

33. See, e.g., Lucian of Samosata, *Dialogues of the Courtesans* 5; §289: "We've been hear-ing . . . that you live with each other, and do goodness knows what together" (292); "What did she do? How? That's what I'm most interested to hear" (Macleod, *Lucian*, vol. 7, 379, 385); and Seneca the Elder, *Controversiae* 1.2.23 (upon finding his wife in bed with another woman, a husband "looked at the man [i.e., the other woman] first, to see whether he was natural or sewed on"). Translation my own.

34. Put grammatically, how does a temporal ablative absolute (the "after a degrading de-vice was produced for their double sexuality" clause) fit with the following clause beginning with "as though" (Latin: *velut*)?

35. *Chronicarum passionum* 4.9; §131: *Non enim hoc humanos ex natura venit in mores.* "For it was not due to a natural disposition that this entered into human customs" (for this interpretation, see Schrijvers, *Erklärung*, 12f).

In his discussion on the etiology of *molles* (see below), Soranos notes that medical thinkers who held that homoeroticism was passed on through the seed did not "blame nature," since they do not seem to have found homoerotic behavior among animals (*Chronicarum pas-sionum* 4.9; §§135f). Some ancient writers asserted in the strongest terms that same-sex

later point he refers to other medical leaders who believe that once these defects have entered the human race, they become hereditary, and humanity cannot purge itself of them.[36] Within this context, the phrase "having been nourished by shameful custom" (*consuetudo turpis*) suggests human responsibility for the disease. "Custom" must mean that human practice, rather than organic causes, created the disease or that human practice exacerbated an organic abnormality,[37] while "shameful" (*turpis*) conveys the moral condemnation associated with the disease.[38]

Thirdly, Soranos characterizes *tribades* as women who "rejoice in the outrage to their own sex." "Outrage" (*iniuria*) can be a legal term referring to sexual assault, or to an act calculated to injure someone's reputation or feelings. For example, Seneca the Elder uses the term *iniuria*[39] to describe a rapist's behavior.[40] The text implies that *tribades* are like rapists in that they ravish their own sex, destroying the qualities associated with be-

---

sexual behavior is absent in the animal world. Plutarch explicitly refers to the lack of female homoerotic behavior in animals: οὔτ' ἄρρενος πρὸς ἄρρεν οὔτε θήλεος πρὸς θῆλυ μῖξις; "no sexual intercourse between male and male, nor between female and female" (*Moralia: Beasts Are Rational* 990D–991A, quote 990D). See also Plato, *Nomoi* 1.2; 636B–C; 8.5.1; 836B–C; Philo, *De animalibus* 49 (extant only in Armenian: see Abraham Terian, *Philonis Alexandrini De animalibus: The Armenian Text with an Introduction, Translation, and Commentary* [Studies in Hellenistic Judaism; Chico, CA: Scholars Press, 1981] 89, 239). See Urs Dierauer, *Tier und Mensch im Denken der Antike: Studien zur Tierpsychologie, Anthropologie und Ethik* (Amsterdam: Grüner, 1977) 63, 272. Other ancient writers were aware of its existence among animals. (E.g., Pliny, *Naturalis historia* 10.80.166 [on female doves and other female birds mating with one another]; Aelian, *Varia historia* 1.15 [see also Aelian, *De natura animalium* 15.11, who states that the land-marten was once a human being with unnatural erotic desires]; Clement of Alexandria, *Paidagōgos* 2.10.83.1–88.4. Dierauer, *Tier und Mensch*, neglects to mention the ancient authors who were aware of same-sex behavior among animals.) The view of these physicians also raises the interesting question of how thinkers in this period saw human beings in relation to animals. For example, the jurist Ulpian (2d/3d C.) viewed animal behavior as normative in the case of female-male couplings (*Corpus Iuris Civilis, Digesta* 1.1.1.3). In the context of defining natural law, Ulpian derives the human institution of marriage (*matrimonium*) from the "conjunction of male and female" (*maris atque feminae coniunctio*) in the animal world. On Ulpian's definition, see Michael Bertram Crowe, *The Changing Profile of the Natural Law* (The Hague: Nijhoff, 1977) 44–46. The Justinian *Institutes* repeated Ulpian's influential definition of natural law (1.2 *proem*).

36. *Chronicarum passionum* 4.9; §§135f.

37. See (Pseudo)Aristotle, *Problemata* 4.26; 880a, for habit or custom (ἔθος) causing male passivity or exacerbating it in the case of a man who is lustful and effeminate (probably biologically, i.e., with spermatic ducts leading to the anus, instead of to the penis).

38. Mustio uses the term *turpitudo* in his translation of Soranos's *Gynaikeia* to refer to the sexual behavior of women with an overly large clitoris.

39. Schrijvers attributes the term *iniuria* to the concept of natural law, which he calls a "widespread concept." A concept of natural law may in fact be implicit in the text, but even if it is not, "outrage" as a criminal act fundamentally aimed at dishonoring another person makes sense here (Schrijvers, *Erklärung*, 35).

40. Seneca the Elder, *Controversiae* 1.5.1.

ing a woman, even if it is their own womanliness that they have destroyed. "Their own sex" is perhaps intentionally ambiguous, conveying both that *tribades* bring outrage and shame upon all womankind by their behavior and that they damage their own feminine identity.

Up to this point I have discussed questions internal to the passage on *tribades*. Now I wish to raise larger questions about the etiology of homoeroticism, the applicability of the extended discussion of soft and passive men to women, and homoeroticism as a category in ancient medical writing.

One major area of debate regarding homoerotic sexual behavior was and continues to be its origins. Soranos mentions two theories on the etiology of the disease of *molles*, which probably apply also to *tribades*. He quotes the pre-Sokratic philosopher Parmenides, who argues in his work *On Nature* that if at conception the forces found within the seed of the man and that of the woman " 'clash and do not build a unity in the melded body, then the *Dirae* (Furies) will distort the sex of the offspring with the double seed.' "[41] An important background point here is that Parmenides assumes

41. *Chronicarum passionum* 4.9; §135: *pugnent, / nec faciant unam permixto in corpore, Dirae / nascentem gemino vexabunt semine sexum.* I am following Schrijvers's suggestion that *dirae* may be *Dirae*, i.e., the Furies (Schrijvers, *Erklärung,* 42f, 45f). Caelius Aurelianus gave the Parmenides quote in Latin verse, since the Greek original quoted in Soranos was in verse. See Hermann Diels, *Die Fragmente der Vorsokratiker,* ed. Walther Kranz, 2 vols. (7th ed.; Berlin: Weidmann, 1954), 1:244f; Parmenides B18 (cf. 227; Parmenides A54). For a retroversion of the whole fragment into Greek, see Hermann Diels, *Parmenides Lehrgedicht* (Berlin: Reimer, 1897) 44. Diels assumes that Parmenides was referring to the origin of effeminate men and masculine women who did not engage in same-sex love or to hermaphrodites, and that Soranos misinterpreted Parmenides. Ulrich von Wilamowitz-Moellendorff, *Sappho und Simonides: Untersuchungen über griechische Lyriker* (Berlin: Weidmann, 1913) 72, n. 1, disagrees, referring as a parallel to Plato's *Symposion* 191E, in which Aristophanes discourses on the original double human beings, consisting of two women, two men, and a woman and a man, who then split apart and are the origin of women attracted to women, men attracted to men, and women and men attracted to each other. Wilamowitz-Moellendorff argues that Parmenides may have inspired Plato to write about ἑταιρίστριαι (women attracted to other women), and that there is no reason to doubt that Soranos correctly interpreted Parmenides. He correctly points out that Diels does not have any textual evidence for the hermaphrodite theory. However, Wilamowitz-Moellendorff incorrectly rebukes Diels for not referring to Plato's *Symposion* 191E as the background of Phaedrus, *Liber Fabularum* 4.16 (quoted by Diels as an example of *molles* and *tribades* being hermaphrodites, which, Diels argues, could have been Soranos's understanding; I believe that Phaedrus is speaking of same-sex love). Wilamowitz-Moellendorff's rebuke is unfounded, because Phaedrus writes that Prometheus placed female genitals on male bodies and vice versa, whereas Plato has Aristophanes describe round double beings who were split apart and now seek partners of the original gender: female/female, male/male, and male/female. Wilamowitz-Moellendorff is confusing two different models for explaining the origin of same-sex love. Schrijvers follows Wilamowitz (Schrijvers, *Erklärung,* 46, 69, n. 88), while, e.g., Uvo Hölscher still follows Diels (*Parmenides: Vom Wesen des Seienden* [Frankfurt: Suhrkamp, 1969] 58).

On Parmenides, see also: Schrijvers, *Erklärung,* 52–62; Erna Lesky, *Die Zeugungs- und*

that both the female and the male contribute a seed at conception, hence the possibility of "double seed" (*geminum semen*) in the offspring.[42] According to Parmenides, as interpreted by Soranos, the condition of soft and passive men originates at conception and is the result of the female and male seeds asserting themselves as independent forces throughout the life of the individual and causing them to desire both active and passive sexual experiences ("both kinds of love").[43]

Vererbungslehre der Antike und ihr Nachwirken (Abhandlungen der geistes- und sozial-wissenschaftlichen Klasse 19; Wiesbaden: Akademie der Wissenschaften und der Literatur in Mainz, 1950) 40–50; Kathleen Freeman, *Ancilla to the Pre-Socratic Philosophers* (Oxford: Blackwell, 1956) 41–46; Kathleen Freeman, *The Pre-Socratic Philosophers* (Oxford: Blackwell, 1946) 140–52. Lesky argues that the two fragments of Parmenides relating to theories of conception (B17 and B18) contradict each other. Freeman argues that in Parmenides' original poem, the portion called the "Way of Opinion," of which this fragment is a part, does not represent the views of Parmenides himself, but that it does represent the most plausible view of the world that could be arrived at by relying on sense perception, which is contained in the best-established views of prior philosophers. Parmenides utterly rejects sense perception as leading to truth (*The Pre-Socratic Philosophers*, 143–46).

42. Compare, e.g., Aristotle, who assumes that only the male seed is pure seed, since only male seed has the principle of soul, which the menstrual discharge does not, even though it is also seed (*Generation of Animals* 2.3; 737a). Not everyone in the ancient world shared Aristotle's view. For an analysis of some of Galen's criticisms of Aristotle, particularly with respect to the transmission of parental traits to the offspring, see Michael Boylan, "The Galenic and Hippocratic Challenges to Aristotle's Conception Theory," *Journal of the History of Biology* 17 (1984) 83–112, esp. 105f. For an overview of ancient concepts of conception, see Lesky, *Die Zeugungs- und Vererbungslehren der Antike;* and Thomas Laqueur, *Making Sex: Body and Gender from the Greeks to Freud* (Cambridge, MA: Harvard University Press, 1990).

43. *Chronicarum passionum* 4.9; §135: *utraque Venus.* The reader may wonder what *both* kinds of love are, since other ancient authors knew of many sexual positions and possibilities for human pairings. "Both kinds of love" could mean love for women and love for men or it could mean active love and passive love. (See *Chronicarum passionum* 4.9; §137: *gemina luxuriae libido dividitur, animo eorum nunc faciendo nunc patiendo iactato;* "the sexual desire [of these persons] assumes a dual aspect, in which the soul is excited sometimes while playing a passive role and sometimes while playing an active role" [ET: Drabkin, *On Acute Diseases and On Chronic Diseases,* 905]). In the larger picture of ancient Mediterranean concepts of sexuality, active and passive are more fundamental categories than male and female and make more sense as "both kinds of love." If a woman has sex with a man, she is the passive one (since coitus is culturally conceived of as penetration, rather than, for example, as the vagina swallowing or enfolding the penis), while if she has sex with a woman, she can be either active or passive. Thus, for a woman, love with women and love with men is not two kinds of love, but three. The case is the same for a man, who is the active partner with a woman and the active or passive partner with another male. The point of comparison in *On Chronic Diseases* 4.9 is between passive men and active women, not between men who have sex with men and women who have sex with women (but, of course, women can be active only with other women). The implication is that proper sexual behavior for a free adult male is active, while the proper sexual role of all females is passive.

See also the Hippokratic corpus, *Peri diaitēs* (*Regimen*) 1.28f. There the author describes three types of male and three types of female offspring that can result from the mixing of

Soranos, or, more strictly, Caelius Aurelianus, presents a second opinion
on the etiology of this disease. He states that, "many leaders of the other
sects" (i.e., unspecified schools of medical thought) see this condition as
an innate or inherited disease, one which is passed on from generation to
generation by way of the seed.[44] These medical thinkers must have seen
male passivity and female desire for other women as arising from something analogous to a mutated gene, induced by "shameful custom" and
henceforth hereditary. This must mean that a passive father or homoerotically inclined mother passes on the condition to the child. If a father passed

female and male seeds. The assumption is that both the mother and the father secrete minus-
cule bodies. The male categories are: (1) men "brilliant in soul and strong in body" (ἄνδρες
λαμπροὶ τὰς ψυχὰς καὶ τὸ σῶμα ἰσχυροί)—when the mother and the father secrete male
bodies; (2) brave (ἀνδρεῖοι) men, less brilliant than the first type—when the mother secretes
a female body and the father a male one and the male one gains mastery; (3) men-women
(ἀνδρόγυνοι)—when the mother secretes a male body and the father a female one and the
male gains mastery (the author of this portion of the Hippokratic corpus does add that
the mixing of the parts of water, nourishment, education, and habits also contribute to
the level of manliness). The female categories are: (1) women who are very female and fair
(θηλυκώτατα καὶ εὐφυέστατα)—when the mother and the father secrete female bodies;
(2) women bolder than the first type, but modest (θρασύτεραι . . . κόσμιαι)—when the
mother secretes a female body and the father a male one and the female gains mastery;
(3) mannish women (ἀνδρεῖαι) who are bolder (τολμηρότεραι) than the other two types—
when the mother secretes a male body and the father a female one and the female gains mastery. This model is similar to that of Parmenides in that gendered behavior is seen to result
from the contributions of the mother and the father at conception. Note that the third type
of man, the man-woman, does not parallel the third type of woman, the mannish (or courageous) woman. Linguistically, type three on the female side, the ἀνδρεῖαι, parallels type two
on the male side, the ἀνδρεῖοι. Further, if the man-woman is a hermaphrodite, why is the
hermaphrodite categorized as male (here and in other ancient texts)? The author does not
present ἀνδρεῖαι as female hermaphrodites. This asymmetry demonstrates once again that
male and female are not precisely parallel categories in the ancient world. Fridof Kudlien dates
this portion of the Hippokratic Collection to the end of the 4th C. BCE (Der Kleine Pauly, s.v.
"Hippocrates"). For additional discussion of male and female typologies, see Maud W. Gleason, "The Semiotics of Gender: Physiognomy and Self-Fashioning in the Second Century
C.E.," in Before Sexuality: The Construction of Erotic Experience in the Ancient Greek World,
ed. David M. Halperin, John J. Winkler, and Froma I. Zeitlin (Princeton: Princeton University
Press, 1990) 389–415.

44. Chronicarum passionum 4.9; §§135f: Multi . . . sectarum principes genuinam dicunt
esse passionem (ET: Drabkin, On Acute Diseases and On Chronic Diseases, 905). Schrijvers
points out that On Acute Diseases and On Chronic Diseases elsewhere mentions heredity as a
cause of disease only for diseases of the joints and feet (arthritis and podagra; Chronicarum
passionum 5.2; §§29f), but does not take up the theory. Schrijvers suggests that Soranos was
as hesitant about the inheritance theory for the disease of molles as he was about the inheritance theory for arthritis and podagra. Schrijvers proposes that Soranos's line of reasoning
must have been that even those leaders of other sects who assume inheritance as the cause
of the disease also assume that the human race, rather than nature, is at fault (Schrijvers, Erklärung, 47).

it on to his son, would a mother have passed it on to her daughter? Since this could happen only if the mother had a seed through which to pass it, then those medical writers who saw the seed itself as containing homoerotic "genetic material" must have believed that the woman had a seed. Or could a soft, passive father cause a daughter to become a *tribas*? If these medical writers held that the woman had a seed, could her seed cause a son to become a soft, passive male? Alternatively, instead of interpreting this text as presupposing a female seed, we can construe it as compatible with those ancient theories of biological conception that posit that only the male parent contributes a seed. In this case, the tendency toward deviant behavior would be passed through the one seed, that is, the male one. Without further sources, these questions must go unanswered. What is clear is that for Parmenides the lifelong condition of male passiveness and softness originated from the circumstances of conception, that is, a lack of mingling of the female and male seeds, while for many other medical thinkers the seed itself contained the inclination in this direction. Both views suggest that homoeroticism is a lifelong condition.

At the beginning and end of the discussion of *tribades*, Soranos equates soft and passive men with *tribades*. Are they alike in every way? Presumably their respective practices are not in accordance with nature (*non . . . ex natura*), and are characterized by unrestrained lust. Further, Soranos views homoeroticism as a disease of the mind,[45] rather than of the body,[46] for both men and women.[47] According to *On Chronic Diseases*, practicing

45. An important parallel to Soranos's view that homoerotic behavior is a disease of the mind (*mens* or *animus*) is the astrologer Ptolemy's position that it is a disease of the soul (*psychē*) for both women and men. Ptolemy breaks the soul down into the active, thinking part and the passive, nonthinking part. He sees excesses and deficiencies in matters relating to femaleness and maleness to be a perversion of the passive, nonthinking part of the soul (*Tetrabiblos* 3.14; §171). Ptolemy describes treatments that are effective with diseases of the soul that involve both its active and its passive part; these diseases include epilepsy and insanity, which are curable, depending on the particular configuration of the stars, with medical treatments, diet, drugs, oracles, or divine aid (3.14; §§169f). In contrast, Ptolemy does not mention treatments or cures for homoerotic behavior, which for him is a disease only of the passive part of the soul. Ptolemy agrees with Soranos that homoerotic behavior is not a bodily disease, although he sees no cure to this behavior and categorizes it as a disease of the nonrational, nonintellectual part of the soul (not the *mens* or the *animus* as in Soranos). Since Ptolemy was active in or around Alexandria at the same time that Soranos lived there (early 2d C.), we may be seeing in these points of overlap and disagreement reflections of debates on homoeroticism in the intellectual circles of Alexandria at this time.

46. *Chronicarum passionum* 4.9; §131: *corruptae mentis vitia*; "defects of a depraved mind"; §132: *malignae ac foedissimae mentis passio*; "disease of an ill-disposed and shameful mind."

47. *Chronicarum passionum* 4.9; §133: *Sic illi comparatione talium animi passione iactari noscuntur*; "Thus, the effeminate men, like the *tribades*, are afflicted by a disease of the mind." Schrijvers observes that the argument against a bodily cause for the disease is not a very pol-

"both kinds of love" is a lifelong disease. The disease manifests itself in men differently in different stages of life. Boys, who do not possess virile powers, and old men, whose virile powers have waned, will tend to play the passive role in same-sex intercourse, while men in the prime of life who are afflicted with this disease will alternate between the active and passive roles.[48] In this text, male passivity at any age signals a disease.[49] What this implies for the *tribades* is unclear, since women are never supposed to take an active role or to have virile powers. Can we infer that *tribades* are principally younger, adult women, since they, like men in the prime of life, are excited by both the active and the passive roles? The author does not seem to have thought about whether the disease of *tribades* presents itself differently at different times in a woman's life.

While these points seem to apply equally to *molles* and *tribades*, the chapter is asymmetrical, primarily focusing on the men, mentioning women only for comparative purposes. This asymmetry parallels the asymmetry inherent in the greater attention given to men throughout the literature of the Roman period. Therefore, the reader cannot know whether or not everything Soranos says about men applies equally to women.

David M. Halperin uses *On Chronic Diseases* 4.9 to support his argument that homosexuality did not exist as a category before the nineteenth century.[50] Halperin argues that the author classifies *molles* and *tribades* together not because they are both sexually oriented toward the same sex, but rather because they both engage in sex-role reversals or because they both alternate between the characteristics and sexual practices culturally defined as feminine and those defined as masculine.

Halperin points out that Caelius Aurelianus at another point in his translation of Soranos does not define adult men's sexual attraction toward boys

---

ished one and suggests that Caelius Aurelianus may have omitted part of Soranos's discussion (Schrijvers, *Erklärung*, 37; see above, n. 11). Another explanation for the lack of polish is Soranos's own ambivalence concerning the etiology of same-sex love. This ambivalence is evidenced in the contradiction between the presentation of *tribades* as suffering from a disease of the mind and that of women with masculine desires suffering from an overly large clitoris, a disease of the body.

The Roman jurist Ulpian (2d/3d C.) holds that a man may divorce an insane woman (*furiosa*), but that she may not divorce him on account of her insanity (*dementia*) (*Corpus Iuris Civilis, Digesta* 24.2.4; Theodor Mommsen and Paul Krueger, eds. *The Digest of Justinian*, trans. Alan Watson, vol. 2 [Philadelphia: University of Pennsylvania Press, 1985] 715f. Did the medical description of *tribades* as suffering from a mental illness have the effect of removing from women so diagnosed their legal power under Roman law to divorce their husbands? We can only speculate.

48. *Chronicarum passionum* 4.9; §137.

49. This includes sexually passive boys, who are "afflicted by this disease" (*Chronicarum passionum* 4.9; §137: *pueros hac passione iactari*).

50. David M. Halperin, *One Hundred Years of Homosexuality: And Other Essays on Greek Love* (New York: Routledge, 1990) 22–24.

as diseased.[51] From this Halperin deduces, "There is nothing medically problematical, then, about a desire on the part of males to obtain sexual pleasure from contact with males—so long as that desire respects the proper phallocentric protocols (which, as we shall see, identify 'masculinity' with an insertive sexual role)."[52] This may be true for men[53] (although not for boys).

Women, however, cannot both respect phallocentric protocols and obtain sexual pleasure from contact with other females. Caelius Aurelianus and Soranos do not assume that any forms of sexual attraction between females are healthy. The same phallocentric protocols that define men as the penetrators define women as the penetrated. Women who derive sexual pleasure from contact with women, that is, outside the realm of male penetration, have to be medically problematic.[54] Halperin correctly recognizes that the text is concerned with reversing proper sex roles or with alternating between behaviors and characteristics proper to women and to men

51. *Acutarum passionum* 3.18; §§180f.

52. Halperin, *One Hundred Years,* 23. For a similar view, see John Boswell's statement, "No ancient writers appear to have considered homosexual attraction itself pathological, but some did regard passive sexual behavior in adult males as 'sick,' possibly due to their attitudes toward female sexuality" (Boswell, *Christianity, Social Tolerance, and Homosexuality,* 53). Much of the following critique applies not only to Halperin, but also to Boswell. Boswell's statement makes clear that he was construing "homosexuality" as male.

53. Soranos focuses his attention in this chapter on the passive partner; we cannot exclude the possibility that he held a view like that of his contemporary, the Stoic philosopher Epiktetos (1st/2d C.), who argued that both the active male (ὁ διατιθείς) and his passive partner (ὁ τὰ τοῦ κιναίδου πάσχων) lose their manhood (*Discourses* 2.10.17; W. A. Oldfather, ed. and trans., *Epictetus,* vol. 1 [LCL; Cambridge, MA: Harvard University Press, 1972] 278f).

54. One might argue that the "passive" partners of *tribades* conform to phallocentric protocols, since they maintain feminine sexual practices. We have, however, no positive evidence that passive sexual behavior by adult women in relations with other adult women was societally acceptable. Soranos and Caelius Aurelianus do not provide such evidence. While Caelius Aurelianus's discussion of male satyriasis, i.e., a constriction of the male organs, does assume that healthy men will be attracted to boys, Soranos's discussion of female satyriasis does not assume that even healthy women might be attracted to some females, nor do Caelius Aurelianus's and Mustio's (probably 5th or 6th C.) translations of Soranos on this point: Soranos, *Gynaikeia* 3.3; §25; Johannes Ilberg, ed., *Sorani Gynaeciorum libri iv* (*Corpus Medicorum Graecorum* 4; Leipzig/Berlin: Teubner, 1927) 109.1–8; Caelius Aurelianus, *Gynaecia* 2.23; 69v; 354–59; Miriam F. Drabkin and Israel E. Drabkin, eds., *Caelius Aurelianus Gynaecia: Fragments of a Latin Version of Soranus' Gynaecia from a Thirteenth Century Manuscript* (Supplements to the Bulletin of the History of Medicine 13; Baltimore: Johns Hopkins Press, 1951) 75; and Mustio, 2.3.25; Valentin Rose, ed., *Sorani Gynaeciorum: Vetus Translatio Latina* (Leipzig: Teubner, 1882) 57. Both translations speak of the female satyriasis patients having "an insatiable desire for men" (*insatiabili virorum desiderio*). Ann Ellis Hanson points out that this recognition of hypersexuality in women is a post-Hippokratic development (also the case with gonorrhea, an excessive flow of the seed) (in *Before Sexuality: The Construction of Erotic Experience in the Ancient Greek World,* ed. David M. Halperin, John J. Winkler, and Froma I. Zeitlin [Princeton: Princeton University Press, 1990] 333).

respectively. The problem is that according to Halperin's interpretation, there is no way for women to have sexual contact with other women other than to take on male sex roles or to alternate between characteristics and practices proper to women and those proper to men. Further, Caelius Aurelianus's chapter explicitly defines the passivity of boys as diseased.[55] Thus, while adult men's desire for boys may be seen as healthy, boys' passive sexual behavior is not. In sum, Halperin is incorrect in reading *On Chronic Diseases* as unconcerned about same-sex love per se. For women, the text's several strategies of classification—role reversal, alternation between properly female and properly male characteristics and practices, and sex of the sexual partner—all coincide. According to the text, female homoeroticism *is* role reversal; it is for a woman to adopt male characteristics and male sexual practices. The homoerotically inclined male has the acceptable outlet of attraction toward a boy, but his female counterpart has no such option. All systems of classification combine to constrict her and to guide her into submissive female behavior. For males, while the adult man's desire for a boy may conform to phallocentric protocols, his passive boy partner's desires and behaviors do not. Thus, according to the system of *On Chronic Diseases*, there exists no same-sex encounter in which both partners are disease-free, which means that the same-sex factor is an important classificatory principle.

In sum, the evidence I have presented shows that Caelius Aurelianus and therefore presumably Soranos employed the technical terms *molles, subacti,* and *tribades* to indicate a medical diagnosis. While the precise content of these terms is specific to the Roman world, they illustrate an ancient medical system of diagnostic classification that is based upon a complex interplay between biological sex and active-versus-passive sexual behaviors. Active and passive, the fundamental categories, function differently for women than for men in this medical system in that any woman who sexually expresses her love for another woman is considered pathological, whereas male attraction to boys is not (at least the attraction of the free, upper-class males envisioned as the recipients of learned medical care). That this classification system differs from that developed in the nineteenth century does not mean that it is any less medical.

Clitoridectomy for Women with Masculine Desires

In his treatise on gynecology (*Gynaikeia*), Soranos advocates the surgical removal of part of a woman's clitoris if it is "overly large,"[56] a condition

55. *Chronicarum passionum* 4.9; §137: *Pueros hac passione iactari.*

56. Note that the following discussion is about selective clitoridectomy connected with a socially unacceptable behavior, not about ritual clitoridectomy (see below for the exception, namely the Egyptian practice described by Philoumenos and abstracted by Aetios of Amida),

that he correlates with unrestrained sexual behavior. Soranos's description of clitoridectomy clearly indicates that an "overly large" clitoris was of medical concern not because the women were complaining of pain or of any type of dysfunctionality, but rather because of his concern about maintaining social structures. A woman who possesses the physical means by which to penetrate another person is unacceptable in a culture that conceives of the sexually active role as properly restricted to males.

The *Gynaikeia* as a whole deals with questions ranging from the anatomy of the female reproductive organs, the qualities of a good midwife, and how to care for a newborn infant to dysmenorrhea, difficult labor, and uterine growths. The Greek original of this portion of the *Gynaikeia* is no longer extant, but a fifteenth-century Greek index of chapter headings records the section's title as: "Concerning an Immensely Great Clitoris and Clitoridectomy."[57] We can accurately reconstruct the main elements of Soranos's original thanks to three later texts. Two Latin translations preserve the content of the section, one by a man named Mustio,[58] and an-

---

on which see: Jonathan P. Berkey, "Circumscision Circumscribed: Female Excision and Cultural Accommodation in the Medieval Near East," *International Journal for Middle East Studies* 28 (1996) 19–38; Esther K. Hicks, *Infibulation: Female Mutilation in Islamic Northeastern Africa* (New Brunswick, NJ: Transaction, 1996); Hanny Lightfoot-Klein, *Prisoners of Ritual: An Odyssey into Female Genital Circumcision in Africa* (New York: Harrington Park, 1989); Awa Thiam, "Women's Fight for the Abolition of Sexual Mutilation," *International Social Science Journal* 98 (1983) 747–56; Janice Boddy, "Womb as Oasis: The Symbolic Context of Pharaonic Circumcision in Rural Northern Sudan," *American Ethnologist* 9 (1982) 682–98; and Harriet Lyons, "Anthropologists, Moralities, and Relativities: The Problem of Genital Mutilations," *Canadian Review of Sociology and Anthropology* 18 (1981) 499–518.

57. Ilberg, *Sorani Gynaeciorum libri iv*, p. xx:139. Περὶ ὑπερμεγέθους νύμφης καὶ νυμφοτομίας (see also *Gynaikeia* 4.9 [25]; Ilberg, *Sorani Gynaeciorum libri iv*, 147.2).

58. Mustio is also called Muscio in the manuscripts. Valentin Rose, ed., *Sorani Gynaeciorum: Vetus Translatio Latina* (Leipzig: Teubner, 1882) p. 106 (139); 2.76:

XXV *De inmoderata landica*
quam Graeci yos nymfin appellant.

Turpitudinis symptoma est grandis yos nymfe. quidam vero adseverant pulpam ipsam erigi similiter ut viris et quasi usum coitus quaerere.

curabis autem eam sic. supinam iactantes pedibus clusis myzo quod foris est et amplius esse videtur, tenere oportet et scalpello praecidere, deinde conpetenti diligentia vulnus ipsum curare.

Myzo = Greek μύδιον. The shift from the 2d pers. sing. (*curabis*) to the pl. participle (*iactantes*) is probably due to a 1st pers. pl. in Soranos's original. Paulus of Aegina, who uses the 1st pers. pl., is most likely closer to Soranos on this point.

XXV. Concerning an Excessive Clitoris,
which the Greeks call *nymphē*

other probably by Caelius Aurelianus.[59] While these two translations differ considerably in formulation, they contain the same basic components. In addition to these two Latin versions of Soranos, Paulus of Aegina (7th C.)

> A large clitoris is a symptom of turpitude; in fact they strive to have their own flesh stimulated just like men and to obtain sexual intercourse, as it were.
>
> Now, you will perform the surgical operation on her in the following way. Placing her lying on her back with the feet closed (i.e., together), one should hold in place in a small forceps that which protrudes and appears to be larger (than normal) and cut it back with a scalpel; then one must attend to the wound itself with competent diligence.

Mustio's work is an epitome for midwives of a gynecological handbook that circulated under the name of Soranos. Mustio seems to have drawn this piece from Soranos's *Gynaikeia*. On Mustio, see, in addition to Rose, ed., *Sorani Gynaeciorum*, IV–VIII; Drabkin and Drabkin, *Caelius Aurelianus Gynaecia*, viii–xii; and Martin Schanz, *Geschichte der römischen Litteratur*, vol. 4/2, revised by Carl Hosius (Handbuch der Altertumswissenschaft 8.2; 4th rev. ed.; 1935; reprint, Munich: Beck, 1980) 289–91; §1132. Mustio may have lived in the 5th or 6th C., possibly in Africa. Schanz and Hosius consider him to have been a careful translator.

See also the edition and Italian translation by Rino Radicchi, *La "Gynaecia" di Muscione: Manual per le osetriche e le mamme del VI sec. d. C.* (Pisa: Editrice Giardini, n.d.) 190 (Radicchi prints the same text as the one I have reproduced here), 205; see also Rino Radicchi, *Introduzione e considerazioni sulla "Gynaecia" di Muscione (VI sec. d. C.) e studio dei suoi codici* (Scientia Veterum 118; Pisa: Editrice Giardini, 1968).

59. Drabkin and Drabkin, *Caelius Aurelianus Gynaecia*, p. 113: 74r–74v; 1391–1401:

2.112. *De immodica landica.*

Quibusdam landicis horrida comitatur magnitudo et feminas partium feditate confundit et, ut plerique memorant, ipse adfecte tentigine virorum similem appetentiam sumunt et in venerem coacte veniunt.

*suppina denique mulier locanda est conductis femoribus, ne febre feminini sinus distantiam sumant. tunc [in] midio est tenenda superflua atque pro modo alienitatis sue scalpello precidenda. si enim plurimum extenditur porrecta longitudine sequetur * * atque ita inmodice decissionis largo fluore afficit patientem. set post cirurgiam erit adhibenda cohercens atque * * curatio.*

For *feditate*, read *oe*, and for *ipse, adfecte*, and *sue*, read *-ae*. For *febre*, read *fibrae*. For *set*, read *sed*. *Midio* = Greek μύδιον.

2.112. Concerning an Immoderate Clitoris

An uncouth size is present in certain clitorises and brings women into disorder by the deformity of the (private) parts and, as most people say, those same women, affected by the lust [or: erection] (typical) of men, take on a similar desire, and they approach sexual intercourse (i.e., with men) only under duress.

If it comes to that, the woman is to be placed lying on her back and with the thighs closed, lest the viscera of the feminine cavity become distended. Then-

includes a description of a clitoridectomy in his treatise on surgery that closely resembles those found in Mustio and Caelius Aurelianus and probably also derives from Soranos.[60]

the excess part is to be held in place in a small forceps and cut back with a scalpel in proportion to its unnaturalness (i.e., unnatural size). For if the entirety of it is extended (and) cut with its length stretched out. . . . And thus it produces an excessively harmful effect on the patient by the copious discharge (resulting from) the cutting back. But after the surgery a strict (and confining) treatment is to be applied.

The early medieval compiler of this text drew upon the prior translations of Caelius Aurelianus and of Mustio. Miriam and Israel Drabkin assume that Caelius Aurelianus is the translator of the present passage, which makes sense, since it is obviously not by Mustio.

This is a discrete unit in the Mustio text edited by Valentin Rose and in the medieval compilation edited by Miriam and Israel Drabkin. In both cases the context is uterine cancer and uterine growths.

The term *tentigo* in the first full sentence has both the narrower meaning of "swelling" or "stiffness," and, since these can refer to a male erection, the extended meaning of "lecherousness" or "lust" (see Lewis and Short, s.v. *tentigo*). Martial refers to the *tentigo* of the *tribas* Philaenis. Juvenal uses *tentigo* to refer to the sexual arousal of the wife of the Emperor Claudius, who, he says, used to go out at night and play the role of a common prostitute to satisfy her excessive sexual desires. After a night of such activity, "still burning with the hard-on (*tentigo*) of her stiff womb," she went away (Juvenal, *Saturae* 6.129; ET: Amy Richlin, *The Garden of Priapus: Sexuality and Aggression in Roman Humor* [New Haven: Yale University Press, 1983] 107). See also Amy Richlin, *Juvenal Satura VI* (Bryn Mawr Latin Commentaries; Bryn Mawr, PA: Bryn Mawr College, 1986) 47, where she notes, "*tentigo*, 'stiffness,' often used of male erection. A rare allusion to physical manifestations of female sexuality."

60. I. L. Heiberg, ed., *Paulus Aegineta*, vol. 1 (*Corpus Medicorum Graecorum* 9.1; Leipzig: Teubner, 1921) p. 112.21–27; *Epitomae medicae* 6.70:

Περὶ νυμφοτομίας καὶ κερκώσεως

Ὑπερμεγέθης ἐνίαις γίνεται νύμφη καὶ εἰς ἀπρέπειαν αἰσχύνης ἀπαντᾷ· Καθὼς δέ τινες ἱστοροῦσιν ἔνιαι διὰ τοῦ μέρους καὶ ὀρθιάζουσιν ἀνδράσιν ὁμοίως καὶ πρὸς συνουσίαν ὁρμῶσιν. διόπερ ὑπτίας ἐσχηματισμένης τῆς γυναικὸς μυδίῳ κατασχόντες τὸ περιττὸν τῆς νύμφης ἐκτέμωμεν σμίλῃ φυλαττόμενοι τὸ ἐκ βάθους αὐτὴν ἐκτέμνειν, ἵνα μὴ ῥυαδικὸν ἐκ τούτου γένηται πάθος.

Concerning Clitoridectomy and a Growth at the Opening of the Uterus

An immensely great clitoris occurs in some women; the presenting problem is shameful impropriety. According to what some people report, some women even have erections similar to men on account of the (bodily) part and are eager for sexual intercourse. Wherefore, when the woman has been placed lying on her back, while holding in place the superfluous part of the clitoris with a small forceps, we cut it out with a scalpel, avoiding cutting deeply into the clitoris, lest a condition of excessive flux should result from that.

There follows a description of the surgical removal of a growth at the opening of the uterus, and then a discussion of warty excrescences. These and several of the other topics treated in

The Mustio text is entitled, "Concerning an Excessive (*inmoderata*) Clitoris, Which the Greeks Call *nymphē*,"[61] while the other version is called "Concerning an Immoderate (*immodica*) Clitoris." Both terms referring to the size of the female organ can also mean intemperance or lack of restraint.[62] Thus, the Latin titles subtly suggest that the size of this body part can affect a woman's behavior. Further, moral and aesthetic disgust permeates all versions in terms such as: "turpitude," "disorder," "disgrace," and "shameful impropriety." While these terms of moral condemnation relate to the size of a woman's clitoris, the authors clearly associate this physical condition with culturally problematic sexual behavior. Specifically, they speak of these women as capable of taking the active, penetrative role, thus equating a large clitoris with a male penis. In this text, female sexual behavior is viewed within the framework of male sexual autonomy. Outside of this phallocentric sexual framework a large clitoris, which neither assists nor hinders a woman in performing the large range of nonpenetrating sexual stimulations, would not be seen as a problem.[63]

---

the chapters that follow overlap precisely with both Mustio and the 13th-C. manuscript that includes Caelius Aurelianus. This overlap would indicate a use of common sources. What precedes the passage on clitoridectomy in Paulus, however, differs from the other two. Clitoridectomy follows the chapters on eunuchs and on hermaphrodites. Paulus states that female hermaphrodites often have a growth similar to the male member and to male testicles. Thus, he may be viewing women with larger than average clitorises as a type of hermaphrodite.

Francis Adams takes this text as referring to the type of woman described by Martial: "Martial, in more than one place, makes allusion to unnatural practices connected with an enlarged clitoris" (*The Seven Books of Paulus Ægineta: Translated from the Greek with a Commentary*, 3 vols. [London: Sydenham Society, 1844–47], 2 [1846] 382).

61. Soranos uses the term νύμφη for clitoris (*Gynaikeia* 1.3; §18; Ilberg, *Sorani Gynaeciorum libri iv,* 12.19–22; see also the edition, translation, and commentary by Paul Burguière, Danielle Gourevitch, and Yves Malinas, *Soranos d'Éphèse: Maladies des femmes*, vol. 1, *Texte établi, traduit et commenté* [Paris: Les Belles Lettres, 1988] 15 [numbered there as *Gynaikeia* 1.5; §18]).

62. Ann Ellis Hanson states that "[a]n enlarged clitoris is a sign of hypersexuality in a woman" (in *Before Sexuality: The Construction of Erotic Experience in the Ancient Greek World*, ed. David M. Halperin, John J. Winkler, and Froma I. Zeitlin [Princeton: Princeton University Press, 1990] 333). To document this view she refers to *Priapea* 78, a poem that refers to cunnilingus and to the clitoris (*landica*), as well as to a Latin inscription (*CIL* 11.6721 [5]). The inscription is found on one of the Perusine *glandes.* (The Perusine *glandes* are siege bullets, several of which are inscribed with proper names accompanied by an image of a phallus or the word "anus.") Inscription 5 refers to the "clitoris of Fulvia" ([*la*]*ndica Fulviae*). Neither the poem from the *Priapea*, nor the inscription expressly states that the *landica* is enlarged, but the poem certainly implies hypersexuality, and the military nature of the inscription may imply an enlarged *landica*, if an enlarged *landica* is symbolic of greater aggression.

63. Ancient writers were aware of nonpenetrative clitoral sexual stimulation. Rufus of Ephesos, for example, a Greek medical writer (ca. 100 CE), mentions the verb κλειτοριάζειν, which he defines as "to touch it [i.e., the clitoris] licentiously" (*Peri onomasias* 111; Ch. Daremberg and Ch. Émile Ruelle, eds. and French trans., *Œuvres de Rufus d'Éphèse* [Paris, 1879; reprint, Amsterdam: Hakkert, 1963] 147). This raises the question whether all touch-

The text makes the most sense if it is referring to women seeking intercourse with other women. A large clitoris poses a problem to Soranos and his translators and adapters because it makes women like men. Caelius Aurelianus and Paulus of Aegina explicitly refer to a female erection. With the exception of anally or orally penetrating men with this erect female organ, the only plausible use of such an erection is the penetration of a woman.[64] Female sexual behavior is thus seen through male eyes. Penetration constitutes the only sexual activity worthy of note; therefore, any perceived female ability to penetrate must be prevented through surgical intervention.

Possession of a female organ that can function like a male organ, resulting in women's desire to behave sexually as if they were men, occurs in all of the versions of the text and must, therefore, have been present in the Soranos original. In order to arrive at the conceptualization of the clitoris as penis-like, these medical writers had to break from standard medical understanding. According to the principle of analogy, articulated by Herophilos of Chalcedon (3d C. BCE) and adopted by the leading medical writers of the Roman period, the female reproductive organs are analogous to the male ones, only inside, rather than outside, the body. Thus, the ovaries correspond to the testicles, the endometrium to the scrotum, the "neck of the uterus" or vagina to the penis, and the external female genitalia to the prepuce or foreskin.[65] Notice that the vagina, not the clitoris, is like the

---

ing of the clitoris was considered licentious and underscores that the essential issue here is really female pleasure.

A similar definition of κλειτοριάζειν as licentious occurs elsewhere; see, e.g., the Suda, s.v. Κλειτοριάζειν; see also κλειτορίζεσθαι in the Suda, s.v. Μύρτον (Ada Adler, ed., *Suidae Lexicon* [Lexicographici Graeci 1; pt. 3; Stuttgart: Teubner, 1933] 132, 428). The second-century grammarian Pollux of Naukratis, however, defines κλειτορίζειν (alternate spelling) simply as "stroking the clitoris" (Eric Bethe, ed., *Pollucis Onomasticon* [Lexicographici Graeci 9; pt. 1; Leipzig, 1900; reprint, Stuttgart: Teubner, 1967] 137). Since Pollux uses Rufus of Ephesos as a source, he may be consciously making the term neutral rather than negative.

64. If the penetration of men were implied, then the women would be like men, and their penetrated male partners would be considered effeminate within this cultural framework. Martial depicts the *tribas* Philaenis as one who "buggers boys" and "quite fierce with the erection of a husband, bangs eleven girls each day" (*Epigrammata* 7.67.1–3: *Pedicat pueros tribas Philaenis / et tentigine saevior mariti / undenas dolat in die puellas* [W. M. Lindsay, ed., *M. Val. Martialis: Epigrammata* (2d ed.; Oxford: Clarendon, 1929)]). See Judith P. Hallett, who, even without the aid of these medical texts, was able to identify the motif in Roman satire of a *tribas* having the physical ability to penetrate genitally, "Female Homoeroticism and the Denial of Roman Reality in Latin Literature," *Yale Journal of Criticism* 3 (1989) 209–27, esp. 215–19.

65. Herophilos, Fragment 61 (*apud* Galen, *De semine* 2.1) (Heinrich von Staden, ed. and trans., *Herophilus: The Art of Medicine in Early Alexandria* [Cambridge: Cambridge University Press, 1989] 183–86; discussion on pp. 167–69). See also Erna Lesky, *Die Zeugungs- und Vererbungslehren der Antike und ihr Nachwirken* (Abhandlungen der geistes- und sozialwissenschaftlichen Klasse 19; Wiesbaden: Akademie der Wissenschaften und der Literatur in Mainz, 1950) 184f and passim.

penis. And yet the clitoridectomy texts assume that an overly large clitoris is a penis-like organ, capable of an erection.

All of the versions describe essentially the same surgical procedure. The woman is to be placed lying on her back with her legs together. The medical practitioner holds the excess part of the clitoris with a small forceps and then cuts back the clitoris with a scalpel. Caelius Aurelianus and Paulus of Aegina acknowledge that the surgery can be dangerous to the patient and warn against cutting in too deeply, lest an uncontrollable discharge result. Mustio and Caelius Aurelianus prescribe postsurgical care.

The reader must ask at whose request such brutal surgery took place. Did a husband who suspected his wife of having a relationship with a woman bring her in to have surgery performed? Would a brothel owner maintain control of a prostitute by ordering the operation? Did a medical practitioner (perhaps a midwife, i.e., a woman) insist that this was the necessary therapy for a turpitudinous woman? This text is addressed to the medical practitioner. How much control would such a person have? Would the medical practitioner inform the woman precisely what procedure was about to take place? While the ancient versions of the text do not give us answers to these questions, they invite us to pose them. Further, Soranos and his translators had a long-term effect on the medical treatment of women. From the Middle Ages through the modern period medical writers and practitioners in the Arab world and in Europe have instructed surgeons on how to perform the selective clitoridectomy on a woman with an "overly large clitoris" (see fig. 12 for evidence of the practice in 17th-C. Europe).[66] We need a proper and complete history of the selective cli-

66. These include the writers Albucasis and Avicenna (for exact references see Francis Adams, *The Seven Books of Paulus Ægineta: Translated from the Greek with a Commentary*, 3 vols. [London: Sydenham Society, 1844–47], 2 [1846] 382); and François Thevenin, Roderico à Castro, Fabricius ab Aquapendente, Johannes Scultetus (Johann Schultes), Pierre Dionis, Lorenz Heister, and Isaac Barker-Brown (for exact references see James V. Ricci, *The Development of Gynæcological Surgery and Instruments: A Comprehensive Review of the Evolution of Surgery and Surgical Instruments for the Treatment of Female Diseases from the Hippocratic Age to the Antiseptic Period* [Philadelphia: Blakiston, 1949; reprint: San Francisco: Norman, 1990] 113–295.

On the clitoris generally, see Thomas W. Laqueur, "Amor Veneris, vel Dulcedo Appeletur," in *Fragments for a History of the Human Body: Part Three*, ed. Michel Feher with Ramona Naddaff and Nadia Tazi (New York: Zone, 1989) 90–131. Laqueur is at great pains to argue that Western medical practitioners did not perform clitoridectomies until the nineteenth century, at which time they were quickly condemned for so doing. The Western European sources cited by Ricci, however, as well as sources cited by Laqueur himself, demonstrate that Laqueur errs in his opinion. Some of the Western medical writers do argue that an overly large clitoris occurred more frequently among Arabians and Egyptians than among Europeans. Lorenz Heister, for example, writes that the clitoridectomy was seldom performed on Europeans, because European women with this condition hide it "either through lust, modesty or a dread

toridectomy in Western Europe, Southwestern Asia, and Northern Africa (preferably grouped together, in order to ascertain whether or not the selective clitoridectomies of these three regions all ultimately derive from the sources I have discussed above). Perhaps future research on these and other sources will allow us to create a fuller picture of the social history of medicine.

Aetios of Amida, a Christian physician writing in Greek in the early sixth century, also wrote about the clitoridectomy, using as a source Philoumenos, a second-century medical writer.[67] Aetios describes the problem somewhat differently from those writers dependent upon Soranos. He holds that an overly large clitoris "leads to unseemliness and shame" and that the constant rubbing of the clitoris against one's garments "stimulates a desire for intercourse."[68] He does not describe a masculine desire or a physical erection, although "unseemliness and shame" could include these and certainly imply a tone of moral condemnation. Aetios then describes the Egyptian custom of amputating the clitoris of young girls before they

---

of the knife" (*A general system of surgery, in three parts. Containing the doctrine and management I. of wounds, fractures, luxations, tumors, and ulcers, of all kinds. II. of the several operations performed on all parts of the body. III. of the several bandages applied in all operations and disorders . . . to which is prefixed an introduction, concerning the nature, origin, progress, and improvements of surgery* [4th ed.; London: Printed for W. Innys, 1750] pt. 2, sect. 5, p. 197, chap. 148 [cited by Ricci, *Development*, 209f, 267, n. 195]). But if the women about whom Heister writes had "a dread of the knife," they must have known about the procedure, perhaps having heard of women on whom a surgeon had performed it. Further, Laqueur reports on a clitoridectomy performed on a 17th-C. *tribas* who had dressed in men's clothing, served in the military, and had sexual encounters with other women, as well as a clitoridectomy performed on a 17th-C. nun near Pavia. Laqueur unconvincingly attributes the former clitoridectomy solely to the cross-dressing—leaving unexplained the account of her sexual encounters, while he classifies the second as a freak occurrence, because the surgeon later confessed that he had not known the "doctrine of the clitoris" (pp. 115f, 130, n. 82). Laqueur also refers to the French surgeon Ambroise Paré, who prescribes clitoridectomy for a woman whose clitoris swells to such an extent that she can engage in sexual activity with another woman (pp. 116f, 131, n. 83f).

For a critique of Laqueur and a different theory concerning the clitoris, see Valerie Traub, "The Psychomorphology of the Clitoris," *GLQ* 2 (1995) 81–113.

On the clitoris in the Hippokratics and Aristotle, see Lesley Ann Dean-Jones, *Women's Bodies in Classical Greek Science* (Oxford: Clarendon, 1994) 78–80.

67. Aetios of Amida, *Biblia iatrika* 16.115; Skevos Zervos, ed., *Gynaekologie des Aëtios: sive sermo sextus decimus et ultimus* (Leipzig: Fock, 1901) pp. 152.13–153.10; German trans. by Max Wegscheider, *Geburtshülfe und Gynäkologie bei Aëtios von Amida* (Berlin: Springer, 1901) pp. 130f; 16.106; ET of the 1542 Latin trans. of Cornarius by James V. Ricci, *Aetios of Amida: The Gynaecology and Obstetrics of the Sixth Century, A.D.* (Philadelphia: Blakiston, 1950) pp. 107f; 16.103. On Aetios, see also M. Wellmann, PW 1, s.v. "Aetios" (1894) 703f.

68. Aetios of Amida, *Biblia iatrika* 16.115: εἰς ἀπρέπειαν καὶ αἰσχύνην γίνεται . . . τὴν πρὸς συνουσίαν ὁρμὴν ἐπεγείρει (Zervos, *Gynaekologie des Aëtios*, 152.18f; 152.20).

reached the age of marriage.[69] Rather than lying face up, the young girl is to be placed in a chair with a robust young man standing behind to steady her. From that point on, the procedure is similar to that described by Soranos. The surgeon grasps hold of the clitoris with a forceps and cuts off the upper portion, taking care not to cut too deeply. Aetios notes that it is easy to cut off too much, which will result in a discharge. He then describes the postsurgical care in some detail.

As for Soranos, it is not surprising to find him prescribing a clitoridectomy for women who behave like men, since he describes soft men and *tribades* as diseased in *On Chronic Diseases*. Both his treatise on gynecology and his *On Chronic Diseases* contain strong terms of moral revulsion (the "shameful custom" of the *tribades* [consuetudo turpis] and "turpitude" [turpitudo]). In *On Chronic Diseases*, however, Soranos explicitly says that the soft men and the *tribades* are victims of an affliction of the mind and that there is no bodily treatment. It is the mind that must be controlled.[70] Here, Soranos advises a bodily treatment, namely surgery, for women who behave like men. These treatments seem to contradict each other. Soranos may intend the clitoridectomy for women whom he imagines to be physically capable of penetrating others, whereas he prescribes mind control for women whom he imagines to have a mental illness that has behavioral implications. The root problem with both types of women is their active (i.e., masculine) sexual desire. Perhaps there is not even a contradiction at all, since the discussion of the mental disease could be meant to cover those cases of masculine, that is, active, women who do *not* have an enlarged clitoris. Since Soranos discusses the two diseases in two separate places with no cross-reference, we cannot definitively resolve the conflict.

Whether treated medically by mind control or clitoridectomy, the presenting problem for the women in both passages is in fact a social one: women are behaving like men in that they are successfully obtaining sexual arousal and are seeking to play the active role in a sexual encounter with another person. A culture that cannot tolerate female assertiveness in sexual matters will probably try to control female homoerotic behavior by whatever means, even when these means conflict at the theoretical level (whether the disease is of the body or of the mind), and the measures taken will also affect women who are attracted to men. We do not know the circumstances under which a woman would be given a clitoridectomy or who

69. Strabo states that the Egyptians circumcize the males and excise (ἐκτέμνω) the females, as is the law among the Jews (*Geography* 17.2.5). He also describes a group of people called "Meat-Eaters" in the region of the Red Sea who mutilate the sexual glands of the men and who excise the women in the Jewish fashion (16.4.9: Ἰουδαϊκῶς). Strabo's view of the excision of women as a Jewish custom is puzzling.

70. *Chronicarum passionum* 4.9; §133.

would make this decision, but the possibilities for social control through denial of female pleasure are obvious.[71]

The Medical Heritage of Female Homoeroticism

In addition to the discussions of soft men and *tribades* and the clitoridectomy, Soranos makes brief mention of two other issues of possible relevance to female homoeroticism. First, he touches again on the origin of masculine women in a discussion of the popular belief that if a wet-nurse who had borne a son nursed a baby girl, the girl would become more masculine, and vice versa. Soranos rejects this view as absurd,[72] but the belief is fascinating testimony to ancient views about gender. Perhaps some people saw such "cross-gender milk" as the cause of masculine women and effeminate men and rejected the view that homoerotic or bisexual orientation comes through the seed or through the nonmingling of the female and male seed.[73]

Second, Soranos appeals to cultural stereotypes about gender in describing "mannish women." He refers to mannish women at several points when discussing menstruation, and states that women may fail to menstruate if they are too young or too old, pregnant, mannish, barren singers, or athletes.[74] Soranos writes that one can ascertain through examination the cause of amenorrhea. On mannish women he writes that medical practitioners can "recognize . . . mannish women from their appearance, and habits and manner of life by questioning" the women,[75] but he does not describe these habits or manner of life. His description in *On Chronic Dis-*

71. A worthwhile comparison to the clitoridectomy is the castration of men, which Paulus of Aegina describes shortly before the section on clitoridectomy. Paulus expresses great hesitation about the operation, saying that he is describing the procedure only because high-ranking persons often force surgeons to perform castrations against their will. None of the descriptions of the clitoridectomy contain any hint of hesitation about violating the integrity of a woman's body (*Epitomae medicae* 6.68; I. L. Heiberg, ed., *Paulus Aegineta* [Corpus Medicorum Graecorum 9/1; Leipzig: Teubner, 1921] 111.18–112.5).

72. *Gynaikeia* 2.12 [32]; §20 [89]; Ilberg, *Sorani Gynaeciorum libri iv*, 68.26–69.5; ET: Temkin, *Soranus' Gynecology*, 94. Soranos gives the parallel of twins, one male and one female, who drink the same milk, and also mentions animals feeding their female and male young with the same milk.

73. See Clement of Alexandria, *Paidagōgos* 1.6, for an extended discussion of milk as a gendered theological metaphor (with the church as the mother and Christ as the holy milk). See the insightful discussion by Denise Kimber Buell, "Procreative Language in Clement of Alexandria" (Ph.D. diss., Harvard University, 1995) chap. 5.

74. *Gynaikeia* 3.1; §7: ἀνδρώδεις (Ilberg, *Sorani Gynaeciorum libri iv*, 97.23; ET: Temkin, *Soranus' Gynecology*, 133).

75. *Gynaikeia* 3.1; §8: τὰς δὲ ἀνδρώδεις συγκρίνομεν ἐκ τῆς ὄψεως, τὸ δὲ ἐπιτήδευμα καὶ τὸν βίον ἐκ τῆς ἀνακρίσεως (Ilberg, 98.5f; ET: Temkin, 134).

eases of *tribades* as displaying masculine characteristics and of soft men as effeminate makes it quite possible that "mannish women" (*andrōdeis*) are *tribades*. The masculine behavior attributed to women in the passage on clitoridectomy (striving to have their own flesh stimulated just like men, a desire similar to men, and having an erection) could be what Soranos envisages under "habits and manner of living."[76] Soranos does not suggest a treatment for the amenorrheic mannish women. He emphasizes that the singers and the athletes require no treatment, since they have no disease, but that leading a less athletic life will make their bodies more feminine, which aids them in conceiving.[77] Thus, singers and athletes are apparently also mannish, but their mannishness can be easily reversed by exercising less; in this case Soranos does prescribe a treatment. Becoming feminine, that is, less athletic, makes conception possible. Does Soranos not propose a therapy for the women he calls mannish because he considers their condition to be permanent or does he, at this point, not consider their condition to be a disease? Or did mannish women perceive amenorrhea to be less of a problem for them since fewer of them had a desire to conceive? Regardless, in this passage, Soranos identifies and categorizes mannish women according to their mode of living and appearance.

While mode of living and appearance may serve as identifying markers for Soranos, he attempts to explain the origins of lifelong orientations using ancient theories of procreation. Parmenides thought that female and male seeds warring at conception and never mingling properly caused the offspring (presumably both the female and the male) to desire both kinds of love, probably active and passive. The leaders of several medical schools argued that the homoerotic orientation (of men, also of women?) was a disease that had made its way into the human race and could now be passed on through the seed containing this orientation.

Soranos himself describes *tribades* and soft men as suffering from a dis-

---

76. On mannish women with amenorrhea, see also: *Gynaikeia* 1.6; §29: τὰς οὖν πλείονας τῶν μὴ καθαιρομένων εὐτονωτέρας θεωροῦμεν, ὥσπερ τὰς ἀνδρώδεις τε καὶ στείρας (Ilberg, 19.29f; ET: Temkin, 26: "Now we observe that the majority of those not menstruating are rather robust, like mannish and sterile women"; see also the edition, translation, and commentary by Paul Burguière, Danielle Gourevitch, and Yves Malinas, *Soranos d'Éphèse: Maladies des femmes*, vol. 1, *Texte établi, traduit et commenté* [Paris: Les Belles Lettres, 1988] 25 [numbered there as *Gynaikeia* 1.8; §29]; see further *Gynaikeia* 1.4; §23; Ilberg, 15.25; ET: Temkin, 19f). Soranos also connects mannishness with sterility in *Gynaikeia* 1.9; §34; Ilberg, 23.23–30; ET: Temkin, 32, but he notes that Diokles reports that women who are masculine-looking are more likely to conceive: *Gynaikeia* 1.9; §35: ἀρρενωποί (Ilberg, 24.17–19; ET: Temkin, 33) (cf. Aristotle, *Generation of Animals* 2.7; 747a, who speaks of masculine-looking women [ἀρρενωποί] who do not menstruate and effeminate men [ἄνδρες θηλυκοί] who have thin, cold semen).

77. *Gynaikeia* 3.1; §9; Ilberg, 98.26–28; ET: Temkin, 135.

ease of the soul, not of the body, which makes women take on male characteristics and desire sex with both women and men, and which makes men become effeminate in behavior and in dress. He prescribes mind control as the treatment. Elsewhere, Soranos recommends the surgical extirpation of the clitoris in women whose overly large clitorises lead them to male sexual desire and physical response.

What is clear is that Soranos believes that medical practitioners can and should control active female sexual behavior. Both methods raise the larger questions of the relationship between female sexual activeness and social control and of the moral values inherent in medical treatments. Caelius Aurelianus adopts both the mind-control and the surgery models as his own. Mustio and Paulus of Aegina agree with the anatomical model and adopt the recommendation of surgery. Aetios of Amida, abstracting Philoumenos, describes the clitoridectomy for women whose overly large clitorises lead them to shameful and unseemly behavior. According to these models, for a woman to be overly masculine sexually, that is, to take the active role in sexual relations, is a disease that can and should be treated. This is of cultural significance for women as a whole, because it means that all women are thereby confined to a passive role. This material demonstrates that the modern medical diagnosis of love between women as pathological has ancient antecedents.

6

Unnatural Love: Classifying Dreams

The ancient literature of dream interpretation constitutes yet another source for understanding Roman-period attitudes toward female homoeroticism. But ancient dream interpreters understood and interpreted dreams very differently from the way we understand this process today. Artemidoros of Daldis in Lydia (2d C. CE), the fullest available witness of the rich literature of dream interpretation in the Greek and Roman worlds, exemplifies these cultural differences. When explicating ancient interpretations of dreams in a manner appropriate to their culture, we face an even greater challenge than trying to interpret ancient dreams themselves. While Freud and Jung continue to influence contemporary Western dream analysis, dream interpreters in the Roman world did not share the same interpretive priorities and principles.[1] For example, although they believed that some dreams emanated from individual hidden anxieties, they showed little interest in them and focused instead on dreams that could predict the future. Further, while the sexual meaning of dreams arouses great interest in our culture, Roman-period interpreters seldom derived a sexual meaning from dreams. And when they encountered dreams with explicit sexual content, they often interpreted them as referring to such nonsexual areas of life as business, children, or civic affairs. Artemidoros included dreams about sexual relations between women among the sexual dreams he interpreted. In what follows, I explore how Artemidoros classified female homoeroticism within his interpretive framework and discuss

1. For a stimulating discussion of the problems of seeing Artemidoros as an ancient predecessor to Freud and of using Freudian theory to interpret ancient dreams, see S. R. F. Price, "The Future of Dreams: From Freud to Artemidoros," in *Before Sexuality: The Construction of Erotic Experience in the Ancient Greek World*, ed. David M. Halperin, John J. Winkler, and Froma I. Zeitlin (Princeton: Princeton University Press, 1990) 365–87.

how this framework represents persistent cultural norms about gender and sexuality.

Artemidoros drew upon earlier written sources[2] and upon his own extensive empirical research in order to systematize dream interpretation in his five-volume *Oneirokritika* ("The Classification of Dreams"),[3] which contains numerous examples of dreams accompanied by his interpretation of them. He wrote in the rhetorically polished, Atticizing style (i.e., imitating classical Attic Greek) popular among the educated elite of his day, but occasionally employed the terminology of his less elite sources, such as astrological writings and writings from other arcane disciplines. Roger Pack argues that "[t]he majority of Artemidorus' friends and clients had a rather modest social standing,"[4] which means that in Artemidoros we have the

2. Artemidoros states that he tried to procure every available book on dream interpretation (*Oneirokritika* 1. proem; p. 2.11–13). Claes Blum argues that Artemidoros may have drawn especially upon the Stoic philosopher Poseidonios [and on Hermippos of Berytos] (Claes Blum, *Studies in the Dream-Book of Artemidorus* [Uppsala: Almqvist and Wiksells, 1936] 59–71); but A. H. M. Kessels argues that Poseidonios and Artemidoros did not work with the same classification system and that Artemidoros was not a Stoic ("Ancient Systems of Dream-Classification," *Mnemosyne* 4.22 [1969] 389–424, esp. 391–99). Tertullian, a Christian contemporary of Artemidoros, was familiar with the five-volume work on dream interpretation by Hermippos of Berytos (*De anima* 46), so Tertullian and Artemidoros may have had at least one source in common. Since Hermippos of Berytos's work is not extant, we cannot know whether it included material on sexual dreams similar to that found in Artemidoros. Tertullian's stance toward predictive dreams is similar to that of Artemidoros, i.e., he believes in them and tries to refute those who do not.

3. Scholars usually translate the title as "The Interpretation of Dreams." My translation is more in line with Luther H. Martin's proposal of "A Taxonomic Science of Dreams." Martin argues that "interpretation" implies too much of a Freudian understanding of dreams ("Artemidorus: Dream Theory in Late Antiquity," *Second Century* 8 [1991] 97–108, esp. 107).

Roger A. Pack, ed., *Artemidori Daldiani Onirocriticon Libri V* (Leipzig: Teubner, 1963); ET: Robert J. White, *The Interpretation of Dreams: Oneirocritica by Artemidorus* (Park Ridge, NJ: Noyes, 1975). In what follows, my translation is generally based upon that of White. An early Arabic translation of books I–III of the *Oneirokritika* has been edited by Toufic Fahd, *Artémidore d'Éphèse: Le Livre des songes, traduit du grec en arabe par Hunayn B. Isḥāq* (Damascus: Institut Français de Damas, 1964). The first three books of the *Oneirokritika* seem to have been meant for the general public, while the last two were addressed to Artemidoros's son to teach him how to be a better dream interpreter (probably the reason why the Arabic translation includes only the first three books). On Artemidoros generally, see: Michel Foucault, *The History of Sexuality*, vol. 3, *The Care of the Self*, trans. Robert Hurley (French original, Paris: Éditions Gallimard, 1984; New York: Random House, 1986) 1–36; Roger Pack, "Artemidorus and His Waking World," *Transactions and Proceedings of the American Philological Association* 86 (1955) 280–90; and Blum, *Studies in the Dream-Book of Artemidorus*, esp. 47–71. For overviews of dreams in this period, see Patricia Cox Miller, *Dreams in Late Antiquity: Studies in the Imagination of a Culture* (Princeton, NJ: Princeton University Press, 1994); and John S. Hanson, "Dreams and Visions in the Graeco-Roman World and Early Christianity," *ANRW* II.23.2 (Berlin: De Gruyter, 1980) 1395–1427.

4. Pack, "Artemidorus," 287; see 285–87.

rare chance to read reports of the experiences of the Roman world's non-elite population.

While Artemidoros presents his own assessment of particular dreams, the system within which he classifies and organizes the dreams represents the norms of his culture, rather than his own original thought. Scholars as diverse as Roger Pack, Michel Foucault, and John Winkler agree on this point. Roger Pack, editor of the best critical edition of the *Oneirokritika*, writes, "No doubt most of the social attitudes reflected in the *Oneirokritika* are not original with its author, but they are his in that he gives them a silent endorsement. When set forth tersely, according to the traditional formula, they are more likely to have been drawn from his sources."[5] John Winkler calls Artemidoros's work, "uniquely informative about the perceived public meanings of sexual activity. Artemidoros' empirical stance allows us to grasp a general semantics of sex in the ancient world usually obscured by the tendentious treatment of the moralists."[6] Winkler is referring here to Artemidoros's categorization of sexual behavior, which derived from his culture. Even though Artemidoros interpreted sexual dreams as having nonsexual meanings, he showed great interest in the taxonomy of the sexual behavior found in dreams. Winkler also contrasts the tone of the *Oneirokritika* with "the elite and intellectualist biases which typify so much ancient writing."[7]

Further, Artemidoros placed great emphasis on the empirical method and collected his data in marketplaces and festivals in several areas of the Roman Empire.[8] Thus, the dream material itself typifies what early Christians may have heard or experienced. Artemidoros is particularly helpful for his picture of the social attitudes that shaped life for large numbers of people throughout the Roman Empire. Early Christians were the heirs to

5. Ibid. Michel Foucault is in line with this view when he makes Artemidoros the reference point for sexuality in this period because Artemidoros's work represents "current modes of valuation and generally accepted attitudes. . . . One can thus expect this text by Artemidoros to provide evidence of a rather widespread moral tradition, which was doubtless rather deeply rooted in the past" (Foucault, *History*, 3:9). John Boswell has criticized Foucault for giving Artemidoros such a prominent place in his work: "Artemidorus' dream book had no influence either on the sexuality of the age or on subsequent discourse about it. The interpretation of dreams was a recondite specialty, about as influential as urology journals today" (*New York Times Book Review*, January 18, 1987, p. 31). Boswell misses Foucault's point, which is that the social attitudes found in Artemidoros are not his individual creation, but rather representative of broader cultural streams.

6. John J. Winkler, *The Constraints of Desire: The Anthropology of Sex and Gender in Ancient Greece* (New York: Routledge, 1990) 43. Winkler's entire chapter on the *Oneirokritika* is superb (pp. 17–44).

7. Ibid., 43.

8. *Oneirokritika* 1. proem. Blum argues that Artemidoros modeled his methods of dream interpretation on the three methods of the Empirical School of medicine, namely, experience, transmitted experience, and analogy (Blum, *Studies*, 88–91).

these attitudes. If scholars are correct about the enduring nature of the social attitudes found in the *Oneirokritika*, then this second-century document sheds light on how we can understand the first-century writings of the New Testament.

The *Oneirokritika* consists of a systematic presentation and a methodical exposition of dreams. Artemidoros divides them into two types: *enhypnia* and *oneiroi*. *Enhypnia* are anxiety dreams or petitionary dreams; they indicate a present state of affairs. Whereas anxiety dreams were of the greatest interest to Sigmund Freud, and, in his wake, to us moderns, Artemidoros dismisses *enhypnia* as nonsignificative.[9] *Oneiroi*, dreams that predict the future, are his real interest and the subject of his handbook. *Oneiroi* fall into two categories: *theorēmatikoi*, dreams in which the dream image corresponds exactly to a future event (e.g., a man suffers a shipwreck in a dream and then in a waking state), and *allēgorikoi*, dreams in which an image signifies a future event.[10] For Artemidoros, virtuous, serious people do not have dreams about present events (*enhypnia*), but only about future ones (*oneiroi*), especially dreams that directly predict future events (*theorēmatikoi*) and thus do not require professional dream interpreters. Accordingly, Artemidoros devotes the bulk of the *Oneirokritika* to allegorical *oneiroi*, since people themselves cannot understand them without assistance. He methodically classifies these dreams and describes how to discern what they predict.

Throughout the five books of the *Oneirokritika*, Artemidoros's main goal is to teach people how to predict accurately the results of allegorical dreams. His primary tool for explaining allegorical dreams is the "juxtaposition of similarities":[11] for example, the head in a dream corresponds to one's father and the foot to a slave.[12] In addition, he employs a grid of six criteria established by former dream interpreters and uses them to evaluate dreams as auspicious or inauspicious, saying, "it is a basic principle that all imagery that is in accordance with [1] nature, [2] law (or convention) (*nomos*), [3] custom (*ethos*), [4] occupation, [5] names or [6] time is good, but that whatever is contrary to them is bad or inauspicious."[13] Artemidoros asserts that what is from nature must always remain the same but does not explain what he means by this.[14] Custom, or unwritten law, is

9. *Oneirokritika* 1.6; ἀσήμαντα (Pack, *Onirocriticon*, 15.22f).
10. *Oneirokritika* 1.2; 4.1.
11. *Oneirokritika* 2.25; Pack, *Onirocriticon*, 144.12.
12. *Oneirokritika* 1.2.
13. *Oneirokritika* 4.2; Pack, *Onirocriticon*, 245.2–4; cf. *Oneirokritika* 1.3.
14. *Oneirokritika* 4.2: τὰ μὲν οὖν φύσει δεῖ κατὰ ταὐτὰ καὶ ὡσαύτως ἔχειν (Pack, *Onirocriticon*, 242.21f). A. J. Festugière notes that Plato (*Phaedo* D 2 and 5f) uses this same formula to refer to nontemporal reality, i.e., being in itself (*Artémidore: La clef des songes* [Paris: Librairie Philosophique J. Vrin, 1975] 220, n. 8).

what people have agreed upon, while laws (*nomoi*) are what people have written down out of fear that others will transgress them. (Examples of the unwritten laws are marriage and attraction to and intercourse with women.)[15] Time, occupation, and names are subdivisions of nature, law, and custom.[16] An auspicious dream is generally in accordance with nature and law, but not always. For example, a potter dreamed of beating his mother, which is illegal. But the mother signified the earth and the beating represented the shaping of the clay. This dream predicted that the man would make many objects.[17]

Throughout the *Oneirokritika*, Artemidoros assumes an adult male client and thus probably an adult male reader; examples involving male dreamers predominate.[18] Only two examples of female dreams appear among the dozens of varieties described in the section on sexual intercourse (1.78–80). Probably Artemidoros had carried out less investigation of sexual dreams by women (or women did not share their sexual dreams with him) because his clients were largely men. (Perhaps women shared their dreams more with one another or consulted female dream interpreters.)[19] A female's intercourse with a male (heterosexual relations) occurs under the category "natural, legal, and customary": "[A dream of] being possessed by someone with whom one is familiar, whatever his character, means profit for a woman."[20] The verb used for "to possess," *peraino*, apparently means "to penetrate." Artemidoros assumes here and elsewhere a strict disjuncture between the active male and the passive female sexual roles. Further, whereas Artemidoros subdivides the dreams of men penetrating a large variety of partners into numerous categories (gender, age,

15. *Oneirokritika* 1.8; 4.2; Pack, *Onirocriticon*, 17.8f; 243.4.

16. For a more detailed explanation, see *Oneirokritika* 4.2; Pack, *Onirocriticon*, 242.16–245.24, as well as Foucault, *History*, 3:15f.

17. *Oneirokritika* 4.2; Pack, *Onirocriticon*, 245.9–12.

18. Artemidoros describes dreams in which a male dreamer has intercourse with a variety of partners. Dreams by a female about her intercourse with equivalent partners cannot be substituted and the same interpretations applied to them. For example, Roman law strictly prohibited a female slaveowner from having sexual intercourse with her male slave. Therefore such intercourse cannot be classified under the legal category. In contrast, Artemidoros properly classifies intercourse between a male owner and his male or female slave as legal, since Roman law did not prohibit such intercourse. A second example is the husband dreaming of intercourse with his wife, which represents either his craft or occupation or that over which he presides or rules (οὗ προΐσταται καὶ ἄρχει [*Oneirokritika* 1.78 (Pack, *Onirocriticon*, 86.25)]), just as he presides and rules over his wife. Since wives in Roman society did not have the legal right to rule over their husbands, a wife's dream about intercourse with her husband presumably could not signify her craft or occupation or that over which she ruled.

19. For an example of a female dream interpreter, see *IG* III.162 (dated to 127/8 or 128/9 CE). See Winkler, *Constraints*, 39.

20. *Oneirokritika* 1.78: περαίνεσθαι δὲ ὑπό τινος γνωρίμου γυναικὶ μὲν [ἡδὺ καὶ] λυσιτελές, οἷος ἂν ᾖ ὁ περαίνων (Pack, *Onirocriticon*, 88.25–27).

and relative legal and social status of the partner, precise sexual position, etc.), a female's dream about sexual relations with a man is given a blanket signification: it is always auspicious for a woman to dream of being penetrated by a man known to her. Female-female sexual relations fall under the category "unnatural" and will be discussed shortly. With these two exceptions, Artemidoros focuses on men and their dreams.[21]

The first and second books of the *Oneirokritika* treat dreams about the human life span from birth to death. A chapter on sexual intercourse (1.78–80) falls at the center and contains sexual dreams that Artemidoros categorizes as either: (1) natural, legal (or conventional),[22] and customary; (2) illegal (or unconventional) (*para nomon*); and unnatural (*para physin*). Dreams in each of these categories can be auspicious or inauspicious. For example, if a healthy man dreams of intercourse with a deity, this unnatural sexual pairing nonetheless portends auspicious events: his superiors will assist him. Conversely, if he dreams of intercourse with a woman who is old, ugly, living in pain, and unwilling to submit to the intercourse, such conventional behavior bears an inauspicious meaning: failure in the man's undertakings. Note that the meanings of these sexual dreams are nonsexual. Thus, several factors are operative here: societal definitions (such as of "law"/"convention" or "nature"), interpretation of details in the dream, and the dream interpreter's evaluative system. Artemidoros's original contribution lies in his interpretive and evaluative methods; his threefold division into legal, illegal, and unnatural is one common to the larger society and provides a particularly clear map of Artemidoros's and his society's attitudes toward sexual relations.

Artemidoros's first category of sexual dreams includes intercourse with a man's wife or mistress, prostitutes, a woman whom the dreamer does not know, his male or female servant, a woman known to him and well-acquainted with him, the penetration of a female dreamer by a man known to her, intercourse between a man and an active male lover, and masturbation (i.e., for a man to stroke his own penis). The illegal category consists primarily of incest: penetrating one's son (distinguished as to age), being

---

21. Women's dreams occur rarely throughout the whole work. See Winkler, *Constraints*, 39.

22. Winkler translates νόμος as "convention" and ἔθος as "habit" (ibid., 35, 36, 37, and passim). I translate νόμος as "law" and ἔθος as "custom," because Winkler's translation does not sufficiently distinguish between νόμος and ἔθος. Since, however, the translation of νόμος as "law" does not work in all cases, in what follows I sometimes translate it as "convention." Artemidoros employs his terms ambiguously. For example, he subdivides those things in life that exist "by law"/"by convention" (νενομισμένα) into "custom"/"habit" (ἔθος)—which is itself an "unwritten law"—and "laws" (νόμοι) (*Oneirokritika* 4.2; Pack, *Onirocriticon*, 242.19–243.4).

penetrated by one's son, having intercourse with one's daughter (distinguished as to age and marital status), intercourse with one's sister (which is not discussed, since it has the same meaning as with one's daughter), penetrating one's brother, penetrating one's friend, having intercourse with one's mother (in a variety of positions, with a living or a dead mother, with a mother from whom one is estranged), and having fellatio with one's mother or with a variety of other people (both as the passive and the active partner in the act). The unnatural category includes: masturbation (i.e., for a man to "have sex with himself"—not differentiated from stroking his own penis), kissing one's own penis, practicing fellatio with oneself, a woman playing the active or the passive role with another woman, sexual intercourse with a female or male deity, intercourse with a corpse (both active and passive—Artemidoros does not explain the mechanics of this latter category), and intercourse with an animal (both active and passive).

Notice that same-sex sexual acts occur in all three categories. For a man to penetrate his male servant is natural, legal, and customary, as it is for the man to be penetrated by a richer, older man. Both dreams are good omens. Penetration by a household slave or a younger or destitute man is inauspicious, but these still fall under the legal category. A father's active or passive sexual intercourse with a son is illegal, as is penetrating a brother or a friend and having active or passive fellatio with male (and female) partners. In the unnatural category, same-sex possibilities include a woman having active or passive intercourse with another woman and a man having active or passive intercourse with a male deity or with a corpse.

Artemidoros's system is not totally decipherable or consistent, which gives rise to certain questions. What if the richer, older man (or the younger or destitute man) of the conventional category were a friend of the dreamer, which would put the intercourse into the unconventional category? Friendship for Artemidoros apparently implies a similar social status (i.e., not "richer, older" or "younger or destitute"), an equality that penetration destroys. Perhaps the dominance of penetration makes a friendship between two adult males of equal status impossible. (In this case, *para nomon* must mean "unconventional" rather than "illegal." Second-century Roman law, at any rate, did not consider sexual relations between two consenting adult free males illegal.) Further, why is Artemidoros so opposed to fellatio, while admitting anal intercourse with one's male slave or with another man into the legal category? And why does masturbation fall under both categories one and three? Another dilemma is Artemidoros's claim on the one hand that the animal world is his model for what is natural—since animals have intercourse in one habitual position—and that human beings invented the other positions out of wantonness, licentiousness, and drunkenness, and, on the other hand, his classification of anal penetration (slave; richer and older man; younger or destitute man) as natural, legal, and customary.

While we cannot answer these questions, attention to the active/passive dichotomy and to status differences helps in sorting out Artemidoros's distinctions. For example, he uses the verb *perainō* for active sexual intercourse, or penetration; and *perainomai* for being penetrated.[23] In a heterosexual union, the "wife represents either the craft or occupation of the dreamer, from which he derives pleasure, or whatever he controls or governs, as he does his wife."[24] The wife is at the center of the natural, legal, and customary category. The other unions of that category are generally socially unequal: man/mistress; man/prostitute; man/woman he does not know; man/woman he does know; man/female or male slave; man/richer, older man; man/younger or destitute man. The unions between males and females are unequal because of the social, political, and economic inequality between women and men in this period. The sexual union of a free male with a female or male slave is unequal due to the difference in status. Economic and age differences characterize the inequality in the male/male relations cited.[25]

The illegal (or unconventional) category contains primarily incestuous relationships. Artemidoros distinguishes between penetrating and being penetrated, and among sons and daughters of different ages, but the inequality inherent in father-son, father-daughter, brother-sister, and mother-son incest (and in brother-brother incest when there is an age difference) is not an organizing principle. At issue is consanguinity, rather than power imbalance. Why is male friend (*philos*) in this category? Could Artemidoros be classifying penetrating a friend as unconventional precisely because that act destroyed the equality that should exist between free male friends? The section on fellatio is somewhat of an excursus, for the act of fellatio, rather than the partner, is unconventional according to Artemidoros.[26]

23. The verbs "to mingle" (μίγνυμι) and "to have sexual intercourse" in the sense of "to be with" (σύνειμι) occur for both the passive and the active partners.

24. *Oneirokritika* 1.78; Pack, *Onirocriticon*, 86.22–26; ET: White, *Oneirocritica*, 58.

25. Man/enemy also falls under category one, and it could represent an equal relationship. But the system is not absolutely precise and consistent, since man/brother is mentioned in both the legal and the illegal categories.

26. Again, the meaning "unconventional" must apply, since Roman law did not oppose fellatio.

Although Artemidoros does not say so explicitly, fellatio seems to be on the border between unconventional and unnatural. He lists masturbation (presumably this is the meaning of "mingling with oneself," but he could mean anal sex with oneself) as the first form of unnatural intercourse, and then goes on to kissing one's penis and practicing fellatio with oneself. Artemidoros describes masturbation in the legal category as manual stimulation; he interprets the hands as attendants to the penis and the act as signifying possession of a female or male slave.

Finally and most important for this discussion: why is female-female intercourse categorically included under "unnatural," whereas intercourse between human men falls into the conventional and unconventional categories? Intercourse with a deity, a corpse, or an animal could be unnatural because each of these represents another kind of being, another realm, but that would not explain the presence of woman/woman intercourse in this category.

Artemidoros refers to woman/woman intercourse in the second dream by a woman in the section on sexual intercourse. The passage reads:

> If a woman dreams that she possesses another woman, she will share her secrets with the woman she has possessed. But if she is not familiar with the woman whom she possesses, she will attempt futile projects. But if a woman dreams that she is being possessed by another woman, she will be divorced from her husband or become a widow. She will learn besides the secrets of the woman with whom she has had sexual intercourse.[27]

Artemidoros describes female/female relations in culturally male terms, using the active/passive dichotomy. When Artemidoros otherwise uses the verb for "to possess" (*perainō*), he apparently means "to penetrate." Here he presents the same schema that he uses for male/male relations: if *a* possesses *b*; if *a* is possessed by *b*. He therefore seems to be thinking of some form of penetration with the women as well. In each case, the active woman shares her secrets with the passive woman; the active partner gives the secrets, and the passive one receives them. In contrast, the male dreamer enters into the secrets of the familiar woman about whom he has had a sexual dream (legal category).[28] There, the man enters into, that is, receives, the secrets of the passive female, whereas here the active female imparts her secrets.[29] The futile projects could refer to business activities or other types of undertakings, including public ones.

Thus, he describes masturbation in the first category as a servile act, that is, as symbolizing an unequal social relation. The forms of masturbation in category three are kissing one's penis and practicing fellatio with oneself. The precise reasons for seeing fellatio as unconventional and unnatural are puzzling. See Winkler, who refers to the general societal disgust in which fellatio was held (Winkler, *Constraints*, 38).

27. *Oneirokritika* 1.80: γυνὴ δὲ γυναῖκα ἐὰν περαίνῃ, τὰ ἑαυτῆς μυστήρια τῇ περαινομένῃ κοινώσεται. ἐὰν δὲ ἀγνοῇ τὴν περαινομένην, ματαίοις ἐπιχειρήσει πράγμασιν. ἐὰν δὲ γυνὴ ὑπὸ γυναικὸς περαίνηται, χωρισθήσεται τοῦ ἀνδρὸς ἢ χηρεύσει· τὰ μέντοι μυστήρια τῆς μιγνυμένης οὐδὲν ἧττον μαθήσεται (Pack, *Onirocriticon*, 97.9–14; ET: White, *Oneirocritica*, 65).

28. *Oneirokritika* 1.78; Pack, *Onirocriticon*, 88.20f.

29. Suzanne MacAlister interprets Artemidoros as associating secrets with the female body and the feminine, as opposed to the masculine public sphere ("Gender as Sign and Symbolism in Artemidoros' *Oneirokritika*: Social Aspirations and Anxieties," *Helios* 19 [1992] 147).

Maud W. Gleason notes that Polemo, a second-century physiognomist, describes a female

Why is woman/woman intercourse unnatural for Artemidoros? Woman/woman relations occur in the text just after a man kissing his penis or practicing fellatio with himself and just before intercourse with deities, corpses, and animals. Relations with deities, corpses, and animals may be classified as unnatural because these beings represent other realms. Sex between a man and a deity, a corpse, or an animal is a union between two radically different spheres of existence. Is oral masturbation unnatural because one is too much like oneself, since one person cannot represent a human social hierarchy? This would mean that natural sexual relations are those between beings within the same realm but differing from one another in some fundamental way, such as gender, age, legal status, or social status. That is, natural sexual relations represent and create human social dominance and hierarchy. Does woman/woman intercourse follow upon oral masturbation because women are too much like each other and therefore do not represent a human social hierarchy?

No distinction is made as to rich or poor women, young or old, slave or free, characteristics that would differentiate the female partners from each other (as male/male relations had been differentiated). Androcentric systems of social classification typically do not contain the same gradations for women as for men, often because they do not bother to classify some types of women, such as slave women, poor women, or old women. In some ways, such women are off the scale of what constitutes womanhood, since they are not the wives of the adult, free men who create the classificatory systems (obviously some free men had old wives, but the young, sexually receptive, and childbearing woman is the dominant image of woman here; the system did not compensate for difference in this case). In this way, two women (read: "free, adult women who could be the wives of the intended readers") engaged with each other do not represent a social hierarchy and are therefore too much like each other. Or perhaps a woman's sexual love with another woman cannot be natural because one of the women is taking the active role and thereby usurping the natural role of the man.

An alternative interpretation is that woman/woman intercourse is unnatural because Artemidoros senses that the verb "to penetrate/possess" does not accurately describe the sexual relations that women generally have

---

as one who hides what she is thinking ("The Semiotics of Gender: Physiognomy and Self-Fashioning in the Second Century C.E.," in *Before Sexuality: The Construction of Erotic Experience in the Ancient Greek World*, ed. David M. Halperin, John J. Winkler, and Froma I. Zeitlin [Princeton: Princeton University Press, 1990] 391f). If Artemidoros were following this line of thinking, the woman's sharing of her secrets would constitute nonfeminine behavior.

We cannot know whether having a woman share her secrets with another woman portends a good or bad outcome.

with one another, that female/female relations are outside of the category of penetration. This would explain why penetration of a male friend is unconventional, but not unnatural (because men naturally penetrate), whereas female/female relations are so anomalous that they are unnatural.[30] For a man to penetrate his slave is natural, legal, and customary because it is male penetration (and hence, natural) of a person of lower status to whom he has legal access.

John Winkler's interpretation accords well with what I have presented here. His principal thesis in interpreting Artemidoros's treatment of sexual dreams is that "nature" really means "culture," that Artemidoros defines as natural those values long held by his culture to be proper. Sexual relations between women are a prime example for Winkler of nature meaning culture:

> The basic idea seems to be that unnatural acts do not involve any representation of human social hierarchy. . . . Sex between women is here viewed as not intrinsically equipped to display the hierarchy of its participants. . . . Sexual relations between women are here classed as "unnatural" because "nature" assumes that what are significant in sexual activity are (i) men, (ii) penises that penetrate, and (iii) the articulation thereby of relative statuses through relations of dominance. . . . Woman-woman intercourse is "unnatural" only and exactly insofar as it lies outside that determinate field of meaning. The "unnatural" is meaningless: "nature" once more turns out to stand for "culture."[31]

The single element common to all of the types of sexual relations found in the unnatural category is that they do not recreate a human social hierarchy. Artemidoros's concepts of natural and unnatural are in line with Ptolemy, Soranos, and those other authors investigated in this book for whom natural sexual relations are intrinsically unequal. We need to know the patterns of social dominance within Artemidoros's culture in order to understand why it is natural, legal, and customary for a man to penetrate his male slave, but unnatural for two women to be sexual with each other. Although Artemidoros describes female/female sexual relations within an active/passive framework by using the verb "to possess/to penetrate"

---

30. See also *Oneirokritika* 2.12: Ὕαινα δὲ γυναῖκα σημαίνει ἀνδρόγυννον ἢ φαρμακίδα καὶ ἄνδρα κίναιδον οὐκ εὐγνώμονα (Pack, *Onirocriticon*, 125.4f): "The hyena signifies an androgynous woman or a witch and a man who is an unreasonable [i.e., probably in the sense of "outrageous"] *kinaidos*." Translation my own.

See *Oneirokritika* 5.65, in which Artemidoros speaks of a "notorious *kinaidos* . . . who is both effeminate and androgynous." Translation my own.

31. Winkler, *Constraints*, 38–40.

(*perainō*), his classification of these relations as solely unnatural reveals that female homoeroticism finds no place in his cultural schema with its requisite patterns of social dominance. Thus, in Artemidoros's eyes, female penetration is not real penetration, and female homoeroticism is a pale and futile imitation of male sexual behavior.

Illustrations

Fig. 1. Plate from the Greek Island of Thera. Ca. 620 BCE. CE 34. Discussion on p. 57.

Fig. 2. Attic Red-figure *Kylix*. Ca. 515–495 BCE. R207. Apollodoros. Discussion on p. 57.

Fig. 3. Attic Red-figure Type B *Kylix*. Ca. 470–460 BCE. Perhaps by the Boot Painter. Collection of the J. Paul Getty Museum, Malibu, California. Accession Number 83.AE.251. Discussion on pp. 57–58.

Figs. 4, 5. Attic Red-figure Type C Amphora. Ca. 490 BCE. Attributed to the Flying-Angel Painter. Discussion on p. 58.

Fig. 6. Apulian *Pelike* from Taranto, Italy, Ca. 350 BCE. Discussion on p. 58.

Fig. 7. Augustan funerary relief of two women with their right hands clasped in the classic gesture of ancient Roman married couples. 27 BCE–14 CE. British Museum Sculpture 2276. *Corpus Inscriptionum Latinarum* 6/3.18524. Discussion on pp. 59–60.

Fig. 8. Oval lead tablet from Hermoupolis Magna (known today as el-Ashmunen), Upper Egypt. 3d/4th C. CE. Inscribed with a Greek love spell to attract Gorgonia to Sophia. Biblioteca Medicea Laurenziana, Florence, Italy. *PSI* 28. By permission of the Ministero per i Beni Culturali e Ambientali. All rights reserved. Discussion on pp. 81–90.

Fig. 11. Close-up of the tablet B illustrated in fig. 10. Line 4: the Greek letter H. Discussion on pp. 94–96.

Figs. 9, 10. Two lead tablets from Panopolis (known earlier as Achmim), Upper Egypt. Probably 2d C. CE. Originally fastened together to form a diptych and inscribed with a Greek love spell to attract Nike to Pantous/Paitous. The spell is possibly homoerotic. *Suppl. Mag.*, 1.37 Archäologisches Institut of the University of Heidelberg. Discussion on pp. 90–96.

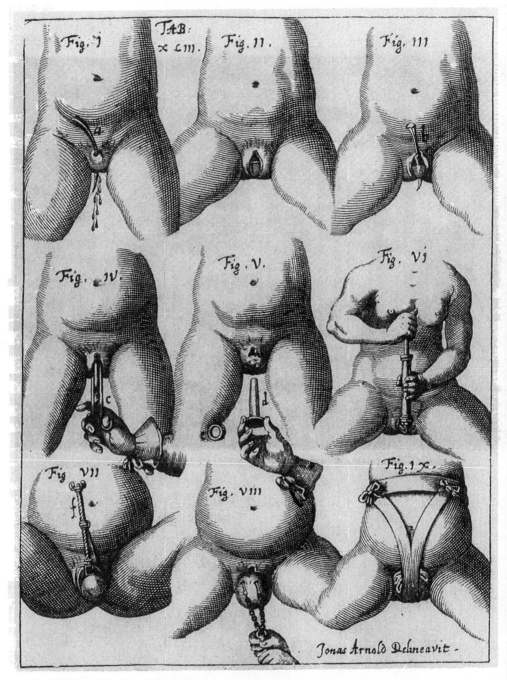

Fig. 12. Illustration from a seventeenth-C. surgical textbook. Figure IV illustrates a clitoridectomy on an adult woman, demonstrating that the clitoridectomy described by Soranos (1st /2d C. CE) continued to be carried out for many centuries. Johannes Scultetus, *Wundarztneyisches Zeughauß* (Frankfurt: 1666). Discussion on pp. 162–71.

PART TWO

Early Christian Responses to
Female Homoeroticism

Introduction: Of British Schoolteachers
and Romans 1

The place: Edinburgh, Scotland. The time: 1811. Miss Marianne Woods and Miss Jane Pirie, two schoolteachers accused of having had a sexual relationship with each other, deny the charges and sue their accusers for libel. The schoolteachers' lawyer tries to discredit Miss Jane Cumming, the young school girl who claims that she has observed Miss Woods and Miss Pirie having sex together. The lawyer, Mr. Clerk, argues that Miss Cumming is an unreliable witness because she is of illegitimate birth, colored, and a native of India. The defendants in the libel suit have to produce evidence that sexual relations between women are even possible. That evidence includes Paul's Letter to the Romans 1:26, as well as some of the passages discussed in part I of this book (Lucian, Martial, Juvenal, Phaedrus). Upon appeal, the House of Lords decides in 1819 in favor of the schoolteachers. Several of the lords claim that, while such lascivious behavior might exist in Miss Cumming's native India, a British woman is incapable of such an act.

In other words, the schoolteachers won their case on the grounds that sexual contact between two women, or in any case, between two British women, was impossible. Their lawyer conceded that the ancients mentioned sexual relations between two women, but that these always included the use of a penetrating object. Since the schoolgirl had never alleged the use of an artificial instrument, then no sexual act could have taken place. Concerning the New Testament, Mr. Clerk argued that, if it referred to relations between women, then an artificial instrument must be involved, but that Rom 1:26 more likely referred to sodomy between a woman and a man.[1]

---

1. For a full account of the proceedings, see Lillian Faderman, *Scotch Verdict* (New York: Quill, 1983) esp. 211f, 220f; Lillian Faderman, *Surpassing the Love of Men: Romantic Friendship*

In many ways, this case epitomizes a centuries-old debate on whether a woman is even capable of sexually loving another woman. The British lawyer argued that the primitive, dark-skinned women of the East might engage in such vile activities, but that British women were quite simply incapable of it. As we saw above, in the ancient world, members of the Roman upper class believed that Greek women in their licentiousness might resort to such activities, but that this behavior had no history among virtuous Roman matrons. Similarly, Jews warned the daughters of Israel not to walk in the ways of the Canaanites and the Egyptians, among whom women even married other women.

And the focus on an artificial instrument is both ancient and modern. Male lawyers, judges, poets, and theologians wonder again and again: "What could women ever possibly do together without one?" Across centuries these men share a fundamental assumption about female sexuality, namely that female pleasure requires a penis. Throughout Western history we find the male creators of culture and of ideology wavering between assuming that sexual relations between women do not exist at all—indeed cannot exist—and imagining that if they do, then the women must be capable of penetration, whether with an appendage on their own bodies, such as an enlarged clitoris, or with an imitation penis or other penetrating object.

We have seen authors of the Roman period presenting female homoeroticism as imitative of phallocentric sexuality. Nevertheless, people in the Roman world must have had a harder time denying its very existence than the citizens of nineteenth-century Edinburgh. Astrologers spoke about *tribades* on street corners. Dream interpreters told about female homoerotic dreams in marketplaces throughout the Roman world. Roman poets satirized *tribades*, while physicians attempted to cure them. Rabbis debated whether Jewish women who had sexual relations with other women could eat the priestly offerings. The scribes of Egypt wrote love spells for women to attract and bind other women to them. In sum, early Christianity was born into a world in which people from various walks of life acknowledged that women could have sexual contact with other women. The cities in which Paul of Tarsus, Clement of Alexandria, and John Chrysostom lived, taught, wrote, and preached were not the Edinburgh of the nineteenth century.

I will demonstrate in the coming chapters that early Christians shared certain fundamental assumptions about sexual relations and gender with their contemporaries and viewed female homoeroticism negatively for rea-

---

and Love between Women from the Renaissance to the Present (New York: William Morrow, 1981) 147–54.

sons similar to those of their contemporaries. As we have seen, nearly all of the extant Roman-period sources on female homoeroticism condemn it, defining it as monstrous, unnatural, diseased, and more. Similarly, early Christian sources strongly condemn sexual love between women. And while early Christians promoted somewhat different sexual behaviors from those of their pagan and Jewish contemporaries—such as a greater focus on celibacy—early Christians nevertheless conceptualized female homoeroticism in many of the same ways we have already seen in this book. These similarities across ethnic and religious lines reveal a set of assumptions about gender and the erotic common to shapers of culture throughout the Roman world.

Against the background of the preceding chapters, we are not surprised to learn that the apostle Paul speaks of a married woman as a woman "under a man" (*hypandros*) or that he describes man as the head of woman.[2] Within the Roman world, a wife, even if she is "under a man," had rights and responsibilities. For example, within ancient Jewish law, a woman had the right to sexual intercourse, in order that she might have pleasure and bear children, upon whose financial support she depended in her old age. Similarly, Paul reminds married couples of their mutual right to sexual intercourse.[3] He even goes a step further by speaking of a woman's authority over (*exousiazō*) her husband's body, although, for social, economic, and political reasons, women had far less power actually to exert such authority than men.

On the whole, we can characterize Paul's understanding of women as both culture-bound and forward-looking. Paul did call for gender differentiation in hair style and for the veiling of women, and possibly called for the silence of women in the church. He apparently assumed a one-seed theory of conception based on female passivity; thus, Paul calls a wife her husband's "vessel."[4] But he also worked closely with women colleagues, such as the teacher Prisca; the apostle Junia; his fellow workers Euhodia and Syntyche; his fellow laborers Tryphaina, Tryphosa, and Persis; Phoebe, minister of the church in Kenchraia; and more.[5] Paul expressed respect for the labor and leadership of these women within the church and expressed a vision of women and men being one in Christ.[6] Within this larger picture of Paul's complex theological understanding of gender, I classify Paul's

2. Rom 7:2; 1 Cor 11:3.
3. 1 Cor 7:1–5.
4. 1 Cor 11:2–16; 14:33b–36; 1 Thess 4:4. See esp. O. Larry Yarbrough, *Not Like the Gentiles: Marriage Rules in the Letters of Paul* (SBL Dissertation Series 80; Atlanta: Scholars Press, 1985) 68–73.
5. Acts 18:2, 18, 26; Rom 16:1f, 3f, 7, 12; 1 Cor 16:19; and Phil 4:2f.
6. Gal 3:28.

condemnation of sexual relations between women as based upon the assumption widely shared within the Roman world that nature calls for men to be superordinate and active and for women to be subordinate and passive.

In the coming pages I devote far greater attention to Paul than to any other author in this book for one very simple reason: Paul has held greater authority within Western culture than any other author I discuss. While Martial or Juvenal, as upper-class Roman men, had a far greater impact on their own world than did Paul, a little-known provincial from an obscure eastern cult, Paul's influence exceeded their own in subsequent centuries. And of Paul's various letters, his Letter to the Romans has had the greatest impact of all. The most authoritative theologians within Christian history have commented on it: Origen, Augustine, Martin Luther, John Calvin, and Karl Barth. Vivid interest in Paul's Letter to the Romans continues today, as marked by the publication of dozens of commentaries and scholarly studies each year. Because of the influential character of Paul's Letter to the Romans and the plethora of commentaries on it, I have structured my discussion of Paul's condemnation of sexual love between women (Rom 1:26) in three chapters.

The general reader may be surprised at the change of pace in the coming three chapters. Some readers may ask themselves why I go into such detail on individual words and points that seem peripheral to the subject of sexual love between women. Consulting the select annotated bibliography at the back of this book can help readers to understand why I do this. The annotated bibliography can give readers a sense of the intensity and variety of commentary on Rom 1:26f. Interpreters have read these verses in vastly different ways. Some believe that Paul condemns nothing, others that he condemns bestiality or anal intercourse, and yet others that he condemns heterosexuals having homosexual experiences. Some think that Paul defined same-sex sexual relations as sin, others that he saw these to be a result of sin, while others claim that Paul is merely pointing out societal disapproval of them. How to get out of this morass? The only way out of it is through it. Some interpretations have stronger evidence to support them. We need to examine each verse, weigh each argument, and consider several interpretive frameworks. In this painstaking process, we will discover that the contradictory interpretations result, in part, from the varying ways in which people understand Paul's theology, from their selection of ancient texts against which to read Paul, from their analysis of the structure of Romans 1 and of Romans as a whole, and from their assessment of Paul as an authority for the churches today.

In order to provide readers with a solid basis for interpreting Paul's teaching on homoeroticism and for bringing that interpretation into church and public policy debates about lesbians, gay men, and bisexuals, I have engaged a broad range of Pauline interpretation. A detail within Rom 1:18–32 that is irrelevant for one interpreter is central for another. A thorough reading of the three chapters on Paul will enable readers to debate Paul's teaching on same-sex love with persons from various schools of thought.

In the first of the chapters on Romans, I consider the letter as a whole and describe how different interpretations of the whole of Romans affect our reading of Paul's castigation of female homoeroticism. I then proceed to a verse-by-verse commentary on Rom 1:18–32, which forms the immediate context of Rom 1:26. Finally, in the third chapter I employ the study of intertextuality to help us reconstruct how Paul's earliest readers may have read him. I achieve this by presenting texts that Paul's earliest readers may have known and of which we find echoes in Romans 1.

After interpreting Paul, I test my interpretation of him by examining other early Christian condemnations of female homoeroticism. Early Christian apocalyptic visions of hell, as well as Tertullian, Clement of Alexandria, Hippolytos on the Naassenes, John Chrysostom, Shenute, and Augustine, replicate many of the images and concepts we have already encountered: the active/passive distinction, the natural versus the unnatural, female subordination, lack of focus on procreation in the condemnation of female homoeroticism (with a corresponding centrality of the male seed), and a struggle to fit female homoeroticism within an asymmetrical phallocentric construction of sexuality.

Early Christian theology does, however, give rise to specifically Christian angles on same-sex love. Early Christians mention female homoeroticism together with male homoeroticism more frequently than other ancient authors. Their visions of homoerotic women and men together in one pit in hell illustrates this tendency. By considering homoerotic women and men together, early Christians may have played a crucial—and as yet unrecognized—role in the development of the concept of homosexuality. Further, the early Christian creation of widespread monastic communities, which provided favorable conditions for same-sex love, led early Christian writers to a heightened awareness of homoerotic attraction. In contrast, classical Greek writers may have known about same-sex love occurring in women's quarters but paid it little attention. And while one strand of rabbinic tradition condemns sexual love between women as harlotry, the majority tradition does not. These rabbis did not overly concern themselves with the female romantic friendships that may have existed in polygynous marriages and other homosocial environments. Such church fathers as John Chrysostom, Shenute, and Augustine, did, however, cast their gaze on women's church communities and attempt to regulate them.

In all of this discussion, the figure within early Christianity most strikingly absent is Jesus of Nazareth himself. We know of no saying attributed
to Jesus, either within the New Testament or within any of the many ancient gospels not included in the canon, in which he comments on sexual
love between men or between women. Such love was apparently not a major concern to him. In spite of this, the early church set itself on a path that
in the late twentieth century has resulted in opposition to lesbian, gay, and
bisexual civil rights and ecclesial recognition as a hallmark of most forms of
Christianity.

Paul's Letter to the Romans: Interpretive Frameworks and Female Homoeroticism

aul explicitly addresses female homoeroticism only once, in his Letter to the Romans (1:26f),[1] in which he speaks of women who give up natural intercourse for unnatural and of men who analogously reject natural intercourse with women and become enflamed with passion for other males.

Even though Paul restricts his comments on homoeroticism to this and one other passage (1 Cor 6:9f, which refers to sexual relations between males), his views have deeply impressed themselves on Western culture. The following American colonial statute from New Haven (and the many others that have placed the death penalty on male-male sexual relations throughout history) illustrates this legacy: "If any man lyeth with mankinde, as a man lyeth with a woman, both of them have committed abomination, they both shall surely be put to death. Levit. 20. 13. And if any woman change the naturall use, into that which is against nature, as Rom. 1. 26. she shall be liable to the same sentence, and punishment."[2] Paul's influence, however, is by no means limited to the past. Christian opponents of lesbian and gay civil rights today—whether from within the Roman

---

1. For the text of Rom 1:18–32, see below, pp. 215f.

2. The original statute appeared in *New Haven's Settling in New England: And Some Lawes for Government* (London: printed by M.S. for Livewell Chapman, 1656). The whole of *New Haven's Settling* is reprinted in J. Hammond Trumbull, ed., *The True-Blue Laws of Connecticut and New Haven and the False Blue-Laws* (Hartford: American, 1876) 199; and quoted and discussed in Jonathan Ned Katz, *Gay/Lesbian Almanac: A New Documentary* (New York: Harper and Row, 1983) 101f, 676f, n. 30. Katz notes that this law, dated to March 1, 1656, was one of the few that placed the death penalty on women's "changing the 'natural use.'" He states that the statute remained in effect for ten years, until Connecticut, whose sodomy statute applied only to men, annexed New Haven.

Catholic hierarchy or from within fundamentalist or mainstream Protestantism—often cite Rom 1:26f in support of their views.

Because of its canonical status, Paul's condemnation of female and male homoeroticism enjoys a privileged and authoritative position not only within the church, but also, through its long-lasting influence, on the laws and culture of the Western world. In countries with a majority-Christian culture, very few people can actually cite Rom 1:26f, but most know that many Christians condemn lesbians and gay men as sinners. And, whereas Christian influence on questions of foreign or economic policy has waned to the point of negligibility, many politicians and private citizens alike continue to grant considerable authority to church teachings on sexuality and family life. While church doctrine on homoeroticism has undergone some change over time, it ultimately derives from the Bible. Thus, whether or not Western people have ever heard of Paul's Letter to the Romans, it affects their lives.

The Letter to the Romans has enjoyed particular prominence among Protestant theologians ever since the Reformation initiated by Martin Luther, owing to the reformers' strong emphasis on doctrines that they found in Romans (such as justification[3] by faith, rather than by works, or predestination). The rise of historical-critical biblical scholarship has also strengthened the impact of Romans, since virtually all scholars agree that Romans is one of the earliest writings within the New Testament and that Paul himself (rather than one of his students or later followers) composed the letter. The letter's theological complexity has added to its fascination and attracted literally hundreds of scholarly interpreters.

How does Paul's condemnation of homoeroticism fit into the larger theological purposes of this influential early Christian document? Scholars have given very different answers to this question, depending on their interpretive approach to the Letter to the Romans as a whole. In this chapter I will show how a scholar's interpretation of Paul's view of homoeroticism differs according to that interpretive approach. To do this, I will examine and critique several different approaches to Romans. First, I will treat two literary approaches, and second, I will present and critique several interpretive frameworks for explaining the overall theological and conceptual themes of Romans. Because Paul's Letter to the Romans contains a number of apparent contradictions, we may need more than one model of interpretation in order to address the multilayered arguments found within it. In the following two chapters, I first present a verse-by-verse commen-

3. "Justification" (e.g., Rom 3:20, 28) refers to human beings being made right with God, being cleared of blame by God, whereas "righteousness" (e.g., Rom 1:17) signifies God's fair and just treatment of human beings.

tary and then several reconstructions of how the earliest readers of Romans may have understood the letter. I shall draw upon each of the readings presented in this chapter as I offer my own historical and theological interpretation of Rom 1:18–32. Rather than aiming to establish a single correct interpretation or the original authorial intent—which would be impossible goals—I put forth interpretations that are plausible within the letter's earliest cultural and intellectual context.

Literary Approaches to Romans

Some interpreters attempt to understand Paul's Letter to the Romans through literary means, utilizing such methods as ancient rhetorical theory, epistolary theory, and genre criticism for analyzing Paul's arguments.[4]

I find genre analysis to be the most fruitful of these methods for interpreting Romans, specifically David Aune's classification of Romans. He has defined it as a speech of exhortation (*logos protreptikos*) cast into the frame of a letter.[5] Aune argues that exhortation, or protreptic, is concerned with how to persuade (*protrepō*) or to dissuade. Protreptic is also rooted in philosophy, where it can be paired with censure in order to bring people to the truth.[6] The literary genre of the speech of exhortation likely draws upon these traditions of protreptic. No ancient theorist, however, describes the speech of exhortation, and only a few examples of it are known.[7]

For Aune, Paul taught and argued with people in order to convert them

4. In addition to these approaches, the tools of modern rhetorical theory—with its emphasis on persuasion and the relationship between the author and the audience—may also help us to understand Romans. Such theory could assist us because whether or not Paul studied formal rhetoric, he clearly wanted to persuade his readers. Unfortunately, since no one has yet undertaken a thorough analysis of the entire Letter to the Romans on the basis of contemporary rhetorical theory, I cannot employ it here. Rhetorical analysis needs to be based on the whole of a work and not just on one part of it.

Antoinette Clark Wire describes one hindrance to applying contemporary rhetorical criticism to the Pauline letters, namely the dogmatic theological position of many contemporary interpreters that Paul is always right: "Because an argument Paul makes cannot be rejected as unconvincing, it also cannot convince. In this way the authority we [Christians in the twentieth century] attribute to Paul prevents him from persuading us. . . . Understanding Paul's letters as argument may be possible in the church only when there is a shift in its view of the Bible's authority. . . . Paul's letters' authority depends on free assent to Paul's arguments because they are convincing" (Antoinette Clark Wire, *The Corinthian Women Prophets: A Reconstruction through Paul's Rhetoric* [Minneapolis: Fortress, 1990] 10). I fully agree with Wire that we need to study how Paul tried to persuade his readers and to consider the possibility that he did not always convince them.

5. David E. Aune, "Romans as a *Logos Protreptikos*," in *The Romans Debate*, ed. Karl P. Donfried (rev. and exp. ed. of the 1977 ed.; Peabody, MA: Hendrickson, 1991) 278–96.

6. Ibid., 279f.

7. E.g., Aristotle, *Protreptikos*; Cicero, *Hortensius*; and Iamblichos, *Protreptikos*.

and modeled himself upon philosophers who exhorted people to take up the philosophical way of life. He believes that Paul developed some portions of Romans orally in his public ministry, including that on homoeroticism, and later combined them into a written exhortation in order to persuade people to believe his understanding of the gospel and to behave in accordance with it.

Aune views Rom 1:16–4:25 as a textual unit that functions as a protreptic *elenchos* ("censure," "argument of disproof" or "of refutation"), which contains elements of diatribe (a dialogical style of admonition), and may exemplify the way that Paul dealt with outsiders.[8] Within this broad censure, Rom 1:16–32 is a narrative describing how God handed over to vice primitive people who knew God but became idolaters.[9] In contrast, Aune sees Rom 5:1–8:39 as a positive *endeiktikos* ("demonstration," "argument of proof") focusing on insiders. Thus, in Aune's view, Paul gives the Roman Christians concrete examples of the ways in which he preached the gospel to a variety of people in different settings, refuting the life practices of outsiders and demonstrating the value to insiders of particular life choices.[10]

Epistolary theorist Stanley Stowers represents a variation of this view in that he sees Romans as a protreptic letter.[11] (Thus, in contrast to Aune, Stowers views Romans as originally and intrinsically a letter, rather than as a speech or series of speeches cast into the framework of a letter.) He notes that the Stoic philosopher Epiktetos, a contemporary of Paul, describes the protreptic style as characterized by "[t]he ability to show to the individual, as well as to the crowd, the warring inconsistency in which they are floundering about, and how they are paying attention to anything rather than

8. Notice that Aune's first textual unit (1:16–4:25) nearly overlaps with Jewett's first proof (1:18–4:25). Karl Donfried finds significant common ground between the analyses of Jewett and Aune, especially with respect to structure (in *The Romans Debate*, lvii–lxi).

9. Aune, "Romans," 291. The other units are: Romans 9–11 (digression) and Rom 12: 1–15:13 (paraenetic section). The epistolary frame is Rom 1:1–15 and 15:14–16:27.

10. Aune, "Romans," 296.

11. Stanley K. Stowers, *Letter Writing in Greco-Roman Antiquity* (Philadelphia: Westminster, 1986) 112–14. Stowers succinctly defines Romans as "a protreptic letter that makes central use of indirect admonition by means of censorious address to imaginary interlocutors in the style of the diatribe (2:1–5, 17–29; 9:19–20; 11:13–25; 14:4, 10)" (Ibid., 128). An example of an ancient protreptic letter with parallels to Romans is the pseudonymous Cynic epistle of Anacharsis to Croesus (Anne M. McGuire, trans., in *The Cynic Epistles*, ed. Abraham J. Malherbe [Missoula, MT: Scholars Press, 1977] 47–51; translation reprinted in Stowers, *Letter Writing*, 118–21).

See also Stanley K. Stowers, *A Rereading of Romans: Justice, Jews, and Gentiles* (New Haven: Yale University Press, 1994), which appeared just as this manuscript was ready to go to press.

what they truly want. For they want the things that conduce to happiness, but they are looking for them in the wrong place."[12] While Paul and other Christians might argue that salvation, rather than happiness, is what people really want, Stowers suggests that the protreptic style, as defined by Epiktetos, would clearly appeal to early Christians, who were strongly interested in moral exhortation.[13] Paul's assertion that these people claim to be wise, but are really fools (v. 22)[14] could exemplify "the warring inconsistency in which they are floundering about." And we could interpret the whole of Rom 1:18–32 as describing confused people, who do not do what they really want, assuming that people truly want to be in right relation to God. In this reading, falsely directed attention includes homoeroticism, an example of a distraction from what is central in life.[15]

The classification of Romans as protreptic makes sense of certain elements of Romans 1. Specifically, the category "censure" (elenchos) clarifies its individual polemical features, such as the condemnation of idolatry and of homoeroticism. Interpreted as part of a censorious exhortation, the homoeroticism of Romans 1 emerges clearly as a behavior absolutely opposed to Paul's understanding of the gospel.[16] Thus, the protreptic category helps us to recognize the condemnation of homoeroticism as simultaneously theological and ethical, since within protreptic it makes no sense to distinguish sharply between theology (teachings about God and about the human relation to the divine) and ethics (teachings about moral behavior). As an element of a protreptic work, homoeroticism is a theological issue in that it results from human beings turning away from God, and an ethical one in that humans who have turned away from God falsely direct their erotic impulses.

An alternate, but related, way to interpret Romans is to employ ancient rhetorical theory. Commentators who work with ancient rhetorical the-

---

12. *Discourses* 3.23.34; W. A. Oldfather, ed. and trans., *Epictetus: The Discourses as Reported by Arrian, the Manual, and Fragments* (LCL; Cambridge, MA: Harvard University Press, 1928) 182f.

13. In addition to Romans, see such other early Christian examples of protreptic as *Epistle to Diognetus* and Clement of Alexandria, *Protreptikos*.

14. Cf. 1 Cor 1:26–31, in which Paul expresses his deep suspicion of worldly wisdom.

15. Stowers argues that the protreptic elements of Romans include Paul's introducing the Roman congregation to his understanding of the gospel, presenting himself to them as a teacher, and censuring them for attitudes that prevent them from accepting his gospel (*Letter Writing,* 114; on elements of admonition see also 128; and Stanley Kent Stowers, *The Diatribe and Paul's Letter to the Romans* [SBLDS 57; Chico, CA: Scholars Press, 1981]).

16. The advantages of Aune's interpretation apply also to that of Stowers, and the differences between a protreptic letter and a protreptic speech in an epistolary framework are irrelevant for Romans 1.

ory ask whether Paul studied formal rhetoric and used it in his Letter to the Romans. Some interpreters say that he did, especially since educated people in the Roman world often used formal rhetoric to persuade others. A lawyer defending or accusing a person in a law court used *forensic* (judicial) rhetoric to persuade a judge concerning the justice or injustice of the person's past actions. A politician employed *deliberative* (advising) rhetoric to persuade an assembly to take or not to take a future action, such as going to war. And when people wanted to praise what was honorable or to lay blame for what was shameful in the present, they crafted their speech using *epideiktic* (demonstrative or panegyric) rhetoric. Such ancient rhetorical theoreticians as Aristotle, Cicero, and Quintilian defined these three species or genres of formal rhetoric and gave instructions on how to construct the subunits necessary for each genre, while noting that the genres often overlapped.[17] An ancient author, such as Paul, could implement these three modes of persuasion in a variety of oral and written genres.[18]

Some problems do, however, inhere in applying ancient rhetorical theory to the New Testament. First, ancient rhetoricians discuss only some types of persuasive speaking and writing. Beyond the three main species, they pay only peripheral attention to other types, such as exhortation. If Paul had a purpose other than those of the three rhetorical genres, then formal rhetoric would not have suited his purposes in Romans. Further, scholars have difficulty classifying ancient literature according to the three main species, since rhetorically trained authors sometimes combined elements of each, and ancient theorists in fact recognized that these rhetorical genres are constructs and can overlap. Finally, we are not even certain whether Paul was particularly well trained in formal rhetoric beyond the elementary techniques of rhetoric that children learned in school.

On the other hand, even with these problems, ancient rhetorical theory could nevertheless help to illuminate Romans. Robert Jewett builds the case for applying ancient rhetorical criticism to Pauline studies by drawing upon ancient school exercise handbooks, rather than just on Aristotle, Cicero, and Quintilian; Paul probably used such handbooks in his own early elementary education, but may never have studied the more learned representatives of formal rhetoric.

Jewett holds that Romans contains epideiktic rhetoric (giving praise or blame), used to reinforce values held by the community to which Paul was

---

17. Quintilian, *Institutio Oratoria* 3.4.16.

18. For suggestions as to how the early church developed its own forms of rhetoric beyond those outlined by the classical rhetoricians, see, e.g., Burton Mack, *Rhetoric and the New Testament* (Minneapolis: Fortress, 1990) 94–97.

writing.[19] According to his reading, Paul was trying to foster support among the Roman Christians for his goal of "world unification through the gospel,"[20] and was seeking the Roman Christians' cooperation in his future missionary activities. For Jewett, Romans consists of an introduction (*exordium:* 1:1–12), a narration of some background information (*narratio:* 1:13–15), a thesis statement (*propositio:* 1:16f),[21] a series of four different proofs of the thesis (*probatio:* 1:18–15:13), and a conclusion (*peroratio:* 15:14–16:27). Rom 1:18–32 begins the first proof (1:18–4:25). In this first proof, which is a confirmation (*confirmatio*) of the letter's main thesis that the gospel embodies God's righteousness, Paul shows that God impartially grants righteousness to both Jews and gentiles by faith. Paul's overall focus is on gentile believers who praise the God of Israel by coming to the gospel (Rom 15:7–13), rather than, for example, on God's righteousness being disclosed apart from the Jewish law (Rom 3:21), as earlier generations of commentators have argued. For Jewett, rhetorical analysis shows that Paul's theological vision was to unify God's world on the basis of the gospel, transcending Jewish and other cultural barriers. Further, according to Jewett, rhetorical criticism demonstrates the coherence of Paul's theological argument, which culminates in the last chapters (sometimes called ethical or practical), rather than in earlier ones (sometimes called doctrinal or theological). Thus, rhetorical criticism, by providing an outline for Rom 1:18–15:13 as a series of four proofs of the thesis in Rom 1:16f, enables us to see the inextricable link in Romans between theology and ethics and between faith and tolerance.[22]

In this interpretation, homoeroticism is an elaboration on the "human distortion" that shows the presence of God's wrath.[23] The mention of ho-

<del></del>

---

19. Robert Jewett, "Following the Argument of Romans," in *The Romans Debate*, ed. Karl P. Donfried (rev. and exp. ed. of the 1977 ed.; Peabody, MA: Hendrickson, 1991) 265–77. Other scholars also classify Romans as epideiktic rhetoric: Marty Y. Reid, "A Rhetorical Analysis of Romans 1:1–5:21 with Attention Given to the Rhetorical Function of 5:1–21," *Perspectives in Religious Studies* 19 (1992) 255–72; Wilhelm Wuellner, "Paul's Rhetoric of Argumentation in Romans: An Alternative to the Donfried-Karris Debate over Romans," in *The Romans Debate*, ed. Donfried, 128–46; and George A. Kennedy, *New Testament Interpretation through Rhetorical Criticism* (Chapel Hill: University of North Carolina Press, 1984) 152–56.

20. Jewett, "Following the Argument," 276.

21. Rom 1:16: "For I am not ashamed of the gospel; it is the power of God for salvation to everyone who has faith, to the Jew first and also to the Greek. (17) For in it the righteousness of God is revealed through faith for faith; as it is written, 'The one who is righteous will live by faith' [Hab 2:4]."

22. Jewett, "Following the Argument," 276f.

23. Ibid., 273.

moeroticism helps to prove the thesis of Rom 1:16f, namely that the gospel embodies God's righteousness, by confirming that God impartially judges all people, in this case, those who suppress the truth about God.

Not all interpreters who employ rhetorical criticism classify Romans as epideiktic. For example, François Vouga defines Romans as an apology (forensic rhetoric), that is, a judicial defense speech.[24] Currently, however, more interpreters favor the epideiktic classification for Romans. Contemporary interpreters also dispute how to classify Rom 1:18–32, whether as part of a proof or as a statement of the facts of the case.

From the standpoint of Romans 1, classifying Romans as protreptic is more convincing than classifying it as epideiktic, since the category "censure" (*elenchos*) better explains the polemical tone of Romans 1 than does the category "proof" (*confirmatio*).[25] Since, however, Paul had probably not advanced beyond the intermediate level in either rhetorical theory or in philosophy, he may have combined techniques and genres from both

24. François Vouga, "Römer 1,18–3,20 als narratio," *Theologie und Glaube* 77 (1987) 225–36. Vouga does not explicitly classify Romans as forensic rhetoric, but rather disputes Kennedy's claim that it is epideiktic (George A. Kennedy, *New Testament Interpretation through Rhetorical Criticism* [Chapel Hill: University of North Carolina Press, 1984] 152–56) and states that Romans is an apology (Vouga, "Römer 1,18–3,20," 225). Since Vouga aims to define the rhetorical elements of Rom 1:18–3:20, I am assuming that he means "apology" in the sense used by the rhetoricians, i.e., a defense speech in the forensic rhetorical mode, rather than in the sense used within genre criticism. (An example of the genre "apology" would be Josephus, *Against Apion*, which is a defense of Judaism against a detractor, Apion. Ancient apologies, in the sense in which genre critics employ the term, do not necessarily employ the techniques of forensic rhetoric.) Vouga would strengthen his argument if he defined what he means by "apology," why he applies it to Romans, and if he gave reasons for Romans being forensic rather than epideiktic rhetoric (if he indeed views it as forensic). He uses "rhetoric" almost in a generic sense, ignoring the distinctive ancient categories.

In Vouga's view, Rom 1:18–3:20 is the *narratio* (statement of the facts of the case), namely that all people have sinned. Homoeroticism, then, is one of the facts demonstrating human sinfulness and disobedience. Since a forensic *narratio* had a different function from an epideiktic one (see Jewett, who defines Rom 1:13–15 as the *narratio* of an epideiktic composition ["Following the Argument," 272]), and since the *narratio* occurred only rarely in deliberative rhetoric, we need a reasoned classification of the rhetorical genre of Romans in order to assess Vouga's divisions. Because ancient rhetoric taught people to compose for specific purposes and settings, defining a pericope as a *narratio* requires naming its purpose and setting.

See also Jean-Noël Aletti, who defines Rom 1:18 as the *propositio* (thesis), 1:18–32 as the *narratio*, 2:1–3:19 as the *probatio* (proof), and 3:20 as the *peroratio* (conclusion) ("Rm 1,18–3,20: Incohérence ou cohérence de l'argumentation paulinienne?" *Biblica* 69 [1988] 47–62). Aletti is equally vague about the specific type of rhetoric Paul uses in Romans, but seems to classify it as forensic.

25. Robert Jewett classifies Rom 1:18–4:25 as *confirmatio* ("Following the Argument," 273). By classifying Romans as epideiktic, however, Jewett does recognize the blaming aspects of the letter, although he does not emphasize these.

rhetoric and philosophy, not using either in a sufficiently technical fashion to lead to a consensus in current scholarship.[26] In what follows, I interpret Romans 1 as censure aimed to exhort people to the life suited to belief in Christ.[27]

Interpretive Frameworks for Romans 1:18–32

Romans is a complex theological document that lends itself to multiple interpretations, and Rom 1:18–32 contains some specific exegetical problems that contribute to this lack of consensus. At first glance the passage seems to be about sinful gentiles who, although capable of perceiving the true God in nature, instead turned away and worshiped idols.[28] But, surprisingly, Paul does not use the words "sin," "gentile," "nature,"[29] or "idol" in 1:18–32. The word "idol" does not present a major problem, since the text explicitly describes the images that the people worshiped. But what of the other terms? Is the passage about nature?[30] Is it about gentiles? Is it even about sin? Further, does Paul, for whom the gospel of Jesus Christ is so central, really believe that gentiles can know the true God independently of the gospel?[31] These latter three questions have particularly occupied scholars.

Interpreters often debate the main point of the beginning chapters of Paul's Letter to the Romans. A traditional view is that Romans 1 focuses on the sins of the gentiles, while Romans 2 discusses the sins of the Jews, leading up to the claims in Rom 3:9 and 3:23 that all human beings are under the power of sin and have sinned. In this schema, homoeroticism in

---

26. The problems of strict classification also lie in the ancient sources. E.g., Quintilian refers to the view of the rhetorician Anaximenes that oratory is divided into two (rather than three) genres, forensic and public, of which there are seven species, including exhortation. For his part, Quintilian classifies Anaximenes's species of exhortation as deliberative rhetoric (*Institutio Oratoria* 3.4.9). Since scholars classify Romans either as epideiktic or forensic, but not as deliberative, viewing the hortatory aspects of Romans in the light of deliberative rhetoric (in line with Quintilian) does not seem to be a plausible alternative to classifying Romans as protreptic.

27. I also recognize, along with Jewett and others, the centrality of God's righteousness in Romans 1–4.

28. This common-sense reading may, in part, be conditioned by traditional interpretations.

29. Paul uses ποιήματα, rather than φύσις, to designate what God has created (Rom 1:20). He, of course, does use παρὰ φύσιν and φυσικὴ χρῆσις in vv. 26f.

30. On φύσις see Helmut Koester, "*Physis*," *TWNT* 9 (1973) 246–71; or *TDNT* 9 (1974) 251–77. The interpreters whom I discuss immediately below do not consider the absence of φύσις in Rom 1:18–23.

31. I mean "gospel" in the Pauline sense of Christ's death for the sins of humanity and his resurrection (1 Cor 15:1–11).

Rom 1:26f counts as quintessential gentile degeneracy. More recent interpreters in this vein generally modify this schema by noting that Romans 1 does not specifically use the term "gentile"; they see Romans 1 as speaking generally about God's wrath. In this model, homoerotic behavior is a human failing, rather than a specifically gentile one, although Paul echoes typical Jewish antipagan polemics in selecting same-sex love as an example. According to a second view, divine impartiality (Rom 2:11) is the central theological point of these chapters and same-sex sexual expression is divine punishment for the primal sin of exchanging "the truth about God for a lie" (Rom 1:25). In a third interpretation, honor and shame are central for Paul's culture and to his Letter to the Romans. Homoeroticism in this schema poses a threat to the clearly defined sex roles characteristic of honor-and-shame cultures. It is thus principally a societal, rather than an individual, problem. By avoiding homoeroticism, the early Christians could define themselves over and against the outside society.

Each of these interpretations has a valid textual base and good supporting evidence. In what follows I will summarize one example of each in greater detail, noting its strengths and weaknesses. Since more than one textual interpretation can be valid (which is not to say that all readings are tenable), I will draw upon this plurality of interpretations in my commentary in the next chapter, which is in line with my goal of establishing plausible readings of Romans 1 that explain its coherence within Romans and its relationship to its culture.

The nineteenth-century commentators William Sanday and Arthur Headlam, who exemplify the traditional interpretation, argue that Rom 1:18–3:20 is a unit on the human inability to become righteous in God's sight. For them, Paul first describes the moral failure of the heathen in Rom 1:18–32, makes a transition to the Jews in 2:1–16, and then describes the moral failure of the Jews in 2:17–29.[32] In Rom 3:1–8 Paul responds to casuistical objections, while in Rom 3:9–20 he closes the whole argument by asserting a "Universal Failure to Attain Righteousness."[33] This unit is framed both by Rom 1:16f, which states the thesis that humans can attain righteousness not through their own work, but rather through faith; and by Rom 3:21–26, which shows how God's righteousness manifests itself.

For Sanday and Headlam, Rom 1:26f describes the moral corruption that God hands down as punishment for idolatry. They argue that heathen

32. William Sanday and Arthur C. Headlam, *A Critical and Exegetical Commentary on the Epistle to the Romans* (International Critical Commentary; 5th ed.; Edinburgh: Clark, 1902) 39–68.
33. Ibid., 68–81.

deities allowed their followers "to follow their own unbridled passions."[34] Of 1:26 they write, "God gave them up to the vilest passions. Women behaved like monsters who had forgotten their sex."[35] Thus, Sanday and Headlam understood same-sex sexual expression to be behavior typical for idol-worshipers and therefore Rom 1:26f to epitomize gentile sinfulness.

Pagan deities, however, were actually not as tolerant of sexual love between women as Sanday and Headlam would have us believe. As we saw above, even Aphrodite was displeased with Bitto and Nannion,[36] and Isis remedied the situation of the "monstrous" love which Iphis bore for Ianthe by changing Iphis into a male.[37] Further, the image of monstrous women who had forgotten their feminine sex also correlates closely with what pagans were writing about women who had sexual relations with other women. Thus, while Sanday and Headlam may be correct in arguing that same-sex love epitomizes gentile sinfulness for Paul, their sharp distinction between pagan and Pauline views on female homoeroticism is historically inaccurate.

Like other contemporary interpreters of Romans, I am hesitant to follow Sanday and Headlam's view that Rom 1:18–32 is about the "failure of the gentiles," since the text does not speak of "gentiles," but rather of "humans" (v. 18; NRSV: "those"). The parallel treatments of idolatry in the Wisdom of Solomon and Romans 1 have led both ancient and modern readers to see Paul as focusing in Romans 1 on gentile failure to attain righteousness.[38] However, I believe that Paul consciously avoids the term "gentile," while at the same time speaking about these people in a way reminiscent of the ways in which his Jewish contemporaries spoke about gentiles. This rhetorical strategy allows Paul to establish consensus with Jewish-Christian readers, as well as with the *former* pagans of the Roman Christian congregation—in short, with everyone.

Recognizing this as Paul's strategy, Ulrich Wilckens has modified the traditional approach by arguing that Rom 1:18–32 describes the situation of gentiles and Jews, but his interpretation does not represent a departure from the traditional approach. He takes Rom 1:18 (the revelation of God's wrath) as the antithesis to Rom 1:16f (salvation to those who have faith). All are under the wrath of God, because all, without exception, have sinned. Wilckens sees Rom 1:18 and 3:9–20 (that Jews as well as gentiles

34. Ibid., 50.
35. Ibid., 40.
36. Asklepiades in *Anthologia Graeca* 5.207 (206).
37. Ovid, *Metamorphoses* 9.666–797.
38. Sanday and Headlam's extensive chart of the precise Greek parallels between Wisdom and Romans supports their "gentile" interpretation (Sanday and Headlam, *Commentary*, 51f).

are guilty before God) as framing Rom 1:18–3:20, which is about Jews and gentiles being under God's wrath. He believes that in Rom 1:19–32 Paul condemns gentile ungodliness in a very Jewish fashion, which leads the Jewish reader to agree with him and to think that Paul is speaking about gentiles. Paul's word choice of "humans" rather than "gentiles" in Romans 1 is actually a skillful rhetorical device, because when discussing Jewish sinfulness in Romans 2, Paul retroactively shows that the condemnation of Romans 1 includes the Jewish reader. In Rom 3:1–8 Paul responds to hypothetical Jewish objections and in 3:9–20 affirms that Jews and gentiles are guilty before God. Thus, for Wilckens, Rom 1:18–32 is the first stage of the argument for the central theme of the justification of the ungodly (both Jews and gentiles), which Rom 3:21–5:21 addresses.

Wilckens describes the homosexuality of vv. 26f as "unsatisfied emptiness, which sexual egoism, bestial lust, leaves behind"[39] and as a prime example of the misery of ungodliness. In Wilckens's understanding, Paul draws upon Jewish tradition in his use of homosexuality as epitomizing gentile degeneracy. Wilckens cites examples of Jewish authors condemning sexual relations between males,[40] but does not discuss female homoeroticism at all.

Wilckens's interpretation is generally judicious, especially in his close attention to the actual wording of the text. Thus, he entitles Rom 1:18–32 "The Revelation of the Wrath of God," which approximates Paul's opening statement in 1:18, rather than, for example, "Gentile Sinfulness." He recognizes the verbal and substantive overlap between Rom 1:18–32 and both Jewish Wisdom literature (polemic against idol worshipers) and Jewish apocalyptic thinking (image of God's wrath as a judgment). Nevertheless, Wilckens's exegesis of Rom 1:26f suffers from two shortcomings. First, he apparently assumes that Jews viewed homoeroticism as epitomizing gentile degeneracy. In fact, Jewish sources show this to be true only for male homoeroticism. The few extant Jewish sources on female homoeroticism generally discuss it as a Jewish rather than gentile problem. [41] Secondly, Wilckens does not delve into the question of the meaning of "natural" and "unnatural."

Jouette Bassler has pioneered the second major interpretation by argu-

39. "[I]n der unbefriedigten Leere, die der sexuelle Egoismus, die tierische ὄρεξις . . . hinterläßt" (Ulrich Wilckens, *Der Brief an die Römer*, vol. 1 [Evangelisch-Katholischer Kommentar zum Neuen Testament 6; Zurich: Benziger, 1978; Neukirchen-Vluyn: Neukirchener Verlag, 1978] 110).

40. Ibid., 109f. In contrast to what he writes in the text, Wilckens argues in a footnote that modern medical and psychoanalytic research on the origins of homosexuality mean that one should no longer simply morally condemn it (n. 205).

41. See above for my discussion of these Jewish sources.

ing that the central theological point of Rom 1:16–2:29 is divine impartiality. She uses literary criteria to make the case that Rom 2:11 ("For
God shows no partiality") summarizes Rom 1:16–2:11 and introduces
Rom 2:12–29.[42] She outlines the *inclusio* or ring structure of Rom 1:16–
2:11, which has as its theme corresponding or exact retribution.[43] In contrast to the traditional view, Bassler further argues that a word chain[44] running from Rom 1:32 to 2:3 smoothly joins chapters 1 and 2. (A clear
break at the end of chapter 1 would support the view that Romans 1 deals
with the sins of the gentiles, while Romans 2 focuses on the sins of the
Jews.) In addition, she identifies a second word chain,[45] which sets off
Rom 2:12–29 as a separate unit built upon Paul's affirmation of divine
impartiality in Rom 2:11. In Bassler's view, Rom 3:9 ("all, both Jews and
Greeks, are under the power of sin") does not function as a summary of
the beginning chapters of Romans (as in the universal human sinfulness
model). Rom 3:9 cannot express the main point of Romans 1–2, since
Rom 1:18–2:9 allows for the possibility that gentiles will keep the law
(and are therefore not under sin), while Rom 3:9–18 holds that all, *without exception*, stand condemned as sinners. In Bassler's framework, Romans 1–2 presents God as an impartial judge of human beings on the basis
of their works, whereas Rom 3:21–31 describes God as impartial in grant-

---

42. Jouette M. Bassler, "Divine Impartiality in Paul's Letter to the Romans," *NovT* 26
(1984) 43–58; and Bassler, *Divine Impartiality: Paul and a Theological Axiom* (SBLDS 59;
Chico, CA: Scholars Press, 1982) esp. 121–70. In what follows, I refer to Bassler's article, i.e.,
the more recent statement of her thesis. See *Divine Impartiality* for more extensive discussion
of several of her points.

43. Bassler, "Divine Impartiality," 45–49 (chart on p. 47). Bassler is building upon
E. Klostermann, "Die adäquate Vergeltung in Rom 1,22–31," *ZNW* 32 (1933) 1–6. Klostermann argues that Rom 1:22–31 is based upon the ancient legal concept of *ius talionis*
(corresponding or exact retribution: "an eye for an eye and a tooth for a tooth"). Thus, Klostermann sees the structure to be:

vv. 22f ("exchanged glory [δόξα]"—sin)
v. 24 ("degrading [ἀτιμάζεσθαι]"—retribution)
v. 25 ("exchanged [μετήλλαξαν] . . . truth . . . for a lie"—sin)
vv. 26f ("exchanged [μετήλλαξαν] . . . natural intercourse for unnatural"—retribution)
v. 28 ("they did not see fit [οὐκ ἐδοκίμασαν]"—sin)
v. 28 ("God gave them up to things that should not be done [ἀδόκιμον νοῦν]"—
retribution).

Klostermann's principal argument for this structure consists of hellenistic Jewish examples
of the *ius talionis* principle expressed with the techniques of Greek rhetoric.

Klostermann's parallels are suggestive, but not conclusive. Philologically, his focus on the
above-mentioned Greek terms as the key structural elements are less convincing than the
(μετ)ἀλλάσσω/παραδίδωμι pairs of vv. 23f, 25f, 26, 28.

44. "Practicing—doing" (πράσσειν—ποιεῖν).

45. "Apart-from-the-law—law—circumcision—uncircumcision" (ἀνόμως—νόμος—πε-
ριτομή—ἀκροβυστία).

208
CHAPTER EIGHT

ing salvation on the basis of faith. She believes that Paul's goal in using the concept of divine impartiality toward Jews and gentiles is the elimination of social distinctions between Jews and gentiles in the community.

The strengths of Bassler's argument are that she can clearly document the ring structure and the word chains that she uses in support of seeing Rom 2:11 as central; that she is able to explain why Paul presupposes a judgment according to works for believers (which those who focus on justification by faith have difficulty explaining); and that she is able to account for the centrality of the Jew-gentile theme throughout Romans. The weaknesses of her argument are that the conflict between Rom 1:18–2:29 and 3:9 (whether gentiles can keep the law or whether they have failed and are under sin) remains in any case; that a Jewish-Christian from this time period could have read Rom 1:18–32 in the light of Wisdom as referring to the sins of gentiles, which she does not refute; and that the reader could deduce from the abrupt change of style at 2:1[46] that another group of persons is now being addressed, which the word chain of 1:32–2:3 does not alter. Further, the ring structure does not include Rom 1:21–32 (these verses fall within the hole at the center of the ring), yet they are the prime candidates for being summed up in 3:9, since they enumerate actual sins.[47] In other words, although Bassler clearly demonstrates the centrality of divine impartiality in Romans 1–3, she fails to counter the view that universal human sinfulness is also central and that the echoes of the Wisdom of Solomon validate reading Rom 1:18–32 as referring to gentile sin (as does the discussion of idolatry within Rom 1:18–23 itself). In line with her emphasis on divine impartiality rather than human sinfulness, Bassler devotes virtually no attention to homoeroticism.

Halvor Moxnes offers a third interpretation by arguing that honor and shame are central categories of Paul's society and of his Letter to the Romans.[48] For Moxnes, the people of Romans 1 did not grant to God the honor required by God's power and divinity, but rather claimed for themselves the honor of being wise. In response to this insubordination, God put humanity to shame.[49] Moxnes interprets Rom 1:26f in light of Paul's honor-and-shame culture:

46. Rom 1:18–32 is in the third person and a narrative style, whereas at Rom 2:1 Paul changes to the second person and a dialogical style.
47. Bassler herself calls them sins ("Divine Impartiality," 48), which is the term used in Rom 3:9.
48. Halvor Moxnes, "Honor, Shame, and the Outside World in Paul's Letter to the Romans," in *The Social World of Formative Christianity and Judaism: Essays in Tribute to Howard Clark Kee*, ed. Jacob Neusner et al. (Philadelphia: Fortress, 1988) 207–18.
49. V. 24: ἀτιμάζεσθαι; v. 27: ἀσχημοσύνη.

> Paul does not here discuss homosexuality as an ethical issue in our
> sense of the term when we discuss same-sex relationships. To Paul the
> issue was much more basic: it was one of sex roles and borders be-
> tween genders. In most honor-and-shame cultures there is a strong
> emphasis upon clearly defined sex roles. A blurring of such roles is
> perceived as a threat.[50]

The interpretive framework of honor-and-shame theory gives Moxnes a
way of explaining the prominent location of homoeroticism within Romans 1, where Paul singles it out from among the transgressions for special mention. Honor and shame, while linked with right and wrong, are
not inherently ethical categories. Rather, honor and shame are linked to
society, since societal evaluation helps to determine a person's honor and
shame. Moxnes's view, based on anthropological theory, that sex roles[51]
and gender boundaries are the root issue of Rom 1:26f, coincides with my
own research in this book.

Concerning female homoeroticism, Moxnes writes, "In a significant
departure from the almost complete silence on female homosexuality in
antiquity, Paul also speaks of women breaking with sex roles (1:26)."[52]
Moxnes, like others, is apparently unaware of the ancient sources on female
homoeroticism,[53] but his interpretation of Romans 1 is nevertheless quite
compatible with these ancient sources.

In Moxnes's view, Paul himself underscores the importance of honor
and shame by opening his argument with the words, "I am not ashamed
of the gospel" (Rom 1:16) and by using various terms for honor and
shame throughout Romans.[54] In this interpretation, honor and shame are
central to Romans 1, and Romans 1 is central to Paul's Letter to the Romans as a whole. Drawing upon anthropological research on honor and

50. Moxnes, "Honor," 213.
51. Moxnes uses the term "sex roles." I prefer the term "gender roles," which designates
socially constructed male and female roles. I use "sex" in the sense of physical difference.
Thus, "sex differences" are physical, while "gender differences" are cultural, and "gender
roles" are based upon culturally constructed gender differences.
52. Moxnes, "Honor," 213.
53. My 1985 article, "Paul's Views on the Nature of Women and Female Homoeroticism," in *Immaculate and Powerful*, ed. Clarissa W. Atkinson, Constance H. Buchanan, and
Margaret R. Miles (Boston: Beacon, 1985) 61–87 (abstracted in *NTA*), which refers to many
of these sources, would have been available to Moxnes when he was writing his article.
54. Moxnes includes the terms τιμή ("honor"), δόξα ("glory," "honor"), δοξάζω ("to
praise," "to honor"), ἔπαινος ("praise"), ἐπαινέω ("to praise"), καύχημα ("boast"),
καύχησις ("boasting"), καυχάομαι ("to boast"), ἀσχημοσύνη ("shameless deed"), ἀτιμία
("dishonor," "shame"), ἀτιμάζω ("to dishonor," "to treat shamefully"), ἐπαισχύνομαι
("to be ashamed of"), and καταισχύνω ("to put to shame") ("Honor," 217, n. 15).

shame,[55] Moxnes believes these categories "represent the value of a person in her or his own eyes but also in the eyes of his or her society."[56] His analysis builds upon the work of Unni Wikan, who has argued that shame is more central than honor in contemporary Mediterranean and Middle Eastern culture. Moxnes adapts this insight to Romans by claiming that, for Paul, honor and shame pertain to different spheres: honor to the public sphere over which the Christians have no control, and shame to the private sphere of gender roles and sexual behavior, which they can regulate.

In Paul's social context, the highly stratified Roman world, honor was linked to the ability to wield power. Moxnes interprets Rom 13:1–7 (on being subject to the governing authorities and paying taxes) as a call to Christians to accept the given order in the public sphere and to grant honor to the powerful. In contrast, shame pertains to the private sphere of gender roles and sexual behavior (as in Rom 1:24–27 or Rom 6:19–23, on the Christians' former life of impurity, of which they are now ashamed). I believe, however, that we should be cautious of assigning gender and sexual relations to the private sphere in the ancient world.[57]

Moxnes argues that Paul is thus encouraging the Christian community to integrate itself into Roman society by accepting its system of honoring the powerful (whose honor depends on society's granting it). In turn, the Christian community will receive praise from the powerful (Rom 13:1–7). On the other hand, Paul exhorts the community to distinguish itself from the world around it by avoiding acts that Paul deems shameful, such as homosexuality.

Moxnes sees these societal categories of honor and shame embedded within a theological context. For him, Paul's main theme in Romans is the power of God (and not righteousness or justification, as some claim). In the divine sphere, as in the human one, power is linked to honor. Thus, ultimately, all honor comes from God. Paul can live free of shame in the gospel (Rom 1:16), because Paul believes that God is powerful. Moxnes interprets Paul to mean that God grants people honor, which means that they do not need to be ashamed of the gospel, even though society may see the gospel as shameful.[58]

55. See esp. Unni Wikan, "Shame and Honour: A Contestable Pair," *Man* 19 (1984) 635–52; J. G. Peristiany, ed., *Honour and Shame: The Values of Mediterranean Society* (London: Weidenfeld and Nicolson, 1965); and J. A. Pitt-Rivers, *The People of the Sierra* (New York: Criterion, 1954).

56. Moxnes, "Honor," 208.

57. See, e.g., Diodoros of Sicily, who depicts gender as something that is recognized publicly, in this case, in court (32.10.2–10). The astrologer Ptolemy of Alexandria describes a type of sexual behavior as public (*Tetrabiblos* 4.5; §187).

58. Moxnes does not stick closely to his own distinction between shame as private and honor as public. (The gospel is presumably public.)

Moxnes's anthropological approach helps him to explain why idolatry and homoeroticism are the first sins that Paul mentions in Romans, to recognize the centrality of gender in homoeroticism, and to relate Romans to the cultural values of Paul's world. On the other hand, when Moxnes draws upon Unni Wikan, he misinterprets her at several points. For example, when Wikan says that shame and honor are not a binary pair, she means that shame is far more central than honor in the Mediterranean world and the Middle East, because people use "shame" far more frequently in daily speech.[59] Shame thus better conveys the native's perspective, while honor is more of an anthropologist's analytical construct. Moxnes misleadingly appeals to Wikan's insight when he argues that Paul places honor in the public sphere (e.g., Romans 13) and shame in the private sphere (e.g., Romans 1 and 6); for Wikan, honor and shame do not correspond to these separate spheres.

Further, Wikan strongly challenges the current definition of honor (value in one's own and in others' eyes) by pointing out that we have to establish precisely who the relevant "others" are, which Moxnes neglects to do. The women of a woman's world may assess value in a different way and on different grounds than the men of a man's world.[60] Wikan also questions the relationship between value in one's own eyes and value in the eyes of one's society. She argues that a person's own self-assessment may outweigh society's evaluation of her or him. In contrast, Moxnes unquestioningly accepts the traditional anthropological definition of honor.

Moxnes may exaggerate the centrality of "honor" and "shame" in Romans by including Greek terms in his list that may not be relevant at all. How do we know, for instance, that such terms as "to boast" and "boasting" would have been terms involving honor and shame in the ancient world? Unni Wikan, in contrast, defines the precise meaning of different Arabic terms for "shame" and "honor" used today in the Middle East, which is linguistically more responsible.[61]

Finally, if shame and honor are not a binary pair, then I question the

59. Wikan, "Shame and Honour," 635–52, esp. 637f.
60. E.g., in her research in Sohar, Oman, Wikan found that while female sexual purity may be a central male value, hospitality is central for women. Further, the women's world consists of small groups of neighbors and kinswomen who know each other well, while the men's world is one large group of a few friends and many strangers. Thus, the women of a neighborhood may respect a woman in spite of her adultery, because they know her and value her hospitality. In contrast, men who are relative strangers may have to base their assessment of a person on the one or two things they know about him or her ("Shame and Honour," 639–49).
61. Moxnes also assumes a common Mediterranean culture, whereas Wikan is less global and more differentiated. She notes, for example, differences between Cairo and Oman in the way in which people talk about each other. Instead of speaking of an "honor-and-shame

category "honor-and-shame" society. But let us grant for a moment Moxnes's view of Roman society as an honor-and-shame society, which, as such, rejected homosexuality as a blurring of gender boundaries.[62] If so, then how could the early Christians distinguish themselves from the surrounding world by avoiding homosexuality? The ancient sources show us that people in the Roman world did condemn female homoeroticism as a blurring of gender boundaries, and that this prevailing ideology cut across religious lines—pagan, Jewish, and Christian. Therefore, these sources require the opposite conclusion, namely, that Christians shared with many of their neighbors an assessment of homoeroticism as shameful.

These different models of interpretation correlate with differences in the interpreters' theological emphases. First, those focusing on human sinfulness in Romans 1–3 usually see it as the basis of Paul's doctrine of justification by faith and not works (Rom 3:21–26). Martin Luther found Paul's teaching on justification by faith (i.e., that human beings can be justified or brought into right relation with God by belief in Christ) to be a powerful antidote to a Roman Catholic emphasis on individual merit and on remission of the punishment due to sin by means of indulgences. If sin and justification are central, then homoeroticism, in this context, stands as a primary example of sin—specifically, of what it means not to be in right relation to God.

Secondly and in contrast, seeing divine impartiality as central to Romans 1–2 represents a larger shift in Pauline studies away from a focus on human responses toward God or Christ. Current Pauline scholars tend, rather, to emphasize God's righteousness and Christ's faithfulness toward humanity. In this perspective, homoeroticism exemplifies God's justice and fairness as fitting punishment for the crime of turning away from the true God toward images.

The third interpretation represents an attempt to depart from an individualistic theological focus on faith and justification and to move toward an understanding of Romans based on the values that Paul shared with his society. In this interpretation, Paul is urging the early Christians, as a group, to set a boundary between themselves and the world around them. For Paul, homosexuality epitomizes the shameful moral corruption of the godless. When people do not give honor to God, God hands them over to this shameful act.

---

culture," she tries to discern the complex ways in which various peoples of the Mediterranean world and the Middle East describe and respond to shame and express respect (Ibid., 647f).

62. Roman society could have rejected same-sex sexual expression as a blurring of gender boundaries even if it were not to have been an honor-and-shame society. My point here is to test the logic of Moxnes's position.

Thus, these interpretations each emphasize a different central theological aspect of Rom 1:18–32: the sinfulness of the gentiles (Sanday and
Headlam), the sinfulness of all human beings (Wilckens), the wrath of God
(Wilckens), divine impartiality (Bassler), and the social constructs of honor
and shame (Moxnes). Yet each interpreter leaves significant exegetical
problems unsolved: the lack of the term "gentile" in Romans 1 (Sanday
and Headlam); the precise determination of non-Christian views on female
homoeroticism (Sanday and Headlam, Wilckens, Bassler, Moxnes); the
apparent contradiction between Rom 2:14, which assumes that some gentiles follow the law, and Rom 3:9, 23, according to which everyone is under sin (Bassler); the relationship to Jewish discussions of idolatry (Bassler);
and which Greek terms within the text designate the values that signify an
honor-and-shame society (and whether, independently of Romans, we can
so designate the Mediterranean world) (Moxnes). No one interpretation
solves all the problems.

Further, these New Testament interpreters do not treat the question of
nature as an exegetical problem in Romans 1, which I consider to be crucial
to the interpretation of the passage. Even today, theologians, ethicists, and
the public at large continue to debate what is natural and unnatural sexual
behavior, often with appeal to Romans 1. In order to comprehend why
Paul condemns sexual relations between women, the questions of natural
theology and natural law, as well as the range of meaning of "unnatural"
and "natural" (Rom 1:26f), need to be addressed.

In the following chapter, I will treat the above-mentioned exegetical
problems as necessary to elucidate Rom 1:26. I am not adopting a single
model of interpretation. Rather, my research questions require the multiple
perspectives of the literary and interpretive approaches of prior exegetes.

Since Paul sought to persuade his readers by means of the rhetorical and
literary conventions of his time, I analyze Rom 1:18–32 in light of these
conventions, more specifically in light of Romans as protreptic. Because I
take universal human sinfulness, the wrath of God and divine impartiality
as central theological themes of Romans 1–3, I examine how, for Paul,
female homoeroticism exemplifies human sinfulness, how it has resulted
from the wrath of God against human beings who have turned away from
God, and how God, as an impartial judge, can decree death for a woman
who engages in sexual relations with another woman. I also utilize anthropological insights to understand why Paul classifies homoeroticism as "impurity." Like Moxnes (although for different reasons), I conclude that for
Paul and his earliest readers, homoeroticism constituted a blurring of gender boundaries.

Thus, I build upon prior genre criticism, theological exegesis, analysis of
literary structures, and anthropological interpretation. Using the methods

of philology and comparative textual analysis, I will fill in gaps left by prior researchers, most prominently the meanings of "nature" and of "unnatural" and how the understandings of female homoeroticism in the Roman world shaped Paul's understanding of it. Finally, I demonstrate how nature and gender are deeply theological concepts in Romans.

9

Romans 1:18–32: A Commentary

In Romans 1:18–32, Paul describes the state of the miserable human beings who have turned away from God:

18 For the wrath of God is revealed from heaven against all ungodliness and wickedness of those who by their wickedness suppress the truth. 19 For what can be known about God is plain to them, because God has shown it to them. 20 Ever since the creation of the world God's eternal power and divine nature, invisible though they are, have been understood and seen through the things God has made. So they are without excuse; 21 for though they knew God, they did not honor God as God or give thanks to God, but they became futile in their thinking, and their senseless minds were darkened. 22 Claiming to be wise, they became fools; 23 and they exchanged the glory of the immortal God for images resembling a mortal human being or birds or four-footed animals or reptiles.

24 Therefore God gave them up in the lusts of their hearts to impurity, to the degrading of their bodies among themselves, 25 because they exchanged the truth about God for a lie and worshiped and served the creature rather than the Creator, who is blessed forever! Amen.

26 For this reason God gave them up to degrading passions. Their women exchanged natural intercourse for unnatural, 27 and in the same way also the men, giving up natural intercourse with women, were consumed with passion for one another. Men committed shameless acts with men and received in their own persons the due penalty for their error.

28 And since they did not see fit to acknowledge God, God gave them up to a debased mind and to things that should not be done.

29 They were filled with every kind of wickedness, evil, covetousness, malice. Full of envy, murder, strife, deceit, craftiness, they are gossips, 30 slanderers, God-haters, insolent, haughty, boastful, inventors of evil, rebellious toward parents, 31 foolish, faithless, heartless, ruthless. 32 They know God's decree, that those who practice such things deserve to die—yet they not only do them but even applaud others who practice them.

This passage, which contains Paul's only explicit reference to female homoeroticism, presents complex exegetical challenges, many of which remain unresolved despite the variety of interpretations proposed by New Testament scholars and theologians. In this chapter and the next, I will investigate and propose solutions to these problems, first by a verse-by-verse reading and commentary on Romans 1:16–32 and then by a discussion of various possible influences on Paul and his earliest readers.

The central question of my investigation is: what are natural and unnatural intercourse? In what follows I will argue that Paul condemns sexual relations between women as "unnatural" because he shares the widely held cultural view that women are passive by nature and therefore should remain passive in sexual relations. Like the hellenistic- and Roman-period authors surveyed above, he views sexual relations as asymmetrical, so that a sexual encounter necessarily includes an active and a passive partner. Egalitarian, mutual relationships were not part of the dominant cultural discourse of the time. According to this literature, a woman cannot naturally assume the active role, thus rendering natural sexual relations between women impossible.

But in order to understand Paul's view fully, we first need to understand its context within Romans and within the Roman world. Paul condemns unnatural sexual relations as part of his description of God's wrath against idol worshipers, whom God has handed over to all manner of evil deeds, including same-sex love (Rom 1:18–32). The larger context of the passage is Paul's claim that all human beings, both Jews and non-Jews, are under sin (Rom 3:9: "we have already charged that all, both Jews and Greeks, are under the power of sin"; see also Rom 3:23). This claim, for which Paul presents his case in Rom 1:18–3:20, serves to demonstrate the human need for justification by faith.[1]

As a Jewish thinker who believed in Christ, Paul needed to work out the precise relationship between observance of the Jewish law and belief in Christ. And as a person who wanted to bring the message of Christ to gentiles unfamiliar with the Jewish law, he argued that nature could help

---

1. Justification by faith means that God will declare blameless those who believe in Christ on the basis of their faith, rather than because of their actions.

gentiles know God's will for them. Rom 1:18-32 has a complex interrelationship with Jewish law and with contemporaneous discussions of nature and of natural law. The passage echoes—perhaps surprisingly—concepts and commandments of the book of Leviticus, and also contains significant overlap with postbiblical Jewish legal thinking. But Paul appeals to an audience that includes both gentiles and Jews and argues that the works of creation give *all* human beings the capability of knowing the true God and that there is a decree of God known to *all* people. Paul may draw upon natural law theory within a framework similar to that of Philo of Alexandria, for whom the law of Moses is in perfect accord with a law of nature.

By means of introduction, I will briefly comment on Paul's mission and the Roman congregation and then give a verse-by-verse exegesis of Rom 1:18-32. In the next chapter, I will focus on themes of significance to the passage as a whole: the question of natural law, the meaning of nature, relationship to Jewish law, relationship to Wisdom of Solomon, and how sources on female homoeroticism from the cultural environment can help us to understand Paul's condemnation.

Paul's Letter to the Romans is a deeply partisan document, an impassioned appeal for one man's understanding of Christ, God, sin, salvation, and human existence. Paul of Tarsus lived his life in dialogue and dispute, and Romans bears testimony to that. He wrote the letter between 54 and 58 CE, possibly from Corinth, to a Christian community or communities[2] that he had not founded. Others had laid the groundwork, formed the community, set the terms of the internal debates. Planning to visit this community, Paul crafted his letter with diplomatic sensitivity. The modern reader can detect indications of the care that Paul took to present his understanding of the gospel in a way that would be convincing to the Roman congregation.

Breaking down the barriers between Jews and gentiles was a central focus of Paul's entire ministry throughout the eastern Roman Empire. Paul's letters contain numerous impassioned discussions of the barriers to Jewish-gentile harmony, such as circumcision, dietary laws, and the Jewish law as a whole. Paul did not, however, call for radical changes in such other areas as slavery and the condition of women. I believe that Paul wrote to the Romans because he felt that Jews and gentiles were equal before the God of Jesus Christ and could be equally justified through faith in Jesus Christ, and because he hoped that Christian communities would uphold this prin-

2. As Peter Lampe points out, the Roman Christians may have worshiped in several different house churches, rather than forming a single congregation ("The Roman Christians of Romans 16," in *The Romans Debate*, ed. Karl P. Donfried [rev. and exp. ed. of the 1977 ed.; Peabody, MA: Hendrickson, 1991] 229f).

ciple. Paul's promotion of the traditional gender values of the Roman world through his condemnation of same-sex love contrasts with his anxiety-provoking blurring of the boundaries between Jews and gentiles. As strongly as he insists that same-sex sexual mingling makes one deserving of death, so too does he insist that Jewish-gentile intermingling befits a congregation's life in Christ.

The addressees of the Letter to the Romans are the members of the church in Rome, which was diverse in several respects.[3] Judging by the specific names mentioned in Romans 16, the congregation included both Jews (Prisca, Aquila, Andronikos, Junia, and Herodion) and gentiles (most of the other names, such as Apelles, Tryphaina, Tryphosa, and Hermas, are probably those of gentiles, but we cannot be sure). At several points in the letter, Paul seems to speak separately to the Jews in the congregation (e.g., Rom 2:17; 7:1) or to the gentiles (e.g., Rom 11:13). The community may also have included members of different social strata; some of the names of Romans 16 occurred as slave names in antiquity and may be names of slaves or former slaves (e.g., Persis, Tryphosa). Both women and men were active as members and leaders. Of the twenty-six Christians whom Paul greets by name in Rom 16:3–16, nine are women. Paul employs titles of leadership or technical terms for community-building work for several of these women (he applies the technical term "apostle" to Junica, "fellow worker" to Prisca, and "to labor" to Mariam, Tryphaina, Tryphosa, and Persis). Understanding the composition of Paul's audience will help us better discern Paul's line of argumentation.

The community may have been involved in considerable internal conflict before Paul wrote his letter to them. The Roman emperor Claudius (41–54) had recently expelled some Jews from the city of Rome, probably those involved in conflicts within Roman synagogues over the messiahship of Jesus.[4] Perhaps some Jewish-Christians preached and taught about Jesus as

3. Some interpreters believe that Romans 16 was originally a separate letter later added to Romans 1–15 (e.g., Helmut Koester, *Introduction to the New Testament*, vol. 2, *History and Literature of Early Christianity* [German original, Berlin: DeGruyter, 1980; Philadelphia: Fortress, 1982] 52f, 138f; Ernst Käsemann, *Commentary on Romans* [Grand Rapids, MI: Eerdmans, 1980] 421–28); but, in line with a growing consensus among scholars, I maintain the integrity of Romans (see, e.g., Peter Lampe, "The Roman Christians of Romans 16," in *The Romans Debate*, ed. Karl P. Donfried [rev. and exp. ed. of the 1977 ed.; Peabody, MA: Hendrickson, 1991] 216–30; Harry Gamble, *The Textual History of the Letter to the Romans* [Studies and Documents 42; Grand Rapids, MI: Eerdmans, 1977]; Wolf-Henning Ollrog, "Die Abfassungsverhältnisse von Röm 16," in *Kirche: Festschrift für Günther Bornkamm zum 75. Geburtstag*, ed. Dieter Lührmann and Georg Strecker [Tübingen: Mohr (Siebeck), 1980] 221–44).

4. See Suetonius, *Claudius* 25.4 (Claudius expelled the Jews from Rome, because they were stirred up over "Chrestus" [probably a misunderstanding of "Christus"]); Cassius Dio, *Roman History* 60.6.6 (in the year 41 Claudius barred the Jews from assembling, rather than

messiah during synagogue worship services—to the consternation of others who did not accept Jesus as messiah. Maybe they argued about circumcision or Jewish dietary laws or the Jewish law as a whole. Paul wrote his Letter to the Romans after Nero (54–68) had allowed these exiles to return, at which time tensions must have still been very high.

Members of this community must have appropriated Paul's letter in a variety of ways, depending on their own educational level and background. Some members may have attained a high level of Jewish learning through studying the Greek-language Jewish Bible, the Septuagint, and through learning how to interpret it by means of one of the sophisticated philosophical methods of the day (such as the allegorical interpretation practiced by Philo of Alexandria). Since both Jews and non-Jews in the Roman world read the Septuagint, this knowledge could have been pervasive in the community. These hearers of the Letter to the Romans could have recognized in it echoes of the Wisdom of Solomon. Other members may have, like Paul, had a Pharisaic background. Perhaps they knew Hebrew and methods of interpreting the Jewish law similar to those we find in the Mishnah and the Talmud. These hearers, who had studied Leviticus and its detailed teachings concerning holiness, purity, impurity, and abomination, would have been attuned to the overlap in content and terminology between Romans 1 and Leviticus 18 and 20. Some members may have had knowledge of Stoic philosophy, including its teachings about natural law. Since Stoic philosophy enjoyed broad appeal, knowledge of it extended beyond the limits of the philosophically trained, much as popular psychology's influence today goes far beyond those who have academic training in psychology. These hearers may have discerned an overlap between Romans 1 and 2 and Stoic natural law theory and concepts of nature. In what follows, I comment upon Romans 1:16–32 (vv. 16f provide the necessary background for understanding vv. 18–32), particularly in light of the varying intellectual frameworks in which members of Paul's earliest audience may have read it.

Commentary on Romans 1:16–32

The Letter to the Romans served to introduce Paul and his message to the Roman community of those who believed in Christ. Rom 1:16–32, which

---

expel them); and Acts 18:2 (Aquila and Priscilla met Paul in Corinth, to which they had come after Claudius had expelled the Jews from Rome). Claudius probably expelled only some of the Roman Jews, since if he had expelled all of them, we would expect such Jewish sources as Flavius Josephus to mention that fact. See Wolfgang Wiefel for an evaluation of these somewhat divergent sources ("The Jewish Community in Ancient Rome and the Origins of Roman Christianity," in *The Romans Debate*, ed. Karl P. Donfried [rev. and exp. ed. of the 1977 ed.; Peabody, MA: Hendrickson, 1991] 85–101); see also the literature cited by Wiefel.

follows upon the greetings and other preliminaries, opens the body of the letter with a statement of the main thesis and with the first arguments demonstrating God's impartiality and universal human sinfulness. Romans 1: 16f contains this thesis, of which 1:18–32 is the first part of the explication.

Romans 1:16f.[5] *For*[6] *I am not ashamed of the gospel; it is the power of God for salvation to everyone who has faith, to the Jew first and also to the Greek. (17) For in it the righteousness of God is revealed through faith for faith; as it is written, "The one who is righteous will live by faith."* [Hab 2:4] These verses, which form the transition from the opening to the body of the letter,[7] contain the principal thesis of the Letter to the Romans: belief in Christ makes salvation accessible to everyone. Everyone is subsumed under the categories "Jew" and "Greek," since for Paul "Greek" means "gentile."[8]

Paul does not explicitly state the object of the faith, Jesus Christ, until Rom 3:22. The text only indirectly refers to Christ with the term "gospel" and with the bold statement that the righteousness of God is revealed in the gospel.[9] The general focus on God, rather than Christ,[10] enables Paul to achieve his goal for the first three chapters, namely, to demonstrate divine impartiality and universal human sinfulness, before and outside of Christ.

In Rom 1:17 and throughout Romans, Paul employs scriptural quotations and allusions to draw a tight connection between the revelation of God in Christ and God's revelation in Jewish scripture.[11] In Rom 1:16f, however, the text is silent about the works of the law (Rom 3:20) as an

---

5. Rom 1:16: Οὐ γὰρ ἐπαισχύνομαι τὸ εὐαγγέλιον, δύναμις γὰρ θεοῦ ἐστιν εἰς σωτηρίαν παντὶ τῷ πιστεύοντι, Ἰουδαίῳ τε πρῶτον καὶ Ἕλληνι. 17 δικαιοσύνη γὰρ θεοῦ ἐν αὐτῷ ἀποκαλύπτεται ἐκ πίστεως εἰς πίστιν, καθὼς γέγραπται· ὁ δὲ δίκαιος ἐκ πίστεως ζήσεται [Hab 2:4]. The LXX of Hab 2:4 has ἐκ πίστεώς μου, that is, that the righteous one will live by faith in God. In the Hebrew: the righteous one will live by her or his "faithfulness" (בֶּאֱמוּנָתוֹ).

6. The "for's" (γάρ) of vv. 16f indicate causal relationships. Paul plans to preach the gospel in Rome, *for* he is not ashamed of the gospel (Rom 1:11–15). He is not ashamed, *because* it is the power of God. The gospel is the power of God, *for* in it God's righteousness is revealed.

7. Jouette M. Bassler argues that these verses are the first two of an *inclusio* extending through 2:11 ("Divine Impartiality in Paul's Letter to the Romans," *NovT* 26 [1984] 43–58, esp. 45–49).

8. See 1 Cor 1:23f.

9. I mean "gospel" in the specifically Pauline sense, for which see Helmut Koester, *Ancient Christian Gospels: Their History and Development* (Philadelphia: Trinity Press International, 1990) 1–48, esp. 4–9.

10. For a christological interpretation, see Ulrich Wilckens, *Der Brief an die Römer*, vol. 1 (Zurich: Benziger, 1978; Neukirchen-Vluyn: Neukirchener Verlag, 1978) 120.

11. Paul employs the Jewish division of scripture into the law (i.e., the Pentateuch) and the prophets (i.e., the historical writings and the prophets) in Rom 3:21. The Jewish canon

alternative to belief as a basis for salvation. The Jewish law gradually makes its way into the argument; beginning in Rom 2:12 (on sin and the law), the law occurs frequently up through Romans 8. Since the necessity of the Jewish law was a point of contention, Paul's silence on the Jewish law until 2:12 is a wise rhetorical technique, for it allows him to establish consensus with his readers before addressing the heavily disputed topic.

Verse 17 speaks first of God and then of a human being and of human behavior, a pattern that the following verses continue. As the following chapters of Romans show, the righteous "one" of v. 17 includes both the Jew and the Greek of v. 16.

Romans 1:18.[12] *For*[13] *the wrath of God is revealed from heaven against all ungodliness and wickedness of those who by their wickedness suppress the truth.* Is the righteousness of God revealed in the gospel, *since* the wrath of God is revealed from heaven? This would mean that God's righteousness (v. 17) can be revealed because God's judgment of human sinfulness is also revealed. Notice that God's wrath is revealed "from heaven," whereas God's righteousness is revealed "in it," that is, in the gospel. The progression is logical and not temporal; both times "is revealed" is in the present passive tense.

How is God's wrath revealed from heaven? There has been no earthly catastrophe, such as a devastating earthquake or the destruction of a city or enslavement of a people that might be called a sign of God's wrath. Paul may be working within the framework of the Jewish apocalyptic movement, which speculated about the coming wrath of God.[14] A more plausible explanation, however, is that God's wrath is revealed through the human behavior described in vv. 24-32. This would mean that God's handing idolaters over to wretched deeds *is* the revelation of God's wrath against those who suppress the truth.

"Ungodliness and wickedness." "Ungodliness" is a lack of piety and "wickedness" a lack of virtue.[15] Lack of reverence for God and lack of human virtue are interconnected in this text from the very beginning. The verb "to suppress" implies that human beings are agents who can know

---

of Paul's time did not necessarily include the third division, the writings, which were still fluid at the time of Paul.

12. Rom 1:18: Ἀποκαλύπτεται γὰρ ὀργὴ θεοῦ ἀπ' οὐρανοῦ ἐπὶ πᾶσαν ἀσέβειαν καὶ ἀδικίαν ἀνθρώπων τῶν τὴν ἀλήθειαν ἐν ἀδικίᾳ κατεχόντων.

13. The "for" (γάρ) of this verse is puzzling. "But" (δέ) would seem more appropriate, yet the text has "for" and demands explanation as it stands.

14. For the influence of apocalyptic thinking on Paul's theology, see J. Christiaan Beker, *Paul the Apostle: The Triumph of God in Life and Thought* (Philadelphia: Fortress, 1980) 135-81.

15. In Greek ἀσέβεια and ἀδικία both have an alpha-privative, which produces alliteration.

the truth and actualize it in human behavior. The text describes persons with intellectual and moral capabilities, who could have known better, foreshadowing the dishonor and shame attributed to them when they practice homoeroticism. Who are these people? The text has *"all* ungodliness and wickedness of those who . . . ,"* not "the ungodliness and wickedness of *all* people." At v. 18, readers who worship the God of Israel and follow God's commands can assume that the text refers to *other* people, to the ungodly and the unrighteous, but not to themselves. This assumption gains support through Paul's skilled use of literary allusions, in particular to traditional Jewish descriptions of the folly of idolatry. Only toward the end of the argument in Rom 3:9 does Paul say that "all, both Jews and Greeks, are under the power of sin."

Romans 1:19f.[16] *For what can be known about God is plain to them, because God has shown it to them. (20) Ever since the creation of the world God's eternal power and divine nature, invisible though they are, have been understood and seen through the things God has made. So they are without excuse.* How could people have known better? By what means could they have recognized the true God? Rom 1:19f provide justification for the revelation of God's wrath. In order to show that the human actors of v. 18 are "without excuse," Paul must show that they can know truth. In order to establish that these people knew the truth, but suppressed it, Paul employs natural theology in Rom 1:18–32.[17]

Excursus: The Debate on Natural Theology

Scholars have long debated whether or not Paul uses natural theology.[18] Natural theology is the belief that all humans can know God through ob-

---

16. Rom 1:19: διότι τὸ γνωστὸν τοῦ θεοῦ φανερόν ἐστιν ἐν αὐτοῖς· ὁ θεὸς γὰρ αὐτοῖς ἐφανέρωσεν. 20 τὰ γὰρ ἀόρατα αὐτοῦ ἀπὸ κτίσεως κόσμου τοῖς ποιήμασιν νοούμενα καθορᾶται, ἥ τε ἀΐδιος αὐτοῦ δύναμις καὶ θειότης, εἰς τὸ εἶναι αὐτοὺς ἀναπολογήτους.

17. Cf. Gal 4:8–11, in which Paul presupposes that the Galatians did not know God before they came to faith in Christ. The reasons for this discrepancy between Galatians and Romans are unclear.

18. See James Barr, "Biblical Law and the Question of Natural Theology" in *The Law in the Bible and in Its Environment*, ed. Timo Veijola (Publications of the Finnish Exegetical Society 51; Helsinki: Finnish Exegetical Society, 1990) 1–22; James Barr, "La foi biblique et la théologie naturelle," *ÉTR* 64 (1989) 355–68; William Vandermarck, "Natural Knowledge of God in Romans: Patristic and Medieval Interpretation," *TS* 34 (1973) 36–52; David M. Coffey, "Natural Knowledge of God: Reflections on Romans 1:18–32," *TS* 31 (1970) 674–91; Dieter Lührmann, *Das Offenbarungsverständnis bei Paulus und in paulinischen Gemeinden* (Neukirchen-Vluyn: Neukirchener Verlag, 1965) esp. 21–26; Rudolf Bultmann, "Der Begriff der Offenbarung im Neuen Testament," in *Glauben und Verstehen*, vol. 3 (essay

serving nature.[19] I hold that Paul does use natural theology to argue that all human beings have sinned and that this universal human sinfulness establishes the need for justification through faith in the crucified and resurrected Christ. Natural theology enables Paul to accuse human beings and from there to build his own Christocentric theology. Despite the importance of natural theology in Paul's argument, Paul does not use it as the foundation of his own theology or ethics.[20] Natural theology implies that all human beings can know God through nature, without having had Christ preached to them; thus, people ultimately do not need Christ. Paul's theology, however, is opposed to any theology that would make Christ unnecessary. Natural theology, therefore, is a building block in Paul's theology that establishes the sinfulness of all people, and thus their need for Christ.

When Catholic and Protestant theologians have debated the meaning of natural theology, Rom 1:19f has been the main biblical text under dispute. Since the First Vatican Council, the Roman Catholic church has officially taught a "natural theology," that "God, the beginning and end of all

---

originally published in 1929; Tübingen: Mohr [Siebeck], 1962) 1–34; Heinrich Ott, "Röm. 1, 19ff. als dogmatisches Problem," *TZ* 15 (1959) 40–50; H. P. Owen, "The Scope of Natural Revelation in Rom. i and Acts xvii," *NTS* 5 (1958–59) 133–43; Hans Bietenhard, "Natürliche Gotteserkenntnis der Heiden?" *TZ* 12 (1956) 275–88; A. Feuillet, "La connaissance naturelle de Dieu par les hommes," *Lumière et Vie* (B) 14 (1954) 63–80; Hannelis Schulte, *Der Begriff der Offenbarung im Neuen Testament* (Beiträge zur evangelischen Theologie 13; Munich: Kaiser, 1949) esp. 20–27, 34–43; Edmund Schlink, "Die Offenbarung Gottes in seinen Werken und die Ablehnung der natürlichen Theologie," *TBl* 20 (1941) 1–14; Heinrich Schlier, "Über die Erkenntnis Gottes bei den Heiden (Nach dem Neuen Testament)," *EvT* 2 (1935) 9–28; Gerhardt Kuhlmann, *Theologia naturalis bei Philon und bei Paulus* (Neutestamentliche Forschungen, ser. 1, Paulusstudien 7; Gütersloh: Bertelsmann, 1930) esp. 39–53; Anton Fridrichsen, "Zur Auslegung von Röm 1,19f.," *ZNW* 17 (1916) 159–68; Heinrich Daxer, *Römer 1,18–2,10 im Verhältnis zur spätjüdischen Lehrauffassung* (Naumburg: Pätz, 1914).

19. See Ulrich Wilckens, who points to ancient Stoic parallels for natural theology (e.g., Kleanthes, *Hymn to Zeus* [*apud* Stobaios, *Anthologion* 1.25,3–27,4]), while demonstrating that Paul's apocalyptic context makes his statements about God ultimately very non-Stoic (*Brief an die Römer*, 1:99f).

20. Günther Bornkamm convincingly argues that, although Rom 1:18–32 has close parallels with Stoic philosophy and hellenistic Judaism, Paul's purpose is not to deduce God's existence through observing the world, but rather to reveal what the world is really like through God's revelation ("Die Offenbarung des Zornes Gottes," in *Das Ende des Gesetzes*, vol. 1, *Paulusstudien* [Beiträge zur evangelischen Theologie 16; Munich: Kaiser, 1952] 9–34).

See 1 Cor 1:21 ("For since, in the wisdom of God, the world did not know God through wisdom, God decided, through the foolishness of our proclamation, to save those who believe"), which makes clear that Paul gives priority to the revelation in the gospel over any human ability to know God.

things, can be known with certainty by the natural light of human reason from the works of creation."[21] Rom 1:20 constitutes the principal biblical support for this position. Protestants have traditionally rejected this emphasis on human reason.[22] Protestant theologian Karl Barth, for example, uses the term "intellectual work-righteousness" to describe natural theology.[23] "Intellectual work-righteousness" is a play on "work-righteousness," a derisive term that Protestants have traditionally leveled at Catholics, who, in the eyes of many Protestants, focus too strongly on gaining merit for heaven (grace) by means of good works. For Barth, the belief that we can know God through reason and through the works of creation constitutes "intellectual work-righteousness," because direct human access to knowledge of God places humans too much at the center of theology. Barth believes that we know God only through Christ, and that we are saved by believing in Christ. If human beings can know God with certainty without Christ, then Christ is not at the center of theology. For Barth, people recognize God's *existence* through God's *actions* in human history, with God's central action in history being Christ. This argument also locates the Bible as the central source for knowledge of God's actions.

If Christ and the Bible have been central for Protestants, defining the relationship between human reason and belief has been central for Catholics. The First Vatican Council was reacting to Immanuel Kant's view that humans cannot prove the existence of God. Instead of adopting Kant's

21. *Deum, rerum omnium, principium et finem, naturali humanae rationis lumine e rebus creatis certo cognosci posse* (Heinrich Denzinger and Adolf Schönmetzler, *Enchiridion Symbolorum* [34th ed.; Freiburg im Breisgau: Herder, 1967] no. 1785; see also no. 1806, in which those who say otherwise are anathematized).

22. A number of Protestant exegetes have commented on the problem of natural theology presented by Rom 1:19f. For example, Wiard Popkes tries to solve this problem by seeing Rom 1:18–32 as a juridical speech leading up to Paul's actual interest, which is to declare the Torah-observant Jew to be without salvation ("Zum Aufbau und Charakter von Römer 1.18–32," *NTS* 28 [1982] 490–501). In other words, Popkes implicitly argues that Rom 1:19f gives no warrant for natural theology, because it is one small piece of a larger argument focusing on the salvation of Jews, rather than of gentiles. Popkes correctly recognizes that Rom 1:18–32 can refer to gentiles or to humanity generally (and therefore theoretically to Jews). But even if his view were correct that Rom 1:18–32 merely prefaces what follows, defining vv. 19f as just one small piece of an argument does not nullify their presence and role within that argument. Moreover, Rom 1:18–32 does not merely preface what follows. Rom 3:9–30, which demonstrates that Paul was concerned with both gentile and Jewish sinfulness and salvation, supports my interpretation on that point.

23. Karl Barth, in *Natural Theology: Comprising "Nature and Grace" by Professor Dr. Emil Brunner and the Reply "No!" by Dr. Karl Barth*, trans. Peter Fraenkel (London: Centenary, 1946) 102. Barth's German original appeared in 1934 as part of the Confessing Church's response to Hitler. Barth defended his view (that true knowledge of God can come only through Jesus Christ and scripture) not only over against his fellow Protestant Brunner, but also against Roman Catholic theologians and those Germans who hailed Hitler as a savior of the German nation.

critique, it continued in the tradition of Thomas Aquinas, who elevated human rationality and argued that humans can prove the existence of God. The Catholic optimistic view of human rationality, however, does not mean that Vatican I claimed that people actually know God by means of human reason. Rather, it claimed that people have the ability to do so. In this, the Vatican I aligned itself with Paul, who claimed that people knew God.[24] Whereas for Protestants God's revelation in the Bible is the ultimate authority, for Vatican I God's revelation as interpreted by the pope and the bishops is the highest authority, and not individual human reason. In other words, even though Vatican I stressed the human ability to know God, it—like Paul—did not consider such knowledge sufficient.

This Roman Catholic/Protestant debate about the knowledge of God and Rom 1:19f highlights tensions within the larger text of Romans itself. On the one hand, Rom 1:18-32 contains no mention of Christ.[25] To be sure, the very first verses of the Letter to the Romans (Rom 1:1-6) mention Christ, and Paul's theology clearly centers on Christ as the means to salvation. But Rom 1:18-32 refers to people who had the ability to perceive God, not Christ, and who chose to worship a work of God, rather than God directly. Speaking about Christ's suffering, death, and resurrection, or even about Christ's teachings, would not demonstrate Paul's introductory point (Rom 1:18) that the people's wickedness has evoked God's anger. Rather, the value as a means to salvation of believing in Christ only becomes clear once the readers recognize that, outside of Christ, all people are under the power of sin. In other words, in order to make his point that belief in Christ is necessary, Paul must demonstrate universal sinfulness *without* appealing to Christ. Paul begins by setting up recognition of a creator through observing the things around oneself (Rom 1:18-32) as the most basic form of knowledge about the divine that people can have. He then turns to the Jewish law (Rom 2:12-3:20), a more advanced form

24. Joseph A. Fitzmyer has described the relationship between the two as follows: "Vatican I was dealing with the capability [*potentia activa*] of the human mind to know God. Paul rather speaks of a de facto situation: God is intellectually perceived and known from created things; he also describes the actual 'godlessness and wickedness' of pagan humanity and its failure to acknowledge God properly. From this de facto situation the council moved a step farther and argued for the capability" (*Romans: A New Translation with Introduction and Commentary* [Anchor Bible; New York: Doubleday, 1993] 277).

25. Barth does not claim that Rom 1:18-32 literally names Christ. His commentary on Romans consists of theological reflection on the way in which Paul's Letter to the Romans speaks to people today. He quite consciously did not write a historical-critical commentary. Barth interprets Rom 1:18-20 as referring to the ways we do not let God into our lives. When Barth speaks of our relationship to God without Christ, he refers generally to people's unwillingness to accept the healing, salvific crisis that knowledge of God can bring. Since the contemporary reader is able to know Christ through the Bible and Christian preaching, the historical situation of those about whom Paul speaks is of less interest to him (*Der Römerbrief* [1922; reprint, Zurich: EVZ, 1967] 19-22).

of religious knowledge. Only then does Paul speak of faith in Jesus Christ (Rom 3:22). Thus, Paul presupposes that all people can know God through God's created works, that is, through nature. But knowledge of God (and even living according to God's will) is not sufficient for salvation. For Paul, both Jews and non-Jews can attain salvation through belief in Christ.

This text does not speak about God's act of sending Christ (as in Rom 8:3), and it does not speak about God acting in history at all (e.g., the delivery of the Israelites from Egypt, the giving of the law, the fall of Jericho). A Protestant interpreter who attempts to find such self-revealing divine actions in Rom 1:18-32 does not have a textual basis for this assertion.[26]

Karl Barth argues that one can find natural theology in Rom 1:19f only by interpreting it atomistically, that is, by severing it from its context, the revelation of the gospel of Jesus Christ. For Barth there is only one revelation, but it has two sides, composed of lightness and darkness or shadow. The revelation of God's wrath in Romans 1 upon the gentiles and in Romans 2 upon the Jews represents the shadow side of the revelation of God's grace, namely the justification of believers (Rom 1:16f; 3:21f).[27]

To his credit, Barth keeps his focus on Paul's main theological point,

26. Ulrich Wilckens agrees with Barth that theological discussion of the knowledge of God has to be oriented toward God's actions, rather than God's existence, but I do not see that either Wilckens or Barth has a textual basis for this claim in Romans. Wilckens believes that the general biblical focus on God's actions, rather than God's existence, is also present in Rom 1:19f in that ποιήματα ("things God has made") result from God's creative activity. He argues that Rom 1:20 differs from hellenistic Jewish discussions of knowing God as an artist from the things that God has created (e.g., Wis 13:1, 5) in that Rom 1:20 uses the instrumental dative (τοῖς ποιήμασιν), whereas the hellenistic Jewish sources use ἐκ plus the genitive (meaning that a person recognizes God *from* those things, rather than by means of God's creative works). He also takes δύναμις ("power") in v. 20 to be the power of God's actions (*Brief an die Römer*, 1:106, 119f).

Wilckens's arguments are not convincing. Scripture does present God as acting in history, but Wilckens places quite a heavy theological burden on a fairly minor grammatical difference. Perceiving God by means of the things God has made (Rom 1:20) is very similar to perceiving God "from the greatness and beauty of created things" (Wis 13:5). Further, while δύναμις may refer to God's actions, the text does not state these actions (with the exception of the revelation of God's wrath).

David Novak has recently argued that Barth's interpretation of Rom 1:19-21 is plausible in light of the view of some ancient rabbis that gentiles are prohibited from practicing idolatry or from committing murder ("Before Revelation: The Rabbis, Paul, and Karl Barth," *JR* 71 [1991] 50-66).

27. Karl Barth, *Church Dogmatics*, I/2, trans. G. T. Thompson and Harold Knight (German original, Zollikon: Verlag der Evangelischen Buchhandlung, 1938; Edinburgh: Clark, 1956) 303-7; II/1, trans. T. H. L. Parker et al. (German original, Zollikon: Verlag der Evangelischen Buchhandlung, 1946; Edinburgh: Clark, 1957) 118-23.

belief in Jesus Christ. How idol worshipers can know God is clearly part of a larger argument within Romans, rather than the main point or even a separate point. Barth overlooks natural theology as a crucial step in Paul's argument that all people are under sin, but that everyone can be justified through faith in Christ. In order to accuse gentiles of having sinned (Rom 3:9, 23), Paul has to grant that the gentiles have had access to knowledge of God and to knowledge of right and wrong. Thus, while natural theology and natural law are only part of a larger argument, they are a necessary part.

The cognitive language used in these and the following verses favors the official Roman Catholic interpretation of Rom 1:20 ("what can be known [about God]," "have been understood and seen" [literally: perceived], "knew," "thinking," "senseless," "wise").[28] But the cognitive language plays a different role in Rom 1:18–32 than in the decree of the First Vatican Council. Since Paul attempts to explain the process by which human beings have come to sin, rather than the process by which human beings can know God, we can never know whether Paul felt that human reason and the works of creation alone serve as a sufficient basis for knowledge of God. The First Vatican Council attempts to define how human beings can know God. In contrast, Rom 1:18–32 describes the miserable situation of human beings who know God, but have turned away from God. In spite of this difference, Vatican I has a firm textual base ("the invisible aspects of God, being understood, are perceived in the things that have been made")[29] and correctly interprets Paul as teaching that human beings can perceive the invisible aspects of God through the works of creation, without having observed or learned about God's actions in history and without having had Christ preached to them.

Interpreting Rom 1:18–32 in line with natural theology deemphasizes the centrality of Christ, which many Protestant interpreters deem essential to Pauline thought. One could then argue that knowing God through the works of creation is enough for salvation, that humans do not also need Christ. An abstract philosophy could replace theology and even the Bible. How could this be Pauline theology, the Pauline gospel? This uneasiness is well founded, since Christ, not philosophy, is so central in Paul's theology. Nevertheless, the passage stands, without Christ and with the affirmation that humans can know God through observing the world. How and whether human beings can know the divine or even of its existence and how and whether human beings can know how to lead an ethical life are the most fundamental problems facing theology. Paul's theology does not

28. [T]ὸ γνωστὸν (τοῦ θλιβερεοῦ), νοούμενα, καθορᾶται, γνόντες, διαλογισμοί, ἀσύνετος, σοφοί.

29. This more literal rendering of the τὰ ... ἀόρατα αὐτοῦ ... τοῖς ποιήμασιν νοούμενα καθορᾶται of Rom 1:20 makes the role of human reason clearer than the NRSV.

solve these problems, but rather contains tensions and inconsistencies concerning knowledge of God and concerning how to know God's will for
human behavior.

Natural theology, then, serves as a prerequisite for Paul's use of natural
law, which I will discuss in connection with v. 32. People can know "God's
decree" (Rom 1:32), because "what can be known about God is plain to
them" (Rom 1:19). This is a God accessible to everyone, even those to
whom the gospel has not been preached.

"What can be known about God." Although some have suggested that
this means that God's invisible being can be perceived as a whole, the
grammar supports the more usual interpretation of the part of God that
can be known, namely "God's eternal power and divine nature" (v. 20).[30]

"Because [or: "for"[31]] *God has shown it to them."* The "for's" continue;
here the causal relationship to "is plain to them" presents no problems.
People can know God through the created things, as v. 20 shows. Thus,
the text focuses on God as creator, and the pattern of divine action and
human response (v. 20) continues.

*"[For][32] God's eternal power and divine nature, invisible[33] though they
are, have been understood and seen."* V. 20 states more specifically the
meaning of v. 19. The created things make understanding possible and the
invisible visible. Did everyone understand? The absence of a subject with
the passive participle, "having been understood," leaves this question unanswered. People are without excuse because at least some have understood, which demonstrates the possibility of understanding.

"Ever since the creation of the world." Knowledge of God has thus been
available to humans before the giving of the law or the coming of Christ.
This universal accessibility means universal accountability.

"Through the things God has made." This term raises more questions
than it answers. Does the text refer to an order of creation that will lead
the careful observer to recognize that a higher power must have created it?

30. I agree with most interpreters, who view τὸ γνωστὸν τοῦ θεοῦ as a partitive genitive.
In contrast, Wilckens and Ernst Käsemann take the phrase to mean God's knowability, implying that human beings have access to God as an invisible being (Wilckens, *Brief an die Römer*,
1:105; see Käsemann, *Commentary on Romans*, ed. and trans. Geoffrey W. Bromiley [German
original, Tübingen: Mohr (Siebeck), 1973; Grand Rapids, MI: Eerdmans, 1980] 39–42).

31. Notice that the NRSV translates διότι as "for" and γάρ as "because."

32. I include "[For]" here to indicate the presence of the Greek γάρ, even though the
NRSV does not. This is the final "for" of the sequence that begins in v. 18 ("For the wrath of
God . . .").

33. A rhetorically artful paradox builds on two uses of the root "to see," an adjective used
as a noun (literally: "the invisible things"; NRSV: "invisible though they are") and a verb
("have been seen": the ἀ-όρατα contrasts with καθ-ορᾶται). The rhetoric is heightened by
the participle "having been understood" (NRSV: "have been understood": νοούμενα).

Are all beings, including animals and humans, "things God has made?" If so, how do we explain that animals and humans perform acts deemed by Paul to be unnatural and resulting from turning away from God, such as same-sex sexual activity? If humans are under the power of sin, can they be a source of knowledge of God? Perhaps some human behaviors provide knowledge of God, but how can people distinguish between human modes and actions that bear testimony to God and those that witness to the power of sin? Concerning animals, even if Paul did not know of or did not accept the view that animals do engage in same-sex sexual activity, other animal behaviors, such as violence and killing one another, raise the question of how humans can discern God's existence from observing animals.

The same problems remain, even if we read the text in a more general way—that is, that the simple existence of the things that have been made leads one to ask who made them. For example, the winds, the rain, and the sun may lead to knowledge of God and of God's power to nourish life on earth. But what about destructive earthquakes or violent animals and humans? The hypothetical ancient reader may have assumed that God caused or created earthquakes and so forth, but would she or he have recognized in these natural phenomena the eternal aspects of God, namely God's eternal power and divinity?

"So they are without excuse." This language of a law court reminds us that God is judge,[34] and draws the reader back again to the "wrath of God," in this case, to the punishment for the wrongdoing.

In sum, vv. 19f deal with the most fundamental theological problem faced by human beings: how can we know the divine? Paul's brief, paradoxical assertion that the created things show the invisible aspects of God does not settle that question. The theological debates about natural theology and Rom 1:18–20 highlight a tension in Paul's letters between his assertion in Romans 1 that humans can understand God's power and deity by means of the works of creation (as if the works of creation were sufficient to know God) and the Christocentrism of the rest of Paul's theology. Unresolved questions about how to know God lead to problems about how to know God's will, for example, concerning sexual behavior. After his explanation of why people were "without excuse," Paul moves to an accounting of the apparent results of turning away from the knowable God.

Romans 1:21.[35] *[F]or though they knew God, they did not honor God as God or give thanks to God, but they became futile in their thinking, and their*

---

34. Ἀναπολόγητοι. An ἀπολογία is a speech on behalf of the defendant, while the κατηγορία is a speech accusing the defendant, although these terms have other meanings as well.
35. Rom 1:21: διότι γνόντες τὸν θεὸν οὐχ ὡς θεὸν ἐδόξασαν ἢ ηὐχαρίστησαν, ἀλλ' ἐματαιώθησαν ἐν τοῖς διαλογισμοῖς αὐτῶν καὶ ἐσκοτίσθη ἡ ἀσύνετος αὐτῶν καρδία.

senseless minds were darkened.[36] In v. 20 Paul has asserted that God's power and deity have been understood and perceived; that is now no longer a debatable point. The text circles back to the "ungodliness"[37] of v. 18, which in Greek denotes impious behavior toward the deities, not lack of belief in them. These people actually knew God, but did not worship God in a fitting manner. The text does not specify legitimate forms of worship, as the verbs "to honor" and "to give thanks" might lead us to expect. V. 23 spells out only the illegitimate ones.[38] The "they" are always an amorphous group, called "those who" (literally: "people") in v. 18 and thereafter designated only by third-person plural pronouns or inclusion in third-person plural verb forms. Paul leads the reader who believes that she or he does worship God properly into setting up a "we/they" dichotomy, which is radically called into question by his sharp rebuke to "you" in Rom 2:1, directly after Rom 1:32.

Romans 1:22.[39] *Claiming to be wise, they became fools.* This verse repeats the charge of intellectual vacuousness made in v. 21. These two verses have a loose chiastic structure, that is, they form an X-shaped literary figure:

a: they became futile
b: in their thinking (v. 21)
b': claiming to be wise,
a': they became fools (v. 22).

This structure emphasizes the futility and folly by placing them first and last. The phrase "claiming to be wise" evokes once again (see v. 21) the image of intellectual debate and speculation. Paul's generally negative stance toward intellectuals and intellectualism is apparent here.[40]

---

36. "Senseless" (ἀσύνετος) implies lack of intelligence, as well as a lack of moral quality. The darkness evokes images of the sun becoming dark, of the darkness of the depths of the sea or the darkness of death. By describing their minds as darkened, Paul suggests the confusion of living in an unenlightened state.

37. Ἀσέβεια.

38. Many gentiles in the Roman world were attracted to Judaism, expressing their interest by attending synagogue services, donating synagogues (e.g., a Roman centurion [Luke 7: 2–5], and Tation [*Corpus Inscriptionum Iudaicarum* 738]), or by actually converting. Jewish forms of worship included scripture reading, prayers, songs (such as the Psalms), blessings, animal sacrifice in the temple, observance of festivals and the sabbath, and the following of dietary laws. While Paul may not find all of these forms equally valid for those who believe in Christ (e.g., dietary laws; see Rom 14:13–23), forms like these may have been what a Jewish-Christian such as Paul would expect of gentiles who came to believe in God independently of Christ.

39. Rom 1:22: φάσκοντες εἶναι σοφοὶ ἐμωράνθησαν.

40. Compare in particular 1 Cor 1:18–2:5 on the wisdom of this world and how God shames the wise through what is foolish, i.e., the cross.

Romans 1:23.[41] *[A]nd they exchanged the glory of the immortal God for images resembling a mortal human being or birds or four-footed animals or reptiles.* Structurally, this verse marks the first of a series of exchanges, each of which results in God handing them over:

> v. 23: "they *exchanged* the glory of . . . God for images"
> v. 24: "God *gave them up* . . . to impurity"
> v. 25: "they *exchanged* the truth about God for a lie"
> v. 26: "God *gave them up* to degrading passions"
> v. 26: "their women *exchanged* natural intercourse for unnatural."
> v. 28: "God *gave them up* to a debased mind and to things that should not be done."

The phrasing of v. 23 recalls "the things God has made" of v. 20 and the creation language in Genesis 1.[42] V. 25 charges that they "worshiped and served the creature rather than the Creator," while v. 23 names the creatures whom they worshiped, and through whom they could have known the Creator.

Paul draws upon motifs of Jewish antipagan polemic. Both the Wisdom of Solomon (hellenistic or early Roman period) and Philo of Alexandria (ca. 20 BCE-ca. 45 CE) explicitly polemicize against Egyptian animal worship.[43]

---

41. Rom 1:23: καὶ ἤλλαξαν τὴν δόξαν τοῦ ἀφθάρτου θεοῦ ἐν ὁμοιώματι εἰκόνος φθαρτοῦ ἀνθρώπου καὶ πετεινῶν καὶ τετραπόδων καὶ ἑρπετῶν.

42. LXX of Gen 1:26: God proposes to create a human being (ἄνθρωπος) κατ᾽ εἰκόνα . . . καὶ καθ᾽ ὁμοίωσιν. Πετεινός occurs in Gen 1:20, 21, 22, 26, 28, 30; τετράπους in Gen 1: 24; and ἑρπετός in Gen 1:20, 21, 24, 25, 26, 28, 30. M[orna] D. Hooker has emphasized Paul's indebtedness in Romans 1 to the Genesis accounts of the creation and fall of Adam ("Adam in Romans i," *NTS* 6 [1960] 297-306; "A Further Note on Romans i," *NTS* 13 [1966-67] 181-83).

43. Wis 15:18f. Philo of Alexandria also singles out the Egyptians for scorn on account of their animal worship (*On the Decalogue* 76-80; *On the Contemplative Life* 8f: for humans to worship animals is for rulers and masters to worship beings which are by nature obedient and slavish [τὰ ὑπήκοα φύσει καὶ δοῦλα]). In other words, Philo bases his denunciation on a presumed universal social order in which humans are masters and animals are slaves.

Owing to the close parallels between hellenistic Jewish writings and Rom 1:18-2:29 and to the difficulty in harmonizing the concept of the law present in Romans 2 with that found elsewhere in Romans, E. P. Sanders takes 1:18-2:29 as slightly altered Jewish homiletical material incorporated by Paul into his letter (*Paul, the Law, and the Jewish People* [Minneapolis: Fortress, 1983] 123-35).

For examples of images in ancient Jewish art, see: Estelle Shohet Brettman, *Vaults of Memory: Jewish and Christian Imagery in the Catacombs of Rome* (Boston: International Catacomb Society, 1985); James Stevenson, *The Catacombs: Life and Death in Early Christianity* (Nashville: Nelson, 1978) esp. 56f; Lee I. Levine, ed., *Ancient Synagogues Revealed* (Jerusalem: Israel Exploration Society, 1981) 8 (Hammath-Tiberias) and passim; Hershel Shanks, *Judaism in Stone: The Archaeology of Ancient Synagogues* (New York: Harper and Row;

Throughout the Roman world religious people venerated statues and images of deities, but animals and animal heads particularly characterize Egyptian religious iconography.[44]

But educated readers might also recognize in Rom 1:18–23 scriptural allusions to ancient Israelite veneration of images. For example, Psalm 106: 19f refers to the golden calf: "They made a calf at Horeb and worshiped a cast image. They exchanged the glory of God for the image of an ox that eats grass."[45] And Deut 4:16–18 warns the Israelites not to make idols for themselves "in the form of any figure—the likeness of male or female, the likeness of any animal that is on the earth, the likeness of any winged bird that flies in the air, the likeness of anything that creeps on the ground, the likeness of any fish that is in the water under the earth."[46] In other words, ancient readers could recognize Paul's anti-idolatry polemic as directed not only against gentiles, but also against Jews.

Romans 1:24.[47] *Therefore God gave them up in the lusts of their hearts to impurity, to the degrading of their bodies among themselves.* Turning away from the truth about God constitutes the principal—and primal—human sin in Rom 1:18–32. In Rom 1:18, Paul first assesses the fundamental transgression theologically ("ungodliness," "wickedness," "suppress the truth") and in v. 23 and v. 25 describes it in detail (worshiping images in the form of humans or animals, thus serving creature, not creator). Similarly, Paul does not describe the exact nature of the degradation in v. 24, but only its theological character ("lusts," "impurity"). Vv. 26f and 29–31 supply the concrete details.

The text flows from human action to divine counteraction to human action. This movement demonstrates how Paul explains God's wrath. Once humans, in their ungodliness and wickedness, had repudiated God, embracing instead images of mortal human beings or animals, then God proceeded accordingly and turned them over to impurity and dishonor.

Washington, DC: Biblical Archaeology Society, 1979) 89–95 (Dura-Europos) and passim; Michael Avi-Yonah and Ephraim Stern, eds., *Encyclopedia of Archaeological Excavations in the Holy Land*, 4 vols. (English ed., Englewood Cliffs, NJ: Prentice-Hall, 1975–78), vol. 1, s.v., "Beth-Shean"; vol. 4, s.v., "Tiberias, Hammath."

44. Animals also play a role in Greek and Roman religion, of course, as, e.g., the snakes that were an integral part of the Roman *lararium* (a chapel within a Roman house dedicated to the protective house deities) demonstrate (see esp. Pompeii). (I thank Prof. John Lanci for suggesting this point.)

45. "[T]he glory of God" (NRSV) is text-critically uncertain: MT: כְּבוֹדָם; LXX (105:20): τὴν δόξαν αὐτῶν or τὴν δόξαν αὐτοῦ.

46. See also Jer 2:11; 10:14.

47. Rom 1:24: Διὸ παρέδωκεν αὐτοὺς ὁ θεὸς ἐν ταῖς ἐπιθυμίαις τῶν καρδιῶν αὐτῶν εἰς ἀκαθαρσίαν τοῦ ἀτιμάζεσθαι τὰ σώματα αὐτῶν ἐν αὐτοῖς.

We can imagine the scenes conjured up by the text: an Egyptian priest worshiping a jackal-headed deity, a Greek woman bringing drink-offerings to a temple of Aphrodite, a festival for Artemis of Ephesos, a slave attending to the household shrine. The implied Jewish reader visualizes these scenes as epitomizing gentile ungodliness and wickedness: of course these people are impure. God's wrath against them is certainly justified. Paul's rhetoric confirms the Jewish reader's religious belief of gentile impurity. Since the gentile Christians in the Roman community had presumably left behind their former religious practices, they too may be defining themselves over and against impure gentiles.[48]

The phrase, "to impurity," poses an interpretive puzzle. While purity and impurity are central categories for Pharisaic and for rabbinical thought, Paul emphasizes strongly that they do not apply to food.[49] Why, then, does he employ "impurity" here with respect to the dishonoring of the body? Paul does maintain the concepts of impurity and holiness for the Christian congregation at other points in his letters.[50] The sexual impurity in question in Romans relates to gender differences, which Paul upholds at crucial points, whereas impurity in food relates to distinctions between Jews and gentiles, which Paul radically rejects.[51]

Further, why does Paul define homoeroticism as "impurity," whereas Leviticus describes it as an "abomination?" Since the Septuagint sometimes uses the Greek word for "impurity" to translate the Hebrew word usually rendered into English as "abomination,"[52] Paul's usage may not be

48. See, e.g., the mishnaic tractate ʿAboda Zara, which sets forth guidelines for dealing with non-Jewish religious practitioners.

49. Rom 14:14–23; 1 Cor 8:1–13; 10:23–11:1; Gal 2:11–14.

50. E.g., Rom 6:19 (contains the double juxtaposition of impurity/iniquity with righteousness/sanctification); 1 Cor 7:14 (juxtaposition of unclean with holy); 1 Thess 4:7 (contrasts impurity with holiness). I am using "unclean" as a synonym for "impure" and "holiness" as a synonym for "sanctification."

Michael Newton concurs that Paul upholds purity regulations in sexual matters (*The Concept of Purity at Qumran and in the Letters of Paul* [Cambridge: Cambridge University Press, 1985] 102–4).

51. See Halvor Moxnes, "Social Integration and the Problem of Gender in St. Paul's Letters," *Studia Theologica* 43 (1989) 99–113. Moxnes describes gender as "the difference which remains."

52. For "abomination," Lev 18:22 and 20:13 have תּוֹעֵבָה, which the LXX renders as βδέλυγμα. In the LXX, "impurity" (ἀκαθαρσία) usually translates טֻמְאָה. The Greek term for "impurity" (ἀκαθαρσία) can, however, also translate the Hebrew word for "abomination" (תּוֹעֵבָה, as in Prov 6:16; 24:9; see also Prov 3:32; 16:5; 17:15; 20:10 for ἀκάθαρτος as a translation for תּוֹעֵבָה). Within the Hebrew text of Leviticus, the nouns "abomination" (תּוֹעֵבָה) and "impurity" (טֻמְאָה) and the verb root for "to be impure"/"to defile" (ט.מ.א) overlap somewhat. See, e.g., Lev 18:27, in which "all these abominations" (כָּל־הַתּוֹעֵבֹת הָאֵל) refers back to transgressions defined as "impurity" or "abomination," as well as to others.

problematic, but it does raise the question of his precision with legal vocabulary. In the end, however, philological detail will not help us to understand Paul's use of "impurity" as much as a more systematic approach, such as that offered by anthropology.

Excursus: An Anthropological Understanding of Impurity

Anthropologist Mary Douglas has greatly advanced our understanding of purity, impurity, and holiness by insisting that we study these systematically. Douglas's analysis of ancient Israelite concepts of purity helps us to understand why Paul uses the term "impurity" (*akatharsia*) in Rom 1:24 and then proceeds to condemn homoeroticism. Douglas's explanation of the impurity of animals in Leviticus 11 and Deuteronomy 14 contrasts with earlier piecemeal explanations, such as medical materialism, according to which Moses was trying to improve the Israelites' health and hygiene by prohibiting animals that could harbor diseases. Douglas takes a cue from the first Genesis creation narrative, noting that each type of animal has a form of locomotion proper to its kind: "two-legged fowls fly with wings" through the air; "scaly fish swim with fins" in the water; and "four-legged animals hop, jump or walk" on the earth.[53] Animals that do not fit into these categories are unclean for human consumption. For example, four-footed animals that fly, such as insects (Lev 11:20, 23), cross the boundary between two-legged animals that fly with wings and four-legged animals that hop, jump, or walk. Since insects' mode of locomotion does not conform to that of one of the delineated categories, insects are impure; touching their carcasses renders an Israelite impure (Lev 11:24f). Locusts, on the other hand, which have jointed legs above their feet, move about on the earth by jumping and therefore qualify as four-legged animals that jump on the earth. Israelites may eat locusts, since they conform to one category and thus are clean.

Douglas argues that the biblical purity rules "set up the great inclusive categories in which the whole universe is hierarchised and structured."[54] In her view, the laws concerning clean and unclean animals correspond

---

53. Mary Douglas, *Purity and Danger: An Analysis of the Concepts of Pollution and Taboo* (London: Routledge and Kegan Paul, 1966) 55. See the important correction to Douglas's view of the creation myth as the conceptual model for demarcating and defining the universe in Howard Eilberg-Schwarz, "Creation and Classification in Judaism: From Priestly to Rabbinic Conceptions," *History of Religions* 26 (1987) 357–81, esp. 358–62. Eilberg-Schwarz argues that the authors of Leviticus tried to link the dietary laws to the creation account (rather than that the creation myth gave rise to the dietary laws). The priestly writers (P) composed both Gen 1:1–2:4 and Leviticus.

54. Mary Douglas, in her critique and commentary to *The Idea of Purity in Ancient Judaism: The Haskell Lectures, 1972–1973* by Jacob Neusner (Studies in Judaism in Late Antiquity 1; Leiden: Brill, 1973) 139.

to the laws concerning pure and common people, as well as to the laws on blemished and unblemished sacrificial victims, priests, and women. Through this system of purity regulations, ancient Israelites created worship in their daily lives: at their tables and in their beds, as well as on their altars. For Douglas, this system of clear and distinct categories invited people to meditate on God's oneness, completeness, and purity.[55]

Douglas summarizes: "[I]n general the underlying principle of cleanness in animals is that they shall conform fully to their class. Those species are unclean which are imperfect members of their class, or whose class itself confounds the general scheme of the world."[56]

This description fits ancient homoeroticism perfectly. Homoerotically involved women do not conform fully to the class of women, since they take on the active sexual roles that many authors of the Roman period describe as unnatural or monstrous for women. In fact, they form a class of their own, often called *tribades*. This class of women "confounds the general scheme of the world," because women should, by nature, passively and subordinately receive the male organ. Passive, receptive, soft men likewise fail to conform to what should constitute the perfect class of men: active, insertive, and hard. To define as impurity this blurring of gender boundaries is to solidify the boundaries themselves. According to Douglas, not only the ancient Israelites, but also some other cultures, have created purity systems in order to demarcate and map the world around them. I am applying her insight about purity to Paul's use of "impurity" in Rom 1:24 and simply stating the obvious: homoeroticism is fundamentally about gender. Impurity applied to gender thus means that people are not maintaining clear gender polarity and complementarity.[57]

55. Douglas, *Purity and Danger,* 57. Douglas does not explain how the purity system led to awareness of God's purity. Why would a pure God create impure animals? Why would a binary system lead to recognition of God's oneness?

56. Ibid., 55.

57. L. William Countryman, also drawing upon Douglas's theories, argues that Paul explicitly defines homosexual acts as impurity, rather than as sin, a category reserved for the idolatry (Rom 1:18–23) and social disruption (some of the sins of Rom 1:28–32) for which the homosexual acts are recompense. In his view, Paul does not require gentiles to keep a Jewish purity code. For Countryman, homosexual behavior, as impurity, demarcates gentile from Jewish culture; Paul treats homosexual acts as "an integral if unpleasingly dirty aspect of Gentile culture" (p. 117), which means that Paul's words do not relate to today's ecclesiastical situation, since we no longer accept the purity code underlying them (L. William Countryman, *Dirt, Greed, and Sex: Sexual Ethics in the New Testament and Their Implications for Today* [Philadelphia: Fortress, 1988] 109–23; quote on p. 117). Countryman reasons that Paul includes a purity concern at the beginning of Romans to persuade his Jewish readers of his understanding of the gospel by inviting them to feel superior to impure gentiles, while at the same time not alienating his gentile readers, who already know from prior contacts with him (see Romans 16) that he rejects Jewish dietary laws for gentiles (e.g., Rom 14:14). I agree with Countryman on the centrality of purity for understanding homoeroticism and that Paul

Authors of the Roman period describe women who have sexual relations with other women as both anomalous (their behavior is contrary to the order of nature) and ambiguous (they can be interpreted as feminine or as masculine). Douglas outlines four ways in which a variety of cultures respond to anomaly and ambiguity. First, people may reduce ambiguity by deciding on one or another interpretation of the ambiguous event or phenomenon. I think here of Lucian of Samosata, whose character Megilla protests, "Don't make a woman out of me. . . . My name is Megillos, and I've been married to Demonassa here for ever so long; she's my wife."[58] Lucian has Megilla/os reduce the gender ambiguity by claiming to be a man. Second, people may physically control the existence of anomaly. The selective clitoridectomy for women with masculine desires comes to mind here. Third, Douglas suggests that "a rule of avoiding anomalous things affirms and strengthens the definitions to which they do not belong." By depicting women's active love for women as monstrous and unnatural, ancient authors strengthen and affirm the definition of woman as passive, subordinate, and deriving their identity principally from men. Fourth, cultures may define anomalous events as dangerous.[59] The Levitical definition of male-male sexual relations as an abomination, which the Israelites must

---

was inviting his Jewish readers to feel superior to gentiles when reading Romans 1. I also agree that the concept of impurity inherent in Paul's words should not form the basis of contemporary sexual ethics. Countryman's sharp distinction between sin and impurity, however, does not hold up. He argues that homosexual acts were a purity issue for Leviticus (which is almost correct: Paul does call such relations an "impurity" but, strictly speaking Lev 18:22 and 20: 13 define sexual relations between males as an "abomination," rather than an "impurity"), but "impurity" (or "abomination") and "sin" are not mutually exclusive categories. Further, in Rom 3:9, 23 Paul applies the category "sin" to both Jews and gentiles, which I understand to refer back to the preceding chapters; Countryman does not discuss Rom 3:9, 23. Finally, the structure that Countryman proposes (Rom 1:18–23: about sin; Rom 1:24–27: about impurity, not sin; and Rom 1:28–32: about sin) would be more convincing if the text contained stronger markers indicating that the middle section concerns itself with mere impurity, rather than serious sin. In contrast, I see the three units as substantially interconnected, and I do not see indications in the text that Rom 1:26f defines the recompense for *both* the idolatry of Rom 1:18–23 and the social disruption of Rom 1:28–32.

Countryman defines the incest case in 1 Cor 5:1–5 as principally an issue of sexual property and secondarily a purity concern. His recognition of the sexual property aspect helps to explain the relation of 1 Cor 5:1–5 to 1 Cor 5:9–6:11 (Ibid., 197–202). Countryman's thought-provoking and helpful book would be even stronger if he more consistently delineated the connections between sexual purity and sexual property by applying gender analysis to the texts.

58. Lucian of Samosata, *Dialogues of the Courtesans* 5; §291; M. D. Macleod, ed. and trans., *Lucian*, vol. 7 (LCL; Cambridge, MA: Harvard University Press, 1961) 382f.

59. For these four responses (and a fifth, which does not apply here, namely that "ambiguous symbols can be used in ritual . . . to enrich meaning or to call attention to other levels of existence"), see Douglas, *Purity and Danger*, 39f.

purge by executing the two males, exemplifies this response.[60] Romans 1 extends the danger signal to sexual relations between women as well. Douglas notes that describing an event as dangerous helps to ensure conformity. Thus, taking seriously Paul's description of homoeroticism as "impurity" helps us to see it as a societal, rather than a private concern.

"The lusts of their hearts." The Greek word for "lusts," *epithymiai*, can also mean "desires," especially sexual desires. Paul does, however, often associate *epithymiai* with sin, transgression of the law, or vice.[61] As modern readers steeped in popular psychology, we may find this negative assessment of desire surprising or even offensive. Not so ancient readers influenced by Stoic philosophy, which devoted much attention to the means of extirpating or rooting out the passions.[62] And Philo of Alexandria calls desire "the source of all evils."[63]

Perhaps the NRSV committee, by rendering *epithymiai* as "lusts," wanted to suggest that Paul opposes uncontrolled or excessive sexual desires, but not healthy, moderate desires. "Desires," a term with a broader scope than "lusts" and not restricted to uncontrolled or excessive desires, is probably the better translation. In contrast to the Stoics, however, Paul does not present a concrete plan on how to deal with desire. For Paul, desire is a theological problem—the result of refusing to worship the true

60. The danger of crossing the gender boundaries also appears in Deut 22:5: "A woman shall not wear a man's apparel, nor shall a man put on a woman's garment; for whoever does such things is abhorrent to the LORD (תּוֹעֲבַת יהוה) your God." Philo, when commenting on this commandment, stresses that the law was intended to distinguish sharply between the domestic life of a woman and the civic life of a man and to guard against mannish women and womanish men (*On the Virtues* 18-21). See also 1 Cor 11:2-16 (on veiling and female and male hairstyles).

61. Rom 6:12; 7:7f; 13:14; Gal 5:16. See also Gal 5:24: "And those who belong to Christ Jesus have crucified the flesh with its passions and desires." On the increasing tendency within paganism to see desire negatively, see Aline Rousselle, *Porneia: On Desire and the Body in Antiquity*, trans. Felicia Pheasant (Oxford: Basil Blackwell, 1988).

62. The Stoics believed that the passions, unlike the appetites (e.g., thirst), have a cognitive base, which humans can alter, thereby curing themselves of the passions. The Stoics counted four basic emotions (concrete episodes of passion): delight (ἡδονή), desire or longing (ἐπιθυμία), distress (λύπη), and fear (φόβος), for all four of which they developed therapeutic methods of extirpation. The cured person, freed of concern about externals, could pursue virtue and carry out duty in all serenity. For a thorough and sympathetic philosophical analysis, followed by critical questions, see Martha Nussbaum, "The Stoics on the Extirpation of the Passions," *Apeiron* 20 (1987) 129-77; see also her compendious study *The Therapy of Desire: Theory and Practice in Hellenistic Ethics* (Princeton, NJ: Princeton University Press, 1994). See further Nicholas P. White, "Two Notes on Stoic Terminology," *American Journal of Philology* 99 (1978) 115-19. For numerous references to the Stoic use of ἐπιθυμία in a negative sense, see BAGD, s.v. ἐπιθυμία.

63. *On the Special Laws* 4.84.

God. The cure for lust or desire presumably lies in correct worship, in other words, in behavior or action.

"To the degrading of their bodies among themselves." The term for "degrade" (*atimazō*) can also be rendered "dishonor."[64] For Paul, treatment of female and male bodies should differ, especially with respect to honor. Paul asks in 1 Cor 11:14, "Does not nature itself teach you that if a man wears long hair, it is degrading (*atimia*) to him?" This required gender differentiation in hair length points to bodily appearance as a primary basis for distinguishing between women and men. According to the theological anthropology of 1 Cor 11:3, the man is head of woman. Short hair and the lack of a veil signify the male body, as God's image and glory (1 Cor 11:7); the opposite conditions, long hair and veil, apply to the female body, marking the woman's subordinate status as the glory of man (1 Cor 11:7). In this hierarchical framework, a noncompliant woman brings shame (*kataischynō*) upon her husband.[65] Paul, however, seems to use the term *atimazō* ("to degrade" or "to dishonor") to refer to both females and males, as if the women had honor to lose. Does Paul mean that the women of v. 26 have lost honor or rather that they have brought shame upon men?

Romans 1:25.[66] *[B]ecause they exchanged the truth about God for a lie and worshiped and served the creature rather the Creator,*[67] *who is blessed forever! Amen.*[68] V. 25 parallels v. 23. The beginning of v. 25 repeats the

64. Ἀτιμάζεσθαι. The articular infinitive in the genitive is consecutive, i.e., the *result* of God's having turned them over to impurity is that they dishonor or degrade their bodies among themselves.

65. Some anthropologists have argued that men's honor derives from women's sexual conduct and that women really cannot achieve honor for themselves; see Unni Wikan, "Shame and Honour: A Contestable Pair," *Man* 19 (1984) 635–52, for citations and a rebuttal of this position.

66. Rom 1:25: οἵτινες μετήλλαξαν τὴν ἀλήθειαν τοῦ θεοῦ ἐν τῷ ψεύδει καὶ ἐσεβάσθησαν καὶ ἐλάτρευσαν τῇ κτίσει παρὰ τὸν κτίσαντα, ὅς ἐστιν εὐλογητὸς εἰς τοὺς αἰῶνας, ἀμήν.

67. "To worship" signifies expressing the feelings of awe, fear, and respect due to a deity, while "to serve" denotes the carrying out of religious, especially cultic, duties, such as offering sacrifice in a temple. "Creature" here probably refers to the images of v. 23. There is a certain irony here, in that an image is a creation of a human being; it is a creation of a creature. This evokes the memory of such texts as the Wisdom of Solomon, with its bitingly sarcastic depiction of a woodcutter carving a cast-off piece of a tree into the likeness of a human or an animal, painting it, setting it up, and praying to it (Wis 13:11–19). See also Rom 1:20 ("things . . . made").

68. A traditional Jewish doxology follows directly upon the heels of charges of false worship. For the Jews among Paul's readers, the effect is complete. This familiar Jewish liturgical form shows them that Paul is speaking of the God of Israel. Since the Jewish readers know that they worship the God of Israel, that is, the true God, they "know" that Paul is speaking of the

substance of v. 23: human beings, who were capable of knowing God's power and divine nature, *exchanged* the knowledge of the truth (see also vv. 18, 20) for a lie. This repetition in the text underscores the profundity and dreadfulness of that fundamental exchange. After giving a summary statement in v. 24 of the result of the terrible deed of exchanging the glory of God for an image, Paul returns to the deed once again, paraphrasing it. "Glory" becomes "truth," and "image" becomes "lie." Rom 1:18-32 does not proceed in a linear or logical fashion. Rather, the progression in the text is lack of progression; everything leads back to that one, fatal human action. For this reason, attempts to discern a linear outline fail. Nor is the text circular. Instead, it forms a spiral, beginning with the human rejection of the true God, climbing to God's response, and then winding back again to the human turn toward falsehood. While circling back upon itself, it simultaneously progresses forward. Only after the passage makes the spiral-progression clear (specifically, the causal relationship between the human action and the divine response), can it proceed to the content of the impurity.

Romans 1:26.[69] *For this reason God gave them up to degrading passions. Their women exchanged natural intercourse for unnatural.*[70] How could a good God hand people over to behaviors that are deserving of death (v. 32)? The spiral movement of the text illustrates human accountability and God's impartiality through the image of God as judge and bailiff. God reacts to humans having turned away from the truth by handing them over into the custody of degrading passions.[71] Is God thereby unfair or cruel?

---

gentiles here. The mention of images of humans and of animals, of impurity, and of dishonor in vv. 23f has already directed the intended Jewish readers toward gentiles and their false worship. The familiar Jewish prayer introduces a note of proper Jewish piety into the text. The very mention of the Creator deserves a prayer. What a contrast to the meaningless prayers to idols! The prayer emphasizes the scandalous nature of the false worship.

69. Rom 1:26: Διὰ τοῦτο παρέδωκεν αὐτοὺς ὁ θεὸς εἰς πάθη ἀτιμίας, αἵ τε γὰρ θήλειαι αὐτῶν μετήλλαξαν τὴν φυσικὴν χρῆσιν εἰς τὴν παρὰ φύσιν.

70. For scholarly discussion of Rom 1:26f specifically and of the Bible and homosexuality generally, as well as of ecclesiastical stances on same-sex love, see my Select Annotated Bibliography.

71. Paul J. Achtemeier describes God's punishment for idolatry as permissiveness, that is, God allows rebellious human beings to have their own way. Achtemeier recognizes homo-eroticism as a question of the order of society, rather than simply a private matter. He sees Paul's focus in Romans 1 as abuse: "abuse of the created order of male and female . . . abuse of creation . . . abuse of one another as creatures" (*Romans* [Interpretation; Atlanta: John Knox, 1985] 40f). I agree with Achtemeier on Paul's societal focus, but I believe that the possibilities for abuse inherent in families with women and children (and in Paul's world, also slaves) subordinated to a father far outweigh the abuses that may occur when strict gender boundaries are blurred and homoeroticism is accepted.

Not within the framework of this text, as vv. 19f establish. Paul dovetails the ability to know God with a requirement to recognize and worship that God without exception.

Vv. 19–26a both expand and explicate v. 18. With the second part of v. 26, the text moves forward. We begin to learn the meaning of impurity and the degrading passions. Paul's suspension of details for several verses may signal disgust concerning the degrading acts. Even here as the actions of the women begin to come to light, Paul favors roundabout description. Only the discussion of men's passion for other men in v. 27 is genuinely explicit. The fourth-century church father John Chrysostom, commenting on this passage, claimed that this type of sexual contact is more shameful for women than for men, since women ought to be more modest than men.[72] This commonly held cultural assumption about female shame may help to explain why Paul mentions women first and why he does not spell out the exact form of their sexual contact. Perhaps, as for many other writers throughout history, female homoeroticism is unspeakable for Paul, making him hesitant to describe it precisely.

Another explanation for mentioning women first could be that homoeroticism represents an overturning of the order of creation. According to Genesis 2, to which Paul refers in 1 Cor 11:8f, God created woman from man and for man. Women in relationships with other women defy the created order of "woman from man" and "woman for the sake of man."

"*Their women.*"[73] The text speaks of "their" women, which points to the group nature of the transgression. Rather than the image of isolated individuals worshiping idols, the text evokes a picture of groups engaging

72. John Chrysostom, *In Epistolam ad Romanos*, Homily 4, *PG* 60.417; ET: John Boswell, *Christianity, Social Tolerance, and Homosexuality: Gay People in Western Europe from the Beginning of the Christian Era to the Fourteenth Century* (Chicago: University of Chicago Press, 1980) 360.

73. The Greek term for "women" in v. 26 is actually "females" (θήλειαι). "Females" is reminiscent of Gen 1:27 ("male and female God created them"), just as the terms "human being," "birds," "four-footed animals" and "reptiles" (all found in Rom 1:23) occur at a number of points in Genesis 1. Perhaps Paul is indirectly alluding to an order of creation, which is certainly at the forefront of what has just been said in Rom 1:18–25, but why then does he—in contrast to the creation narrative in Genesis 1 (see specifically Gen 1:27)—mention women first? (See Gal 3:28 and Mark 10:6, which preserve the order of Gen 1:27.) Otto Michel suggests that Paul's placing the women first could derive from the Genesis account of the sin of Eve and of Adam (*Der Brief an die Römer* [Kritisch-Exegetischer Kommentar über das Neue Testament 4; 5th reworked ed.; Göttingen: Vandenhoeck and Ruprecht, 1978] 105). C. E. B. Cranfield argues that mentioning the women first allows Paul to discuss the men at greater length in the second part of the sentence. He also notes that the terms "males" and "females" make clear Paul's focus on sexual differentiation (*A Critical and Exegetical Commentary on the Epistle to the Romans*, vol. 1 [International Critical Commentary; Edinburgh: Clark, 1975] 125).

in such religious practices. Jewish readers would think of groups of pagans. Thus, "their" women connotes the wives and daughters of the gentiles.

The relativizing "their" occurs only for the women (the text does not speak of "their" men). Indeed, it is a logical term in male-dominated societies, in which women belong to men and are seen in relation to them. This qualifying of women underscores their subordinate status within this culture.

"Exchanged natural intercourse for unnatural."[74] If we read Rom 1:26f in light of a broad variety of ancient sources on sexuality and gender roles, "natural" intercourse means penetration of a subordinate person by a dominant one.[75] Sexual relations between women confounded societal categories of gender that classify all females as passive, subordinate recipients of penetration. In this framework, all female-female sexual relations were inherently unnatural. Roman-period authors (e.g., Seneca the Elder, Martial, Soranos, Lucian) frequently depicted women who had sexual relations with other women as having become like men, that is, as trying to transcend the passive, subordinate role accorded to them by nature by attempting to take on a dominant, penetrating role.

"Exchanged" implies that the women were capable of natural intercourse, just as those who "exchanged the glory of the immortal God for images" (v. 23) were capable of knowing and worshiping the true God.[76]

---

74. John Boswell argued that παρὰ φύσιν means "*beyond* nature in the sense of 'extraordinary, peculiar,' " since παρά can mean "in excess of" in addition to "contrary to." He also held that παρὰ φύσιν does not refer to a transgression against natural law, a concept which was not fully developed at that time (*Christianity, Social Tolerance, and Homosexuality*, 111–14). The context within Romans 1, however, makes clear the condemnatory character of Paul's statement, and παρὰ φύσιν far more frequently means "contrary to nature" than "beyond nature." In Boswell's favor, however, is Origen's commentary on Romans (extant only in the Latin translation of Rufinus), which, with the exception of one manuscript, reads *extra naturam*, rather than *contra naturam* (on Rom 1:26–2:1; 1.22 [19]; Caroline P. Hammond Bammel, ed., *Der Römerbriefkommentar des Origenes: Kritische Ausgabe der Übersetzung Rufins: Buch 1–3* [Vetus Latina: Aus der Geschichte der lateinischen Bibel 16; Freiburg: Herder, 1990] 92; see also Caroline P. Hammond Bammel, *Der Römerbrieftext des Rufin und seine Origenes-Übersetzung* [Vetus Latina: Aus der Geschichte der lateinischen Bibel 10; Freiburg: Herder, 1985] 165, 289, 460). For further discussion of the meaning of παρὰ φύσιν, see Richard B. Hays, "Relations Natural and Unnatural: A Response to John Boswell's Exegesis of Romans 1," *Journal of Religious Ethics* 14 (1986) 187, 196–99. In contrast to Boswell, I hold that Paul was participating in the natural law debate, but παρὰ φύσιν is only one piece of the evidence for that (see below).

75. Most Greek and some Roman authors did classify the penetration of certain categories of subordinate males, such as a boy or a slave, as natural, but Jewish authors, in line with Leviticus, did not.

76. *Testaments of the Twelve Patriarchs*, a Jewish work from around the second century BCE, uses similar arguments and terminology. Jacob's son Naphtali warns his sons before he dies about the gentiles, who "changed the order." These gentiles "forsook the Lord" and

Some scholars have argued that "exchanged" in v. 26 and "giving up" in v. 27 show that the text speaks of heterosexuals committing homosexual acts, rather than of homosexual persons per se, on the grounds that Paul presupposes their ability to engage in "natural intercourse."[77] Proponents of this position hold that Paul's words do not address the situation of lesbians and gay men today, who may feel that they cannot engage in heterosexual intercourse, since their homosexuality is innate to their being. Other interpreters hold that such a distinction is alien to Paul, and indeed to his whole culture, and that Paul completely condemned homosexual acts.[78]

Neither group's position precisely suits Paul's culture—or our own. On the one hand, the evidence from ancient astrology and medicine establishes that some people in the Roman world conceptualized a congenital sexual orientation, although sexual orientation was far more complicated than simply "homosexual" or "heterosexual" and could include the categories active or passive, public or private, orientation toward persons richer or poorer, higher or lower in status, and—in the case of men—attraction toward boys or toward males of any age.[79] On the other hand, Paul may have accepted such a view, but, like the medical teachers cited by Soranos, he may have seen the inherited condition as an inherited disease, brought on

---

worshiped sticks and stones and patterned themselves after wandering spirits. Naphtali tells his sons not to "alter the Law of God by the disorder of your actions," not to "become like Sodom, which departed from the order of nature" (*Testament of Naphtali* 3:4: μὴ γένεσθε ὡς Σόδομα, ἥτις ἐνήλλαξε τάξιν φύσεως αὐτῆς [M. de Jonge, ed., *Testamentum XII Patriarcharum* (2d ed.; Leiden: Brill, 1970) 54; ET: *OTP,* 1:812]); see also 4:2. "Sodom" may refer to male-male relations. Learned Jewish readers may have recognized this common Jewish view of gentiles: they have turned away from the true God to worship idols, and they lead a disorderly life. See Lewis John Eron, "Early Jewish and Christian Attitudes toward Male Homosexuality as Expressed in the Testament of Naphtali," in *Homophobia and the Judaeo-Christian Tradition*, ed. Michael L. Stemmeler and J. Michael Clark (Gay Men's Issues in Religious Studies Series 1; Dallas: Monument, 1990) 25–49; and L. William Countryman, *Dirt, Greed, and Sex: Sexual Ethics in the New Testament and Their Implications for Today* (Philadelphia: Fortress, 1988) 63f, who argues that "become like Sodom" may refer to any kind of prohibited sex.

77. See, e.g., Klaus Wengst, "Paulus und die Homosexualität," *Zeitschrift für Evangelische Ethik* 31 (1987) 77; John J. McNeill, *The Church and the Homosexual* (3d exp. ed. of 1976 ed.; Boston: Beacon, 1988) 53–56; Boswell, *Christianity, Social Tolerance, and Homosexuality,* 109; and Else Kähler, "Exegese zweier neutestamentlicher Stellen (Römer 1,18–32; 1. Korinther 6,9–11)," in *Probleme der Homophilie in medizinischer, theologischer und juristischer Sicht,* ed. Theodor Bovet (Berne: Haupt, 1965; Tübingen: Katzmann, 1965) 31.

78. See, e.g., Hays, "Relations Natural and Unnatural," 200; and Derrick Sherwin Bailey, *Homosexuality and the Western Christian Tradition* (London: Longmans, Green, 1955) 38.

79. For an example of this spectrum, see Ptolemy, *Tetrabiblos* 4.5, who argues that these orientations are set at birth by the configuration under which one is born.

by "shameful custom," or like the astrologers, as innate, but nevertheless unnatural.[80]

With respect to our own world, both proponents and opponents of same-sex love debate its etiology. Since the nineteenth century, advocates of the decriminalization of homosexual acts and of civil rights for and religious acceptance of lesbians and gays have often argued that homosexuality is an innate, rather than a freely chosen condition.[81] Such advocates argue that if homosexuality is congenital, it cannot be a moral issue; rather, religious communities can and should accommodate homosexual relationships on an equal footing with heterosexual ones. Many lesbians, however, argue quite differently, claiming lesbian existence as a choice and a political act within the current conditions of patriarchy.[82] Such women challenge theologically justified male dominance as a root cause of discrimination against lesbians and of violence toward women and children, so that religious institutions cannot accommodate lesbians within existing theology. Lesbians have principally formulated this position outside of a church con-

80. Horst Balz recognizes this possibility when he argues that Paul would have seen congenital homosexuality as a very clear sign of the forsakenness of the gentiles ("Biblische Aussagen zur Homosexualität," *Zeitschrift für Evangelische Ethik* 31 [1987] 65).

81. See the recent neuroscientific studies on differences between gay and heterosexual men in the size of the bundle of nerve fibers linking the left and right hemispheres of the brain (e.g., Laura S. Allen and Roger A. Gorski, "Sexual Orientation and the Size of the Anterior Commissure in the Human Brain," *Proceedings of the National Academy of Sciences of the USA* 89 [1992] 7199-202), and on differences in the hypothalamus of the brain (e.g., Simon LeVay, *The Sexual Brain* [Cambridge, MA: MIT Press, 1993]; and Simon LeVay, "A Difference in Hypothalamic Structure between Heterosexual and Homosexual Men," *Science* 253 [1991] 1034-37). Some point to these studies as proof that homosexuality is innate. Such a conclusion is, however, premature for several reasons: (1) the studies did not include the examination of lesbian brain specimens (corresponding to the general lack of medical research on women); (2) the studies have not yet been large-scale; and (3) the brain differences could be behaviorally induced, rather than genetic. Scientists dispute whether the fact that the gay men in LeVay's study had died of AIDS affected the research results. For further critique of LeVay, see Bonnie Spanier, "Biological Determinism and Homosexuality," *NWSA Journal* 7:1 (1995) 54-71.

On the question of a genetic component to sexual orientation, see Dean Hamer and Peter Copeland, *The Science of Desire: The Search for the Gay Gene and the Biology of Behavior* (New York: Simon and Schuster, 1994).

For a survey of the neurological and genetic evidence, see Simon LeVay and Dean H. Hamer, "Evidence for a Biological Influence in Male Homosexuality," *Scientific American* (May 1994) 44-49; for a critique, see William Byne, "The Biological Evidence Challenged," *Scientific American* (May 1994) 50-55.

82. E.g., Adrienne Rich, "Compulsory Heterosexuality and Lesbian Existence," *Signs* 5 (1980) 631-60 (see also the responses by Martha E. Thompson [*Signs* 6 (1981) 790-94], and by Ann Ferguson, Jacquelyn N. Zita, and Kathryn Pyne Addelson [*Signs* 7 (1981) 158-99]); and Monique Wittig, *The Straight Mind and Other Essays* (Boston: Beacon, 1992) esp. 9-45.

text, in which lesbian voices are heard even less frequently than those of gay men. And bisexual women and men oppose discrimination while not claiming that they are incapable of heterosexual relations.

Thus, both arguments fall short (that Paul condemns only heterosexuals committing homosexual acts and not homosexuals per se, and that the distinction between sexual orientation and sexual acts would have made no sense to him). Paul could have believed that *tribades, kinaidoi,* and other sexually unorthodox persons were born that way and yet still condemn them as unnatural and shameful, this all the more so since he is speaking of groups of people rather than of individuals.[83]

Further, even if Paul condemned only homosexual acts committed by heterosexual persons, many lesbians in the church, who feel that they have *chosen* to love women, as well as all bisexuals, would fall under that condemnation and are thereby not helped by this interpretation. In sum, the category of the innate homosexual who is thereby free of shame and whose sexuality counts as natural does not fit the Roman world and does not address the self-understanding of many contemporary lesbian, bisexual, and gay[84] Christians.

I believe that Paul used the word "exchanged" to indicate that people knew the natural sexual order of the universe and left it behind. Paul uses the plural throughout Rom 1:18–32, showing the communal aspect of the behavior: as a people, they suppressed the truth about God, and as a people they changed their form of sexual behavior.[85] In other words, I see Paul as condemning all forms of homoeroticism as the unnatural acts of people who had turned away from God.

Does "natural intercourse" (*physikē chrēsis*) here mean heterosexual intercourse? If so, does it include all types of heterosexual relations? Are sexual position, age, and consent relevant categories? For example, would that include heterosexual intercourse in any position, including anal intercourse? Would sexual relations between a minor girl and an adult man be

83. This could mean that female-female and male-male sexual relations entered the human race at some historical point as a result of idolatry and would thus be in line with the medical teachers cited by Soranos who argue that the condition of the pathic male, and probably of the tribadic female, entered the human race owing to "shameful custom" at a prior point (Caelius Aurelianus, *Chronicarum passionum* 4.9; §§135f).

Richard Hays uses the helpful term "mythico-historical event" for the exchange of the truth about God for a lie ("Relations Natural and Unnatural," 200), which stresses the communal nature of the initial transgression that led to the homoerotic behavior.

84. Some gay men may also understand their sexual orientation as a choice, but the predominant gay male position is the innateness of homosexuality.

85. Paul mentions the societal toleration necessary to sustain such changes in v. 32, lending support to the communal interpretation.

included? Would heterosexual rape constitute natural intercourse? Does "natural intercourse" imply the subordination of women?

A main purpose of this book is to outline what Paul and his culture meant by "natural intercourse" and why they categorized sexual relations between women as "unnatural."[86] The Greek term for "intercourse," *chrēsis*, literally means "use." Greek authors from the classical period through late antiquity use both the noun *chrēsis* and the verb *chraomai* ("to use") in a sexual sense.[87] A man "uses" or "makes use of" a woman or a boy. "Their women" exchanged the culturally accepted form of men "using" them for another form of sexual contact. As the subject of an active verb, "their women" acted as agents in changing their form of sexual contact.

86. Richard Hays correctly argues against John Boswell that Rom 1:26f condemns sexual relations between women and between men (rather than referring to persons who are not homosexual committing homosexual acts, which are unusual or peculiar but not contrary to nature). I agree with Hays that Romans 1 concerns itself with humanity's rebellion against God, and that, for Paul, same-sex sexual expression constitutes a "flouting of sexual distinctions that are fundamental to God's creative design" ("Relations Natural and Unnatural," 191). Hays's argument loses its strength, however, because he fails to define those sexual distinctions for Paul and his contemporaries and to ask why ancient authors view such distinctions as natural. Hays concedes that, for Paul, nature "appeals to an intuitive conception of what ought to be, of the world as designed by God" (p. 194). In other words, Paul has constructed a concept of nature; he has intuited the kinds of sexual distinctions demanded by God. Hays further recognizes that Jewish and non-Jewish hellenistic thinkers shaped Paul's understanding of nature. Yet Hays says nothing of these thinkers' concept of nature as gendered or of their call for sexual distinctions based upon female inferiority. For example, Josephus describes the Jewish law as promoting the "natural" (κατὰ φύσιν) union of husband and wife and prohibiting relations between males (*Against Apion* 2.199, cited by Hays, p. 193). But in describing the natural union of husband and wife, Josephus emphasizes that the woman is "inferior in every respect to the man" (χείρων . . . ἀνδρὸς εἰς ἅπαντα) and that women are to be subordinate to their husbands (*Against Apion* 2.201). By atomistically citing several ancient authors' views that male-male relations are unnatural, Hays actually distorts the picture for the modern reader, who may not know the extent to which concepts of female inferiority shaped these authors' understandings of natural relations between women and men. Further, Hays treats female and male homoeroticism as if they were the same, which the ancient sources do not. Hays's lack of an accurate and complete historical base seriously hinders his ethical endeavor of suggesting a proper role for Rom 1:26f in contemporary theology. Hays criticizes Boswell for never questioning "the truth or authority of Scripture" (p. 210). But, ultimately, Hays attributes full truth and authority not only to Paul, but also to Paul's culture, because while he recognizes Paul's condemnation of homoeroticism as not original, but rather shared with his culture, he does not question—or even describe—the gender arrangements of that culture.

87. LSJ, and BAGD, s.v. χρῆσις and χράομαι. A later author, Pseudo-Lucian (ca. 4th C. CE), shows that in his time at least, *chrēsis* could include both coitus and anal intercourse (*Erōtes* 25 [comparison of sexual intercourse with a boy and intercourse with a woman]; see also *Erōtes* 27 [using a woman like a boy, i.e., having anal intercourse with her]).

The active verb (*metēllaxan*) with a feminine subject (*hai thēleiai*) is striking. The specific verbs for sexual intercourse are usually active when they refer to men and passive when they refer to women. Thus, a man penetrates (*perainei*) a woman, while a woman is penetrated (*perainetai*) by a man. Ancient Greek authors also applied an active verb to male animals having intercourse or to male human beings having intercourse with animals. Thus, a male animal or male human being mounts (*ocheuei*) his animal partner, while a female animal or female human being is mounted (*ocheuetai*) by her animal partner. The case is the same for marriage: a man marries (*gamizei*) a woman, while a woman is married (*gamizetai*) by a man. Some verbs, such as "to mingle" (*mignymi*), do occur in the active for both women and men, but the more common pattern is to use an active verb for the male and a passive one for the female.

"To exchange" is, of course, not a verb that means "to have sexual intercourse" or "to marry." Nevertheless, in the context of the widespread cultural view of women as sexually passive, for women actively to "exchange natural intercourse for unnatural" stands out.

The text leaves open a range of possible meanings for the new form of sexual behavior: sexual relations with other women, anal heterosexual intercourse, cunnilingus or fellatio, coitus in an unacceptable position, or sexual relations with animals or corpses. To ascertain the viability of this spectrum, two steps are necessary: (1) defining "natural intercourse" in contrast to "unnatural intercourse" within Paul's culture; and (2) seeing if the context within Rom 1:24–27 can help to limit the meaning within this text.[88]

The Jewish philosopher Philo of Alexandria, a contemporary of Paul, serves as a good guide to what a diaspora Jew considered unnatural sexual relations.[89] Philo gives a systematic overview of the biblical laws concerning prohibited sexual relations in his treatise *On the Special Laws*. These in-

88. This procedure will yield a range of meanings appropriate to Rom 1:26f. In addition to these two steps, I have also considered the use of παρὰ φύσιν and κατὰ φύσιν elsewhere in Paul's writings. They occur in Rom 11:21–24; in these verses Paul employs the image of grafting wild olive branches onto a cultivated olive tree to describe the relation of gentiles who believe in Christ (wild olive branches) to the Jewish people (a cultivated olive tree). Paul defines the process of grafting as "contrary to nature" (παρὰ φύσιν). Some scholars have used the Pauline usage of παρὰ φύσιν in Rom 11:24 to interpret the same phrase in Rom 1:26, concluding that the phrase in Rom 1:26 does not contain a condemnatory nuance (e.g., Daniel A. Helminiak, *What the Bible Really Says about Homosexuality*, with a foreword by John S. Spong [San Francisco: Alamo Square, 1994] 65f). This interpretation is methodologically problematic, however, because the two contexts differ so sharply.

89. Henry Chadwick notes significant overlap between Philo's writings and Rom 1:18–32 on a variety of questions ("St. Paul and Philo of Alexandria," *Bulletin of the John Rylands Library* 48 [1965–66] 286–307, esp. 292–94).

clude incest, adultery, pederasty, the rape of a widow, the rape of a virgin, and others. At only three points does Philo use or imply the term "contrary to nature" (*para physin*): (1) of relations between a man and a woman during her menstrual period; (2) of relations between a man and a boy; and (3) of relations between one species of animal and another (thereby implying that relations between a human being and an animal are also contrary to nature). He also calls those who have intercourse with barren women (such as men who marry sterile women and refuse to divorce them) "enemies of nature."[90] With respect to menstruation, Philo argues that nature purges the womb as if it were a field of arable land. The man, like a good farmer, must wait for the right time to sow his seed, thereby respecting the "law of nature."[91]

Philo's concerns for procreation[92] and for clarity with respect to one's gender or species seem to govern his categorizations. Male sexual relations with a menstruating woman, a boy, or a sterile woman will not result in a pregnancy. Sexual relations with an animal or between two animals might produce a half-breed. In the case of sexual relations between two males, between a human and an animal, or between two species of animal, ambiguity equally troubles Philo. He calls the boy partner of same-sex relations an "androgyne," and he accuses the adult male of teaching the boy "unmanliness and softness."[93] Similarly, he refers to the mythological Minotaur (offspring of a human woman and a bull)[94] as a "half-beast" and to the mule as a "mixed animal."[95]

By analogy, "unnatural" relations in Rom 1:26 could refer to menstruants having sexual relations, women having sexual relations with other women, and women having sexual relations with animals. Yet two principal differences distinguish Paul from Philo: (1) Paul does not follow all of the

90. *On the Special Laws* 3.7–82.
91. *On the Special Laws* 3.32f.
92. See also Clement of Alexandria, who justifies naturalness via procreation (e.g., *Paidagōgos* 2.10).
93. *On the Special Laws* 3.37–42. See Dorothy Sly, *Philo's Perception of Women* (Brown Judaic Studies 209; Atlanta: Scholars Press, 1990) 211f. For Philo's use of "male" and "female," see also R. Melnick, "On the Philonic Conception of the Whole Man," *Journal for the Study of Judaism* 11 (1980) 1–32; and Richard A. Baer, *Philo's Use of the Categories Male and Female* (Arbeiten zur Literatur und Geschichte des hellenistischen Judentums 3; Leiden: Brill, 1970).
94. Philo's use of Greek mythology to illustrate a point of Jewish law is striking.
95. *On the Special Laws* 3.43–50. The first-century Jewish historian Josephus also groups together sexual relations with a menstruant (literally: "a woman defiled by the things according to nature," i.e., that menstruation is nature's doing), with animals, and between males (*Antiquities* 3.12.1; §275). While Josephus does not call these three "contrary to nature," the constellation could indicate that he, like Philo, considered them to be such.

Pentateuchal laws and nowhere mentions menstruation as an issue for the Pauline communities;[96] and (2) Paul expresses virtually no interest in procreation[97] and was himself unmarried (1 Cor 9:5). (Paul actually expresses ambivalence about any form of sexual expression.)[98] Therefore, while Paul's categorization of sexual relations into "natural" and "unnatural" may coincide with that of Philo, Paul may have had a narrower concept of "unnatural." Concretely, Paul may have classified sexual relations with a menstruant as unnatural, but probably because of ritual impurity rather than for reasons of procreation. On the other hand, Paul taught that believers in Christ could dispense with at least some of the Mosaic law, which may have included the menstrual laws. The first readers of Romans, namely the members of the Roman congregation, may not have known Paul well enough to know his views on procreation or the Mosaic law. Thus, the Jewish-Christians among them may have had a Philo-like view of unnatural relations and have understood Paul's reference as applying equally to sexual relations during the menstrual period, sexual relations between women, and sexual relations between women and animals.

Most interpreters believe that v. 26 speaks about sexual relations between women, although a few suggest bestiality or anal intercourse.[99] I

96. Theoretically, menstruation could have posed a significant purity problem for the Pauline communities, since Paul encouraged celibacy and gave guidelines for temporary celibacy within marriage (1 Corinthians 7). Women who are less frequently pregnant obviously menstruate more often.

97. Klaus Wengst emphasizes Paul's recognition of sexual activity as a way of satisfying sexual needs (1 Cor 7:2–5, 9, 36) and the absence of reproduction as an issue in Pauline thought ("Paulus und die Homosexualität," *Zeitschrift für Evangelische Ethik* 31 [1987] 76). In a similar vein, Derrick Sherwin Bailey recognizes that the Bible never gives lack of population growth as an argument against homosexuality (*Homosexuality and the Western Christian Tradition* [London: Longmans, Green, 1955] 58). In contrast, Peter von der Osten-Sacken argues that Paul would have defined as unnatural *coitus interruptus* (Genesis 38) and medicinal birth control, but does not give reasons ("Paulinisches Evangelium und Homosexualität," *Berliner Theologische Zeitschrift* 3 [1986] 39).

98. See, e.g., 1 Cor 7:1 (which I take as Paul's words, rather than as the Corinthians'), 7:8, 32–40.

99. James Miller has argued that Rom 1:26 probably refers to heterosexual anal or oral intercourse. Miller points both to the minimal evidence within Paul's social environment for a concept of homosexuality common to both females and males and to the relative paucity of ancient discussion of female homoeroticism to support his view that Paul would not have conceptualized homosexuality as both a female and male phenomenon ("The Practices of Romans 1:26: Homosexual or Heterosexual?" *NovT* 37 [1995] 1–11).

Miller's argument has several weaknesses. He does not cite a single ancient source that defines anal intercourse as "unnatural." Herodotos 1.61 speaks of "illegal" or "unconventional" (οὐ κατὰ νόμου) intercourse, not of intercourse that is contrary "to (natural) law," as Miller claims (p. 9). Although Miller claims that Pseudo-Phokylides 189 refers to "unnatural" forms of intercourse with one's wife (pp. 7f), it in fact refers to unspecified "shameful" (αἰσχυντοί) forms of intercourse. And Miller correctly recognizes that "*Pseudo-Phocylides* stands as a

argue that "unnatural intercourse" refers specifically to sexual relations between women, because (1) the "likewise" (*homoiōs*) of Rom 1:27 serves to specify the meaning of Rom 1:26; and (2) other ancient sources depict

---

lone Jewish voice against heterosexual perversion, and is not specific" (p. 10). Later rabbinic discussions testify to a general acceptance of anal intercourse with one's wife. Although a few rabbis forbid it, according to halakhah a man may have intercourse with his wife in whatever way he wishes (see *b. Nedarim* 20a-b; *b. Sanhedrin* 58b). And since Miller concedes that anal intercourse between women and men generally carried no stigma in pagan Roman society, he has thus given his readers no source from which Paul might have derived an unnaturalness of anal intercourse with a woman. Miller treats oral intercourse even more briefly and cites no sources that define it as unnatural and no evidence that Paul's earliest readers took Rom 1:26 as a prohibition of oral intercourse. Beyond that, Miller cites only a portion of the ancient sources that mention female and male homoeroticism together and neglects the extracanonical early Christian ones entirely (including those that take Rom 1:26 as referring to sexual contact between women). Miller could have had access to some of these sources through my earlier articles: "Patristic Interpretations of Romans 1:26," in *Studia Patristica XVIII: Papers of the Ninth International Patristics Conference, Oxford 1983*, vol. 1., *Historica-Theologica-Gnostica-Biblica*, ed. Elizabeth A. Livingstone (Kalamazoo, MI: Cistercian, 1985) 287–91; and "Paul's Views on the Nature of Women and Female Homoeroticism," in *Immaculate and Powerful*, ed. Clarissa W. Atkinson, Constance H. Buchanan, and Margaret R. Miles (Boston: Beacon, 1985) 61–87. Further, Miller claims that "likewise" (ὁμοίως) in the *Testament of Naphtali* 3:5, which links unnatural same-sex sexual practices (those of the Sodomites) with unnatural heterosexual ones (those of the Watchers of Gen 6:1–4), shows that "likewise" (ὁμοίως) in Rom 1:27 could also link heterosexual with homosexual practices. He thereby overlooks the fact that the ancients would not have classified the Watchers' intercourse with human women as "heterosexual." Intercourse between the Watchers, who were sons of God, and human women transgressed the order of nature by crossing the boundary between the human and the divine. The *Testament of Naphtali* 3:4f constitutes a closer parallel to Artemidoros, *Oneirokritika* 1.80, than to Rom 1:26f. Artemidoros classifies both sexual relations between women and sexual relations between a human and a deity as unnatural.

Peter J. Tomson suggests that Paul was referring to anal intercourse, called in Rabbinic terminology שלא כדרכה (literally: "not according to her manner") (Peter J. Tomson, *Paul and the Jewish Law: Halakha in the Letters of the Apostle to the Gentiles* [Compendia Rerum Iudaicarum ad Novum Testamentum 3.1; Assen / Maastricht: Van Gorcum; Minneapolis: Fortress, 1990] 94; see also Hermann Strack and Paul Billerbeck, *Kommentar zum Neuen Testament aus Talmud und Midrasch*, vol. 3: Paul Billerbeck, *Die Briefe des Neuen Testaments und die Offenbarung Johannis* [Munich: Beck, 1926] 68f). Tomson overlooks, however, that the rabbinic concept of דרך refers simply to what is customary and thus implies far less than the Greek concept of φύσις. Tomson is on a weak footing by appealing to the rabbinic phrase שלא כדרכה, while not mentioning that the majority of the ancient rabbis allow intercourse שלא כדרכה.

Klaus Haacker has argued that Rom 1:26 condemns intercourse beween women and animals (prohibited in Lev 18:23; 20:15f; see also Philo, *On the Special Laws* 3.43–50), while Rom 1:27 condemns intercourse between men (prohibited in Lev 18:22). Haacker reasons that Paul's nonspecific formulation in v. 26 must refer to a phenomenon familiar to his readers and points out that the Jewish scriptures, as well as early Jewish and the earliest Christian writings, fail to condemn sexual relations between women, whereas Lev 18:23 and 20:16 do condemn sexual relations between animals and women (Klaus Haacker, "Exegetische Gesichtspunkte zum Thema Homosexualität," *Theologische Beiträge* 25 [1994] 174f).

In response I would argue that: (1) female homoeroticism was sufficiently discussed in the

sexual relations between women as unnatural (Plato, Seneca the Elder, Martial, Ovid, Ptolemy, Artemidoros, probably Dorotheos of Sidon). One further possibility is sexual relations between a woman and a corpse, which Artemidoros calls "unnatural," but—in contrast to same-sex sexual relations—Paul does not explicitly mention intercourse with corpses, during menstruation, or with animals.

Numerous texts discussed throughout this book yield the following picture. Many inhabitants of the Roman world viewed asymmetrical sexual relations as the norm, that is, one active, superordinate person with a passive, subordinate partner. Notice that males can be either active or passive (such as when they are boys or slaves), whereas females are always supposed to be passive. The division between active and passive is, therefore, not a biological one. In my assessment, the shapers of Paul's culture saw any type of vaginal intercourse, whether consensual or coerced, as natural,[100] such

Roman world, both within Judaism and outside of it, for Paul and his readers to be familiar with it; (2) ὁμοίως makes more sense if both verses refer to homoeroticism, than if v. 26 refers to bestiality and v. 27 to sexual relations between males; (3) the phrase "the degrading of their bodies among themselves" (v. 24: ἐν αὐτοῖς) suggests interhuman, rather than human-animal contact; (4) if Paul had meant bestiality, he could have been more explicit (whereas his lack of explicitness in v. 26 on homoeroticism is balanced by the vivid description in v. 27 on homoeroticism); and (5) Haacker's arguments could as easily apply to a menstruating woman's having sexual relations (prohibited in Lev 18:19; 20:18; defined as against the law of nature by Philo, On the Special Laws 3.32f), which means that no single nonhomoerotic meaning would have jumped out at the ancient reader.

Derrick Sherwin Bailey suggests the possibility of a heterosexual interpretation for v. 26, noting that Ovid and Apuleius (and Martial) "describe the reverse of the supposedly 'natural' coital position" (Homosexuality and the Western Christian Tradition [London: Longmans, Green, 1955] 40, n. 1). The categorization of certain forms of intercourse as unnatural is Bailey's, rather than Ovid's, Apuleius's or Martial's. Rather, Ovid advises women to adopt sexual positions which display the more attractive parts of their bodies and hide the less attractive ones; e.g., he counsels a small woman to ride astride the man. Ovid describes none of these various positions as unnatural. In this context, he also counsels women to feign an orgasm (Ars amatoria 3.769–808). Apuleius describes both frontal vaginal intercourse and anal intercourse ("playing the part of a boy") without evaluative comment (Metamorphoses 2.17; 3.20). Similarly, Martial includes anal heterosexual intercourse in the epigram cited by Bailey without categorizing it as unnatural (Epigrammata 9.67). In the end, however, Bailey concludes that homosexual acts are the more likely referent in Romans 1:26.

A. M. J. M. Herman van de Spijker states that v. 26 probably refers to general, heterosexual, promiscuous unchastity, since the question of female homosexuality would have been alien to Paul's thinking; he gives no reasons to support this assumption (Die gleichgeschlechtliche Zuneigung: Homotropie: Homosexualität, Homoerotik, Homophilie—und die katholische Moraltheologie [Olten: Walter, 1968] 84).

On the use of the Greek verbs πυγίζω (to have anal intercourse) and λαικάζω (to fellate), see David Bain, "Six Greek Verbs of Sexual Congress (βινῶ, κινῶ, πυγίζω, ληκῶ, οἴφω, λαικάζω)," Classical Quarterly 41 (1991) 51–77, esp. 67–70, 74–77.

100. Athenaios (late 2d/early 3d C.) explicitly contrasts pederasty, which he calls "unnatural" (παρὰ φύσιν), with a Spartan general's seizure of 200 of the enemy's most eminent

as between an adult man and woman married to each other, an adult man
and free woman not married to each other,[101] an adult man and a slave
woman or slave girl, an adult man and his daughter, or an adult woman
and her son.[102] The type of sexual relations engaged in by women most
often called "contrary to nature" (*para physin*) in the Roman world is
sexual relations between women.[103] The materials found in Part I docu-

---

and beautiful matrons and virgins, which Athenaios defines as "natural" (κατὰ φύσιν) (*Deipnosophistai* 13.605d–e; Charles Burton Gulick, ed. and trans., *Athenaeus*, vol. 6 [LCL; Cambridge, MA: Harvard University Press, 1937] 262–65).

101. Some may have seen intercourse between a man and a married woman as unnatural, because it disturbed a man's control over his house; the followers of Zeno of Kition, the
founder of Stoicism, held this view (in Origen, *Contra Celsum* 7.63; *SVF* 1.58.11–15; Fragm.
244). See Helmut Koester, "*Physis*," *TWNT* 9 (1973) 265; or *TDNT* 9 (1974) 271.

102. With the exception of intercourse between a mother and her son, which Jewish law
prohibits (Lev 18:7), Jewish law generally allows the aforementioned types of intercourse,
albeit with some restrictions. Thus, a married man who has intercourse with the wife of an
Israelite male is liable to the death penalty for adultery (Lev 20:10; Deut 22:22), but if he
sleeps with a foreigner's wife, a prostitute, his own slave girl or slave woman, or his own daughter, there is no penalty. These do not constitute adultery against his own wife, and he has not
infringed upon the rights of another male Israelite. In other words, my examples are not only
natural in terms of the philosophical thought of the Roman period, but most are also legal
under Jewish law. Other legal systems operative in Paul's day, such as Roman law, also gave
free men the freedom to engage in a variety of sexual relations without penalty.

103. Other writers of this period employ φύσις and παρὰ φύσιν when debating gender
questions, e.g., Plutarch, *Moralia: The Dialogue about Love* 761E (love can lead women
to courageous acts beyond nature, even to die); Soranos, *Gynaikeia* 3.1.2.2 (against those,
such as Aristotle and Zeno the Epicurean, who argue that females are by nature different from
males); and 3.5.1.5 (female medical conditions are not generically different from those
of men, but only in a specific and particular way, since the male nature is the same as the female
nature).

Several writers of this period use παρὰ φύσιν in a Stoic sense: e.g., Philo, *On the Posterity
and Exile of Cain* 53.1 (unspeakable unnatural desires); *On Abraham* 27 (unnatural movement of the mind or soul); *On the Decalogue* 142 (desire is the hardest of all the passions that
move and shake the soul to an unnatural state); *On the Decalogue* 150 (without philosophical
reasoning, desire will distort life's affairs to a state of unnaturalness); *On the Special Laws* 4.79
(passion as an irrational and unnatural movement of the soul); Epiktetos, *Discourses* 4.6.11
(living unnaturally); and Plutarch, *Moralia: Advice about Keeping Well* 125C (the body moved
to pleasures by the mind's desires as unnatural).

Some authors define disease as παρὰ φύσιν, e.g., Plutarch, *Moralia: Table-Talk* 731E (unnatural conditions, such as diseases, are part of nature); Soranos, *Gynaikeia* 1.1.2.2 (division
of gynecology into the natural, i.e., anatomy and physiology; and the unnatural, i.e., diseases);
1.28.5.3 (some medical teachers argue that menstruation is unnatural, because it is due to an
ulcerated uterus); and 3.6.2.7 (do not treat premenstrual or postmenopausal women for lack
of menstrual flow or their natural condition will become unnatural, i.e., pathological).

Other notable uses of παρὰ φύσιν in this period include: Philo, *On the Contemplative Life*
70 (the Therapeutai and Therapeutrides consider the ownership of slaves as contrary to nature); Philo, *On the Eternity of the World* 31–34 (in the world everything is ordered according
to a natural arrangement [τάξις]; if anything is destroyed, it must have been arranged unnaturally); Plutarch, *Moralia: On the Eating of Flesh* 134B (emetics and cathartics as unnatural);

ment this point. The "natural relations" that the women gave up include a wide variety of heterosexual relations, such as marital relations, adultery, rape, incest, prostitution, and sexual relations between an adult male and a minor girl.

Further, the authors reviewed above illustrate a concern with anomaly and ambiguity when evaluating relations between women or between women and animals. Some ancient authors describe a woman who had relations with another woman as having become like a man. She was both anomalous and ambiguous by deviating from the norm of a culturally defined femaleness; in other words, her gender was ambiguous. A human being who copulated with an animal in Greek mythology maintained her or his human gender identity, that is, either "mounted" the animal or "was mounted" by it. But the mythological offspring of women who had intercourse with beasts were anomalous in that they deviated from the norms of both human and animal identity, and ambiguous in that they were neither fully human nor fully animal, but rather "half-beasts." Paul's description of man as head of woman and his call for strict gender differentiation in dress and hairstyle (1 Cor 11:2–16) demonstrate that he shares this concern over anomaly and ambiguity. Gender ambiguity is also the best framework within which to view Paul's understanding of unnatural relations in Romans 1.[104]

In sum, while ancient Jewish-Christian readers may have read Rom 1:26 in light of the other Philonic possibilities for unnatural relations, namely intercourse with a menstruating or barren woman, Paul's failure to mention the menstrual laws and barrenness make these less plausible readings. In fact, Paul does not use procreation as an argument against any kind of sexual behavior, including same-sex love. Rom 1:27, which discusses sexual relations between males, further delimits the range of plausible interpretations of the "unnatural" sexual relations of the women in v. 26. Although other ancient sources do condemn male-male sexual relations as nonprocreative (e.g., Philo), those on female homoeroticism do not attack women involved in relationships with other women for not bearing

---

993D–E; 995B, D (unnaturalness of eating meat); and 996B (we pay more attention to avoiding acts contrary to custom than those contrary to nature, such as eating meat).

104. Other scholars have implicitly or explicitly recognized this. See Richard B. Hays, "Relations Natural and Unnatural: A Response to John Boswell's Exegesis of Romans 1," *Journal of Religious Ethics* 14 (1986) 191 ("[r]ebellion . . . made palpable in the flouting of sexual distinctions that are fundamental to God's creative design"); Simon Jan Ridderbos, "Bibel und Homosexualität," in *Der homosexuelle Nächste: Ein Symposion*, with contributions by Hermanus Bianchi et al. (Hamburg: Furche, 1963) 60–62 (the issue is the boundaries between the sexes); Greg L. Bahnsen, *Homosexuality: A Biblical View* (Grand Rapids, MI: Baker, 1978) 55–57 (God ordained a specific distinction between male and female).

children, but rather for lives that are shameful, impure, unnatural, and monstrous.

Romans 1:27.[105] *[A]nd in the same way also the men, giving up natural intercourse with women, were consumed with passion for one another. Men committed shameless acts with men and received in their own persons the due penalty for their error.*[106] This verse makes explicit what v. 26 leaves open, namely the precise nature of the unnatural acts. The phrasing is parallel: just as the females exchanged natural intercourse for unnatural, so too do the males give up the natural use of women.

The Greek word *homoiōs*, translated here as "the same way," establishes as parallel the actions of the women and the men, which, I argue, means that both groups engaged in homoerotic behavior.[107] Rhetorically, the text elicits greater suspense from the reader by delaying its explanation of the women's "unnatural relations" until v. 27; here, the text defines "natural intercourse" as that between a man and a woman and its opposite as male-male relations. The possible interpretation of the women's unnatural relations as bestiality thus produces a strained reading in light of v. 27. Why would Paul have used "in the same way" (*homoiōs*) if the unnatural relations of the women were with animals, while those of the men were with

---

105. Rom 1:27: ὁμοίως τε καὶ οἱ ἄρσενες ἀφέντες τὴν φυσικὴν χρῆσιν τῆς θηλείας ἐξεκαύθησαν ἐν τῇ ὀρέξει αὐτῶν εἰς ἀλλήλους, ἄρσενες ἐν ἄρσεσιν τὴν ἀσχημοσύνην κατεργαζόμενοι καὶ τὴν ἀντιμισθίαν ἣν ἔδει τῆς πλάνης αὐτῶν ἐν ἑαυτοῖς ἀπολαμβάνοντες.

106. Robin Scroggs argues that Paul must be referring to pederasty, since that was the principal form of homosexuality in Graeco-Roman antiquity. In his view, Paul's condemnation of sexual relations between males is in line with other thoughtful writers of his time who recognized the dehumanizing aspects of pederasty. Scroggs amply documents the existence of pederasty and the opposition to it in Roman-period sources. If however, the dehumanizing aspects of pederasty motivated Paul to condemn sexual relations between males, then why did he condemn relations between females in the same sentence? Scroggs concedes that ancient authors normally did not assume a pederastic model for female-female relations. Scroggs discusses female homoeroticism only very briefly in an appendix, but maintains his thesis concerning pederasty even though the sources on women do not support it (*The New Testament and Homosexuality: Contextual Background for Contemporary Debate* [Philadelphia: Fortress, 1983] esp. 109-18, 140-44).

Simon Jan Ridderbos has suggested that Paul may be thinking of cultic prostitution ("Bibel und Homosexualität," in *Der homosexuelle Nächste: Ein Symposion*, with contributions by Hermanus Bianchi, et al. [Hamburg: Furche, 1963] 59-62), but his proposal has not gained acceptance, since the Roman-period sources on homoeroticism do not focus on cultic prostitution.

107. The Greek phrase ὁμοίως τε καί as a whole places the actions of the women parallel to those of the men. Both Nestle-Aland 26th edition, and the United Bible Societies' 4th edition construe v. 26b and v. 27a as one sentence. Thus, if "unnatural" were to mean a different type of sexual act for the women than for the men, this would mean a shift of meaning in mid-sentence.

other men? The reading that best takes into account the parallel structure of v. 26b and v. 27a is that both verses refer to same-sex relations.

An ancient reader familiar with Stoic thought could have read Rom 1: 24–27 within a Stoic framework. Rom 1:24 speaks of God handing people over to "desires" (*epithymiai*), while v. 26 speaks of "passions" (*pathē*) and of "unnatural [*para physin*] intercourse," and v. 27 describes men "consumed with passion [*orexis*] for one another." Such a reader would have seen God as reason itself and humans who are subject to passion as not living in accordance with nature. This reader could have been Jewish, such as Philo of Alexandria, who drew heavily upon Stoic thought.[108]

Diogenes Laertios (ca. early 3d C. CE) cites the definition of passion (*pathos*) offered by Zeno of Kition (the founder of Stoic philosophy; ca. 333/332–262 BCE) as "an irrational and unnatural [*para physin*] movement of the soul or an impulse in excess."[109] Because the Stoics viewed nature as imbued with rationality, "irrational" and "unnatural" are essentially synonymous. For the Stoic, one can know how to live in accordance with nature by observing it.

Diogenes describes desire (*epithymia*) as "irrational longing" (*alogos orexis*) and as one of the four passions, noting that the type of desire known as *erōs* does not affect morally virtuous people, that is, that they do not have erotic desire (which is based upon physical beauty).[110] Even without knowing the precise type of erotic desire, the Stoic reader would know that passions themselves are contrary to nature, contrary to divine rationality.

Owing to this overlap of terminology and conceptualization, Paul's text could have been understandable to a person familiar with Stoic philosophy. Theologically, of course, Paul's position differs considerably from that of the Stoics, since he insists on the necessity of Christ for human salvation, rather than the sufficiency of nature.

"The men, giving up natural intercourse with women, were consumed with passion for one another." The text repeats "the natural intercourse" (*hē physikē*[111] *chrēsis*) found in v. 26 and specifies it as the natural use of the female.

---

108. See Thomas H. Tobin, *The Creation of Man: Philo and the History of Interpretation* (Catholic Biblical Quarterly Monograph Series 14; Washington, DC: Catholic Biblical Association of America, 1983) 79–87 and passim.

109. Diogenes Laertios 7.110. Diogenes notes that the Stoics Zeno, Chrysippos, and Hekato all composed treatises entitled "On the Passions" (7.110f). Andronikos of Rhodes did as well.

110. Diogenes Laertios 7.113.

111. This term does not occur in the LXX at all, and φύσις occurs only rarely and has no precise Hebrew equivalent, demonstrating that the inspiration for Paul's concept of nature must have come from Greek-speaking Judaism or other Greek thought.

What Paul had left open in the first part of the sentence with the women, he now defines for the men and thereby retroactively for the women. In this rhetorically effective way, the text defines "natural intercourse with women" as the alternative to intercourse with men. If another type of "unnatural intercourse" were meant, such as anal intercourse with women, we would expect a distinction between natural intercourse with women and unnatural intercourse with *women*, which the text does not state.

"Consumed with passion" also translates as "to be enflamed with desire." [112] The negative connotation of *orexis* ("passion" or "desire") extends across Stoic thought and the Jewish literature most likely known to Paul, such as the Wisdom of Solomon and Sirach. [113] Whether we read *orexis* in a more Stoic or a more Jewish sense, it evokes the image of men enmeshed in a spiral of wrong behavior. Thus, while they actively give up sexual intercourse with women, their burning desire (*orexis*) for other males arises passively as a desire apparently beyond their control. [114]

The text alternates between depicting those who suppress the truth as actively undertaking an action (suppressing the truth, not honoring God, exchanging the glory of God for images) and as passively acted upon (God gave them up to impurity, God gave them up to degrading passions). This alternating culpability centers around the women's giving up natural intercourse for unnatural and the men's relinquishing of natural intercourse and being consumed with passion for one another. The text gives us mixed signals. Abandoning natural intercourse, although expressed with active verbs ("exchanged," "giving up") results from God's action of handing women and men over to degrading passion. Even as subjects of active verbs, humans passively receive divine action. The passive verb "were consumed" is thus a passive act within a larger passive scenario; the men of v. 27, already in a state of being given over by God to impurity (v. 24), are consumed with passion. They gave up natural relations because God handed them over, and they were consumed because they gave up natural relations.

Throughout this interplay of action and counteraction, the reader can lose sight of the precise moral culpability. Is their only sin the primal sin of turning away from God? Or is their sexual behavior also a sin? Rom 1:18-32 does not contain the word "sin" at all, but it would be a mistake to assume the absence of the concept, especially as it figures prominently in

112. Passive voice. This verb occurs in other texts of this period with a sexual meaning; see BAGD, s.v. ἐκκαίω.

113. Wis 14:2; 15:5; Sir 18:30; 23:6.

114. We cannot know whether Paul would have similarly employed both active and passive verbs for the women if he had spelled out their exchange in greater detail.

the subsequent part of the argument: "all, both Jews and Greeks, are under the power of sin" (Rom 3:9).[115] Further, Rom 1:31 speaks of a decree of God according to which people who do the things of the preceding verses deserve to die, which demonstrates that they are morally responsible for these behaviors.[116] Thus, even though the unnatural intercourse ensues from God's action, the text presents those who engage in it as guilty and deserving of death.

"Men . . . with men." The Greek term for "men" is literally "males," which includes males of all ages. This language calls to mind both Gen 1:27 (that God created humanity "male and female") and Lev 18:22; 20:13 (on lying with a male as with a woman). Romans, like Leviticus, condemns same-sex relations between males of all ages, not only pederasty. Like Leviticus, it demonstrates that the category of male homoeroticism existed in antiquity. Just as Lev 20:13 categorically places under the death penalty sexual intercourse between any two males, so too does Rom 1:27 condemn sexual acts on the basis of the partner's gender. I suggest that Paul, like Philo and many other Greek-speaking diaspora Jews, considered male-male intercourse a transgression of social roles, which he would understand as dictated by nature. The passive male has allowed himself to play the part of a woman, while the active male has taught his partner effeminacy and participated in his becoming effeminate.

Robin Scroggs has argued that in Rom 1:27 Paul was opposing the principal form of homosexuality known in the Roman world, namely pederasty.[117] Scroggs and Victor Furnish[118] believe that Paul's condemnation of sexual relations between males constituted a humanitarian opposition to the inhumane and humiliating institution of pederasty. If Paul directed

115. Interpreters disagree on whether Paul presents homoeroticism as a result or as a manifestation of sin (e.g., Abraham Smith, "The New Testament and Homosexuality," *Quarterly Review* 11:4 [1991] 18–32), or as itself a sin (e.g., Greg L. Bahnsen, *Homosexuality: A Biblical View* [Grand Rapids, MI: Baker, 1978] 49 ["both sin and punishment for sin"], 59). L. William Countryman argues that Paul treated homosexuality as an "unpleasingly dirty aspect of Gentile culture," which was not in itself sinful (*Dirt, Greed, and Sex: Sexual Ethics in the New Testament and Their Implications for Today* [Philadelphia: Fortress, 1988] 117).

116. William Countryman disputes that Rom 1:31 refers back to vv. 26f on the argument that the demonstrative τοιαῦτα ("such things") must "refer to the nearest possible antecedent," i.e., only to the vice list in vv. 28–30 (*Dirt, Greed, and Sex*, 116). "Such things" clearly includes the behaviors mentioned in vv. 28–30. Since, however, the demonstrative pronoun does not have a limit on how many words back its antecedent can extend, there is no grammatical reason why τοιαῦτα does not also include the vices of vv. 26f, especially because the content of the vice list of vv. 28–30 begins with vv. 26f.

117. Robin Scroggs, *The New Testament and Homosexuality: Contextual Background for Contemporary Debate* (Philadelphia: Fortress, 1983).

118. Victor Paul Furnish, *The Moral Teaching of Paul* (Nashville: Abingdon, 1979) 52–83.

Rom 1:27 mainly against pederasty out of humanitarian concern for the passive boy partner, several interpretive problems emerge. Why does Paul apply the phrase "deserve to die" (Rom 1:32) to all of the foregoing acts, not distinguishing between victims and perpetrators? Ancient Jewish readers would probably have assumed the boy partner's culpability, since Lev 20:13 commanded the death penalty for both males. Contrary to Scroggs and Furnish, Philo actually assumed that his readers would judge the boy deserving of death, but might not condemn the active partner (probably because the active partner remained culturally masculine). For this reason, after condemning the passive boy partners as "rightly judged worthy of death by those who obey the law, which ordains that the man-woman who debases the sterling coin of nature should perish unavenged, suffered not to live for a day or even an hour, as a disgrace to himself, his house, his native land and the whole human race," Philo feels constrained to add that the active partner is also subject to the same penalty.[119] For Philo, whereas a death penalty for the boy is obvious, the same penalty for the pederast (*paiderastēs*) requires explanation. Philo explains the pederast's culpability as pursuing "an unnatural [*para physin*] pleasure," "destroying the means of procreation" and becoming leader and teacher in "the grievous vices of unmanliness [*anandria*] and effeminacy [*malakia*]."[120] Paul's ancient Jewish readers would have had similar views and assumptions about pederasty similar to Philo's, that is, many would have condemned the passive boy partners as soft, effeminate, unmanly androgynes. Rom 1:27, like Lev 18:22 and 20:13, condemns all males in male-male relationships regardless of age, making it unlikely that lack of mutuality or concern for the passive boy were Paul's central concerns.

"Committed shameless acts." Since the Greek word for "shameless acts" is a singular noun (*aschēmosynē*), it could also translate as "indecency" or "disgraceful conduct." Strikingly, the Septuagint translation of Leviticus 18 and 20 uses *aschēmosynē* thirty-two times, although not with respect to sexual relations between males, but rather in connection with incest.[121] A learned Jewish reader could have noticed the Levitical language in Romans and associated it with the various forms of illicit sexual activity prohibited in Leviticus. Romans does not specify what the men did with other men, which could include anal intercourse, fellatio, and manual stimulation of the penis, all of which are documented in ancient sources.

"Received in their own persons the due penalty for their error." "Due pen-

---

119. *On the Special Laws* 3.37–39; F. H. Colson, *Philo*, vol. 7 (LCL; Cambridge, MA: Harvard University Press, 1937) 498f.

120. *On the Special Laws* 3.39; Colson, *Philo*, vol. 7, 498–501.

121. Lev 18:6–19 (twenty-four times); 20:11–21 (eight times). In each case ἀσχημοσύνη translates עֶרְוָה.

alty" is particularly enigmatic here. Did Paul envisage a venereal disease resulting from these men's sexual activity with other males? [122] Or was their becoming effeminate the penalty? Or perhaps Paul saw these men's sexual activity itself as the penalty for their idolatry? Philo of Alexandria may be referring to a similar phenomenon when he describes the passive partners in male same-sex relations as "habituating themselves to suffer from the disease of effemination," that is, physical softness and a passive sexual role (or: "a feminine disease," that is, a disease that women contract) and the active partners as becoming sterile.[123] In this sense, we could construe the behavior *itself* as diseased. Similarly, as we saw above, some ancient medical writers defined willing male receptive sex as diseased. As the text allows for several interpretations, any of the above options are plausible.

Romans 1:28.[124] *And since they did not see fit to acknowledge God, God gave them up to a debased mind and to things that should not be done.* Each time that Paul describes God giving them up, he describes the same primal sin in a distinct manner (vv. 23f: exchanging the glory of God for images; vv. 25f: worshiping and serving the creature rather than the Creator; and v. 28: not seeing fit to acknowledge God). The text describes God's action of giving them up in three different ways:

v. 24: "to impurity . . . to the degrading of their bodies";
v. 26: "to degrading passions";
v. 28: "to a debased mind and to things that should not be done."

Reading each of these as a variation on the same theme fits with the spiral structure of the text from v. 24 through v. 32. Each of the three (impurity, degrading passions, and a debased mind) leads to one or more results. Whereas impurity results in bodily degradation, degrading passions cause women and men to exchange natural intercourse for same-sex intercourse, and, when God hands them over to a debased mind, they do "things that should not be done." Vv. 29–31 spell out these things in the form of a vice list. This helical structure of vv. 24–32 means that the unnatural intercourse of vv. 26f refers not only to the "degrading passions" of v. 26, but also to the "impurity" and to the "degrading of their bodies among themselves" of v. 24, as well as "the things that should not be done" of v. 28. Paul strategically employs a variety of terms that might repel the reader

122. Based on the theory of pre-Columbian syphilis, R. R. Willcox, a venereologist, has suggested that the Bible provides evidence for the existence of syphilis ("Venereal Disease in the Bible," *British Journal of Venereal Diseases* 25 [1949] 28–33). Perhaps Paul is speaking of a disease of whose history we do not yet have a full picture.

123. Philo, *On the Special Laws* 3.37; *On Abraham* 135f.

124. Rom 1:28: Καὶ καθὼς οὐκ ἐδοκίμασαν τὸν θεὸν ἔχειν ἐν ἐπιγνώσει, παρέδωκεν αὐτοὺς ὁ θεὸς εἰς ἀδόκιμον νοῦν, ποιεῖν τὰ μὴ καθήκοντα.

("impurity," "degrading," "debased," etc.) and names a number of actions that the reader might abhor (same-sex love, murder, strife, etc.) in order to drive home the point that once these people turned away from the true God, they committed one iniquity after another.

"And since they did not see fit to acknowledge God, God gave them up to a debased mind." This cognitive language[125] echoes that of vv. 19-22, reminding the reader again that these people committed their principal error with their minds. Despite their theological aptitude, they refused to revere God as God. Since their minds generated the error, their minds suffer the consequences of becoming disreputable and discredited, and they manifest this debasement through their bodies.

"Things that should not be done." Ta kathēkonta ("things that should be done") is a technical term within Stoic philosophy, sometimes translated as "duty."[126] Diogenes Laertios attributes the singular of this term, "that which should be done" (*to kathēkon*) to the founder of Stoic philosophy, Zeno, and defines it as "an action in itself suited to nature's conditions," while specifying "things that should be done" as those that "reason [*logos*] prevails upon us to do."[127]

An ancient reader well-versed in Stoic philosophy could interpret this clause to mean that the "things that ought to be done" accord with nature, which is itself imbued with divine reason. Such a reader would view the people who have turned away from the divine as performing deeds contrary to nature and against divine reason. Paul's use of "things that ought to be done" and other terms popular within Stoic philosophy ("passions," "unnatural," "desire" [NRSV: "lust"]) increases the persuasiveness of his argument since it enables ancient readers familiar with Stoic philosophy to read Rom 1:24-32 in that light and to find a common basis of understanding.[128]

125. δοκιμάζω ("see fit"), ἐπίγνωσις ("knowledge," "recognition"; ἔχειν ἐν ἐπιγνώσει means "to acknowledge").

126. See Nicholas P. White, "Two Notes on Stoic Terminology," *American Journal of Philology* 99 (1978) 111-15.

127. Diogenes Laertios 7.108: τὸ καθῆκον . . . . ἐνέργημα δ' αὐτὸ . . . ταῖς κατὰ φύσιν κατασκευαῖς οἰκεῖον . . . . Καθήκοντα . . . ὅσα λόγος αἱρεῖ ποιεῖν (R. D. Hicks, ed. and trans., *Diogenes Laertius*, vol. 2 [LCL; Cambridge, MA: Harvard University Press, 1925] 212, 214). Diogenes lists examples of τὰ καθήκοντα: honoring one's parents, brothers, and native land and having social relations with one's friends.

128. Hans Lietzmann suggests that the vice catalogue in Rom 1:29-31 is actually more Stoic than biblical in its orientation (*An die Römer* [Handbuch zum neuen Testament 8; 5th ed.; Tübingen: Mohr (Siebeck), 1971] 35f). Anton Vögtle hotly disputes this point, seeing the Stoic influence as formal and superficial and noting that there is little verbal overlap between the vice catalogue in Romans 1 and Stoic vice catalogues and that Paul uses such terms as ἐπιθυμία and ἀνελεήμων in a non-Stoic sense (*Die Tugend- und Lasterkataloge im Neuen Testament* [Münster i. W.: Aschendorff, 1936] 206-17). Siegfried Wibbing empha-

Romans 1:29-31.[129] *They were filled with every kind of wickedness, evil, covetousness, malice. Full of envy, murder, strife, deceit, craftiness, they are gossips, (30) slanderers, God-haters, insolent, haughty, boastful, inventors of evil, rebellious toward parents, (31) foolish, faithless, heartless, ruthless.* This type of list, known as a vice list or vice catalogue, is common in ancient literature.[130] Since many of the individual elements of this list occur in other ancient vice lists, we can assume that Paul was familiar with this literary form and actually composed his from one or more vice lists known to him.

Among the vice lists in Paul's other letters, only this one breaks with his convention of including sexual transgressions.[131] The list in 1 Cor 6:9-11, for example, includes "fornicators" (*pornoi*), "adulterers" (*moichoi*), "weak/soft persons" or "men who assume a passive sexual role with other men" (*malakoi*),[132] and "those who have sex with men" (*arsenokoitai*).[133] Gal 5:19-21 refers to "fornication" (*porneia*) and "licentious-

---

sizes the parallels between the New Testament vice lists and those found in the Qumran documents (*Die Tugend- und Lasterkataloge im Neuen Testament* [Berlin: Töpelmann, 1959] esp. 92-94).

129. Rom 1:29: πεπληρωμένους πάσῃ ἀδικίᾳ πονηρίᾳ πλεονεξίᾳ κακίᾳ, μεστοὺς φθόνου φόνου ἔριδος δόλου κακοηθείας, ψιθυριστὰς 30 καταλάλους θεοστυγεῖς ὑβριστὰς ὑπερηφάνους ἀλαζόνας, ἐφευρετὰς κακῶν, γονεῦσιν ἀπειθεῖς, 31 ἀσυνέτους ἀσυνθέτους ἀστόργους ἀνελεήμονας· Some ancient witnesses either replace πονηρίᾳ by πορνείᾳ or add πορνείᾳ before πονηρίᾳ but the witnesses without πορνείᾳ are more reliable. Perhaps early scribes noticed the lack of sexual sins in vv. 29-31.

130. E.g., Philo, *On the Sacrifices of Abel and Cain* 32; Diogenes Laertios 7.111-14.

131. See in the undisputed letters of Paul: Rom 13:13; 1 Cor 5:10f; 2 Cor 12:20f; Gal 5:19-21.

132. For the meaning "passive male partner" for μαλακός see, e.g., Vettius Valens, *Anthologiai* 2.37.54; see also *Anthologiai* 2.38.82 (David Pingree, ed., *Vettii Valentis Antiocheni Anthologiarum libri novem* [Leipzig: Teubner, 1986] 108.3; 115.31f; see also appendix I.384.11). Philo of Alexandria connects μαλακία (*On the Special Laws* 3.40) and μαλακότης (*On Abraham* 136) to passive men. For the view that μαλακοί does not refer to homosexuality, see L. William Countryman, *Dirt, Greed, and Sex: Sexual Ethics in the New Testament and Their Implications for Today* (Philadelphia: Fortress, 1988) 117-20; and Boswell, *Christianity, Social Tolerance, and Homosexuality,* 338-41.

133. For the dispute concerning the meaning of this term (including whether it refers to both women and men or only to men), see: Dale B. Martin, "*Arsenokoitês* and *malakos:* Meanings and Consequences," in *Biblical Ethics and Homosexuality: Listening to Scripture,* ed. Robert L. Brawley (Louisville, KY: Westminster/John Knox, forthcoming); D. F. Wright, "Translating ΑΡΣΕΝΟΚΟΙΤΑΙ (1 Cor. 6:9; 1 Tim. 1:10)," *Vigiliae Christianae* 41 (1987) 396-98; William L. Petersen, "Can ΑΡΣΕΝΟΚΟΙΤΑΙ be translated by 'Homosexuals'? (I Cor. 6.9; I Tim. 1.10)," *Vigiliae Christianae* 40 (1986) 187-91; David F. Wright, "Homosexuals or Prostitutes? The meaning of ΑΡΣΕΝΟΚΟΙΤΑΙ (1 Cor. 6:9, 1 Tim. 1:10)," *Vigiliae Christianae* 38 (1984) 125-53; and Boswell, *Christianity, Social Tolerance, and Homosexuality,* 341-53. See also David E. Malick, "The Condemnation of Homosexuality in 1 Corinthians 6:9," *Bibliotheca Sacra* 150 (1993) 479-92.

ness" (*aselgeia*); [134] it also lists "impurity" (*akatharsia*), which, as in Rom 1:24-27, may include a "degrading" of the body, such as same-sex sexual activity. The vice list of Rom 1:29-31 probably lacks mention of sexual vices because Rom 1:24-27 explicitly and expansively addresses improper sexual behavior.[135] In other words, the content of vv. 24-27 belongs with the vice list of vv. 29-31, but Paul highlights the sexual vices by lifting them out of the list for fuller discussion.[136]

Why does Paul give special prominence to unnatural sexual intercourse, rather than simply list it in the vice catalogue? Perhaps he, and his readers, connected same-sex love with the urban center of Rome, since the sexually unorthodox can have greater visibility and cultural influence when present in larger numbers. As the sources on female homoeroticism discussed in Part I illustrate, Rome was a center of debate and discussion about same-sex love. With this reading, we can compare Paul's situation to that of a person writing to an audience in San Francisco or New York today; such an author would be aware of the large lesbian, gay, and bisexual communities there.[137] Paul explicitly condemns homoeroticism in his letters to the Romans and the Corinthians, but does not mention it when he writes, for example, to the backwoods of Galatia. Today also, a person writing to such rural areas as South Dakota or Idaho might be less likely to mention same-sex love than when writing to a city where homoeroticism was part of the public discourse. If the composition of Rom 1:24-31 reflects the reputation of the city of Rome, then Paul may be doing one of two things: (1) counting on the Roman congregation to agree with him about the iniquitous behavior of the city, thereby building their consensus with him; or (2) attempting to persuade members of the congregation not to practice acts of same-sex love and to oppose them actively (see v. 32 on those who "even applaud others who practice them"). 1 Corinthians 5 illustrates how Paul responded to an actual case of a Christian practicing a type of sexual intercourse prohibited by Levitical law. In 1 Cor 5:5 Paul recommends handing over to Satan the man living with his father's wife, and in 1 Cor 5: 13 he quotes Deut 17:7: "Drive out the wicked person from among

134. See the Greek fragment of Dorotheos of Sidon that refers to the birth of "licentious persons" in *Dorothei Sidonii Carmen Astrologicum*, ed. and trans. David Pingree (Leipzig: Teubner, 1976) 343.

135. Other commentators agree on this point; see, e.g., Ulrich Wilckens, *Brief an die Römer*, 1:113.

136. See 1 Thess 4:3-7 for a similarly full description of behaviors, rather than just a list.

137. Of course, our sources on homoeroticism are predominantly from the cities, especially Rome, which correlates with the greater literary production of the cities. This means that we have more extant discussion of all aspects of urban life. For the view that urban societies, including those within Western history, may be more tolerant toward same-sex love than rural ones, see Boswell, *Christianity, Social Tolerance, and Homosexuality*, 35-37 and passim.

you." According to 1 Cor 5:11, "the wicked person" is the fornicator, the greedy person, the idolater, the reviler, the drunkard, and the robber. Excluding them from the community includes refusing to eat with such people.[138] Perhaps Paul would have had a similar response to a Christian engaging in same-sex love.

If specific circumstances in Rome are not behind Paul's emphasis on sexual vices, then he may simply be employing a traditional Jewish anti-idolatry diatribe, which, like any polemic in this period, typically includes charges of sexual misconduct. In this case, Paul would be using Jewish anti-gentile polemic in order to obtain a common base of agreement with Jewish-Christians (who have learned this attitude toward gentiles from early childhood)[139] and with gentile-Christians (who may feel secure in scorning their religious past, since they are no longer idolaters). From this consensus, Paul can go on to address the more divisive issues, such as the role of the Jewish law or the salvation of those Jews who do not accept Christ.

We might also consider an intermediate position, namely that Paul employs traditional Jewish anti-gentile polemic and that he adapts it to the Roman situation by giving special prominence to same-sex sexual contact.

While we cannot definitively establish Paul's strategy in composing Rom 1:24-31 as he did, we can say with certainty that Rom 1:29-31 is the only Pauline vice list that does not contain any sexual vices. Rom 1:24-27 does speak of some things that occur in Pauline vice lists elsewhere, namely "impurity" (see Gal 5:19) and male homoerotic activity (see 1 Cor 6:9). "Licentiousness" (Gal 5:19) may be a further point of overlap, since some ancient authors call homoeroticism licentious behavior.[140] For Paul, "licentiousness" may have implied homoeroticism, especially since the Galatians vice list does not specifically list same-sex sexual behaviors. In Rom 1:29-31, Paul alters his usual practice of including sexual vices in his lists, but he has compensated for this by naming sexual misconduct in Rom 1:26f, three verses before the beginning of the vice catalogue. This observation confirms my reading of Rom 1:24-31 as a spiral-like unit of composition, based upon repetition and expansion.

138. See Peter von der Osten-Sacken, "Paulinisches Evangelium und Homosexualität," *Berliner Theologische Zeitschrift* 3 (1986) 38f.

On 1 Cor 5:1-5, see Adela Yarbro Collins, "The Function of 'Excommunication' in Paul," *Harvard Theological Review* 73 (1980) 251-63.

139. Several postbiblical Jewish works connect idolatry with vice, including sexual vice, e.g., 2 Enoch 10 (the J manuscript is more explicit than the A manuscript); Jubilees 20 and 22; Testament of Jacob 7; *Testaments of the Twelve Patriarchs*, Judah 23.

140. E.g., Pseudo-Lucian, *Erōtes* 28 (τριβακὴ ἀσέλγεια).

Romans 1:32.[141] *They know God's decree, that those who practice such things deserve to die—yet they not only do them but even applaud others who practice them.* "Such things" likely refer to all of the behaviors described or listed in vv. 18–31, rather than just to the vices of vv. 29–31. In addition, a number of questions arise from this verse. What is God's decree? And how have those who worship idols come to know it? Does death refer to a death penalty or to an eternal death, that is, being denied eternal life in the world to come? Does this penalty of death apply to all of the aforementioned vices equally, to envy as well as to murder, to gossip as well as to God-hating?

"They know God's decree." The text once again picks up the cognitive language of vv. 18–22. There the people could have known "what can be known [*gnōston*] about God," and, in fact, they did know (*gnontes*) God. But, just as they did not "see fit to acknowledge God" (*echein en epignōsei;* v. 28), so too "they know [*epignontes*] God's decree," but do not follow it. Again and again the text underscores the capacity of these people to know God and God's will.

"God's decree" must signify some form of natural law, the only form of ethical injunction that everyone, including idol worshipers, can know.[142] The idol worshipers' knowledge of God's decree in the form of natural law corresponds to their knowledge of God through observing nature (Rom 1:19f). I will expand upon natural law below at greater length. This decree cannot be the Jewish law, because the people who venerated their deities in the form of animals and human beings did not know the law of Moses.

"That those who practice such things deserve to die." Death could mean a ruling in the end-time, at the final judgment, barring them from eternal life. Death could also mean the death penalty on this earth.[143] We cannot know what Paul meant; ancient readers could take it either way. We cannot know whether this death penalty applies equally to all of the aforementioned vices, although Paul seems to imply that it does.

---

141. Rom 1:32: οἵτινες τὸ δικαίωμα τοῦ θεοῦ ἐπιγνόντες ὅτι οἱ τὰ τοιαῦτα πράσσοντες ἄξιοι θανάτου εἰσίν, οὐ μόνον αὐτὰ ποιοῦσιν ἀλλὰ καὶ συνευδοκοῦσιν τοῖς πράσσουσιν.

142. Rudolf Bultmann's view of "God's decree" as the ethical part of the Mosaic law does not explain how the idol worshipers could have known it (*Theology of the New Testament*, trans. Kendrick Grobel, vol. 1 [New York: Scribner's, 1951] 260 [German original, *Theologie des Neuen Testaments* (6th ed.; Tübingen: Mohr [Siebeck], 1968) 261]).

143. Philo, *On the Special Laws* 3.38f, describes the death penalty for male-male sexual relations in the most vivid of terms.

Conclusion

Rom 1:26f serves Paul's principal arguments in Romans 1–3, namely that all humans have sinned and that God impartially punishes and rewards both Jews and gentiles. These arguments each build up the case for one of Paul's main theological points in Romans: belief in Christ can save everyone, first the Jew and then the gentile. To this end, Paul argues that all humans need salvation, because all are sinners, and that God, that is, the God of Jesus Christ, deals justly with everyone, giving preference neither to Jew nor to gentile. In order to establish that all people can know right from wrong, Paul argues that the world around them provides everyone with the necessary ingredients to gain knowledge of God through observation (natural theology) and that everyone has access to the contents of a divine decree (natural law). Homoeroticism is the second example in Romans of a human behavior that runs counter to this universally known decree of God. Having lifted up same-sex love as a particular example of degrading passions and impurity, Paul then merely lists other nonsexual sins or vices.

For Paul, same-sex love in Rom 1:26f is a sin against the social order established by God at creation, and not just a private sin against a system of private morality as contemporary Christians may understand. Paul envisages a social order in which Jew and gentile are no longer relevant categories and attempts to break down the boundaries distinguishing them (e.g., circumcision and dietary laws). In contrast, within this same social order Paul deems necessary a natural, and therefore immutable, gender boundary. Those who do not confine themselves within these demarcated areas break down the required gender polarity and gender distinctions, thereby becoming impure. Accordingly, a woman or a man who physically expresses love and affection toward a person of the same sex behaves unnaturally and deserves to die. And the God who does not show partiality toward persons on the basis of whether they are Jewish or gentile *does* show partiality toward those who love or wish to marry persons of the same sex. Concretely, a Jewish-Christian woman need not marry a circumcised Jewish man, but, if she marries, she must marry a man. Crossing the boundary of circumcision no longer jeopardizes one's salvation, but crossing the gender boundary makes a person deserving of death.

Thus, within Paul's theology the famous verse, "There is no longer Jew or Greek, there is no longer slave or free, there is no longer male and female; for all of you are one in Christ Jesus" (Gal 3:28), has quite different implications for the first and third pairs.[144] While all six categories of per-

---

144. The distinctions between "slave and free" fall into yet a third category and would require additional and extensive analysis. For a study of the slave imagery in a christological

sons can gain salvation, Paul systematically works to dismantle the distinctions between Jew and Greek in the early Christian communities, but continues throughout his works to attribute religious significance to gender boundaries, as in the cases of same-sex love and of hairstyle and veiling (1 Cor 11:2–16). Rom 1:26f stands in tension with Gal 3:28: in Rom 1:26f maleness and femaleness are of ultimate significance, whereas in Gal 3:28 they are of no significance.

Paul's distinction between "natural" and "unnatural" intercourse serves as a window to his vision of gender and sexuality. I understand "natural intercourse" in Rom 1:26 to signify any kind of male-female intercourse, regardless of the age or consent of the female. In the light of the male-male relations of Rom 1:27, I read "unnatural intercourse" in v. 26 to refer to sexual relations between women. Since the text of Romans itself does not contain sufficient clues to the precise meaning of "unnatural," I undertook broader philological study and analysis of other representations of female homoeroticism, a topic that scholars have previously almost totally overlooked. Such study and analysis have revealed that Roman-period authors saw women who had sexual relations with other women as going beyond the passive, subordinate sexual role accorded to them by nature, and they often described them as taking on an active role, thereby becoming like men.

Against this background, we can recognize a range of early Christian exhortations to women to subordinate themselves to their husbands as supporting a social model that includes the condemnation of sexual love between women. For example, the author of the Epistle to the Ephesians puts forth the model of a household in which wives, children, and (female and male) slaves are subject to husbands, parents, and masters (Eph 5:21–6:9).[145] The author allegorizes Christ's relationship to the church as that between a bridegroom and bride. He urges wives to model their subjection to their husbands on their subjection to the Lord. Slaves are to obey their masters "with fear and trembling" as they obey Christ. Husbands are to love their wives, as Christ loves the church, fathers are not to provoke their children, and masters are not to threaten their slaves. Christian clergy often read this influential text at wedding ceremonies.

A love relationship between two women runs absolutely counter to this passage. Not only does the envisaged household have no room for a rela-

---

hymn adapted by Paul and its social effects, see Sheila Briggs, "Can an Enslaved God Liberate? Hermeneutical Reflections on Philippians 2:6–11," in *Interpretation for Liberation*, ed. Katie Geneva Cannon and Elisabeth Schüssler Fiorenza (Semeia 47; Atlanta: Scholars Press, 1989) 137–53.

145. See also Col 3:18–4:1; 1 Tim 2:11–15; Tit 2:3–10; and 1 Pet 2:11–3:12.

tionship between women, but such love confounds its very structure. According to the theology of Ephesians, reverence for Christ calls for hierarchically organized households. We have seen that authors from the cultural environment of early Christianity had great difficulty conceptualizing love between women in any consistent way. Similarly, the theology of Ephesians has no place for a female romantic relationship. Who would be subordinate to whom? Since the two women cannot base their love on that between Christ as a bridegroom and the church as a bride, their love for each other undermines the very theology of Ephesians. And what of the men who see themselves as destined to become husbands and fathers, destined to love their wives as Christ loved the church? If women refuse to take on the roles of subordinate wives and mothers, how can these men fulfill their divinely ordained roles? In this book I have focused on early Christian texts that deal specifically with female homoeroticism, but numerous early Christian texts contributed to the ancient cultural construction of females as subordinate to males, which is the cultural view that made sexual love between women a thing to be despised.

Female-female and male-male sexual relations in the Roman world and in Rom 1:26f are both parallel and not parallel to one another. They both exemplify homoeroticism, but they differ socially, since, within this gender hierarchy, a man loses status in adopting a passive role,[146] while a woman theoretically gains status by giving up a passive role.[147] Paul's description of the man as head of woman (1 Cor 11:3) and his use of the term *hypandros* ("under a man") for a married woman (Rom 7:2) demonstrate Paul's acceptance of certain fundamental assumptions of his highly gendered culture. Therefore, Paul's condemnation of sexual relations between women embodies and enforces the assumptions about gender found in nearly all the Roman-period sources on female homoeroticism.

As I have demonstrated, Paul did not invent the concept of "natural intercourse," but rather adopted it from his culture and gave it a theological foundation. While Asklepiades, Seneca, Pseudo-Phokylides and Dorotheos of Sidon fully represent hellenistic and Roman understandings of natural and unnatural relations, the influence of that model has come down to us on the stream of early Christian teachings, of which the Bible has been the most authoritative.

146. Within Greek-speaking Judaism, a man may also lose status by teaching effeminacy and unmanliness to the passive male partner.

147. This theoretical rise in status is the very reason that these ancient authors categorically condemn female homoeroticism. Since the culture had difficulty envisaging nonpenetrating female-female relationships, we cannot determine the exact status of all nonpenetrating women, i.e., the "passive" partners, involved in same-sex relationships. For further discussion, see Part I.

Intertextual Echoes in Romans 1:18–32

Well-educated ancient readers would have recognized echoes of other ancient texts when reading Romans 1, as well as terminology from the cultural and philosophical discussions of their day. Readers versed in Stoic thought, including Jews, could have read Romans 1 in a Stoic mode, noticing the concept of natural law inherent in the text, as well as the negative references to passion and desire. Some may have connected Rom 1:27 with Levitical prohibitions (Lev 18:22; 20:13) and Rom 1:26 with postbiblical Jewish condemnations of sexual relations between women. Likewise, they may have heard echoes of the Wisdom of Solomon or similar Jewish anti-idolatry polemic. In what follows, I shall explore several of the intellectual frameworks within which ancient readers may have read Romans 1. As with any text, Paul's Letter to the Romans is culturally multifaceted, making it possible to view the text from several angles. This method will help us to see how Paul's text relates to the culture of his time.

Natural Law

Was Paul familiar with the concept of natural law current in his time?[1] And did he draw upon it to serve his larger theological goals? The evidence that

---

1. Origen, the earliest commentator on Romans, believes that Paul refers to natural law (*naturae lex*) with the term νόμος and to Mosaic law with the term ὁ νόμος (on Rom 3:21–24: 3.4 [7]; Caroline P. Hammond Bammel, ed., *Der Römerbriefkommentar des Origenes: Kritische Ausgabe der Übersetzung Rufins: Buch 1–3* [Vetus Latina: Aus der Geschichte der lateinischen Bibel 16; Freiburg: Herder, 1990] 232). Origen lived ca. 185–ca. 253; his Romans commentary is extant only in the Latin translation by Rufinus (ca. 345–410). Origen's philological distinction may or may not be correct (cf. William Sanday and Arthur C. Headlam, *A Critical and Exegetical Commentary on the Epistle to the Romans* [International Critical

Paul knew and worked with natural law theory consists of: (1) his reference to idol-worshipers "know[ing] God's decree" (Rom 1:32);[2] (2) his statement concerning gentiles who "by nature do what the law requires" (Rom 2:14f);[3] and (3) his belief that all people can know God through God's created works—that is, without any particular revelation or missionary activity (Rom 1:20). This last concept corresponds to the philosophical model inherent in natural law theory: human beings can determine proper ethical behavior (which theologians define as God's will) by observing nature.

Two principal reasons mitigate against assuming that Paul employs natural law theory:[4] (1) his profound ambivalence toward legal thinking as a viable form of ethical discourse (see, e.g., Rom 10:4: "Christ is the end of the law"), and (2) the absence of the term "law of nature" (*nomos physeōs*) in his extant letters. As to the first argument, despite Paul's ambivalence toward the Jewish law, at the practical level he draws directly upon it.[5] The second argument presents a more serious hindrance to the case for natural

---

Commentary; 5th ed.; Edinburgh: Clark, 1902] 58), but the point is Origen's belief that Paul spoke of a law of nature.

Tertullian (ca. 160–after 220) also holds that Paul refers to natural law (*lex naturalis* and *natura legalis*) in Romans (*De Corona* 6.1 [CChr; Aem. Kroymann, ed., *De Corona, Tertulliani Opera* 2,2 (Turnhout: Brephols, 1954)] 1046f).

Adolf Bonhöffer disputes that Paul taught natural law and emphasizes the differences between Stoic thinking and that of Paul on this point (*Epiktet und das Neue Testament* [Gießen: Töpelmann, 1911] 151–55). Bonhöffer argues that Paul's goal was to show that both gentiles and Jews are under sin, rather than that the gentiles can fulfill a natural law. I agree, but I see natural law as necessary to that enterprise.

2. Rom 2:26 speaks of the uncircumcised keeping δικαιώματα τοῦ νόμου ("the requirements of the law"), and in Rom 8:4 Paul states, "so that the just requirement of the law (τὸ δικαίωμα τοῦ νόμου) might be fulfilled in us." Each of these cases apparently refers to the Mosaic law, but those observing it are, quite strikingly, the uncircumcised (Rom 2:26) and those "who walk not according to the flesh, but according to the Spirit" (Rom 8:4). In other words, a broader—or different—concept of the law than the Mosaic law may be present in Rom 2:26 and 8:4 as well.

3. Friedrich Kuhr argues convincingly that "gentiles" means non-Christian gentiles, rather than gentiles who believe in Christ, as some interpreters hold. Kuhr holds that Paul makes use of the Stoic concept of natural law in Rom 2:14f, but only for the purpose of demonstrating gentile accountability, and that he then puts it aside as he proceeds into his own theological argument ("Römer 2.14f. und die Verheissung bei Jeremia 31.31ff.," *ZNW* 55 [1964] 243–61).

4. Since Rom 2:12 (on people sinning apart from the law [ἀνόμως] or under the law [ἐν νόμῳ]) refers to the Jewish law, I do not take it as a hindrance to interpreting Paul in light of natural law theory. Rom 2:14 (on gentiles doing by nature what the law requires) shows that Paul is at great pains to show that those who do not consider themselves as following a law do actually follow one.

5. Peter J. Tomson, *Paul and the Jewish Law: Halakha in the Letters of the Apostle to the Gentiles* (Compendia Rerum Iudaicarum ad Novum Testamentum 3.1; Assen/Maastricht: Van Gorcum; Minneapolis: Fortress, 1990); Bernadette J. Brooten, "Paul and the Law: How

law theory in Rom 1:18-32. Nevertheless, the absence of a term does not de facto imply the absence of a concept.

I am working with a fairly strict and limited concept of natural law, as defined by the philosopher Gisela Striker: "the rules of morality conceived of as a kind of legal system, but one that has not been enacted by any human legislator."[6] She points out that some have conflated natural justice (i.e., that communities aim at the common good) with natural law and on this basis have been able to find "natural law" in Plato and Aristotle. Striker argues that the early Stoics[7] invented natural law to solve two problems: (1) the problem of objectivity, that is, the threat to morality posed by the lack of an objective, universally accepted understanding of justice; and (2) the problem of congruence, or whether human beings will be happy if they do what is just. The Stoics held that divine rationality permeates nature and that all human beings can live in accordance with nature by learning its laws. Further, nature provides a universal norm for justice, and those who live in accordance with it will be happy.

By the time of Paul, some thinkers had altered the Stoic concept of natural law by placing it within a Platonic framework. For example, Cicero (106–43 BCE) and Philo speak of a transcendent God who legislates natural law,[8] whereas the Stoics view the divine as part of the well-ordered, rational, material universe. Platonism allowed Philo (and subsequent Christian theologians) to harmonize natural law with his biblical belief in a divine creator. Richard Horsley argues that this Platonic reshaping of the Stoic concept of natural law occurred within a broader eclectic philosophical movement expounded, for example, by Antiochos of Askalon (2d/1st C. BCE), a teacher of Cicero.[9]

Because sexual order and marriage figure prominently in ancient natural

---

Complete Was the Departure?" *Princeton Seminary Bulletin*, Supp. Issue, no. 1 (1990) 71– 89. (Examples include 1 Cor 5:1–5; 14:34.)

6. Gisela Striker, "Origins of the Concept of Natural Law," in *Proceedings of the Boston Area Colloquium in Ancient Philosophy*, vol. 2, ed. John J. Cleary (Lanham, MD: University Press of America, 1987) 79–94, quote on p. 79 (response by Brad Inwood, pp. 95–101).

7. Chrysippos (281/77–208/04 BCE) particularly shaped this development.

8. For Philo on natural law, see André Myre, "La loi de la nature et la loi mosaïque selon Philon d'Alexandrie," *ScEs* 28 (1976) 163–81, who argues that Philo sees natural and Mosaic law as in harmony with each other, but not identical. See also David Winston, "Philo's Ethical Theory," in *ANRW* II.21.1 (Berlin: De Gruyter, 1984) 381–88.

9. Richard A. Horsley, "The Law of Nature in Philo and Cicero," *HTR* 71 (1978) 35–59.

Helmut Koester, on the other hand, has argued that Philo of Alexandria is the principal originator of the understanding of natural law that later became so important in Western Christian history and has stressed that the term *nomos physeōs* is actually quite rare before Philo ("NOMOS PHYSEOS: The Concept of Natural Law in Greek Thought," in *Religions in Antiquity: Essays in Memory of Erwin Ramsdell Goodenough*, ed. Jacob Neusner [Studies in the History of Religions (Supplements to Numen) 14; Leiden: Brill, 1968] 521–41).

law theories and concepts of nature, a solid understanding of ancient theories of natural law is necessary to evaluate properly Paul's teachings about sexuality, especially his condemnation of same-sex love.[10] "Sexual perversion" constitutes one principal indicator of the disruption of the natural order. Paul's focus on same-sex love as a paradigmatic example of disordered human behavior agrees with the prominence assigned to sexual behavior in ancient natural law theory.[11]

In the Roman world neither natural law theory nor its applications were monolithic. Since Paul's principal concern was how human existence can be made right with God (his doctrine of justification), he greatly adapted the natural law theory of the philosophers. Where the Stoics started with the problems of objectivity and congruence, Paul began with sin and salvation. But like the Stoics, he addressed the problem of objectivity. While Philo used natural law theory to demonstrate the universal applicability of the law of Moses, Paul used it to relativize Mosaic law. Paul's use of natural law enabled him to establish a common ground of understanding with members of the Roman congregation well versed in Stoic or Philonic-like discussions of natural law.

If Paul uses the concept of natural law, what problem is he trying to solve

10. The Roman jurist Ulpian (2d/3d C.) writes: "*Jus naturale* is that which nature has taught to all animals; for it is not a law specific to humankind but is common to all animals—land animals, sea animals, and the birds as well. Out of this comes the union of man and woman which we call marriage [*hinc descendit maris atque feminae coniunctio, quam nos matrimonium appellamus*], and the procreation of children, and their rearing. So we can see that the other animals, wild beasts included, are rightly understood to be acquainted with this law" (*Corpus Iuris Civilis, Digesta* 1.1.1; Theodor Mommsen and Paul Krueger, eds.; Alan Watson, trans., *The Digest of Justinian*, vol. 1 [Philadelphia: University of Pennsylvania Press, 1985] 1f (translation adapted for gender-specific language); see also *Corpus Iuris Civilis, Institutiones* 1.2. proem; Paul Krueger, ed., *Corpus Iuris Civilis*, vol. 1, *Institutiones* (Berlin: Weidmann, 1911; reprint, Zurich: Weidmann, 1973) 1. For other applications of natural law, see: *Corpus Iuris Civilis, Digesta* 1.1.4 (Ulpian: that according to natural law, all would be born free); 1.5.24 (Ulpian: that a child born out of wedlock belongs to his or her mother); and 1.8.2f (Marcianus: that air, flowing water, the sea, and the shores of the sea belong to all people in common; Florentinus: that pebbles, gems, and whatever we find on the shore belong to all people in common).

11. See Paul's contemporary, Philo of Alexandria, who describes men engaging in male-male sexual relations as having shaken off the yoke of natural law (*On Abraham* 135: ὁ τῆς φύσεως νόμος; F. H. Colson, ed. and trans., *Philo*, vol. 6 [LCL; Cambridge, MA: Harvard, 1966] 70).

This focus on sexual behavior in natural law theory continues into the Middle Ages. See, e.g., Thomas Aquinas, who classifies coitus as part of natural law (*Summa Theologica* I-II. Q 94. a 2). Aquinas defines contraception, masturbation, homoeroticism, and bestiality as contrary to nature and therefore worse than adultery, fornication, incest, and rape, which are sinful, but according to nature (II-II. Q 154. a 12). For a brief discussion and critique, see Lisa Sowle Cahill, *Women and Sexuality: 1992 Madeleva Lecture in Spirituality* (New York: Paulist, 1992) 8–10.

with it? Theologically, Paul's concept of justification requires that people need salvation. Paul needs to answer the question how gentiles can sin if they do not know the God of Israel or the law of Moses. Natural law provides an instrument whereby to judge the gentiles. Paul builds his argument in successive stages. First, everyone can learn universally valid rules of morality through observing nature; since everyone can know what is good, everyone is capable of sin. The Jewish law represents the next, more advanced form of religious knowledge (Rom 2:12–3:20). Notably, natural law also enables Paul to remove the Mosaic law from center stage. If gentiles can instinctively fulfill natural law, then people do not need to study the Mosaic law to gain salvation. Only then does Paul speak of faith in Jesus Christ (Rom 3:22). Natural law thus allows Paul to present his message of justification to the gentiles.[12] For homoeroticism, natural law theory enables Paul to argue that everyone can recognize it as wrong, just as everyone can recognize God. He preempts a gentile attempt to argue that differences in sexual practice may be culturally based.

Nature

Although Paul states that the women gave up "natural intercourse" (*physikē chrēsis*, Rom 1:26) for "unnatural" intercourse (*hē para physin* [*chrēsis*]) and that the men likewise gave up "the natural use of women"

12. For further discussion of natural law, see Robert P. George, ed., *Natural Law Theory: Contemporary Essays* (Oxford: Clarendon, 1992); Charles E. Curran and Richard A. McCormick, eds., *Natural Law and Theology* (Readings in Moral Theology 7; New York: Paulist, 1991); Lloyd L. Weinreb, *Natural Law and Justice* (Cambridge, MA: Harvard University Press, 1987); Russell Hittinger, "The Recovery of Natural Law and the 'Common Morality,'" *This World* 18 (Summer 1987) 62–74; Milner S. Ball, "Law Natural: Its Family of Metaphors and Its Theology," *Journal of Law and Religion* 3 (1985) 141–65; Harold E. Remus, "Authority, Consent, Law: *Nomos, Physis*, and the Striving for a 'Given,'" *Studies in Religion/Sciences Religieuses* 13 (1984) 5–18; Alan F. Johnson, "Is There a Biblical Warrant for Natural-Law Theories?" *Journal of the Evangelical Theology Society* 25 (1982) 185–99; Marcel Boivin, "Natural Law and Cultural Norms," *African Ecclesiastical Review* 20 (1978) 230–35; Klaus Bockmühl, "Natural Law," *Christianity Today* (November 18, 1977) 59f; Michael Bertram Crowe, *The Changing Profile of the Natural Law* (The Hague: Nijhoff, 1977); Theodor Herr, *Naturrecht aus der kritischen Sicht des Neuen Testamentes* (Abhandlungen zur Sozialethik 11; Munich: Schöningh, 1976); Roger A. Couture, "The Use of *Epikeiea* in Natural Law: Its Early Developments," *Église et Théologie* 4 (1973) 71–103; David Greenwood, "Saint Paul and Natural Law," *BTB* 1 (1971) 262–79; John L. McKenzie, "Natural Law in the New Testament," *Biblical Research* 9 (1964) 3–13; B. G. Skinner, "New Testament Ethics and Natural Law," *CQR* 165 (1964) 8–16; Alexander Passerin d'Entrèves, *Natural Law: An Introduction to Legal Philosophy* (London: Hutchinson, 1951); and Ernst Troeltsch, "Christian Natural Law" and "Stoic-Christian Natural Law and Modern Secular Natural Law," in *Religion in History: Ernst Troeltsch*, trans. James Luther Adams and Walter F. Bense (Fortress Texts in Modern Theology; Minneapolis: Fortress, 1991) 159–67; 321–41.

(*hē physikē chrēsis tēs thēleias,* Rom 1 : 27), evidence internal to Rom 1 : 18 –
32 does not sufficiently show the meaning of "nature." Two potential
meanings of "nature" may elucidate Paul's concept of nature in Rom 1 :
18 – 32: (1) as the order of creation, and (2) as the gendered nature of
human beings. I will now turn to these two meanings within the Roman-
period debates and discussion on nature, with particular attention to how
they shape views about gender and sexual behavior and how they might
influence a reading of nature in Romans 1.[13]

NATURE AS THE ORDER OF CREATION

"Nature" in Romans 1 could mean an order established by God at creation.[14] Strikingly, the beginning of the passage (vv. 18 – 23) does not contain the term "nature" (*physis*). Rather, Paul uses a more creation-oriented
term, "the things which have been made" (*ta poiēmata*). Instead of
speaking of nature as an entity identifiable with the divine (e.g., Stoic
thought), the text speaks of God, God's power, and what God has created.
If God creates nature (Rom 1 : 18 – 23), then nature requires a theocentric
interpretation: "contrary to nature" means "contrary to God." Just as human beings can perceive God's "eternal power and divine nature" in "the
things God has made" (Rom 1 : 20), so too can they presumably perceive

13. For a helpful overview of the range of meanings of φύσις in this period, see Helmut
Koester, "*Physis,*" *TWNT* 9 (1973) 246 – 71; or *TDNT* 9 (1974) 251 – 77.

For an insightful treatment of the origins of the concept of nature within Greek thought,
see G. E. R. Lloyd, *Methods and Problems in Greek Science* (Cambridge: Cambridge University
Press, 1991) 417 – 34. Lloyd, a historian of ancient science and philosophy, entitles his chapter
"The Invention of Nature" to indicate that Greek thinkers, far from agreeing on the concept
of nature or what was natural, debated the subject and polemicized against their rivals. The
relationship between νόμος ("law," "convention") and φύσις particularly shaped the debate.
Thus, some viewed νόμος as specific to individual societies and φύσις as common to all beings,
including humans; others devalued νόμος as *mere* convention (set up by the weak to protect
themselves), arguing that, according to nature, the stronger should justly have more than the
weak; others highly valued νόμος as that which sets humans off from other animals; and still
others, such as Plato, see νόμος and φύσις as very close to one another (i.e., that the same
creative intelligence at work in nature should shape the ideal human legislator's laws). The
tension between what is and what ought to be also spurred on debate. E.g., Aristotle's thinking contains a tension between nature as what is always or generally true and nature as the
τέλος ("goal," "end"). Thus, Aristotle argues against those who hold slavery to be unnatural,
asserting that distinguishing between ruler and ruled is natural (as in soul /body, humans/
other animals, male /female); slavery thus corresponds to the goal of being human, to the ideal
of human life (*Politika* 1.2.7 – 23; 1254a – 1255b; Lloyd deduces that τέλος is in the background here).

Lloyd's analysis of the earlier Greek material helps us to understand the possibility of more
than one reading of nature in the Roman world, which was heir to the earlier debates.

14. V. 20: "Ever since the creation of the world . . . the things God has made"; v. 25: "and
[they] worshiped and served the creature rather than the Creator."

God's "decree" for human behavior (Rom 1:32) in these created things. But how can people distinguish natural from unnatural intercourse by observing the things that God has made? Some thinkers in the Roman world derived a heterosexual norm for humans from the presumed exclusive heterosexuality of animals.[15]

In fact, the animal world complicates the picture rather than clarifying it. "Contrary to nature" could mean "contrary to animal behavior," but how animals behaved was a subject of controversy in the ancient world. Plato refers in passing to the "nature of animals" (*hē tōn thēriōn physin*), namely that a male animal does not touch another male sexually, since that would not be in accordance with nature.[16] Aristotle, on the other hand, records same-sex sexual contact among animals, noting that female doves will first kiss and then mount one another if males are not present.[17] The Jewish hortatory poem by Pseudo-Phokylides gives the lack of male-male intercourse among animals as a reason for humans to avoid it,[18] and the Jewish philosopher Philo of Alexandria (1st C.) contrasts the temperate and chaste sexual life of animals with human vice, including male-male relations.[19] Some decades later, the philosopher Plutarch denies male-male and female-female mating among animals,[20] while his contemporary Pliny the Elder describes female-female mating (resulting in infertile eggs) not only among doves, but also among hens, partridges, peahens, geese, and ducks.[21] Knowledge of same-sex mating among animals continued beyond the first century. For example, Claudius Aelian (2d C.) repeated Aristotle's

15. For further discussion of same-sex mating among animals, see John Boswell, *Christianity, Social Tolerance, and Homosexuality: Gay People in Western Europe from the Beginning of the Christian Era to the Fourteenth Century* (Chicago: University of Chicago Press, 1980) 12f, 152–56; and Urs Dierauer, *Tier und Mensch im Denken der Antike: Studien zur Tierpsychologie, Anthropologie und Ethik* (Amsterdam: Grüner, 1977) 63, 272.

16. *Nomoi* 8.5.1; 836C.

17. *History of Animals* 6.2; 560b.30–561a.3. Aristotle's work does contain a ranking of animals according to how they give birth (he ranks viviparous above oviparous animals; *Generation of Animals* 1.18–2.1; 723a.25–734a.16; see also 3.1; 751a.14–18 and contrast *History of Animals* 6.2; 560b.10–17).

18. *The Sentences of Pseudo-Phokylides* 190f; P[ieter] W. van der Horst, ed. and trans., *The Sentences of Pseudo-Phocylides: With Introduction and Commentary* (Leiden: Brill, 1978) 100f, 237–39.

19. *De animalibus* 49 (extant only in Armenian: see Abraham Terian, *Philonis Alexandrini De animalibus: The Armenian Text with an Introduction, Translation, and Commentary* [Studies in Hellenistic Judaism 1; Chico, CA: Scholars Press, 1981] 89, 239).

20. *Beasts Are Rational; Moralia* 990D; see also *Moralia* 990E, in which Plutarch recognizes that cocks do mount one another, but states that a prophet or seer will declare such an event to be an important and terrible omen. Notice that Plutarch parallels female-female and male-male mating, demonstrating that some concept of homosexuality, however unlike our own, did exist in this period.

21. *Naturalis Historia* 10.80.166.

view concerning female-female mating among doves.[22] And the medical writer Soranos (2d C.; extant in a 5th C. translation) refers to other medical theorists who do not "blame nature" for passing on at conception male passivity (and possibly the condition of being a *tribas*), since they do not find such behavior among animals.[23] In addition to the philosophical and scientific debate, Ovid's poetry (1st C. BCE) also contains echoes of this debate in his story of a young woman who has fallen in love with another young woman. She bemoans her situation and exclaims that, among animals, females are not seized with passion for other females.[24] And Pseudo-Lucian (probably early 4th C.), author of *Erōtes*, a disputation about the different types of love, bitingly argues that animals, who observe the law of nature and the doctrines of providence, do not practice male-male intercourse.[25] In other words, before, during, and after Paul's time, the jury was out concerning whether animals practiced same-sex mating.

We cannot know Paul's views on this debate. Further, we do not discern how—or even whether—debate on animal behavior influenced Paul's thinking about the order of creation.[26] However, since "the things that have been made" (v. 20) obviously include animals, it is plausible to see animal behavior as leading to knowledge of God and of proper human behavior. Therefore, Paul may be deriving a heterosexual norm from animal behavior.

Nature could also mean an order of creation as laid down in the Genesis creation narratives. The first creation narrative, that of Genesis 1, composed by the Priestly writer, does not define male and female as oriented to one another. Gen 1:27 ("male and female God created them") describes the existence of the two sexes, but does not specify any form of sexual contact as in accordance with God's will or against it.[27] Even Gen 1:28 ("Be fruitful and multiply") does not limit human sexual contact, but rather implies the necessity of *at least* one type, namely reproductive sexual intercourse. The second creation narrative (that of the Yahwist), however,

---

22. *Varia Historia* 1.15; see also *De natura animalium* 15.11.

23. Caelius Aurelianus, *Chronicarum passionum* 4.9; §§135f.

24. *Metamorphoses* 9.731–34.

25. *Erōtes* 22: ἡ τῆς φύσεως νομοθεσία (M. D. MacLeod, ed. and trans., *Lucian*, vol. 8 [LCL; Cambridge, MA: Harvard University Press, 1967] 184f). See also Clement of Alexandria, *Paidagōgos* 2.10.83.1–88.4.

26. For a survey of the role of animal behavior in philosophical discourse from early Greek writers through Roman-period Stoicism, see Dierauer, *Tier und Mensch im Denken der Antike*.

27. Peter Stuhlmacher interprets the behavior described in Rom 1:26f as the gentiles profaning themselves "(in a sinful reversal of Gen. 1:27f.) in lesbian love and sodomy" (*Paul's Letter to the Romans: A Commentary*, trans. Scott J. Hafemann [Louisville, KY: Westminster/John Knox, 1994] 37).

specifies the woman as the helper of the man (Gen 2:18), and derives male-female relations from the woman's creation from the man: "Therefore a man leaves his father and his mother and clings to his wife, and they become one flesh" (Gen 2:24). Strictly speaking, a woman's desire for her husband results not from an order of creation, but rather from the sin. After the woman has eaten from the fruit, God says to her: "your desire shall be for your husband, and he shall rule over you" (Gen 3:16). Paul explicitly refers to the second Genesis creation narrative to support his argument that women should wear long hair and veils, while men should wear short hair and be unveiled: "Indeed, man was not made from woman, but woman from man. Neither was man created for the sake of woman, but woman for the sake of man" (1 Cor 11:8f). Therefore, the naturalness of the marriage of woman to man, derived as it is from the creation of woman out of man, may provide the key to understanding "nature" in Romans 1, and ancient readers familiar with Genesis could have read Romans 1 in this way. The order of creation would then refer to the priority of man over woman,[28] which women who love other women and men who love other men do not preserve.

NATURE AS THE GENDERED NATURE OF HUMAN BEINGS

Paul's use of "nature" could also mean the particular nature of man and the particular nature of woman. Extant contemporaneous sources, which may not represent Paul's world as a whole, tilt the debate strongly in favor of sharp gender differentiation and gender asymmetry and, thus, distinct male and female natures.

We must remember, however, that the cultures of the Roman world defined gender differently than we do.[29] The highly differentiated social and

28. 1 Cor 11:8f; see also 1 Cor 11:3 (on the man as head of woman), as well as Paul's concession in 1 Cor 11:11f. ("Neverthless, in the Lord woman is not independent of man or man independent of woman. For just as woman came from man, so man comes through woman; but all things come from God.").

On 1 Cor 11:2–16, see esp. the differing interpretations by Daniel Boyarin, "Paul and the Genealogy of Gender," *Representations* 41 (1993) 1–33; Antoinette Clark Wire, *The Corinthian Women Prophets: A Reconstruction through Paul's Rhetoric* (Minneapolis: Fortress, 1990) 116–34; Lone Fatum, "Women, Symbolic Universe and Structures of Silence: Challenges and Possibilities in Androcentric Texts," *Studia Theologia* 43 (1989) 61–80; and Elisabeth Schüssler Fiorenza, *In Memory of Her: A Feminist Theological Reconstruction of Christian Origins* (New York: Crossroad, 1983) 226–36.

29. I am distinguishing between the cultural category "gender" and the physical category "sex." For an analysis of the physical category "sex" as likewise culturally determined, see Thomas Laqueur, *Making Sex: Body and Gender from the Greeks to Freud* (Cambridge, MA: Harvard University Press, 1990), who describes the historical shift from the ancient one-sex biological model (woman as an imperfect version of man, having the same organs, only inter-

economic structures of the Roman world were important organizing categories in that world, and understandings of gender were interconnected with status expectations. For example, some ancient Mediterranean ethnic groups held that women should generally remain indoors. But even such an apparently universal norm did not pertain to slave women or to free women of the lowest social level, since they de facto did not classify such women as "women." We must be cautious, therefore, when applying gender analysis to the socially and economically stratified Roman world. While the authors that I discuss in this book come from a range of social strata, with the New Testament representing the nonelite strata, the majority of the extant sources represent the elite.

The extant sources give evidence of the concept of distinctive male and female natures. The Stoic philosopher Epiktetos (ca. 55–ca. 135) provides a philosophical view that different types of beings have different natures, that a horse, for example, does not have the same nature as a dog. In other words, when speaking of a particular being, one can speak of "its nature."[30] The concept of a feminine nature that differs from that of man occurs in earlier Greek literature.[31]

In the Roman period, philosophers heatedly debate the question of distinctive female and male virtues. The first-century CE Stoic philosopher Musonius Rufus, for example, argues that women and men possess the same virtues (including "courage" [*andreia*]) and that women should study philosophy, just as men do.[32] Epiktetos speaks of natural distinctions

---

nal, rather than external) to the currently prevailing two-sex model. Aristotle's view that woman is an imperfect man corresponds to Galen's belief that women are physiologically identical to men, but with the organs inside, i.e., that women's reproductive organs are lesser male organs inverted (pp. 25–35).

30. Epiktetos, *Discourses* 3.1.3–4. See also G. E. R. Lloyd, *Methods and Problems in Greek Science* (Cambridge: Cambridge University Press, 1991) 424f, who notes that earlier Greek writers often used animals as models for human behavior, attributing set characteristics to specific species (such as courage to the lion or cunning to the fox), which meant that one animal species might have a permanent characteristic, while individual humans within one species (i.e., the human species) may have characteristics corresponding to those of one specific animal (such as courage or cunning).

31. See, e.g., Sophokles, *Trachiniai* 1062; Thukydides, *Historiai* 2.45.2; Xenophon, *Lakedaimoniai* 3.4. Thukydides uses the term "female virtue" (γυναικεία ἀρετή).

For earlier Greek philosophy, cf. Plato, *Politeia* 456A (that women and men have the same nature with respect to guardianship of the state, except that one is weaker and the other stronger) and Aristotle, *Politika* 1.2.12; 1254b (that, by nature, the male is superior and the female inferior, the male the ruler and the female the ruled). On the shift in male representations of women from the pre-Sokratics to Plato and then Aristotle, see Page duBois, *Sowing the Body: Psychoanalysis and Ancient Representations of Women* (Chicago: University of Chicago Press, 1988) esp. 169–83; see also Nicholas D. Smith, "Plato and Aristotle on the Nature of Women," *Journal of the History of Philosophy* 21 (1983) 467–78.

32. Musonius Rufus 3f.

between women and men, which humans ought not try to alter, of which
male hairiness is a principal example. In addressing a man who plucks out
his hairs, Epiktetos writes, "Man, what reason have you to complain
against your nature? Because it brought you into the world as a man?"[33]
Formulators of later legal documents appeal to the "weak nature" of
women as an argument in favor of particular governmental support of
women.[34]

Diodoros of Sicily, an elder contemporary of Paul's, tells a story about a
hermaphrodite that strikingly illustrates common understandings of masculinity and femininity in Paul's time.[35] Most important for this study, the
story reveals the cultural grounding of gender coding in this case of biological uncertainty.

The story takes place in Arabia just before the death of Alexander. The
protagonist, named Herais, began life as the daughter of a Macedonian
man, Diophantos, and an Arab woman. When Herais reached a marriage-
able age, Diophantos gave her a dowry and married her to a man named
Samiades. When they had lived together for a year, Samiades took a long
journey away from home. Meanwhile, Herais became ill with a strange disease. A tumor that had developed near her genitals eventually burst and
male genitals appeared. When Herais recovered from the illness she continued to behave as a woman, that is, wearing female clothing, leading a
domestic mode of life, and conducting herself in accordance with her subjection to a man.[36] Those close to her assumed that she must have had
"masculine [presumably anal] intercourse"[37] with her husband prior to
the illness, since they did not know how a hermaphrodite could have had
"natural intercourse."[38]

---

33. Epiktetos, *Discourses* 3.1.30: ἄνθρωπε, τί ἔχεις ἐγκαλέσαι σου τῇ φύσει; ὅτι σε ἄνδρα ἐγέννησεν; (W. A. Oldfather, ed. and trans., *Epictetus* [LCL; Cambridge, MA: Harvard
University Press, 1928] 14f). Note that ἄνθρωπος seems to mean "male human being" here,
which is one of its common meanings. The alternative explanation is that the man in question
is fighting against his *human* nature, which includes a distinction between male and female.
Oldfather notes that this use of the personal pronoun with φύσις is not in accordance with
prior Greek usage (pp. 12, 15).

34. See, e.g., Papyrus London 3.971,4 (3d/4th C. CE; διὰ ἀσθένειαν τῆς φύσε[ως]—
the document apparently concerns the appointment of a guardian for the property of a
woman); and Papyrus Oxyrhynchus 1.71 (303 CE; τὸ τῆς φύσεως ἀσθενές; the petitioner, a
widow Aurelia, appeals to the prefect in the matter of dishonest overseers of her property).

35. Diodoros of Sicily 32.10.2–10; Francis R. Walton, ed. and trans., *Diodorus of Sicily*,
vol. 11 (LCL; Cambridge, MA: Harvard University Press, 1957) 446–53.

36. Diodoros of Sicily 32.10.4: ἡ ἄλλη ἀγωγὴ οἰκουρὸς καὶ ὕπανδρος (Walton, *Diodorus* 448).

37. Diodoros of Sicily 32.10.4: ἀρρενικαὶ συμπεριφοραί; this presumably means anal
intercourse, such as men might have with each other.

38. Diodoros of Sicily 32.10.4: ἡ κατὰ φύσιν ἐπιπλοκή.

When Samiades returned, Herais avoided him out of shame.[39] Her father was too ashamed to say the reason, and finally Samiades became so angry that he took Diophantos to court, because Herais would not show herself to him. Herais, the subject of the dispute (whom the text refers to literally as *sōma*, "body," a term used especially, but not exclusively, of slaves), appeared on the scene, and the jurors debated whether her husband or her father should rule over[40] her. When the court had found that a married woman was obligated to follow her husband, Herais became bold, unloosed her garment, and displayed her male nature, that is, male genitals,[41] to the assembly. She protested against their forcing a man to cohabit with a man. Now that her shame had been revealed publicly, Herais took a number of steps to become a man. First, Herais exchanged her female garments for those of a young man. Next, she underwent an operation to make the male genitals fully normal, for which the physicians received much credit. Herais then changed her name to that of her father, Diophantos, enrolled in the cavalry, and fought in the royal forces. Herais's new identity took a toll on Samiades; He was so ashamed of his unnatural marriage (*ho para physin gamos*) that he committed suicide. Diodoros remarks in closing that she who had been a woman took on male honor and daring,[42] while the man had been weaker-minded than a woman, presumably in committing suicide.

The story turns on Herais's physical transformation from a woman into a man, an accident of nature.[43] Yet the sudden appearance of the male organs did not effect an immediate change in Herais's life. She continued to behave as a dutiful, homebound, subordinate wife. Her public exposure in court, not the mere fact of male genitalia, signaled her metamorphosis into a man; her exchange of garments concretized the shift. Having spoken publicly, she became a public male, that is, a man.

Although the story purports to be about body parts, it contains numer-

---

39. Diodoros of Sicily 32.10.5: διὰ τὴν αἰσχύνην (Walton, 448).

40. Diodoros of Sicily 32.10.5: κυριεύειν (Walton, 450).

41. Diodoros of Sicily 32.10.6: τὸ τῆς φύσεως ἄρρεν (Walton, 450).

42. Diodoros of Sicily 32.10.9: δόξα καὶ τόλμα (Walton, 452).

43. Strikingly, Diodoros uses φύσις both in a physical and in a more extended sense. Φύσις designates both male genitals (32.10.6: τὸ τῆς φύσεως ἄρρεν [Walton, 450]) and female genitals (32.10.7: φύσις θηλεία [Walton, 450]; see also 32.11.1), as well as normal human anatomy, as in the case of Diodoros's description of the membrane encasing the male organ before it burst forth as "contrary to customary nature" (32.10.7: παρὰ τὸ σύνηθες τὴν φύσιν [Walton, 450]). In another story Diodoros emphasizes that a hermaphrodite "shares a common nature" (32.12.2: ἀνδρόγυνος [used as a synonym for ἑρμαφρόδιτος (32.10.4)] ... ὁμοίας κεκοινωνηκώς φύσεως [Walton, 456]), i.e., a human, albeit dimorphic, nature, with himself and his readers. On φύσις and the Latin *natura* in the sense of "genitals," see John J. Winkler, *The Constraints of Desire: The Anthropology of Sex and Gender in Ancient Greece* (New York: Routledge, 1990) 217–20.

ous societal assumptions about proper female and male behavior and about gender-specific virtues.[44] The definitions of gender roles present in this story do not receive Diodoros's special attention, because they enjoyed broad cultural support. To be a woman is to exist in the private realm, under the control of a father or a husband. A woman need not appear in court, since male jurors can decide her fate quite well without her, the only question being which man has jurisdiction over her. When Herais becomes Diophantos she immediately undertakes military ventures, displaying her masculinity through public deeds and public renown. Masculinity is strength; femininity is weakness. When the boundary between masculine and feminine is blurred, as in the case of a hermaphrodite, father, daughter, and husband all feel shame. Was Samiades mainly ashamed that his wife had male genitals and that he still loved her?[45] Or was he also ashamed that she joined the cavalry and fought for the king? Alternatively, was he ashamed that he had had sex with someone who turned out to be male?

A strict boundary divides the male nature from the female one in this story, so that even hermaphrodites do not represent a genuine mingling of female and male natures. Diodoros does apply the term *dimorphos* ("two-formed") to the hermaphrodite Herais/Diophantos in the sense that that person had two forms,[46] but these occur successively, not simultaneously. Diodoros describes women who become men when male genitals burst forth as breaking sharply with their female past. Nature may deceive us for a time, but, ultimately, nature does not blur the boundaries, creating an intermediate, androgynous being. Herais goes from her subordinate status to become a warrior, from woman to man. In another story, a woman, Kallo, puts aside her loom-shuttles and other instruments of female work, changes her name to Kallon, and assumes male garments and status when the surgeon brings the male genitals to the surface.[47] Diodoros repeatedly stresses that we are not left with ambiguous beings, part man and part woman, anomalies who, in Diodoros's perception, understandably evoke hatred and horror. He shows how to integrate hermaphrodites into a strictly gender-dimorphic society by enabling them to take on the societal

---

44. See Thomas Laqueur, *Making Sex: Body and Gender from the Greeks to Freud* (Cambridge, MA: Harvard University Press, 1990) esp. 1–24.

See also Johann Weyer's 1583 treatise on dealing with witches, which speaks of the clitoris as like a penis and describes women who have become men when male organs burst forth upon their bodies. He notes that women have the potential to become men (through their clitorises), but not vice versa, since nature does not move toward the less worthy (*De praestigiis daemonum* 4.24; ET: John Shea et al., trans., *Witches, Devils, and Doctors in the Renaissance: Johann Weyer, De praestigiis daemonum* [Medieval and Renaissance Texts and Studies 73: Binghamton, NY, 1991] 344–45).

45. Diodoros of Sicily 32.10.9.

46. Diodoros of Sicily 32.10.2, 8.

47. Diodoros of Sicily 32.11.4.

role appropriate either to their underlying female or underlying male nature, rather than ignorantly ostracizing or punishing them.[48]

Thus, even in the case of a hermaphrodite, Diodoros insists that each person be of one gender. He implicitly defines such societal practices as gender-specific clothing and work or female submissiveness and male involvement in war as intrinsic to human nature, which he divides into male and female natures. The common ground between hermaphrodites and "the rest of us" is that their human nature is also either male or female.[49]

Against this background, "unnatural" and "natural" in Rom 1:26f would mean, respectively, contrary to or in conformity with female and male nature. The content of these natures corresponds to specific cultural norms and practices. Female submissiveness to a man constitutes part of the female nature (see Rom 7:2 on a married woman as *hypandros*),[50] and therefore, a woman who loves another woman is not living in accordance with her nature, which for Paul is God-given. Similarly, a man who himself submits to a man (thereby becoming *hypandros*) contravenes his male nature. Even if he does not himself play the passive sexual role, thereby confounding his own male nature, he can transgress male nature by causing another man to submit to him.

The understanding of nature as gendered human nature could complement understanding nature as the order of creation. While we cannot ascertain the precise role the animal world played in Paul's view of the created order, especially whether animals serve as models for human behavior, Paul could be visualizing God as having established an immutable order at creation, and he may be seeing this order as intrinsically gendered, especially since Roman-period authors almost uniformly describe nature as hierarchically gendered.[51] Since Paul's condemnation of female homoeroticism as unnatural corresponds closely to that of his contemporaries, we have every reason to expect that for Paul nature entailed a gender hierarchy.

48. He even gives two examples in which people burned hermaphrodites alive (Diodoros of Sicily 32.12.2).

49. For an analysis of the late twentieth-century medical response to hermaphrodites, see Suzanne J. Kessler, "The Medical Construction of Gender: Case Management of Intersexed Infants," *Signs* 16 (1990) 3–26. The phenomenon of intersexed infants poses a challenge to a two-gendered society: "Moreover, in the face of apparently incontrovertible evidence—infants born with some combination of 'female' and 'male' reproductive and sexual features—physicians hold an incorrigible belief in and insistence upon female and male as the only 'natural' options" (p. 4). Kessler observes that medical professionals rely on cultural understandings of gender to manage such cases.

50. On Rom 7:2, see Elizabeth A. Castelli, "Romans," in *Searching the Scriptures*, vol. 2, *A Feminist Commentary*, ed. Elisabeth Schüssler Fiorenza with the assistance of Ann Brock and Shelly Matthews (New York: Crossroad, 1994) 283f.

51. We need to remember, however, the controversial origins of the concept of nature in Greek thought: "the theorists . . . did not (so much) discover nature. . . . Rather they created,

Romans 1:26f and Jewish Law

Natural law gives Paul a framework in Romans 1 within which to evaluate the moral behavior of gentiles, but the problem of the Jewish law is far more central within Paul's theology as a whole.[52] Paul, as a former Pharisee

---

they invented, their own distinctive and divergent ideas, often in direct and explicit confrontation with their rivals. The concept was forged in controversy" (G. E. R. Lloyd, *Methods and Problems in Greek Science* [Cambridge: Cambridge University Press, 1991] 431f).

Others have recognized the controversial character of the concept of nature. See, e.g., Klaus Wengst on Rom 1:26f: "Könnte es nicht auch sein, daß etwas als 'natürlich' behauptet wird, was sich bei näherem Hinsehen lediglich als eine bestimmte gesellschaftliche *Konvention* entpuppt?" ("Paulus und die Homosexualität," *ZEE* 31 [1987] 75). See also John J. Winkler, who titles his discussion of Artemidoros's categories of sexual intercourse "For 'Nature,' Read 'Culture' " (*The Constraints of Desire: The Anthropology of Sex and Gender in Ancient Greece* [New York: Routledge, 1990] 17). Both scholars implicitly refer to the Greek debate on the boundaries between νόμος and φύσις.

52. Of any aspect of Judaism, the law is certainly one to which Paul devoted much original thought. Interpreters writing within a wide variety of theological frameworks have long recognized the tensions in Paul's thought concerning the Jewish law. On the surface, it is difficult to reconcile such views as: Christ as the end of the law (Rom 10:4); sin as dead without the law (Rom 7:8); law as having come to increase the trespass (Rom 5:20); the law as unnecessary in dietary matters (1 Cor 8, 10; Gal 2:11–14; Romans 14); and circumcision as unnecessary (Gal 5:2–12; Rom 2:25–29; 1 Cor 7:19, etc.), with Paul's affirmation that he upholds the law (Rom 3:31) or that "the law is holy, and the commandment is holy and just and good" (Rom 7:12). Some scholars maintain that there are genuine inconsistencies in Paul's thought. Heikki Räisänen, for example, sees a development in Paul's thinking; at first the law was an *adiaphoron* (an indifferent matter) for Paul, but later, pressure from his Jewish-Christian opponents drove him to argue for the total abrogation of the law (*The Torah and Christ* [Publications of the Finnish Exegetical Society 45; Helsinki: Kirjapaino Raamattutalo, 1986]; and *Paul and the Law* [WUNT 29; Tübingen: Mohr (Siebeck), 1983]). E. P. Sanders argues that Paul held that people are not admitted into the body of Christ by the law, but that Christian conduct must be scripturally based (*Paul and Palestinian Judaism: A Comparison of Patterns of Religion* [Philadelphia: Fortress, 1977]; and *Paul, the Law, and the Jewish People* [Philadelphia: Fortress, 1983]).

Others argue that a deeper look at Paul's letters reveals a center to his thinking through which one can interpret the seemingly inconsistent passages. For example, Ernst Käsemann ("The Righteousness of God in Paul," *New Testament Questions of Today*, trans. W. J. Montague [Philadelphia: Fortress, 1969] 168–82; and *Perspectives on Paul*, trans. Margaret Kohl [Philadelphia: Fortress, 1971]); and Peter Stuhlmacher (*Gerechtigkeit Gottes bei Paulus* [FRLANT 87; 2d ed.; Göttingen: Vandenhoeck and Ruprecht, 1966]), see justification by faith or the justification of the godless as the center of Pauline thought, while W. D. Davies (*Paul and Rabbinic Judaism: Some Rabbinic Elements in Pauline Theology* [4th ed.; Philadelphia: Fortress, 1980]; and *Jewish and Pauline Studies* [Philadelphia: Fortress, 1984]); and Joseph A. Fitzmyer (*Paul and His Theology: A Brief Sketch* [2d ed.; Englewood Cliffs: Prentice Hall, 1989]) see Christ as its center. Krister Stendahl argues that Western theologians have read Paul too individualistically and so have missed that Paul's primary concern was with the salvation of the gentiles as a group of people, rather than with any individual agonizing over the Jewish law. According to Stendahl, Paul held that Jews may keep the law, but that gentiles

282
CHAPTER TEN

trained in the Jewish law,[53] quotes from the Bible frequently. Although
very ambivalent toward the Jewish law, Paul's departure from it was by no
means complete or uniform. While Paul broke sharply with Jewish dietary
laws and with the commandment of circumcision in order to open Jesus-
believing congregations to gentiles, in several other areas, especially gender roles and gender relations, Paul continued to be indebted to the Torah
as a practical guide. Concepts and precepts of the Book of Leviticus constitute the background of Paul's teaching at several points, including at
Rom 1:24–27.

Rom 1:26f reflects the Jewish legal thinking concerning same-sex love
that was developing in the Roman period. While the Jewish scriptures
do not explicitly condemn sexual relations between women, postbiblical
Jewish writings (e.g., the Jerusalem Talmud, which attributes a debate on
whether to proscribe female homoerotic relations to first-century rabbinical schools) do, which makes Paul's condemnation quite in line with postbiblical Jewish discussion.

Rom 1:26–32 directly recalls Lev 18:22 ("You shall not lie with a male
as with a woman; it is an abomination")[54] and 20:13 ("If a man lies with
a male as with a woman, both of them have committed an abomination;
they shall be put to death; their blood is upon them.")[55] Even though
Romans 1 does not explicitly cite Leviticus 18 and 20, they overlap at three

---

need not keep it (*Paul among Jews and Gentiles and Other Essays* [Philadelphia: Fortress,
1976]). Johan Christiaan Beker has suggested that a model of coherence and contingency can
help us to see the structure of Paul's thought. Beker argues that Paul used an apocalyptic
framework as a means by which to interpret the Christ-event (Christ is "the proleptic fulfill-
ment of the triumph of God") and that Paul applied this to the situations of particular communities (*Paul the Apostle: The Triumph of God in Life and Thought* [Philadelphia: Fortress,
1980] 351; and "Paul's Theology: Consistent or Inconsistent?" *NTS* 34 [1988] 364–77
[argues against the very concept of "center"]). See also Joseph Plevnik, "The Center of Pauline Theology," *CBQ* 51 (1989) 461–78.

For discussion of Paul's closeness to the Jewish law, see Bernadette J. Brooten, "Paul and
the Law: How Complete was the Departure?" *Princeton Seminary Bulletin*, Supp. Issue, no.
1 (1990) 71–89; and Peter J. Tomson, *Paul and the Jewish Law: Halakha in the Letters of the
Apostle to the Gentiles* (Compendia Rerum Iudaicarum ad Novum Testamentum 3.1; Assen /
Maastricht: Van Gorcum; Minneapolis: Fortress, 1990). Tomson surprisingly makes only one
brief mention of Rom 1:26f in his survey (p. 94).

53. Phil 3:5f: "circumcised on the eighth day, a member of the people of Israel, of the
tribe of Benjamin, a Hebrew born of Hebrews; as to the law, a Pharisee . . . as to righteousness
under the law, blameless" (κατὰ νόμον Φαρισαῖος . . . κατὰ δικαιοσύνην τὴν ἐν νόμῳ γε-
νόμενος ἄμεμπτος).

54. MT: וְאֶת־זָכָר לֹא תִשְׁכַּב מִשְׁכְּבֵי אִשָּׁה תּוֹעֵבָה הִוא LXX: καὶ μετὰ ἄρσενος οὐ κοιμηθήσῃ
κοίτην γυναικός· βδέλυγμα γάρ ἐστιν.

55. MT: וְאִישׁ אֲשֶׁר יִשְׁכַּב אֶת־זָכָר מִשְׁכְּבֵי אִשָּׁה תּוֹעֵבָה עָשׂוּ שְׁנֵיהֶם מוֹת יוּמָתוּ דְּמֵיהֶם בָּם LXX: καὶ ὃς ἂν
κοιμηθῇ μετὰ ἄρσενος κοίτην γυναικός, βδέλυγμα ἐποίησαν ἀμφότεροι· θανατούσθωσαν,
ἔνοχοί εἰσιν.

points: (1) Romans 1 and Leviticus 18 and 20 use similar terminology;[56] (2) both Romans and Leviticus contain a general condemnation of sexual relations between men;[57] and (3) both describe those engaging in such relations as worthy of death.

The postbiblical Jewish scholar Philo of Alexandria discusses male-male sexual relations[58] in a way that resembles Rom 1:27 on three counts: (1) both Paul and Philo condemn such relations; (2) both call them "unnatural" (para physin); and (3) both describe a physical effect of such relations on the participants' bodies. Further, both Philo and Paul link gender differentiation with dress and hairstyle,[59] and Philo describes the men of Sodom, who had sexual relations with each other, as having shaken off the yoke of natural law.[60]

In contrast, Roman law in this period did not contain a general condemnation of sexual relations between men. Only during the Christian Roman Empire, under the influence of Christian scripture and theology, can we be certain that there was such a law.[61] Therefore, Paul did not simply adopt

56. "Shameless acts"/"nakedness." The Greek term for the men's "shameless acts" of Rom 1:27 (ἀσχημοσύνη) occurs twenty-four times in Leviticus 18 and eight times in Leviticus 20, always as a translation of עֶרְוָה (NRSV: "nakedness").

"Impurity" (ἀκαθαρσία). Rom 1:24 describes the behavior of those who have turned away from God as "impurity" (ἀκαθαρσία). The Hebrew noun most frequently translated as ἀκαθαρσία in the LXX is טֻמְאָה. The noun טֻמְאָה occurs in Lev 18:19, for which the LXX has ἀκαθαρσία. (The LXX also has ἀκαθαρσία as a translation for נִדָּה in Lev 20:21). Hebrew verbs derived from the same root as טֻמְאָה i.e., verbal forms derived from ט·מ·א, occur ten times in the immediate vicinity of Lev 18:22 and 20:13 (Lev 18:20, 23, 24 [twice], 25, 27, 28, 30; 20:3, 25; NRSV: "defile," "become defiled"). The LXX renders the various verb forms of ט·מ·א in Leviticus 18, 20 as μιαίνω and ἐκμιαίνω and in one case as ἐν ἀκαθαρσίᾳ (Lev 20:25). In sum, although the actual noun ἀκαθαρσία occurs only twice in Leviticus 18, 20, the Hebrew root often rendered as ἀκαθαρσία or ἀκάθαρτος occurs frequently in those two chapters.

"Male" (ἄρσην). Rom 1:27 has ἄρσενες, and the LXX renders זָכָר as ἄρσην in Lev 18: 22; 20:13.

57. I.e., Leviticus and Romans do not explicitly limit their condemnations to prostitution or coercive sexual relations with another man.

58. On the Special Laws 3.37-42; On Abraham 133-36; On the Contemplative Life 59-63.

59. On the Special Laws 3.37; 1 Cor 11:2-16.

60. On Abraham 135: ὁ τῆς φύσεως νόμος (Colson, Philo, vol. 6 [1966] 70).

61. The lex Scantinia, mentioned by M. Caelius Rufus, Suetonius, Juvenal, Tertullian, Prudentius, and Ausonius and understood by some scholars to have outlawed sexual relations between free males, is shrouded in mystery. The text of the law is not extant. Amy Richlin argues "that the law penalized the free male who willingly let himself be penetrated" ("Not Before Homosexuality: The Materiality of the Cinaedus and the Roman Law Against Love Between Men," Journal of the History of Sexuality 3 (1993) 523-73 (quotation on p. 530). Saara Lilja suggests that it "might have been the law by which Domitian forbade castration" or that it might be "the anonymous law mentioned by Quintilian which prohibited the rape of freeborn minor youths" (Homosexuality in Republican and Augustan Rome [Commenta-

Roman law as his teaching. Paul's teaching is a specifically Jewish one, framed in Jewish terms. The general condemnation of sexual relations between men, combined with the view that such relations are deserving of death, coincides more closely with Leviticus than with any other known source, except Philo, who himself depends upon Leviticus.

Current ethical and theological categories may unduly shape our historical assessment of Paul's use of the Jewish law. Most Christian theologians and ethicists today would argue that only some of the commandments of the Pentateuch, such as the love commandment, are incumbent upon Christians. Interpreters have traditionally distinguished between moral and ritual laws and held that only the moral commandments of the Jewish law pertain to Christian ethics.[62] Christian thinkers quite appropriately search scripture for guidelines for Christian behavior, selecting passages that seem more relevant to today's situation than others. In fact, if theologians and ethicists did not select from among biblical commandments and distinguish as to their relative validity, we would be attempting to recreate ancient patriarchal, slaveowning, peasant societies in today's world. Even then, inconsistent values would remain, since the Bible contains laws enacted during different time periods, representing changing societal conditions within the biblical period itself. Thus, theologians, eth-

---

tiones Humanarum Litterarum 74; Helsinki: Societas Scientiarum Fennica, 1983] 121). John Boswell proposes that the *lex Scantinia* may have "protected minor and infant males from involuntary prostitution or castration" (*Christianity, Social Tolerance, and Homosexuality*, 65–69; quotation on p. 67). Boswell also discusses other sources adduced in favor of the argument that male same-sex relations were illegal under Republican and early Imperial Roman law and deems them inapplicable (63–69). For further discussion of the *lex Scantinia* and of other Roman laws relevant to male same-sex relations, see Ramsay MacMullen, *Changes in the Roman Empire: Essays in the Ordinary* (Princeton, NJ: Princeton University Press, 1990) 184, 348.

Sextus Empiricus states without further explanation that intercourse between males is forbidden by law among the Romans (*Outlines of Pyrrhonism* 1.152).

The Theodosian Code 9.7.3 contains a law from the year 342 outlawing marriages between males, which had apparently been legal up to that point (see Boswell, *Christianity, Social Tolerance, and Homosexuality*, 123, n. 9).

62. E.g., Jost Eckert, *Die urchristliche Verkündigung im Streit zwischen Paulus und seinen Gegnern nach dem Galaterbrief* (Biblische Untersuchungen 6; Regensburg: Pustet, 1971) 135, 159; Wolfgang Schrage, *Die konkreten Einzelgebote in der paulinischen Paränese: Ein Beitrag zur neutestamentlichen Ethik* (Gütersloh: Gerd Mohn, 1961) 231–33; Herman Ridderbos, *Paulus: Ein Entwurf seiner Theologie*, trans. Erich-Walter Pollmann (Dutch original, 1966; Wuppertal: Brockhaus, 1970) 103f, 199. These and other interpreters generally see the ritual and cultic commands as intrinsically inferior to the lofty moral ideals enshrined in the moral commands of the Pentateuch.

See Leander Keck, "Paul as Thinker," *Interpretation* 47 (1993) 27–38, esp. 33. Keck states that Paul ignores the distinction between moral and cultic laws, which assumes that such a distinction existed.

icists, and all Christians need to use discretion in applying biblical commandments to Christian life today. This necessary use of discretion in using the Bible as a resource for today's ethical decisions is very different, however, from the historical judgment that Paul distinguished between moral and ritual laws or that those categories would have made sense to Jews in the Roman world.

Some scholars maintain that the Jewish law consists of two clear and distinct categories: moral commands (e.g., the ten commandments,[63] "[y]ou shall not abuse any widow or orphan,"[64] and "love your neighbor as yourself")[65] and cultic or ritual commands (e.g., "[y]ou shall observe the festival of unleavened bread,"[66] "[y]ou shall also make curtains of goats' hair for a tent over the tabernacle,"[67] and "[w]hen any man has a discharge from his member, his discharge makes him ceremonially unclean.")[68] Those holding this theory believe that the moral commandments have eternal validity, while the ritual ones are specific to the ancient Israelite cult and therefore not valid for Paul or for Christians today.

Based on this theory, many interpreters of Paul assume that (1) all regulation of sexual behavior belongs to the sphere of morals and that (2) while Paul departed from the Torah's ritual commandments, he adhered to the law's moral commandments in his writings. This assumption has hindered the search for an explanation of Paul's condemnation of same-sex relations, since those who hold that homosexual relations are immoral find it self-evident that Paul would condemn them. Further, this dual assumption has meant that commentators have seldom wondered about the possible relationship between Rom 1:24-27 and the Jewish law.

Jews in the Roman period employed a variety of categories for classifying the law. They divided the Torah into "positive" and "negative," "time-bound" and "non-time-bound" commandments;[69] they also made some distinction between "greater" and "lesser" commandments, while insisting that Jews need to follow all of the commandments.[70] To be sure, they also divided transgressions into those by a human being against God and those by a human being toward one's neighbor.[71] One could argue that

63. Exod 20:2-17; Deut 5:6-21.
64. Exod 22:22.
65. Lev 19:18.
66. Exod 23:15.
67. Exod 26:7.
68. Lev 15:2.
69. See, e.g., *m. Qiddušin* 1:7.
70. See Ephraim E. Urbach, *The Sages: Their Concepts and Beliefs*, trans. Israel Abrahams (Jerusalem: Magnes, 1975) 342-65. (See also Matt 5:19; 22:34-40.)
71. *M. Yoma* 8:9. I thank my colleague Prof. Arthur Green of Brandeis University for challenging me to think further about this point.

this constitutes a distinction between "ritual" and "moral," but the neighbor/God distinction might still differ from our own culture's understanding of those categories. For example, this distinction does not clarify whether the abomination committed by a male who lies with another male constitutes an abomination principally against one's neighbor ("ethical"?) or principally against God ("ritual"?). Jews in this period gave special prominence to the decalogue (the ten commandments), although they did not employ the category "moral" to distinguish the decalogue from the other commandments. For example, Philo of Alexandria's treatise *On the Decalogue* illustrates the centrality of the ten commandments among Jews in the pre-Christian period. That Philo organizes his treatise on the other commandments, *The Special Laws*, around the ten commandments, also underscores the importance of the decalogue. In addition, ancient Samaritan synagogues often contained inscriptions of the decalogue, which demonstrates that in the reading of the Pentateuch the ten commandments played a special role.[72]

In order to ascertain the methods of categorization Paul used in reading the Pentateuch, we must test ancient Jewish categories before applying modern Christian ones. The divisions into negative and positive commandments, into time-bound and non-time-bound ones, and even into transgressions against God and transgressions against one's neighbor do not occur in the Pauline letters.[73] The centrality of the decalogue, on the

72. The ancient Samaritan religion, like ancient Judaism, grew out of preexilic Israelite religion. "Judaism" derives from "Judea," the center of postexilic Judaism, whereas "Samaritan" derives from "Samaria," the hill country to the north of Judea. On the decalogue in Samaritan synagogues, see Gottfried Reeg, *Die antiken Synagogen in Israel*, pt. 2, *Die samaritanischen Synagogen* (Beihefte zum Tübinger Atlas des vorderen Orients, ser. B [Geisteswissenschaften] no. 12/2; Wiesbaden: Reichert, 1977) 545–50 (see also the entries for each of the sites at which an inscription of the decalogue has been found). The Samaritan liturgy and the early medieval piyyutim (liturgical poetry) also included the decalogue. The Samaritan emphasis on the decalogue could be indirect evidence for Jewish thinking before the early Christians began to argue that only the decalogue had ongoing validity. Jews increasingly insisted viv-à-vis the Christians that all commandments must be followed, while Samaritans maintained the older emphasis on the decalogue. Thus, the Samaritan religion, which claimed (and claims) to preserve preexilic Israelite customs, could be a clue to what Judaism was like before its encounter with Christianity.

There are also internal, exegetical reasons for assuming that even within the Pentateuch itself (at least in its final shaping in D and P), the decalogue has a more foundational nature than the other commandments. See Patrick D. Miller, *Deuteronomy* (Interpretation; Louisville, KY: Knox, 1990) 66–70; and Patrick D. Miller, "The Place of the Decalogue in the Old Testament and Its Law," *Interpretation* 43 (1989) 229–42.

73. Paul does stress love of neighbor at various points (e.g., Rom 13:9; Gal 5:14), but he also interweaves proper behavior toward God and proper behavior toward one's neighbor, as in Rom 1:18-32. Paul's vice lists also interweave such sins as "idolatry" and "sorcery" with "anger" and "envy" (e.g., Gal 5:19-21).

other hand, appears at several points in Paul's Letter to the Romans, and Paul assumes its ongoing validity.[74] Interpreters have usually not perceived a contradiction between Paul's doctrine of justification by faith and his acknowledgment of the decalogue's validity, because they often anachronistically classify the decalogue as moral law, rather than ritual law, and some assume that Paul understood the decalogue to be a fundamental guide for Christian living, rather than a path to salvation.[75]

Paul's thought pattern may resemble that of Philo of Alexandria, who distinguishes between the ten commandments, which summarize the other commandments and which were given by God directly, and the special commandments, which were given by God through the prophet Moses.[76] Paul's statement in Rom 13:9 that the love commandment sums up the other commandments, of which he gives four examples from the decalogue, does not render invalid the individual commandments of the decalogue. Indeed, he alludes to each of these four examples elsewhere.[77] The term "summarize"[78] does not mean "replace." Thus, Paul could be adapting the model of some commandments as summaries of others by defining the love commandment as the summary of all of the commandments.

One might object that Paul's clear and unambiguous upholding of the love commandment[79] supports the position that he viewed dietary laws and circumcision as ritual—that is, related to the religious rites of a particular people and having no bearing on universal moral questions. Paul does explicitly contrast circumcision with the love commandment in Gal 5:13f, lending further support to this distinction. At this one point in Galatians, the moral/ritual distinction seems to make sense, but we need to

---

74. Rom 2:21f: "you, then, that teach others, will you not teach yourself? While you preach against stealing, do you steal? You that forbid adultery, do you commit adultery? You that abhor idols, do you rob temples?" Rom 7:7: "What then should we say? That the law is sin? By no means! Yet, if it had not been for the law, I would not have known sin. I would not have known what it is to covet if the law had not said, 'You shall not covet.' " Rom 13:8–10: "Owe no one anything, except to love one another; for the one who loves another has fulfilled (πληρόω) the law. The commandments, 'You shall not commit adultery; You shall not murder; You shall not steal; You shall not covet'; and any other commandment, are summed up (ἀνακεφαλαιόω) in this word, 'Love your neighbor as yourself.' Love does no wrong to a neighbor; therefore love is the fulfilling of the law." For the individual commandments of the decalogue, see Exod 20:1–17; Deut 5:6–21. The love command is found in Lev 19:18.

75. E.g., Ernst Käsemann, *Commentary on Romans*, ed. and trans. Geoffrey W. Bromiley (Grand Rapids, MI: Eerdmans, 1980) 361f.

76. *On the Decalogue* 18–20. Philo calls the ten commandments κεφάλαια and κεφαλαιωδέστερα (in comparison with the special laws).

77. See Rom 1:24, 29; 1 Cor 6:9f.

78. Ἀνακεφαλαιόω.

79. Rom 13:8–10; Gal 5:14: "For the whole law is fulfilled (πληρόω) in one word, 'You shall love your neighbor as yourself' " (Lev 19:18).

288
CHAPTER TEN

consider additional evidence and explore other explanations that make
sense of the Pauline treatments of the law.

The Book of Leviticus, replete with commands usually considered ritual,
is actually Paul's source for the love commandment in Gal 5:13. In fact,
Leviticus influences Paul's thought at a number of points, as I shall demonstrate with several examples. I shall further argue that ritual and morality
are not the organizing principles of the Levitical legislation on incest and
male-male sexual relations. Instead, the key concepts internal to the text of
Leviticus are holiness, impurity,[80] defilement,[81] shame[82] and abomination,
and it is impossible to distinguish between "moral" and "ritual" uses of
these.[83] These concepts, rather than ritual/moral distinctions, shape Paul's
use of Leviticus.

Paul's pattern of speaking about sanctification and impurity strongly
echoes Leviticus, which consists principally of what many scholars would
call "ritual law." At first glance, the Levitical concern with priestly rituals,
holy things and impurities, purification rites, and separation of the people
of Israel from the surrounding peoples all seem antithetical to Paul's
gospel, which is based on table fellowship among Jews and gentiles and
diametrically opposed to purification rites and to any strict, detailed observance of ritual law. Paul even states in a highly un-Levitical fashion,
"Everything is indeed clean" (Rom 14:20). On the other hand, consider
1 Thess 4:3-5, 7:[84]

> For this is the will of God, your sanctification (*hagiasmos*): that you
> abstain from fornication; that each one of you know how to take a
> wife for himself [or: how to control your own body] in holiness (*hag-
> iasmos*) and honor, not with lustful passion, like the Gentiles (*ethnē*)

80. The terms "holy" (ἅγιος), "impurity" (ἀκαθαρσία), and "impure" (ἀκάθαρτος) occur more frequently in Leviticus than in any other book of the LXX.
81. The Hebrew verb is ט·מ·א, while the Greek equivalent is μιαίνειν.
82. The LXX renders עֶרְוָה, ("nakedness") as ἀσχημοσύνη ("shame") in Leviticus 18 and
20, which gives this Greek term a slightly different nuance than it usually has. The LXX's
extensive use of "shame" in the Levitical verses immediately preceding or following the prohibition of male-male relations may have influenced Paul.
83. For example, Lev 18:20 defines sexual intercourse with a kinsman's wife as defilement,
and Lev 20:21 describes intercourse with the wife of one's brother as impurity, yet most
Christian interpreters would regard these acts as moral, and not merely ritual, transgressions.
84. Philip Carrington, *The Primitive Christian Catechism: A Study in the Epistles* (Cambridge: Cambridge University Press, 1940) esp. 16-21; and Edward Gordon Selwyn, *The
First Epistle of St. Peter* (London: Macmillan, 1946) 369-75, propose that Leviticus 17-19
or 17-20 forms the background of 1 Thess 4:1-12. They posit the existence of an early
Christian neo-Levitical catechism, transformations of which can be found in 1 Thess 4:1-12
and in 1 Peter.

who do not know God. . . . For God did not call us to impurity (*aka-tharsia*) but in holiness (*hagiasmos*).[85]

Compare Lev 20:23, 26 (I refer to the Greek translation, since Paul wrote in Greek):

You shall not follow the practices of the nation [LXX: "nations," *ethnē*] that I am driving out before you. Because they did all these things, I abhorred them. . . . You shall be holy (*hagioi*) to me; for I the LORD am holy (*hagios*), and I have separated you from the other peoples to be mine.[86]

Both passages share the common focal point of holiness, defined as closeness to God and separation from those who do not worship God, and both passages contain divinely sanctioned disdain for gentiles.[87]

To be sure, other aspects of Lev 20:22-26 represent that which Paul most passionately and explicitly opposes (e.g., the distinction between clean and unclean beasts, birds, and other animals), or which he deems irrelevant (e.g., the possession of the land). Nevertheless, both share this fundamental scheme of a nation holy to its God, not following the practices of the peoples.

Paul also uses concepts that recall Leviticus in Rom 6:19-23 (on yielding one's members to impurity or to righteousness for sanctification) and in 1 Cor 7:14 (on the children of a believer and a nonbeliever being impure or holy). Further, "impurity" occurs twice in vice lists in conjunction with "sexual immorality/fornication" and "licentiousness" (Gal 5:19; 2 Cor 12:21), so that, for Paul, impurity probably relates to sexual activity. Levitical background also appears in 1 Cor 5:1-5,[88] in which Paul di-

---

85. See O. Larry Yarbrough, *Not Like the Gentiles: Marriage Rules in the Letters of Paul* (SBLDS 80; Atlanta: Scholars Press, 1985) 65-87. Yarbrough's discussion of the meaning of σκεῦος as "wife," rather than "body" is especially convincing and complete (pp. 68-73). He does not devote similar attention to the background of the holiness/impurity complex.

86. See also Lev 19:2.

87. Other elements in 1 Thessalonians reminiscent of Leviticus 17-26 include: brotherly and sisterly love (1 Thess 4:9: φιλαδελφία; see Lev 19:18: ἀγαπήσεις τὸν πλησίον σου) and the image of walking to describe human conduct (1 Thess 4:1, 12: περιπατέω; see Lev 18:3: τοῖς νομίμοις αὐτῶν οὐ πορεύσεσθε; see also Leviticus 26 for the image of walking in God's statutes). Both of these are, of course, relatively widespread within Judaism.

88. 1 Cor 5:1-5: It is actually reported that there is sexual immorality among you, and of a kind that is not found even among pagans; for a man is living with his father's wife. And you are arrogant! Should you not rather have mourned, so that he who has done this would have been removed from among you?

For though absent in body, I am present in spirit; and as if present I have already pronounced judgment in the name of the Lord Jesus on the man who

rects the congregation to deliver to Satan a man living with the wife of his father (*gynē patros*). Paul exhorts the Corinthians to remove the man from the midst of the congregation. Lev 18 : 8 reads, "You shall not uncover the nakedness of your father's wife [LXX: *gynē patros*]; it is the nakedness of your father." Lev 20 : 11 describes the penalty, "The man who lies with his father's wife has uncovered his father's nakedness; both of them shall be put to death, their blood is upon them."[89] Interpreters have never been particularly surprised to find Paul in conjunction with Levitical law in the cases of forbidden sexual relations between two men and between a man and his father's wife, probably because such relations are generally perceived as pertaining to moral, rather than ritual, law. The categories moral and ritual, however, do not help to explain the Levitical legislation on incest.

Holiness, shame, impurity, defilement, and abomination are the categories operative in Leviticus 18 and 20.[90] An impure or abominable sexual act defiles all participants, and the holiness of the community requires that the community be cleansed of their presence, regardless of whether they were forced to participate or even had the capability to consent. Lev 18 : 8 and 20 : 11 occur in the larger context of incest prohibitions,[91] which is also the context of the prohibition of sexual relations between males.[92] Lev 20 : 13 does not distinguish among intercourse between consenting adult males, between an adult and a minor, and between one adult and another nonconsenting adult. The victim of homosexual rape and the child victim of pederasty face execution along with their perpetrators. Similarly, the penalties for incest, which include death, apply not only to consenting adults, but also to the child victims and to their adult perpetrators. Age and consent do not occur as relevant categories in this material, which they should if we were to consider them relevant to our own morality. Further, father-daughter incest constitutes a striking omission to this legislation.

---

has done such a thing. When you are assembled, and my spirit is present with the power of our Lord Jesus, you are to hand this man over to Satan for the destruction of the flesh, so that his spirit may be saved in the day of the Lord.

89. Roman law prohibits a marriage beween a man and his stepmother, which Paul may also have known.

90. I am focusing on the final redactional shape of these chapters, which is the shape that is relevant for Paul. For a study of the preredactional stage or stages of Lev 18:22 and 20:13, see Saul M. Olyan, "'And with a Male You Shall Not Lie the Lying Down of a Woman': On the Meaning and Significance of Leviticus 18:22 and 20:13," *Journal of the History of Sexuality* 5 (1994) 179–206.

91. Lev 18:6–18; 20:11–21.

92. Lev 18:22; 20:13.

Mother-daughter and father-son incest are also excluded; the prohibition is articulated in the second person masculine singular and the object is always a female. Father-daughter incest could possibly be included under the prohibition against taking "a wife and her mother also" (Lev 20:14; see also Lev 18:17), which requires the burning of all three. Thus, if a father raped his minor daughter, the perpetrator, the victim and the nonperpetrator mother would all be burned, since the man's sex with his daughter would constitute taking her as his wife.[93] Father-son incest could, of course, be categorized as relations between two males, in which case the adult perpetrator and the victim, his son, would both have to be executed (Lev 20:13).

Just as Leviticus requires the death penalty for sexual behaviors that are perceived to defile the participants and thereby the community as a whole, so too Paul calls upon the congregation to remove from its midst a man practicing a behavior prohibited by Leviticus, and he orders the man's deliverance over to Satan, a drastic removal from his spiritual community (1 Cor 5:2, 5).[94] Since Paul does not mention the father's wife, she is presumably not a member of the congregation. Note that Paul's judgment does not reflect moral categories that we might employ today, such as coercion or consent. In fact, Paul does not divulge the process whereby he arrived at his decision. He may have known the precise circumstances. We do not. For example, the father's wife could have initiated intercourse with her stepson while he was still a minor, and the present relationship could, therefore, continue what we would call an earlier victimization of the man while he was still a boy. In sum, ascertaining the ancient organizing principles of prohibited sexual behaviors requires great care and further re-

93. Judith Romney Wegner notes that the omission of father-daughter incest from Leviticus 18 and 20 also occurs in the Mishnah's lists of incestuous relationships in *m. Keritot* 1:1; *m. Sanhedrin* 7:4; and *m. Makkot* 3:1. She points out that consanguinity is not the primary issue, but rather whether the women prohibited to a particular man are "*the sexual property of other men*" (*Chattel* or *Person? The Status of Women in the Mishnah* [New York: Oxford University Press, 1988] 28 [emphasis Wegner's]). She does note that by mishnaic times father-daughter incest was prohibited under reference to Lev 18:17 (*m. Sanhedrin* 9:1).

Deut 22:25-27, on the rape of an engaged woman in the open country (who is not punished), does not contradict my reading of Lev 18:17 and 20:14 or Lev 18:22 and 20:13. The Deuteronomic legislation does withhold punishment from this category of rape victim, but does not carry that over to other rape victims. E.g., Deut 22:22 concerns prohibited sexual intercourse between a married Israelite woman and another man. "[B]oth of them shall die." The law foresees no exception in the case of rape.

94. In 1 Cor 5:6-8, Paul carries the image of the community requiring cleansing further into the image of the leaven and the lump of dough, which is a ritual image drawn from Passover practices.

search.[95] The Levitical legislation on incest and homosexual relations, as well as Rom 1:24–27 or 1 Cor 5:1–5, both of which have clear precedents in Leviticus, are not elucidated by the distinction between ritual and moral categories.

The Levitical code aims to ensure the holiness of the people of Israel, not to secure the rights or liberties of individuals. This focus on the group rather than the individual helps to explain some penalties that we could not explain in terms of human rights or morality. For example, while many people today oppose lesbian and gay rights and support sodomy statutes, few would argue that a boy raped by an adult male should be punished together with the adult. And even people with no sympathy for animal rights might find it strange to kill an animal with whom a human has had intercourse (Lev 20:15f), since we do not attribute moral agency to animals. But if these laws address the problem of the holiness of the group, rather than of individual moral agency or individual human rights, then such penalties make sense. Within the value system of Leviticus, a conflict between the group's need to maintain its holiness and the desire of an individual to live may result in society's killing a hapless individual defiled by

95. Source-critical and tradition-historical studies of Leviticus 18 and 20 have often proceeded from anachronistic assumptions that have hindered progress in uncovering the ancient organizing principles. For example, Karl Elliger assumes that father-daughter incest must have originally been prohibited in a statement just preceding 18:10 and was accidentally deleted through a transmission error ("your sister, the *daughter* of your father" occurs in v. 9; a scribe could have deleted an adjacent verse concerning the daughter through homoeoarcton; that is, because both verses [the allegedly missing verse and 18:10] had "daughter" at or close to the beginning, the scribe erred and copied just one of the "daughter" verses); he further argues that a series of eleven elements, as in Lev 18:7–17a, does not conform to the standard form for a series of apodictic laws, which often occur in sets of twelve. "Denn es ist schwerlich zu bestreiten, daß vor v. 10 das entsprechende Verbot über die Tochter ausgefallen ist, natürlich infolge Homoiarkton. . . . Daß sich ungesucht die bei solchen Reihen apodiktischer Rechtssätze beliebte Standardzahl 12 ergibt, darf als weiteres Zeichen für die Einheit und einstmalige Selbständigkeit der vv. 7–17a gebucht werden" ("Das Gesetz Leviticus 18," *Zeitschrift für die alttestamentliche Wissenschaft* 67 [1955] 2; see also *Leviticus* [Handbuch zum Alten Testament 1/4; Tübingen: Mohr (Siebeck), 1966] 234, 238). The thesis of accidental omission is not convincing. If father-daughter incest were central to the legislation, then why would not a later redactor (of a text assumed by Elliger and other scholars to have passed through multiple stages of redaction) have noticed the omission and reinserted it? Elliger's second argument, concerning the standard sets of twelve apodictic laws, would be easier to evaluate if he had presented a thorough argument, complete with an overview of the parallels. His assumption that father-daughter incest must have been present in the text prevents an analysis of why, in fact, it is not. See also Henry Sun, "An Investigation into the Compositional Integrity of the So-Called Holiness Code (Leviticus 17–26)" (Ph.D. diss., Claremont Graduate School, 1990), who argues that the absence of father-daughter incest is intentional, rather than accidental, and is based on the rights of a father over his daughter. Sun also questions the existence of a Holiness Code as a distinct unit.

circumstances beyond his or her control. The group's survival takes precedence over the individual's survival. Although Paul's theological framework differs greatly from that of Leviticus, he inherits one aspect of this very ancient system of group holiness when he adopts Levitical positions on male-male relations and intercourse with one's father's wife, namely that a prohibited sexual act can constitute impurity, regardless of the circumstances.

Of any passage in the Pauline corpus, 2 Cor 6:14–7:1 stands out as the most replete with the language of separation, holiness, impurity, and defilement.[96] Some scholars categorize it as a later interpolation;[97] some classify it as a pre-Pauline fragment inserted into 2 Corinthians;[98] while others treat it as an integral part of the letter.[99] If it is a later interpolation, then some early Christians were able to convince congregations and later scribes that Paul could have preached a theology of holiness versus defilement, of separation from uncleanness, and of the lack of fellowship between light and darkness.

In the light of Paul's other use of Jewish law and of Levitical concepts, 2 Cor 6:14–7:1 could have looked quite Pauline to early scribes. I propose as a methodological principle that scholars discussing possible interpolations and pseudepigraphic writings need to raise the historical question of what helped an interpolation or pseudepigraphic writing to become accepted as genuine, and not stop with the questions of authenticity.

What does the Levitical background of Romans mean for our interpre-

---

[96.] 2 Cor 6:14–7:1: Do not be mismatched with unbelievers. For what partnership is there between righteousness and lawlessness? Or what fellowship is there between light and darkness? What agreement does Christ have with Beliar? Or what does a believer share with an unbeliever? What agreement has the temple of God with idols? For we are the temple of the living God; as God said, 'I will live in them and walk among them, and I will be their God, and they shall be my people. Therefore come out from them, and be separate from them, says the Lord, and touch nothing unclean; then I will welcome you, and I will be your father, and you shall be my sons and daughters, says the Lord Almighty.' Since we have these promises, beloved, let us cleanse ourselves from every defilement of body and of spirit, making holiness perfect in the fear of God.

97. E.g., Joachim Gnilka, "2 Cor 6:14–7:1 in the Light of the Qumran Texts and the Testaments of the Twelve Patriarchs," in *Paul and the Dead Sea Scrolls*, ed. J[erome] Murphy-O'Connor and James H. Charlesworth (New York: Crossroad, 1990) 48–68.

98. E.g., Elisabeth Schüssler Fiorenza, *In Memory of Her: A Feminist Theological Reconstruction of Christian Origins* (New York: Crossroad, 1983) 194–96.

99. Peter J. Tomson, *Paul and the Jewish Law: Halakha in the Letters of the Apostle to the Gentiles* (Compendia Rerum Iudaicarum ad Novum Testamentum 3.1; Assen/Maastricht: Van Gorcum; Minneapolis: Fortress, 1990) 198f.

tation of it? The concept that some sexual acts defile the participants serves as a basis for the Levitical prohibitions against certain sexual relations. That the intercourse is an abomination has nothing to do with consent or coercion, categories that most ethicists today consider central for moral discourse. Likewise for Paul, consent and coercion do not play a role in his condemnation of homoeroticism. A concern for the holiness and purity of the Israelites as a group guides the Levitical code; similarly, Paul wants the Christian community to be holy and to avoid the impurity that exemplifies gentile life. As I have outlined above when discussing anthropological research on impurity, classifying certain phenomena as impure enables a society to create order for itself. When Paul defines homoeroticism as impure, he—like Leviticus—is helping to maintain strict gender differentiation. Rom 1:26f, like the biblical source with which it most overlaps, defies classification as either moral or ritual.[100] Reading Rom 1:24–27 against the background of Leviticus and of such postbiblical Levitical interpreters as Philo of Alexandria helps us to recognize how these verses both reflect and help to create a particular social order.

Wisdom of Solomon 12:23–15:19 and Romans 1:18–32

Rom 1:18–32 resembles traditional Jewish depictions of idolatry, such as Wis 12:23–16:4, which presents idolatry as the source of other sins (especially of sexual sins). Using this familiar theme strategically, Paul gains a rhetorical advantage by establishing consensus with his readers. His contemporary Jewish-Christian readers of Rom 1:18–32 would have recognized the antipagan polemic but considered themselves exempt from his condemnations; likewise, Gentile-Christian readers would rest assured that they had transcended their life of gentile impurity. But his claim in the following chapters that all, both Jews and gentiles, are under sin, would have surprised readers. Thus, while he employs an anti-idolatry polemic in Romans similar to that of the Wisdom of Solomon, his application of it differs in that it serves rhetorically to convict his readers rather than identify sinfulness in others.

The Wisdom of Solomon (especially 12:23–15:19) overlaps with Romans 1 not only in content, but also in terminology.[101] Given the problems

---

100. Strikingly, idolatry (Rom 1:18–24) also defies classification as ritual or moral. What better constitutes ritual than worship and what could be—for Paul—more fundamental to the moral life than worship? Rom 1:18–27, then, is of one piece, drawing upon very ancient concepts for creating order within society through separating and distinguishing categories of beings.

101. E.g., αἰσχύνομαι, ἀδίκως/ἀδικία, ἀσέβεια, δικαιοσύνη, δύναμις (of God), εἰκών, ἐπίγνωσις/ἐπιγινώσκω, κτίσμα/κτίσις, μάταιος/ματαιόω, ὄρεξις, φθαρτός. Notice also that Wisdom uses βδέλυγμα (12:23; 14:11), and Romans has ἀκαθαρσία. Both terms can translate the Hebrew term תּוֹעֵבָה.

with dating,[102] we cannot be certain that Paul knew Wisdom, but the similarities mentioned below point to his familiarity with common understandings of idol worship found in Jewish apologetic thinking.[103]

Like Paul, the author of Wisdom paints a negative picture of idol worshipers. Wisdom sarcastically depicts a craftsman carving a statue in human or animal form, covering its blemishes with paint, and fastening it in a niche with iron so that it will not fall, for the craftsman knows that the statue cannot help itself. Then the craftsman prays to the thing he has made from a useless piece of wood:

> For health he appeals to a thing that is weak;
> for life he prays to a thing that is dead;
> for aid he entreats a thing that is utterly inexperienced;
> for a prosperous journey, a thing that cannot take a step;
> for money-making and work and success with his hands
> he asks strength of a thing whose hands have no strength.
>
> (Wis 13:18f)

These powerful juxtapositions pervade this section of the Wisdom of Solomon,[104] ironically contrasting the lifelessness and impotence of the idol with the worshiper's need for life and help. The learned reader of Romans could remember such juxtapositions when reading about the images of humans and birds and animals and reptiles (Rom 1:23), whether from Wisdom itself directly or from other Jewish anti-idol literature, sermons, or discussions.[105]

Wisdom of Solomon locates the origins of idols in a statue set up by a grieving father to his dead child and an image of a king whose subjects

102. The Wisdom of Solomon is difficult to date and was a disputed part of Jewish scripture in Paul's time. David Winston assigns it to the reign of Gaius 'Caligula' (37-41 CE) (*The Wisdom of Solomon* [Anchor Bible 43; Garden City: Doubleday, 1979] 23), while Dieter Georgi argues for the late 2d C. BCE (*Unterweisung in lehrhafter Form: Weisheit Salomos* [Jüdische Schriften aus hellenistisch-römischer Zeit 3; Gütersloh: Gütersloh/Gerd Mohn, 1980] 395-97).

103. Philo treats nature worship and idolatry at several points (*On the Decalogue* 52-75; *On the Special Laws* 1.13-27; for further references and discussion, see Winston, *Wisdom,* 248f).

104. This section on idolatry occurs in what interpreters generally agree is the third major part of Wisdom, namely, chapters 11-19 (Winston, *Wisdom,* xv; Georgi, *Unterweisung,* 393). In what follows, I am working with the assumption of the literary integrity of the document. Winston argues for single authorship (Winston, *Wisdom,* 12-14), while Georgi posits school authorship over a period of time (Georgi, *Unterweisung,* 392-95). Thus, even with Georgi's view, redactional changes are internal to the same school.

105. Such a Jewish reader of Romans, may also, however, have seen images in Jewish catacombs and synagogues.

wished to honor him.[106] Wisdom simultaneously explains why people
would create images—grief and honor are not in themselves evil[107]—and
divests the images of any religious significance. Although part of creation,
the idol is still an abomination,[108] which will be destroyed.[109]

Regardless of the motivation, the consequences of venerating images[110]
are unambiguously evil:

> For the idea of making idols was the beginning of fornication, and the
> invention of them was the corruption of life (Wis 14:12).[111]

By venerating images, these people brought sin, especially sexual sin,
into the world: impure lives and marriages, murder, adultery, and other
vices and confusions, including "sex perversion" or "interchange of sex
roles."[112] Rom 1:18–32 also identifies idolatry as the origin of sin, espe-

---

106. Wis 14:12–21. Cf. Euhemeros of Messene (4th/3d C. BCE), the author of a ro-
mance (only fragmentarily extant) describing Uranos, Kronos, and Zeus as early kings who
had been deified; for references, see Heinrich Dörrie, *Der Kleine Pauly*, s.v., "Euhemeros."

107. To be sure, monarchs commanded their images to be worshiped, and ambitious
craftsmen promoted such worship and foisted it on the people with a less than noble intent
(Wis 14:16–27).

108. Wis 14:11 (βδέλυγμα).

109. Wis 14:11 (ἐπισκοπή).

110. Wisdom includes discussion of both the veneration of images and the veneration of
the stars and other elements. The nature worshipers, such as practitioners of astrology, receive
a mixed judgment. Those "who were ignorant of God were foolish by nature" (Wis 13:1:
Μάταιοι μὲν γὰρ πάντες ἄνθρωποι φύσει, οἷς παρῆν θεοῦ ἀγνωσία). They are both "little
to be blamed" (Wis 13:6) and "not . . . to be excused" (Wis 13:8), for they could have known
better, because they had the ability to investigate the world. They could have discovered the
Creator through observing the beauty of creation (Wis 13:5–9). Thus, Wisdom employs a
kind of natural theology. (Georgi considers Wis 13:1–9 to be a diatribe taken over from
hellenistic Jewish apologetics added by the final redactor [Georgi, *Unterweisung*, 447].)

111. Wis 14:12: Ἀρχὴ γὰρ πορνείας ἐπίνοια εἰδώλων, εὕρεσις δὲ αὐτῶν φθορὰ ζωῆς.

112. Wis 14:24–26: γενέσεως ἐναλλαγή. This term, literally "variation" or "interchange" of "generation" or "kind," could mean same-sex relations. Γένεσις is strange here
and seems to be the wrong word. The word γένος includes the meanings of "sex," and "gender" and is what we might expect (see Winston, *Wisdom*, 280). Notice the verbal similarity to
Rom 1:26: their females μετήλλαξαν natural relations for unnatural. The "disorder of marriages" (v. 26: γάμων ἀταξία) is also striking. Could it include a change of gender roles within
marriage? On the whole, the vice list in Wis 14:24–26 has a concern for purity and order,
especially in sexual relations: "pure marriages" (γάμοι καθαροί), "confusion over what is
good" (θόρυβος ἀγαθῶν), "pollution of souls" (ψυχῶν μιασμός), "sex perversion" (γενέσεως ἐναλλαγή), "disorder in marriage" (γάμων ἀταξία), "adultery" (νοθεύω, μοιχεία),
and "licentiousness" (ἀσέλγεια). L. William Countryman disputes that Wis 14:24–26 refers
to same-sex relations (*Dirt, Greed, and Sex: Sexual Ethics in the New Testament and Their
Implications for Today* [Philadelphia: Fortress, 1988] 63); and Derrick Sherwin Bailey expresses uncertainty on the matter (*Homosexuality and the Western Christian Tradition* [Lon-
don: Longmans, Green, 1955] 45–48).

cially sexual sin. Wisdom of Solomon deems both idols and idol worshipers accursed.[113]

In distinction from Romans, Wisdom of Solomon sees knowledge of God as a protection against sin, whereas according to Romans, everyone is able to know God, but that knowledge does not protect them against sin. Wisdom maintains a strict Jew/gentile dichotomy; the term "we" in the text denotes those who belong to God and excludes idol worshipers.[114] Romans startles its readers by bridging this dichotomy. Although all can know God, that knowledge does not protect them against sin. Indeed, "all, both Jews and Greeks, are under the power of sin" (Rom 3:9) and "all have sinned and fall short of the glory of God" (Rom 3:23).

Wisdom of Solomon uses no names of persons, peoples, or places, creating an aura of universalism. The strong biblical allusions and traditional language in Wisdom allow Jewish readers to identify themselves as the "we" and gentiles as the idol worshipers, but it is important to remember that the text does not refer explicitly to Jews or to Israelites, but only to gentiles.

Like Wisdom, Paul employs universalistic, nonspecific language in Rom 1:18–32 (e.g., no references to Jews or gentiles), but, unlike Wisdom, Paul does not present knowledge of God as "complete righteousness" (Wis 15:3)[115] or as protection against sin. This difference becomes a rhetorical tool in Paul's overall strategy. Rom 1:18–32 presupposes that the reader familiar with the Septuagint can recognize the anti-idolatry polemic from the Wisdom of Solomon and other Jewish sources and believe that knowledge of the God of Israel and belonging to the God of Israel protects the Jewish people (which encompasses Jewish-Christians). The reader will recollect that idol worshipers are the enemies, the oppressors of the Israelites.[116] The text of Romans unfolds to catch such a reader off guard with the rhetorical twist in Rom 2:1:

> Therefore you have no excuse, whoever you are, when you judge
> others; for in passing judgment on another you condemn yourself,
> because you, the judge, are doing the very same things.

The Wisdom of Solomon expresses praise, and implicitly, gratitude, to God that "we," who worship God rather than idols, will not sin, and the reader of Rom 1:18–32 has every reason to expect the same argument here. Jews,

113. Wis 13:10; 14:8.
114. Wis 15:2f: "For even if we sin we are yours, knowing your power; but we will not sin, because we know that you acknowledge us as yours. For to know you is complete righteousness, and to know your power is the root of immortality."
115. ['O]λόκληρος δικαιοσύνη.
116. Wis 15:14.

including Jewish-Christians, will not assume that they have suppressed the truth about God for a lie or "exchanged the glory of the immortal God for images" (Rom 1:23). Then Paul surprisingly accuses the accuser. Paul uses content and language similar to the Wisdom of Solomon to his rhetorical advantage by leading a Jewish reader to think of the sinner as "the other" throughout Rom 1:18–32 until Romans 2, in which Paul sharply accuses Jews of transgressing the law and praises gentiles for fulfilling the law. Paul even goes so far as to say that gentiles can "do by nature what the law requires" (Rom 2:14).

The Wisdom background of Romans 1 helps us better to understand Paul's condemnation of homoeroticism by bringing into focus the stark polemic at work here. This polemic functions to set a clear boundary between those who worship the God of Israel (for Paul, both Jews and Christians) and all who observe pagan religious practices (whether pagan or not). This pattern of strict boundary-setting is interconnected with other types of dichotomies, such as can be found in sex and gender roles.[117] Boundary differentiations of various types occur as a matter of course in polemically conceived arguments, and these passages in Romans and Wisdom are no different. Paul's very selection of homoeroticism, in all of its boundary-confusing aspects, is particularly suited to elucidate the chaos that results when people fail to observe proper religious practices. Reading Romans 1 in light of Wisdom helps us to discern the extent and character of the polemic that ancient readers familiar with the Septuagint would have recognized and to conceptualize Paul's condemnation of female homoeroticism as a question of religiously defined social order.

The echoes of the Wisdom of Solomon in Romans 1 show that Paul is theologically indebted to his Jewish education. Establishing a Jewish (or non-Jewish) background, in my view, does not decrease or increase the theological value of any passage within the New Testament. Whether a theological or ethical teaching originated within early Christianity, or was adopted by early Christians from their cultural and intellectual environment, does not alone determine that teaching's validity for the churches today.

How Other Ancient Sources on Sexual Love Between Women Can Help Us Understand Paul's Condemnation

Roman-period authors treat female homoeroticism somewhat differently from male homoeroticism, which is in keeping with the very different treatment of women and men in the Roman world. Rom 1:26f, like other an-

---

117. Paul does not uphold strict boundaries in every aspect of his teachings. E.g., he assumes in 1 Cor 14:23 that nonbelievers will be entering into the Corinthian worship services.

cient sources, partially places female "unnatural" sexual behavior parallel to male "unnatural" sexual behavior and partially treats it differently. Paul mentions the women first and with less specificity than the men. Other sources from Paul's time display a similar tension in depicting female and male homoeroticism, such as by setting up a literary parallelism that breaks down upon inspection (e.g., Dorotheos of Sidon) or by describing male homoeroticism at greater length than female (e.g., Pseudo-Phokylides and Dorotheos of Sidon). Artemidoros's classification of male homoeroticism as natural or illegal and of female homoeroticism as unnatural, which may be based upon older traditions, further exemplifies the asymmetrical treatment of sexual love between women and between men.

Paul's description of the divine disapproval of sexual love between women also finds its counterpart in hellenistic and early imperial sources. The poet Asklepiades represents sexual love between women as unpleasing to Aphrodite. Similarly, Ovid has Isis save the day by changing a young woman into a man to transform the "monstrous" and "unnatural" love between two women into an acceptable form of love. Thus, Paul's theological presentation of sexual love between women as contrary to God's plan for humanity finds precedent in pagan thought.

Paul's depiction of sexual love between women as a result of idolatry resembles the Roman representation of such love as foreign. While Roman authors present it as Greek, Paul connects it with paganism generally. His allusion to deities in the form of animals particularly leads the reader to Egypt. Egyptian and non-Egyptian sources that postdate Paul (Sifra, erotic spells, Ptolemy of Alexandria, Clement of Alexandria, and Iamblichos) confirm the image of Egypt as a region that tolerated female romantic friendship and even woman-woman marriage.

The use of "females" and "males," rather than the more common "women" and "men," suggests that both Paul and Pseudo-Phokylides were extending the Levitical prohibition of male-male coupling (18:22; see also 20:13) to include women.

Roman-period sources are especially helpful in interpreting Paul's use of "unnatural." A variety of contemporaneous sources represent sexual love between women as unnatural, involving women who are masculine, women who do not conform to their "naturally" passive roles (e.g., Phaedrus, Martial, Pseudo-Phokylides, Dorotheos of Sidon, Manetho).

A survey of ancient sources further suggests that for Paul, as for nearly all of his contemporaries, neither female-female pederasty nor female procreation was at stake in condemnations of female homoeroticism. The relative lack of these motifs further confirms the centrality of gender transgression in Paul's and other ancient rejections of female same-sex sexual transgression.

Conclusion

A Jewish woman, dark and noble, stands tall, listening intently to the letter from Paul of Tarsus being read aloud for the first time in a Roman house church. When she hears his words about males becoming enflamed with passion for one another, she thinks of Leviticus, a text she has heard read aloud in the synagogue so many times since she was a child.

An old blind man who has worshiped many gods in his life is seated on a bench a few feet away from her and pays equal attention to the words. For a moment, his mind wanders to the days of his youth, when, as a slave, he read aloud to his master; he can remember reading a Stoic discussion on natural law to his master, a Roman lawyer.

His wife, about fifty years old, tries hard to stay awake, crouched in the corner, her belly protruding beneath her stained ochre-colored dress. She has just come from working all day at their *taberna*, a tiny corner stall where she serves her customers hot dishes from deep earthenware bowls set into the counter. At the words, "unnatural intercourse," her head jerks upright. She may be illiterate, but she understands human nature, and she's seen all kinds at her food stall. Two young women had come to her shop that day, their arms around each other. After they left, one of her regular customers, already a little drunk at mid-day, had muttered aloud, "Those girls should be married and pregnant. Why don't their fathers marry them off? It just isn't natural. The things you see these days! Why, what do they do? Strap something on?" The shopkeeper, red in her wrinkled face, had cut him off, "Why you never mind. It's not what you think. Those girls are very pious. Now, can I get you some more fish sauce?" The shopkeeper knows the girls as virgins and, like herself, followers of Christ. She strains to hear what Paul has written about unnatural intercourse.

The most learned person in the assembly, a short Jewish man from Alexandria, educated in grammar and rhetoric, recognizes Paul's allusions to Jewish writings against gentile idolatry. He will be delivering a sermon when the reading of Paul's letter is over, and in his mind he goes over how he might bring in the Wisdom of Solomon. In listening, he feels increasingly confident that his superior rhetorical and biblical training will enable him to convince the congregation of the rightness of his views concerning the law of Moses and Jesus Christ—over those of Paul.

The earliest hearers of Paul's Letter to the Romans partook of the same culture as he, and many could recognize the allusions he made. At a distance of over nineteen hundred years, we have to reconstruct academically what his first hearers knew experientially from their own culture: from Jewish literature, from the philosophy discussed in the marketplaces and lecture halls, and from what people said on the streets and in the corner taverns. After they read his letter, they probably talked about it. (Scripture and rabbinic literature are both filled with people of various backgrounds talking to one another about religious matters.) Maybe the Jewish woman explained to the older gentile couple what she knew about Levitical law, about purity and holiness. The tavern keeper must have put in her two cents about what is natural for women and men respectively, probably only to be interrupted by the learned Alexandrian, who may have explained philosophically why it is unnatural for a free woman to rule over a free man. Perhaps he had heard that Paul promoted celibacy and disagreed, arguing that marriage better protects against licentiousness than celibacy. And perhaps women who loved, or had loved, other women were also among Paul's first hearers. Did they listen silently, feeling guilty and afraid that the congregation would find out? Or did they speak up, confident in their love for one another and for Christ? We cannot know. Their voices are absent.

We do know that Rom 1:18-32 sounds very much like other ancient Jewish anti-idolatry polemics, as exemplified in the Wisdom of Solomon. And we can recognize "natural" and "unnatural" as categories born of controversy, as the result of disputes about social order and as attempts to create clarity in a world in which women and men, by their behavior, were blurring societally ordained gender roles. We can see Paul's condemnation of homoeroticism as part of an unfolding legal discussion of the meaning of Levitical concepts in the Roman world. Further, we can discern significant overlap between Paul's condemnation of homoeroticism and that of Philo of Alexandria, for whom males in same-sex relationships either lose their masculinity or teach others effeminacy.

Most important, by his very condemnation of sexual love between women as unnatural, Paul demonstrates that he is a man of the Roman world. Depending on their social circumstances and regional and ethnic background, Paul's earliest readers may have recognized love between women as a practice of Roman matrons, Greek prostitutes, daughters of Jewish priests, or Egyptian women seeking the aid of magicians. They may have read or heard of physicians who tried to stop such love by means of clitoridectomy, astrologers who explained a woman's orientation toward other women as both caused by the stars and unnatural, or satirists who described *tribades* as monstrous and unnatural. Far from being the product of thoughtful philosophers concerned about encouraging sexual relationships that respect the full humanity of each partner, the Roman-period opposition to sexual love between women grew out of the view of women as inferior, unfit to rule, passive, and weak. Paul's condemnation of female homoeroticism has helped to maintain this view.

Reading Rom 1:18-32 against the background of other writings with which Paul's earliest readers could have been familiar has helped us to see how Paul tried to persuade his readers: by alluding to Jewish antipagan polemic, by appealing to nature, by referring to a divine decree accessible even to idol worshipers, by condemning a behavior prohibited by the Jewish law in language reminiscent of Leviticus. Paul has persuaded generations of Christians for hundreds of years. These Christians have categorized love between women as sinful, unnatural, and shameful. Since Christianity has become the basis for much of Western culture, our legal and popular ethics reflect these attitudes.

I have argued that Paul's condemnation of homoeroticism, particularly female homoeroticism, reflects and helps to maintain a gender asymmetry based on female subordination. I hope that churches today, being apprised of the history that I have presented, will no longer teach Rom 1:26f as authoritative.[118]

118. In this book I have focused on female homoeroticism. Male homoeroticism raises some of the same questions, as well as some different ones, which I cannot subsume under my discussion of women.

11

Tortures in Hell: Early Church Fathers
on Female Homoeroticism

In the prior chapters I have argued that Paul's first-century readers would have read his condemnation of female homoeroticism both in the context of a larger cultural pattern of asymmetry in sexual relations (active/passive; superordinate/subordinate) and in the context of his emphasis on gender differentiation in physical appearance as a means of enforcing gender boundaries. I have further argued that these readers would have interpreted Paul as viewing homoerotic behavior as contrary to natural law and therefore worthy of death. In this chapter I shall demonstrate that Christian interpretations of Rom 1:26f in the second through fifth centuries and discussions of female homoeroticism from the same time period corroborate my arguments.

The sources that I discuss in this chapter confirm that certain features of Graeco-Roman culture remained constant over a period of centuries—particularly the conceptualization of sexual relations as asymmetrical and unequal. Paul's readers of the second through the fifth centuries validate the appropriateness of reading Paul within the cultural and intellectual frameworks within which I have interpreted him. Early Christian depictions of homoerotic women suffering tortures in hell for their sin correspond to Paul's view that such women are deserving of death in God's judgment. As in Romans 1, several such depictions classify homoerotic women and men as two relatively parallel groups, which was unusual in the Roman world. Early church writers describe female homoeroticism in terms of gender transgression and insist that both female partners are culpable. Gender boundaries enforced through dress codes (with explicit appeal to 1 Cor 11: 2–16) form an important framework for these discussions of sexual love between women, as does a gendered understanding of nature. Natural law and natural theology also play a role in early patristic interpretations of Romans 1.

These early patristic discussions also echo images of *tribades* from the larger cultural context of ancient Christianity: the image of the masculine woman and the insinuation of a connection between *tribades* and prostitutes or between *tribades* and castrated men. We also find an intriguing reference to woman-woman marriage in second-century Egypt that, taken together with non-Christian references to the same phenomenon, may point to an actual historical practice. This material thereby completes the quilt that I have been piecing together throughout this book and demonstrates the close connections between early Christianity and its cultural environment in the construction of gender and of female sexuality.

Apocalyptic Visions of God's Punishment for Sexual Relations Between Women

Several apocalyptic texts paint in vivid colors a picture of the teaching we found in Paul's Letter to the Romans: that women and men who cross gender boundaries in their sexual behavior deserve an extreme form of punishment, since they have committed a grave transgression of God's law. In narrative form they depict how Paul's early Christian readers visualized the results of divine judgment, how these early readers pictured the eschatological effects of God's wrath. Taking the form of guided tours through hell,[1] these texts (precursors of and an inspiration to Dante) present themselves as first-person accounts narrated by persons who either had a vision of hell or who had died and gone to hell and then had the good fortune of being raised to life again. In each case, the narrator tells of horrendous tortures suffered by sinners. Since the souls of these sinners cluster together with other souls suffering punishment for the same sin, the narrator describes tableau-like scenes of sinners enduring punishments commensurate to their particular sin: false witnesses suffer the punishment of biting through their tongues and having flaming fire in their mouths; the merciless rich lie dressed in filthy rags on glowing hot pebbles; blasphemers hang by their tongues above a blaze of fire. From apocalypse to apocalypse the precise punishments differ, but the principle of a punishment suitable to the particular sin remains constant.

This principle of commensurate punishment, reminiscent of Paul's statement that on the day of wrath "God will repay according to each one's

1. See Martha Himmelfarb's definitive study, *Tours of Hell: An Apocalyptic Form in Jewish and Christian Literature* (Philadelphia: University of Pennsylvania Press, 1983). In contrast to Albrecht Dieterich, who posited an Orphic-Pythagorean background to the earliest Christian tour of hell (which is found in the *Apocalypse of Peter*) (*Nekyia: Beiträge zur Erklärung der neuentdeckten Petrusapokalypse* [Leipzig: Teubner, 1893]), Himmelfarb, by delineating the literary interrelationships among all of the extant documents and fragments, has established the close connections among the various Jewish and Christian apocalyptic depictions of hell (see esp. pp. 127–68 and the "Family Tree for Tours of Hell" chart on p. 171).

deeds" (Rom 2:6), offers insight into early Christian conceptualizations of female homoerotic behavior. Although Paul did not describe the final judgment day or human suffering in hell, his thinking was apocalyptic in its orientation toward a future judgment and a second coming of Christ. For this reason, the apocalypses that I will discuss exhibit a certain compatibility with Romans 1. But whereas Paul referred obliquely to "the wrath of God" and to these people's deserving to die, the early Christian apocalyptic visions contain concrete details of the postmortem punishments.[2] These details denote the relative gravity of the sin in the eyes of the authors of the apocalyptic accounts and how these authors conceptualized female homoerotic behavior.

WOMEN CASTING THEMSELVES OFF A CLIFF IN HELL: THE *APOCALYPSE OF PETER*

In the earliest extant Christian apocalypse, the *Apocalypse of Peter*,[3] which was fairly widely known in the early church and was considered authoritative scripture by some,[4] homoerotically behaving men and women cast

2. Notice that Paul says that people who have engaged in the prohibited behaviors deserve to die, whereas the apocalypses focus on the postmortem punishment. The authors of these apocalypses apparently interpreted Paul's phrase, "deserve to die," eschatologically.

3. See Richard J. Bauckham, "The Apocalypse of Peter: An Account of Research," in *ANRW* II.25.6 (Berlin: De Gruyter, 1988) 4712–50, esp. 4738; and Himmelfarb, *Tours of Hell*, 8–10. Researchers date the *Apocalypse of Peter* to the first half of the second century CE based on its probable dependence on the Gospel of Matthew and 4 Ezra and its use by Clement of Alexandria and *Sib. Or.* 2. Interpreters dispute its provenance.

In addition to the Greek original and the Ethiopic translation that I discuss here, see also the medieval Garshuni version (Arabic in Syriac characters) of the *Apocalypse of Peter*, which contains a revelation to Peter about the evils of the end time: "A father will marry a woman, and his son her daughter; a man will marry two sisters, and men will marry men as if they were women. Males will debase themselves with males and females with females, and they will own one another" (A. Mingana, *Woodbrooke Studies: Christian Documents in Syriac, Arabic, and Garshūni, Edited and Translated with a Critical Apparatus*, vol. 3 [Cambridge: Heffer, 1931] fasc. 7, p. 277 [see also p. 245: "when you see women dressed in men's dresses and *vice versa*, know that the time is at hand, and that the hour of judgment is come"]).

4. Clement of Alexandria wrote a commentary on it as part of his scriptural commentary (see Eusebios, *Ekklēsiastikē Historia* 6.14.1; see Clement's quotations of it in *Eklogai* 41, 48, and 49); and the Canon Muratori and Codex Claromontanus count it as canonical. The fifth-century writer Sozomen states that churches in Palestine read it as scripture (*Ekklēsiastikē Historia* 7.19). Eusebios counts it among the non-genuine books of the disputed category, which he classifies as higher than the heretical works (*Ekklēsiastikē Historia* 3.25). For further references both to Eastern and Western church writers, see Dennis D. Buchholz, *Your Eyes Will Be Opened: A Study of the Greek (Ethiopic) Apocalypse of Peter* (SBLDS 97; Atlanta: Scholars Press, 1988) 20–42; and Bauckham, "The Apocalypse of Peter," 4739f. See also Annewies van den Hoek, "Clement and Origen as Sources on 'Noncanonical' Scriptural Traditions during the Late Second and Early Third Centuries," *Originiana Sexta*, ed. Gilles Dorival (Louvain: Peeters, 1995) 93–113.

themselves down from a high, overhanging cliff, whereupon their tormen-
tors force them to go up again and be cast down again. The *Apocalypse*
describes the men who are tortured in this way as "those who defile their
bodies, behaving like women," and the women with them as "those who
have sex with one another as a man (does) with a woman." [5]

In the *Apocalypse of Peter*'s hell these women and men reproduce what
they ostensibly did during their lifetimes: turn themselves upside down,
again and again. (The text does not specify whether they cast themselves
headfirst or feetfirst; by "turn themselves upside down" I mean that they
alternate between standing atop the cliff and falling to the ground below.)
Because the men behaved as women, and the women likewise took on male
roles, their torturers now force them to cast themselves off a cliff. [6] Since
the *Apocalypse of Peter* presents each punishment as commensurate to the
crime, I interpret this punishment to mean that just as these men and
women reversed their proper roles during their lifetimes, so too must they
now pursue a ceaseless process of going up and coming down, going up
and coming down again, reversing their direction just as they reversed the
gendered order of society. Two centuries later, John Chrysostom said of

5. *Apocalypse of Peter* (Greek Akhmim fragment) 17: Ἄλλοι ἄνδρες καὶ γυναῖκες ἀπὸ
κρημνοῦ μεγάλου καταστρεφόμενοι ἤρχοντο κάτω καὶ πάλιν ἠλαύνοντο ὑπὸ τῶν ἐπικει-
μένων ἀναβῆναι ἄνω ἐπὶ τοῦ κρημνοῦ καὶ κατεστρέφοντο ἐκεῖθεν κάτω, καὶ ἡσυχίαν οὐκ
εἶχον ἀπὸ ταύτης τῆς κολάσεως. οὗτοι δὲ ἦσαν οἱ μιάναντες τὰ σώματα ἑαυτῶν ὡς γυναῖκες ἀναστρεφόμενοι . . . αἱ συγκοιμηθεῖσαι ἀλλήλαις ὡς ἂν ἀνὴρ πρὸς γυναῖκα (Oscar
von Gebhart, ed., *Das Evangelium und die Apokalypse des Petrus: Die neuentdeckten Bruch-
stücke* [Leipzig: Hinrichs, 1893] 52 [pp. 19f of the manuscript]). M. R. James, the first English translator of the work, did not translate the portion beginning with "those who defile,"
but rather wrote: "[These were guilty of lewdness.]" (J. Armitage Robinson and Montague
Rhodes James, *The Gospel According to Peter and the Revelation of Peter* [London: Clay, 1892]
51). Such circumlocutions, common in the nineteenth century, have made research on ancient
sexual mores and values infinitely more difficult.

The ancient Ethiopic translation, considered by some scholars to be closer to the original
than the Greek Akhmim fragment, is more vague than the Greek at this point. Dennis Buchholz translates (10:4): "These are they who cut their flesh, sodomites and the women who
were with them. And in it are those men who, like (with) women, defile one another" (Buchholz, *Your Eyes Will Be Opened,* 215). C. Detlef G. Müller renders the same passage as: "These
are they who have cut their flesh as apostles of a man, and the women who were with them . . .
and thus are the men who defiled themselves with one another in the fashion of women"
(Wilhelm Schneemelcher, ed., *New Testament Apocrypha,* trans. R. McL. Wilson, vol. 2 [rev.
ed. of the collection initiated by Edgar Hennecke; Tübingen: Mohr (Siebeck), 1989; Cambridge: Clarke, 1992] 631). The "women who were with them" could be homoerotically
behaving women or women of some other type who associated themselves with homoerotic
men. See also Hugo Duensing, "Ein Stücke der urchristlichen Petrusapokalypse enthaltender
Traktat der äthiopischen Pseudoklementinischen Literatur," *ZNW* 14 (1913) 65–78, who
notes that the text is totally corrupted at this point (p. 71).

6. The cliff might be an allusion to the Leukadian Cliff, off which later legend has Sappho
casting herself; see, e.g., Ovid, *Heroides* 15; and Plutarch, *Centuria* 1.29.2.

same-sex erotic love: "Whenever God forsakes someone, all things are turned upside down."[7]

In the *Apocalypse of Peter*, only passive male homoerotic participants occupy a place in hell, not their active male partners (only the passive males behave "like women");[8] however, *both* female partners, active and passive, apparently deserve this punishment, since both women count as sinners. I base this interpretation on three observations about the text. The first clue lies in the verb "to have sex with" (*synkoimaomai*):[9] unlike Greek verbs meaning "to penetrate" that occur in the active for men and the passive for women,[10] this verb occurs elsewhere for both female and male sexual behavior and thus encompasses both an active and a passive sense. Second, the term for "with one another"[11] implies that both partners in the female homoerotic activity are now undergoing punishment. Third, whereas the text describes the men as "like women," it describes the women behaving "as a man [does] with a woman,"[12] emphasizing the behavior rather than the gender role. This text does not depict the female sinners as like men, but rather as engaging in the sexual act in which a man engages with a woman, which probably implies the penetration of one woman's vagina or genital-to-genital contact. Thus, the *Apocalypse of Peter* presumes that both of the female participants deserve the punishment of hell.

Like other texts we have seen from the Roman world, the *Apocalypse of Peter* may presume either an organic or an artificial penetrating device on the part of one of the female participants. The phrase "those [f.] who have sex with one another as a man [does] with a woman" may indicate the presence of such a device.[13] Thus, the *Apocalypse of Peter* apparently shares the widespread ancient view that homoerotic women imitate men: just as men penetrate either females or males, so too do homoerotic women penetrate other women. In one of his fictitious legal controversies, the Elder Seneca (1st C. BCE–1st C. CE), depicts a man who finds his wife in bed with another woman as looking first to the "man" to ascertain "whether he was natural or sewed on."[14] The first-century CE Latin poet Martial

---

7. John Chrysostom, *Commentary on Romans, Homily* 4; *PG* 60.417 mid.

8. On passive males as a category in Roman society, see Amy Richlin, "Not Before Homosexuality: The Materiality of the *Cinaedus* and the Roman Law against Love between Men," *Journal of the History of Sexuality* 3 (1993) 523–73.

9. Passive with an active sense.

10. E.g., περαίνω, περαίνομαι.

11. [Ἀ]λλήλαις.

12. [Ὡ]ς ἂν ἀνὴρ πρὸς γυναῖκα.

13. The presence of both women in hell and the possibility of a device raises the question whether the author conceived of the women taking turns, which would have run contrary to the prevailing ancient understandings of sexual behavior.

14. *Controversiae* 1.2.23.

writes of Bassa, a woman who engaged in sex with other women, that "her monstrous lust imitates a man," and of Philaenis that "she buggers the boys," as if she had the means wherewith to penetrate them.[15] In the second century Lucian of Samosata has one of his characters refer to women in Lesbos who have faces like men and are unwilling to endure a passive sexual role with men, instead approaching only women, as if they themselves were men. Lucian also speaks of women who kiss like men and who have something in place of the male genitals.[16] Thus, the phrase in the *Apocalypse of Peter*, "as a man [does] with a woman," shows how the work is interwoven into the texture of its society.

In addition to the portrayal of women as imitators of men, the *Apocalypse of Peter*'s theoretical significance lies in its linking of male and female homoeroticism, since the *Apocalypse* thereby bears witness to an early Christian category of homoeroticism. Both the penetrated males and the penetrating females and their female partners suffer the same punishment in the same region of hell.[17] Passive males and both passive and active homoerotic females thus form a triad of unorthodox alternatives to the penetrating male and his passive female partner. This pairing of female and male homoeroticism, not universal in the Roman world, recalls Paul's Letter to the Romans, in which Paul mentions both female and male homoeroticism.

Like Paul, the author of the *Apocalypse of Peter* discusses homoeroticism in the context of idolatry.[18] In the Greek fragment containing the scene of the passive males and the homoerotic females, the text locates the punishment site for those who had fashioned images near the cliff from which the aforementioned women and men cast themselves down. The Ethiopic version of the *Apocalypse of Peter* presents the punishment of idol worshipers right before that of the men who defile themselves with one another.

Thus, the *Apocalypse of Peter* echoes themes found in Paul and in the Roman world at large: the deity (whether Aphrodite or the God of Israel) does not approve of homoerotic women, who deserve a severe punishment for doing what men do.

15. *Epigrammata* 1.90; 7.67.

16. Lucian of Samosata, *Dialogues of the Courtesans* 5; §§289–92.

17. Strikingly absent, however, are males who penetrate other males; such males do not "behave like women." Perhaps the text implies the presence of these men, since they cause other males to behave like women, but it does not explicitly mention them.

18. The *Apocalypse of Peter* also resembles Romans 1 in its reference to defilement. Although the Greek word for the men's defilement of themselves (μιαίνω) is not that used by Paul for "impurity" (ἀκαθαρσία), it connotes impurity.

WOMEN BURNING IN HELL: THE *ACTS OF THOMAS*

The second earliest Christian apocalypse, the *Acts of Thomas*, probably written in the early third century in Syria,[19] contains an account of a visit to the underworld[20] similar to the vision in the *Apocalypse of Peter*.[21] According to the *Acts of Thomas*, those (both women and men) who have "exchanged the intercourse of man and woman" or "who change the intercourse that has been appointed by God" will suffer in hell. I interpret these phrases as referring to homoeroticism, because they echo the conceptualization found both in Rom 1:26f and in the larger culture that homoerotically behaving persons exchange/change the type of intercourse willed by God and laid down in nature. (Theoretically, "exchanged" could refer to other unorthodox forms of sexual contact, such as anal intercourse or oral-genital contact, but then the phrase "of man and woman" would make little sense.) As in other Christian sources, divine displeasure at this human change of a sexual act ordained by God results in God's wrathful punishment. Two different versions of the *Acts of Thomas*, however, describe very different forms of punishment.

The *Acts of Thomas* was composed in Syriac, a dialect of Aramaic, and is

19. See Han J. W. Drijvers, in *New Testament Apocrypha*, ed. Wilhelm Schneemelcher, trans. R. McL. Wilson, vol. 2 (rev. ed. of the collection intitiated by Edgar Hennecke; Tübingen: Mohr [Siebeck], 1989; Cambridge: Clarke, 1992) 323.

20. The account is embedded within the story of a young man who has killed a young woman out of anger because she refused to enter into a celibate marriage with him. He defends his deed on the grounds that "she would not obey me, to keep herself chaste." The apostle Thomas, who condemns the murder, enables the man to raise the woman from the dead. Upon returning to life, she recounts what she saw in the underworld. An ugly black man (notice the negative depiction of the black man, which raises the question of its racial implications; early Christian literature often depicted the devil as black) took her to see groups of dead souls in a series of chasms suffering tortures appropriate to their deeds on earth. The young woman was apparently about to be handed over to one of these tortures, since she was "one of the sheep that have gone astray," but her being raised from the dead saved her from that fate. Thomas successfully uses the opportunity to preach repentance to his followers (*Acts of Thomas* 6.51–61 [48–58]; Richard Adelbert Lipsius and Maximilian Bonnet, eds., *Acta Apostolorum Apocrypha*, vol. 2/2 [Darmstadt: Wissenschaftliche Buchgesellschaft, 1959] 167–78; ET: Schneemelcher, *New Testament Apocrypha*, 2:360–64).

21. Like the vision in the *Apocalypse of Peter*, this account contains a series of images of dead persons grouped according to their sins and suffering punishments suited to their transgressions on earth. Both the *Apocalypse of Peter* and the *Acts of Thomas* drew on earlier traditions, especially Jewish apocalyptic traditions about the underworld (see Himmelfarb, *Tours of Hell*, 132f). For discussion of whether the *Acts of Thomas* is dependent on the *Apocalypse of Peter* and for a review of the less convincing theory that the *Acts of Thomas*, the *Apocalypse of Peter*, and other early Christian apocalypses are dependent on an earlier Orphic-Pythagorean description of a visit to the underworld, see Richard J. Bauckham, "The Apocalypse of Peter: An Account of Research," in *ANRW* II.25.6 (Berlin: De Gruyter, 1988) 4726–33.

now extant in both Syriac and Greek versions.[22] Because the Greek translation (which may on the whole be closer to the original Syriac composition than the reworked Syriac version we now have) contains an enigmatic punishment for homoeroticism, at this point in the text the Syriac may be more reliable. First I will discuss the Syriac version and then the more puzzling Greek version.

In the Syriac version of the *Acts of Thomas*, the young woman who visited the underworld describes the first group of souls that she saw as follows: "And he made me look down into each of the pits; and I saw the first pit, and as it were fire was blazing in its midst, and wheels of fire were revolving in its midst; and he said to me: 'Into this torment are destined to come those souls which transgress the law, which change the union of intercourse that has been appointed by God.'"[23] The Syriac version lists souls who have not preserved their virginity as next in line for this punishment, thus linking two sexual transgressions to the same torture. Fire as torture had long since captured the ancient imagination.[24] It may be reminiscent here of the biblical punishment visited on Sodom. Because of fire's widespread use for a variety of sins, however, we cannot deduce anything particular about the author's view of homoeroticism, other than its gravity as a sin.

In contrast to this fiery punishment in the Syriac *Acts of Thomas*, the Greek version of the *Acts of Thomas* depicts those who exchanged or perverted "the intercourse of man and woman" as suffering the enigmatic punishment of inhabiting a chasm together with their newborn children: "[new-born] infants heaped one upon another and struggling with one

22. Interpreters generally agree that the *Acts of Thomas* were originally written in Syriac (for the most recent articulation of this case, see Harold W. Attridge, "The Original Language of the Acts of Thomas," in *Of Scribes and Scrolls: Studies on the Hebrew Bible, Intertestamental Judaism, and Christian Origins Presented to John Strugnell on the Occasion of His Sixtieth Birthday*, ed. Harold W. Attridge, John J. Collins, and Thomas H. Tobin [Lanham, MD: University Press of America, 1990] 241–50), but disagree on whether or not the extant Greek version is a translation of a Syriac text older than the extant Syriac. The Greek could be a reworking of the original Syriac or the extant Syriac could be a reworking of the original Syriac. See Himmelfarb, *Tours of Hell*, 11f; and A. F. J. Klijn, *The Acts of Thomas: Introduction—Text—Commentary* (Supplements to *Novum Testamentum* 5; Leiden: Brill, 1962). Klijn argues that "the Greek version goes back to a stage of the Syriac version earlier than known from the Syriac version in the available MSS" (pp. 13f), but that in the tour of hell, "the Syriac version of this description is the original one and . . . the Greek version of the Acts added the different punishments from a different source" (pp. 252f).

23. *Acts of Thomas* 6.55; ET: William Wright, trans., *Apocryphal Acts of the Apostles: Edited from Syriac Manuscripts*, vol. 2 (London, 1871; reprint, Amsterdam: Philo, 1968) 195. See also Klijn, *The Acts of Thomas*, 94; based on the translation by Wright.

24. See Himmelfarb, *Tours of Hell*, 106–15, who classifies fire as an environmental punishment (in contrast, e.g., to hanging punishments).

another as they lay upon them. . . . 'These are their children, and therefore are they set here as a testimony against them.' " [25] Several solutions to this enigma are possible.

The presence of the infants leads Martha Himmelfarb to suggest that the parents have perhaps committed abortion or infanticide, since other apocalypses include infants accusing their parents of abortion and infanticide.[26] As an alternative explanation, Himmelfarb suggests that the parents committed adultery. Thus, Himmelfarb interprets "perverted the intercourse of man and woman" as "committed abortion and infanticide." Her solution to the interpretive problem makes sense from the standpoint of the punishment (the presence of the accusing infants). Unless, however, we construe abortion and infanticide as perverting the procreative purpose of intercourse, her proposal does not adequately address the meaning of the sin, since neither abortion nor infanticide perverts the act of male-female intercourse.

Alternatively, the children could represent the fruit of "proper" intercourse between married women and men in which the souls had engaged, in addition to their prohibited homoerotic activity. The image of the struggling infants could represent the chaos and confusion resulting from homoerotic behavior or the shame and failure of the man in his role as husband and father. Or perhaps these children resulted from an unorthodox type of female-male intercourse that the author saw as perverted. Or

---

25. *Acts of Thomas* 6.55 (52); Lipsius and Bonnet, eds., *Acta Apostolorum Apocrypha*, vol. 2/2:172; ET: Schneemelcher, *New Testament Apocrypha*, 2:362. The *New Testament Apocrypha* renders μεταλάσσω as "pervert," whereas I translate it as "exchange" in order to make clear the connection with Romans 1. Theoretically, the clause could refer to a type of intercourse other than same-sex, but its similarity to Rom 1:26f makes that implausible. Further, referring to other unorthodox forms of sexual contact, such as anal intercourse or oral-genital contact, with the prepositional phrase "of man and woman" would make little sense.

The Ethiopic work *Barlâm and Yĕwâsĕf*, which contains a reworking of the story found in the *Acts of Thomas*, depicts a double punishment—one similar to that found in the Greek *Acts of Thomas* and one similar to that of the Syriac version—but it refers only to male homoeroticism (B 247a1–2/A170a1): "I saw before me a pit of blazing fire. Here there were wheels which went round, and to these wheels were bound souls which shrieked and cried out, but there was none to deliver them. And the black man said, 'These are the souls of people like thyself [presumably in the sense of "human beings like youself" B.B.], who when their days [upon earth] have come to an end, are delivered over to this punishment, for being men they made themselves to be as women.' And I also saw little children, one above the other. And the black man answered and said unto me, 'These are the children of those souls, and God hath placed them here to disgrace them' " (Ernest A. Wallis Budge, *Barlâm and Yĕwâsĕf [Barlaam and Josaphat]: Being the Ethiopic Version of a Christianized Recension of the Buddhist Legend of the Buddha and the Bodhisattva*, vol. 2 [Cambridge, 1923; reprint, Amsterdam: Philo, 1976] 335).

26. Himmelfarb, *Tours of Hell*, 96.

maybe the infants are struggling to gain the recognition of those who should have been their parents, had the potential parents not engaged in homoerotic behavior. None of these suggestions adequately explains this anomalous punishment.

I propose a text-critical solution to the mismatch between sin and punishment. An early copyist or the person translating the *Acts of Thomas* from Syriac into Greek may have mistakenly skipped over one category of sinner and one punishment and put together a sin and a punishment that did not originally belong together. In the present Syriac version, the category of sinners immediately following those who "change the union of intercourse that has been appointed by God" consists of men and women who commit adultery, young men who have sex with prostitutes, and virgins who have broken their virginity.[27] The present Syriac version does not describe the precise tortures reserved for this latter group of sinners. Perhaps the Syriac version used by the Greek translator described their punishment as their children accusing them, and the Greek translator applied the punishment for the fornicators to those who engage in perverse sexual relations. In this solution, the fiery punishment of the extant Syriac text may have been the original punishment found in the earlier Syriac version now lost to us.[28] I therefore take the fiery punishment of the Syriac *Acts of Thomas* as original.

In contrast to the punishment, the sins in both the Syriac and the Greek versions are nearly identical (Syriac: "the souls . . . which change the union of intercourse that has been appointed by God"; Greek: "the souls that exchange the intercourse of man and woman").[29] With respect to the sin, the *Acts of Thomas* echoes Paul's condemnation of homoeroticism in several ways. First, the term in the Greek version for "exchange" is *metallassō*, a verbal root used three times in Romans 1 to describe the exchanges made by those "who suppress the truth" (Rom 1:18): "they exchanged (*allassō*) the glory of . . . God for images" (Rom 1:23); "they exchanged (*metal-*

27. Syriac *Acts of Thomas* 6.56. ET: William Wright, trans., *Apocryphal Acts of the Apostles: Edited from Syriac Manuscripts*, vol. 2 (London: 1871; reprint, Amsterdam: Philo, 1968) 195. I thank Prof. Harold Attridge for suggesting this point to help me to refine this text-critical argument.

28. Alternatively, an early Syriac scribe could have noticed a mistake (the unsuitable punishment) in the original Syriac text and corrected it.

29. Syriac *Acts of Thomas* 6.55; ET: Wright, *Apocryphal Acts of the Apostles*, 2:195. See also Klijn, *The Acts of Thomas*, 94; based on the translation by Wright.

Greek *Acts of Thomas* 6.55 (52): αὗται [i.e., the souls] εἰσιν αἱ μεταλλάξασαι ἀνδρὸς καὶ γυναικὸς τὴν συνουσίαν (Richard Adelbert Lipsius and Maximilian Bonnet, eds., *Acta Apostolorum Apocrypha*, vol. 2/2 [Darmstadt: Wissenschaftliche Buchgesellschaft, 1959] 172; translation my own; for the context: ET: Schneemelcher, *New Testament Apocrypha*, 2: 362).

lassō) the truth about God for a lie" (Rom 1:25); and "[t]heir women exchanged (*metallassō*) natural intercourse for unnatural" (Rom 1:26). Second, as in Romans 1 (and as in other tours of hell), the souls depicted in the *Acts of Thomas* experience God's wrath in the form of a punishment. According to Romans, they "deserve to die" (Rom 1:32), and in the *Acts of Thomas* they suffer the "punishment and destruction" to which they were handed over in the days of reckoning.[30] According to the *Acts*, some of the suffering souls "are entirely consumed" in the process of their punishments, while others suffer first one punishment and then another, presumably first for one category of sin and then for another.[31]

Third, like Romans the *Acts of Thomas* apparently refers to both women and men. In a rare move for the ancient world, the *Acts of Thomas* encompasses both homoerotic women and men under one gender-neutral phrase ("the souls . . . that change/exchange the intercourse"). Further, since the word for "intercourse" in the Greek version (*synousia*) denotes coming together or commingling, rather than penetration, it can refer to sexual acts by either females or males. Moreover, the phrases "of man and woman" and "appointed by God" can apply either to women exchanging intercourse with men for that with women or vice versa. Thus, like Paul, the *Acts of Thomas* depicts female and male homoeroticism as an exchange within the divine order that God will severely punish.

WOMEN RUNNING IN A RIVER OF FIRE: THE *APOCALYPSE OF PAUL*

The *Apocalypse of Paul*, a third-century[32] detailed description of what the author imagines that Paul saw when caught up in paradise (2 Cor 12:1–7), depicts not only heaven, but also afterlife tortures in hell corresponding to earthly sins. In a fashion similar to the *Apocalypse of Peter* and the *Acts of Thomas*, the *Apocalypse of Paul* presents a series of persons suffering punishments. Among the groups of people whom Paul sees in hell are "men and women covered in dust, and their faces were like blood, and they were in a pit of tar and brimstone, and they were running in a river of fire." The angel serving as Paul's guide explains, "They are those who have committed the iniquity of Sodom and Gomorrah, men with men. Therefore

---

30. Greek *Acts of Thomas* 6.55 (52): ἐν ἡμέραις ἀριθμοῦ παρεδόθησαν εἰς κόλασιν καὶ ἔκτριψιν (Lipsius and Bonnet, *Acta Apostolorum Apocrypha*, vol. 2/2:172; ET: Schneemelcher, *New Testament Apocrypha*, 2:362). This phrase is missing in the Syriac version.

31. Syriac *Acts of Thomas* 6.57; ET: Wright, *Apocryphal Acts of the Apostles*, 2:196. See also Klijn, *The Acts of Thomas*, 95; based on the translation by Wright.

Greek *Acts of Thomas* 6.57 (54); Lipsius and Bonnet, *Acta Apostolorum Apocrypha*, vol. 2/2:173; ET: Schneemelcher, *New Testament Apocrypha*, 2:363.

32. I am accepting the dating of Himmelfarb, *Tours of Hell*, 16–18.

they pay the penalty unceasingly."[33] It is puzzling that the text explicitly refers to both men and women, but then describes their sin as "men with men." Judging by the parallels in the *Apocalypse of Peter* and the *Acts of Thomas*, the women's sin in the *Apocalypse of Paul* is probably sexual contact with other women.[34] On the other hand, since the author of the *Apocalypse of Paul* was probably familiar with the *Apocalypse of Peter*,[35] he or she must have described in general terms a sin that was quite clear in the earlier apocalypse. Thus, the "men and women" of the *Apocalypse of Paul* shows a connection to the tradition (according to which both homoerotic women and men will suffer punishment in the afterlife for their behavior), while the phrase "men with men" either includes female homoeroticism or refers only to male homoeroticism as the more commonly discussed of the two types.[36]

These early Christian apocalypses, while they differ on the punishments, share the vision of God punishing homoerotic women—apparently both female partners (not just the "active" one)—by means of a severe torture: a cycle of ceaselessly falling off a steep cliff and then going up to be cast down again; living in a pit of fire; or running in a river of fire. They dramatize Paul's teaching in Romans: that people who transgress God's decree deserve God's wrath. While these apocalyptic visions purport to give us a window into the world of the dead, they actually expose the priorities and fears of the early Christians who wrote and read these visions of hell.

Patristic Writers of the Second and Third Centuries
WOMEN WHO DEFY NATURE AND THE SOCIAL ORDER:
TERTULLIAN OF CARTHAGE

While the apocalyptic visions of hell confirm that early Christians saw sexual relations between women and between men as deserving of ignominious punishment, the well-educated North African church writer

33. *Apocalypse of Paul* 39; ET: Hugo Duensing and Aurelio de Santos Otero, in *New Testament Apocrypha*, ed. Wilhelm Schneemelcher, trans. R. McL. Wilson, vol. 2 (rev. ed. of the collection initiated by Edgar Hennecke; Tübingen: Mohr [Siebeck], 1989; Cambridge: Clarke, 1992) 733.

34. Notice that the Ethiopic translation of the *Apocalypse of Peter* is similarly vague. See above, n. 5.

35. The two works show great similarities in their descriptions of hell. See Duensing and Otero, in *New Testament Apocrypha*, ed. Schneemelcher, 2:714.

36. This is particularly true of the Jewish literature known to the author of the *Apocalypse of Paul*. Other apocalypses that depict punishment for male homoeroticism include: the *Ethiopic Apocalypse of Baruch* (ET: Wolf Leslau, trans., *Falasha Anthology* [Yale Judaica Series 6; New Haven: Yale University Press, 1951] 71); and the Elijah fragment found in the *Pseudo-Titus Epistle* (pederasty, although not distinguished as to the sex of the child) (ET: Schneemelcher, *New Testament Apocrypha*, 2:64).

Q. Septimius Florens Tertullianus (ca. 160–after 220) confirms the centrality of nature, natural law, and social order in early Christian discussions of female homoeroticism. Like the ancient astrologers, Tertullian classified homoerotic women either with prostitutes or with castrated men—traitors to the stratified social order of Tertullian's world. As in the Roman world at large, Tertullian closely associated homoeroticism with transgressions against the gendered dress codes of his society, and he appealed to Paul's teachings to support his own.

Tertullian argues that Paul bases his prohibition of a headdress for men and requirement of a veil for women on natural law (1 Cor 11:14). Indeed, Tertullian believes that natural law, which is identical with God's law, surrounds human beings and is engraved on "natural tablets," apparently in the phenomena of the natural world.[37] He also discerns the concept of natural law at work in Rom 2:14,[38] claiming that Paul "suggests both natural law and law-full nature."[39] For the lawyer and theologian Tertullian, God, nature, and law are fully intertwined.

Tertullian presents Paul as a protector and advocate of nature when in Rom 1:26f Paul "asserts that males and females altered among themselves the natural use of a creature to an unnatural use" as divine retribution for their idolatry.[40] Just as the tablets of nature teach us that bareheaded women and men with head-coverings contradict God's law, so too do they prohibit same-sex sexual expression. On several key points, Tertullian's close reading of Romans 1–2 and 1 Cor 11:2–16 yields an interpretation similar to what I have presented in the preceding chapters. Tertullian recognizes a connection between Rom 1:26f and 1 Cor 11:2–16. He discerns a use of natural theology and natural law in Paul: human beings can know both God (natural theology) and God's will (natural law) through observing nature. For Tertullian, persons who thoughtfully observe nature will not deviate from the gendered dress and sexual codes of the world that he and Paul share.

---

37. *De Corona* 6.1; Jacques Fontaine, ed., *Q. Septimi Florentis Tertulliani:* De Corona (Paris: Presses Universitaires de France, 1966) 85f; Aem. Kroymann, ed., *De Corona, Tertulliani Opera* 2,2 (CChr; Turnhout: Brepols, 1954) 1046. In the treatise *De Corona* (dated to 211, i.e., within Tertullian's "Montanist" period) Tertullian opposes soldiers wearing honorific military crowns on their heads and believes that Christians should not serve in the military at all.

38. "When Gentiles, who do not possess the law, do instinctively what the law requires, these, though not having the law, are a law to themselves."

39. *De Corona* 6.1: [L]*egem naturalem suggerit et naturam legalem* (Fontaine, *Q. Septimi Florentis Tertulliani,* 86; Kroymann, *De Corona,* 1046).

40. *De Corona* 6.1: *naturalem usum conditionis in non naturalem masculos et feminas inter se demutasse affirmans ex retributione erroris in uicem poenae, utique naturalibus patrocinatur* (Fontaine, *Q. Septimi Florentis Tertulliani,* 86f; Kroymann, *De Corona,* 1046f).

Dress codes and sexual mores constitute important theological themes throughout Tertullian's writings. Like other early Christians and their non-Christian contemporaries, Tertullian debated whether women should be veiled, and at what age; whether men should shave; whether women should braid their hair or wear pearls; and even whether men should wear boots or sandals. He issued a particularly rigorous call for Christians to look different from the world around them and to separate themselves from many of its activities.[41] Because Tertullian believed that Christianity should regulate all the details of one's daily life, he wrote treatises promoting the veiling of young girls (*De Virginibus Velandis*), opposing the use of cosmetics by Christian women (*De Cultu Feminarum*), and denouncing Christian attendance at the theater, circus, gladiatorial fights, and chariot races (*De Spectaculis*). He even composed an entire treatise (*De Pallio*) to justify his having exchanged the Roman toga, the garment of elite Roman males, for the *pallium*, a more comfortable Greek cloak and the international mark of a philosopher.[42]

The question of nature (*natura*) versus custom (*consuetudo*) lies at the core of Tertullian's treatise *On the Pallium*.[43] For Tertullian, nature is unchangeable, while custom can change.[44] His concern is to distinguish between forms of dress that outrage nature and those proper changes of dress that do not contradict nature. In *On the Pallium*, Tertullian classifies his change from the toga to the *pallium* as a proper change of custom, contrasting his own appropriate change with those of persons who contradict

41. See Margaret R. Miles, "Patriarchy as Political Theology: The Establishment of North African Christianity," in *Civil Religion and Political Theology*, ed. Leroy S. Rouner (Boston University Studies in Philosophy and Religion 8; Notre Dame, IN: University of Notre Dame Press, 1986) 169–86, esp. 172–77. Miles points out that "Tertullian is the only North African Christian leader who wrote pointedly against the leadership of women in Christian churches" (p. 172) and demonstrates that his preoccupation with women's appearance derives from his concern for the danger to male salvation ostensibly posed by the sight of unveiled women.

42. Jean-Claude Fredouille notes, however, that by Tertullian's time the toga—because of its cumbersomeness—had become increasingly unpopular among Romans (*Tertullien et la conversion de la culture antique* [Paris: Études Augustiniennes, 1972] 448–52).

43. Suggested dates for *De Pallio* range from 193 through 211. Fredouille has argued that it may be Tertullian's last work (*Tertullien et la conversion de la culture antique* [Paris: Études Augustiniennes, 1972] 444). Thus, it is unclear whether Tertullian wrote *De Pallio* during his "Catholic" or his "Montanist" period (and Fredouille disputes whether such a clear distinction is even possible).

44. In *De Pallio* 4.2, Tertullian expresses this theme succinctly: "Let custom show loyalty to time, nature to God" (*Det consuetudo fidem tempori, natura deo* [A. Gerlo, ed., *De Pallio, Tertulliani Opera* 2,2 (CChr; Turnhout: Brepols, 1954) 742]).

Tertullian argues for a particular relationship between nature and custom as a point in his overall attempt to demonstrate Christianity's superiority as a philosophy over pagan philosophy. (See Fredouille, *Tertullien*, 462–68, who defines the genre of *De Pallio* as *laudatio* and argues that Tertullian used this genre to affirm this superiority.)

nature by failing to dress in accordance with their gender or their social status.

Tertullian peppers his treatise with examples of persons who ignore such dress codes. He expresses great dismay at seeing former slaves dressed as equestrians (Roman citizens of the class of knights), branded slaves as gentlemen, clowns as urban dwellers, buffoons as lawyers, and corpse-bearers, pimps, and gladiator trainers wearing the same garments as his elite Roman male readers.[45] He disdains men who wear effeminate boots and scorns men who depilate the hair of their arms or use tweezers to pluck out the hairs of their beards. Tertullian derides matrons who appear in public without their stolas. (Roman law reserved to elite married citizen women the privilege of wearing this long overgarment as a visible symbol of their social status and gender.)[46] He also complains of other women of the upper strata who further violate the dress code by adopting a low-status physical appearance inappropriate to their elite womanliness: "Look at the streetwalkers, the shambles of popular lusts; also at the *frictrices*;[47] and, if it is better to withdraw your eyes from such shameful spectacles of publicly slaughtered chastity, yet do but look with eyes askance, (and) you will at once see them to be matrons!"[48]

45. Tertullian also derides Alexander the Great for having worn trousers, the dress of those whom he had conquered. He thus picks up on a charge leveled against Alexander even during his own lifetime.

46. Roman law distinguished among the dress of Roman matrons—the stola—and the dress of slaves, that of prostitutes, and that of other women (Ulpian, *Corpus Iuris Civilis, Digesta* 47.10.15.15). Thus, like the toga, the stola signified the Roman citizen class.

47. Several early modern European writers refer to *fricatrices* (presumably a variant spelling of *frictrices*). E.g., Johann Weyer, in his *De praestigiis daemonum*, a 1583 treatise on how to deal with witches, writes about women in the city of Fez (Morocco) who claim to be the mouthpiece of demons: "But those of sounder judgment rightly call these women *Sahacat*, which in Latin would be *Fricatrices* [women who rub], because they have sexual relations among themselves in a damnable fashion—I would use more respectable language if I could. If on occasion attractive women come to them, the witches are inflamed with love just as young men are for girls, and, in the guise of the demon, they ask that the women lie with them as payment" (*De praestigiis daemonum* 3.25; ET: John Shea et al., trans., *Witches, Devils, and Doctors in the Renaissance: Johann Weyer, De praestigiis daemonum* [Medieval and Renaissance Texts and Studies 73: Binghamton, NY, 1991] 249). Note Weyer's use of the Arabic term, *sahāqa*, the same word used by the Arabic translator of the astrologer Dorotheos of Sidon.

See also L. J. K. Mende, *Ausführliches Handbuch der gerichtlichen Medizin für Gesetzgeber, Rechtsgelehrte, Aerzte und Wundärzte*, pt. 4 (Leipzig: Dyk, 1826) 512; and Theo van der Meer, "Tribades on Trial: Female Same-Sex Offenders in Late Eighteenth Century Amsterdam," *Journal of the History of Sexuality* 1 (1991) 438, and the sources that they cite.

48. De Pallio 4.9: *Aspice lupas, popularium libidinum nundinas, ipsas quoque frictrices, et si praestat oculos abducere ab eiusmodi propudiis occisae in publico castitatis, aspice tamen uel sublimis, iam matronas uidebis* (A. Gerlo, ed., *De Pallio, Tertulliani Opera* 2,2 [CChr; Turnhout: Brepols, 1954] 745; ET: S. Thelwall, in Alexander Roberts and James Donaldson, eds., ANF 4, p. 10).

By speaking of prostitutes who turn out to be matrons, Tertullian seems to be alluding to some elite women's responses to the Emperor Augustus's laws, which severely restricted sexual behavior. While these laws allowed elite men access to prostitutes, slaves, and other lower-strata women, they restricted elite women to marital relations.[49] In order to achieve sexual freedom, some women officially registered as prostitutes, a strategy that Augustus's successor, Tiberius, soon foreclosed by prohibiting such registration.[50] By alluding to this historical situation, Tertullian calls to the mind of early-third-century Carthaginian readers the image of the highly ordered first-century Roman society whose stratification Augustus was attempting to maintain or restore. (Augustus's strict sexual legislation was aimed at raising the number of legitimate births in the upper social and economic strata in order to produce more elite Romans who could rule the empire.) Tertullian thereby reminds his reader that such matrons upset a highly stratified society and actively undermined Augustus's attempt at propagating the upper class.

Frictrices—women who have sexual relations with other women—and prostitutes epitomize for Tertullian Roman matrons betraying the privileges and boundaries of their status. Perhaps as in the astrological thought known in Tertullian's time,[51] Tertullian mentions prostitutes together with *frictrices* because both terms signify women as public, sexual beings—a far cry from the ideal of the chaste Roman matron sitting at home spinning wool for her family's garments (an ideal for elite Roman wives). The Latin term *frictrices* parallels the Greek word *tribades*, although the word *frictrix* (sing.) occurs much less frequently than *tribas*. As I discussed in the introduction to this book, *frictrix* may derive from *frico* ("to rub"), just as *tribas* may derive from *tribō* ("to rub").

The inclusion of *frictrices* in this treatise on dress implies that the elite male Carthaginian reader could recognize them on the street, just as he could recognize prostitutes. Perhaps *frictrices* wore a certain kind of dress or hairstyle, such as the short hair under the wig of Megilla/Megillos in Lucian's *Dialogues of the Courtesans*. Or maybe their public expression of affection gave these women the visibility that elicited Tertullian's disdainful

---

49. *Corpus Iuris Civilis, Digesta* 48.5.6. See Susan Treggiari, *Roman Marriage: Iusti Coniuges from the Time of Cicero to the Time of Ulpian* (Oxford: Clarendon, 1991) 60–80, 277–98, for further sources and discussion. See also Sarah B. Pomeroy, *Goddesses, Whores, Wives, and Slaves: Women in Classical Antiquity* (New York: Schocken, 1975) 160.

50. Tacitus, *Annales* 2.85.1. See Treggiari, *Roman Marriage*, 297, for further sources and discussion.

51. E.g., Dorotheos of Sidon, 2.4.21; David Pingree, ed. and trans., *Dorothei Sidonii Carmen Astrologicum* (Leipzig: Teubner, 1976) 48 (Arabic); ET: Pingree, *Carmen Astrologicum*, 202.

response. In any case, for Tertullian, the appearance of Roman matrons as prostitutes and *frictrices* does not constitute a proper development in custom, but an offense to the natural order.

In *On the Resurrection of the Flesh* (*De Resurrectione Carnis*),[52] Tertullian derides homoerotic women as outsiders to polite society. In this polemical treatise, Tertullian grapples with the theological problem of the relationship between the soul and the body and argues that the dead will rise at the end time.[53] He argues against the view that because the soul alone bears moral responsibility and the body is merely a vessel that contains the soul, the body is free of moral responsibility and thereby of moral constraints.[54] Since his presentation is polemical, we cannot be sure that any ancient person actually held that view. Tertullian accepts the Platonist view that the body is a vessel for the soul and also agrees with his opponents that at the final judgment, God will judge the soul alone, and not the body. But Tertullian rejects the absolute body/soul dualism that he attributes to Platonist Gnostics. Therefore he holds that the body will bear some moral culpability on the final judgment day.

To prove that bodies can indeed be judged, he argues that human beings pass judgment even on inanimate objects and illustrates his analogy with the example of drinking cups.[55] According to Tertullian, we would not want to take a sip from a drinking cup from which a *frictrix*, a castrated chief priest of the deity Cybele, a gladiator, or a hangman has drunk, thereby infecting it with their breath, any more than we would want their kisses.[56] In contrast, we want a drinking cup that has no reproach on it, and we may even honor such a cup by decorating it with a crown or with flowers. Thus, in Tertullian's view, we do pass judgment on vessels; our judgment implies their responsibility. Therefore, even if the body is a vessel, it still bears responsibility for its actions.

52. The suggested dates of *De Resurrectione Carnis* range from 210 through 217, i.e., within Tertullian's "Montanist" period.

53. Like the medical writer Soranos, Tertullian presents the soul as physical, a kind of blueprint of the body.

54. For more on the ancient discussion about the relationship between the soul and the body, see Galen, *Quod animi mores corporis temperamenta sequantur* 9.805 (Johannes Marquardt, Iwan Mueller, Georg Helmreich, eds., *Claudii Galeni Pergameni: Scripta minora*, vol. 1 (Leipzig: Teubner, 1884) 64.19–65.4; Albinus, *Didaskalikos* 28.182.10–12; and Philo, *On the Special Laws* 2.229f; as well as Dietmar Wyrwa, *Die christliche Platonaneignung in den Stromateis des Clemens von Alexandrien* (Arbeiten zur Kirchengeschichte 53; Berlin: De Gruyter, 1983) 230–32 (I thank Annewies van den Hoek for these references).

55. *De Resurrectione Carnis* (also termed *De Resurrectione Mortuorum*) 16.6.

56. *De Resurrectione Carnis*, 16.6: *sed frictricis uel archigalli uel gladiatoris aut carnificis spiritu infectum* (J. G. Ph. Borleffs, ed., *De Resurrectione Mortuorum*; *Tertulliani Opera* 2,2 [CChr; Turnhout: Brepols, 1954] 939). Note that there is a text-critical problem; *frictricis* is an emendation from *fictricis*, which would make no sense.

In this context, the term *frictrix* connotes the dregs of society, those people whom members of polite society utterly shun. The first two groups, *frictrices* and castrated Cybele priests, fail to conform fully to their gender.[57] (Recall that ancient astrologers sometimes classified *tribades* together with castrated men.)[58] Unlike hermaphrodites or eunuchs whose slaveowners have castrated them and whose ambiguous gender status derives from nature or from other human beings, *frictrices* and castrated priests bear responsibility for their sexual unorthodoxy and gender ambiguity. The second two groups, gladiators and hangmen, deal with criminal death on the margins of society. Tertullian achieves his rhetorical effect by playing on his elite reader's sentiments about gender, death, and crime; to Tertullian and his implied readers, homoerotic women, castrated pagan priests, gladiators, and hangmen are despicable people.

The lives of *frictrices* epitomized the opposite of the rigorous Christian life that Tertullian envisaged for his female followers. Whereas he set forth as an ideal a silently praying, secluded virgin veiled from a young age,[59] *frictrices*—like prostitutes—moved freely in public. Like unveiled women, homoerotic women transgressed natural law—God's law. For Tertullian, *frictrices* belonged to the demimonde of castrates, hangmen, and gladiators—persons marginal to polite society. Because *frictrices* did not conform to the culturally determined gender definitions, Christian society and elite Roman society had no place for them.

WOMEN WHO MARRY OTHER WOMEN: CLEMENT OF ALEXANDRIA

Clement of Alexandria stayed closer than Tertullian to the traditional values of procreation and marriage, which he saw as a duty necessary for maintaining society.[60] Both thinkers, despite their different views on the value of procreation versus celibacy, condemned female homoeroticism, which demonstrates that the rejection of female homoeroticism does not directly relate to whether an author had a positive or negative view of sexuality, of marriage, or of the human body. Like other authors of the Roman period, Clement defined relations between females and between males as unnatural (*para physin*); his discussion also overlaps conceptually with non-Christian discussions of homoeroticism. Throughout his writings, Clement explicitly delineated the connections among nature, gender roles, and the active/passive dichotomy.

57. On the *galli* as gender-variant men who may have engaged in homoerotic activity, see Randy P. Conner, *Blossom of Bone: Reclaiming the Connections between Homoeroticism and the Sacred* (San Francisco: HarperSanFrancisco, 1993) 99–125.

58. E.g., Ptolemy, *Tetrabiblos* 4.5; §187.

59. *De Virginibus Velandis.*

60. *Strōmateis* 2.23.140.

Clement drew upon both Paul, whom he frequently quoted, and the *Apocalypse of Peter*, about which he wrote a commentary,[61] and which he considered scripture.[62] Thus, Clement knew that Paul condemned female and male homoeroticism as unnatural, and that the *Apocalypse of Peter* depicted homoerotic women and men as suffering in hell. Like Paul (and Tertullian), Clement called for strict gender differentiation in physical appearance. His own condemnation draws upon those found in Paul and the *Apocalypse of Peter*.

Clement not only knew the scriptures of the early church, but he was also exceptionally well versed in the whole of Greek literature, and the extensive library resources of ancient Alexandria gave him access to a broad range of that literature.[63] Clement viewed Greek philosophy as a preparation for the Greeks to receive the gospel, just as the Mosaic law prepared the Hebrews to receive it.[64] Consequently, in addition to Christian sources, Clement also drew upon non-Christian literature to support his view of same-sex sexual behavior as unnatural, and he explicitly quotes Plato on this subject.[65] In addition to frequent references to Plato, Aristotle, Zeno, Musonius Rufus, and numerous other philosophers whose views shaped early Christian thinking about gender, Clement's work also cites or alludes to bodies of literature and topics discussed elsewhere in this book: Parmenides,[66] the Anthologia Palatina,[67] Plutarch,[68] astrology,[69] dream interpretation,[70] and magic.[71] For example, in the area of astrology (to which, Clement maintains, Egypt had given birth,)[72] Clement refers explicitly to the astrological books of Hermes,[73] perhaps an early form of the *Book of Her-*

61. Eusebios, *Ekklēsiastikē Historia* 6.14.1.

62. *Ek tōn Prophētikōn Eklogai* 41.

63. Annewies van den Hoek notes that Clement cited Alexandrian writers with particular frequency: "Clement's Alexandrian identity is primarily determined by the presence of one or more libraries—probably including a Christian one—and by his reading list, which had a strongly local bias" ("How Alexandrian Was Clement of Alexandria? Reflections on Clement and His Alexandrian Background," *Heythrop Journal* 31 [1990] 179–94, quotation from p. 191).

64. *Strōmateis* 1.5.28.

65. Plato, *Nomoi* 8.5.1; 838E, in Clement, *Paidagōgos* 2.10.83.3.

66. *Strōmateis* 5.2.15.5; 5.9.59.6; 5.14.112.2; 5.14.138.1; 6.2.23.3.

67. *Strōmateis* 4.8.62.3; 4.22.142.1; 5.11.68.4.

68. Passim.

69. *Protreptikos* 6.67.2; *Strōmateis* 1.14.65.1; 1.16.74.2; 2.1.2.4; 6.4.35.4.

70. *Strōmateis* 1.16.74.1.

71. *Protreptikos* 4.58.3 (here Clement refers explicitly to magical "incantations" [ἐπαοιδαί], a term used frequently in the love spells themselves); *Strōmateis* 3.2.11.1 (here Clement accuses magicians of promoting deviant forms of sexual behavior, in this case, incest and having wives in common).

72. *Strōmateis* 1.16.74.2.1.

73. *Strōmateis* 6.4.35.4.

mes Trismegistos.[74] Although he does not refer to them directly, he probably knew of such second-century writers as Ptolemy of Alexandria, the leading natural scientist of Clement's Alexandria; Soranos, who had studied in Alexandria; Artemidoros of Daldis; and Lucian of Samosata. Thus, it is not surprising that Clement's condemnation of male and female homoeroticism reveals concepts of gender very close to those of other authors discussed in this book.

Clement's views on female-female marriage are rooted in his basic understanding of nature. In his work on Christ as a tutor to the Christian believers (the *Paidagōgos*), Clement describes women who, contrary to nature (*para physin*), behave like men (*andrizontai*),[75] and marry other women (both actively and passively, i.e., with both the active and passive participles of "to marry" [*gamousai* and *gamoumenai*]). According to Clement, female-female marriage is an "unspeakable practice," a result of a luxury that confounds nature's clearly gendered order.[76] In this order, males are naturally active and females naturally passive. Thus, Clement depicts woman-woman marriage as "unnatural," both for the women taking the active role in marrying (*gamousai*), as well as for those who assume the role of a bride in woman-woman marriages (*gamoumenai*). In my discussion of Clement, I first analyze the understandings of gender, marriage, and nature in this passage on women's unnatural marriage to other women and within Clement's work as a whole and then turn to the historical question of the woman-woman marriages mentioned by Clement.

74. Clement actually considered astrology useful under some circumstances (*Strōmateis* 2.1.2.3.)

75. Clement uses this term elsewhere in the positive sense of "to act bravely," "to behave manfully" (*Strōmateis* 2.12.55.3 [quotation from the *Shepherd of Hermas*]; 7.10.59.5).

76. *Paidagōgos* 3.3.21.3: "[Luxury] confounds nature; men passively play the role of women [literally: "suffer the things of women"], and women behave like men in that women, contrary to nature, are given in marriage and marry (other women)"; συγχεῖ τὴν φύσιν, τὰ γυναικῶν οἱ ἄνδρες πεπόνθασιν καὶ γυναῖκες ἀνδρίζονται παρὰ φύσιν γαμούμεναί τε καὶ γαμοῦσαι γυναῖκες (Otto Stählin, ed., *Clemens Alexandrinus*, vol. 1 [GCS; 3d ed.; Berlin: Akademie, 1972] 249).

Nature is central to Clement's discussion of sexual relations, which is striking when we notice that Clement sometimes seems to avoid the use of φύσις in other areas. Annewies van den Hoek has observed that, in contrast to Philo, who viewed the law of Moses as the law of nature, Clement (and other early gentile Christians) lacked a law of nature in written form. She posits that for this reason Clement often avoids φύσις (Personal correspondence, November 7, 1989). He apparently also avoided φύσις because some Gnostics believed in a "'natural theology' of salvation, in which only a few are elected to be saved even long before they were born." In contrast, she notes that when speaking about theological anthropology or gender, "he is apparently much less afraid and more inclined to go with traditional Stoic terminology" (Personal correspondence, September 10, 1994). For extensive analysis of Clement's reshaping of Philonic thought, see Annewies van den Hoek, *Clement of Alexandria and His Use of Philo in the* Stromateis: *An Early Christian Reshaping of a Jewish Model* (Leiden: Brill, 1988).

Clement's view, as a Christian, of what it means to be a human male or female—his theological anthropology—shapes his condemnation of female homoeroticism. For him, the Genesis creation narratives lay the framework for understanding nature as gendered, while Christ's maleness further helps to delineate human nature. The reference to woman-woman marriage occurs within an extended discussion of men who embellish themselves by means of cosmetics, jewelry, or delicate clothing, and by shaving or depilating their hair.[77] Clement particularly opposes shaving off one's beard or depilating one's bodily hairs. He argues that men must display their greater physical similarity to Christ by wearing beards, which symbolize men's stronger nature,[78] their male nature,[79] and their right to rule.[80] He further claims that when woman was created from the rib of man, all softness was taken out of man, while the softer Eve was created to receive the male seed, to help man, and to keep his house for him.[81] Notice that Clement's call for strict gender differentiation in physical appearance resembles Paul's argument in 1 Corinthians 11 in that both writers use the creation narrative of Genesis 2 as a theological source.

Clement derides men who turn away from their male nature and imitate women by assuming a softer appearance or by receiving the male seed from another male. He expresses particular scorn for public displays of male softness and male homoeroticism, an attitude that we have seen in the astrologer Ptolemy and elsewhere: "He who denies his masculinity in broad daylight will certainly prove himself to be a woman at night."[82]

77. *Paidagōgos* 3.3.21. On Clement's similarity to the ancient physiognomists, see Maud W. Gleason, "The Semiotics of Gender: Physiognomy and Self-Fashioning in the Second Century C.E.," in *Before Sexuality: The Construction of Erotic Experience in the Ancient Greek World*, ed. David M. Halperin, John J. Winkler, and Froma I. Zeitlin (Princeton: Princeton University Press, 1990) 399–402.

78. *Paidagōgos* 3.3.19.1: the beard is a "symbol of the stronger nature"; σύμβολον τῆς κρείττονος φύσεως (Otto Stählin, ed., *Clemens Alexandrinus*, vol. 1 [GCS; 3d ed.; Berlin: Akademie, 1972] 247).

In contrast to this view, some early Christians depicted Christ as beardless. See, e.g., the sixth-century mosaic image of Christ Militant in the Archiepiscopal Chapel in Ravenna, Italy (reproduced in Jaroslav Pelikan, *Jesus Through the Centuries: His Place in the History of Culture* [New Haven: Yale University Press, 1985] following p. 30).

79. *Paidagōgos* 3.3.19.3: τῆς ἀνδρώδους φύσεως σύμβολον (Stählin, *Clemens Alexandrinus*, 1:247).

80. *Paidagōgos* 3.3.18.1. In *Paidagōgos* 1.5.18.4 Clement emphasizes Christ's maleness with reference to Ephesians 4:15. Stoic philosophers also opposed men cutting their beards, e.g., Musonius Rufus 21.

81. *Paidagōgos* 3.3.19.1.

82. *Paidagōgos* 3.3.20.3: ὁ γὰρ ὑπὸ τὰς αὐγὰς τὸν ἄνδρα ἀρνούμενος πρόδηλός ἐστι νύκτωρ ἐλεγχόμενος γυνή (Stählin, *Clemens Alexandrinus*, 1:248). On the necessity for strict gender differentiation in clothing, see also *Strōmateis* 2.18.81.3f, in which Clement paraphrases Philo of Alexandria's interpretation of Deut 22:5 (*On the Virtues* 18–20). For a discussion of Clement's subtle shift, see van den Hoek, *Clement of Alexandria*, 76f.

On the surface, the requirements for female and male dress and sexual behavior appear to parallel each other. Men are to wear beards and not to depilate other body hairs, to dress in plain clothing, and to orient themselves sexually toward their wives alone. Similarly, women, whose skin is naturally soft and hairless, should wear clothing that is plain (although their clothing may be softer than men's) and they are to orient themselves sexually toward their husbands alone. Clement does not employ a double standard in terms of adultery: he requires strict monogamy of both husband and wife. The system of thought seems parallel: men are not to give up their masculinity by assuming a female appearance and taking a sexually receptive posture, and women are not to take on a male appearance and a sexually active role vis-à-vis other women.

But a deeper look at the structure reveals a fundamental asymmetry between Clement's views of woman and of man. While Clement denounces both male and female homoeroticism, his reasons for doing so are markedly different for men than they are for women. He derides homoerotic men for taking on a female sexual behavior (they "suffer the things of women"), whereas he describes the women in terms of a socially accepted institution—marriage. The masculine roles assumed by the women enjoyed a social status in Clement's world that the female roles taken on by the men did not. He heaps scorn upon men who deny the stronger male nature that equips them for ruling, since these passive men are giving up a great deal of social prestige by so doing. He cannot, or does not, heap the same kind of scorn upon the women. What, indeed, were the women giving up by marrying other women? Unlike the homoerotic men, they were not giving up a greater similarity to Christ or the right to rule or to be strong. Instead, through their behavior these women implicitly rejected their roles as receivers "of the [male] seed" [83] and as helpers and housekeepers for their husbands. Clement does not deride these women for wanting to give up their passive role. Instead, he subsumes woman-woman marriage under "licentiousness," "lechery," and "lawlessness," and expresses great concern at how common it, along with male passiveness and female and male prostitution, had become in the cities.

We can visualize this asymmetry better by outlining what a symmetrical picture might look like: all homoerotic males and females would stand equally under censure and would receive equal time in the text. Clement would deride both men and women for giving up social status. Alternatively, the passive homoerotic male and the active homoerotic female would suffer equal disapprobation, while their active male and passive female partners respectively would count as natural men and women. Since, however, Clement and his society valued penetration by males more highly

83. *Paidagōgos* 3.3.19.1: ὑποδοχὴ σπέρματος (Stählin, *Clemens Alexandrinus*, 1:247).

than any other sexual act, they abhorred the triad of (1) passive males,[84] (2) passive homoerotic females, and (3) active homoerotic females.[85] These three categories have in common their nonparticipation in the cultural ideal of sexual relations.[86]

This underlying gender asymmetry helps us to understand why Clement describes both the passive and active female partners as behaving contrary to nature and as "behav[ing] like men" (*andrizontai*). Their masculine behavior apparently lies in the fact that they do not assume the female role with a man. In other words, proper female passiveness is passiveness vis-à-vis a man. If a woman is bride to a woman, she does not serve as receptacle to the male seed, nor does she act as helper and housekeeper to a man.

In fact, the male seed is central to this whole discussion.[87] For Clement, "The male seed contains within itself nature's thoughts [i.e., something like the genetic material necessary for the formation of a human being]. To shame nature's thoughts by irrationally bringing them on unnatural paths, is totally godless."[88] The wife is "the receptor of the husband's seed, which in Clement's eyes is already the whole person"[89] and which signifies for Clement men's participation in God's creative power.[90] In this focus on procreation, Clement differs from Paul, who wrote little that would promote procreation,[91] although Clement's concept of the wife as the recipi-

84. Clement and other authors of his time devoted more attention to passive males than to any other homoerotically inclined person. Presumably, they believed that if men maintained their role as penetrators, women would acquiesce to a passive role, since women's weaker social and economic status gave them little alternative.

85. I derive the categories of passive and active females from the passive and active participles of "to marry." While the verb γαμέω/γαμέομαι does not in itself denote the sexual act, the active and passive forms of this verb do denote gender roles that include sexual expectations. Normally in antiquity, a woman "was married" by a man who penetrated her as a result of marrying her.

86. Clement's strong focus on procreation does, however, lead him to chastize men who practice any insertive, but nonprocreative, sexual behavior (e.g., *Paidagōgos* 2.10.83.3; 2.10.87.3; 2.10.88.3; 2.10.90.1–4).

87. See Denise Kimber Buell, "Procreative Language in Clement of Alexandria" (Ph.D. diss., Harvard University, 1995). Buell analyzes how Clement uses "procreation as a metaphor to describe the origins and organization of the universe."

88. *Paidagōgos* 2.10.83.3: συνεσπαρμένους ἔχουσαν τῆς φύσεως τοὺς λογισμούς· τοὺς δὲ κατὰ φύσιν λογισμοὺς ἀλόγως εἰς τοὺς παρὰ φύσιν καταισχύνειν πόρους ἄθεον κομιδῇ (Stählin, *Clemens Alexandrinus*, 1:208).

89. Donald Kinder, "Clement of Alexandria: Conflicting Views on Women," *Second Century* 7 (1989–90) 216; see *Paidagōgos* 2.10.94.4.

90. *Paidagōgos* 2.10.91.2. See also *Paidagōgos* 2.10.94.4, in which Clement describes the loss to a human being through the ejaculation of his seed. Since Clement is working with the one-seed theory of conception, that loss applies only to the male. The concept of loss underscores the significance of the male seed.

91. On this point, Clement is closer to Philo of Alexandria, whom he frequently quotes. See van den Hoek, *Clement of Alexandria*.

ent of the male seed coincides with Paul's views (1 Thess 4:3–8).[92] Like others of his time, Clement compares the man to a farmer sowing his seed and the woman to a field ready to receive it. Clement is apparently following the one-seed theory of conception (rather than the two-seed theory held by such thinkers as Parmenides, with whom Clement was familiar), according to which only the male has a seed. Because a man should avoid wasting the precious male seed, he should avoid intercourse with men, with boys, with females who cannot conceive (menstruants, pregnant women, girls, and barren women),[93] and with androgynes (according to Clement, this last form of intercourse is impossible anyway).[94] Out of respect for his participation in God's creative act, he should also avoid intercourse with any females other than his wife. The purpose of sexual intercourse is to plant the male seed at the right time in the right place: "to have sexual intercourse for any purpose other than generating children is to violate nature."[95]

The uterus, in contrast, identifies women as God's helpers.[96] Clement discusses how the uterus—through its desire to be filled—proves that intercourse has a good purpose. When pregnant, the opening to the uterus is shut, thereby foreclosing any improper desires for nonprocreative intercourse.[97] Through his guidelines for sexual behavior, Clement seeks to promote male participation in God's creative power by means of proper implantation of his seed and female assistance by means of receiving the male seed.

In addition to ancient agrarian images for procreation, Clement's writings also echo Stoic concepts. His term for "irrationally" (*alogōs*) literally means "without the *logos*," not in accord with divine reason.[98] For the

92. This is a disputed passage. I am following the translation of 1 Thess 4:4 as "that each one of you know how to take a wife for himself in holiness and honor" (NRSV alternate rendering). The Greek word for "wife" is σκεῦος (literally: "vessel"). The image of woman as a vessel ready to receive the male seed presupposes the theory that only the male has a true seed.

93. Female barrenness posed more of a problem for Philo than for Clement.

94. *Paidagōgos* 2.10.87.3.

95. *Paidagōgos* 2.10.95.3. See John Boswell's discussion of this formulation, known as the "Alexandrian rule" (*Christianity, Social Tolerance, and Homosexuality: Gay People in Western Europe from the Beginning of the Christian Era to the Fourteenth Century* [Chicago: University of Chicago Press, 1980] 147).

96. *Paidagōgos* 2.10.93.1.

97. *Paidagōgos* 2.10.88.2; 2.10.93.1.

98. *Paidagōgos* 2.10.83.3: "To shame nature's thoughts by irrationally bringing them on unnatural paths, is totally godless." Clement refers several times to the Stoic maxim to live in accord with nature (*Strōmateis* 2.19.101.1; 2.21.129.1; 5.14.95.1; see also *Paidagōgos* 1.13.101–3).

Stoics, reason (*logos*)—which is divine—imbues nature. In Clement's thought, Christ is the *logos*. To shame nature's thoughts, to deprive them of their honor, thus runs counter to Christ and is indeed godless.

Clement's thinking about procreation accords with his teachings about marriage. For him, nature allows people to enjoy lawful unions for the purpose of procreation. Clement saw these lawful unions as fundamentally asymmetrical. A husband was the head of his wife, and she had to be subservient to him.[99] As a preventive against adultery, women were to shut themselves in their houses, avoiding unnecessary contact with any nonrelatives.[100] If her husband behaved abusively toward her, a wife had to endure the abuse and had no option to leave.[101] The wife may "never do anything against his will, with the exception of what is contributing to virtue and salvation."[102] Like Philo, Clement assumes that males have been allotted

---

99. *Strōmateis* 4.8.63.5.

100. *Strōmateis* 2.23.146.1.

101. *Strōmateis* 2.23.145.3. Clement presupposed, with Matthew, that only the husband may inititate divorce (Matt 5:32; 19:9).

102. *Strōmateis* 4.19.123.2. For further discussion, see Kinder, "Clement," 213–20. Kinder points out that Clement's assumption of women's weakness is in line with the philosophical tradition of his time, especially with Stoicism. Kinder cites as one example Musonius Rufus, who recommends that women study philosophy and that daughters receive the same education as sons, and who holds that women, like men, "have a natural inclination toward virtue" (Musonius Rufus 3: "That Women Too Should Study Philosophy" and 4: "Should Daughters Receive the Same Education as Sons?" Cora Lutz, ed. and trans., *Musonius Rufus: "The Roman Socrates"* [Yale Classical Studies 10; New Haven: Yale University Press, 1947] 38–49). Kinder points out that Musonius nevertheless holds that women are generally better suited to remain indoors and to serve their husbands (Musonius Rufus 3; Lutz, *Musonius Rufus*, 42f) and that he maintains the classical distinctions between stronger and weaker, ruler and ruled, and superior and inferior (Musonius Rufus 12; Lutz, *Musonius Rufus*, 86–89; Kinder, "Clement," 217–19). Kinder, however, overstresses the similarities between Musonius and Clement. Musonius presupposes, but does not justify, gender differentiation in spheres of work (women indoors; men outdoors), and believes that these spheres can change. Further, Kinder does not mention the context or rhetorical import of Musionius's "ruler-ruled" schema. Musonius employs that categorization in the context of attempting to convince men not to have sex with their female slaves—an unusual appeal in the ancient world. To drive home his point, Musonius appeals to male slaveowners by asking what they would think if their wives had relations with male slaves. Rather than assume the "ruler-ruled" schema as natural or immutable, Musonius argues that if men "expect to be superior to women" (εἴπερ καὶ προεστάναι ἀξιοῦνται τῶν γυναικῶν), then their morality must exceed that of women (Musonius Rufus 12; Lutz, *Musonius Rufus*, 88f). Clement, in contrast, gives theological and scriptural reasons for women's subordination to their husbands.

Musonius and Clement do, however, overlap in their views on sexual relations. Musonius sees sex within marriage for the purpose of procreation as the only legitimate form of intercourse, and—like Clement—rejects sexual relations between males as "contrary to nature" (παρὰ φύσιν; Musonius Rufus 12; Lutz, *Musonius Rufus*, 86f).

an active role and females a passive or suffering role in life; this view forms an important basis for Clement's teachings about marriage.[103]

On the other hand, Clement fully accepts Christian women as equal in the faith to Christian men and stresses that the *Logos,* Christ, is the trainer of both men and women.[104] He particularly praises women's courage in martyrdom.[105] He rejects the view of some of his contemporaries that women have a separate nature from men. Since women and men share one nature, he writes, both are obligated to pursue virtue, and both are capable of attaining it.[106] He argues that women and men have both the same virtue and the same feeling of shame.[107] This common quest for virtue results in Clement's teaching that women should study philosophy.[108] While wives do not share social equality with their husbands, they do share a common nature and a common quest. In contrast to early Christian ascetics, some of whom saw sex as impure, Clement championed marriage as a Christian institution. For him, if a man was sanctified, then so was his seed.[109] In support of his promarriage position, Clement maintained that even Paul was married.[110]

Just as Clement promoted traditional marriage with its gender role differentiation, he also opposed radical ideas of human equality, which he connected with sexual libertinism. For example, a Christian group known as the Karpokratians (the followers of Karpokrates and of his son Epiphanes) promoted such equality, and Clement excoriated them for their alleged sexual profligacy. He particularly attacked Epiphanes, who in his work "On Justice," maintained the equality of all earthly beings, on all of whom the sun shines equally. Karpokrates "does not distinguish between rich and poor, people and ruler, foolish and wise, females and males, free and slave."[111] He also refused to treat animals differently from humans.

103. *Paidagōgos* 3.3.19.2: τὸ δρᾶν αὐτῷ [i.e., the man] συγκεχώρηται, ὡς ἐκείνῃ [i.e., the woman] τὸ πάσχειν (Stählin, *Clemens Alexandrinus,* 1:247).

104. *Paidagōgos* 1.4. In line with his view that women and men share one nature, Clement speaks of "human nature" (*Paidagōgos* 1.12.100.3).

105. See Annewies van den Hoek, "Clement of Alexandria on Martyrdom," in *Studia Patristica,* vol. 26, ed. Elizabeth A. Livingstone (Louvain: Peeters, 1993) 324–41.

106. *Strōmateis* 4.8.59.1–3.

107. *Paidagōgos* 1.4.

108. *Strōmateis* 4.8.62.4–63.1; 4.8.67.1–3.

109. *Strōmateis* 3.5.46.5.

110. *Strōmateis* 3.6.53.1f, in which Clement refers to Phil 4:3.

111. *Strōmateis* 3.2.6.1f (see the whole of 3.2.5–11 for the full discussion of the Karpokratians). Clement's categories are close to those found in Aristotle, *Politika* 1.1–2; 1252a–1255b. For a full treatment of Clement's use of Aristotle, see Elizabeth A. Clark, *Clement's Use of Aristotle: The Aristotelian Contribution to Clement of Alexandria's Refutation of Gnosticism* (New York: Edwin Mellen, 1977). Clark has ascertained that Clement based his thinking upon the Stoic teaching that we should live according to nature, but altered it by empha-

According to Karpokratian tenets, this basic equality of all beings engenders a communist mode of life practiced with respect to both property and reproduction. Clement reports on the Karpokratian view that God gave males greater desire in order to preserve the species and that therefore males should not restrict themselves to their own wives. According to Clement, for Karpokrates equality ostensibly consisted in having all wives in common. Clement argues that Epiphanes misunderstood Plato concerning having women in common, since Plato meant that anyone could choose from among all the virgins, but that the chosen one would then belong to that man. Because sexual libertinism belongs to the stock polemical epithets hurled by ancient writers against Jews, Christians, and pagans of all types, we have to view Clement's charge with some skepticism. The charge of radical equality, in contrast, is quite rare and therefore more historically plausible. Perhaps Clement employed the common charge of sexual libertinism to discredit the Karpokratian stand on equality. For our purposes, what is striking is Clement's sharp rejection of such an egalitarian view.[112]

Clement's opposition to the equality of all beings (as seen in his opposition to Karpokrates' views) and his view of same-sex sexual mingling as unnatural lead him into logical difficulties when he confronts the problem of sexual unorthodoxy among animals. Animals would best conform to Clement's view of nature if they did not engage in any sexual behaviors that Clement deems unnatural in humans. At one point he claims sexual propriety in animals, arguing that the animal worship of the Egyptians is better than the Greeks' worship, because—unlike the Greek deities—animals at least do not commit adultery or seek unnatural pleasures.[113] Ancient understandings of the hare and the hyena, however, challenged Clement's faith in the sexual decorum of animals.[114] He deals with the "facts" that the hare has as many anuses as its age (which it uses for sexual lasciviousness) and that the hyena changes its sex every year by claiming

---

sizing the Aristotelian doctrine of the mean. This intertwining of the natural and the avoidance of extremes is particularly evident in Clement's teachings about marriage and proper sexual behavior.

112. For more on the Karpokratians, see Morton Smith, *Clement of Alexandria and a Secret Gospel of Mark* (Cambridge, MA: Harvard University Press, 1973) 295–350; and Alain Le Boulluec, *La notion d'hérésie dans la littérature grecque IIe–IIIe siècles* (Paris: Études augustiniennes, 1985), vol. 2:299–301, 322f; see also vol. 1:104f, 130.

113. *Protreptikos* 2.39.4.

114. See, e.g., the *Epistle of Barnabas* 10.6f (that the hare has an anus for each year of life and that the hyena changes its sex each year). See also Pliny, *Naturalis Historia* 8.81.217–20; Claudius Aelian, *De natura animalium* 1.25, as well as Mary Pendergraft, "'Thou Shalt Not Eat the Hyena:' A Note on 'Barnabas' *Epistle* 10.7," *Vigiliae Christianae* 46 (1992) 75–9.

these beliefs as the basis for Moses' prohibition of hare and hyena meat
(Moses, that is, the Pentateuch, actually does not prohibit the eating of
hyena meat).[115] Eating the flesh of these animals is prohibited in order to
keep humans from becoming like them. Clement adds, however, that he
does not believe that these animals truly change their nature, since "nature
can never be forced to change."[116] In a stunning twist of logic, Clement
then argues that hyenas practice unnatural intercourse by means of a small
body part that looks like an anus, but is not.[117] Thus, Clement walks a
tightrope of citing animal behaviors that he finds offensive and unnatural
and arguing that nature really does not allow unnatural phenomena.

The hyena serves as a cipher for Clement of that which humans should
not imitate: lack of gender differentiation and indiscriminate coupling. In
his discussion on the hyena, Clement cites Plato on love for boys[118] and
Paul (Rom 1:26f). The example of the hyena aids Clement in interpreting
Rom 1:26f, because the hyena stands for idolatry (if we follow Clement's
imprecise conflation of two texts in Jeremiah).[119] Thus, the hyena symbolizes same-sex love and idolatry—the central themes of Rom 1:18–27.

Just as Clement derives prohibitions for specific human behaviors from
Moses' alleged prohibition of hyena flesh, so too does the hare serve as a
bugbear for human sexual ethics. According to Clement, two characteristics of the hare led Moses to prohibit hare meat: the hare's rear-approach
intercourse (which presumably reminded Clement of sexual contact between men and boys) and its frequent pregnancies.[120] Clement allegorically
interprets Moses as counseling humans to refrain from "excessive desires,
intercourse with a pregnant woman, same-sex sexual contact, corruption
of children [usually understood as boys], adultery, and licentiousness."[121]

---

115. Lev 11:6 and Deut 14:7 prohibit eating the flesh of the hare. Clement follows Barnabas in erroneously assuming that the Bible prohibits eating the flesh of the hyena. John
Boswell suggested that ὗν (the accusative of "pork") in Deut 14:8 resembles ὕαινα (the
nominative of "hyena"; the accusative of "hyena" is ὕαιναν) and could have led to the confusion (*Christianity, Social Tolerance, and Homosexuality*, 138, n. 5). The author of the *Epistle
of Barnabas* made the original error. Since Clement's Greek was so good, and he surely would
have known the difference between the two, he probably depended upon Barnabas's citation
and did not check the biblical reference himself.

116. *Paidagōgos* 2.10.84.1.

117. *Paidagōgos* 2.10.86.1. Both the female and male hyenas ostensibly possess this anus-
like body part that allows for anal-like, nonprocreative sexual intercourse, and which symbolizes the hyena's desire for frequent, nonprocreative, indiscriminate intercourse.

118. Plato, *Phaidros* 254A-E; in Clement, *Paidagōgos* 2.10.86.2.

119. Clement quotes Jeremiah as follows: σπήλαιον ὑαίνης γέγονεν ὁ οἶκός μου (*Paidagōgos* 2.10.87.4; Otto Stählin, ed., *Clemens Alexandrinus*, vol. 1 [GCS; 3d ed.; Berlin: Akademie, 1972] 210). In the LXX Jer 7:11 has: σπήλαιον λῃστῶν ὁ οἶκός μου and 12:9 has:
σπήλαιον ὑαίνης.

120. *Paidagōgos* 2.10.83.5.

121. *Paidagōgos* 2.10.88.3.

The Greek term that I have translated as "same-sex sexual contact" (*allē-lobasiai*)[122] must refer to both female and male homoeroticism for several reasons. First, when Clement speaks of male-male sexual relations, he usually either uses a term that includes the word "male" in it, such as *arreno-mixia* ("male-mingling"), or he speaks of "pederasty" or of the "corruption of children."[123] Second, the word *allēlobasia* literally means "going into one another" (in a sexual sense). Whereas in our world, we might think of "one another" as referring to persons of the opposite sex, in the sexually segregated environment envisaged by Clement and experienced by his readers, "one another" would be the persons of one's own environment—for women, other women, and for men, other men. Clement speaks of those who sexually encountered one another by remaining within their own sphere, rather than crossing the boundary to encounter the opposite sex. Third, ancient linguistic parallels support this interpretation.[124] *Allēlobasiai* thus bears witness to an emerging early Christian category of homoeroticism. Perhaps Paul's condemnation of both female and male same-sex sexual contact contributed to the development of this general category—quite rare in the ancient world. Who would have imagined that a rabbit could have given so much to sexual ethics?[125]

As the foregoing discussion has demonstrated, Clement bases his very firm views as to what constitutes nature on a variety of sources: the creation narrative of Genesis 2, biblical prohibitions of certain foods, the one-seed theory of conception, Plato, Paul, and Clement's own observations and

122. Otto Stählin renders ἀλληλοβασίαι as "gleichgeschlechtlicher Verkehr" (*Des Clemens von Alexandreia Der Erzieher* [Bibliothek der Kirchenväter 2d ser. 8.2; Munich: Kösel, 1934] 96). Claude Mondésert translates it as "l'homosexualité" (Claude Mondésert and Henri-Irénée Marrou, *Clément d'Alexandrie: Le Pédagogue*, vol. 2 [SC 108; Paris: Les Éditions du Cerf, 1965] 173). John Boswell translated the term as "reversal of roles in intercourse" (*Christianity, Social Tolerance, and Homosexuality*, 358). LPGL, s.v., has "reciprocal intercourse." In a sense, these translations are all saying the same thing: same-sex sexual contact is a reciprocal role reversal, since it does not conform to the culturally required gender asymmetry. In male homoeroticism, one partner reverses his normal role, while in female homoeroticism, both partners fail to conform to the cultural norm.

123. *Paidagōgos* 2.10.86.2; 87.3; 88.3.

124. Since, according to a search of the *Thesaurus Linguae Graecae*, this is the only occurrence of ἀλληλοβασία in all of ancient Greek literature, we need to draw upon relevant parallels to understand it. Clement's use of ἀλληλίζω to refer to a male hyena's assuming a passive sexual role (presumably with another male) would confirm the interpretation of ἀλληλοβασία as same-sex sexual encounter (*Paidagōgos* 2.10.88.3). Paul's use in Rom 1:27 of "for one another" (εἰς ἀλλήλους) to designate the men who became inflamed with homoerotic passion may have partially inspired Clement's use of ἀλληλοβασία here. Note also that the medieval scholion (cited below, n. 142) on Clement, *Paidagōgos* 2.10.86.3 uses the phrase ἀλλήλαις βαίνουσαι for female same-sex encounters.

125. See Boswell, *Christianity, Social Tolerance, and Homosexuality*, 142f and passim, for the influence of these ancient views of the hare (and the hyena) on medieval discussions of same-sex love.

thoughts. In Clement's system of thought, woman-woman marriage is un-natural because: it defies God, who created woman from man in order for her to receive man's seed and to help him; it prevents the male seed from finding a proper field; humans should not imitate such lascivious animals as the hare; Paul called female homoeroticism unnatural; and the uteri of the two women are calling out to be filled with the male seed. Thus, a close analysis of Clement's brief condemnation of woman-woman marriage gives us insight into his theological understanding of maleness and femaleness. In Clement's theology, man's greater similarity to Christ and the leadership role granted him by God (according to Genesis) rendered woman-woman marriage theologically counter to God's plan for human-ity. The lack of a male head and the absence of proper female passivity puts woman-woman marriage outside the bounds of Clement's theology.

Throughout this chapter I focus principally on patristic representations of female homoeroticism and analyze how these representations relate both to that of Paul and to those of other ancient writers. I will now shift gears and engage in the reconstruction of women's history in antiquity. The extant material teaches us much more about ancient male under-standings of female homoeroticism than it does about female homoerotic practice. But woman-woman marriage is one subject about which we have historical evidence. In analyzing the ancient evidence for woman-woman marriage, I utilize diverse sources to reconstruct historically a social practice.

For years I believed that Clement's reference to marriage between women was metaphorical, but I now take Clement seriously as a historical source for woman-woman marriage.[126] My reasons are threefold: (1) sev-eral of Clement's contemporaries refer to woman-woman marriage; (2) ac-cording to Roman, Greek, and Egyptian law, marriage was a matter of private law; and (3) in second-century Alexandria, marriage took a variety of forms.

I shall briefly expand upon these three reasons. First, the astrologer Ptol-emy of Alexandria, an elder contemporary of Clement, states that women born under a particular constellation have sexual relations with other women, with whom they play a male sexual role, and whom they call their "lawful wives."[127] Another second-century author, Iamblichos, describes in a novel what may have been the marriage of an Egyptian queen, Bere-

---

126. See Mary Rose D'Angelo, "Women Partners in the New Testament," *Journal of Feminist Studies in Religion* 6:1 (1990) 65–86, for a study of committed relationships be-tween women in the New Testament. (D'Angelo does not argue that these women had mar-ried their partners, but I refer to her work here because ancient marriage between women existed on a continuum that also included female friendship.)

127. Ptolemy, *Tetrabiblos* 3.14; §172.

nike, to a woman named Mesopotamia, with whom she had fallen in love.[128] The Sifra, a rabbinical commentary on Leviticus, takes Lev 18:3 ("You shall not do as they do in the land of Egypt . . . and you shall not do as they do in the land of Canaan") as including a prohibition of marriage between women.[129] In other words, three different ancient sources, probably all from the second century, connect female-female marriage with Egypt, which could indicate that Clement was speaking literally when he wrote of female-female marriage. Another second-century source, Lucian of Samosata, also refers to two women cohabiting (*syneinai*—a term used in marriage contracts). One of the women, Megilla, calls herself by the masculine name "Megillos" and says that she married (*gameō*) Demonassa a long time ago and that Demonassa is her wife (*emē gynē*).[130]

Second, in contrast to modern Western legal systems, in which a bride and groom must appear before a public official and sign a public document, a woman and a man in the Alexandria of Clement's time could create a legally valid marriage through a private ceremony or simply by living together. While they could also draw up several types of documents acknowledging details of the union, these documents, even when placed in public archives, were a matter of private law.[131] The parties themselves created the marriage; public officials did not need to ratify or register it.

But how can we ever imagine that women could marry women in a period in which so many people opposed female homoeroticism, as the sources amply document? And how could a woman-woman marriage fulfill the goal of procreation so central to the concept of marriage in this period? In order to answer these questions and to interpret these second-century sources on woman-woman marriage properly, we need to remind ourselves of the great diversity of social institutions and competing legal systems in the Roman world.

128. This fragment of Iamblichos, *Babyloniaka*, was preserved in the *Bibliothēkē* of the tenth-century patriarch Photios. See René Henry, ed. and trans., *Photios: Bibliothèque*, vol. 2 (Paris: Les Belles Lettres, 1960) 44–46. See also the critical edition of the fragments of Iamblichos by Elmar Habrich, *Iamblichi Babyloniaciorum Reliquiae* (Leipzig: Teubner, 1960) 58–65. See John Boswell, *Same-Sex Unions in Premodern Europe* (New York: Villard, 1994) 82f.

129. J. H. Weiss, ed., *Sifra* (Vienna: Schlossberg, 1862), on Lev 18:3 (*Aharei Mot, Parasha* 9).

130. Lucian of Samosata, *Dialogues of the Courtesans* 5; §291. See Boswell, *Same-Sex Unions*, 82.

131. At the time of Augustus, some of the leading Alexandrians practiced a more solemn form of marriage in which the parties drew up their contracts before a board of the priests of a female deity. This form of marriage, which gave a higher legal status to the offspring, falls into the realm of public, rather than private, law. See Hans Julius Wolff, *Written and Unwritten Marriages in Hellenistic and Postclassical Roman Law* (Haverford, PA: American Philological Association, 1939) 37–40.

Within Roman law, if we examine only *matrimonium*, we arrive at a falsely narrow picture, since *matrimonium* was not accessible to large numbers of people in the early Roman Empire, most notably slaves and soldiers. Slaves could create a marriage-like union called *contubernium*. *Contubernium* also designated the union of a master and his female slave or the union between a freedperson and a slave. Roman soldiers often formed unions with non-Roman women in the regions in which they served on military duty, but Roman law barred them from *matrimonium*. Further, an elite citizen male could enter into a marriage-like relationship with a lower status woman, a woman socially ineligible for *matrimonium* with him. The Romans called such a union *concubinatus*. Given the large slave population in the Roman Empire and the stringent eligibility requirements for *matrimonium*, Roman jurists would have classified as *matrimonium* only a minority of the sexual unions in existence. Jurists focused their attention on *matrimonium*, because the Roman state thereby promoted its interest in creating the next generation of elite citizen rulers and in regulating the transmission of property from one generation of elites to the next.[132] Since these interests did not touch slaves and the other lower-status persons who comprised the majority of the population of the early Roman Empire, these groups created types of unions far less frequently documented in ancient juridical sources. While procreation was central to *matrimonium*, since *matrimonium* concerned the reproduction of the citizen elite, other types of unions may have placed less emphasis on procreation. For example, a concubine provided a man with sexual pleasure, but since any children she might bear had no claim on his property, she had no legal incentive to bear them. Culturally, participants in unions other than *matrimonium* may have strived to imitate that institution. But perhaps this imitation included forms that Roman jurists would have found grotesque but unworthy of legal scrutiny. For example, two Roman freedwomen may have mustered the financial means to create a common living arrangement and decided to call themselves married. Perhaps the Augustan funerary urn depicting two freedwomen with their right hands clasped testifies to such a self-understanding.[133] A Roman jurist would have paid no more attention

132. For a magisterial study of *matrimonium*, see Susan Treggiari, *Roman Marriage: Iusti Coniuges from the Time of Cicero to the Time of Ulpian* (Oxford: Clarendon, 1991). See her comments on *contubernium*, pp. 52–54; on *concubinatus*, pp. 51f; on soldiers being debarred from *matrimonium* until the time of Claudius, pp. 46f and 66f. See also Boswell, *Same-Sex Unions*, 28–52 (on male-female marriage in the Graeco-Roman world), 53–107 (on same-sex unions in the Graeco-Roman world).

133. *Corpus Inscriptionum Latinarum* 6/3.18524. Mary Rose D'Angelo first introduced this inscription into the discussion of the lesbian continuum ("Women Partners in the New Testament," *Journal of Feminist Studies in Religion* 6:1 [1990] 65–72).

to freedwomen designating themselves as married than to persons living in some unusual type of *contubernium*. Other freedpersons and slaves may, however, have taken the union as seriously as some forms of *contubernium* or *concubinatus*.

Within Roman Egypt, however, only part of the population created marriages and marriage-like arrangements according to Roman law. Native Egyptians, Greeks,[134] Jews, and others living in Roman Egypt created sexual unions in accordance with their own diverse legal traditions. For example, Greek-speakers in Roman Egypt often entered into "unwritten marriage."[135] Through cohabitation they created these undocumented marriages that were no less valid than documented ones. The background of cohabitation as the essential element of marriage provides a further model for interpreting the sources that speak of women marrying other women. The women mentioned by Clement, Ptolemy, Iamblichos, Lucian, and the Sifra may have created marriages by forming a household, that is, by living under one roof.[136]

The ethnic diversity of Roman Egypt and the concomitant diversity of legal practice can serve as a reminder of the lack of a monolithic cultural ideology. According to the prevailing cultural ideology that I have documented throughout this book, people would have seen woman-woman marriage as unnatural, monstrous, licentious, and more. But the homoerotic love spells discussed above document a countercultural current. Woman-woman marriage may represent a further countercultural current or another branch of the same one. The women who commissioned the erotic spells may have called their partners "wives" and have entered into long-term relationships with them. Alternatively, the women commissioning erotic spells may have located themselves on the adventurous end of a spectrum that extended to low-profile, socially adaptive woman-woman marriage. While we can only speculate on these questions, the ancient references to woman-woman marriage suggest the existence of female homoerotic relationships that enjoyed some level of tolerance. Even a minimal tolerance helps to explain the vociferousness of Clement and of the other ancient opponents of sexual love between women.

People familiar with the practice of woman-woman marriage known in several African societies today might identify ancient marriages between women with this contemporary practice, but I would argue against too

134. Or Macedonians, i.e., the descendants of the Macedonians who had come to Egypt in the wake of Alexander the Great.

135. Ἀγράφως συνεῖναι. See Wolff, *Written and Unwritten Marriages*.

136. Or, alternatively, they could have drawn up contracts to document their union and to attempt to protect their property rights. Such contracts, like those between women and men, would have been in the sphere of private law.

hastily making such an identification. Nigerian scholar Ifi Amadiume has criticized Western feminists for attributing a sexual character to Igbo woman-woman marriage in contemporary Nigerian society, rather than recognizing its economic nature.[137] In contrast, the ancient sources describe second-century Egyptian woman-woman marriage in sexual rather than in economic terms. A better understanding of women's economic circumstances in second-century Egypt would help us to discern the economic aspects of the ancient woman-woman marriages. In-depth research on the fragmentary evidence for women's economic circumstances in second-century Egypt is greatly needed and would enable us to understand better the institution of woman-woman marriage as part of Egyptian culture.

Woman-woman marriage exemplified for Clement the antithesis to the proper Christian life. He believed that Christ, by means of his exhortations, can cure the unnatural passions of the soul.[138] By engaging in sex for a purpose other than procreation, these women violated nature. Since God had created nature,[139] and since Christ could have cured them of their unnatural passions, their marriages insulted both God and Christ. In Clement's view, these women should have been living lives of obedience to Christ and submissiveness to their husbands, assisting God in his creativity by presenting their uteri to be filled with the male seed. Clement's teachings on female homoeroticism thereby promote a particular social order and thereby contribute to the subordination of all women, regardless of their sexual inclinations or behavior.

137. Ifi Amadiume, *Male Daughters, Female Husbands: Gender and Sex in an African Society* (London: Zed, 1987). I accept Amadiume's criticism of white Western feminists, who have often studied and written about African women for the purpose of furthering white Western feminist goals. Her own presentation of Igbo women in her hometown of Nnobi is exemplary both for the model of scholarship it presents and in the details of the research. But her criticism of such Western lesbians of African descent as Audre Lorde requires revision. Amadiume criticizes Black lesbians for "using such prejudiced interpretations of African situations to justify their choices of sexual alternatives which have roots and meaning in the West. Black lesbians are, for example, looking into African women's relationships and interpreting some as lesbian. . . . How advantageous is it for lesbian women to interpret such practices as woman-to-woman marriages as lesbian (see Lorde 1984)" (p. 7). Audre Lorde speaks of Black women bonding together in support of one other, using such examples as African cowives (about whom she assumes that they bond together "in relationship to one man"), the Amazon warriors of ancient Dahomey, and the West African Market Women Associations. Lorde does speak of sexual contact between African women, but she does not present woman-woman marriage as always lesbian and does not overlook the economic character of such marriage (*Sister Outsider: Essays and Speeches* [Trumansburg, NY: Crossing, 1984] 49f).

138. *Paidagōgos* 1.2.6.1.

139. *Strōmateis* 1.19.94.2.

Excursus: Ancient Marginal Notes on Clement

Medieval scribes often commented on ancient authors by making notes in the margins, thereby creating annotated editions of the works they were transcribing. According to a marginal note on Clement's term for "behave like men" (*andrizontai*), Clement is referring here to "abominable *tribades*, whom they also call *hetairistriai* and Lesbians" (Greek: *Lesbiai*).[140] With this note, the anonymous author of this comment thereby tied Clement's presentation of female homoeroticism into the larger cultural matrix, reminding the reader of the *tribades* mentioned by the astrologers, Soranos, and others and of the *hetairistriai* referred to by Plato and by Lucian of Samosata. This note also demonstrates the existence of a cultural category of homoerotic women (and not just of individual female homoerotic acts). By connecting the terms *tribades, hetairistriai,* and *Lesbiai* to the word *andrizontai,* this commentator interpreted female homoeroticism as I have in this book: women transgressing the social norms for what constitutes proper female behavior and behaving like men.

This usage of "Lesbian" for a homoerotically behaving woman is the oldest known attestation of "Lesbian" with this meaning. "Lesbian" is thus the oldest of any of the terms currently used for persons in same-sex relationships. ("Gay" is several hundred years old, while "homosexual" is a nineteenth-century invention.)[141] Further research on the term "Lesbian" could help in reconstructing women's history in the Middle Ages and beyond and could help us to understand earlier cultural constructions of female homoeroticism.

In another marginal note on Clement's *Paidagōgos,* the anonymous commentator refers to an early Christian writer named Anastasios. The note about Anastasios was written in the margin of Clement's text at the point at which Clement quotes Rom 1:26. According to this anonymous commentator, Anastasios interpreted Rom 1:26 as follows: "Clearly they [that is, the "females" of Rom 1:26] do not go into one another [f.], but rather offer themselves to the men."[142] Anastasios apparently disputed the possibility of sexual relations between women at all. Perhaps Anastasios was referring to prostitution; as we have seen elsewhere, other ancient authors

140. Scholion to *Paidagōgos* 3.3.21.3: τὰς μιαρὰς τριβάδες λέγει, ἃς καὶ ἐταιριστρίας καὶ Λεσβίας καλοῦσιν (Otto Stählin, ed., *Clemens Alexandrinus,* vol. 1 [GCS; 3d ed.; Berlin: Akademie, 1972] 337). The term μιαραί can also mean "polluted" or "defiled" in a ritual sense, which ties in with Paul's use of ἀκαθαρσία in Rom 1:24.
141. See John Boswell, *Christianity, Social Tolerance, and Homosexuality,* 42f.
142. Scholion to *Paidagōgos* 2.10.86.3 (quotation of Rom 1:26f): οὐκ ἀλλήλαις βαίνουσαι δηλαδή, ἀλλὰ τοῖς ἀνδράσιν οὕτω παρέχουσαι ἑαυτὰς (Stählin, *Clemens Alexandrinus,* 1:331).

connected prostitution with female homoeroticism. According to the marginal note, Anastasios had made this comment in an exegetical study of the Corinthian correspondence. It would be wonderful to know with reference to which passage in 1 or 2 Corinthians Anastasios commented on the question of Rom 1:26. I have argued a close conceptual connection between Rom 1:26f and 1 Cor 11:2-16. Whether Anastasios made this connection or not we cannot know, but the possibility is intriguing.

Heretics Who Promote Equality: Hippolytos on the Naassenes

According to the early church writer Hippolytos of Rome (ca. 170-236),[143] a Christian Gnostic[144] group known as the "Naassenes"[145] saw male-female intercourse as wicked and filthy and believed that Paul's words in Rom 1:20-27 contained "their whole hidden and unspeakable mystery of blessed pleasure."[146] The Naassenes were one of the earliest known Gnostic groups, one of the groups that founded the Gnostic movement. As Gnostics, they saw this carnal world as evil and as inferior to a higher, spiritual world from which they believed human beings had come and to which they endeavored to return. Gnostics believed that they had within themselves the knowledge (*gnōsis*) of their otherworldly origin. The specific Naassene version of Gnostic doctrine emphasized gender differentiation as a characteristic of the lower, earthly realm, and intercourse between women and men as the human practice associated with gender differentiation.[147] Since the Naassenes aimed to overcome these differences and to

143. Hippolytos wrote *The Refutation of All Heresies* between 222 and 235 (Luise Abramowski, *Drei christologische Untersuchungen* [BZNW 45; Berlin: De Gruyter, 1981] 55, n. 103). In *The Refutation of All Heresies* 5.6.3–11.1, he describes the Naassenes, whom Abramowski argues flourished during Hippolytos's time (*Drei christologische Untersuchungen*, 20).

144. Hippolytos, *The Refutation of All Heresies* 5.6.4; 5.11.1. Luise Abramowski postulates that the self-designation "Gnostic" in 5.6.4 may be an editorial addition by a pre-Hippolytos, Christian Gnostic redactor of the Naassene source used by Hippolytos. In other words, the Naassenes may not have explicitly called themselves "Gnostic." Nevertheless, Abramowski, like other interpreters, considers the Naassenes Gnostic. In her assessment, both the pre-Hippolytos redactor and the redactor's sources were Christian Gnostic and influenced by classical Greek philosophy (*Drei christologische Untersuchungen*, 53–55).

145. The name "Naassene" derives from the Hebrew word for "serpent" (נָחָשׁ), because the Naassenes apparently gave special honor to the serpent of Genesis 3 (Hippolytos, *The Refutation of All Heresies* 5.6.3f). Rather than see the serpent as the downfall of humanity, they probably honored the serpent as a giver of wisdom and knowledge (γνῶσις).

146. Hippolytos, *The Refutation of All Heresies* 5.7.18f: ὅλον . . . τὸ κρύφιον αὐτῶν καὶ ἄρρητον τῆς μακαρίας μυστήριον ἡδονῆς (Miroslav Markovich, ed., *Hippolytus, Refutatio omnium haeresium* [Patristische Texte und Studien 25; Berlin: De Gruyter, 1986] 147).

147. Clement of Alexandria actually holds a similar position, except that Clement values gender differentiation and procreative intercourse, rather than rejecting them (*Paidagōgos* 1.4.10).

enter into a higher world without gender, they rejected sexual relations between women and men. They may have seen same-sex love as an ideal or they may have rejected all sexual intercourse as characteristic of this lower, carnal, earthly sphere of being.

The precise views of the Naassenes on same-sex relations are difficult to ascertain, because Hippolytos, our only source for the Naassenes, was polemicizing against them. Moreover, recent scholars who have attempted to reconstruct from Hippolytos's *Refutation of All Heresies* the original Naassene source upon which he based his critique have concluded that one or more Gnostic editors had already redacted it before it came into Hippolytos's hands.[148] A prior Christian Gnostic editor (or editors) had apparently compiled a number of Gnostic sources, bringing the Naassene teachings into line with those of other Gnostic groups and embellishing the primary sources by adding in relevant scriptural quotations. Given this multilayered texture of Hippolytos's polemic against the Naassenes, we have difficulty knowing precisely who saw male-female intercourse as wicked and filthy and why, and exactly who saw in Rom 1:20–27 a "mystery of blessed pleasure" and what that meant. In what follows, I shall briefly outline the features of the original Naassenes' theological thought that one or more pre-Hippolytos Gnostic editors may have embellished with this unusual, positive interpretation of Rom 1:20–27.

In my distinction between the views of the Naassenes and those of their editor or editors, I am building upon the studies of other scholars. The work of Josef Frickel, who has painstakingly reconstructed the Naassene writing against which Hippolytos was polemicizing, helps us to ascertain the Naassenes' particular theological views.[149] Luise Abramowski's work gives us further help in sorting out which views to attribute to the Naas-

148. On the composite character of Hippolytos's *The Refutation of All Heresies*, see Josef Frickel, *Hellenistische Erlösung in christlicher Deutung: Die gnostische Naassenerschrift: Quellenkritische Studien—Strukturanalyse—Schichtenscheidung—Rekonstruktion der Anthropos-Lehrschrift* (NHS 19; Leiden: Brill, 1984); and Luise Abramowski, "Ein gnostischer Logostheologe: Umfang und Redaktor des gnostischen Sonderguts in Hippolyts 'Widerlegung aller Häresien,'" in Luise Abramowski, *Drei christologische Untersuchungen* (BZNW 45; Berlin: De Gruyter, 1981) 18–62.

149. I am following Josef Frickel's reconstruction of the original Nassene writing, which he based on a source-critical investigation of Hippolytos's *The Refutation of All Heresies* 5.6.4–10.2. He has isolated a hypothetical original text by applying the standard criteria of source criticism: differences in literary style among the several redactional layers, literary seams (abrupt changes, inconsistencies, breaks), and differences in worldview and theology. I am attributing to the Naassenes those teachings that Frickel includes in his reconstruction of the Naassene writing. See Frickel's reconstruction of the Greek text of the original Naassene writing and his German translation of it: *Hellenistische Erlösung in christlicher Deutung: Die gnostische Naassenerschrift: Quellenkritische Studien—Strukturanalyse—Schichtenscheidung—Rekonstruktion der Anthropos-Lehrschrift* (NHS 19; Leiden: Brill, 1984) 214–51.

senes and which views to a specific level of Hippolytos's multilayered source.[150]

For the Naassenes, androgyny characterized the world above. As an example of this androgyny, they honored a primal human being named Adamas who was both male and female.[151] Because this primal human was both male and female, they prohibited sexual intercourse between women and men.[152] In addition to the masculine-feminine Adamas, Jesus' saying "Do not throw that which is holy to dogs or your pearls to the swine" (Matt 7: 6) gave them further support for prohibiting sexual intercourse between women and men.[153]

Beyond this, the Naassenes reinterpreted in a Christian Gnostic fashion the traditional Phrygian Attis legend,[154] according to which Attis died from having castrated himself. In the Naassene reinterpretation, Attis had thereby passed from the earthly parts of the world below to the eternal substance of the world above—a world where "there is neither male nor female" (Gal 3:28).[155]

According to Hippolytos, the Naassenes took Rom 1:20–27 to refer to

150. Luise Abramowski, "Female Figures in the Gnostic *Sondergut* in Hippolytus's *Refutatio*," in *Images of the Feminine in Gnosticism*, ed. Karen L. King (Philadelphia: Fortress, 1988) 136–52; and "Ein gnostischer Logostheologe: Umfang und Redaktor des gnostischen Sonderguts in Hippolyts 'Widerlegung aller Häresien,' " in Luise Abramowski, *Drei christologische Untersuchungen* (BZNW 45; Berlin: De Gruyter, 1981) 18–62.

151. Hippolytos, *The Refutation of All Heresies* 5.6.5. Adamas had originated everything that exists (5.7.14; see also 5.5.5, in which Hippolytos states that one of their hymns contained reference to a father and a mother who emanated from and through this androgynous being).

For further examples of the Gnostic view of an androgynous primal human being, see the *Revelation of Adam* 64:6–28f; and *Poimandrēs* (Hermetic Tractate 1) 15 (in *The Gnostic Scriptures*, trans. Bentley Layton [Garden City, NY: Doubleday, 1987] 55, 455).

152. Hippolytos, *The Refutation of All Heresies* 5.7.14.

153. Hippolytos, *The Refutation of All Heresies* 5.8.33. The Naassenes did not, however, impute binding authority to any one set of scriptures or traditions, but rather drew upon Homer, the mysteries of Isis, the legends of Osiris and of Attis, as well as writings now found within the New Testament and such extracanonical gospels as the Gospel of Thomas and the Gospel According to the Egyptians.

154. Phrygia is a region in Asia Minor (today's Turkey).

155. Hippolytos, *The Refutation of All Heresies* 5.7.15. Frickel attributes the description of the "new humanity" (Eph 2:15; 4:24) as both masculine and feminine (5.7.15) to a Christian Gnostic editor whom Frickel designates as the *"Pneuma*-Gnostic" editor (in contrast to a chronologically earlier *"Anthropos*-Gnostic" editor) (Frickel, *Hellenistische Erlösung*, 178). With Luise Abramowski, however, I believe that distinguishing between two levels of pre-Hippolytos Gnostic editorial activity is stretching the method of source criticism beyond its limit. (See Abramowski, "Female Figures," 136, n. 1.) Arguing for one pre-Hippolytos Gnostic editor, however, may be plausible. Abramowski correctly points out that Frickel has not sufficiently engaged her scholarship on the Naassene writing (p. 136, n. 1).

Hippolytos also states that the Naassenes attend the mysteries of the Great Mother and a "mystery of blessed pleasure,"[156] but both Frickel and Abramowski argue that a pre-Hippolytos Gnostic editor added this interpretation of Rom 1: 20–27 to the original Naassene writing.[157] Whether created by the Naassenes themselves or by a Gnostic editor of the original Naassene writing, this unusual interpretation of Rom 1:20–27 deserves our attention. In the eyes of the Naassenes or the later Gnostic editor of their writing, the "unnatural intercourse" of Rom 1:26 was good, since in their eyes "natural" signified fleshly or carnal, as opposed to spiritual. The Greek word in Rom 1:27 that we usually translate as "shameless acts" (*aschēmosynē*), that is, the men's sexual acts with other men, presented ancient Gnostic interpreters with a special challenge. They chose another of the usual meanings of this Greek word, namely "formlessness" (that is, without *schēma*). By focusing on the word for "form" (*schēma*), they found in the *aschēmosynē* of Rom 1:27 a scriptural basis for their doctrine of "the primal, blessed, formless substance, which is the cause of all forms in the things that are formed."[158] In other words, the substance that gave rise to earthly creatures had no form itself, although it gave form to that which it created. Instead of seeing in *aschēmosynē* the depths of shamefulness, they found in it their ideal of formlessness.

In addition to their teaching concerning a blessed, formless substance, these ancient Gnostics also found in Rom 1:27 a scriptural basis for the doctrine of baptism.[159] Perhaps they took the word translated by the NRSV as "due penalty"[160] in "received in their own persons the due penalty for their error" in its other, more positive sense of "recompense" or "re-

---

behave like the castrated men there in that they strictly urge their followers to abstain from intercourse with women (*The Refutation of All Heresies* 5.9.11), but Frickel attributes this polemical statement to Hippolytos (*Hellenistische Erlösung*, 114, n. 584).

156. Hippolytos, *The Refutation of All Heresies* 5.7.18f.

157. Abramowski suggests that the phrase "their whole hidden and ineffable mystery of blessed lust" (her translation) is a summarizing remark of the redactor who had edited the Naassene source used by Hippolytos ("Female Figures," 148).

Frickel attributes it to the "*Pneuma*-Gnostic" editor (*Hellenistische Erlösung*, 178f).

158. This is an etymological play on words: ἀσχημοσύνη . . . ἡ πρώτη καὶ μακαρία . . . ἀσχημάτιστος οὐσία, ἡ πάντων σχημάτων τοῖς σχηματιζομένοις αἰτία (Hippolytos, *The Refutation of All Heresies* 5.7.18; Miroslav Marcovich, ed., *Hippolytus, Refutatio Omnium Haeresium* [Patristische Texte und Studien 25; Berlin: De Gruyter, 1986] 147; ET: Werner Foerster, *Gnosis: A Selection of Gnostic Texts*, trans. R. McL. Wilson, vol. 1 [Zurich: Artemis, 1969; Oxford: Clarendon, 1972] 266; see also the French translation with notes: A. Siouville, trans., *Hippolyte de Rome: Philosophoumena ou Réfutation de toutes les hérésies* [Milan: Arché, 1988] 131; Siouville thinks that Hippolytos incorrectly attributed this interpretation of ἀσχημοσύνη to the Naassenes).

159. Hippolytos, *The Refutation of All Heresies* 5.7.19. Frickel also attributes this segment to the "*Pneuma*-Gnostic" editor (*Hellenistische Erlösung*, 178f).

160. Ἀντιμισθία.

quital." If baptism is "recompense" or "requital," it could constitute religious compensation for human error. Gnostics placed great emphasis on baptism, since they closely associated it with receiving knowledge (*gnōsis*). For the Gnostic exegete whose views Hippolytos found in his source, at baptism a person was introduced into "unfading pleasure."[161]

According to this Gnostic interpretation, then, Paul's words in Rom 1: 20–27 had a deeper meaning to which these ancient interpreters had access through their Gnostic mode of interpretation. While such a reading seems strange to the modern reader, we have to remember that throughout history Jews and Christians have often read their respective Bibles allegorically, arguing that the text means something other than what it seems to mean, that it contains a deeper meaning. (Clement's interpretation of the Mosaic prohibition of hare meat would be one such example.) Thus, as strange as it seems to us to interpret Paul as speaking about an "unspeakable mystery of blessed pleasure" in Rom 1:20–27, second-century people could have seen at least the interpretive method as culturally plausible.

Some ancient Gnostics (whether the Naassenes themselves or the person or persons who edited their writing), then, rejected "natural intercourse" and found a positive basis for their doctrines in those words of Paul that others have interpreted as a condemnation of same-sex love. But does this mean that they actually promoted the practice of same-sex love? We can interpret the evidence in two ways. The Naassenes or their Gnostic editor or editors, who rejected male-female intercourse as belonging to the carnal realm of existence here below, may have promoted same-sex love as characteristic of the androgynous spiritual realm above this earth. Seeing homoerotically active persons as androgynous would fit in with the Graeco-Roman conception of *tribades* as masculine women and of passive males as androgynous. A Gnostic stress on the strict division of the universe into the realm above and that below and the characterization of the realm above as transcending gender differences, combined with the prohibition of gender differentiated sexual intercourse, could have led them to promote same-sex love. They could have seen it as expressing in the lower realm what the Naassenes knew about the higher realm: that the blessed Adamas of the realm above is both masculine and feminine, thereby obviating sexual intercourse between women and men.[162] The reported male-male sexual

161. Hippolytos, *The Refutation of All Heresies* 5.7.19.
162. One might wonder whether androgyny hinders same-sex love, since androgynous persons have no reason to prefer a person of the same gender (gender no longer being a relevant category). But, just as people in Graeco-Roman culture linked gender differentiation with sex between women and men, they also linked androgyny with same-sex love. For the view that the Naassenes may have engaged in cultic homoeroticism, see Randy P. Conner, *Blossom of Bone: Reclaiming the Connections between Homoeroticism and the Sacred* (San Francisco: HarperSanFrancisco, 1993) 127–29.

practices of other Gnostic groups could constitute further evidence in support of Naassene same-sex sexual practices.[163]

Alternatively, these Gnostics may have rejected all sexual intercourse as carnal, finding in the "unnatural [intercourse]" of Rom 1:26 a reference to a spiritual act, rather than a physical, carnal one.[164] In support of this interpretation is the fact that Hippolytos at no point charges the Naassenes with same-sex sexual practices, which would certainly have served his polemical purposes. These Gnostics may have taken "unspeakable mystery of blessed pleasure" in an esoteric Gnostic sense no longer accessible to us. For example, for another second-century Gnostic named Ptolemy, "pleasure" and "the blessed" were mythical aeons who had emanated from the "Word" united with "life."[165]

While we cannot know whether unorthodox sexual practices accompanied the early Gnostics' unorthodox interpretation of Rom 1:20–27, their testimony provides evidence for lively debates in the early church concerning Paul's words and concerning how Christians should view human gender.

Church Awareness of Sexual Love Between Women in the Fourth and Fifth Centuries

As Christianity established itself throughout the Roman Empire, Christian values and Christian conceptualizations of the body and of gender increas-

163. Epiphanios (ca. 315–403), a church father who wrote against heretical groups, describes some Gnostics as engaging in male-male sexual intercourse (Epiphanios, *Panarion* 26.11.8; 26.13.1; ET: Bentley Layton, trans., *The Gnostic Scriptures* [Garden City, NY: Doubleday, 1987] 212f).

164. According to Hippolytos, the Naassenes interpreted Matt 3:10 ("every tree therefore that does not bear good fruit is cut down and cast into the fire") as referring to a being who "is unfruitful when he is fleshly and carries out the 'desire of the flesh' [Gal 5:16]" (*The Refutation of All Heresies* 5.8.31). Josef Frickel attributes this passage to the original Naassene writing (*Hellenistische Erlösung*, 225, 244).

Further, according to Hippolytos, the Naassenes—like other Gnostics—divided human beings into three categories. They classified themselves as spiritual (πνευματικοί), apparently because they consisted of spirit, soul, and flesh. Others they classified as either animate (ψυχικοί, that is, consisting of soul and flesh) or fleshly (σαρκικοί, that is, consisting only of flesh). In accordance with this division of humanity, they categorized the forms of mystic initiation into lesser and greater. In contrast to the lesser mysteries associated with birth in the flesh, they praised the higher form of initiation into "the house of God" (Gen 28:17) reserved for spiritual persons like themselves (Hippolytos, *The Refutation of All Heresies* 5.8.44). See Frickel's reconstruction of the relevant portion of the Naassene writing and his commentary on it (*Hellenistische Erlösung*, 200–207, 227f, 246).

165. Epiphanios of Salamis cites Iranaios of Lyons (writing ca. 180), who describes Ptolemy's mythical system of thought (in Epiphanios, *Panarion* 31.9.1–31.32.9; ET of Irenaios of Lyons, *Against Heresies* 1.1.2 in *The Gnostic Scriptures*, trans. Bentley Layton [Garden City, NY: Doubleday, 1987] 282f).

ingly shaped the larger culture. For example, asceticism blossomed in the deserts of Egypt, the mountains of Syria, and in even in the great cities of the empire as ascetic women and men created living arrangements ranging from single-sex communities to celibate marriages.[166] And as single-sex communities spread, same-sex romantic friendship found new homes in which to flourish.

But even as Christians enjoyed increasing opportunities to shape the world around them, they maintained their legacy of Graeco-Roman culture. In what follows, I shall demonstrate how the late fourth-century church father John Chrysostom discusses female homoeroticism in categories reminiscent of earlier centuries and in continuity with non-Christian descriptions of it. I shall then briefly review two further late antique church fathers who demonstrate an awareness of female homoeroticism in monastic communities, Shenute of Atripe and Augustine of Hippo.

"NATURE KNOWS HER OWN BOUNDARIES":
JOHN CHRYSOSTOM ON ROMANS I : 26F

In the late fourth century, John of Antioch (347–407), nicknamed "Chrysostom" ("golden mouth") owing to the rhetorical skills that kept listeners enraptured for two-hour sermons, preached an entire homily on Rom 1:26f.[167] In it he speaks of the natural asymmetry of the sexes, of the differing natures of women and men, of the interrelationship between nature and law, of punishment in hell, of "all things [being] turned upside down,"[168] and of "nature know[ing] her own boundaries."[169] On each point, he shows knowledge of the early Christian and other ancient discussions of homoeroticism that I have discussed earlier in this book.

The entire structure of Chrysostom's homily reflects his asymmetrical conceptualization of the sexes. He devotes far greater attention to "male mania"[170] than to sexual relations between females, and claims that, compared with male homoeroticism, it is "far more disgraceful when even women seek after these sexual connections, since they ought to feel more shame than men."[171] In fact, for Chrysostom, in contrast to Clement of

166. Non-Christians in this period also promoted the ascetic life, but Christian forms of asceticism were probably more widespread.
167. John Chrysostom was born in Antioch in Syria. For an English translation of his fourth homily on Romans, see NPNF 11.355–59. For a partial translation, see Boswell, *Christianity, Social Tolerance, and Homosexuality,* 359–62. For an analysis of the homily and of contradictions between this homily and other passages in Chrysostom, see Boswell, 156f.
168. *PG* 60.417mid.
169. *PG* 60.420mid.
170. *PG* 60.416bot–417top: ἡ κατὰ τῶν ἀρρένων μανία.
171. *PG* 60.417mid: καὶ τὸ δὴ τούτων ἀτιμότερον, ὅταν καὶ γυναῖκες ταύτας ἐπιζητῶσι τὰς μίξεις, ἃς ἀνδρῶν μᾶλλον αἰδεῖσθαι ἐχρῆν.

Alexandria, women have a different nature from men.[172] These differing natures lead to very different social roles. Basing himself upon the second Genesis creation narrative, he argues that by nature, man was assigned to be an instructor to woman, and woman commanded to be a helper of man.[173]

In Chrysostom's eyes, "male mania" and its female counterpart have destroyed the natural creation order laid down in Genesis so that instead of the sexes behaving in a friendly way to each other, they engage in war (*polemos*) against each other and even in a war with members of their own sex. Women, he says, insulted (*hybrizō*) other women, and not only men.[174] This war between the sexes, and even within the same sex, has resulted in social chaos. They have overturned the social order: "Whenever God forsakes someone, all things are turned upside down."[175]

The image of social disorder and abandonment of gender roles is reminiscent of the *Apocalypse of Peter*'s punishment of turning oneself upside down, again and again.[176] Being turned upside down implies a boundary transgression, and Chrysostom stresses just that: "nature knows her own boundaries."[177]

Thus, in nature, which sets boundaries between the sexes and between their roles, homoeroticism does not occur. Chrysostom expresses his nay vote in the ancient debate on same-sex coupling among animals by excoriating homoerotic humans as "more irrational than mindless beings [i.e., animals] and more shameless than dogs."[178]

In fact, Chrysostom, known to contemporary readers for his virulently anti-Jewish statements, imprecates the women and men spoken of in Rom 1:26f in a whole series of invectives: "how many hells will suffice for

172. *PG* 60.419bot.
173. *PG* 60.417bot. See Gen 2:18, 20. Cf. Clement of Alexandria, *Paidagōgos* 3.3.19.1. Chrysostom takes the active/passive distinction as a cultural given (see, e.g., *PG* 60. 419mid), but does not accord it as prominent a place in his discussion as some other ancient authors.
174. *PG* 60.418mid.
175. *PG* 60.417mid: ἀλλ' ὅταν ὁ Θεὸς ἐγκαταλίπῃ, πάντα ἄνω καὶ κάτω γίνεται. The disorder resulting from same-sex love extends not only to human society, but to the earth as well. Chrysostom points out that God's destruction of Sodom by fire meant that the womb of the earth in that city could no longer serve as a receptacle to the seed. In other words, since Sodom's men wasted their seed by implanting it into men, its fields became as infertile as the men's seed. People in the Roman world applied the agrarian metaphor of sowing a field to human procreation. Chrysostom is drawing a full circle by applying the gendered human metaphor back to agriculture. In his image, the feminine womb of the earth no longer serves as proper passive receptacle to the male seed (*PG* 60.420mid).
176. *Apocalypse of Peter* (Greek Akhmim fragment) 17.
177. *PG* 60.420mid.
178. *PG* 60.420mid.

such people?" [179] "not only was their dogma satanical, but their way of life was also diabolical"; [180] "whatever transgression you speak of, you will name none equal to this lawlessness"; [181] and "there is nothing more irrational and grievous than this outrage." [182]

Chrysostom sees homoeroticism as worse than prostitution: prostitution—although lawless—is at least natural. [183] He thereby distances himself from the classification of prostitutes with homoerotic persons found in Tertullian and the ancient astrologers. Chrysostom carries this line of thinking a step further and describes "this mania" as inexpressibly "worse than fornication." [184] Why is it worse? Because a homoerotically behaving man has thereby positioned himself on the boundary between masculinity and femininity, but has not truly taken on a female nature, even though he has lost his male nature. For this ambiguous gender status, he, as in the days of Leviticus, "deserves to be driven out and stoned to death by both men and women." [185]

In addition to the sin language of ancient Judaism and early Christianity, Chrysostom also adopts the disease language found in ancient medical writers and astrologers. [186] In contrast to the astrological affirmation of the diseased behavior as caused by the stellar and planetary configuration at the time of one's birth and in contrast to the medical debates about the etiology of the disease of male passivity and female bisexuality, Chrysostom stresses most emphatically that "changing implies possession." [187] From Paul's use of the verb "to change" Chrysostom deduces that these persons changed from the natural sexual intercourse of which they were fully capable to the unnatural, lawless variety. Chrysostom has thus entangled himself in a dual and somewhat contradictory conceptualization: homoeroticism as both a sin and a disease.

To the categories of sin and disease, Chrysostom adds another component when he defines same-sex love as the luxuriant practice of the effete rich. Unlike Tertullian, who had appealed to his elite Roman readers by classifying *frictrices* on the margins of society together with prostitutes, gladiators, hangmen, and castrated pagan priests, Chrysostom casts homoerotically active persons as indulging themselves in a luxury (*tryphē*). [188]

179. *PG* 60.420top.
180. *PG* 60.417mid.
181. *PG* 60.419mid.
182. *PG* 60.419bot.
183. *PG* 60.419mid.
184. *PG* 60.419bot.
185. *PG* 60.419bot.
186. *PG* 60.418.
187. *PG* 60.417top. See Boswell, *Christianity, Social Tolerance, and Homosexuality*, 109.
188. *PG* 60.420bot. Cf. Clement of Alexandria, who also applies the term τρυφή to homoeroticism (*Paidagōgos* 3.3.21.3).

He ends the homily with a clarion call to "lay aside gilded garments and take up virtue," which fits in with his attempts to make Christians concerned about the massive numbers of urban poor in late fourth-century Antioch.[189] On the other hand, he also compares homoerotically active persons with thoughtless slaves who have gone to the marketplace and forgotten what they were supposed to do there. Such slaves have to be beaten.[190] These seemingly contradictory images of homoerotic persons— marginal, despised people; wealthy persons in gilded garments; slaves who need to be beaten—nevertheless share one thing: they all designate the social Other.

Chrysostom drives home the point of social otherness and the disruption of the social order by means of the categories of law and nature. Recall Artemidoros's classification system: (1) natural, legal, and customary; (2) illegal or unconventional; and (3) unnatural. Unlike Artemidoros, Chrysostom classifies both male and female homoeroticism as both illegal/unconventional and unnatural. But Chrysostom shows an awareness of a tripartite division even when he applies the categories of illegal and unnatural to homoeroticism: "For the intercourse engaged in by them [i.e., female prostitutes], even if illegal, is at least natural. But this [i.e., homoeroticism] is both illegal and unnatural."[191] Like Artemidoros, Chrysostom has a middle category (between natural and unnatural) of illegal but natural. (Chrysostom differs from Artemidoros, of course, in that he classifies all homoeroticism as unnatural, and not just female homoeroticism.) Throughout the homily, Chrysostom repeatedly stresses that homoeroticism falls into the unnatural and lawless category, rather than into the middle one. To do this, he links the unnaturalness and the lawlessness of same-sex sexual expression, claiming, for example, that the persons whom Paul castigates in Rom 1:26f "both dishonored nature and trampled on the laws."[192] Perhaps Chrysostom feels a special need to draw members of his audience away from the view that same-sex sexual love is merely lawless or unconventional (like prostitution or other fornication), but still natural. (Some may, for example, have followed Artemidoros's thought that only female homoeroticism is unnatural, while male homoeroticism is natural, since it preserves a human social hierarchy.) By linking

189. *PG* 60.422mid. See Peter Brown, *The Body and Society: Men, Women, and Sexual Renunciation in Early Christianity* (Lectures on the History of Religions, n.s. 13; New York: Columbia University Press, 1988) 310–22.

190. *PG* 60.420bot; 421top.

191. *PG* 60.419top: Ταῖς μὲν γὰρ εἰ καὶ παράνομος, ἀλλὰ κατὰ φύσιν ἡ μίξις· αὕτη δὲ καὶ παράνομος, καὶ παρὰ φύσιν.

In this context, ancient Athenian legal tolerance and even public promotion of same-sex love proves an embarrassment for Chrysostom, since he concedes the Athenians' wisdom, while criticizing them for making a law of same-sex love.

192. *PG* 60.418top. See also 418bot and 419mid.

the two categories of illegal/unconventional and unnatural, he stresses the social dimension of unnaturalness. Unnaturalness is not a private matter, but rather a public concern, a matter of laws and social conventions.

Chrysostom, superbly trained in the art of rhetoric by the great rhetorician Libanius, recognizes that the concept of nature gave greater force to Paul's condemnation of female homoeroticism.[193] He comments that "nature" enabled Paul to achieve two potentially conflicting goals with respect to female homoeroticism: to speak chastely and to sting the hearer.[194] Paul needed to chastise the practitioners of immoral behavior, but he had to be careful of speaking too explicitly about their sexual transgressions. On the assumption that Paul had to speak chastely about the women because women ought to feel more shame than men, he argues that "nature" served as a kind of veil or curtain to maintain female shame. Chrysostom implies that Paul could use nature as a rhetorical veil, because Paul's audience knew about unnatural and natural sexual relations between women, that it was aware of sexual love between women.

Chrysostom pursues the same rhetorical strategy as Paul. He speaks more explicitly about "male mania" than about its female counterpart, cloaking in modesty and shame his description of sexual love between women. In spite of his circumlocutions, a contemporary reader can see that his audience was familiar with both female and male homoeroticism and apparently even attracted to it.[195] In fact, he has to go to great lengths to dissuade them from it. He even agrees with his intended audience's assumption that people who engage in same-sex sexual expression actually have pleasure. In fact, Chrysostom does not dispute that they have pleasure or even that pleasure is good; rather, he seeks to persuade them that it is the wrong kind of pleasure.[196]

HOMOEROTICISM IN A MONASTIC SETTING: SHENUTE OF ATRIPE

Shenute of Atripe (4th–5th C.), the influential head of a large Egyptian monastic community, repeatedly warned his monks and nuns against sexual expression of any kind. Several thousand male and female ascetics found a spiritual home in the White Monastery, located on the western bank of the Nile river not far from Akhmim/Panopolis, which flourished under Shenute's leadership in the years following 383. In his writing on

194. *PG* 60.417mid.
195. On Chrysostom as a witness for same-sex love among Christians in Antioch, see Boswell, *Christianity, Social Tolerance, and Homosexuality*, 131f.
196. *PG* 60.417mid ("genuine pleasure is that which is according to nature"), 419top (assumption that such persons had pleasure); 422mid ("virtue and the pleasure that comes from it").

the monastic life, Shenute straightforwardly enumerates the ways in which ascetic women and men can violate their vow of celibacy. These include female and male homoerotic contact between adults, sexual contact between adult women and men, the sexual use of children, and masturbation. Shenute pronounces a curse upon any adult who undertakes any of these activities.

Shenute's general curse on adult sexual contact is gender-inclusive: "Those who will lie down on a mat, being two, or those who will lie entirely close to one another that they might grope or touch each other entirely in lustful passion, they, whether a man or a woman shall be accursed."[197] This general formulation includes sexual contact between a woman and a man, between two men, and between two women. Similarly: "Those, whether a man or a woman, who will continue walking, approaching their neighbor, having lust for him in their heart, they shall be accursed."[198] If "neighbor" here can mean both a man and a woman, Shenute is again referring to both same-sex and opposite-sex sexual attraction.

In his discussion of the sexual use of girls and boys, Shenute explicitly names both adult women and men as initiators:

> Cursed is she, namely a woman among us, who will pursue young girls and anoint them and who is filled with a passion or who [. . .] them with a lustful passion and a laziness and a laughter and a vain deceit. . . .
>
> Those, then among us or among you [women] who will touch some boys or girls whether they are sleeping or awake and those who touch them that they might know that they are mature, they are accursed whether a man or a woman.[199]

Unlike others in antiquity, such as Philo of Alexandria, who condemn both the adult and the child involved in pederasty, Shenute censures only the adult. He thus holds the adult solely responsible for the sexual use of a child. His condemnation of women who initiate sexual contact with children (both girls and boys) breaks the usual pattern of the ancient world in

197. Shenute, *De vita monachorum* 21; J. Leipoldt, ed., *Sinuthii Archimandritae Vita et opera omnia*, vol. 4, with the assistance of E. W. Crum (*Corpus Scriptorum Christianorum Orientalium 73/Scriptores Coptici* 5; Paris: Gabalda, 1913; reprint, Louvain: Secrétariat du Corpus SCO, 1954) 124. I express gratitude to Michael Foat, Ph.D. candidate in the religion department of Brown University, who is preparing a doctoral dissertation on Shenute and kindly provided me with these references. I cite Foat's own original translations throughout this section.

198. Shenute, *De vita monachorum* 21; Leipoldt, *Sinuthii Archimandritae Vita*, 124.

199. Shenute, *De vita monachorum* 26; Leipoldt, *Sinuthii Archimandritae Vita*, 169–70, 171.

several respects. Recall that one of the few positive assessments of female homoeroticism, that by Plutarch in his *Life of Lykurgos*, describes sexual contact between an adult woman and a girl. Plutarch praises the unequal relationship between a woman and a girl, modeled on the unequal relationship of male-male pederasty.[200] In contrast, Shenute condemns both female and male homoerotic pederasty.[201]

Shenute's warnings to his fellow monastics give insight into the daily circumstances of life in a fourth-century Upper Egyptian monastery. We have seen female homoerotic love spells from Upper Egypt ranging in date from the second through the fourth centuries, as well as evidence for marriage between women in second-century Egypt. The women entering Shenute's monastery entered it from a world in which people knew of, practiced, sometimes tolerated, and sometimes condemned sexual love between women. Shenute's warnings demonstrate his awareness that the women entering the White Monastery brought with them the various possibilities for sexual contact practiced in the world outside its walls. His straightforward presentation of the possible sexual temptations facing a woman provides evidence that some women may have felt—and acted upon—these temptations.

LET NUNS GO OUT IN GROUPS OF THREE: AUGUSTINE OF HIPPO

At the same time as Shenute was warning his fellow monastics in Upper Egypt about a variety of sexual temptations within the monastery, his contemporary Augustine (354–430),[202] Bishop of Hippo (known in Algeria today as Bône/Annaba) also showed awareness of homoeroticism within monastic life. Augustine explicitly warns the nuns in a convent previously headed by his sister that the love that they bear to each other must be spiritual rather than carnal. He criticizes immodest women who shamefully engage in erotic activity with other women. Augustine criticizes homo-

---

200. Plutarch, *Lives, Lykurgos* 18.9.

201. For a condemnation of male-male pederasty, see *De vita monachorum* 25: "Cursed is he who will kiss his neighbor or a boy with lustful passion" (Leipoldt, *Sinuthii Archimandritae Vita,* 169). "Neighbor" would refer to a fellow monastic, presumably male, but perhaps also female.

Shenute elsewhere condemns sexual contact between adult monastics: "Cursed is he who will touch his neighbor or who will approach him in the latrines or in the places of his lying, who gropes for him or who touches him with evil desire" (*De vita monachorum* 25 [Leipoldt, *Sinuthii Archimandritae Vita,* 169]). He also pronounces accursed a person who masturbates: "Cursed is he who will touch himself with his own hands to do evil things" (*De vita monachorum* 25 [Leipoldt, 169]).

202. See the definitive biography on Augustine by Peter Brown, *Augustine of Hippo* (Berkeley: University of California Press, 1967). For Augustine's understanding of the body, see Margaret R. Miles, *Augustine on the Body* (Missoula, MT: Scholars Press, 1979).

erotic activity on the part of married women or of girls who intend to marry, but he deplores such behavior when practiced "by widows or by virgins dedicated by a holy vow to be handmaids of Christ."[203] Thus, Augustine takes for granted that women will be sexually attracted to other women. His instructions to nuns concerning their going to the public baths give us a sense of one setting in which such homoerotic activity might occur. He tells the nuns to go to the public baths only once a month and then only in groups of three or more. In fact, he says, nuns should always go out in groups of three or more whenever they need to leave the convent. Further, the sister who has to go outside of the convent for whatever reason should go with whomever the prioress orders, rather than being allowed to pick those with whom she wishes to go.[204] The specificity and detail of these instructions demonstrate Augustine's consciousness of female romantic friendships among monastic women.[205]

203. *Epistle* 211.14 (*PL* 33.964bot). This epistle (written in 423) has played an important role throughout church history, because it has often formed the basis for ecclesiastical regulations of women's monastic communities.

204. *Epistle* 211.13 (*PL* 33.963bot).

205. Ancient burial inscriptions demonstrating that early Christians occasionally buried two or more women together could bear witness to special friendships among early Christian women, both within and outside monastic settings. Valerie A. Abrahamsen has argued that three of these inscriptions (nos. 1–3 below) constitute evidence for Christian same-sex unions ("Same-Sex Couples at Philippi: Evidence from Basilica Burials," paper presented at the American Academy of Religion/Society of Biblical Literature Triregional Meeting, Boston, MA, March 31, 1995), but I interpret them more conservatively. (She has also raised the possibility that the inscriptions commemorate same-sex missionary couples [*Women and Worship at Philippi: Diana/Artemis and Other Cults in the Early Christian Era* (Portland, ME: Astarte Shell, 1995) 155, 158.) These inscriptions include:

(1) A 4th/5th-C. epitaph (no longer extant) inscribed on a marble stele with a pediment found on the eastern periphery of the Greek city of Philippi: "+ + +/+Resting place belonging to Posidonia, deacon, and Pancharia, most humble canoness; +" Greek: + + +/+ Κοιμ(ητήριον) διαφέρ/οντα Ποσιδω/νίας διακ(ονίσσης or ονος) κ(αὶ) Πα/νχαρίας ἐλα-χ(ίστης)/κανονικῆς + (Denis Feissel, *Recueil des inscriptions chrétiennes de Macédoine du iii* au vi* siècle* [Bulletin de Correspondance Hellénique, supp. 8; Athens: École Française d'Athènes, 1983] no. 241, pp. 204f; see also Paul Lemerle, *Philippes et la Macédoine orientale à l'époque chrétienne et byzantine: Recherches d'histoire et d'archéologie* [Bibliothèque des Écoles Françaises d'Athènes et de Rome 158; Paris: De Boccard, 1945] 92–94 [Lemerle notes that a law promulgated by Theodosius in 390 required deaconesses to be at least sixty years of age and to have borne children (*Codex Theodosianus* 16.2.27), but that other laws set age forty as a minimum; the requirement of children obviously requires a woman to have been in a sexual relationship with a man, which is one of the reasons that I hesitate to accept Abrahamsen's interpretation]; Abrahamsen, *Women and Worship*, 89).

(2) A 5th-C. inscription found in the Extra-Muros Basilica in Philippi: "Resting place of Euhodiana and Dorothea"; Greek: Κυμ(ητήριον) Εὐοδιάνις κὲ Δωροθέας (for a brief mention of the inscription, see Ch. Bakirtzis, "Ἐκθέση Παλαιοχριστιανικῶν Ἀρχαιοτητῶν στὸ Μουσείο Φιλιππῶν," *Athens Annals of Archaeology* 13 [1980] 95; for the transcription, see Abrahamsen, *Women and Worship*, 158).

Augustine also expresses concern about male homoerotic relationships in monastic settings, couching this concern in terms of gender distinction with respect to hair and headdress. Monks, he writes, should maintain their masculine identity even when celibate. (Like many others in the ancient world, Augustine assumes that passive men have become like women.) As part of maintaining their masculinity, monks should avoid long hair, which could create the impression that they are available to be bought. Similarly, Augustine insists that women should veil themselves, for woman, unlike man, does not show through her body that she is made in the image of God. He bases his call for this gender differentiation in appearance on

---

(3) A 5th/6th-C. inscription (no longer extant) found in the cemetery of Hagia Triada in Edessa in Macedonia: "+ + +Memorial shrine of Theodosia, deacon, and of Aspelia and of Agathoklea, virgins"; Greek: + + +/Μημόριον Θεο/δοσίας διακόνου/ καὶ Ἀσπηλίας/ καὶ Ἀγαθοκλή/ας παρθένον. Line 5: read παρθένων (Feissel, *Recueil des inscriptions*, no. 20, pp. 39f).

(4) A 5th/6th-C. inscription of uncertain origin (no longer extant), perhaps from Hagia Triada in Edessa, which is inscribed on a plaque of blue shale: "Memorial shrine of Kalimera and Akylina and Apantia, perpetual virgins"; Greek: [Μημ]όριον/ Καλιμέρας/ κ(αὶ) Ἀκυ-λίνα[ς κ(αὶ)]/ Ἀπαντίας/ ἀειπαρθενο[ν] (Feissel, *Recueil des inscriptions*, no. 23, p. 42).

These and other similar inscriptions could attest merely to an early church practice of bury-ing more than one unrelated person together in a common grave. Supporting this interpreta-tion is the fact that several of the women bear official church titles: "deacon," "canoness," "virgin," and "perpetual virgin," the latter two of which definitely imply celibacy, although Euhodiana and Dorothea's burial inscription does not contain a title indicating a commitment to celibacy. An inscription commemorating a male cantor and a male architect, along with the wife of the architect, lends further support for my more conservative interpretation (5th–6th-C. Edessan epitaph; Feissel, *Recueil des inscriptions*, no. 25, p. 43).

Alternatively, these inscriptions could commemorate a companionship that had existed among the women buried together. The formulations resemble the burial inscriptions of men and women buried together, as well as those of two men buried together (e.g., Feissel, *Recueil des inscriptions*, nos. 28 [5th/6th-C. Edessan epitaph for a man and a woman]; 242 [5th/6th-C. Philippian epitaph for a man and his wife]; 16, 17, 26 [5th/6th-C. Edessan epitaphs for two men]; 235 [4th-C. Philippian epitaph for two male presbyters]; and 236 [4th/6th-C. Philippian epitaph for two male presbyters]).

The witness of the 4th/5th-C. church fathers Shenute and Augustine, as well as of later sources, demonstrates that homosocial Christian environments provided women with the op-portunity for romantic friendships, which cannot be excluded in the case of these inscriptions. On romantic friendships between Christian women in homosocial environments, see: E. Ann Matter, "My Sister, My Spouse: Woman-Identified Women in Medieval Christianity," *Journal of Feminist Studies in Religion* 2:2 (1986) 81–93; republished in *Weaving the Visions: New Patterns in Feminist Spirituality*, ed. Judith Plaskow and Carol P. Christ (San Francisco: Har-per and Row, 1989) 51–62; Monika Barz, Herta Leistner, and Ute Wild, *Lesbische Frauen in der Kirche* (2d reworked ed.; Stuttgart: Kreuz, 1993) 139–93; John Boswell, *Christianity, Social Tolerance, and Homosexuality,* 220f.; Judith C. Brown, *Immodest Acts: The Life of a Lesbian Nun in Renaissance Italy* (New York: Oxford University Press, 1986); and Rosemary Curb and Nancy Manahan, eds., *Lesbian Nuns: Breaking Silence* (Tallahassee, FL: Naiad, 1985).

the theological proposition that man is meant to rule and woman to be subordinate.[206] In his insistence upon short hair for men and veiling for women, as well as in the theological justification for this insistence, Augustine echoes Paul in 1 Cor 11:2–16.

In spite of Augustine's awareness of female romantic friendship, he interpreted Rom 1:26 as referring to unnatural sexual relations between a female and a male, rather than to female homoeroticism. For him "unnatural" means that which does not allow for procreation, such as anal intercourse. He defines anal intercourse between a husband and a wife as "unnatural and grossly wicked," since it is nonprocreative.[207] (In this, Augustine was at direct odds with contemporaneous rabbis, who allowed anal intercourse within marriage.)

We have to understand Augustine's interpretation of Romans 1 within the context of his debate with the Pelagians, specifically with the excommunicated and exiled Pelagian bishop, Julian of Eclanum (southern Italy). Julian apparently used Rom 1:26f to demonstrate that marital sexual intercourse is good and that what is born from it is good, since in that verse Paul rejects unnatural intercourse between men and defines natural intercourse as the sexual use of women. Augustine retorts that Paul does not speak of "conjugal use," but rather of "natural" use. Had Paul spoken of conjugal use (in contrast to unnatural use), argues Augustine, then Paul would have meant to include (and thereby to condone) anal intercourse and other marital sexual contact involving nonprocreative body parts. (Augustine thus categorizes anal intercourse as conjugal, but not natural.) Since, however, Paul contrasts natural and unnatural sexual relations, his condemnation includes such conjugal practices as anal intercourse. With

206. *De opere monachorum* 32.40: *illa regit, haec regitur; illa dominatur, haec subditur* (Joseph Zycha, ed., *Sancti Aureli Augustini De fide et symbolo . . .* [CSEL 41; Prague: Tempsky, 1900] 594; see also *PL* 40.580mid); see the larger context of 31.39–32.40 (CSEL 41.590–94; *PL* 40.578–80). For an extensive analysis of Augustine's theological anthropology of woman, see Kari E. Børresen, *Subordination and Equivalence: The Nature and Rôle of Woman in Augustine and Thomas Aquinas*, trans. Charles H. Talbot (Washington, DC: University Press of America, 1981) 1–140.

207. *De nuptiis et concupiscentia* 20.35 (Carl F. Urba and Joseph Zycha, eds., *Sancti Aureli Augustini: De perfectione iustitiae hominis . . .* [CSEL 42; Prague: Tempsky, 1902; reprint, New York: Johnson, 1968] 289); see also *De bono coniugali* 11f (Joseph Zycha, ed., *Sancti Aureli Augustini: De fide et symbolo . . .* [CSEL 41; Prague: Tempsky, 1900] 202–4). See Boswell, *Christianity, Social Tolerance, and Homosexuality,* 161, n. 99.

Joseph A. Fitzmyer incorrectly interprets Augustine when he writes, "He [i.e., Augustine] granted that a husband and wife could have intercourse that was unnatural, but that has nothing to do with this statement of Paul [in Rom 1:26]" (*Romans: A New Translation with Introduction and Commentary* [Anchor Bible; New York: Doubleday, 1993] 287). In both *De nuptiis et concupiscentia* 20.35 and *De bono coniugali* 11f, Augustine quite explicitly connects Rom 1:26 with anal intercourse.

this interpretation, Augustine attempts to refute the Pelagians' positive view of marital cohabitation and their claim that children are good. He ultimately aims to show that even children born within wedlock are conceived in original sin. Anal intercourse, which in his eyes is conjugal, but not natural, serves as Augustine's wedge between same-sex and opposite-sex love, a wedge designed to cast a moral shadow over marital cohabitation, thereby refuting the Pelagians' positive assessment of it.[208]

For Augustine, it would be a mistake "to doubt that marriage is not sinful."[209] Focusing on the question of natural versus unnatural, he sets up a small hierarchy of the gravity of several sexual sins: (1a) natural intercourse that goes beyond the marriage pact (i.e., beyond the necessity for procreation called for by the legal arrangement) is pardonable when done with one's wife, and (1b) sinful when done with a prostitute;[210] but (2a) unnatural intercourse is execrable when done with a prostitute, and (2b) even more execrable when done with one's wife; and the wife who allows her husband to have anal intercourse with her (or other sexual contact involving a nonprocreative body part) is more shameful than if she allows him to have such intercourse with another woman.[211] At the root of this hierarchy of sins seems to lie the centuries-old categorization found in

208. *De nuptiis et concupiscentia* 20.35. On the debate between Julian of Eclanum and Augustine, see Peter Brown, *The Body and Society: Men, Women, and Sexual Renunciation in Early Christianity* (Lectures on the History of Religions, n.s. 13; New York: Columbia University Press, 1988) 408–19. Brown characterizes Julian's position in this way: "Julian had to go on to demonstrate that, in strict theory, sexual desire did not have to be renounced at all. It was in no way corrupted. It was both irrational and impious to suggest that the sexual urge, as now used in married intercourse, was in any way different from that which God had first placed in Adam and Eve" (p. 412). Brown describes Augustine's response as follows: "As soon as they had made their own wills independent of the will of God, parts of Adam and Eve became resistant to their own conscious will. Their bodies were touched with a disturbing new sense of the alien, in the form of sexual sensations that escaped their control. . . . Sexual desire was no more tainted with this tragic, faceless concupiscence than was any other form of human activity. But the very incongruities associated with sexual feelings used the human body as a tiny mirror, in which men and women could catch a glimpse of themselves. They saw themselves, from this unexpected angle, as God had first seen the fallen Adam and Eve" (pp. 416–18). See also Elizabeth A. Clark, "'Adam's Only Companion': Augustine and the Early Christian Debate on Marriage," *Recherches augustiniennes* 21 (1986) 139–62. Clark argues that Augustine's focus on sexual relations and procreation, formulated in the midst of theological debate about asceticism and pro-sex Pelagianism, overshadowed his original contributions to the concept of marriage as companionship.

209. *De bono coniugali* 11 (Joseph Zycha, ed., *Sancti Aureli Augusti: De fide et symbolo* . . . [CSEL 41; Prague: Tempsky, 1900] 202).

210. Excessive lust by a husband toward his wife is nevertheless sinful, although far less sinful than if he commits fornication.

211. *De bono coniugali* 11f.

Artemidoros (nature, law, and custom) and the assumption that nature takes precedence over law and custom.[212]

Thus, as in Artemidoros, the unnatural category is further away from the natural, legal, and customary than is that which is illegal or that which contravenes custom. For this reason, "natural" sexual acts with a prostitute are worse than "natural acts" with one's wife, since prostitution lies outside the legal boundaries of marriage, but an "unnatural" sexual act is worse within marriage than outside it, since one is thereby sullying the legal institution of marriage. The unnatural is worse than the illegal: if a man must sin, better that he should commit a natural sexual act outside the legal institution of marriage than an unnatural sexual act within the limits of the law. And if he is going to sin against nature, then he should do it outside the legal realm entirely. Thus, although Augustine differs from Artemidoros as to which sexual acts he classifies as natural, legal, and customary, his assumptions about the relative value of nature, law, and custom coincide with those of Artemidoros.

Augustine brings us to a new stage in early Christian thinking about the erotic. Paul and Tertullian and Clement condemned same-sex love as unnatural, exhorting their followers to live according to an order of creation in which man is head of woman. These three thinkers, even though they differed in their evaluation of marriage, nevertheless all assumed the sanctity of marriages characterized by sexual intercourse between veiled, subordinate wives and husbands who instruct them. Augustine introduces a note of profound sadness into the discussion by claiming that original sin is passed on to a child at the moment of conception. Even a "natural," procreative sexual act between a subordinate wife and a husband who rules over her is deeply disturbed and characterized by sin, since humans cannot totally submit their sexual urges to their will. By asserting that sin imbues even a "natural" sexual act within the legal confines of marriage, Augustine subtly banishes "unnatural" sexual acts even further outside the realm of holiness.

Early Christian writers differed in one important respect from many of their contemporaries: they more frequently classified female and male homoeroticism together. Like Paul before them, by viewing homoeroticism as a transgression worthy of horrendous punishment, these early Christian writers tended to classify the female sin as equal in gravity to the male one. For this reason, they envisaged homoerotic women (apparently both part-

---

212. See *Confessiones* 3.8 on the greater seriousness of crimes against nature (such as those of the men of Sodom), as compared with those against custom and law.

ners) and homoerotic men (or at least the passive male partners) as suffering torture in the same ravine in hell. They also tended to discuss female and male homoeroticism in the same sermon or chapter of a book. Clement of Alexandria witnesses to this tendency through his use of a single term for "same-sex sexual contact." By seeing homoeroticism as a sin committed by women and men alike, early Christians contributed to the development of the concept of a homosexual identity encompassing both women and men.

Even though these Christian writers differed from their contemporaries by viewing homoeroticism as a sin committed by both women and men, they nevertheless shared common cultural understandings of gender and of procreation. For this reason, their responses to sexual love between women differ little in conceptualization from other ancient writers within their culture; these writers all shared an asymmetrical view of the sexes and of sexual love.

One might have assumed that pro-sex pagans accepted sexual love between women, while anti-sex Christians rejected it. This study has shown almost uniform condemnation of such love among ancient writers from all traditions and philosophies. The sources analyzed in this chapter further show that whether a Christian writer promoted celibacy, such as Tertullian or John Chrysostom, or marriage, such as Clement of Alexandria, was not the deciding factor as to whether they would oppose female homoeroticism. Instead of a positive or negative view of sexual intercourse, decisive factors were: that they believed that the natural order included strict gender differentiation in appearance; and that they saw man as head of the woman, man as ruler of the woman, and woman as helper to the man and receptacle to the male seed.

The material I have presented in this chapter shows that a number of early Christian writers knew about and condemned sexual love between women.[213] The reality to which they responded may well have included

213. See also Ambrosiaster (Pseudo-Ambrose), who takes Rom. 1:26 as referring to sexual relations between women (*In Epistulam ad Romanos* on Rom. 1:26; Heinrich Josef Vogels, ed., *Ambrosiastri qui dicitur commentarius in epistulas Paulinas* [*Corpus Scriptorum Ecclesiasticorum Latinorum* 81.1; Vienna: Hoelder-Pichler-Tempsky, 1966] 50f). E. Ann Matter notes that Hincmar of Rheims (9th C.) referred to Ambrosiaster's comments on Rom. 1:26 (*PL* 125.692–93; cited in "My Sister, My Spouse: Woman-Identified Women in Medieval Christianity," *Journal of Feminist Studies in Religion* 2:2 [1986] 89; reprinted in *Weaving the Visions: New Patterns in Feminist Spirituality*, ed. Judith Plaskow and Carol P. Christ [San Francisco: Harper and Row, 1989] 58). For an example of a sixth-century patristic writer who warns about nuns looking lustfully at one another, see Severus (Patriarch of Antioch, 512–18), who first urges the deaconess and archimandritess to keep males of all ages away from the sacred virgins and then writes, "Neither let virgins look freely at one another, but with eyes turned downwards let them say what is needed. The lust of the flesh obtains

woman-woman marriage and the acceptance of female homoeroticism by groups they deemed heretical, such as the Naassenes. In light of the evidence I have presented, one can no longer claim that sexual love between women was unknown in the early church.

---

occasions from the lust of the eyes, as the divine John the Evangelist says in his epistle" (1 John 2:16). E. W. Brooks, ed. and trans., *The Sixth Book of the Select Letters of Severus, Patriarch of Antioch, in the Syriac Version of Athanasius of Nisibis*, vol. 1 (text), pt. 2 (Oxford: Text and Translation Society, 1904) 411; vol. 2 (translation), pt. 2 (Oxford: Text and Translation Society, 1904) 365. I thank Susan R. Holman, doctoral student in religion at Brown University, for this reference.

12

Conclusion

The sources I have examined in this book demonstrate a widespread awareness of sexual love between women among people in the Roman world. This awareness extended from elite authors like Martial and Juvenal to lower-status urban provincials like Paul and Vettius Valens, to such Egyptian villagers as the women who commissioned erotic spells, and finally, to the rabbinic sages whose debates the Sifra and the Babylonian Talmud record. Unlike the sources on male-male couplings, some of which promote and some of which reject such couplings, the ancient sources nearly uniformly condemn sexual love between women. At the same time, they testify to a certain level of tolerance for such love, as in their reference to woman-woman marriage, since any kind of cohabitation requires at least minimal social and economic support.

Gender role transgression emerges as the single most central reason for the rejection of female romantic friendship. Ancient shapers of culture shared Paul's assumption that a married woman was "under a man" and saw homoerotic women as transgressing nature by experiencing pleasure while not under a man. For them, such pleasure was against both nature and divine will.

While both Christian and non-Christian writers described female homoeroticism as a gender transgression, they had difficulty conceptualizing it in terms of the asymmetrical phallocentric cultural idiom of the Roman world. The phallocentric model, which requires a penetrator and a passive, penetrated partner, does not necessarily apply to erotic activity between two women. This difficulty resulted in differing answers as to whether to call both women in an erotic relationship *tribades* or just the "masculine" one, as to whether both partners were culpable, and as to whether one woman penetrated another or whether they "rubbed" in a mutual fashion. Christians and non-Christians alike tried again and again to conceptualize female romantic friendship in terms of an active/passive distinction and the primacy of the phallus, but they never quite succeeded. There was always slippage, inconsistency, and a lack of parallelism to male-male relations. They could never quite fit women's experience into a male mold.

While Roman-period writers depicted female homoeroticism first and foremost as a gender transgression against nature, cultural understandings of social status imbued their concepts of both gender and nature. The association of *tribades* with prostitutes may have evoked images of slave women that served to remind upper-class women that only they were truly women. Tertullian's picture of *frictrices*, hangmen, and gladiators would have constituted a polar opposite to his readers' traditional image of the proper Roman matron wearing her status-identifying stola. In subtle and not so subtle ways, Tertullian and other ancient authors reinforced the ideal of gender-differentiated high-status persons versus gender transgressive, all too public, low-status women: *frictrices/tribades* and prostitutes.

Alternatively, ancient Mediterranean writers associated the sexual freedom to love other women with educated, creative women, most especially Sappho. The tribadic epithet hurled at Sappho served to discredit her among women and thereby to limit women's intellectual and creative role models.

Both associations, that between homoerotic women and prostitutes or other low-status persons and that between homoerotic women and the aristocratic Sappho, functioned to maintain the social order by means of strict gender differentiation. In both lines of thought, the implied ideal was a high-status, truly feminine woman, subservient either to her husband or, in the case of celibate Christian women, to the church.

In spite of this widespread and vociferous opposition to female romantic friendship, the sources testify to the presence of sexual love between women throughout the Roman Empire: among Roman matrons, Alexandrian Greeks, villagers of Upper Egypt, daughters of Jewish priests, and female Christian monastics. As a backlash, the vehement opposition bears testimony to some level of tolerance, apparently extending to woman-woman marriage.

While ancient authors nearly all opposed sexual love between women, they differed greatly as to its causes and treatment. Astrologers saw a variety of sexual orientations as caused by the configuration under which one was born. They nevertheless viewed some orientations, such as female homoeroticism, as unnatural. But apparently they would have counseled such women to accept their lot in life. In contrast, medical writers identified the cause as the anatomical deformity of an overly large clitoris, to be corrected by a clitoridectomy, or as a diseased mind, to be treated by mind control. Christian writers cast the discussion in moral terms and described the behavior as deserving of death and/or punishment in hell.

In spite of the differing etiologies and treatments, the concept of female homoeroticism as unnatural runs like a thread, especially through the Greek sources, both Christian and non-Christian. In contrast to their presentations of male homoeroticism, the sources practically never accuse homoerotic women of sex with children or of failure to procreate. Rather, they implicitly contrast unnatural sex between women with the natural erotic roles: men "do" or "act," while women "suffer" or "are passive." In their view, love between women either confounds this schema or allows women to take an active role, a privilege women ought never to have.

I have interpreted Paul's use of "unnatural" in line with that of his culture. My examination of early Christian interpreters of Paul demonstrates that they too read "unnatural" as denoting women's insubordination.

This collection of ancient sources, never before examined together in one study, establishes the necessity for studying love between women on its own, rather than as a minor subcategory of male homoeroticism. Theories recently put forth by other scholars concerning sexual love between males in antiquity do not stand the test of these sources. This material runs counter to John Boswell's view that premodern Christians accepted love and marriage between women. Further, the ancient sources, which rarely speak of sexual relations between women and girls, undermine Robin Scroggs's theory that Paul opposed homosexuality as pederasty. These sources also contradict Michel Foucault's view that the medicalization of homosexuality—including lesbianism—occurred in modernity. Finally, the astrological evidence for lifelong erotic orientations; the terms *tribas* and *frictrix*, which imply an erotic identity; and the early Christian grouping together of homoerotic males and females, challenge David Halperin's view that the concept of homosexuality did not exist until the nineteenth century. As with other studies on women, examining material relating to sexual love between women in antiquity alters our picture of history as a whole.

This study has demonstrated that ancient commentators on sexual love between women were eminently concerned with maintaining a gender-stratified social order. Through Paul's Letter to the Romans and other early church writings, the principal concepts discussed in this book have come to serve as authoritative for Western cultures, as a source for our ethics. If church people and policy makers continue to base church and social policy on the priority of heterosexual marriage over love between women, we will be perpetuating ancient traditions that have diminished and debased the lives of lesbians, bisexual women, and—indeed—all women. By understanding our past, we may progress toward a more humane future, one in which we acknowledge the sacredness and holiness of a woman expressing her love for another woman.

Appendix:
Select Annotated Bibliography on
Romans 1:26f and the New Testament
and Homosexuality Generally

In addition to the following essays and monographs, see also the comments on Rom 1:26f in the numerous commentaries on Paul's Letter to the Romans.

Bahnsen, Greg L. *Homosexuality: A Biblical View*. Grand Rapids, MI: Baker Book House, 1978 (homosexuality in Rom 1:26f constitutes "both sin and punishment for sin" [p. 49]; Paul opposed all forms of homosexuality, including "secular homosexuality" and what some call "inversion" [pp. 52f]; "God, the creator of man, ... forbids the transgression of certain essential boundaries" [p. 55]; Paul held that homosexuality's "practitioners know that they deserve to die for their disobedience to God's will" [p. 59]; " 'Gay liberation' is symptomatic of a culture abandoned by God to destruction and a church provoking the Lord with abomination" [quote on p. 61] [pp. 47–61]).

Bailey, Derrick Sherwin. *Homosexuality and the Western Christian Tradition*. London: Longmans, Green, 1955 (Paul's condemnation applies to all homosexual acts, whether committed by heterosexuals or homosexuals, since the distinction between inversion and perversion was alien to him; Rom 1:26 may refer to heterosexual "variations in coital position or method" [p. 40], i.e., that the heathen women perverted heterosexuality and their men carried it one step further, but more probably refers to "homosexual practices between females" [p. 40], especially since the sexual variations could also include lesbian practices; the early Christians viewed homosexual acts as representing the sexual degeneracy inevitably resulting from idolatry; the Bible never gives population growth or maintenance as an argument against homosexuality [pp. 37–41, 57–61]).

Balz, Horst. "Biblische Aussagen zur Homosexualität." *Zeitschrift für Evangelische Ethik* 31 (1987) 60–72 (Rom 1:26f concerns a violation against the human body as created by God; these verses are not about heterosexuals performing homosexual acts, nor about cultic activity; homosexuality is more serious than infractions against gender roles; pastorally, love among believers takes precedence over all else in dealing with homosexuals within a congregation).

364
SELECT ANNOTATED BIBLIOGRAPHY

Bartlett, David L. "A Biblical Perspective on Homosexuality." *Foundations* 20 (1977) 133–47 (Paul condemns homosexual *lust*, not ongoing affectional relationships, and bases his condemnation in part on interpretation of the Jewish scriptures, in part on the "common wisdom" of his culture, and in part on his own empirical assessment of homosexuality; as in the case of slavery—which scripture fully condones—our empirical understanding of homosexuality has changed since biblical times; the church today can best follow Paul's basic premise that we cannot earn God's favor by recognizing that "the gifts of God's Spirit are equally available to heterosexual people and to homosexual people" [p. 146]).

Becker, Jürgen. "Zum Problem der Homosexualität in der Bibel." *Zeitschrift für Evangelische Ethik* 31 (1987) 36–59 (Paul's condemnation of homosexuality reflects the Jewish views of his time; he promotes strict monogamy or celibacy; the church cannot accept homosexuality, which is inherently deficient in comparison with heterosexual marriage).

Boswell, John. *Christianity, Social Tolerance, and Homosexuality: Gay People in Western Europe from the Beginning of the Christan Era to the Fourteenth Century.* Chicago: University of Chicago Press, 1980 (Rom 1:26f is not a "clear condemnation of homosexual acts" [p. 110]; rather, Paul condemns homosexual acts undertaken by apparently heterosexual persons, since, as John Chrysostom comments, "Only those possessing something can change it"; *para physin* means "more than" or "in excess of," rather than "in opposition"; "nature" does not refer to natural law, which was not fully developed until centuries later, but rather to the character of a person or group of persons; the terms *pathē* ["passions"], *atimia* ["dishonor"], *planē* ["error"] and *aschēmosynē* [KJV: "that which is unseemly"; NRSV: "shameless acts"] do not signify moral failure; Rom 1:26f did not give rise to Christian antigay feelings [pp. 107–17]).

Boughton, Lynne C. "Biblical Texts and Homosexuality: A Response to John Boswell." *Irish Theological Quarterly* 58 (1992) 141–53 (John Boswell's New Testament exegesis in *Christianity, Social Tolerance, and Homosexuality* is flawed; in Rom 1:26f Paul generally condemns homosexual expression, not only that engaged in by persons "naturally" attracted to the opposite sex; Boswell errs in his view that *malakoi* in 1 Cor 6:9 refers to masturbation and that *arsenokoitai* in 1 Cor 6:9 is ambiguous, as other usage and etymology demonstrate).

Coleman, Peter. *Christian Attitudes to Homosexuality.* London: SPCK, 1980 (Paul may have used Noachide laws, i.e., Jewish precepts incumbent even upon gentiles, in Rom 1:26f as the basis of natural law [pp. 88–93]).

Comstock, Gary David. *Gay Theology Without Apology.* Cleveland, OH: Pilgrim, 1993 (the charges leveled in Rom 1:18–32 resemble the lies heaped upon lesbians and gay men today; there is insufficent evidence to say that Paul was principally targeting pederasty or that he was speaking of heterosexuals indulging in homosexuality; the fact that he also mentions other sins does not diminish his condemnation of homosexuality; "[n]ot to recognize, critique, and condemn Paul's equation of godlessness with homosexuality is dangerous" [p. 43]; in contrast, the Song of Songs provides a good basis for sexual ethics [pp. 27–48]).

Corley, Kathleen E., and Karen J. Torjesen. "Sexuality, Hierarchy, and Evangelicalism." *TSF Bulletin* 10 (1987) no. 4, 23–27 (Paul's condemnation of same-sex love in Rom 1:26f theologically reflects his hierarchical understanding of women and men, a view also found in 1 Corinthians 11; his rejection of sexual love between women relates closely to that found in the Graeco-Roman world as a whole; thus, biblical feminism and lesbianism are closely intertwined; Evangelical churches need to decide whether a hierarchy between the sexes is necessary within sexual relationships and within church structures; the churches should support civil rights for lesbians and homosexuals, but should also examine the theological roots of their own traditional arguments). See also the disclaimer by the president of Fuller Theological Seminary of any link between the article and the seminary in *TSF Bulletin* 10 (1987) no. 5.

Countryman, L. William. *Dirt, Greed, and Sex: Sexual Ethics in the New Testament and Their Implications for Today.* Philadelphia: Fortress, 1988 (Paul defines the deeds in Rom 1:26f as an unclean aspect of gentile culture, but not as sinful; "deserve to die" [v. 32] does not pertain to Rom 1:26f; we cannot make the purity or property systems of antiquity the basis of today's sexual ethics [pp. 109–23, 237–67]).

Edwards, George R. *Gay/Lesbian Liberation: A Biblical Perspective.* New York: Pilgrim, 1984 (the church's use of Rom 1:26f to condemn homosexuality runs counter to the fact that the persons addressed are heterosexuals engaging in homosexual acts, to the passage's nonparaenetic rhetorical context, and to Paul's opposition to legal rectitude throughout Romans [pp. 85–100]).

Furnish, Victor Paul. "The Bible and Homosexuality: Reading the Texts in Context." In *Homosexuality in the Church: Both Sides of the Debate.* Ed. Jeffrey S. Siker. Louisville, KY: Westminster/John Knox, 1994 (people in Paul's world regarded same-sex intercourse as a matter of free choice, rather than as a result of a sexual orientation; the two most visible and debated forms of sexual relations between males were pederasty and master/slave relations; people presupposed that one partner would be active and the other passive; people feared that "homosexual" practice could lead to the extinction of human beings; Philo of Alexandria demonstrates that hellenistic Jews shared these views; 1 Cor 6:9, 1 Tim 1:10, and Rom 1:26f show that Paul also shared them; there is insufficient evidence to posit that Paul's view of same-sex sexual relations was influenced by Leviticus 18, 20, by the story of Sodom, or by creation theology; biblical texts concerning sexuality are influenced by patriarchalism as well as by other assumptions that we can no longer accept; "[t]he *more specifically applicable* an instruction is to the situation for which it was originally formulated, the *less specifically applicable* it is to every other situation" [quote on p. 32] [pp. 18–35]).

Furnish, Victor Paul. "Homosexual Practices in Biblical Perspective." In *The Sexuality Debate in North American Churches, 1988–1995: Controversies, Unresolved Issues, Future Prospects.* Ed. John J. Carey. Symposium Series 36; Lewiston, NY: Mellen, 1995, 253–81 (similar in argument to his essay in Siker, *Homosexuality in the Church*).

Furnish, Victor Paul. "What Does the Bible Say about Homosexuality?" In *Caught in the Crossfire: Helping Christians Debate Homosexuality.* Ed. Sally B. Geis and

Donald E. Messer. Nashville, TN: Abingdon, 1994, 57–66 (similar in argument to his essay in Siker, *Homosexuality in the Church*).

Furnish, Victor Paul. *The Moral Teaching of Paul*. Nashville: Abingdon, 1979 (like Paul, non-Christian moral teachers in the Graeco-Roman world condemned homosexuality as exploitative and growing out of an insatiable lust; the principal sin of Romans 1 is idolatry, not homosexuality; Paul's writings do not yield specific answers to contemporary questions about homosexuality [pp. 52–83]).

Goss, Robert. *Jesus Acted Up: A Gay and Lesbian Manifesto*. San Francisco: HarperSanFrancisco, 1993 (Paul has "no concept of sexual orientation" and "does not understand the social construction of modern sexual identity" [p. 92]; Paul's "linkage of cultic prostitution and idolatry" in Romans 1 does not apply to our situation today [p. 93]; biblical scholars need to address the harmful social effects of literalist biblical interpretation [pp. 87–101]).

Grayston, Kenneth. "Adultery and Sodomy: The Biblical Sources of Christian Moral Judgment." *Epworth Review* 15 (1988) 64–70 (in Romans 1 Paul closely follows the social conventions of his time; Paul's view that God has handed sinners over to destructive forces presumably cancels the obligatory death penalty of Lev 20:13; "unnatural" in Rom 1:26 refers to lesbianism; the love commandment and the principle of mutuality between men and women, rather than specific biblical proscriptions, provide the basis for Christian sexual ethics; in sexual behavior, Christians are to avoid "deception . . . force . . . injury . . . ignorance . . . [and] publicity" [p. 70]).

Haacker, Klaus. "Exegetische Gesichtspunkte zum Thema Homosexualität." *Theologische Beiträge* 25 (1994) 173–80 (Rom 1:26 does not refer to lesbian relationships, but rather probably to bestiality; there is no tradition condemning lesbian love in the Old Testament, in ancient Judaism, or in early Christianity; in contrast, the Old Testament [Lev 18:23, Exod 22:18; and Deut 27:21) and such postbiblical Jewish writers as Philo of Alexandria condemned bestiality, sometimes focusing on sexual relations between women and animals; homosexuality in antiquity bore no special relationship to idolatrous cults; the argument that biblical texts assume that people freely choose homosexual acts, rather than that a homosexual orientation is part of one's destiny, does not hold up for Rom 1:26f and 1 Cor 6:9–11; scripture has ultimate authority, but one must consult the whole of scripture for guidance on this ethical decision).

Hart, Hendrik. "Reply to Wolters." *Calvin Theological Journal* 28 (1993) 170–74 (in response to Wolters's critique [in the same issue], one cannot prove but can plausibly argue that Paul likely used Rom 1:18–32 rhetorically, that Paul did not invent its content, and that its judgment seems to differ from Paul's overall intent; we need to listen to God-fearing homosexuals speak about how they understand the Bible).

Hays, Richard B. "Awaiting the Redemption of Our Bodies." *Sojourners* 20 (1991) no. 6, 17–21; reprinted in *Homosexuality in the Church: Both Sides of the Debate*. Ed. Jeffrey S. Siker. Louisville, KY: Westminster/John Knox, 1994, 3–17 (homosexual intercourse in Rom 1:26f graphically represents "the way in which human fallenness distorts God's created order" [p. 19]; "exchange" in Rom 1:26

cannot refer to heterosexuals engaging in homosexual acts, because Paul and the ancient world had no concept of sexual orientation; Paul was not describing pederasty or exploitation in Rom 1:26f; Rom 2:1 tells us that self-righteous condemnation of homosexuals is as sinful as homosexual behavior itself; Paul's use of *arsenokoitai* in 1 Cor 6:9 linguistically resembles and thereby reaffirms the condemnation of male-male intercourse in Lev 18:22, 20:13; in light of "our culture's present swirling confusion about gender roles" and for a variety of theological reasons, the church should abide by "the univocal testimony of Scripture and the Christian tradition" [p. 21]).

Hays, Richard B. "Relations Natural and Unnatural: A Response to John Boswell's Exegesis of Romans 1." *Journal of Religious Ethics* 14 (1986) 184–215 (Boswell errs in arguing that Paul condemns heterosexuals who commit homosexual acts, rather than persons of homosexual orientation, and that Paul describes these acts as unusual, rather than immoral, since: (1) "sexual orientation" is an anachronism when applied to Romans, (2) *para physin* means "unnatural," rather than "unusual," and (3) Paul attaches a moral judgment to these sexual acts; the people of Romans 1 rebelled against "the male and female roles which are 'naturally' theirs in God's created order"; in assessing homosexuality today, Christians should take account of scripture, tradition, reason, and experience [the Wesleyan quadrilateral]).

Helminiak, Daniel A. *What the Bible Really Says about Homosexuality.* San Francisco: Alamo Square, 1994 (Rom 1:26 may refer to sexual intercourse during menstruation, with an uncircumcised male, while standing up, or in another fashion that was "beyond the ordinary" [*para physin*]; in Rom 1:27 Paul does not ethically condemn male-male sex, but rather merely points out that society disappoves of it; in Rom 1:18–32, "Paul is quoting Jewish prejudice precisely to counter and reject it. . . . is appealing to Jewish self-righteousness. . . . is echoing the Jewish claim to moral superiority" [p. 76]; no one really knows the meaning of *malakoi* and *arsenokoitai* in 1 Cor 6:9 and 1 Tim 1:10).

Heyward, Carter. *Touching Our Strength: The Erotic as Power and the Love of God.* San Francisco: Harper and Row, 1989 (we would do well to focus on justice, rather than the Bible; scripture, which may include extrabiblical writings, can have spiritual authority and can connect us to others who have gone before and bring us into relation with them [pp. 72–86]).

Holter-Stavanger, Knut. "A Note on the Old Testament Background of Rom 1,23–27." *Biblische Notizen* 69 (1993) 21–23 (rather than view Rom 1:26f as Paul's response to pagan culture, one can see Rom 1:23–27 as a negative echo of Gen 1:26–28; Rom 1:23–27 also echoes Deut 4:16–18).

Ide, Arthur Frederick. *Zoar and Her Sisters: Homosexuality, the Bible, and Jesus Christ.* Oak Cliff, TX: Minuteman, 1991 (Paul does not condemn homosexuality; *para physin* in Rom 1:26 means " 'going against that which is cutomarily/socially accepted/acceptable' " [p. 178]; Rom 1:26f is about perversion, i.e., a conscious choice, rather than inversion, which is innate; the pronoun "their" in 1:26 shows that married women are meant, perhaps frustrated housewives; in Rom 1:27 Paul was objecting to heterosexual males engaging in relationships *in*

368

SELECT ANNOTATED BIBLIOGRAPHY

excess [*para physin*] of those with their wives; Paul may not have written Romans; Rom 1:26f may be a forgery [pp. 177–92]).

Kähler, Else. "Exegese zweier neutestamentlicher Stellen (Römer 1, 18–32; 1. Korinther 6,9–11)." In *Probleme der Homophilie in medizinischer, theologischer und juristischer Sicht.* Ed. Theodor Bovet. Berne: Paul Haupt; Tübingen: Katzmann, 1965, 12–43, esp. 30–32 (homosexuality is not the main subject of the passage; Paul is reminding the Christian community of their own past, rather than addressing a current pastoral problem of the Roman congregation; Paul sees only one possibility for homosexuality, namely that people capable of heterosexual relations turn to homosexual ones, whereas today we know more about homosexuality in its various forms).

Kroeger, Catherine Clark, and Richard Clark Kroeger. "What Does the Bible Say about Homosexuality?" In *Caught in the Crossfire: Helping Christians Debate Homosexuality.* Ed. Sally B. Geis and Donald E. Messer. Nashville, TN: Abingdon, 1994, 48–56 (the Genesis creation narratives explain God's plan and purpose for women and men; God gave woman "as a precious gift to Adam" [p. 52]; when men rejected God's precious gift to them, thereby devaluing women and distorting the divine plan, women exchanged natural intercourse for unnatural; in Paul's world, people associated sexual misconduct with paganism).

Lance, H. Darrell. "The Bible and Homosexuality." *American Baptist Quarterly* 8 (1989) 140–51 (modern science helps us to understand that homosexual orientation does not result from disbelief in God; the churches are inconsistent to set aside the New Testament teachings on divorce and remarriage, while maintaining the less clear New Testament teaching on homosexuality).

Malick, David E. "The Condemnation of Homosexuality in Romans 1:26–27." *Bibliotheca Sacra* 150 (1993) 327–40 (Rom 1:26f is not a Pauline imposition "of Jewish customs and rules that no longer apply today" [p. 333]; nor does it describe merely a punishment for a sin, rather than a sin itself; nor is it concerned only with perverted forms of homosexuality).

Martin, Dale. "Heterosexism and the Interpretation of Romans 1:18–32." *Biblical Interpretation* 3 (1995) 332–55 (some modern scholars are being disingenuous by claiming that the normativity of heterosexuality is the biblical view, since their views differ from Paul's mythological assumption that polytheism led to homosexuality and from several of his other views; the most appropriate background against which to read Romans 1 is not Genesis 1–3 [as, e.g., Richard Hays reads it], but rather such Jewish accounts about polytheism's origins as are found in *1 Enoch* and *Jubilees*; in Romans 1 Paul refers specifically to gentile culture, rather than to the human condition generally, and speaks about "gentile ethnic impurity" and not "universal concupiscence" [which represents an Augustinian reading of Romans 1]; the ancients had no notion of a "homosexual orientation"; in antiquity, "unnatural" generally meant "in excess of what is natural," although it could also refer to the disruption of gender hierarchy; misinterpreting Paul as referring to universal human sinfulness, rather than to a gentile practice, constitutes not only heterosexism, but also homophobia; by viewing homosexuality as that which threatens us from within, these scholars provide the theological basis for "polic[ing] our inmost urges and those of our fellow citizens").

McNeill, John J. *The Church and the Homosexual.* 3d exp. ed. of 1976 ed. Boston: Beacon, 1988 (Paul does not address the question of homosexual persons, but rather of persons to whom heterosexuality is natural [pp. 53–56]).

Miller, James. "The Practices of Romans 1:26: Homosexual or Heterosexual?" *Novum Testamentum* 37 (1995) 1–11 (Rom 1:26 probably refers to heterosexual anal or oral intercourse; there is minimal evidence within Paul's social environment for a concept of homosexuality common to both females and males and there is little ancient discussion of female homoeroticism; "likewise" [*homoiōs*] in the *Testament of Naphtali* 3.5, which links unnatural same-sex sexual practices [those of the Sodomites] with unnatural heterosexual ones [those of the Watchers of Gen 6:1–4], shows that "likewise" [*homoiōs*] in Rom 1:27 could also link heterosexual with homosexual practices).

Ridderbos, Simon Jan. "Bibel und Homosexualität." In *Der homosexuelle Nächste: Ein Symposion*, with contributions by Hermanus Bianchi, et al. Hamburg: Furche, 1963, 50–73, 274 (Paul presents an image of a moral degeneracy in which people no longer heed the gender boundaries between male and female; he may be thinking of cultic prostitution; pseudo-homosexuality may be the issue; since the meaning of nature is unclear, the contrary-to-nature argument is not convincing; the church should stop speaking of homosexuals as "them").

Scanzoni, Letha Dawson, and Virginia Ramey Mollenkott. *Is the Homosexual My Neighbor? A Positive Christian Response.* Rev. ed.; San Francisco: HarperSanFrancisco, 1994 ("natural" in Romans 1 may refer to social custom, specifically Jewish social custom; Paul may have singled out homosexual practices to underscore the ritual impurity distinguishing Jews from gentiles; since many Christian heterosexuals practice noncoital sexual acts and since animals engage in same-sex sexual relations, it is difficult to view homosexual acts as unnatural; Paul may have been responding to "an abusive understanding of society, sex, and power" in the Roman world [p. 73]; in 1 Cor 6:9 Paul may have been responding to sexual exploitation; biblical texts do not mention the homosexual condition or "the possibility of a permanent, committed relationship of love between homosexual people that is analogous to heterosexual marriage" [quote on p. 83] [pp. 56–83]).

Scroggs, Robin. *The New Testament and Homosexuality: Contextual Background for Contemporary Debate.* Philadelphia: Fortress, 1983 (since the principal form of homosexuality in the Graeco-Roman world was pederasty, Paul must have been opposing pederasty's more dehumanizing aspects; Paul does not give a reason for his condemnation, which weakens its persuasive appeal; since pederasty is not the principal form of homosexuality in our world, Paul's condemnation does not apply to our situation).

Siker, Jeffrey S. "How to Decide? Homosexual Christians, the Bible, and Gentile Inclusion." *Theology Today* 51 (1994) 219–34; reprinted in *Homosexuality in the Church: Both Sides of the Debate.* Ed. Jeffrey S. Siker. Louisville, KY: Westminster/John Knox, 1994, 178–94 (since Paul was referring principally to pederasty and male prostitution, his words give no guidance on "loving monogamous homosexual adult Christian relationships" [p. 229]; in terms of the church, lesbians and gay men are comparable neither to alcoholics [who need to maintain abstinence to contain their disease], nor to African-Americans, other ethnic minorities, or women [who struggle against discrimination based on their group identity], but rather to gentile Christians, whom the early church decided to include).

Smith, Abraham. "The New Testament and Homosexuality." *Quarterly Review* 11:4 (1991) 18–32 (Paul does not call homoeroticism a sin, but rather defines it as a manifestation of sin; he presupposes a model of homoerotic dominance, specifically pederasty; since the church today need not accept that model, nor the culturally specific view of sex roles inherent in Paul's rejection of homoeroticism, Paul does not give us clear instructions for dealing with homoeroticism today).

Soards, Marion L. *Scripture and Homosexuality: Biblical Authority and the Church Today.* Louisville, Ky: Westminster/John Knox, 1995 (in Rom 1:26f Paul refers to female and male homosexuality "as the clear symptom" of gentile sinfulness [pp. 20f]; "neither Paul nor any other ancient person had a concept of 'sexual orientation' " [p. 22]; "Paul was not concerned with the origins, motivations, or gratifications of homosexual activity, nor were other ancient thinkers interested in these issues" [p. 23]; "Christians who affirm biblical authority. . . . disagree with those who voice and seek approval for homosexual activity" [p. 73]).

Stegemann, Wolfgang. "Paul and the Sexual Mentality of His World." *Biblical Theology Bulletin* 23 (1993) 162–66 (Paul's condemnation of same-sex relations had to do with honor and shame, which in Paul's world were gendered categories; "for Paul, same-sex relations pervert the strictly different sexual behaviors of the sexes, which is 'naturally' given each of them" [p. 165]; like the prohibition to women to speak in church and the call for the veiling of women and for different hairstyles for women and men, Paul's condemnation of same-sex relations is part of the cultural values of the ancient Mediterranean world).

Strecker, Georg. "Homosexualität in biblischer Sicht." *Kerygma und Dogma* 28 (1982) 127–41 (Paul demonstrates that the pagans are both guilty and distant from God through his general condemnation of homosexuality; the background, such as Stoic and Jewish views on marriage or cultic prostitution, is irrelevant for Paul's argument; communal ethics, which limit the individual's possibilities for self-actualization, are at stake here; the Christian community needs to be loving toward homosexuals, while keeping the church as a whole in mind).

Van de Spijker, A. M. J. M. Herman. *Die gleichgeschlechtliche Zuneigung: Homotropie: Homosexualität, Homoerotik, Homophilie—und die katholische Moraltheologie.* Olten: Walter, 1968 (in Rom 1:26, Paul probably condemns general promiscuous unchastity, rather than sexual relations between women, since such relations were alien to Paul's thinking; the homosexual acts condemned by Paul are characterized by egoism, perversion, promiscuity, voluntary exchange of heterosexual relations for homosexual ones, and probably idolatry; the moral order transgressed here is what the church calls natural law [pp. 81–86]).

Von der Osten-Sacken, Peter. "Paulinisches Evangelium und Homosexualität." *Berliner Theologische Zeitschrift* 3 (1986) 28–49 (Paul's mention of female homosexuality shows that he was not simply adopting Jewish and Graeco-Roman rejections of pederasty, but rather condemning homosexual behavior generally;

he would have opposed all nonprocreative sex; just as Paul told the Corinthians to drive out fornicators from their midst [1 Cor 5:9–13], so too would he have probably advised purging the community of a practicing homosexual; the lack of gender polarity in homosexuality is a deficiency; we know more about homosexuality today and should not define it as a sin, a sickness, or a perversion).

Wengst, Klaus. "Paulus und die Homosexualität." *Zeitschrift für Evangelische Ethik* 31 (1987) 72–81 (Paul's connection between idolatry and homosexuality derives from his Jewish tradition and does not apply to Christian homosexuals today; as in 1 Cor 11:14f, "nature" could mean "convention" in Rom 1:26f [cf. Aristophanes' description in Plato's *Symposion* of same-sex love as natural, thus showing that nature is a culturally conditioned category]; Paul does not describe procreation as the principal goal of sexual contact [see 1 Cor 7:2–5, 8, 36], thereby distinguishing between human and animal sexuality; Paul presupposes that these people have, of their own free will, given up their own heterosexuality; responsible sexuality is that which enriches one's partner in her or his humanity and does not harm others).

Wiedemann, Hans-Georg. "Homosexualität und Bibel." In *Die Menschlichkeit der Sexualität.* Munich: Kaiser, 1983, 89–106 (Rom 1:26f, which is principally theological rather than ethical, does not yield a norm for sexual ethics [pp. 99–102]).

Wolters, Albert. "Hart's Exegetical Proposal on Romans 1." *Calvin Theological Journal* 28 (1993) 166–70 (critique of Hendrik Hart's suggestion that in Rom 1:18–32 Paul was presenting a Jewish position with which he disagreed; Hart simply asserts, but does not demonstrate this).

Wright, David F. "Homosexuality: The Relevance of the Bible." *Evangelical Quarterly* 61 (1989) 291–300 (Paul is strongly influenced by the condemnations of homosexuality in Genesis and Leviticus).

See also:

Cahill, Lisa Sowle. "Sexual Ethics: A Feminist Biblical Perspective." *Interpretation* 49:1 (1995) 5–16.

Carey, John J., ed. *The Sexuality Debate in North American Churches, 1988–1995: Controversies, Unresolved Issues, Future Prospects.* Symposium Series 36; Lewiston, NY: Mellen, 1995.

Coleman, P. *Gay Christians: A Moral Dilemma.* London: SCM, 1989.

Fulkerson, Mary McClintock. "Church Documents on Human Sexuality and the Authority of Scripture." *Interpretation* 49:1 (1995) 46–58.

Gramick, Jeannine, and Pat Furey, eds. *The Vatican and Homosexuality: Reactions to the "Letter to the Bishops of the Catholic Church on the Pastoral Care of Homosexual Persons."* New York: Crossroad, 1988.

Gramick, Jeannine, ed. *Homosexuality and the Catholic Church.* Chicago: Thomas More, 1983.

Horner, Tom. *Homosexuality and the Judeo-Christian Tradition: An Annotated Bibliography.* American Theological Library Association Bibliography Series 5; Metuchen, NJ: Scarecrow, 1981.

Horner, Tom. *Jonathan Loved David: Homosexuality in Biblical Times.* Philadelphia: Westminster, 1978.

Melton, J. Gordon, ed. *The Churches Speak on: Homosexuality: Official Statements from Religious Bodies and Ecumenical Organizations.* Detroit: Gale Research, 1991.

Moxnes, Halvor. "Hedningenes synder? Polemikken mot 'homoseksualitet' i Det nye testamente" ["Sins of the Gentiles? The Polemic against 'Homosexuality' in the New Testament"] *Norsk Teologisk Tidsskrift* 94 (1993) 1–34.

Nugent, Robert, ed. *A Challenge to Love: Gay and Lesbian Catholics in the Church.* New York: Crossroad, 1983.

Pronk, Pim. *Against Nature? Types of Moral Argumentation Regarding Homosexuality.* Trans. John Vriend. With a foreword by Hendrik Hart. Grand Rapids, MI: Eerdmans, 1993.

Scroggs, Robin. "The Bible as Foundational Document." *Interpretation* 49:1 (1995) 17–30.

Stemmeler, Michael L., and J. Michael Clark, eds. *Homophobia and the Judaeo-Christian Tradition.* Gay Men's Issues in Religious Studies Series 1. Dallas: Monument, 1990.

Verhey, Allen D. "The Holy Bible and Sanctified Sexuality: An Evangelical Approach to Scripture and Ethics." *Interpretation* 49:1 (1995) 31–45.

Wright, David F. *The Christian Faith and Homosexuality.* Edinburgh: Rutherford, 1994.

Wright, J. Robert. "Boswell on Homosexuality: A Case Undemonstrated." *Anglican Theological Review* 66 (1984) 79–94.

Index of Subjects

Page numbers in boldfont refer to the main discussion of that entry. For further references to specific ancient authors, consult the Index of Premodern Sources. See also the Index of Ancient Women.

à Castro, Roderico, 168n
ab Aquapendente, Fabricius, 168n
'*Aboda Zara,* 233n
abomination, 233–34, **288–93**, 296
abortion, 311
Abrasax, 87–88, 112
active and passive, **1–2**
  experienced by one person, 157
  as more fundamental than male and female, 126–27, 140, 157n
  as male and female, 116, 125, 327–28
  See also gender differentiation; penetration; sexual relations
Adamas, 340, 342
adultery, 247n, 270n, 330
Aelian, Claudius, 39, 273–74
Aetios of Amida, 145–46, **169–70**
age, 290–92. *See also* pederasty
Akrammachammari, 88
Albucasis, 168n
Alkaios of Lesbos, 22n, 37n
Alkiphron, 53–54
altar of Chastity, 48
amenorrhea, 171–72. *See also* menstruation
Ammonios, 32n
Anakreon, 37n
anal intercourse. *See* sexual relations
Anastasios, 337
Anaximenes, 203n

androgynes, 54, 247, 326, 340, 342. See also *androgynos, -on* in Index of Ancient Terms
Andronikos, 218
animals
  as lower than humans, 328
  as model for the natural, 181
  that practice homoeroticism, 154n, 155n, **273–74**
  do not practice homoeroticism, 44, 63, 155, **273–74**, 345
  sexual behavior of, 329–30
  as slaves, 231n
Anoubis, **78–81**, 87, 111–12
Anthologia Palatina, 321
anthropology, **208–13**, **234–37**
Antiochos of Askalon, 269–71
Apelles, 218
Aphrodite, 42, 205
apocalyptic visions, **304–14**
Apollonios Dyskolos, 31n
appearance
  beards, 323
  beauty contest, 53
  cosmetics, 316, 323
  depilation, 323
  gender differentiation in, **323–24**, 352–53
  hair, 52, 63, 323

woman-woman marriage an insult to, 336
  wrath of, 221–22
Gomorra, 313
gospel, 220
Great Mother, 340n–341n
Gregory of Nazianzos, 33

hair. *See* appearance
hare, **329–30**. *See also* animals
Harmachimeneus, 85, 111
Hebrew Bible. *See* Bible
Heister, Lorenz, 168n–169n
Hekate, 112n
Helios, 111
hell. *See* punishments
hens (female-female coupling among), 273.
  See also animals
Hephaistion of Thebes, 31n, 123n, **137–39**
Heqet, 92n
hermaphrodites, 52, 58, 135, 156n, **277–80**
Hermas, 218
Hermes, **78–81**, 111–12
Hermes Trismegistos, Book of, 5, **130–32**, 321
Hermippos of Berytos, 176n
Hermogenes, 31n
Herodas, 108
Herodian, 31n
Herodion, 218
Herophilos of Chalcedon, 167
heterosexuals, 242
Hillel, School of, 66n
Hippokratic Corpus, 144–45, 169n
Hippolytos of Rome, **338–43**
Hitler, Adolf, 224n
holiness, **288–94**
Homer, 32–33
homoeroticism
  as diabolical, 346
  as diseased, 125–27, 138–39, 143–73,
    346
  disgust at, 140
  etiology of in ancient medicine, 156–59
  as exchange, 309–13
  as illegal and unnatural, 347
  as irrational, 346
  as lawlessness, 346
  as luxury, 54–55, 322, 346
  male and female grouped together, 41,
    55–56, 148–63, **322–25**, **331**,
    344–48

and prostitution, 324
and sexual distinctions, 13
as sin in Rom 1:26f, 212
and social order, 239n, 264
as unnatural, 270n
usage of in this book, 8
as worse than prostitution, 346
See also female homoeroticism; male homoeroticism; marriage; nature
"homosexual," 22, 337
homosexuality, 8, 21–22
honor
  in Paul, 288
  and shame, **208–12**
Horace, 34–35
horoscope. *See* astrology
Huna, Rav, 67–69
husbands, 327. *See also* men; gender differentiation; marriage; sexual relations
hyena, **329–30**. *See also* animals
hysterectomy, 18

Iamblichos, **51**, 66, 332–33
Iaō, 87–88, 106, 112
idolatry
  and homoeroticism, 62, 64, 308
  and Romans 1, 203, 208, 211, 231–32
  and sexual vice, 262
  as source of other sins, **294–98**
  hyena as symbolic for, 330
Igbo, 336
impurity
  of food, 233
  gentile religion as, 233
  homoeroticism as, 129, 137
  in Leviticus, 62, **288–93**
  Paul on, **232–37**, 260–62, **288–94**
incest
  in dream classification, 180–82
  father-daughter, 290–92
  and homoeroticism, 131–32
  and magicians, 321n
  as natural, 250–51
    but prohibited, 247, 270n
  in Leviticus 18 and 20, 257, **290–91**
  in Paul, **289–92**
inequality. *See* female homoeroticism; male
  homoeroticism; sexual relations
infanticide, 311
intersexed persons. *See* hermaphrodites

Index of Ancient Women
(Both Historical and Fictitious)

Index of Authors

Boer, Emilie
  on Dorotheos of Sidon, 118 n
  on Hephaistion of Thebes, 138 n
  on Manetho, 123 n
  on Ptolemy, 124 n
  on Vettius Valens, 128 n
Boivin, Marcel, 271 n
Boll, Franz
  on Firmicus Maternus, 132 n
  on Hephaistion of Thebes, 138 n
  on *Suppl. Mag.*, 1. 37, 90 n, 92 n, 93–94, 96
Bolle, Geertje, 19 n
Bonhöffer, Adolf, 268 n
Borell, Brigitte, 90 n
Bornkamm, Günther, 223 n
Børresen, Kari E., 353 n
Boswell, John, 6 n, 9 n, **10–13**
  on "Alexandrian rule," 326 n
  on ancient writings
    on Artemidoros, 177 n
    on Caelius Aurelianus, 148 n
    on Chrysostom, 344 n, 348 n
    on Iamblichos, 51 n, 333 n
    on Lev 18:22; 20:13, 62 n
    on Plato, 41 n
    on Rom 1:26f, 242 n, 364
  on female romantic friendship, 352 n
  on "gay," 22 n, 337 n
  on Greek terms
    on *allēlobasia*, 331 n
    on *arsenokoitēs*, 260 n
    on *malakos*, 260 n
    on *para physin*, 241 n
  on hare and hyena, 330 n–331 n
  on "homosexuality," 21
  on *lex Scantinia*, 284 n
  on passive males, 161 n
  on same-sex coupling among animals, 273 n
  on same-sex unions, **10–13**, 334 n
  on tolerance of female homoeroticism, 361
  on urban life and same-sex love, 261 n
Boughton, Lynne C., 364
Bowra, C. M., 30 n, 37 n
Boyarin, Daniel, 46, 61 n, 65 n, 275 n
Boylan, Michael, 157 n
Bram, Jean Rhys, 118 n, 132 n, 134

Brandt, Paul, 30 n
Braund, Susanna H., 48 n
Bremmer, Jan, 26 n
Brenk, F. E., 31 n
Brettman, Estelle Shohet, 231 n
Briggs, Sheila, 102 n, 265 n
Brinker-Gabler, Gisela, 36 n
Brooten, Bernadette J.
  on John Boswell, 11 n
  on female homoeroticism, 209 n, 249 n
  on Jewish women of the priestly class, 67 n
  on Paul and the Jewish law, 268 n–269 n, 282 n
  on women's history, 25 n
Brown, Judith C., 20 n, 352 n
Brown, Peter, 347 n, 350 n, 354 n
Buchholz, Dennis D., 305 n, 306 n
Buell, Denise Kimber, 12 n, 171 n, 325 n
Bullough, Vern L., 20 n
Bultmann, Rudolf, 222 n, 263 n
Burchfield, R. W., 5 n
Burnett, Andrew, 59 n
Butler, Judith, 17 n, 18 n, 19 n
Byne, William, 243 n

Cahill, Lisa Sowle, 270 n, 371
Calder, W. M., 40 n
Califia, Pat, 19 n
Cameron, Averil and Alan, 37 n
Canavello, Robert, 115 n, 140 n
Cantarella, Eva, 9 n, 30 n, 40 n, 109 n
Carey, John J., 371
Carrington, Philip, 288 n
Cassio, Albio Cesare, 5 n
Cassirer, Ernst, 117 n
Castelli, Elizabeth A., 14 n
Cataudella, Quintino, 33 n
Chadwick, Henry, 246 n
Charlesworth, James H., 117 n
Chauncey, George, 1 n–2 n, 20 n, 143 n
Clark, Elizabeth A., 328 n–329 n, 354 n
Clark, Gillian, 24–25, 26 n
Clark, J. Michael, 372
Coffey, David M., 222 n
Coleman, Peter, 9 n, 364, 371
Comstock, Gary David, 364
Conner, Randy P., 342 n
Copeland, Peter, 243 n

Rich, Adrienne, 10, 13, 19n, 243n
Richlin, Amy
  on David Halperin, 8, 21n
  on Juvenal, 48n, 165n
  on *lex Scantinia*, 283n
  on male domination, 103n
  on passive males, 49n, 134n, 307n
Richter, G. M. A., 57n
Ridderbos, Herman, 284n
Ridderbos, Simon Jan, 252n, 253n, 369
Ritner, Robert, 94n
Roberts, J. R., 20n
Robinson, David M., 31n
Rohde, Erwin, 51n
Roof, Judith, 19n
Rose, Andy, 19n
Rose, Valentine, 164n
Rousselle, Aline, 2n, 56n, 144–45, 237n

Saake, Helmut, 30n
Samois, 19n
Sanday, William, **204–5**, 213, 267n–268n
Sanders, E. P., 231n, 281n
Sandy, Gerald N., 51n
Santos Otero, Aurelio de, 314n
Satlow, Michael L., 9n, 65, 66n, 67n
Scanzoni, Letha Dawson, 369
Schanz, Martin, 132n, 147n, 164n
Scheidweiler, Felix, 37n
Schelkle, Bettina, 19n
Schlier, Heinrich, 223n
Schlink, Edmund, 223n
Schmid, Pierre, 147n
Schmid, Wilhelm
  on Caelius Aurelianus, 147n
  on Dorotheos of Sidon, 118n
  on Hephaistion of Thebes, 138n
  on Ptolemy, 124n
  on Soranos of Ephesos, 146n
  on Vettius Valens, 128n
Schmidt, Peter L., 45n
Schneider-Menzel, Ursula, 51n
Schottroff, Luise, 14n
Schrage, Wolfgang, 284n
Schrijvers, P. H., **147–60**
Schulte, Hannelis, 223n
Schüssler Fiorenza, Elisabeth, 275n, 293n
Scroggs, Robin, 9n, 372

on Paul and pederasty, 13, 253n, 256–57, 361
  on Rom 1:26f, 369
Scully, Diana, 98n, 103n
Sedgwick, Eve Kosofsky, 21n
Segal, Alan F., 110n
Selwyn, Edward Gordon, 288n
Shanks, Hershel, 231n
Shaw, Brent D., 12n
Siker, Jeffrey S., 369
Siouville, A., 341n
Skinner, B. G., 271n
Skinner, Marilyn, 36
Sly, Dorothy, 247n
Smith, A. H., 59n
Smith, Abraham, 256n, 370
Smith, Barbara, 19n
Smith, Morton, 329n
Smith, Nicholas D., 276n
Smith, Richard, 81n
Smith-Rosenberg, Carroll, 20n
Smither, Paul C., 81n
Snyder, Jane McIntosh, 30n, 32n, 34n, 37n, 38n, 40n
Soards, Marion L., 370
Spanier, Bonnie, 243n
Spelman, Elizabeth V., 15n
Stählin, Otto
  on Caelius Aurelianus, 147n
  on Clement of Alexandria, 331n
  on Dorotheos of Sidon, 118n
  on Hephaistion of Thebes, 138n
  on Ptolemy, 124n
  on Soranos of Ephesos, 146n
  on Vettius Valens, 128n
Stanton, Domna, 18n
Stegemann, Wolfgang, 370
Stehle, Eva, 30n, 31n
Stein, Judith, 32n
Stemmeler, Michael L., 372
Stendahl, Krister, 281n–282n
Stevenson, James, 231n
Stigers, Eva Stehle. *See* Stehle, Eva
Stowers, Stanley, **198–99**
Strecker, Georg, 370
Striker, Gisela, 269
Stuhlmacher, Peter, 274n, 281n
Stuiber, Alfred, 145n
Stupperich, Reinhard, 59n

Index of Premodern Sources

Index of Ancient Terms

412
INDEX OF ANCIENT TERMS

natura (*continued*)
  extra naturam, 241 n
  as "genitals," 45 n, 278 n
  homoeroticism and, 44 n, 137
  and law
    lex naturalis, 315 n
    natura legalis, 268 n, 315 n
    naturalis usus, 315 n
  in Tertullian, 315–16
  See also *lex*
prodigiosus, -a, -um, 44 n, 47 n
publica, 39 n
publicus, -a, -um, 132 n
rego, 353 n
subdo, 353 n
subigitatrix, 4 n
subigo
  subactus (pl. *subacti*), 148

tentigo, 164 n–165 n
tribas (pl. *tribades*)
  meanings of, **4–8, 24**
  as bisexual, 150–51
  in Martial, **46–48**
  in Phaedrus, **45–46**
  in Seneca the Elder, **43–44,** 109
  as sex addict, 150, 154
  See also Greek *tribas*
trissatrices, 131 n
turpis, -is, -e, 131 n, 150 n
turpitudo, 163 n
virago (pl. *viragines*), **133–36**
  meaning of, 4–5
  virago meretrix, 135
  virago libidinosa, 136
virilis, -is, -e (*viriles actus*), 123 n, 136 n